KV-372-069

SHELF No.

BEN

302424578Z

VANDERBILT LIBRARY

This book investigates maps and their reflection of and influence on the contemporary society of early modern Britain. It is concerned with rural estate maps, which were primarily drawn to show landownership, and with the surveyors who drew them and the landowners who commissioned them. The links between different aspects of maps and their relation to society are exemplified by a study of the historic county of Cambridgeshire.

The work is based on a carto-bibliography of the estate maps of Cambridgeshire which were drawn by 1836. The book is divided into two parts. The first part examines three main areas: the maps and how map-making grew and changed from 1600 to 1836, the surveyors and the development of the surveying profession, and the landowners and how they used the maps. The second part is a carto-bibliography of 785 estate maps, which were found in 50 repositories. Details are recorded about each map's physical characteristics, the topographical information which it shows, and the amount and type of decoration which the surveyor used.

The study, therefore, is part of a wider concern with the interrelations between maps and society, and with the way they interact and change. These factors can be seen as part of more general developments in the history of cartography, which in turn can be related to broader changes in society in early modern Britain.

MAPS, LAND AND SOCIETY

Estate map of Chippenham drawn by Heber Lands for the Earl of Oxford, 1712

MAPS, LAND AND SOCIETY

A history, with a carto-bibliography of Cambridgeshire estate maps, c. 1600–1836

A. SARAH BENDALL

Fellow and Archivist, Emmanuel College, Cambridge

MAGDALEN COLLEGE LIBRARY

CAMBRIDGE
UNIVERSITY PRESS

Published by the Press Syndicate of the University of Cambridge
The Pitt Building, Trumpington Street, Cambridge CB2 1RP
40 West 20th Street, New York, NY 10011–4211, USA
10 Stamford Road, Oakleigh, Victoria 3166, Australia

© Cambridge University Press 1992

First published 1992

Printed in Great Britain at the University Press, Cambridge

A cataloguing in publication record for this book is available from the British Library

Library of Congress cataloguing in publication data
Bendall, A. Sarah.
Maps, land and society: a history, with a carto-bibliography of
Cambridgeshire estate maps, c. 1600–1836 / A. Sarah Bendall.
p. cm.
Includes bibliographical references and index.
ISBN 0 521 41055 X
1. Real property—England—Cambridgeshire—Maps—History. 2.
Real property—England—Cambridgeshire—Maps—Bibliography.
3. Cambridgeshire (England)—Social life and customs. I. Title.
GA795.C36B46 1992
912.426'5—dc20 91–26284 CIP

ISBN 0 521 41055 X hardback

971306

CONTENTS

Contents

ILLUSTRATIONS

PLATES

FIGURES

TABLES

PREFACE

Estate maps have been a major interest of mine since a day in December 1983, when I had Sunday lunch with a group of friends in a bed-sit in North Oxford. I was hoping to compile a bibliography as part of an M.A. in librarianship, and we were discussing possible subjects for someone with geographical and local historical interests. One of our number had been using Welsh estate maps and described them in such glowing terms that I made up my mind to investigate them further; and so began the project which has resulted in this book.

I quickly discovered the excellent carto-bibliographies of estate maps of Essex, Sussex and Kent, and decided to embark upon one of Cambridgeshire. A pilot study, which formed my M.A. dissertation, showed that I had only discovered the tip of an iceberg. I continued searching for maps, initially part-time and then full-time when I became a Research Student at the Department of Geography, University of Cambridge. My enquiries took me to many places and institutions and everywhere I have been met by great helpfulness and hospitality. On occasion, I have ended up in some unexpected places or positions: I have seen maps in the company of stuffed birds in a museum basement, by climbing a step-ladder to examine a splendid example framed and hung high on a wall, in a Tudor muniment room, and by clambering over the roof-tops to reach the storage place of some archives. I have also made some startling incidental discoveries, and shall never forget the contents of a box described as containing 'miscellaneous items found in the attics': some broken pot, a squashed thimble and a dried-up and very dead mouse.

It soon became apparent that the scope of my study had to be limited in some way, and so I confined myself to rural estate maps of the historic county of Cambridge, drawn up to 1836. This led to some tantalizing omissions, of maps nearly in the county but not quite, of maps drawn in 1837, and of maps of estates in Cambridge itself rather than in the rural county. I have been resolute, so that the contents of the carto-bibliography are clearly defined; the broader areas would be well worth further study some day. I have made every effort to be comprehensive, but maps are still turning up, especially ones in private hands which I did not know of or which only turned up as dusty attics were cleared.

Examining many decorative and not-so-beautiful estate maps clearly told only part of the story: why were these maps drawn as they were, how were they used, who were the map-makers, who commissioned them? It became increasingly clear that such lines of enquiry were essential to an understanding of the maps and their reflection of and influence on the contemporary society of early modern Britain, and that this study could shed light on interactions between many different types of map in a wide range of societies. This book arises from the results of my researches, for which I was awarded a Ph.D. in October 1989.

I have been advised, supported and encouraged by many friends and colleagues in the course of my studies. I particular, I should like to thank Alan Baker, who supervised my Ph.D. thesis, Roger Fairclough and his staff in the Cambridge University Library map room, the staff of the Cambridge County Record Office, the archivists of Cambridge University and Clare, Emmanuel, Gonville and Caius, Jesus, Queens', St John's and Trinity colleges, Cambridge, and all the other archivists and librarians who have helped me in my search for maps and associated documents. I am also indebted to Tony Baggs, Peter Barber, Mark Billinge, Peter Burke, Robin Butlin, Steve Daniels, Robin Glasscock, Brian Harley, Paul Harvey, Anne Holton-Krayenbuhl, Ralph Hyde, Elisabeth Leedham-Green, Chris Lewis, David Moore, Peter Searby and Frances Willmoth for helpful discussions. In addition, P. C. D. Campbell, David Cubitt, Peter Eden, Myles Gleeson-White, Francis Herbert, Donald Hodson, Stuart Mason, Bob Silvester and Ruth Wallis have passed on to me some useful details about maps, surveyors and landowners; I am very grateful to them and acknowledge the information which they provided at appropriate points in the text.

I wish to thank libraries and record offices open to the general public, those who have deposited their archives in them, and the following for allowing me to consult documents in their possession: Professor A. Barton; the Governing Bodies of Cambridge University and the colleges of Christ's, Clare, Corpus Christi, Downing, Emmanuel, Gonville and Caius, Jesus, King's, Pembroke, Peterhouse, Queens', St Catharine's, St John's, Trinity and Trinity Hall; Crichel Estates Ltd; Mr M. G. de Courcy-Ireland; the Dean and Chapter of Ely Cathedral; Major J. C. Francis; Mrs R. Gorton; the National Trust; the Curators of the Bodleian Library, Oxford and the Governing Bodies of Christ Church and Merton colleges; Mrs C. Page-Blair; the Governors of St Bartholomew's Hospital, London; the Spalding Gentlemen's Society; Lord Townshend; the Dean and Canons of Windsor; and the Trustees of the Wisbech and Fenland Museum.

I am grateful to the following for permission to reproduce illustrations: the Bodleian Library, Oxford (Plate 26); the Cambridge Antiquarian Society (Plates 13b and 16b); the Cambridgeshire Collection, Cambridgeshire Libraries (Plates 14b and 15b, c); the Cambridgeshire County Record Office (Plate 1); the Syndics of Cambridge University Library (Plates 4, 8, 9, 21, 22, 26 and 28); the Charterhouse (Plates 6, 7 and 10); the Master and Fellows of Clare College, Cambridge (Plates 12a and 14c); the Master and Fellows of Downing College, Cambridge (Plates 11, 13a and 18a); the Master and Fellows of Emmanuel College, Cambridge (Plate 19); the Master and Fellows of Gonville and Caius College, Cambridge (Plates 14a and 16a); the Reverend Stephen Leeke (Plate 29); the National Trust, Rufford Old Hall (Plate 24); the Master and Fellows of Pembroke College, Cambridge (Plate 15a); Spalding Gentlemen's Society (Plates 17a and 30); Mr Peter Thornhill (Plates 3 and 23); the Victoria and Albert Museum (Plate 2); the General Editor of the Victoria History of the Counties of England (Plate 12b); Wicken Parochial Church Council (Plate 5); the owner of the map illustrated in Plate 27.

Preface

Finally, I acknowledge with thanks financial support from the Economic and Social Research Council and Emmanuel College, Cambridge. I am also grateful for the facilities which have been provided by Emmanuel College and the Department of Geography, University of Cambridge.

ABBREVIATIONS

BL	British Library, Map Library
BLM	British Library, Manuscripts Department
BLO	Bodleian Library, Oxford
BRO	Bedfordshire County Record Office
CCC	Christ's College, Cambridge
CCO	Christ Church, Oxford
CLC	Clare College, Cambridge
COL	Cambridgeshire Collection, Cambridgeshire Libraries
CRC	Corpus Christi College, Cambridge
CRO	Cambridgeshire County Record Office, Cambridge Branch
CUA	Cambridge University Archives (in CUM)
CUL	Cambridge University Library, Map Room
CUM	Cambridge University Library, Manuscripts Room
DCC	Downing College, Cambridge
DEP	Burke, B., 1883. *A Genealogical History of the Dormant, Abeyant, Forfeited, and Extinct Peerages of the British Empire*
DNB	*Dictionary of National Biography*, 1885–1900
ECC	Emmanuel College, Cambridge
EDB	Burke, J. and Burke, J.B., 1844. *A Genealogical and Heraldic History of the Extinct and Dormant Baronetcies of England, Ireland and Scotland*
EDC	Ely Dean and Chapter Records (in CUM)
Eden	Eden, P.G., ed., forthcoming. *Dictionary of Land Surveyors and Local Cartographers of Great Britain and Ireland c.1540–1850*, 2nd ed. by A.S. Bendall
EDR	Ely Diocesan Records (in CUM)
EPR	Ely Probate Records (in CRO)
ERO	Essex County Record Office
ESRO	Suffolk County Record Office, Ipswich Branch
Foster	Foster, J., 1888–92. *Alumni Oxonienses*
GCC	Gonville and Caius College, Cambridge
GHL	Guildhall, London
GLC	Greater London Record Office
HERO	Hertfordshire County Record Office
HRO	Cambridgeshire County Record Office, Huntingdon Branch

JCC	Jesus College, Cambridge
KCC	King's College, Cambridge
LBH	London Borough of Hackney, Health District Archives
LG	*Burke's Genealogical and Heraldic History of the Landed Gentry*, 1952
LPL	Lambeth Palace Library
Lysons	Lysons, D. and Lysons, S., 1808. *Magna Britannia. Vol. 2.i. Cambridgeshire*
MCO	Merton College, Oxford
NRO	Norfolk County Record Office
PB	*Burke's Genealogical and Heraldic History of the Peerage, Baronetage and Knightage*, 1970
PCC	Pembroke College, Cambridge
PRI	In private hands
PRO	Public Record Office
PTC	Peterhouse, Cambridge
QCC	Queens' College, Cambridge
RAY	c/o Lord Townshend, Raynham Hall, Norfolk
RCHM	Royal Commission on Historical Monuments
SCC	St Catharine's College, Cambridge
SJC	St John's College, Cambridge
SPA	Spalding Gentlemen's Society
SRO	Suffolk County Record Office, Bury St Edmunds Branch
TCC	Trinity College, Cambridge
TH	Trinity Hall, Cambridge
VAM	Victoria and Albert Museum, London
VCH	*Victoria History of the Counties of England* (*Cambridgeshire* unless otherwise stated)
Venn	Venn, J. and Venn, J.A., 1922–54. *Alumni Cantabrigienses*
WIN	Dean and Canons of Windsor, St George's Chapel, Windsor
WLT	Wiltshire County Record Office
WM	Wisbech and Fenland Museum
WMP	c/o National Trust, Wimpole Hall
WRO	Warwickshire County Record Office
YAS	Yorkshire Archaeological Society, Leeds

Incomplete classmarks in the Cambridge branch of the Cambridgeshire County Record Office indicate maps which have not yet been catalogued.

CONVENTIONS USED IN TRANSCRIPTION

Spelling and punctuation have been preserved; words in small capitals have been transcribed in lower case.

xxx	expansions of abbreviations (some standard abbreviations have not been expanded)
[ ]	editorial insertions
< >	material deleted in MS
\/	material inserted in MS
{ }	MS defective
( )	parentheses in MS
~	hyphen in MS
' '	former names of features and places (on maps)

DATES

In all cases, the year has been taken as beginning on 1 January; for documents which were drawn up before 1752 and between 1 January and 24 March, the two dates are separated by a slash: e.g. 1601/2.

MAP CODES

Each map is identified by a code, for example BAB78502.

BAB	code for parish
785	add 1000 to give year in which the map was completed, in this case 1785
02	running number for maps drawn in a particular year

Conventions used in transcription

PARISH CODES

ABI	Abington Pigotts	DUL	Dullingham
ARR	Arrington	DUX	Duxford St John
ASH	Ashley cum Silverley	DUY	Duxford St Peter
BAB	Babraham	EAS	East Hatley
BAL	Balsham	ELM	Elm
BAP	Barrington	ELS	Elsworth
BAQ	Bartlow	ELT	Eltisley
BAR	Barton	EYC	Ely College
BAS	Bassingbourn	EYM	Ely St Mary
BEN	Benwick	EYT	Ely Trinity
BOT	Bottisham		
BOU	Bourn	FDI	Fen Ditton
BOX	Boxworth	FDY	Fen Drayton
BRI	Brinkley	FOR	Fordham
BUR	Burrough Green	FOW	Fowlmere
BUW	Burwell	FOX	Foxton
		FUL	Fulbourn
CAL	Caldecote		
CAM	Cambridge	GAM	Gamlingay
CAR	Carlton cum Willingham	GIR	Girton
CAS	Castle Camps	GRT	Grantchester
CAX	Caxton	GRV	Graveley
CHA	Chatteris	GTA	Great Abington
CHE	Cherry Hinton	GTE	Great Eversden
CHF	Chesterton	GTS	Great Shelford
CHG	Cheveley	GTW	Great Wilbraham
CHI	Childerley	GTY	Grunty Fen
CHP	Chippenham	GUI	Guilden Morden
COM	Comberton		
CON	Conington	HAD	Haddenham
COT	Coton	HAP	Hardwick
COU	Cottenham	HAQ	Harlton
COV	Coveney	HAR	Harston
CRX	Croxton	HAS	Haslingfield
CRY	Croydon cum Clopton	HAT	Hatley St George
		HAU	Hauxton
DOD	Doddington	HIL	Hildersham
DOW	Downham	HIN	Hinxton
DRY	Dry Drayton	HIS	Histon

HRN	Horningsea		ORW	Orwell
HRS	Horseheath		OUT	Outwell
			OVE	Over
ICK	Ickleton			
IMP	Impington		PAM	Pampisford
ISL	Isleham		PAP	Papworth Everard
			PAQ	Papworth St Agnes
KEN	Kennett			
KIN	Kingston		RAM	Rampton
KIR	Kirtling		ROY	Royston
KNA	Knapwell			
KNE	Kneesworth		SAW	Sawston
			SHE	Shepreth
LAB	Landbeach		SHI	Shingay
LAW	Landwade		SHU	Shudy Camps
LEV	Leverington		SNA	Snailwell
LIN	Linton		SOH	Soham
LIT	Litlington		STA	Stanground
LLA	Little Abington		STL	Stapleford
LLE	Little Eversden		STM	Steeple Morden
LLG	Little Gransden		STN	Stetchworth
LLP	Littleport		STO	Stow cum Quy
LLS	Little Shelford		STR	Stretham
LLW	Little Wilbraham		SUT	Sutton
LOL	Lolworth		SWB	Swaffham Bulbeck
LSA	Long Stanton All Saints'		SWP	Swaffham Prior
LSS	Long Stanton St Michael		SWV	Swavesey
LSW	Longstowe			
			TAD	Tadlow
MAD	Madingley		TEV	Teversham
MAN	Manea		THE	Thetford
MAR	March		THO	Thorney
MEB	Melbourn		THR	Thriplow
MED	Meldreth		TOF	Toft
MEP	Mepal		TRU	Trumpington
MIL	Milton		TYD	Tydd St Giles
NEA	Newmarket All Saints'		UPW	Upwell
NEC	Newton (near Cambridge)			
NEW	Newton (near Wisbech)		WAT	Waterbeach
			WEC	Welches Dam
OAK	Oakington		WEL	Welney

WEN	Wendy		WIC	Wicken
WEO	Wentworth		WLB	Wilburton
WES	Westley Waterless		WLL	Willingham
WET	Weston Colville		WMB	Wimblington
WEU	Westwick		WMP	Wimpole
WEV	West Wickham		WSM	Wisbech St Mary
WEW	West Wratting		WSP	Wisbech St Peter
WHA	Whaddon		WTC	Witcham
WHR	Whittlesey		WTF	Witchford
WHV	Whittlesford		WYD	Woodditton

Chapter 1

INTRODUCTION

In 1696, Edward Russell, first Lord of the Admiralty and Member of Parliament for Cambridgeshire, began a sweeping series of changes to his property at Chippenham, Cambridgeshire. The result was to give him, as victor of the Battle of La Hogue, a fittingly grand estate: he created a landscaped park, bought up at least 25 cottages, demolished a number of them, reorganized the provision of common lands, and built for his tenants a row of new houses leading up to the lodge gates (Spufford, 1968). This was the first village in England to be created in such a way (Darley, 1980, 61), and was dominated by a 'magnificent mansion' (Lysons, 167). The culmination of the reconstructions was the drawing in 1712 of a splendid map of the new Russell estate.

The map and its context paint a picture of the man and his times. Plate 1 illustrates one of the eight sheets of one of the finest estate maps of Cambridgeshire. Drawn on parchment, this sheet is dominated by the Russell seat and shows the layout of its buildings and gardens. The house is surrounded by a wooded park, ornamented with grazing deer. To the north is shown the newly created model village: the High Street with its cottages, outbuildings, church and school, trees, gardens and adjacent plots of land. The process of the emparkment can be detected in the trees in the park which outline the former High Street and other blocked roads, the outlines of former crofts and two isolated cottages surviving in the south. The map thus accurately shows a wealth of topographical detail.

There is, however, more to discover about the map. Who made it, how and why? Heber Lands, the surveyor, mainly practised in the home counties. In Hertfordshire, he mapped estates at Chipping Barnet in 1713 for Nicholas King and at Ware in 1716 for John Evans (Walne, 1969); he drew a sketch plan of an estate at Wanstead in Essex in 1712, and of Great and Little Burstead for Sir James Lumley in 1720 (Mason, 1990, 32); and Emmanuel College, Cambridge, employed him to map its land in Clapham, Surrey, also in 1720.[1] It was not unusual for surveyors to be employed by both private and institutional landowners. No other maps for the Earl of Orford have been found, and it is not clear why or how Lands came to be employed at Chippenham. Apart from his *Short Treatise of Practical Gauging Shewing a Plain and Easie Method*, published in London by George Sawbridge in 1694, there is no surviving documentation about Lands himself, how much he was paid, what techniques he used or how he learned them. It is, however, possible to suggest that he may have been paid between three and six pence per acre, and that he most probably used a chain, plane table and local assistants to make his map. Evidence for such suppositions is provided in Chapters 4 and 5 of this book. He may well have started his career as an assistant to a surveyor, or

1

perhaps have been trained as a military engineer: he may be the Helier Lands who was nominated for duty as such in the Leeward Islands in 1696 (Porter, 1889, 136) and returned to England between 1697 and 1700 (A. S. Mason, personal communication). The maps themselves indicate that Lands was something of an artist: his Burstead map has a decorative border, scale bar, compass rose and cartouche with the Lumley arms above, and each Chippenham sheet is similarly decorated.

Who was the landowner who commissioned such a map, and why did he do so? Edward Russell, Earl of Orford, Viscount Barfleur and Baron of Shingay, was M.P. for Cambridgeshire from 1695 to 1697, after having represented Launceston (Cornwall) and Portsmouth in Parliament in turn from 1689 to 1690 and from 1690 to 1695. He was High Steward of Cambridge University from 1699 to 1727 and Lord Lieutenant of Cambridgeshire from 1715 to 1727 (*PB*, 226; *DNB*, 49, 429–31; Venn, I, 3, 499). Thus he was a notable and important local figure, who made sweeping changes to his Cambridgeshire estate and left charitable endowments to his tenants when he died in 1727 (Munby, 1967, 29). The 1712 map must have been used for practical purposes: to show the land and changes which had been made. With its use of colour, decoration, Russell coat of arms, and careful depiction of the mansion, local topography, deer park, and, on another sheet, the Lord's shepherd watching flocks on the heath, it is also a statement of the Earl's prestige and influence. It demonstrates his authority over his neighbours and tenants, his ability to create a new landscape and to employ a skilled surveyor to record it.

Estate maps, therefore, tell a story: of a landscape, its maps, their makers and the landowners who employed them. They convey information, ideas and social relationships (Harley, 1987, 35); as early as 1717, John Green said (p.154): 'the Eye will learn more in one Hour by Observation, than the Ear will benefit in a Day by Discourse ... In short, a Draught shews at once what many Words can't express.' It is only in recent years, however, that statements similar to Thrower's (1972, 1) that 'A map is a sensitive indicator of the changing thought of man, and few of his works seem to be such an excellent mirror of culture and civilization' have proliferated in the methodological literature of the history of cartography; the importance of studying maps in their wider sociological context has been emphasized by Woodward (1974) and Blakemore and Harley (1980) among others. Indeed, it has been suggested that the use of maps and their impact within society has become one half of the history of cartography (Blakemore and Harley, 1980, 102).

This book uses rural estate maps to examine further the relation between maps and the cultural and historical environment in which they were produced, viewed and used. At the same time, however, questions such as when and where a map was made, why, by and for whom, how and with what results, remain central to the history of cartography and will also be discussed. The next chapter will suggest how existing work on maps as a means of communication can be used to examine the meaning of estate maps, and following chapters study Cambridgeshire maps, map-makers and landowners in detail.

Chapter 2

ART, MAPS AND COMMUNICATION

ART AND MAPS AS MEANS OF COMMUNICATION

Messages about economic, social and cultural conditions can be communicated in a number of ways, for instance through physical signs, words, numbers and pictures. Maps can be studied as a subset of this last category, and this chapter investigates how methods of study of the relation between art and culture can be adapted to explore the interactions between maps and society.

Communication by pictures

Works of art are means of communication, and Paulson said that every one has a meaning (1975, 8). Indeed, a picture can convey both directly and indirectly a multiplicity of messages about the image which is shown and the cultural concepts upon which its production is based. In *Art and Illusion*, E. H. Gombrich quotes a statement by Ernst Kris (1972, 25): 'We have long come to realize that art is not produced in an empty space, that no artist is independent of predecessors and models, and that he no less than the scientist and philosopher is part of a specific tradition and works in a structured area of problems.' Gombrich proceeds to demonstrate that an artist encodes messages from the visible world: he cannot transcribe what he sees but what he perceives he sees, he starts from ideas and concepts which are derived from contemporary society, and he has to rely upon a vocabulary of conventional forms and representations. Thus, symbolism is inherent in all works of art (Clark, 1976, 3), which were produced by a cultural group as a stimulus to a satisfactory aesthetic experience (Munro, 1970, 9).

To interpret the imagery of a work of art and 'decode the cryptograms on the canvas', however, it is not sufficient to study the intentions of the artist; the painter's skill in suggesting must be matched by the public's skill in taking hints (Gombrich, 1972, 168 and 329). As Baxandall (1972) demonstrated for fifteenth-century Italian paintings, a work of art is the product of a social relationship between the painter and the person who asked for a picture, paid for it and used it. The experiences and perceptions of the beholder of a work of art, and his ability to interpret it, are therefore an equally important area of study.

Both of these groups of people, the painter or artist and his patron or public, worked within their own contemporary, commercial, religious, perceptual and social conventions. These cultural conditions were different from those of today, and therefore to understand the messages which a work of art was intended to communicate it is necessary to use what Gombrich calls 'historical imagination' (Gombrich, 1972, 54). It is not only possible, however, to see how the forms and styles of works of art respond to social circumstances; these means of representation can also give an insight to contemporary society. As Baxandall (1972, 152) said,

A society develops its distinctive skills and habits, which have a visual aspect, since the visual sense is the main organ of experience, and these visual skills and habits become part of the medium of the painter: correspondingly, a pictorial style gives access to these visual skills and habits and, through these, to the distinctive social experience. An old picture is the record of visual activity. One has to learn to read it ...

Panofsky developed an iconographical approach to the study of works of art; his aim was to reveal the meaning hidden behind images which were used. He suggested that there were three levels of meaning, and that they were also stages of interpretation. The first level of meaning was primary or natural subject matter. This consisted of identifying 'pure forms' or artistic motifs which represented natural objects and could be understood through daily experience of similar objects. These primary-level motifs could carry secondary or conventional meaning: their arrangement could be understood as a representation of specific themes and concepts. It was at the third level of meaning, the interpretation of intrinsic meaning or content, that a work of art could be studied in its full historical context. This stage involved the establishment of relations between the philosophical, political and religious ideas in a society, and the form and content of art (Panofsky, 1939).

Baxandall (1985) further developed this way of studying art forms. He saw three-way interactions between the object which is produced, the general and specific situations of the individuals involved in its production and the cultural environment. He was particularly concerned that distinctions be made both between the general cultural environment and the specific conditions which affected commissioning and painting a picture, and also between the conditions of which the artists and their patrons or clients were conscious and those of which they were unaware. Geertz, too, was concerned with placing art in its sociological context; art is a subset of culture and 'a theory of art is thus at the same time a theory of culture'. He recommended a move from the study of signs as means of communication and codes to be deciphered, to a consideration of them as modes of thought and idiom to be interpreted (1983, 109 and 120).

In 1972, Gombrich wrote that it is possible to:

experience vicariously the very process of creation, the virtuoso's control over his medium and that awareness of essentials which makes him cut out all redundancies because he can rely on a public that will play the game and knows how to take a hint. The social context in which this happens has hardly been investigated. The artist creates his own elite, and the elite its own artists.

It is well to remember, though, that this give and take is not confined to the sacred precincts of art [paintings]. Wherever the image is used for communication, we can study that assessment of probable intention and the tests of consistency that lead to interpretation and illusion. (1972, 196)

4

A map is a value-laden image which is used for communication (Mitchell, 1986, 9–14). The theme of this book is to see how the work of such art historians as Gombrich, Baxandall and Panofsky can be applied to the history of cartography, to see how a map can be placed in its cultural context.

Communication by maps

As with pictures, symbols and codes on maps reflect their cultural environment; the need is to discover both the cultural, religious and political circumstances of this environment and the nature of the information to be transmitted and recorded (Delano Smith, 1989, 92). The 'code' of a map image can be seen as all the marks of which it is made up, such as conventional signs, written captions, place-names and the decorative elements of its design. Harley (1983, 35) said that: 'To understand the symbolic message of a map, it is necessary to reconstruct both the code employed by the map-maker and the precise historical context in which it was used.' Ehrensvärd (1987), for example, saw cartography as 'a culturally based means of mediating environmental experience through symbolism', and showed how the changing use of colour on maps can be a revealing indicator of cultural change. Similarly, Delano Smith (1985) stressed the need to understand the purpose and content of a map in order to begin to explain the symbols on it. She showed that there is a great variety of ways in which the cartographer has tried to convey messages to the map user; the methods, which use a combination of words, pictorial and abstract signs, do not develop in a simple way. One approach has been to regard the development of forms of representation from pictures of an object to more abstract symbolism as evolutionary. This evolution has been related to the development of the use of symbols by children (Gerber, 1984; Wood, 1977, 161), and to link pre-scientific cartography with art (Gombrich, 1982, 184; Rees, 1980, 62).

Maps, like pictures, can be read as texts (Harley, 1988a, 75; McKenzie, 1986, 34–7), even though neither present their component features in a logical sequence. This sequence, however, was considered as an essential component of 'language' by Robinson and Petchenik in their study of maps as a system of communication (1976, 50). Despite semantic problems, the value of the textual approach is that it focuses attention on the message and the information to be mapped (Guelke, 1977 and 1979; Head, 1984, 19). Maps are seen as social constructions rather than as mere products of a set of technical processes, and thus the effects of making and using maps in different historical societies can be examined: how have maps influenced ideas, experiences, events and issues (Harley, 1989a)? For example, it is important not to over-stress the planimetric accuracy of a map which may have been drawn to convey a message other than precise areas; it may be more useful to study such features as the general layout of a landowner's estates, the distribution of settlements or the location of rivers and upland areas.

Maps can be seen as part of a continuum of which views, prospects and landscape paintings form a part. Both stem from fifteenth-century discoveries which enabled the expression of an awareness of space, of mapping in terms of coordinates and of perspective painting; artists and cartographers were aware of each other's techniques and could practise each other's art (Sack, 1986, 85–6). Schulz (1978) has shown how Jacopo de' Barbari's 1500 woodcut view of Venice was not simply drawn as a guide to the city or as a factual record of its topography: distortions in the view and its decoration provide a 'visual metaphor for the Venetian state'; the 'map' is a symbol of the city and communicates a message about its size, wealth, and political and commercial power. A few decades later in Cologne, Braun and Hogenberg's *Civitates Orbis Terrarum* (1573–98) combined 'mapped views' and words to describe sixteenth-century European towns, economy and society (Nuti, 1988). Alpers (1983) has demonstrated how seventeenth-century Dutch art and maps both reflect a distinctive system of conventions, metaphors, intellectual assumptions and cultural practices, and she stresses the value of investigating the similarities between these forms of representation. Likewise, both English maps and landscape painting show with similar techniques and iconography the virtues of landed property, military control, imperial might, commercial travel and tourism (Alfrey and Daniels, 1990, vii). Late seventeenth-century prospect paintings were large, six by four feet or more, and prominently displayed to impress visitors with their host's nearby and distant properties. The view would be centred on the mansion and gardens, with the prospect of the rest of the estate and its environs (Daniels, 1990). Thus Jan Siberecht's prospect of Cheveley Park, Cambridgeshire, painted in 1681 and now displayed in Belvoir Castle, fulfilled much the same role as the map of the Cheveley estate which was made nearly one hundred years later in 1775 (CHG77501).[1]

Because of the differences between maps and pictures, however, the methodology of study of cartographic works must be adapted. Maps give information about invariant features of an area; elements such as lighting conditions are not important (Gombrich, 1982, 183). These features are represented by conventional signs rather than by real appearances, and, in general, the symbols are set in a framework constructed by careful surveying to attain a uniform scale (Harvey, 1980, 10). Harley (1985, 33) adapted Panofsky's iconographical approach as a basis for his examination of the reflection of culture in maps and the impact and influence which they had on society; Harley's three levels of meaning overlap and interact. At the primary level of meaning he substituted landscape features for Panofsky's natural objects, and conventional signs for artistic motifs. These signs and features can be understood irrespective of the place which they are representing, just as artistic motifs carry meaning independent from the composition of a particular picture. The spatial arrangement of signs denotes a specific place, the cartographic equivalent of Panofsky's secondary level of meaning, where factual questions are asked about a map and its practical uses. Harley's third level of meaning was reconstruction of the interpretation by groups in contemporary society of the symbolic values of images on maps. Here the combination of signs, decoration and blank spaces on maps can be seen as, for example, expressions of political power. Harley showed how these three levels can be applied to maps of many types and scales (1983, 23–31).

Thus, by adopting concepts which have been developed in the history of art, there has been an emphasis in the history of cartography on how the information shown on a map depends on the context in which it was drawn, and it is possible to start to place a map into this context.

Communication of power

Historians of cartography have increasingly concentrated upon the message and information to be mapped; for example, they search for social forces that have structured cartography and locate the presence of power and its effects in all of map knowledge (Harley, 1989b, 2). Territoriality is a basic geographic expression of influence and power (Sack, 1986, 216). Maps define and represent territory, as is demonstrated in the study of the transformation in North America of native Indian land into Euro-American territory (Boelhower, 1988), and then in the eighteenth century, of colonial holdings into the American nation; Clarke (1988) demonstrated how the cartouches on these later maps were integral to the sheet and were powerful ideological symbols. Harley (1988b) examined maps as a form of political discourse. For example, the Spanish and Portuguese set up complex bureaucratic systems to regulate trade and knowledge about their empires, and maps became highly secret documents (Broc, 1986, 44; Harley, 1988b, 61). At the same time, however, the Portuguese were capable of producing very elaborately decorated charts which their king gave to persons he wanted to honour or impress. Despite the prohibitions and attempts to enforce secrecy, therefore, Portuguese decorative charts were made and sold all over Europe (Quinn, 1986, 247). In France, too, maps expressed power. Konvitz (1987) showed how mapping the nation between 1660 and 1848 corresponded to the same rational purpose as mapping an estate: geodetic measurement, cartographic representation of landforms and synthesis of statistics in thematic maps were all ways of claiming possession and asserting knowledge, and functioned as instruments of control.

Maps were therefore not merely passive reflections of changes in the politico-economic order in Europe (Mukerji, 1983, 129). Indeed, Mukerji (1984) demonstrated how cartographic works reinforced patterns of control in Europe; this was shown by using 12 maps and a title-page to an atlas, drawn between the Middle Ages and the end of the seventeenth century. Maps could show authority: a sixteenth-century Doge of Venice hung a *mappa mundi* and a map of Italy in the anteroom to his audience chamber. This impressed upon waiting visitors the extent of the state's dominion and the unity of the world of which it was a part (Schulz, 1987, 116). At a similar time in England, maps were displayed in the Privy Gallery at Whitehall, where courtiers had little to do other than look and be impressed by the King's knowledge of his realms, depictions of his victories and his wise patronage of the best astronomers, artists and cartographers of the age (Barber, 1985). In the seventeenth century, Samuel Pepys, a governor of Christ's Hospital, was asked:

to get some historian painter to draw a fair Table representing his Majesty and some Chief Ministers of the State, The Lord Mayor, The President and some Governors, and the Children of his Majesty's Royall Foundation: a Ship, Globes, Maps, Mathematicall Instruments, and such other things as may well express his Majesty's Royall Foundation and bounty to his Hospitall.

The painting, by Antonio Verrio, was finished in 1688 and hung in the Hospital's hall (Croft-Murray, 1962, 56).

Globes were also used to show power and, from the sixteenth century, they were increasingly frequently owned by the English landowning classes. Depictions of globes were used in decoration: in the gallery at Little Moreton Hall in Cheshire, for example, are sixteenth-century plasterwork renderings of Destiny and Fortune. Destiny holds aloft the sphere in one hand, and in the other hand she clasps a pair of open dividers; Fortune, blindfolded and balancing on a globe, is impartial, has power over the world and is also unstable (National Trust, 1986, 22).

Silences on maps could also demonstrate power. Maps which showed the authority of the landowning classes, for example, often omitted evidence of rural poverty. Thus Thomas Clay's plan of the manor of Great Bookham, Surrey, in 1614 to 1617 did not show the hovels of landless labourers (Harvey, 1966, 282). Similarly, in eighteenth-century English county atlases, the inclusion of charity schools was the only indication of the less affluent classes of English society (Harley, 1988c). Konvitz (1988) showed how the first national map survey of France, in the eighteenth century, omitted topographic detail and characteristics of landforms and settlements which made places distinctive. This concept of a uniform space influenced the design of the new administrative system in France in 1790.

The cartography of sixteenth and seventeenth-century England can be used to show an increased power of the land. Christopher Saxton, an Elizabethan surveyor, was employed by Thomas Seckford, a Master of the Court of Requests, to map the counties of England and Wales for the Queen and her government. Sheets for individual counties were engraved and printed from 1574 to 1578, and the complete atlas was published in 1579 (Tyacke and Huddy, 1980). The relative importance of patron and monarch over surveyor is demonstrated by Seckford's arms appearing on all of the sheets, the royal insignia on all except the first sheet, but Saxton's name first appearing on the 26th sheet. The presence of the royal arms shows that the maps are the Queen's, they depict her land, and her sovereignty over her kingdom as a whole and over each of its provinces. In subsequent printings of Saxton's work, however, and in later maps by Norden, Camden, Speed and Drayton, the space which is given to the royal arms is progressively reduced. There is increased attention to the land itself and a strengthened sense of local identity with it. For example, arms of local gentry and town plans appear together with the royal arms. The texts which accompany, or are accompanied by, these maps similarly move from a chronicle history of the kings of England to a chorographical description of land by locality and region, with an increased emphasis on individuals, their pedigrees and their private property (Helgerson, 1986). Similarly, the completion of the fen drainage project was marked by a map of the whole Bedford Level by the Surveyor-General, Jonas Moore. The map, produced in about 1658, had the coats of arms of members of the Company around the edge and gave an impression of the success of the drainage and of the competence and importance of the surveyor. However, only one copy of this edition is known to survive; most of the members of the Company were Cromwellians, so after 1660 there was no longer the same desire to display their identities, the coats of arms around the margins of the map were erased and the 1684 edition, with its blank spaces, is much more common (Willmoth, 1990, 132–7). Thus maps, combined with pictures and writings, helped to show the power of the land, and of those who owned it.

Although it is possible to demonstrate how maps were used to show the power of the land in Italy, France and England, the same was not true in the Netherlands, where maps reflected a different cultural system. Here, mapping was part of an impulse to record or describe the land, which was shared by artists, surveyors, printers and the public. The system of landownership in the Netherlands led to weak seigneurial power and a large number of very small landowners, and contemporary maps and prints reflect this. Seats were not expression of wealth and authority, and the Dutch were far more interested in being represented in portraits of themselves, their houses and the pleasures of life (Alpers, 1983, 151). For example, Rembrandt's etching 'The Goldweighers Field' of 1651 was probably drawn when he visited the country house of one of his unpaid creditors. Rembrandt showed the land, churches, towns, trees and grass, and the estate, but this last feature was added almost incidentally (Alpers, 1987, 82).

These examples show how maps, as works of art, were used as a means of communication by contemporary society. Maps, however, make abstractions from reality in a particular way, and the above examples also demonstrate that to interpret a map as a social product, a number of questions which are unique to cartographic art forms need to be asked. For example, what practical purpose did a map serve, what topographical information did it show, was it necessary to give accurate planimetric information, what was a map's history of production and publication, who were the surveyors and how did a map relate to contemporary interests in science and land measuring?

These methodological works and examples of their application, therefore, show that it can be useful to study the interaction between maps and the society which commissioned and produced them. This book shows how it is possible to adopt the iconographical, 'textual', approach, of which Harley is a major exponent, to the study of rural estate maps, and also examines the extent to which Baxandall's methodology can be adapted to the study of maps. It demonstrates how estate maps reflect and affect contemporary society, and how distinctions can be drawn between the general cultural environment and the specific conditions which affect a map's commission. It discusses who were the map-producers and map-users, how the interests of a particular patron affected the type of map which was drawn, how this particular type of map fits into contemporary cartographical developments, and how some of the requests were explicit whilst others were assumed by both patron and map-maker. At the same time, however, one must be very cautious about interpreting past cultures and inferring more about a map than was originally intended, either explicitly or implicitly.

ESTATE MAPS AND THEIR CULTURAL SETTING

Estate maps are defined as maps which were drawn primarily to show an individual's landed property (Wallis and Robinson, 1987, 97), and they are studied here to show how they can be related to their social and historical background, how they reflect this environment and contribute to its change. The extent to which they were drawn for the practical management of estates, to help in processes of emparking and inclosure and to settle legal disputes is investigated. Furthermore, it is shown that they also demonstrated the authority of the landowner, his class and his attitude to the land, as was suggested by Harley (1983, 37), and how they contributed to the maintenance of a social structure based on the land and played a role in the history of agrarian class relations (Harley 1988d, 284). Estate maps have been described in many places and used as sources to answer questions ranging from the nature of field systems and agricultural land use to river channel changes. An examination of these maps in relation to their cultural setting affects their use and interpretation as an historical source.

It has already been demonstrated that estate maps are usually manuscript (Baker and Butlin, 1973, 11), though some printed maps do exist, such as Peter Chassereau's map of John Fenner's estate near Ipswich, Suffolk in 1745 (Mason, 1989, 4), or, more commonly, those which accompany nineteenth-century particulars of sale. They have been drawn to depict urban, rural and industrial areas at a range of scales, but usually at three or six chains to the inch (1:3,168 or 1:6,336). The most detailed maps can show buildings such as houses, churches, inns, schools, farm buildings, pounds and windmills, parks, gardens, orchards, woodland and trees, land quality and a number of other features. The maps may be decorated with a vignette of the manor house or church, the landlord's coat of arms, animals in the park, and elaborate title cartouches, scale bars and compass roses (see, for example, Plates 1, 6 and 17a). This study shows how the type and amount of information drawn on rural estate maps varies with the reasons for their commission and the scale at which they were drawn.

Estate plans were produced by many different societies. Buisseret (1988) has investigated how the differing economic base and social structure of areas of North America gave rise to various types of map, of which the estate plan is only one example. In the Midwest, for example, settlement was preceded by a meticulous government survey, so there was no need for any individual to employ a surveyor to plot his estate, which was usually very small. In South Carolina, on the other hand, the conditions for production of estate plans were very favourable. There was no pre-existing large-scale cartographic coverage, there were prosperous tobacco and rice plantations, and the landowning population was large and educated. Many owners had links with the West Indies, where a large number of estate plans was produced. In colonial Mexico, too, estate plans were drawn to delimit property rights and territories, and many of the plans show the influence of the indigenous, Indian, iconography (Gruzinski, 1988, 61–2). They provide civil, fiscal and secular records of Indian life, and some include genealogies drawn to represent the ownership of land or houses (Glass, 1975, 36–7). In other instances, detailed cadastral registers were kept which recorded field dimensions and shape, soil type and tenure, which could be transformed into maps (Williams, 1984). Jamaica was another colonial society which produced estate maps, partly because eighteenth-century absentee proprietors resident in Great Britain were anxious to be able to picture their plantations. Demand for plans of new and restructured plantations continued well into the nineteenth century as the spread of population through Jamaica continued unabated (Higman, 1988b).

This book looks at rural estate map production in early modern England, and how the production of estate maps increased despite the continued production of many map-less surveys, which has been noted by Andrews (1985, 8) among others. It describes why estates were surveyed and mapped, how the maps which were produced reflect the reasons for their commission, and how these maps and surveys influenced landowners in the ways they thought about their land.

A CASE-STUDY OF ESTATE MAPS OF CAMBRIDGESHIRE

By studying one type of estate map in one geographical region, it has been possible to examine them in detail. In this book, the definition of estate maps by Wallis and Robinson (1987, 97) has been narrowed to maps which were drawn primarily to show the land of up to three landowners. Though this figure is arbitrary, it is precise. It is easy to determine separate estates in maps which show the land of a few people, whereas maps which depict the property of many owners do not usually show areas of land which belong to any one person in an immediately accessible form. Only maps of rural estates have been considered as they demonstrate clearly both the practical and symbolic aspects of mapping; urban estates were usually mapped for other reasons and a different genre of map was the result.

The Tithe Commutation Act of 1836 caused large areas of England and Wales to be mapped at a similar scale to estate maps (Kain and Prince, 1985, 86). The character of subsequent maps of landholdings changed, because much reliance was placed on tithe maps. Therefore, 1836 was chosen as the terminus for the study and for the definition of the area to be examined.

Cambridgeshire was chosen for two main reasons. In the first place, the date and nature of local maps reflects the differences between the fenland north of the county and the higher land to the south (Holderness, 1984). Secondly, as many of the colleges of Cambridge University owned land in the county, there is potential for contrast between private and institutional landowners, who had similar and differing reasons for commissioning estate maps.

To facilitate a study in depth of rural estate maps of Cambridgeshire and to enable general conclusions to be drawn about the relations between maps and contemporary economy and society, a carto-bibliography of all rural estate maps of Cambridgeshire was needed. Carto-bibliographies for other areas already existed, though they are either of maps in one particular local collection, such as a county record office (Emmison, 1947, 1952, 1964 and 1968; Hull, 1973), or of all local or manuscript maps for an area (Nichols, 1980 and 1987; Steer, 1962 and 1968). A comparable listing for Cambridgeshire forms Appendix 2 of this volume.

The history of estate mapping in Cambridgeshire is examined from three angles. First, the study looks at the maps themselves, to show how mapping grew and altered between the earliest, late sixteenth-century, maps and those which were produced in the 1830s. Changes in the number of maps which were produced, in the techniques of presentation of cartographic and topographic information, in the decoration of maps and their accuracy, are related to general and particular social and economic changes. Second, the surveyors of estate maps are examined to demonstrate how the careers of those who practised in Cambridgeshire can be related to the growth of the surveying profession in the county, to national developments in the profession and to contemporary society. The third part of the book looks at the men who commissioned estate maps, to show how landowners' knowledge grew of science, surveying and cartography, and the ways in which their increased awareness of maps is reflected in the reasons for which they were drawn and used.

It is therefore possible to examine the degree to which estate maps can be seen as part of the general interest in maps, property, wealth and power of early modern England, and how these maps affected the changing nature, composition, interests and influence of contemporary society.

Chapter 3

CAMBRIDGESHIRE AND ITS ESTATE MAPS

To analyse characteristics of rural estate maps of a specific area of the United Kingdom and place them in their cultural context, it is first necessary to discuss the contemporary economy and society of the area. Thus, this chapter starts with a description of Cambridgeshire and its social, political and economic development in the early modern period; Fig. 3.1 shows the county, at the western edge of East Anglia, and its extent in 1836 (which remained largely unchanged until 1974). Then national developments in estate mapping are outlined, so as to provide a background for a discussion of changes in mapping activity in the county. Having set the scene, it will be possible to study the estate maps which were produced.

A detailed examination of Cambridgeshire rural estate maps starts with a description of the carto-bibliography. Secondly, the representativeness is determined of the sample which was studied, by examining the survival of the maps. Then, the dates at which maps were drawn, the areas of Cambridgeshire which were mapped at various times and the size of estate and how it changed over time are discussed. A number of factors are examined: techniques of presentation, especially the use of scale, orientation and tables; decoration; and map accuracy. This last section considers both planimetric accuracy, accuracy of the scale bar and north point and the care with which acreages on tables have been added up, and accuracy of topographical, especially architectural, information. For all of these themes, there is discussion of contrasts between dates, areas of the county, different types of landowner and uses for maps. Where possible, results are related to developments elsewhere in the country. Thus the relation is shown between estate maps and more general economic and social changes from sixteenth to early nineteenth-century England.

THE SOCIAL, POLITICAL AND ECONOMIC DEVELOPMENT OF CAMBRIDGESHIRE

The characteristics of Cambridgeshire varied across the county; this section describes them and gives an introduction to the social, political and economic changes which occurred during the early modern period. Further discussion of the changing nature of Cambridgeshire and contrasts between its regions will be found at appropriate places throughout the book.

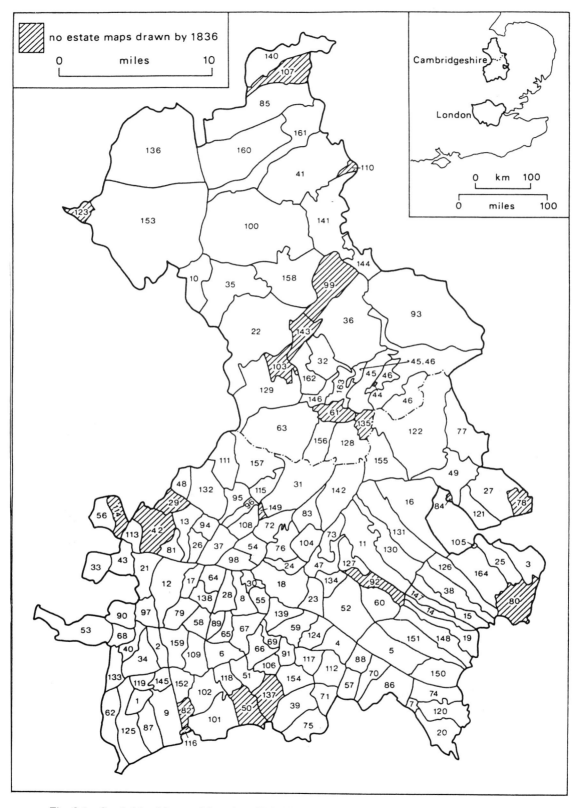

Fig. 3.1. Cambridgeshire parishes in 1836 (Fenland parishes are north of the broken line; upland parishes are to the south).

Key to parishes in Fig. 3.1

	Parish				
1	Abington Pigotts	55	Grantchester	110	Outwell
2	Arrington	56	Graveley	111	Over
3	Ashley cum Silverley	57	Great Abington	112	Pampisford
4	Babraham	58	Great Eversden	113	Papworth Everard
5	Balsham	59	Great Shelford	114	Papworth St Agnes
6	Barrington	60	Great Wilbraham	115	Rampton
7	Bartlow	61	Grunty Fen	116	Royston
8	Barton	62	Guilden Morden	117	Sawston
9	Bassingbourn	63	Haddenham	118	Shepreth
10	Benwick	64	Hardwick	119	Shingay
11	Bottisham	65	Harlton	120	Shudy Camps
12	Bourn	66	Harston	121	Snailwell
13	Boxworth	67	Haslingfield	122	Soham
14	Brinkley	68	Hatley St George	123	Stanground
15	Burrough Green	69	Hauxton	124	Stapleford
16	Burwell	70	Hildersham	125	Steeple Morden
17	Caldecote	71	Hinxton	126	Stetchworth
18	Cambridge	72	Histon	127	Stow cum Quy
19	Carlton cum Willingham	73	Horningsea	128	Stretham
20	Castle Camps	74	Horseheath	129	Sutton
21	Caxton	75	Ickleton	130	Swaffham Bulbeck
22	Chatteris	76	Impington	131	Swaffham Prior
23	Cherry Hinton	77	Isleham	132	Swavesey
24	Chesterton	78	Kennett	133	Tadlow
25	Cheveley	79	Kingston	134	Teversham
26	Childerley	80	Kirtling	135	Thetford
27	Chippenham	81	Knapwell	136	Thorney
28	Comberton	82	Kneesworth	137	Thriplow
29	Conington	83	Landbeach	138	Toft
30	Coton	84	Landwade	139	Trumpington
31	Cottenham	85	Leverington	140	Tydd St Giles
32	Coveney	86	Linton	141	Upwell
33	Croxton	87	Litlington	142	Waterbeach
34	Croydon cum Clopton	88	Little Abington	143	Welches Dam
35	Doddington	89	Little Eversden	144	Welney
36	Downham	90	Little Gransden	145	Wendy
37	Dry Drayton	91	Little Shelford	146	Wentworth
38	Dullingham	92	Little Wilbraham	147	Westley Waterless
39	Duxford St John and St Peter	93	Littleport	148	Weston Colville
40	East Hatley	94	Lolworth	149	Westwick
41	Elm	95	Long Stanton All Saints'	150	West Wickham
42	Elsworth	96	Long Stanton St Michael	151	West Wratting
43	Eltisley	97	Longstow	152	Whaddon
44	Ely College	98	Madingley	153	Whittlesey
45	Ely St Mary	99	Manea	154	Whittlesford
46	Ely Trinity	100	March	155	Wicken
47	Fen Ditton	101	Melbourn	156	Wilburton
48	Fen Drayton	102	Meldreth	157	Willingham
49	Fordham	103	Mepal	158	Wimblington
50	Fowlmere	104	Milton	159	Wimpole
51	Foxton	105	Newmarket All Saints'	160	Wisbech St Mary
52	Fulbourn	106	Newton (near Cambridge)	161	Wisbech St Peter
53	Gamlingay	107	Newton (near Wisbech)	162	Witcham
54	Girton	108	Oakington	163	Witchford
		109	Orwell	164	Woodditton

The landscape of Cambridgeshire

In his *History of the Countryside* (1980, 4–5), Rackham saw Cambridgeshire as typical of one of the two major types of landscape of lowland England:

... there is the Cambridgeshire type of landscape, the England of big villages, few, busy roads, thin hawthorn hedges, windswept brick farms, and ivied clumps of trees in corners of fields; a predictable land of wide views, sweeping sameness, and straight lines ... I call [this] Planned Countryside ... a mass~produced, drawing~board landscape, hurriedly laid out parish by parish under Enclosure Acts in the eighteenth and nineteenth centuries; but occasionally there survive features, notably woods, that the enclosure commissioners failed to destroy.

Defoe described his impressions of this Planned Countryside of Cambridgeshire in the early eighteenth century (1724, 100):

We enter Cambridgeshire out of Suffolk with all the advantage in the world; ... we see a rich and pleasant vale westward, covered with corn~fields, gentlemen's seats, villages, and at a distance, to crown all the rest, that ancient and truly famous town and university of Cambridge; capital of the county.
    ... It [Cambridgeshire] lies on the edge of the great level, called by the people here the fen~country; and great part, if not all, the Isle of Ely, lies in this county and Norfolk. The rest of Cambridgeshire is almost wholly a corn country; and of that corn five parts in six of all they sow, is barley. As Essex, Suffolk, and Norfolk, are taken up in manufacturing, and famed for industry, this county has no manufacture at all; nor are the poor, except the husbandmen, famed for any thing so much as idleness and sloth, to their scandal be it spoken; what the reason of it is, I know not.

A detailed description of Cambridgeshire was given by Postgate (1964) in his examination of local field systems, and his work has formed the basis for much of the present discussion. Postgate divided Cambridgeshire into a number of agricultural regions, based on topography, soils, land use and crops, and in this section distinctions will be drawn between these areas. The main division, as was pointed out by Defoe two hundred years earlier, is between the fenland and the south of the county; this division is shown in Fig. 3.1. The far north of the Isle of Ely, the silt fen area around Leverington, is characterized by narrow parishes which extend from salt marshes and an elongated village site along the Roman Bank in the east to low-lying regularly laid out and drained pastures on the peat fen further inland. The peat fen in the southern part of the Isle has irregularly shaped parishes which share out the limited areas which were not liable to flooding, and nucleated settlements are located on these drier sites (Spufford, 1974, 12). Parishes such as Haddenham and Cottenham, on the margins of the fens, have some of the earliest settlement sites in the county (Postgate, 1964, 88); their villages are typically aligned along the street which leads from the upland arable areas into the fenland pastures.

Parishes in the upland part of Cambridgeshire are smaller: for all of the county, the most common parish size is 1,000–4,999 acres, but whilst 83 % of southern parishes are of this extent, only about half of fenland parishes fall into this range. Similarly, the smaller size of southern parishes is shown by the number of large parishes in the two areas: 0.8 % of southern parishes are larger than 10,000 acres whereas 23 % of fenland parishes exceed this size.

Variations can be seen between these smaller southern parishes. The open chalk regions of central southern Cambridgeshire, of which Thriplow is an example, have nucleated villages in the centres of the parishes. Before inclosure, these villages were surrounded by three or four comparatively large and uniformly sized open fields (Postgate, 1964, 87). To the east, parishes in the south-eastern boulder clay area around Dullingham are elongated so as to provide both arable and downland on the chalk in the north-west and meadow and woodland on the boulder clay soils to the south-east. The protracted process of reclamation from the formerly extensive woodland cover is reflected in small hamlets scattered throughout such parishes as Castle Camps (Postgate, 1964, 9). Finally, in western Cambridgeshire, there are heavy clay soils; parishes are arranged so that they have their share of alluvial meadows and chalk downland (for example, Kingston and Toft), and there are nucleated settlements. In the far west, the 'dairy' parishes such as Croydon, East Hatley and Tadlow have extensive pasture areas.

Demographic and social changes

The population figures for Cambridgeshire reflect the distinction between the fenland north and upland south and the degree to which it was possible to expand the cultivated area. From 1086 to 1801, the population of the fenland showed a marked and continuous growth. Expansion was less marked during the economic stagnation of the fifteenth century, but the revival of agricultural prosperity in the sixteenth and early seventeenth centuries and the systematic drainage of the fens led to renewed rates of population increase. On the other hand, in many of the upland parishes the maximum extent of the cultivated area had been reached by the thirteenth century; the overall population increase was only 13% between 1086 and 1801 and fewer than half of the parishes doubled their populations between these dates. By the sixteenth century, there were still 51 parishes with fewer inhabitants than at the time of the Domesday survey (Postgate, 1964, 128–31). Agricultural depression and emigration were partly responsible for a decrease in the population of the entire county by over 10% in the first half of the eighteenth century (Deane and Cole, 1967, 105). Even the general agricultural progress of the late eighteenth century, with enhanced opportunities for commercial agriculture and improved communications, did not prevent the population of 18 of these 51 parishes declining further by 1801. By the early nineteenth century, however, population levels in the south were increasing: the average population in villages increased from 300 to 700 between 1770 and 1851. Indeed, the overall population growth of 111% in upland Cambridgeshire between 1801 and 1851 was more than that in any other primarily agricultural county (Postgate, 1964, 131 and 285).

As part of these changing population levels, there was also a change in the type of landowner. Cambridgeshire has never been a county with many large landed estates: this can be seen from its position among the counties which had fewest medieval parks (Cantor, 1983, 3). Until the eighteenth century, however, Cambridgeshire had a strong gentry community,

MAGDALEN COLLEGE LIBRARY

typical of a south-eastern Shire county. Except for the Civil War period, when the county was largely Parliamentarian, small county families represented the area in Parliament and there was friendly political rivalry between them (Darby, 1948b, 411). At the end of the seventeenth century, there was a nation-wide population decrease among the aristocracy when the class failed to reproduce itself. This was partly a result of a tendency to marry late and have fewer children and partly from a reluctance to marry at all. The effect upon Cambridgeshire, where, as has been shown, there was also a local demographic crisis in the south of the county, was marked. Elsewhere, new aristocratic communities grew up, but in southern Cambridgeshire the power vacuum was filled by a few magnates (Jenkins, 1984). The most notable of these newcomers to local society were the Yorkes (Earls of Hardwicke) of Wimpole, the Bromleys (later Lords Montfort) of Horseheath and the 6th Duke of Somerset (Hore, 1899, 60–6). The Manners family (Dukes of Rutland), of Cheveley, acquired the Somerset estate by marriage (Gardner, 1851, 27). By the fourth decade of the eighteenth century these families had become established, and their influence is shown by the results of the general elections of 1741 and 1747. As a consequence of these elections, the political history of the county became one of unconcealed rivalry between the aristocratic families of Hardwicke and Rutland (Darby, 1948b, 412). The Rutland family had an ally in John Mortlock, future banker to the University, who in 1784 was returned as Member of Parliament for Cambridge. He was either mayor or deputy mayor from 1785 to 1809 and was a very influential figure (Cam, 1939).

The influence of the Earls of Hardwicke can be seen from developments of their Wimpole estate. This was almost the only estate in the county where ownership of a sufficiently large and unified block of land enabled the layout of an extensive formal landscape; indeed, relatively few landowners in the country were in such a position (Williamson and Bellamy, 1987, 144). The 1st Earl of Hardwicke rebuilt the parish church in 1748 to fit in with the architecture of the hall (Williamson and Bellamy, 1987, 176), and this, together with the creation of an informal landscape by Capability Brown for the 2nd Earl from 1767 to 1772 (*VCH*, 5, 265), demonstrated their power and control in the county. At this time, it was fashionable for the landed elite to hide away evidence of productive agriculture; by the end of the century, however, styles were changing. The 3rd Earl inherited the estate in 1790 and took a great interest in new ideas in farming; he commissioned John Soane to remodel the hall and to design a new Home Farm (National Trust, 1983, 11), and, in the first decade of the nineteenth century, he employed Humphry Repton, who believed a landscaped park should demonstrate an owner's paternalistic role in the rural community and considered farmland to be intrinsically beautiful (Williamson and Bellamy, 1987, 151).

The rivalry and dominance of a few large owners continued into the nineteenth century: in 1829, only 186 proprietors paid more than £20 land tax and in only 37 out of 126 places was one owner responsible for more than half of the total tax paid (Postgate, 1964, 151). In 1860, Cambridgeshire was the county with the fourth lowest number of county families (Walford, 1860). Under 4% of owners in 1874 had estates of more than 500 acres; the largest landowner was the Earl of Hardwicke who owned nearly 19,000 acres scattered among 12 parishes; the Earl and the Duke of Bedford together owned nearly 7% of the county (Postgate, 1964, 152). In 1883, Cambridgeshire was one of the five counties with the lowest proportion of its land area occupied by properties of great landowners (the others were Middlesex, Essex, Herefordshire and Kent), and, with Cumberland, it was the county with the lowest percentage of land owned by the gentry (Clemenson, 1982, 21–2). There were, however, large numbers of small owners; in 1829, 35 % of landowners paid less than ten shillings in land tax, and in 1874, half of the proprietors possessed estates of less than one acre and 73 % owned estates of less than ten acres (Postgate, 1964, 151).

Conversely, Bateman's *The Great Landowners of Great Britain and Ireland* of 1883 shows that, with Middlesex, Cambridgeshire was the highest-ranking county in terms of area occupied by public and institutional owners in 1883 (Clemenson, 1982, 23). The importance of corporate ownership has a long history: the accumulation of church estates was seen by Postgate (1964, 138) as the most significant development in landownership in Cambridgeshire in the Middle Ages. After the Dissolution, ecclesiastical landholding declined and much of the Dean and Chapter of Ely's land was sold during the Commonwealth. The conventual estate of about 2,200 acres, however, was still one of the largest in the county in 1874, and there were small areas of glebe land in most parishes (Postgate, 1964, 145). Collegiate landowners became increasingly important from the fourteenth century. Typically, after an initial period of reliance on its endowment, a college underwent a short but intensive period of estate building. Benefactions were received, occasional purchases were made and land was exchanged so as to consolidate an estate. For example, in 1529 and 1674 Queens' College, Cambridge exchanged property in Guilden Morden (Cambridgeshire) and Eversleigh (Wiltshire) for land in Great Eversden and Kingston, and in the sixteenth century the College made 21 separate purchases of land in Great Eversden. Once the estate had been built up there were few further acquisitions: the last major area of land to be acquired by Queens' College was 98 acres at Haddenham in 1711 (Postgate, 1964, 148). By 1874, 9 % of the southern part of the county belonged to colleges; the largest owners were the Cambridge colleges of King's, Trinity, St John's, Christ's and Gonville and Caius. Many of their estates were widely scattered. For example, St John's College owned land in 34 parishes, Queens' College in 17 parishes and Jesus College in 16. Thus, although collegiate estates were small, they were present in most parishes, and the influence of these landlords was ubiquitous. Colleges were less important owners in the fenland: in 1546, they were only found in five parishes in the Isle compared with 81 parishes in the south. Corporate interest in the fens came to be dominated by the Bedford Level Corporation (Postgate, 1964, 149–50).

Land tenure

The large number of public and institutional landowners affected land tenure: many landlords were absentee and tenant farmers predominated. There were resident landlords, however, in the few country houses and as owner-occupiers of smallholdings. Copyhold tenures were still frequently found as late as the end of the eighteenth century, though leases were becoming increasingly common. Many of these leases were short-term; in 1794, Vancouver studied the tenure of the largest farm in 51 parishes. He found that 20 farms were on 21-year leases, but 23 were held at will. Tenancy-at-will was also found in all of the farms in 14 of the 18 parishes where he noted the conditions of all of the tenancies (1794, 198). In 1811, Gooch similarly found few leases (1811, 38). Leases which were granted by absentee corporate landlords were exceptional; these owners were more concerned with the maintenance of tenure than with maximizing returns from their estates (Postgate, 1964, 163–5). The 1576 Corn Rent Act, which stipulated that one-third of the rent had to be paid either in wheat and malt barley or in cash at the current market value of wheat and malt, safeguarded colleges from the effects of fluctuating price levels (Aylmer, 1986, 535). Typically, colleges let their land for 21 years, with a low annual rent, high entry fine and strict, conservative, farming covenants. By the end of the eighteenth century, as collegiate landlords became more interested in their estates, they increasingly converted their leases to rack rents, which were much more sensitive to market fluctuations (Howard, 1935, 114–15).

Tenurial conditions varied across the county. In the south, especially in the central chalk area, there was relatively strong manorial control and tenant farmers predominated: 84 % of the land tax in 1829 was paid by tenant farmers; owner-occupiers were numerous but they only held small estates. For example, at Melbourn 84 owner-occupiers paid 14 % of the tax, 64 tenants paid the remainder. In the parishes at the fen margins, small owner-occupiers were almost as important as tenant farmers. In Cottenham in 1691, for example, 26 of the 83 holdings were of less than five acres and only four were larger than 50 acres. In 1829, 141 owner-occupiers paid 84 % of the tax. The fenland area, similarly, had a large number of small owners, especially in the silt fen where commoners had acquired holdings during draining and inclosing in the seventeenth and eighteenth centuries; in Tydd St Giles, 28 of the 60 owners in 1874 had holdings of less than ten acres, and only five owned more than 200 acres (Postgate, 1964, 166–8).

Economic changes

These demographic characteristics and tenurial conditions cannot be considered in isolation from changes in agriculture and land use. By the late thirteenth century, the regional pattern of agriculture was well developed. Arable farming was especially important in the south of the county, which was renowned as a granary. There was a flourishing trade in the export of corn both through King's Lynn and down the Lea valley to London, and barley was in especially high demand for the malting markets of Royston, Ware and London. High agricultural prices during the Napoleonic Wars stimulated the conversion of upland heath areas to arable farming. In the early nineteenth century, wheat and barley dominated the upland and accounted for over 60 % of the cropped area of the central chalk area and lower Cam valley, and for over 50 % of the clay areas to the west, east and on the fen margins. As heavy soils were less suitable for grains, oats were also grown in these clay areas. It was only in the fenland, though, that oats were more important than wheat and barley. By 1801, rye was limited to the poorer soils of central and south-eastern upland areas, and nowhere did it account for more than 10% of the cropped area. The depression of 1815 to 1837 led to rural distress of which the riots in Ely and Littleport in 1816 and 1830 were a part. Thereafter, the final upsurge of inclosure, increased tile drainage on clay soils, the introduction of marling in the fens, and the use of four-course crop rotations all stimulated agricultural production (Postgate, 1964, 200–6).

Postgate also described the cultivation of fodder crops and artificial grasses (1964, 207–13). Peas and beans were the main fodder crop; they accounted for over 20% of the sown acreage of heavy soils in the western clay area and in the lower Cam valley and were equal with the major corn crops in 1801. On the lighter soils of central and south-eastern Cambridgeshire, they covered less than 10% of the cultivated area. Turnips were grown from the mid-seventeenth century, but they were never of major importance and in 1801 they covered less than 2,500 acres of the county. They were most common in south-eastern Cambridgeshire; neither the central chalk nor the heavy clay soils were suitable for their cultivation. Potatoes were grown in most parishes, asparagus and other vegetables for export to Cambridge and London were cultivated in the Ely and Waterbeach areas, and onions were grown in the northern fenland. In general, therefore, small acreages of fodder crops were grown on gravel soils in the lower Cam valley, the fen-marginal areas and islands in the fens. The most important area, however, was the fully drained fens, where cole-seed, rape-seed, onions, peas and oats were cultivated (Butlin, 1990a, 65); the Wisbech area in the silt fen accounted for over half of the total acreage of fodder crops in the county in the early nineteenth century. Artificial grasses were also introduced in the seventeenth century; their value as temporary leys in the open fields was especially useful in the central chalk area where natural grazing was scarce. Sainfoin was well suited to the thin dry soils of this region, and improved the value of some land from five to 30 shillings per acre in the early nineteenth century. The peat fens were sources of turf for fuel and housing material (turbary) and sedge (Butlin, 1990a, 73). Industrial crops were cultivated in various parts of the county: saffron was grown in the upland areas in the later eighteenth century, especially around Cherry Hinton, woad and flax were grown in the fens, and Defoe (1724, 417) described the cultivation of hemp: 'Here are the greatest improvements by planting of hemp, that, I think, is to be seen in England; particularly on the Norfolk and Cambridge side of the Fens, as about Wisbech, Well, and several other places where we saw many hundred acres of ground bearing great crops of hemp.'

Pastoral farming was practised throughout the county (Holderness, 1984, 198). Sheep were reared on heathlands and commons in the upland areas and on fattening grounds in the fens. In 1794, over 1,000 sheep per parish were found in the south-eastern boulder clay, southern chalk and fen-marginal regions. Cattle rearing and fattening was most important in the 'dairies' in the west of the county, where in 1750 there were 3,211 acres of pasture land and 1,217 acres of arable: between 200 and 300 head of cattle were reared per parish for the Cambridge and London markets; this was the only part of the county with relatively easy road communication to London. Cattle and horses were also grazed on fen pastures (Butlin, 1990a, 57). Cheese and butter production was important in parishes such as Cottenham, Soham, Waterbeach, Landbeach and Over on the edges of the fens, and fishing and fowling for the London market were extensively practised in the fens themselves; Defoe (1724, 416–17) described the duck decoys, the number of which was 'incredible'.

Agricultural production was affected by reclamation and inclosure. In the sixteenth, seventeenth and eighteenth centuries, most inclosure was piecemeal. Less than 1% of the total area of the county was inclosed in the sixteenth century; in the following century, however, more common land was inclosed than in any other period except for the first three decades of the nineteenth century. These inclosures resulted in an increased food supply, the introduction of new crops, new rotations and an expansion of the market. There was little effect on the central chalk areas, where a shortage of common grazing meant that common land was jealously guarded (Postgate, 1964, 257). Inclosure and reclamation of heathland made some progress in parishes such as Weston Colville, Fowlmere and West Wratting, though, conversely, land in West Wratting and Swaffham Prior was converted to sheep walk in the early eighteenth century (Postgate, 1964, 104). In the western and eastern clay areas, there was piecemeal reclamation of woodland; by 1794, the remnants of a formerly extensive cover had become so scarce and scattered that Vancouver said that 'few woods afforded less matter for observation than those of Cambridgeshire' (1794, 210). It was the drainage of the fens, however, which resulted in the largest-scale conversion of land to private ownership in the seventeenth century. Lack of coordination between owners of small estates, shortage of capital, inadequate means of drainage and legal difficulties of appropriating large areas of common land to individual ownership had made sixteenth-century projects founder (Butlin, 1990a, 60). Under the General Drainage Act of 1600, landlords were empowered to suppress any common rights which stood in the way of drainage; in 1634 the Earl of Bedford and 13 co-Adventurers contracted to drain 95,000 acres and common rights were extinguished over thousands of acres. The scheme was unpopular: it infringed property rights, losses of common rights were inadequately compensated, local inhabitants had to maintain the works, it damaged the natural ecology and reduced stocks of birds and fish. Success was short-lived as drainage failed to allow for shrinkage of the peat: the thinner peats and most fertile soils were blown away and, despite large numbers of windmills, land was frequently flooded (Rackham, 1986, 390). Despite many subsequent attempts, problems of drainage and its management continued until well into the nineteenth century (Darby, 1983).

In 1675, only three counties in England had lower proportions of land inclosed (Gonner, 1912, 167), and the situation had hardly changed by 1800. In 1794, Vancouver said that three-quarters of the county was uninclosed (Vancouver, 1794, 193), and 17 years later Gooch declared Cambridgeshire to be the worst-farmed county in the country, because of the lateness of inclosure (1811, 56). The first parishes to be inclosed by Parliamentary Act were Abington Pigotts in 1770 and Knapwell in 1775; only 2% of parishes, mostly in the east, were inclosed by 1800. Thereafter numbers increased, first in the western clay areas, then in the eastern clay region and finally in the chalk and fen-marginal areas. Fewer Acts were passed during the agricultural depression; numbers increased once again after 1836. By 1847, Cambridgeshire had almost the same proportion of land inclosed as in most Midland counties. Many of the latest Acts were passed for parishes in the Isle of Ely, though as most of the fenland had been inclosed in the seventeenth century, only 7% of the land area was affected (Postgate, 1964, 272–3).

The lateness of inclosure in Cambridgeshire can be attributed to a number of causes, whose relative importance varied over the county. The soil conditions were favourable to grain production, even during periods such as the sixteenth century when elsewhere in the country there was inclosure and conversion to pasture farming; by 1833, when the majority of parishes had been inclosed, there had been hardly any decline in the amount of arable land. Practices in the open fields were flexible: they could accommodate mixed corn crops, pulses and extension of ley farming without needing inclosure (Postgate, 1964, 275). The thin dry soils were unsuitable for the introduction of new root crops, which would have been facilitated by inclosure (Gonner, 1912, 254). In areas where there was a shortage of natural pasture, commoners were determined to maintain their rights and resisted inclosure; where pasture was abundant, common rights were less significant and limited piecemeal inclosures and ley farming removed the incentive for more drastic action; in the fens, there was so much natural grazing that inclosure was not necessary. Thus, much of central Cambridgeshire, which was well suited to corn production and had limited common land and a stagnant population, was inclosed after 1810. Areas which were less appropriate for arable farming were inclosed earlier, such as the 'dairies' in the west and parishes in the boulder clay area in the south-east; 82% of the parishes in this latter region had been inclosed by 1810. Parishes on the margins of the fens were mostly inclosed after 1824, as they had both good arable and pastoral land and a well-balanced economy. Proximity to Cambridge encouraged inclosure as the increased demands of the town, whose population increased by 200% between 1770 and 1851, stimulated agricultural production. Thus parishes in the fenland marginal area which were also within three miles of Cambridge were the ones inclosed before 1824. Landownership and land tenure also affected inclosure: parishes with one large landlord, such as Abington Pigotts, were inclosed early. Conversely, where there were many owner-occupiers, tenant farmers or absentee corporate landlords, inclosure was late. For example, small landowners delayed inclosure at Oakington from 1796 to 1833 (*VCH*, 9, 203), Cottenham, with a large number of small owner-occupiers, was inclosed in 1842 and Caldecote, where Clare College was an important owner, was inclosed in 1845 (Postgate, 1964, 278–91). Soham, with many independent (and, typically, nonconformist) freeholders with very small holdings in the open fields and modest use-rights in commons and fens, was never inclosed at all (Butlin, 1990b, 224).

Industries in Cambridgeshire were few; their scarcity was one of the causes of emigration from the south of the county in the early nineteenth century as the increasing population could not be absorbed (Postgate, 1964, 286). In the fenland, however, there was more available land to accommodate a growing population and retail and handicraft industries developed and diversified (Butlin, 1990b, 219). Industries mainly consisted of stone-quarrying and brick-making (Taylor, 1973, 242); there were also mills for making paper at Sawston and for preparing oil from cole and rape, notably at Whittlesford, Sawston, Hauxton and Shelford, and basket-manufacture (Lysons, 42).

The Lysons' description of Cambridgeshire (p.31) summarizes the characteristics which have been described in this section, first for the upland areas:

Those parts of the county adjoining Suffolk, Essex, and Hertfordshire, have gently rising hills, with downs, and open corn fields; and a considerable portion of wood in the part adjoining Suffolk, from Wood Ditton to Castle~Camps; but in other parts the county is very bare of timber. A great change has been made in this county within the last fifteen years, from the inclosures which have taken place; no fewer than thirty parishes having been inclosed by act of parliament, within that space of time. Gogmagog hills, which begin about 4 miles south~east of Cambridge, though of no great height, yet being the highest in the county, command a very extensive view. There is some pleasing scenery about Linton, Hildersham, and other villages, in the valley through which the Granta runs, between Cambridge and Bartlow, where there is no want of elm trees. The views from the upper part of the Earl of Hardwicke's park at Wimpole are very rich; the park is well wooded, as is also that of Sir Charles Cotton at Madingley, and the Duke of Rutland's at Cheveley.

The fenland, on the other hand, remained an area with many independent smallholders, and was largely pastoral:

The face of the country exhibits considerable variety. The north part, including the isle of Ely, is for the most part fen land, and quite level, intersected with numberless canals and ditches, and abounding with windmills like those of Holland, for conveying the water from the lands, into channels provided for carrying it off to the sea. The inclosures are here mostly formed by ditches, and few trees are to be seen, except pollard willows. There are some rising grounds in this part of the county; the most considerable of them is that on which the city of Ely stands.

Cambridgeshire was therefore a county characterized by a fenland north and upland south, late inclosure, many institutional owners and, from the eighteenth century, only a few large landed private owners, who dominated the local social and political scene. Estate map production occurred in this environment, and was also influenced by national developments in estate mapping.

ESTATE MAP PRODUCTION IN THE BRITISH ISLES

Estate maps were not produced in England until the sixteenth century and did not become at all common until the end of that century. Manorial surveys were carried out throughout the Middle Ages (Emmison, 1963, 35), but Skelton and Harvey (1986) suggest that the idea of drawing local maps developed, independently from these surveys, in the later Middle Ages. The first estate maps can be seen as a combination of both traditions. Events such as the Dissolution of the monasteries and the consequent changes in landownership, sixteenth-century inflation, land sales and inclosure led to the rise in importance of individual proprietorship and the growth of a private property market. From the 1530s, maps began to appear regularly with other more traditional types of document as tools of government and administration (Barber, 1985). Thus the need for boundary definition and the administrative requirements of government led to a demand for surveys (Kiely, 1947, 10; Lynam, 1950; Morgan, 1979, 134). This combined with developments in surveying techniques (stimulated by increasing interest in navigation and developments in the military sciences as well as agrarian changes) (Darby, 1933, 529) to produce a growing number of cartographic surveys

(Beresford, 1971, 47). Estate maps were made from the 1570s; by 1580, the Master of the Rolls, Sir William Cordell, felt the need of a map of his estate at Long Melford in Suffolk. As a result, a magnificent map was drawn by Israel Amyce: on nine sheets of parchment and measuring over eight feet by over six-and-a-half feet, the plan welcomes visitors to Long Melford Hall today (Dymond, 1987). Developments in map-making and surveying continued throughout the seventeenth century, stimulated by increased turnover of land from sequestrations of estates during the Civil War and consequent Restoration land sales with their inevitable legal complications (Phillips, 1979, 20). By the eighteenth century, the idea of local maps had become so widespread that Harley was able to call the period from 1700 to 1850 the 'golden age of the local land surveyor' (1972, 24). For example, samplers of estate maps were embroidered, such as the eighteenth-century one which is illustrated in Plate 2. It is of a farm in the parishes of Stapleford Abbotts and Lambourn in Essex, and it has many typical features which include a decorative title cartouche, a vignette of the farmhouse, a compass rose, an ornamental border, a table of acreages and the names of neighbouring owners.[1] The 1836 Tithe Commutation Act, followed by the six-inch Ordnance Survey maps a few years later, marked the demise of the purpose-made estate plan.

Similar developments can be seen in Ireland, Scotland and Wales. In Ireland, much of the seventeenth-century estate mapping was connected with legal needs for boundary definition. The character of estate maps changed in the eighteenth century as concern with land quality increased. Estate surveys continued to be important until the introduction of the six-inch Ordnance Survey maps from the mid-1820s, when, earlier than in England, it became easier to copy the official survey of the area (Aalen and Hunter, 1964; Andrews, 1967, 275). In Scotland, the period of local estate surveys was more short-lived, with few maps produced before the 1740s and the production of maps closely linked with agricultural improvements (Caird, 1989, 49). There was a brief revival during and immediately after the Napoleonic Wars with a stimulus from inflation and a wartime demand for agricultural produce, but by the 1820s opportunities declined and competition from the Ordnance Survey increased (Adams, 1971 and 1975). In Wales, too, estate mapping developed later than it did in England. Very few of the larger estates whose papers are in the collections of the National Library of Wales were mapped before 1760. During the difficult agricultural conditions of the later eighteenth century, there was more efficient management of property, employment of professional stewards, shorter leases and annual tenancies, all of which stimulated the production of estate maps. Demand for maps continued into the nineteenth century as some estates were broken up and a new class of landowner emerged with estates founded on industrial or commercial wealth (Davies, 1982, 5–15).

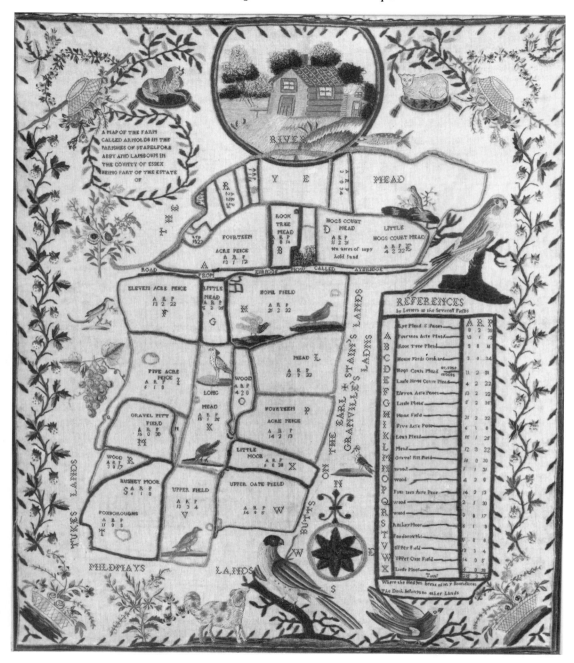

Plate 2. An eighteenth-century sampler of Arnolds Farm, Stapleford Abbotts and Lambourn, Essex.

COMPILATION OF THE CARTO-BIBLIOGRAPHY OF CAMBRIDGESHIRE ESTATE MAPS

The carto-bibliography which forms Appendix 2 provides a database for the study of the characteristics of estate maps of Cambridgeshire, to see how they reflect and influenced contemporary society. To compile the list, enquiries were made at all county record offices and selected libraries in Great Britain, at all of the Oxford and Cambridge colleges, and from some private landowners and solicitors. In all, 785 maps were found in 50 different repositories, the major collections being in Cambridge University Library, the Cambridgeshire County Record Office, in several of the Cambridge colleges (especially Clare, Jesus, Queens', Pembroke, St John's and Trinity colleges) and in the archives of several London-based institutions (notably the Charterhouse, the Corporation of the Sons of the Clergy, and St Bartholomew's and St Thomas' hospitals).

A wide range of information was recorded about each map, so that each sheet could be described as fully as possible and its various features would be available for use in the interpretation of the maps in their sociological context (see Andrews, 1978). A Map Description Form was drawn up to record the information about each map (see Appendix 1). Details were recorded about a map's physical characteristics: its title, surveyor, date, scale, orientation, size and material; the area which it covers; the topographical information which it shows; and the amount and type of decoration which the surveyor used. The precise ways in which the characteristics were described are given on the introductory pages (pp.190–2) of Appendix 2.

SURVIVAL

Any interpretation of the characteristics of estate maps depends very largely upon the representativeness of the sample. Emmison (1974, 62) estimates that over 20,000 estate maps drawn before 1850 survive, but the figure could be much higher. Hindle (1988, 43) suggests about 30,000 are still extant, maybe as many estate plans of Scotland were drawn between 1700 and 1850 (Adams, 1968, 249), and Smith simply says that 'many thousands of estate plans are recorded and more are continually coming to light' (Smith, 1988, 48). Clearly, many plans have been lost and survival is probably selective. Adams (1975, 13) suggests that 90% of the maps drawn of the Hopetoun and Gordon Castle estates survive. For Cambridgeshire, comparison of maps which are currently in repositories with references to maps and their production from estate papers has led to lower estimates of survival. For example, 68% of the maps which were drawn of the Dukes of Bedford's Cambridgeshire estates remain today. The average survival rate for five Cambridge colleges (Clare, Emmanuel, Jesus, Queens' and St John's) is 79%, and this figure conceals a range from 63% of the 78 maps which were drawn for Emmanuel College to 91 % of the 153 maps which were drawn for Jesus College. If discussion is limited to maps which have independent documentary evidence for their existence, the figures are reduced to nearly half overall, and range from one-quarter for Clare College to 71 % for Queens' College. There are occasional references on maps to other plans which have since vanished: for instance, the 1827 map of Haddenham by Alexander Watford junior for Gonville and Caius College (HAD82701) refers to a plan by Mr Waudby which has not been found in the College archives today.

Many factors affected survival: chance is obviously important, as is the quality of past and present estate administration. In one college in Cambridge, for example, the handlist to the archives contains six references to Cambridgeshire maps which were 'not found' in a recent check, giving a loss of one-quarter of the holding within the last few years. The nature of the map should also be considered. Decorative maps could either have been appreciated and treasured by future generations, or forgotten about and lost. Some maps were used for many years after their commission: a map of Radbourne, Warwickshire, drawn in 1634, was still in use a century later (Harvey, 1988). In 1785, William Jemmett was surveying Queens' College's estate at St Nicholas Court in Kent, and he saw a 1670 map of Mr Finch's estate there.[2] For documents to be used, they frequently had to be removed from their storage place and sent to a surveyor: on 17 February 1810, for example, the maps of Queens' College's estate at Eversden were taken by John Hunt for Joseph Truslove,[3] and later in the same year Truslove requested plans and documents of the College's land at Capel in Suffolk.[4] These documents were returned, but others may well have been lost or used so heavily that they disintegrated. Sketch plans of estates were often produced for a particular purpose and then lost or destroyed, and perhaps only a quarter of them still survive. Even if they remain, they are frequently not mentioned in catalogues and lists of archives and so may not have been included in the carto-bibliography in Appendix 2.

THE DEVELOPMENT OF ESTATE MAPPING

In order to study the development of estate mapping, changes in the rate of estate map production are examined and related to local and national developments in the economy, to population levels, to characteristics of society and to reasons for which a map was drawn.

An estate is defined as a continuous area of land, or land in one parish, which belongs to one owner; analysis of dates of map production is of maps of estates rather than of estate maps. The carto-bibliography describes each individual sheet of an estate map as a separate map, unless it has been divided into sheets merely for convenience of storage or because the stitching of parchment has loosened. If each sheet were considered as a map, the distribution of dates would be unrealistically distorted towards the early period of mapping; for example, Merton College, Oxford had its Gamlingay estate mapped in 15 sheets in 1601/2 (GAM60201–15), maps were drawn in 1617 of the Balsham and Castle Camps estates of the Charterhouse in six and five sheets respectively (BAL61701–6, CAS61701–5) and Edward

Russell, Earl of Orford, had his Chippenham estate mapped in eight sheets in 1712 (CHP71201–8). Each of these sets of maps represents one survey.

Fig. 3.2 plots the number of maps of estates against time. The graph of all maps of estates shows the same major periods and rates of map production as that of just the firmly datable maps, except that there is a more marked increase of maps in 1800 as all undated early nineteenth-century maps were counted as having been drawn in that year. Thus subsequent analysis has been based on the larger sample. Eight periods were identified during which map production occurred at similar rates: to 1715, 1716–65, 1766–87, 1788–99, 1800–9, 1810–16, 1817–26 and 1827–36. Periods of major mapping activity were 1766–87, when 2.5 estates were mapped each year, and from 1788, when the rate increased to 7.7 estates a year. Before 1766 far fewer maps were produced, especially in the years before 1600 (0.1 estates a year), between 1617 and 1649 (0.2 estates a year) and from 1688 to 1699 (0.08 estates a year). The same data plotted semi-logarithmically (Fig. 3.3) show the overall trends of the period. There was a roughly exponential increase in map production from 1580 to 1836, with the number of maps increasing tenfold every 140 years. There were three periods during which the rate of mapping activity was different: before 1617, 1688–1712 and 1788–1800.

This exponential increase cannot be related to any one factor. National population increased over the period, except for a slight fall in the second half of the seventeenth century. The rate of increase, tenfold every 310 years was, however, much slower than that of map production (Wrigley and Schofield, 1981, Table A3.1; Fig. 3.4). Local population changes match rates of map production less closely, as the population of Cambridgeshire decreased by over 10% in the first half of the eighteenth century. Thereafter, the population grew though it did not reach national rates of increase until the nineteenth century (Deane and Cole, 1967, 105 and 115). Nor can the exponential growth rate be explained in purely economic terms. Agricultural fortunes in the county largely mirrored national trends, especially in the early nineteenth century (Darby, 1948a, 116). The fluctuation of prices in the seventeenth and eighteenth centuries does not explain the general increase in the number of maps: Fig. 3.5 shows that prices in the Phelps Brown and Hopkins composite unit of consumables remained fairly static from about 1640 to 1750, then there was a period of inflation until about 1810, which was followed by a fall; these trends provide a rough measure of general price changes (Munby, 1989, 25; Phelps Brown and Hopkins, 1962, 193–6). Neither do changes in wages as shown in Fig. 3.6 explain the overall trend: they rose during the seventeenth century and continued to rise until about 1740, declined until about 1810, and then rose again (Wrigley and Schofield, 1981, 642–4).

The development of estate mapping is most probably a reflection of the way in which information and fashions diffuse through society. Many studies have shown that, over time, diffusion rates follow an 'S'-shaped curve. For example, a plot of the dates of the first editions of the large-scale county maps of England and Wales (Fig. 3.7) shows such a curve, with the idea of large-scale county map-making spreading very slowly until the end of the eighteenth century (Rodger, 1972). In the early and middle stages of dissemination, before a phenomenon is widespread, the rate is exponential. This exponential stage has been shown in a study of the growth of map collections (Wolter, 1987), and Harley and Walters (1978, 52) suggested that map collecting increased exponentially at the end of the eighteenth and

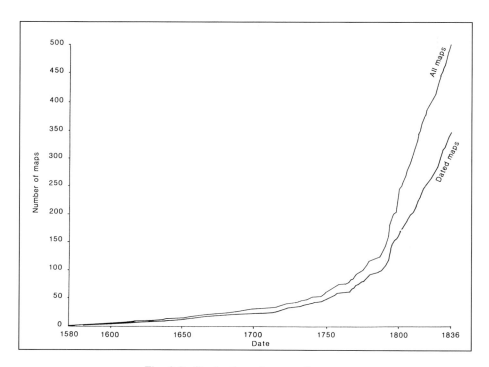

Fig. 3.2. Production of maps of estates.

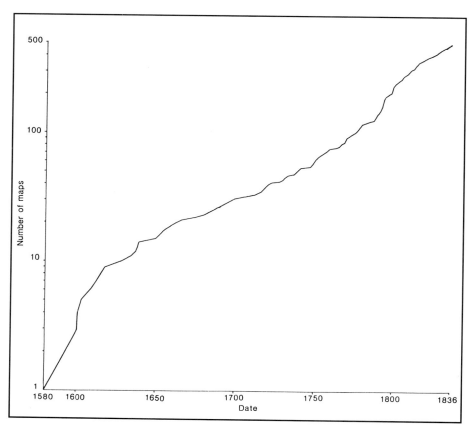

Fig. 3.3. Semi-logarithmic plot of the production of all maps of estates.

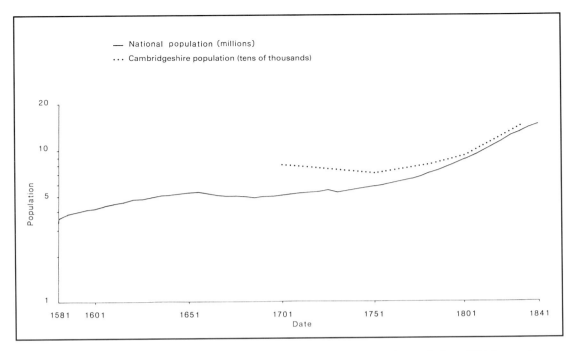

Fig. 3.4. Population increase 1581–1841 (Source for national population: Wrigley and Schofield, 1981, Table A3.1; source for Cambridgeshire population: Deane and Cole, 1962, 103).

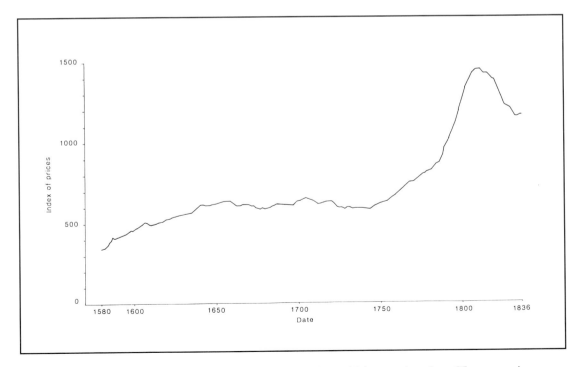

Fig. 3.5. Movement of prices 1580–1836 (The data which are plotted are 25-year moving averages, with the years 1451–75 = 100. Source: Phelps Brown and Hopkins, 1962, 193–6).

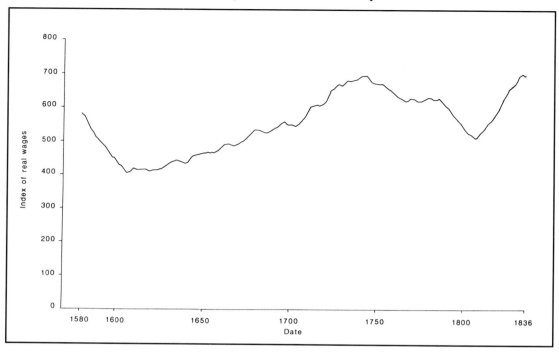

Fig. 3.6. Movement of wages 1580–1836 (The data which are plotted are 25-year moving averages. Source: Wrigley and Schofield, 1981, Table A9.2).

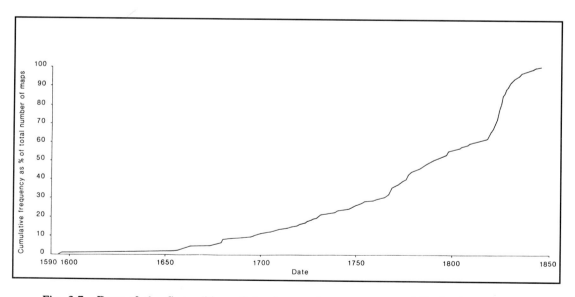

Fig. 3.7. Dates of the first editions of the large-scale county maps of England and Wales (Source: Rodger, 1972).

beginning of the nineteenth centuries. Fig. 3.8 shows that estate mapping in Cambridgeshire was progressing through typical stages of diffusion; by 1836 the rate had not yet slowed down with a consequent flattening of the curve.

Some of the smaller-scale fluctuations in map production can be explained by external events, especially the weather and its effect on harvests, various demographic changes and political developments. Periods of overall economic prosperity when harvests were good could be expected to be more favourable to agricultural activities (Bowden, 1985, 64), which involved surveying and mapping. However, much depended on the size of holding, with smaller farmers much more vulnerable to the vagaries of the weather (Clay, 1985, 176). Some of the bad harvests and economic depressions in Cambridgeshire coincided with periods of reduced map production, such as the 1620s, 1630s and 1690s. As the good harvests of 1741–9 also coincided with a period when fewer maps were drawn, the weather can only be a partial explanation of some of the fluctuations. Decreased map production in the 1630s can also be partly explained by the plague, which was severe in Cambridgeshire from 1600 to 1670 and especially violent in the fourth decade of the century (Hampson, 1948, 101). The Civil War caused more estates to be valued rather than mapped (Thompson, 1968, 25), but in any case Cambridgeshire was largely Parliamentarian so there were few fines and sequestrations of Royalist estates (Darby, 1948b, 410). The national and local demographic crisis among the peerage at the end of the seventeenth century, together with increased tenurial stability, may help to account for reduced rates of mapping at that time (Clay, 1985, 165; Jenkins, 1984, 11; Thompson, 1968, 23). Population continued to decrease in the early eighteenth century, however, when emigration from the county also occurred, whereas the rate of map production was increasing once again at this time.

Landownership influenced the pattern of estate mapping in the county; Fig. 3.9 shows the rate of map production in relation to type of owner. Most maps were drawn for private owners until about 1800. Colleges were also important commissioners of estate maps, however, and they accounted for 34% of maps overall, and other institutional owners for a further 19%. The influence of colleges is especially marked in the period from 1788 to 1800 when map production increased tenfold in 24 years; this can be compared with a tenfold growth in 34 years for all institutional owners and in 110 years for private owners. The growth of interest of landowners, especially colleges, in their estates and the increased use of maps in estate management is discussed in Chapters 6 and 7.

Developments in Cambridgeshire can be compared with those elsewhere; Fig. 3.10 plots the increase in estate map production in Buckinghamshire, Cambridgeshire, Essex, Hertfordshire, Kent and Sussex. Numbers were taken from published catalogues of estate maps (Elvey, 1963; Emmison, 1947, 1952, 1964 and 1968; Hull, 1973; Steer, 1962 and 1968; Walne, 1969). It is possible to establish general trends from these figures despite variations in the types of holding of each record office and its catalogue. For example, some record offices have large collections of photographs of maps which are kept elsewhere, and the catalogues for Essex, Kent and Sussex list maps which are not held in the record office. Collegiate estates are rarely mentioned, so that whilst 53% of the maps of Cambridgeshire are of institutional estates, for other counties this figure probably does not exceed 20%.

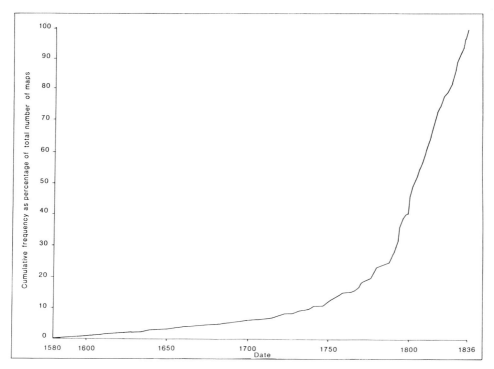

Fig. 3.8. Rate of diffusion of estate maps in Cambridgeshire.

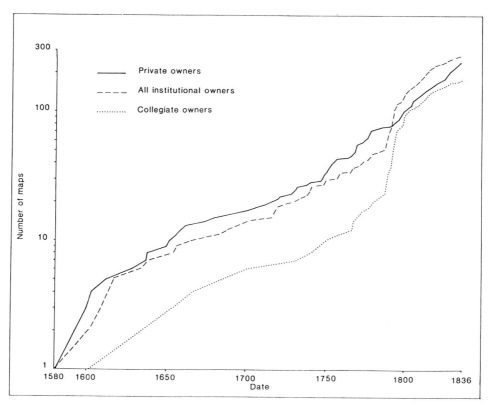

Fig. 3.9. Semi-logarithmic plot of estate map production divided by type of owner.

The overall rate of increase in map production was still exponential and at a similar rate to that of Cambridgeshire, increasing tenfold in about 146 years from 1600 to 1836. It is easier to link some of the smaller-scale fluctuations with external events, as the sample size has increased and the influence of local idiosyncracies is thus reduced. There is still no obvious connection between map production and gross population levels. Links with the economy are more apparent: the poor harvests of 1685–9, 1692–1713 and 1739–40 coincide with declines in map production (though the bad harvests of 1645–51 and 1725–8 did not have similar effects). Years of good harvests, 1652–4, 1685–91 and 1714–49 were years of increased mapping activity. Thus mapping may have been stimulated by favourable economic circumstances. The relation between mapping and the Civil War is more marked: the rate of map production decreased in the 1640s, which agrees with the suggestion made above that sequestrations of land were probably not a great stimulus to mapping, unlike the subsequent sales.

Rates of map production varied from county to county. Fig. 3.11 shows the number of years earlier or later than average that each county had 10%, 25%, 50%, 75% and 90% of its estates mapped. Cambridgeshire was consistently the last county to achieve each marker; only from 1819, when 75% of its estates had been mapped, was it within ten years of the average. In terms of absolute numbers of maps, too, Cambridgeshire was not among the most prolific counties. Before 1700, 37 maps per 1,000 square miles had been drawn; this compares with 125 per 1,000 square miles in Buckinghamshire, 115 in Essex, 84 in Sussex, 77 in Kent and 42 in Warwickshire. Fewer maps were drawn in Hertfordshire (31 per 1,000 square miles), Hampshire (16) and Durham (1) (figures for Warwickshire, Hampshire and Durham are taken from Harvey, 1988). Despite a probable under-representation of collegiate landowners in the carto-bibliographies of all other counties, these figures can be interpreted by patterns of landownership: in Cambridgeshire, there were few large landed estates and many institutions, which started having their estates mapped relatively late. County Durham had a similar pattern: of the four great landowners, two were ecclesiastical who did not commission many estate maps (Harvey, 1988). Likewise 20% of pre-1700 Kentish estate maps were drawn for 14 institutional owners, and mapping started later than in neighbouring Essex, which had some considerable magnates and only six institutional owners who accounted for 10% of maps (Hull, 1987).

An examination of the dates of estate map production, therefore, shows that it increased at a roughly exponential rate. There are no clear links between map production and other developments of the seventeenth and eighteenth centuries except in the most general terms, though periods of economic prosperity were more conducive to mapping. As awareness of maps increased, so more were produced. Much depended on the type of landowner: in Cambridgeshire, with its distinctive pattern of ownership, map production started late and relatively slowly and the importance of colleges, which commissioned more maps for practical reasons and fewer maps for display, was greater than in many other counties.

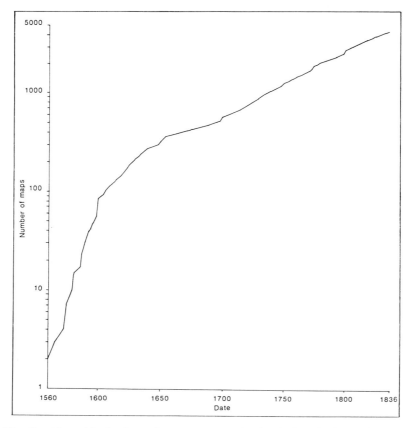

Fig. 3.10. Semi-logarithmic plot of estate map production in Buckinghamshire, Cambridge-shire, Essex, Hertfordshire, Kent and Sussex.

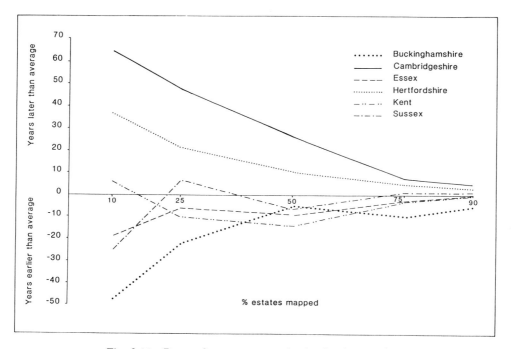

Fig. 3.11. Rates of estate map production in six counties.

AREAS OF CAMBRIDGESHIRE WHICH WERE MAPPED

The dates at which maps were drawn varied across Cambridgeshire and reflected local types of landownership, estates and agricultural regimes. The distribution of parishes for which no estate maps were drawn by 1836 is considered, and then the variation in rates of mapping, estate size and landownership between the fenland and south.

The map of the county in Fig. 3.1 marks parishes for which no estate maps were drawn by 1836. These represent 14% of the parishes: 27% of fenland parishes and 10% of southern parishes. Some of the parishes have distinctive characteristics. There was no major landowner to commission a map in either Welches Dam, which consisted of extra-parochial land and was common land to the surrounding villages, or Grunty Fen, which was common fen. Ely College is a very small parish around Ely Cathedral, of which any maps are more likely to be building plans than estate maps. Apart from these parishes, the others had landownership patterns similar to those of the rest of the county; some had a strong presence of one family whose papers may not have survived or who may not have commissioned maps, others had a mixed pattern of landownership. Some parishes extend into other counties, such as Royston (Hertfordshire), Stanground (Huntingdonshire), and Outwell and Upwell (Norfolk); possibly no maps were drawn of the Cambridgeshire parts of the first three parishes because acreages in the county were small, and consequently the number of map-commissioning landowners was low. The distribution can also be explained by chance loss of documents: St John's College paid £16 for a map of Thriplow in 1806, for example, but no surviving plan was found during the present study.[5]

The south of Cambridgeshire covers about two-thirds of the county whilst about one-third of the land lies in the Isle of Ely. This is reflected in the distribution of estate maps: 80% are of the southern area and 20% are of the fenland. Markedly more maps were drawn of the Isle than the south in 1766–87, when about 40% of the Isle parishes and 23% of southern parishes were mapped; conversely, many more of the southern parts of the county were mapped in 1810–16 (34% of southern parishes, 18% of fenland) and in 1827–36 (40% of southern parishes, 24% of fenland). There is no obvious reason why many fenland estates were mapped in 1766–87; this was not a major period of fen drainage which might have stimulated map-making. The predominance of maps of southern over fenland areas in 1810–16 may reflect inclosure: maps were drawn of 43% of the southern parishes which were inclosed at that time but of none of the fenland parishes. Similarly, 14% of the southern parishes which were inclosed between 1827 and 1836 were mapped, but only one fenland parish.

Differences can be seen between types of landowner: nearly half of the mapped parishes had collegiate owners, and a further 27% of parishes had land belonging to other institutions. Institutional ownership was largely concentrated in the south, and from 1788 to 1826 more of the southern maps were drawn for these owners. Conversely, more of the maps which were drawn for private owners were of the fenland, except for the early period to 1715 and from 1810 to 1816.

Estate size, too, reflects the type of landowner and area of the county. About one-third of the county was mapped for private owners and 12 % for institutional owners. As over half the maps were drawn for institutional owners, their estates were smaller than private ones. The most common size of estate overall was 100–499 acres; fewer-than-average institutional estates were larger than this, with estates of 1,000–4,999 acres as common as those of 100–499 acres (over 20 % in each case). Size of estate varied with part of the county. Fenland estates tended to be much larger: 8 % were larger than 10,000 acres, about 90 % were larger than 100 acres, and estates of 100 to 499 acres were especially common (40 %). Only one map was of an area smaller than one acre. Estate size in the south was smaller and mostly followed the average. Only about 2 % of estates were larger than 5,000 acres and, as in the fenland, the most common size was 100 to 499 acres (29 %). Very few maps covered more than one parish: 2 % of maps were of land belonging to private owners and fewer than 1 % of maps were of institutional owners' estates. Maps of larger fenland estates were more likely to disregard parish boundaries: a maximum of 6 % was reached in 1788–99, while the percentage never exceeded 2 % of maps of smaller southern parishes. This distribution of large and small estates reflects parish size; it has already been shown how southern parishes are smaller than fenland ones and how over four-fifths of southern parishes are of the modal size of 1,000–4,999 acres, whilst only about half of fenland parishes fall into this range.

Estates became smaller over time. After 1787 no estate was larger than 10,000 acres, the differential between fenland and southern estates was less marked and increasing numbers of southern estates were smaller than one acre (2 % by 1810). This increase reflects national trends in size of holding, greater awareness of maps and changing perceptions of their use, and is discussed further in Chapters 6 and 7.

Thus, the estate maps of Cambridgeshire reflect the character of the county and its landowners. More maps were drawn of the smaller parishes of the south, where institutional owners were very important, and estate size declined from 1600 to 1836. It is now necessary to show how landownership affected the techniques which were used to display information on a map.

TECHNIQUES OF PRESENTATION

Techniques of presentation on estate maps changed during the seventeenth and eighteenth centuries so that maps drawn in 1836 hardly resembled those drawn 250 years earlier. The rate of change varied across the country, within a county and from surveyor to surveyor. In this section, the ways in which techniques altered and developed in Cambridgeshire are examined and compared with developments elsewhere. These changes show the influence of different types of landowner in determining the kind of map which was commissioned, and the currency of techniques used by the surveyor who was employed. Four main characteristics of estate maps are discussed: the scale of the maps and how it is represented, orientation, use of tables of explanatory symbols and acreages, and presentation of maps as either single or multiple sheets.

There are three main aspects to a discussion of scale of estate maps: the scale at which a map is drawn, how scale is shown and whether the measurement is customary or statute. There is evidence for use of customary measurements in the county throughout the early modern period, but it is difficult to determine what the customary measure was and where and when it was used. By the end of the thirteenth century, some had come to understand the normal perch as $16\frac{1}{2}$ feet (Jones, 1979, 13), but many other perches existed. A set of maps of Cherry Hinton drawn in 1733 talks of a short pole of 15 feet (CHE73301–4), in Fowlmere a $15\frac{1}{2}$ foot pole was used (Brassley, Lambert and Saunders, 1988, 28) and in Eversden and Harlton in 1763 the local acre was equivalent to only three roods of statute measure.[6] Postgate (1964, 135) found evidence for this last measure in at least 15 places from Melbourn to Ely in the late eighteenth century. Other measures included 16, 18, 20, 22, 24 or 26 feet. For arable land, 16 or $16\frac{1}{2}$ feet became popular, 24 to 26 feet was commonly used for less valuable woodland and assarts (Grierson, 1972, 21), and 18 feet for fenland: a terrier made in 1597 of land in Cottenham on the fen edge uses an 18 foot pole,[7] and ink notes on the scale bar of a map of Thorney in 1731/2 also suggest the use of this customary measure (THO73201).

Customary measures continued to be found in Cambridgeshire at the turn of the eighteenth century: Vancouver commented on the variability of local measures in 1794 (p.10): 'The computed measure in the several open common fields, being extremely various, (seldom exceeding three roads to the acre,) has induced me to reduce the acre, to the legal standard.' From the early seventeenth century, however, estate surveyors said that they used statute measure. At first men such as Thomas Langdon, who mapped Gamlingay for Merton College, Oxford in 1601/2 (GAM60201–16), and John Norden, the surveyor in 1603 of Sir John Spencer's estate at Little Abington (LLA60301), may have mentioned statute measure to emphasize their status as leaders of their profession. During the seventeenth and eighteenth centuries statements of statute measure became more common. It was mentioned less frequently from the late eighteenth century, especially from 1788, probably because its use had become assumed by then. Later use of customary measure, however, was not necessarily an indication of backwardness, as new surveys may have had to be reconciled with previous surveys using older measures (Harley and Stuart, 1982, 52). Because evidence for customary and statute measurements is so patchy, it has been necessary to assume in all subsequent analysis of scales that statute measure has been used, though this may very well not have been so.

The amount of information which can be shown on a map is affected by the scale at which it is drawn. Scales on Cambridgeshire estate maps ranged from under one chain to the inch (1:792) to over 12 chains to the inch (1:9,504), but the most common scale was four chains to the inch, 1:3,168 (11% of the sheets), followed by six chains to the inch, 1:4,752 (10% of sheets) and three chains to the inch, 1:2,376 (8% of sheets). Maps of fenland areas which covered large acreages were drawn at smaller scales; about 8% were drawn at over 12 chains to the inch. Harley and Stuart (1982, 52) found that George Withiell's late seventeenth-century maps of estates in the West Country showed a similar pattern: three chains to the inch was most commonly used, then four and six chains. In seventeenth-century Essex, four chains to the inch was the most common scale of estate maps (Hull, 1987, 242), whilst in the eighteenth century, too, most estate maps were drawn at scales of between three and eight chains to the inch (Mason, 1990, 13). Scales of Cambridgeshire maps changed over time. Over the seventeenth and eighteenth centuries, sheets were increasingly drawn at large scales, which reflected the growing number of maps of small areas. Scales became more variable; most of the maps at four chains to the inch were drawn in 1716–65, and thereafter six and three chains became common. This change may have been caused by a growth in use of maps for specific purposes, for which particularly large or small scales might have been most appropriate.

By the time estate mapping was becoming common in Cambridgeshire, the idea of the scale map was well established. Overall, 63% of maps had a statement of their scale. The percentage of maps with no scale statement increased over time; in 1800–9 about 40% had none, and this increased to nearly 60% in 1817–26. The percentage of maps which had their scale in words was fairly constant, though noticeably fewer used this method of showing scale from 1788–99 (less than 5%) and more used it in 1827–36 (about 20%). Use of a scale bar declined from a maximum of 80% of maps having a bar in 1716–65 to about 30% in 1817–26. Some maps showed scale both in a scale bar and in words: 9% to 1715, 7% in 1716–65 and 16% in 1766–87. Thereafter, the percentage was lower, and no maps used both methods between 1800 and 1809 and from 1817 to 1826.

Part of the changes in use of scale can be explained by landownership. Harvey (1988) has suggested how landowners may have imitated the use of scale statements on Saxton's county maps, which they had recently bought, and caused scale to be given on maps of their estates. Maps which were drawn for private landowners in Cambridgeshire were more likely to show the scale either in words alone or both in words and with a scale bar, and use of a scale bar declined over time. In maps which showed land belonging to institutional owners, giving scale both in words and a bar was more common in the early period to 1715 than in maps drawn for private owners. Scale-less maps were more usually drawn for institutional owners except for 1827–36. Absence of scale partly reflects the type of map which was drawn; maps which were drawn at a specific number of chains to the inch usually gave their scale whereas maps at intermediate scales rarely had a scale statement. Many of this second type of map were little more than sketch maps, they were not drawn for display and they were frequently unsigned. Overall, 51% of maps had no named surveyor; of these maps about half had no scale whereas only about one-quarter of signed maps had no scale.

Techniques of presentation of orientation also changed over time and can again be linked to the type of owner and the reason for which a map was drawn. Overall, 77% of maps gave their orientation in words, or by compass roses or points. Until 1800, over 80% gave their orientation; thereafter the percentage fell, with a trough being reached in 1817–26 when orientation was only given on just over half the maps. The use of cardinal points in the border of a map was always the least popular method, though until 1787 it was fairly common, especially among institutional owners (15%–20% of maps). In the years after 1788, the percentage of maps showing orientation in this way was negligible. Compass roses were the most popular method until 1766 (40% of maps; see, for example, Plate 3); their use declined in the eighteenth century and after 1809 they were very rare. They were less popular among institutional than private owners. Compass points replaced roses (see Plate 4); points became usual among private owners from 1766 and very common after 1788, when institutional owners also had them drawn on maps. From then on, they were almost the sole method of showing orientation, especially among institutional owners, and between 60% and 80% of maps had compass points. As with the use of scale bars, more unsigned than signed maps did not show any orientation: 28% and 19% respectively. After 1810, a greater number of signed maps did not state their orientation. Magnetic north was rarely shown: the only example amongst Cambridgeshire estate maps is Vincent Wing's map of the Duke of Bedford's land at Thorney in 1752–3 (THO75301). Wing may have taken the magnetic variation of 17° westerly from the statement in the *Gentleman's Magazine* for 1749 (p.554); in 1753, the variation was in fact probably about 18° 20' westerly, and by 1767, the date of Walton's copy of Wing's map (THO76701), about 20° 19' westerly (Walker, 1866, 16). Thus, these maps, for display by a private owner, claim a false degree of precision. Nevertheless, maps which were drawn for private owners to display used more up-to-date methods of showing their orientation; no north point was given on some utilitarian sketch maps.

Three kinds of table were used on maps: an explanation or key, a description of tenurial conditions and a list of acreages. Keys to symbols were introduced in the sixteenth century; the first English engraved map with a key was Norden's map of Middlesex in 1588 (Campbell, 1952, 427). The use of keys increased in the seventeenth century (Campbell, 1962, 414), but they were not used on estate maps until the eighteenth century. In Derbyshire, the earliest estate maps that carry legends which refer to non-tenurial features are dated 1723 (Delano Smith, 1985, 29); in Cambridgeshire, only two maps in the carto-bibliography have this type of key. They are a map drawn in about 1750 of the Duke of Bedford's Thorney estate, where a key is given to the symbols used for different types of drainage engine (THO75001), and a map of Wicken drawn by James Parker for the Earl of Bessborough in 1770 which has a more general key (see Plate 5; WIC77001).

Tables which referred to tenurial conditions were much more common. An early example is John Norden's map of Little Abington, 1603, which gives: 'The destinction of the three fermes following by Coulers Leuerers not Leased, with yollow ... Leased to Edmond Marsh being *part* of Cardinalls ... Leased to Buck in the tenure of Leonerd Swan ... Other mens' land in generall thus' (LLA60301). Other examples can be given for the seventeenth and eighteenth centuries; a map of Rampton in the mid-eighteenth century shows by colour the position of each tenant's strips in the open fields, and a key gives the colour assigned to each tenant (RAM75401).

Frequently, tables gave both tenurial conditions and acreages. In 1600–1 John Norden surveyed and mapped the estates of Sir Michael Stanhope in Sutton near Woodbridge, Suffolk. At the beginning of the survey he explains how to use the key, which suggests that tables were still uncommon:

Plate 3.   Estate map of Boxworth drawn by Matthew Hayward for Lady Ann Cutts, 1650,
showing the compass rose, emblematic title cartouche and deer.

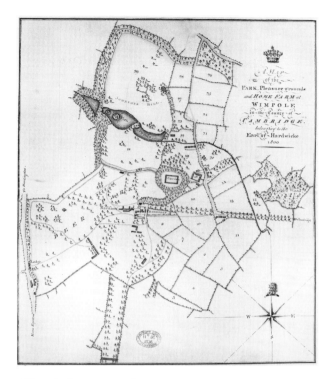

Plate 4. Estate map of Wimpole, drawn for the 3rd Earl of Hardwicke, 1800.

Plate 5. Key to symbols on the estate map of Wicken drawn by James Parker for the 2nd Earl of Bessborough, 1770.

If you desire to know, the conte*n*t or quantities of anie peece of land in anie the Mannors comprehended in theis Mapps, and the value therof, Obserue what letter ther is in that parcell of land and the tena*n*ts name therin, Then refer yow to the table of that Mannor, and in the therde Columne or row, under the title (*Lettres* directory) shall yow finde that be: and righte againste, the same be, in the fowrth rancke or Columne, the content or quantity in the fifte ranck, the tenure, namelie whether Copie Lease or free, or in the Lordes handes, And in the sixth or laste Ranck the yearlie supposed value. And by the Mapps yow may also see the buttes and boundes of anie perticuler parcell of land. On your right hande the mapp is spred before yow is east, on your lefte weste. The upper side from the eye is north, and that nexte the eye southe. If you woulde know the generall content of any mans land Copie Lease or free yow shall finde the quantitie at the foote of the perticular contents, and the yearlie value at the foote of the perticuler values.[8]

So far as Cambridgeshire maps are concerned, 44 % had tables on them, 7 % referred to accompanying terriers and a further 12 % had numbers which probably referred to an accompanying table or terrier. Use of reference tables increased during the seventeenth and eighteenth centuries, peaked in 1788–99 (nearly 70 % of maps) and then declined to under 30 % in 1817–26. References to accompanying terriers decreased over time, whilst references to inclosure awards increased from 1800 and reached a maximum of about 20 % of maps in 1810–16, the time when activities relating to inclosure were greatest. Contrasts can be drawn between private and institutional owners: 35 % of maps drawn for private owners had tables, compared with 55 % of those drawn for institutional owners. Greatest use of tables was later on maps drawn for private rather than institutional owners: 1810–16 instead of 1788–99. References to terriers also peaked later: between 1766 and 1787 nearly half of private owners' maps fell into this category, whereas the maximum percentage of maps drawn for institutional owners in this class was both lower, 37 %, and earlier, 1716–65. Apart from 1810–16, more signed maps had some sort of reference than maps with no named surveyor.

These three main features of estate maps, scale, orientation and reference tables, were not equally important: most maps gave their orientation (77 %), whilst fewer stated their scale or had a reference (63 % in each case). Before 1716, about 90 % of maps had at least one of these features, they became slightly more common until 1816, and then the percentage fell to under 80 % before returning to about 90 % in 1827–36. Some contrasts can be drawn between maps which were drawn for different uses. Only 20 % of maps drawn on leases had statements of their scale, though over 60 % indicated their orientation. By comparison, over half of the maps which accompanied particulars of sale gave their scale and about 65 % had a north point.

Some estate maps, especially the early ones, were in multiple sheets. Until 1715, about 30 % of maps were in more than one sheet, with an average sheet number of eight, and three maps had index sheets. Thereafter, fewer than 16 % of maps were in more than one sheet, the average number of sheets was about four and no maps had index sheets. Except for 1716–87, multiple-sheet maps were more common among institutional than private owners. As with maps in single sheets, scale and orientation became less common as time progressed. Until 1799, more than half of the maps had a scale on all of their sheets, then, except for 1810–16, more than half had no scale. The consistency of scale between sheets decreased: until 1715 nearly three-quarters of the sheets had a scale within $\pm\frac{1}{16}$ in. of each other, then until 1816 about half had a more-or-less consistent scale. Until 1787, over 63 % of all sheets gave their orientation; from 1800 to 1826, the percentage of maps with no statement of orientation exceeded 12%. Fewer maps omitted to state their orientation than their scale: overall, 55% of maps gave the orientation of all of their sheets, 38% had a statement of scale, 18% gave no orientation and 37% did not indicate their scale. The percentage of maps which were signed on all of their sheets decreased from a maximum of 50% in 1766–87 to a minimum of 13% in 1788–99, and the percentage of maps with no named surveyor increased, especially from 1788. Thus, maps in multiple sheets followed the general patterns which have been described for the county.

The number of maps which were unsigned increased to a peak of nearly 80% in 1788–99, and then decreased to about 40% in 1827–36. Many maps with no named surveyor had no scale statement, some had no references and fewer had no indication of orientation. This contrasts with signed maps, where most had no references and the percentages giving no orientation and scale were broadly similar. The increased percentage of unsigned maps with no scale or references in 1766–87 was not paralleled in the maps with a named surveyor. Many of the maps which were drawn for practical purposes were not signed, and none of the maps on leases had a named surveyor. This was probably because the surveyor was employed by those who drew up leases or auctioned land and he was not wholly responsible for the final product. It was not possible for him to demonstrate his skills of map-making and decoration on maps on leases or sale particulars, he was unlikely to attract future work through such maps and so it was not necessary for him to sign them.

The characteristics of estate maps in Cambridgeshire, therefore, changed markedly over time. Some features, such as large multiple-sheet surveys and compass roses, became much less common. By the early nineteenth century, more maps were unsigned and had no indication of their scale or orientation. This probably reflects an increased awareness of maps and their uses; many of these later maps were utilitarian sketch maps rather than grand maps which were hung on walls to show off estates. Even on sketch maps, orientation was often shown whereas scale statements and references were less common. The changes occurred at different times for private and institutional owners. Private owners were more aware of developments in techniques of display, and their maps were more frequently drawn by a named surveyor who introduced new ideas, such as the use of compass points instead of a compass rose, and demonstrated his mathematical prowess by, for example, showing magnetic north (albeit not very accurately). Institutional owners, whose maps were more often drawn for practical purposes, were less likely to have decorative compass roses, and tables were more common. Comparison with other counties was not possible because the published catalogues do not give the necessary level of information. Further analysis of decorative features of maps in the next section, some of which can be compared with other counties, again shows the importance of the landowner in determining the type of map which was drawn.

DECORATION

There are three main aspects to developments in the amount and type of decoration of estate maps: how national fashions affected the style of a map, the presence or absence of decoration, and how ornamentation reflected the reasons for a map's commission. Plates 6 and 7 give an example of how decoration changed: Plate 6 is an early seventeenth-century map of Balsham and Plate 7 is a late eighteenth-century copy of the map. The topographic information is unchanged, but whereas the early map has strapwork ornament typical of its time, the later copy has much simpler decoration. Similarly, the decoration on Leybourn's exemplar of an estate map in 1653 (Plate 26) was replaced by much more restrained ornament in the 5th, 1725, edition.

Decoration of estate maps was affected by national developments in cartographic style, which in turn mirrored trends in other art forms; similar stylistic changes have been described on instrument-maker's trade cards, for example (Crawforth, 1985). Changes in Cambridgeshire were similar to those elsewhere: in the seventeenth century, Elizabethan and Stuart strapwork ornament as shown in Plate 6 gave way to classical motifs (see, for example, the title cartouche to a map of West Wratting in 1719, Plate 8), pendants of fruit and flowers (see Plate 7) and baroque decoration (for example in the title to the map of Rampton in 1754, Plate 9). In the mid-eighteenth century, antique stone slabs and romantic ornament can be found; see, for example, the title cartouche on a tomb to a map of Castle Camps which was drawn in 1741 and is illustrated in Plate 10. The first set of rococo designs was published in England in 1746 (Wills, 1984, 422), and thereafter these ornaments became common with their characteristic frames of moulded wood; Joseph Cole's maps of the Downing estate in 1750 provide early examples of the use of this artistic style on Cambridgeshire estate maps (CRY75001–10, EAS75001–8 and TAD75001–9; see Plate 11). By the end of the eighteenth century, decoration was much more restrained, with plainer borders, and cartouches, if present at all, were very simple (Lynam, 1945, 367–8). Plate 4 is a map of the Wimpole estate of Philip Yorke, 3rd Earl of Hardwicke which was drawn in 1800. Instead of being enclosed in a cartouche, the title is given in decorative lettering, and the compass points and border to the map are plain.

Decoration changed over time, and developments occurred at different times in maps drawn for private and institutional owners. Cartouches were the most popular form of decoration, and were present in over half of the maps drawn before 1766 (and nearly 70 % of maps drawn for private owners before 1715). By 1817, cartouches had become very rare. The scale was surmounted by dividers on nearly half of the pre-1715 maps, after which they disappeared from maps of institutional estates but remained fairly common on maps of private estates until 1766 (about 30 %). Decorative borders were far less common; they can be found on 20 % of maps drawn before 1715, after which date they soon disappeared. Heraldry, which was most popular on maps of private estates between 1716 and 1765 (30 % of maps), lingered on maps for private owners until 1800 but was hardly ever found on maps drawn for

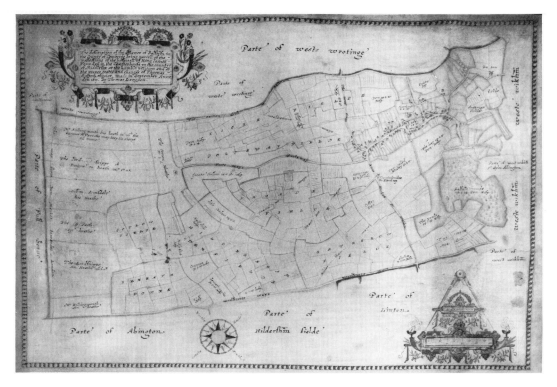

Plate 6. Estate map of Balsham drawn by Thomas Langdon for the Charterhouse, 1617, showing strapwork decoration.

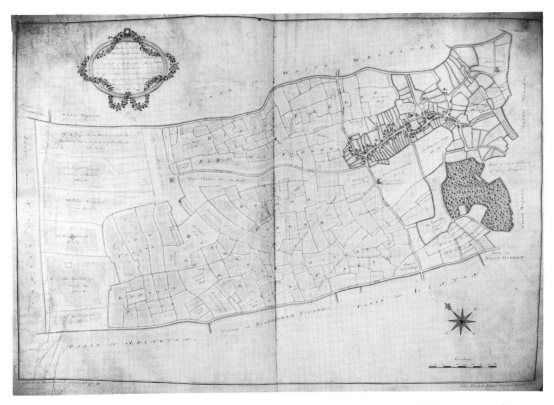

Plate 7. Copy by John Prickett in 1791 of Thomas Langdon's map of the Balsham estate of the Charterhouse.

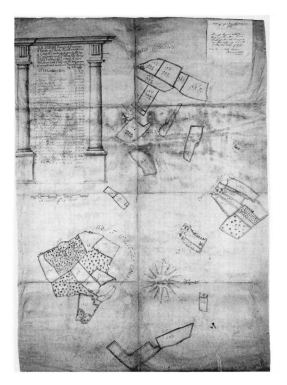

Plate 8. Estate map of West Wratting drawn by Arthur Frogley for the Corporation of the Sons of the Clergy, 1719, showing classical decoration.

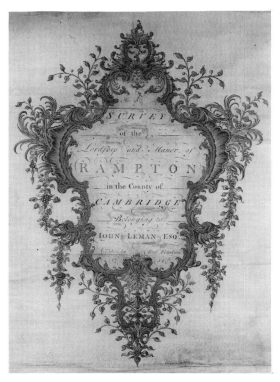

Plate 9. Title cartouche to the estate map of Rampton drawn by Henry Fensham for John Leman, 1754, showing baroque decoration.

institutional owners after 1715. The percentage of maps with no decoration increased so that, overall, over half of the maps were undecorated by 1766. Again, there is a clear contrast between type of owner: over half of the maps drawn for institutional owners were undecorated by 1716 whereas the 50% figure was not reached for maps drawn for private owners until 1800. Thus, the degree of a map's decoration depended on the reasons for which it was drawn; maps which were used to show off a landowner's estate and status were often highly ornamented.

The surveyor who was employed and his desire to advertise his skills also affected decoration. Maps drawn by unnamed surveyors were always far less likely to be decorated; on average, 84% of the unsigned maps were undecorated, and the figure never dropped below 65%. Landowners also demonstrated their ability to employ the best surveyors by the currency of the techniques which were used. For example the Earl of Kildare, an active promoter of new ideas, had his estates mapped. The map of Carton, near Dublin, by Charles Baylie and John Mooney introduced a new technique for showing relief: the spot height (Horner, 1974, 72 and 78).

Changes in the representation of buildings also indicate the quality of the surveyor who was employed. Plan form replaced perspective view of buildings in the eighteenth century; Wyld's *Practical Surveyor* of 1725 was one of the first to show buildings in plan. In Cambridgeshire, plan form was common in maps drawn for private owners from 1716 (20% of maps), and increased rapidly over the next 50 years to 70% of maps. Institutional owners, however, who were less concerned with the currency of the decoration on their maps, were slower to replace perspective with plan, and under half of the houses were shown in plan form until 1788. Some surveyors used both techniques: Thomas Warren, for example, showed buildings at Cheveley Hall in perspective in 1775 (CHG77501), whereas the house at Audley End was shown in plan form in 1783 (Williams, 1966, Plate XVI). Changes were frequently not clear-cut. For example, Joseph Freeman mapped many estates for Queens' College between 1769 and 1783, and ten of the 12 maps used perspective;[9] in his later maps for St John's and Clare Colleges, plan form was much more common but still not universal. Churches were shown in perspective for much longer; nearly half of them were still in perspective in 1827–36. Some private owners had vignettes of the manor house shown in perspective whilst other buildings were in plan. John Mackown, surveyor of Lord Montfort's estate at Horseheath in 1767–70 (HRS77001–7 and SHU77001), for example, advertised in 1766 that he included: 'perspective Drawings of every thing worthy Notice [sic.]';[10] and this form of display continued into the early nineteenth century. Equation of perspective with display needs to be made with care; in Jamaican society, for example, the most important buildings such as the works buildings on coffee plantations, were carefully shown in plan whilst less important houses of both the slaves and landowner were shown in perspective for much longer (Higman, 1986, 76).

Cambridgeshire was one of the earliest counties to have estate maps with buildings in plan form. It cannot compete with Cumberland, however, where Andrew Pellin was asked in 1694 to copy his earlier survey of the town of Whitehaven and to incorporate the more modern method of showing buildings (Tyson, 1986, 174). A map of Sloley, Norfolk, shows buildings in plan form in 1708[11] and in Warwickshire, too, buildings were drawn in plan form by 1710 and the technique was common by 1728 (Pannett, 1985, 74). Elsewhere, development was slightly later: 1721 in Essex, 1731–3 in Worcestershire and 1740 in Gloucestershire, and in Gloucestershire and Essex perspective was more common until 1760 (Smith, 1967, 146).

It is quite clear from this general survey that some maps were drawn for display and that status could be shown in a number of ways: the amount and type of ornamentation, the map-maker who was employed and his methods of display of topographical information. The use of maps as status symbols is further discussed in Chapter 7.

MAP ACCURACY

Several factors determined a map's accuracy, such as the landowner for whom it was drawn and the reason why he commissioned it. In some cases, such as sketch maps, relative rather than absolute locations were more important, and at other times landowners wished to see the area of land round the manor house in greater detail and more accurately than the outlying parts of their estates. There are two main aspects of a consideration of map accuracy: whether the information is correct, and whether it is shown in its correct position. The second problem has two parts: the planimetric accuracy of a map, the extent to which distances and bearings between objects coincide with their true values; and its geodetic accuracy, whether the objects are placed in their correct astronomical position (Laxton, 1976, 38–40). Geodetic accuracy is not a concept of relevance to estate maps, which cover very small areas of the earth's surface. Analysis of a sample of estate maps of Cambridgeshire shows how planimetric accuracy and accuracy of topographical information varied over time.

Planimetric accuracy

The surveying profession was introduced to the concept of planimetric accuracy in its early days, when the practices of unskilled men were often very unsatisfactory. Surveying texts, such as those by Worsop and Agas, discussed the problem, and in the early seventeenth century Norden stressed the advantages of an accurate manorial survey (1610, *2v–*3r):

Lords of Tenants haue due regard of their owne estates, namely of the particulars of all their Tenants lands, and that by a due, true, and exact view and suruey of the same, to the end the Lord bee not abused, nor the Tenants wronged and grieued by false informations, which commonly grow by priuate Intelligencers, and neuer by iust Surueyors. And because the office of a Surueyor (duely waide, [sic.] is an office both necessarie, expedient, and of trust: It behoueth him to bee first honestly and vprightly minded: and next, skilfull and iudicious in the facultie.

Texts continued to discuss the importance of accurate measurement throughout the seventeenth century, and in the early eighteenth century John Green wrote in *The Construction of*

Maps and Globes (1717, 148), that: 'a Map~maker should not take every Map that comes out, upon Trust, or conclude that the newest is still the best, but ought to be at Pains to examine them by the Observations of the best Travellers, that so he may know their Goodness or Defects'. Surveyors in colonial Virginia were allowed a 5% tolerance level in 1710 (Hughes, 1979, 118); in colonial Jamaica, too, there was much concern about map accuracy and legislation to control it (Higman, 1988b, 21). Many eighteenth-century surveying texts described how to check the accuracy of surveying instruments and techniques (for example, Wyld, 1725; Emerson, 1770; Talbot, 1784; Davis, 1798), and in Essex at that time a client might occasionally employ a second surveyor to map a sample of the area and so check the accuracy of a survey (Mason, 1990, 17). There is evidence for a concern about accuracy among Cambridgeshire landowners in the early nineteenth century. In 1808, it was necessary to renew a lease of part of Queens' College's estate at Bermondsey in London. A map which had been made 116 years previously was examined with the lease, it was found that they tallied to within a few inches and so the map was used as the basis for a new survey.[12] Old maps were not always to be relied upon, however: in 1815 the following letter was sent to Emmanuel College from their London agents: 'The old plan [of Hyde Farm, Balham, Surrey] he [William Neale] found so imperfect, that he has taken a new one which I enclose and which shews that it was worth the expence, as it proves the Farm to contain more in quantity.'[13]

An examination of the planimetric accuracy of a map can be very informative. For example, Andrews (1974, 158) studied the accuracy of early seventeenth-century maps of the escheated counties of Ulster and suggested from his results that the maps were plotted from verbal boundary descriptions. He also analysed the accuracy of Henry Pratt's 1697 survey of the estates of Lord Kerry, and demonstrated that the maps were intended to be comprehensive records of boundaries and acreages, but not of antiquities, rivers and roads (Andrews, 1980a, 29). In maps of coffee and sugar plantations in Jamaica, variations in accuracy reflected the relative importance of elements within the plantation. The works were the first buildings to be measured carefully and plotted in plan; measurement of the location and distance of even the landowner's house was of secondary importance (Higman, 1986, 76 and 1987, 18). Another analysis of map accuracy showed other factors which influenced the drawing of a sheet; on a map of Crete which was drawn in 1629, the more strategically important parts of the coast were shown most accurately (Clutton, 1982, 56).

A number of techniques of analysis of the planimetric accuracy of maps have been proposed. Occasionally, studies compare the map to be tested with a contemporary map of the same area; Whittington and Gibson (1986) compared Roy's mid-eighteenth-century military survey of Scotland with contemporary estate plans, for example, but this method makes great assumptions about the accuracy of the contemporary maps. More frequently, methods are based on the principle of comparison of an historical map with a modern map of the same area, though the complexity of the procedure varies. Distances have been compared (Bönisch, 1967; Hooke and Perry, 1976), distortion lattices or displacement vectors, which show distances and directions, have been plotted (Ravenhill and Gilg, 1974; Stone and Gemmell, 1977), Euclidean regression has been carried out (Lloyd and Gilmartin, 1987; Tobler, 1965 and 1966; Waterman and Gordon, 1984), and the similarity between two maps has been examined by bringing them to the same scale photographically and overlaying one on the other (Margary, 1977). Murphy (1978, 92) contrasted four methods of expression of accuracy: standard deviation of the scale factor, average error of distances, root mean square error and Pearson's correlation coefficient. She concluded that the results depended on the method of analysis which had been chosen, but two techniques ranked maps of different accuracy in a logical way: calculation of the root mean square error, the method used by the Ordnance Survey (Harley, 1975, 162), and least squares regression.

Estate maps pose particular problems in assessment of accuracy because they cover small areas and, especially for pre-inclosure maps, very few points can be reliably transferred onto a modern map. The study whose subject approximates most closely to estate maps is Hooke and Perry's calculation of the root mean square error of tithe maps (1976), and their technique was used for the analysis of Cambridgeshire estate maps. Least squares regression is an inappropriate method because it is highly complicated and requires a large number of points for comparison.

Analysis was based on three main assumptions: that the points which were selected for comparison have not changed over time and that they represent the accuracy of all of the map, that the medium on which the map was drawn has not become deformed, and that if a scale had to be calculated, it does not vary over a map. Some previous studies have compared fixed points such as churches, castles and settlements (Laxton, 1976; Ravenhill and Gilg, 1974). Features which may have changed over time were chosen in other examinations (Chardon, 1982; De Boer and Carr, 1969; Lindsay, 1980). In this study, there was little opportunity to choose points as only a few could be transferred onto a modern map; these points included the church, manor house, road junctions, bridges and field boundaries. Whenever possible, a variety of points was selected for comparison. A major disadvantage of this method of point selection was that the points were probably as easy to identify in the past as they are today, and so they could have been the places from which surveying was carried out in the original drawing of the map. Thus, they may reflect the probable maximum accuracy of the map rather than its overall accuracy. As it was difficult both to establish which points were used in the original survey, and to find a sufficiently large sample of points for comparison, the possible use of points as places of survey did not affect the selection of features for comparison. Assumptions were also made about the medium on which the map was drawn. Maps were usually drawn on paper or parchment; over time paper is liable to shrink and parchment to buckle (Carr, 1962, 135). It was not possible to quantify these changes and so it was assumed that they were negligible. Finally, when a map had no scale, one was calculated. This was not straightforward, especially as the scale can vary over a map (Heidenreich, 1975; Stone, 1972). In Norden's map of the Orford area of 1601, for example, the scale varied by up to 100% (Carr, 1962, 136). In this analysis, the scale was determined by measurement between the first two points which were compared.

Blakemore and Harley (1980, 54–70) stress that for a study of map accuracy to be useful, not only is it essential to make clear the reasons for the study and to select appropriate techniques of assessment, but it is also important to remember the reasons for drawing a map and to ask whether a study of its planimetric accuracy is valid. Thus, some maps were excluded from the present study. Sketch maps were not examined as they were never intended to be planimetrically accurate. Tracings from other, usually inclosure, maps were also omitted as they reflected the accuracy of a survey which was not primarily carried out to show an individual's land. Maps on particulars of sale were excluded as they are another distinctive genre, drawn to show land to be auctioned, and this purpose might have affected their accuracy in a unique way. Thus it was not logical to select a sample of maps using random sampling techniques.

The sample was taken from maps in Cambridge University Library, where there are large numbers of copies of maps whose originals are elsewhere, and from photographs in the Cambridgeshire County Record Office of estates belonging to St John's College, Cambridge. The selection consisted of 12% of the sheets, or 13% of the maps, in the carto-bibliography. There was a bias towards the early period: 25% of the seventeenth-century sheets in the carto-bibliography were examined, 16% of those from the eighteenth century and 6% of those from the early nineteenth century.

On each map, one point was selected as the origin and from it were measured coordinates of points on the test map and their equivalents on the 1:10,560 Ordnance Survey sheet. As the map would have been surveyed in imperial units, these units were used for measurement. Readings were repeated until two results within $\frac{1}{16}$in. were obtained, or three measurements had been carried out, whichever number was least. The results were then converted to yards on the ground. The root mean square error, r, was calculated for the eastings and northings, and then the vector, v, of these two errors was determined:

$$r = \sqrt{\left(\frac{1}{n} \sum_{i=1}^{n} x_i{}^2 \right)}$$

where x_i is the error at point i and n is the number of points,

$$v = \sqrt{\left((r_{\text{eastings}})^2 + (r_{\text{northings}})^2 \right)}.$$

Three adjustments to the coordinates of the test map were necessary to obtain the best fit with the Ordnance Survey sheet: for orientation, for horizontal or vertical displacement, and for scale. Adjustments were carried out in this order until the vector was minimized. The resulting vector was divided by the corrected scale of the map to give the normalized error, which enabled comparisons to be made of results for different maps.

The results are given in Table 3.1 and summarized in Table 3.2. The normalized error was 3.77 overall, and this decreased over time from 4.60 in the seventeenth century to 2.63 in the early nineteenth century. Most seventeenth-century maps were accurate, but a few were very inaccurate: 19% of maps had normalized errors of at least twice the mean, and one map had a normalized error of over seven times the mean. Eighteenth-century maps were more accurate, but more were slightly inaccurate with a normalized error greater than average, and again one map had a normalized error of over seven times the mean. Early nineteenth-century maps were the most accurate and had a smaller variation about the mean; the most inaccurate map had a normalized error of under five times the mean. Thus, accuracy increased over time.

Table 3.1. *Results of the measurement of map accuracy*

Map	Orientation given	No. degrees corrected	Scale given	% old scale corrected	Vector (yards)	Normalized error	Table correct	Surveyor	Landowner	Comments
LIN60007	Y in border	+3	Y	-5	63.36	1.91	–	Thomas Waterman?	Ferdinand Parys	
GAM60201	Y in border	+1	Y	-5	73.89	0.62	–	Thomas Langdon	Merton College, Oxford	Summary sheet
GAM60202	Y in border	0	Y	0	19.60	0.67	–	Thomas Langdon	Merton College, Oxford	
GAM60203	Y in border	-1	Y	0	30.29	1.03	–	Thomas Langdon	Merton College, Oxford	
GAM60204	Y in border	0	Y	0	19.74	0.67	–	Thomas Langdon	Merton College, Oxford	
GAM60205	Y in border	+5	Y	0	136.77	4.64	–	Thomas Langdon	Merton College, Oxford	
GAM60206	Y in border	+3	Y	0	28.35	0.91	–	Thomas Langdon	Merton College, Oxford	
GAM60207	Y in border	+3	Y	0	41.66	1.41	–	Thomas Langdon	Merton College, Oxford	
GAM60208	Y in border	+7	Y	0	50.27	1.71	–	Thomas Langdon	Merton College, Oxford	
GAM60209	Y in border	0	Y	0	10.09	0.34	–	Thomas Langdon	Merton College, Oxford	Sheet with village

Map	Orientation given	No. degrees corrected	Scale given	% old scale corrected	Vector (yards)	Normalized error	Table correct	Surveyor	Landowner	Comments
GAM60210	Y in border	+7	Y	0	64.28	2.18	–	Thomas Langdon	Merton College, Oxford	
GAM60211	Y in border	0	Y	0	35.68	1.21	–	Thomas Langdon	Merton College, Oxford	
GAM60212	Y in border	+1	Y	0	12.16	0.41	–	Thomas Langdon	Merton College, Oxford	
GAM60213	Y in border	0	Y	0	29.44	0.95	–	Thomas Langdon	Merton College, Oxford	
GAM60214	Y in border	0	Y	0	29.35	1.00	–	Thomas Langdon	Merton College, Oxford	
GAM60215	N	+17	N	-25	495.53	10.44	–	Thomas Langdon?	Merton College, Oxford?	Rough sketch
LLA60301	Y	(+ -90) -1	Y	0	105.59	3.23	–	John Norden	John Spencer	
CAR61201	Y	-1	Y	-40	450.64	14.60	–	William Norton	Samson Leonard	Buckled; error of 4 central points 9.61
CHP65901	Y	-19	Y	-110	543.84	13.40	–	William Covell	John Clarke	Error of 4 central points 5.73
GRT66601	Y	-3	N	-5	72.07	2.25	–	George Skinner	King's College, Cambridge	
ORW68601	Y	+3	Y	-85	780.29	32.98	–	?	Thomas Chicheley	
CHP71201	Y	+19	Y	0	37.65	0.86	–	Heber Lands	Earl of Orford	

Table 3.1. *(cont.)*

Map	Orientation given	No. degrees corrected	Scale given	% old scale corrected	Vector (yards)	Normalized error	Table correct	Surveyor	Landowner	Comments
CHP71202	Y	+1	Y	+5	184.19	4.49	–	Heber Lands	Earl of Orford	
CHP71203	Y	+9	Y	-5	99.42	2.16	–	Heber Lands	Earl of Orford	Sheet with village
CHP71204	Y	0	Y	+15	116.07	3.16	–	Heber Lands	Earl of Orford	
CHP71205	Y	+21	Y	+5	80.91	1.94	–	Heber Lands	Earl of Orford	
CHP71206	Y	+17	Y	+5	140.06	3.41	–	Heber Lands	Earl of Orford	
CHP71207	Y	+21	Y	-5	167.27	3.37	–	Heber Lands	Earl of Orford	
CHP71208	Y	+9	Y	+5	121.62	2.96	–	Heber Lands	Earl of Orford	
GTA71701	Y	+15	Y	-5	243.17	7.47	–	Benjamin Fallowes	Maximilian Western	Vector if scale in poles as stated 108.89
WEW71901	Y	-1	Y	0	257.39	8.22	N	Arthur Frogley	Corporation of Sons of Clergy	
WEW71902	Y	+7	Y	+15	134.12	1.93	Y	Arthur Frogley	Corporation of Sons of Clergy	Copy by John Newton c. 1811
WLL71901	Y	+13	Y	-5	46.05	1.36	N	Arthur Frogley	Corporation of Sons of Clergy	On same sheet as WL271901
WL271901	Y	+9	Y	+15	128.35	4.69	Y	Arthur Frogley	Corporation of Sons of Clergy	Map of WEW on same sheet as WLL71901
WLL71902	Y	+11	Y	+20	84.69	1.29	N	Arthur Frogley	Corporation of Sons of Clergy	Copy by John Newton c. 1811
WEW73701	Y	-1	Y	0	116.55	2.39	–	John Bowles	Corporation of Sons of Clergy	
CAX75001	Y	(+180) +3	Y	0	79.94	2.50	–	Tycho Wing	Thomas Gape	
RAM75401	Y	+3	Y	0	130.42	5.44	–	Henry Fensham	John Leman	Buckled

Map	Orientation given	No. degrees corrected	Scale given	% old scale corrected	Vector (yards)	Normalized error	Table correct	Surveyor	Landowner	Comments
WLL75401	Y	−7	Y	−5	32.39	1.57	–	William Elstobb	Samuel Knight	
BOT75901	Y	+7	Y	−120	914.75	12.81	Y	Edmund Dipper and Joseph Hickman	'St Bartholomew's Hospital	Error of 3 central points 4.35
MAR76601	Y	+37	Y	0	56.67	0.85	–	?	Sir Robert Bernard	Same surveyor as MAR76602
MAR76602	Y	−3	Y	−5	117.39	1.29	–	?	Sir Robert Bernard	Same surveyor as MAR76601
STN77001	Y	+7	Y	0	94.93	1.85	N	George Salmon	John Fleming	
WIC77001	Y	−1	Y	0	32.48	0.69	–	James Parker	Earl of Bessborough	On same sheet as WI277001 and WI377001
WI277001	Y	−3	Y	−5	129.24	2.62	–	James Parker	Earl of Bessborough	See WIC77001
WI377001	Y	+9	Y	0	25.91	0.55	–	James Parker	Earl of Bessborough	See WIC77001
WMB77501	Y	+5	Y	0	84.01	0.65	Y	J. Porter	John Waddington	Scale given as grid
BAB78501	Y	0	Y	0	28.78	0.43	Y	James Ellis and Simeon King	St John's College, Cambridge	
SOH79002	Y	−13	Y	0	139.49	2.05	Y	Joseph Freeman?	St John's College, Cambridge	

Table 3.1. (cont.)

Map	Orientation given	No. degrees corrected	Scale given	% old scale corrected	Vector (yards)	Normalized error	Table correct	Surveyor	Landowner	Comments
BOU79101	Y	-11	Y	-10	228.12	2.37	Y	Joseph Freeman?	Christ's College, Cambridge	
COU79103	Y	-17	Y	0	100.47	1.11	Y	Joseph Freeman?	St John's College, Cambridge	
GTS79101	Y	-27	Y	+5	364.22	4.54	N	Joseph Freeman?	St John's College, Cambridge	
HRN79101	Y	-15	Y	-25	844.59	8.00	Y	Joseph Freeman?	St John's College, Cambridge	
FDY79201	N	-9	N	-5	269.22	3.76	N	Joseph Freeman	St John's College, Cambridge	
MEB79201	Y	+21	Y	+5	675.60	5.16	N	Nicholas King [and Joseph Freeman?]	St John's College, Cambridge	
BOT79301	Y	0	Y	+20	1,840.59	30.50	Y	Francis Marshall	St Bartholomew's Hospital	Photograph; error of 3 central points 2.40
STM79301	Y	+17	Y	-20	546.32	4.67	N	Joseph Freeman	St John's College, Cambridge	

Map	Orientation given	No. degrees corrected	Scale given	% old scale corrected	Vector (yards)	Normalized error	Table correct	Surveyor	Landowner	Comments
MAR79401	Y	+1	Y	0	11.33	0.32	Y	Joseph Freeman	St John's College, Cambridge	
WET79401	Y	-39	Y	-5	94.72	2.22	Y	Joseph Freeman	St John's College, Cambridge	
FOR79501	Y	+9	Y	0	194.26	2.21	Y	Joseph Freeman?	St John's College, Cambridge	
HIL79501	Y	-11	Y	+5	509.97	16.94	Y	?	Thomas Rumbold Hall	
WLL79501	N	-7	N	0	44.18	1.06	–	Joseph Freeman	Jesus College, Cambridge	
FDI79601	Y	-1	Y	+5	265.37	5.91	Y	Joseph Freeman?	Rev. George Leonard Jenyns	
GUI79701	Y	+7	Y	-10	219.53	6.30	–	John Prickett	Jacob John Whittington	
OVE79701	Y	+3	Y	0	10.14	1.28	Y	Thomas Lovell	Thomas Robinson	
TOF79901	N	-19	N	0	38.30	0.38	N	Joseph Freeman?	St John's College, Cambridge	
SWB80001	Y	+27	Y	0	140.57	1.94	Y	Thomas Norfolk	William Parker Hamond	
WMP80001	Y	+11	N	+10	125.84	1.26	–	?	3rd Earl of Hardwicke	
CHI80201	Y	0	Y	0	28.91	0.45	–	?	Nicolson Calvert	

Table 3.1. (cont.)

Map	Orientation given	No. degrees corrected	Scale given	% old scale corrected	Vector (yards)	Normalized error	Table correct	Surveyor	Landowner	Comments
ICK80301	Y	-3	Y	+15	242.98	4.59	–	Edward Laurence	Percy Charles Wyndham	Copy by W. Haydell
TRU80401	Y	+7	Y	-5	62.50	1.24	–	Edward Gibbons	Francis Charles James Pemberton	Buckled
MAR80501	Y	+5	Y	0	49.48	0.78	Y	William Peak	Hon. General Robert Bernard Sparrow	
WEW80901	Y	+13	Y	+10	541.96	12.35	Y	Thomas Norfolk	John Chester Pern	
HRN81001	Y	-9	Y	-85	774.32	4.79	Y	?	St John's College, Cambridge	
MAD81101	Y	-5	Y	0	47.40	0.66	N	William Custance	Sir Charles Cotton	
WLL81101	Y	-17	Y	0	79.43	2.44	N	?	Corporation of Sons of Clergy	
WEW81501	Y	+9	Y	0	547.24	11.23	N	Thomas Norfolk	Corporation of Sons of Clergy	
CHI81701	Y	+33	Y	0	187.10	2.36	N		Nicolson Calvert	Copy by William Buckland
GTA81801	Y	(+90) -9	N	0	31.16	0.64	Y	Alexander Watford jr	John Mortlock	
CRX82301	Y	0	Y	0	42.81	0.44	–	?	Sir George William Leeds	
RAM82501	Y	0	Y	0	13.36	0.42	–	?	John Mann	
EYM82701	Y	-7	Y	+5	220.34	4.88	–	?	?	

Map	Orientation given	No. degrees corrected	Scale given	% old scale corrected	Vector (yards)	Normalized error	Table correct	Surveyor	Landowner	Comments
HAD82701	Y	-27	Y	-5	107.65	2.22	Y	Alexander Watford jr	Gonville and Caius College, Cambridge	Drawn by James Richardson
LIT82801	Y	+3	Y	+5	88.21	1.49	Y	Alexander Watford jr	John Maryon Wilson	
BAB82901	Y	+5	Y	0	71.91	2.07	–	?	Henry John Adeane	
BOT83301	Y	0	Y	0	39.99	1.25	Y	Thomas James Tatham	St Bartholomew's Hospital	
SOH83301	Y	+9	Y	0	55.72	1.17	–	John Croft	James Drage Merest	
ARR83401	N	+23	Y	0	45.04	1.42	–	Robert Withers	4th Earl of Hardwicke	

Table 3.2. *Summary of the measurements of map accuracy*

Date	Normalized error	% sheets with error greater than mean	% sheets with error greater than 2 x mean	% sheets with error greater than 3 x mean
To 1699	4.60	24	19	10
1700–99	4.08	32	9	7
1800–36	2.63	22	9	9
To 1836	3.77	27	13	8

A few maps were very inaccurate; eight maps had normalized errors of over 10. These were maps of Carlton cum Willingham (1612, CAR61201), Chippenham (1659, CHP65901), Orwell (1686, ORW68601), two maps of Bottisham (1759 and 1793, BOT75901, BOT79301), and maps of Hildersham (1795, HIL79501) and West Wratting (1809 and 1815, WEW80901, WEW81501). For these maps the vectors of distortion were plotted; Fig. 3.12 shows the plot for Carlton cum Willingham. The origin is the church and the figure shows that the centre of the map was more accurately surveyed than the outlying areas. The same was found for the other inaccurate maps. In no case was any one point so inaccurate that the overall accuracy of the map was greatly affected. There did not seem to be any large variation in accuracy between the different types of points which were selected for comparison; some field and parish boundaries were as accurately surveyed as road junctions, bridges, manor houses and churches. One of the maps of Bottisham, BOT79301 in Table 3.1, was a special case as it was a copy in eight photographs of a map in St Bartholomew's Hospital. The high inaccuracy of this map probably reflected difficulty of measurement rather than inaccuracy of survey.

It was possible to see whether the compasses on the maps reflected their true orientation. North points on maps which were drawn in the seventeenth century had to be adjusted by 5°, this correction increased to 10° on eighteenth-century maps and to 11° on early nineteenth-century maps. Before analysis was possible, the compass points on two maps had to be rotated by 90°: John Norden's map of Little Abington of 1603 (LLA60301) and Alexander Watford's map of Great Abington in 1818 (GTA81801), and the compass points on Tycho Wing's map of Caxton of 1749/50 (CAX75001) had to be corrected by 180°. These three surveyors were not merely local men who practised surveying as a side-line, and the maps were all drawn for display. Maybe the surveyors employed draughtsmen to complete and decorate the maps, who may have rotated the compass points by mistake. The duties of assistants to surveyors are further discussed in Chapter 4.

Accuracy of the scale bar and of the addition of acreages on tables were both quite high. On seventeenth-century maps the scale had to be adjusted by 13%, on eighteenth-century

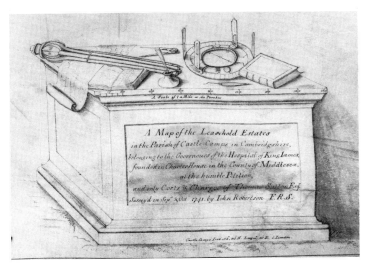

Plate 10. Title cartouche to the estate map of Castle Camps drawn by John Robertson for the Charterhouse, 1741.

Plate 11. Title cartouche to estate map of Grey's Farm, East Hatley, drawn by Joseph Cole for Sir Jacob Garrard Downing, 1750, showing rococo decoration.

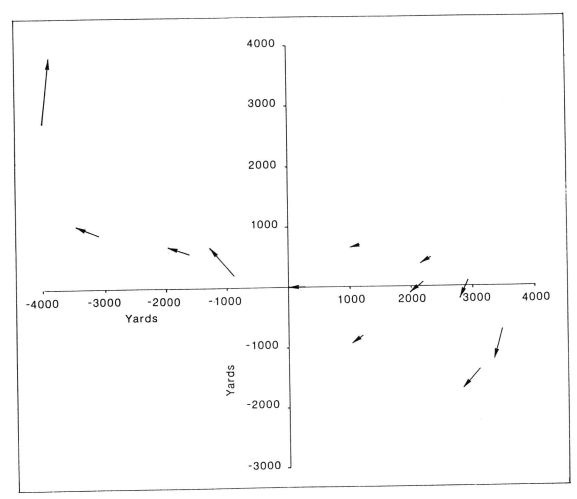

Fig. 3.12. Displacement vectors for the map of Carlton cum Willingham, 1612.

maps by 8% and on early nineteenth-century maps by 6%. The 27 maps in the carto-bibliography which gave their scale both in words and in a bar also showed that scale bars were fairly accurate: one-fifth showed a discrepancy of more than $\pm\frac{1}{16}$ in. between the two scale statements and half were exactly the same. Addition of acreages on tables was checked for the maps in the sample. None of the seventeenth-century maps had tables, 63% of the tables on eighteenth-century maps were correct as were 62% of those on early nineteenth-century maps.

The results varied according to surveyor and landowner. Maps which were drawn for private owners, whose prestige was at stake, tended to be slightly more accurate. This was especially true in the eighteenth century when the error of their maps was 3.15 compared with 4.60 for institutional owners, and in the early nineteenth century when the errors were 2.19 and 3.72 respectively. Although maps which were more decorative were usually signed (68% of the maps in the sample had their surveyor named), these maps were not necessarily more accurate than average (see Table 3.3). Table 3.4 summarizes the accuracy of maps which were drawn by six surveyors, and it shows that individual men produced maps at particular levels of accuracy, and that the consistency of accurate map production varied between surveyors irrespective of the date at which they practised. Some such as Thomas Langdon, whose maps of Gamlingay were drawn in 1601/2, were fairly consistent: the range of errors was 0.34–4.64, the scale had to be corrected by -5% to 0% and the orientation by -1° to 7°. Others were much more variable. Thomas Norfolk's maps, which were drawn between 1800 and 1815, had a range of errors of 1.94–12.35, the scale had to be corrected by 0% to 10%, the orientation by 9° to 27° and one of the three tables was incorrectly added up.

Table 3.3. *Variation over time in the error of signed maps*

Date	Average error	Error of signed maps
To 1699	4.60	2.85
1700–99	4.08	4.18
1800–36	2.63	3.10

Finally, it is possible to see whether acreages were estimated or measured. In the early days of drawing estate maps, acreages were frequently estimated. John Worlidge said in his *Mystery of Husbandry* of 1681 that: 'an Acre is sometimes estimated by the proportion of seed used on it; and so varies according to the richness or sterility of the land' (quoted in Airy, 1909, 268). There is evidence that estimation of area persisted into the nineteenth century in Cambridgeshire. A map of Crown land in Burwell in 1806 (BUW80601) has a table which gives acreages both 'by estimation' and by statute measure. In 1812, a survey of Jesus College's land at Over was carried out to compare the statute and computed measure.[14] Similarly, Alexander Watford surveyed a farm in Barton for the University of Cambridge in

Table 3.4. *Accuracy of surveyors' maps*

Surveyor	Dates of maps	Number of maps	Average error	Range of errors	Correction of scale (a)	Range of (a)	Correction of orientation (b)	Range of (b)
Thomas Langdon	1601/2	14	1.27	0.34–4.64	-0.7%	-5% – 0%	+2°	-1° – +7°
Heber Lands	1712	8	2.79	0.86–4.49	+6.0%	-5% – +15%	+12°	0° – +21°
Arthur Frogley	1719	5	3.80	1.29–8.22	+10.0%	-5% – +20%	+9°	-1° – +13°
Joseph Freeman	1790–99	13	2.91	0.32–8.00	-4.2%	-25% – +5%	-8°	-39° – +21°
Thomas Norfolk	1800–15	3	8.51	1.94–12.35	+3.0%	0% – +10%	+16°	+9° – +27°
Alexander Watford jr	1818–28	3	1.45	0.64–2.22	+3.0%	-5% – +5%	-13°	-27° – -9°

1797, and both he and his son, another Alexander, who resurveyed the property in 1823, probably estimated its acreage. A note on the back of another plan of the farm (BAR80302) says,

Barton Farm Valuation by Watford in 1797 who then made the Quantity of Land 277 A. 1 R. 35 P. In 1823. Mr Watford made it only 249.1.13. Mr Harwood went over all the Land < > Measured every Piece in 1829; & according to his Survey (very accurrately [sic.] particularized in a large Book). The Farm contains only 239 A. 2 R. 26 P. Statute Measure. The Watfords *could* only be Computed Measure but it is difficult to reconcile the difference they make in the Quantity between the years 1797 & 1723 [sic., really 1823] W. C[hristmas].[15]

In some cases it is possible to evaluate accuracy more precisely by comparing acreages with those on early Ordnance Survey maps. Fowler (1936, 41) did this for the 1764 strip map of Eversholt, Bedfordshire, and so did Caird for estate plans of the Western Isles (1989, 74). Similarly, on a map of Great Hazeley in Oxfordshire, surveyed by Joel Gascoyne in 1701, a comparison of some of the acreages of closes with Ordnance Survey area books shows errors of 0.69% and 0.93% (Ravenhill, 1973, 111). Much depended on the landowner: Connor showed this for a map of Whitehill, Oxfordshire, drawn in 1605 (1987, 49). The map is in the style of Thomas Langdon, and it was drawn to show the land which belonged to Corpus Christi College, Oxford and to a local yeoman, Edward Standerd. The College had its land surveyed and each of its strips has the actual area in acres, roods and perches written on. Mr Standerd, however, did not put himself to this expense, and all his strips are nominally of two acres, though in fact from comparison with the College property the areas were probably somewhat less than this. The reason for commissioning a map was also important, as on occasion a rough indication of area was all that was required.

Topographical accuracy

The accuracy of topographical information on maps also varied over time and its study can be as informative as that of planimetric accuracy. In 1948, Beresford compared strips on a 1778 map of Ilmington, Warwickshire with aerial photographs of the area, and he demonstrated that the strips had been accurately drawn on the map. Trees, as sources of timber, were often shown in their correct positions and so provide useful historical evidence. John Say, for example, advertised in 1729 that: 'Timber Trees also taken Account of, put down in the Plan in their exact Place; Oak, and Ash, &c. distinguished by different Colours, if desired.'[16] Similarly, in 1771 Samuel Hervey was instructed: 'in each hedge row or anywhere else if any to note the timbers or trees like for timber therein' in his survey of the Essex estates of George de Horne (Mason, 1990, 10). In Cambridgeshire, a set of estate maps of land belonging to Sir Jacob Garrard Downing in Tadlow, Croydon and East Hatley was drawn in 1750. These maps were carefully drawn and, as comparison with Ordnance Survey maps shows that their topographical information was correct, Rackham (1968) was able to use them to determine the shapes of ponds which have since disappeared.

In this study, analysis was confined to the architectural information which can be derived from churches and houses on maps. Some drawings of buildings are merely conventional symbols, whereas others can be used to determine a wide range of architectural features. For example, a map of part of the Inverary Estate in Scotland, drawn in 1792 by George Langlands, shows cottages with one central door with a single chimney in the middle of the roof, a single window on either side and a small compartment with a small door at each end (Fairhurst, 1968, 183). Roofing materials can be deduced: the maps of Essex which were drawn by the Walker family in the late sixteenth and early seventeenth centuries always distinguish between tile and thatch (Newton, 1969, 4). As buildings on the Walkers' maps were related to the maps' scale, the sheets give information about house size (Edwards and Newton, 1984, 82). Drawings of churches can also be informative; for example, it is possible to see their forms before Victorian restoration (Yates, 1982, 213).

Churches on 21 of the maps of Cambridgeshire were compared with churches today; 17 were shown at their correct stage of architectural development. Some churches were in plan form. For example, Plate 12a shows Downham Church on a map of 1793 and comparison with a modern plan of the church (Plate 12b) shows that apart from recent additions, the two are identical. Alternatively, churches can be in elevation. A drawing of East Hatley Church in 1750 (Plate 13a) is clearly the church which is depicted on an early twentieth-century postcard (Plate 13b); the bellcote was probably added in 1874 (Pevsner, 1970, 334). Similarly, the church at Haddenham on a map drawn in 1827 (Plate 14a) can be compared with a mid-eighteenth-century engraving of the church (Plate 14b). The angle at which the church is viewed in the engraving exaggerates the length of the chancel, whereas the angle from which the church was drawn on the map shortens the chancel. Detail on the tower is not clear, but both plates show the embattled parapet and spire, and the fence which surrounded the church-yard and so are clearly of the same place. Some conventions were followed, however: churches were usually shown from the south side even if the main entrance was on the north, as at Bartlow. Plate 15a shows Bartlow Church from the south on a map which was drawn in 1785. The church is clearly the one shown in Plate 15b, a photograph of the church in the 1920s which shows the main entrance to the church through the north porch, and in Plate 15c, a drawing from an etching of 1832 which demonstrates that there was then no south porch or important entrance on that side of the church, nor had there been previously. Similar cases have been noted by Horner on a 1735 map of Carlow in Ireland (1978, 116) and by Harvey on an Elizabethan map of Sherborne, Dorset (1965, 83). Four maps had conventional symbols for churches: for example Plate 14c, which shows Haddenham Church as it was drawn on a map of 1818, can be compared with Plate 14a, which shows the church in 1827. There is little resemblance between the two churches and Plate 14b shows that the earlier church (Plate 14c) is a conventional symbol. Both of these maps were drawn by Alexander Watford junior, and show that an individual surveyor did not necessarily always show correct drawings of churches. Similarly, Plate 16a shows Alexander Watford's conventional symbol for Teversham Church which does not approximate to the form of the church on a near-contemporary drawing (Plate 16b).

Plate 12a. Downham Church in plan form, on the estate map probably drawn by Joseph Freeman for Clare College, 1793.

Plate 12b. Plan of Downham Church.

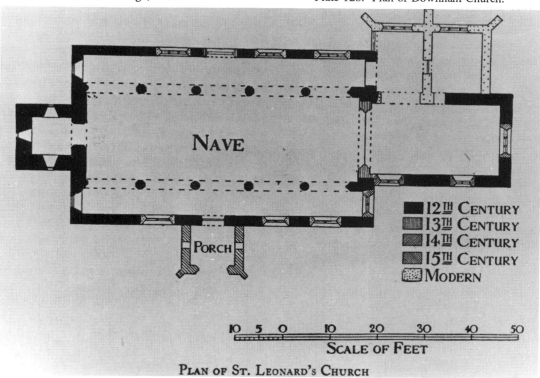

NAVE

PORCH

◼ 12ᵀᴴ CENTURY
▨ 13ᵀᴴ CENTURY
▨ 14ᵀᴴ CENTURY
▨ 15ᵀᴴ CENTURY
▨ MODERN

10 5 0 10 20 30 40 50
SCALE OF FEET

PLAN OF ST. LEONARD'S CHURCH

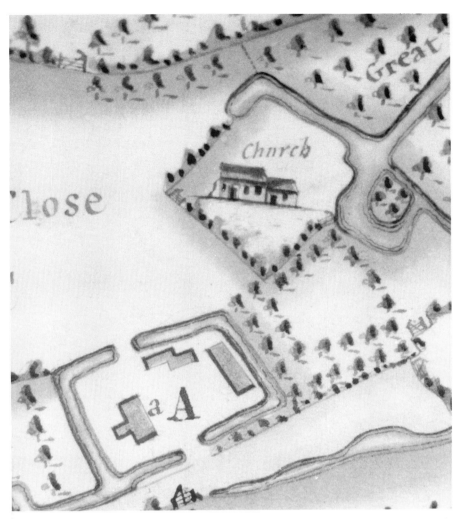

Plate 13a. East Hatley Church and Manor, on the estate map drawn by Joseph Cole for Sir Jacob Garrard Downing, 1750.

Plate 13b. Postcard of East Hatley Church, c. 1910.

Plate 14a. Haddenham Church, on the estate map drawn by
Alexander Watford junior for Gonville and Caius College, 1827.

Plate 14b. Engraving of Haddenham Church by Whiteman and
Bass, c. 1860.

Plate 14c. Haddenham Church,
on the estate map drawn by
Alexander Watford junior for
Clare College, 1818.

Plate 15a. Bartlow Church from the south, on the estate map of Barham Manor, Linton, drawn by Charles Wedge for Sarah Lonsdale, 1785.

Plate 15b. Bartlow Church from the north, c. 1920.

Plate 15c. Bartlow Church from the south, from an etching of 1832.

Plate 16a. Teversham Church, on the estate map drawn by Alexander Watford junior for Gonville and Caius College, 1812.

Plate 16b. Early nineteenth-century drawing of Teversham Church, by R. H. Relhan.

Conclusion

Houses on maps were also compared; for example, William Covell's drawing of Badlingham Hall in Chippenham in 1659 (Plate 17a) shows the same position of the cross-wing, chimneys and entrance as in the manor house in 1987 (Plate 17b), though the dormer windows have been removed. Similarly, the drawing of Mordon Hall Farm in Plate 18a was probably an exact drawing of the farm as it existed in 1751 as, although it does not show a jettied first floor and a door has been removed and a window added, it is obviously the same building as in Plate 18b, a photograph of the farm in 1987. The 1751 map was drawn by Joseph Cole for Sir Jacob Garrard Downing. Downing's estates in Croydon, East Hatley and Tadlow were also mapped by Cole and there is a vignette of each farmhouse (CRY75001–11, EAS75001–8 and TAD75001–9). Many of the buildings on the estate, however, fell into disrepair during the litigation which followed Jacob's death (Henderson, 1982, 22). Thus it is not easy to compare the other drawings with buildings which are still extant today. As architectural changes to houses are less well documented than those for churches, it is more difficult to see from published sources how a building would have looked at the time a map was drawn.

This discussion of map accuracy has considered two main areas: the planimetric accuracy of a map and the accuracy of the topographical information which it contains. Though some of the carefully drawn early maps could be as accurate as those which were drawn in the nineteenth century, in general accuracy increased over time. The increase, however, was not at a uniform rate and in some cases acreages were estimated as late as the nineteenth century. Some maps were drawn as decorative objects to hang on walls and to show the importance of the owner's land; the area around the church and manor was most accurately shown and the manor could be depicted in a perspective drawing. The landowner, surveyor and reasons why a map was drawn all affected the type of map which was produced.

CONCLUSION

This examination has shown that by detailed analysis of a set of maps which cover a particular region it is possible to determine their general characteristics, and to relate these characteristics to local patterns of landownership and reasons for commissioning a map. The overall rate of increase of map production in Cambridgeshire was exponential and probably reflected diffusion of knowledge of maps and their uses. Smaller-scale fluctuations can be related to economic and social events: some good harvests, the Civil War, the interest of colleges in developing their estates in the late eighteenth century and inclosure.

Estate maps can be seen as part of an interest in the land in the seventeenth and eighteenth centuries, and many of the developments and their variations can be explained by the nature of the landowner who had his estates mapped. The unusual character of landownership in Cambridgeshire, with relatively few large landed owners and many institutional estates which were small and largely concentrated in the south of the county, explains the late development of map-making, the areas of the county which were mapped and the type of map which was

Plate 17a. Badlingham Hall, Chippenham, on the estate map drawn by William Covell for John Clarke, 1659.

Plate 17b. Badlingham Hall, 1987.

Plate 18a. Mordon Hall Farm, Guilden Morden, on the estate map drawn by Joseph Cole for Sir Jacob Garrard Downing, 1751.

Plate 18b. Mordon Hall Farm, 1987.

drawn. Private owners were more interested in maps as objects of display and status, their maps were frequently carefully drawn, attributed to surveyors, were accurate and often showed the use of new techniques. Thus, the use of compass points and depiction of buildings in plan form was adopted by private owners earlier than by institutions. Institutional owners were more concerned with the practical management of their estates, though some of their maps, especially the early ones, could also be decorative. As patterns of landownership changed, the number of maps produced for practical purposes grew; these maps were far less decorative and were sometimes merely unsigned sketch maps. The characteristics of landowners in Cambridgeshire, the ways they changed and the reasons for commissioning maps are discussed in further detail in Chapters 6 and 7.

Before considering landowners more fully, however, it is useful to look at the changing status and accomplishments of the surveyors who produced estate maps. The relation between this aspect of social history and maps is examined in the next two chapters.

Chapter 4

ESTATE SURVEYORS AND THEIR EMPLOYMENT

In the history of cartography, as in the graphic arts, literature, or the history of science, biographical research makes an indispensable contribution ... We cannot know too much about the map~maker ... there is a danger in over~reacting to the charisma of prominent men. (Blakemore and Harley, 1980, 33)

In early modern Britain, new groups of men emerged to add to the traditional professions of medicine, law and theology, such ones as architecture, engineering, surveying and teaching. Not until the nineteenth century did these new professions become fully fledged, when a social distinction between the leaders and the led became institutionalized, and a particular expertise, acquired through approved methods of training and practised under the discipline of an accepted code of conduct, was rewarded by a certain status and commensurate level of remuneration and privilege (Buchanan, 1989, 15). The careers of those who surveyed estate maps of Cambridgeshire demonstrate a small part of this overall trend and can be related to the growth of the surveying profession in the county, to national developments in the profession and to other alterations in the society and economy of early modern Britain. Several aspects of surveyors' lives are examined: this chapter describes where and for whom they worked, and how they were employed; the next chapter discusses the pay and status of surveyors in society, the degree to which they depended on surveying for their livelihood, how they learned the techniques which they used and whether their techniques developed and changed. A brief discussion of the rise of the surveying profession in England from the sixteenth to the nineteenth centuries provides a national context for a detailed study of the careers of some local surveyors.

THE SURVEYING PROFESSION IN EARLY MODERN ENGLAND

The central function of a surveyor has always been the overlooking of property and surveyors were employed on estates from medieval times, but a nineteenth-century surveyor would hardly have recognized his medieval predecessor. A medieval surveyor's work consisted of drawing up manorial extents and surveys and he had to select appropriate witnesses, assess and classify their evidence and interpret the customs of the manor (Thompson, 1968, 5). Fitzherbert's *The Boke of Surveyeng and Improvmentes* of 1523, the first English surveying text to be printed, described these tasks:

it is necessary that euery great estate bothe men & women of worship that haue great possessyons of landes and tenementes shulde haue a Surueyour that can extende but and bounde and value them. And therof to make a boke in parchement bearyng a certayne date ... that the lorde his freholders copyeholders nor tenauntes shall neuer lose landes nor rentes customes nor seruyces. (1523, bii)

Techniques of measurement were not mentioned. Simultaneously, surveyors were emerging from amongst Tudor master-masons and military engineers; John Rogers, *par excellence*, served Henry VIII as a working mason, master-mason, architectural and topographical draughtsman, architect, military engineer, hydraulic engineer, building consultant, administrative clerk, military spy, diplomatic attaché, and land surveyor (Shelby, 1967, 3).

As the concept of landed property as a collection of rights gave way to that of ownership of a definable piece of land, it was no longer sufficient to rely upon oral tradition and local knowledge, and the simple 'landmeater' who had accompanied the steward was replaced by a professional surveyor who could prepare a well-executed and ornamented estate plan (Darby, 1933). The early practitioners, who started producing estate maps in the 1570s, came from a variety of backgrounds: the elder Ralph Treswell was a member of the Painter and Stainers' Company (Schofield, 1987), while Ralph Agas was Rector of Gressenhall in Norfolk and then settled at Stoke by Nayland in Suffolk and became agent for Thomas Browne, an absentee royal farmer (Eden A43; MacCulloch, 1975, 281). Map-making spread slowly, and a simple survey, either with a measuring rod or cord or by estimation, was sufficient for many landowners well into the seventeenth century (Taylor, 1947, 130). Written surveys continued to be common: maps were only drawn as part of the surveys in 1631–2 of the manors of Philip, 1st Earl of Pembroke and Montgomery, when there had been extensive changes from inclosure or the exchange of open field lands or commons (Kerridge, 1953, xiii). Similarly, maps were rarely drawn in surveys of Crown lands (Madge, 1938, 139). In about 1616, John Norden advised that plotting whole manors would be too expensive and would double the cost of a survey, though demesnes and improvable wastes should be mapped in all cases (Lawrence, 1985, 54–5).

Early surveyors were not held in high esteem, partly because there was a shortage of skilled men and a number of rogues masqueraded as surveyors. The problem was seriously regarded; Ralph Agas described inaccurate amateur surveys (1596, B2):

And in my comming to London, this last Tearme, I saw a plaine Table man (mary he was a plumber, and had learned from a Painter) in lesse than an acre and halfe, of leuell marrish grounde taken by some foure stations fel short at his cloase two pearches at the least. And an ancient country measurer at the same time, a man highly regarded among his neighbors, for his vndoubted skills differed in one hundred & ten akers, two and twenty at the least, in two seuerall measures, taken and set downe onely by himselfe ... They are termed Surueighors, if they but once shewe forth a plaine table: and are content to arrogate and challenge that name to them selues: but they must turne a new leafe, and take forther an other lesson before they finish a good and perfit Surveigh.

Worsop, too, was concerned and published his *A Discoverie of Sundrie Errours and Faults Daily Committed by Landemeaters* in 1582. He included an early call for some sort of professional organization:

If the skilful in the parts Mathematicall, Legal, and Judicial would frindly, and singly ioyne together to reforme, and instruct each others, and to reduce surueie to a perfect order: without doubt many which now vnderstand but parts, and peeces rightly: but moe things erroniously, or lamely, would in short space proue sufficient men. (1582, K2r)

Complaints continued into the early seventeenth century: the son of Richard Gough of Myddle's great aunt married the daughter of Thomas Spendlove, who was 'a crafty contriveing old fellow, a great surveyor and measurer of Lands'. Gough's schoolmaster called him 'Longo limite mensor', or, the measurer with the long boundary (Gough, 1701, 162).

After this time, there were fewer grumbles as surveyors became more competent through greater practice, though they were mostly still humble men (Phillips, 1980, 100; Woodward, 1978, 160). There were some exceptions: William Fowler, who surveyed estates in Montgomeryshire, Shropshire, Staffordshire and Warwickshire, was the younger son of a small landowning but well-established Staffordshire gentry family (Phillips, 1979, 19). Practical mathematics flourished, and astronomers, astrologers, instrument-makers and mathematical teachers all produced almanacs in which they advertised their services, including land surveying (Capp, 1979, 199). The professions in general prospered in England after the Restoration (Holmes, 1982), and simultaneously there was a stimulus to the nascent surveying profession (Thompson, 1968, 26).

The eighteenth century saw the start of the development of land surveying in Scotland and Wales as agricultural improvements occurred (Adams, 1968, 249; Thomas, 1985, 218). Throughout the kingdom, the profession was still relatively undeveloped and surveyors had to have a variety of alternative occupations as a cushion against variations in demand (Eden, 1973, 474). The eighteenth century was a period when scientific societies were founded and flourished, and land surveyors became involved with them: William Elstobb, a land surveyor and engineer of King's Lynn who mapped land at Carlton cum Willingham and Willingham in Cambridgeshire for the Reverend Samuel Knight (CAR75401 and WLL75401), visited and wrote to the Peterborough Gentlemen's Society. Edward Laurence and John Grundy (see ICK80301 and THO74901 respectively) were members of both the Spalding and Stamford Gentlemen's societies (Evans, 1982, 270 and 277), and Grundy's son, another John, was also a member of the Spalding society (Goshawk, 1948, 89). Surveying was seen as a way for the poor to improve their social status: John Clare, for example, strived for betterment through education (Storey, 1982, 48): 'my pride fancyd itself climbing the ladder of learning very rapidly on the top of which harvests of unbounded wonders was concieved [sic.] to be bursting upon me and was sufficient fire to my ambition ...' (Clare, 1984, 431), and, 'I fancyd too that I was book learnd for I had gotten together by saving a quantity of old books ... I will recollect some of them there was the young mans best companion Arithmetic the last was a favourite with me & I kept it Bonnycastles Mensuration & Wards Mathematics Leybourns & Morgans Dialling ... Martindales Landsurveying & Cockers Landsurveying Hills Herbal Balls Astrology ...' (Clare, 1951, 50). Though Clare found that: 'I was not sufficient to become master of these things [practical mathematics] without better assistance, as a superficial knowledge of them was next to nothing' (1931, 54), others fared better, began to specialize and to continue their climb to a higher status. By the end of the eighteenth century, they were being increasingly used in inclosure and estate management (Beckett, 1989, 593). Many were employed as professional valuers of estates (Andrews, 1985, 253; Eden, 1975, 122), some formed firms of estate agents (Pannett, 1985, 81), and by the nineteenth century surveyors could acquire substantial fortunes.

In 1834, six London surveyors and three friends formed the Land Surveyors' Club; they were all experienced chain surveyors but regarded their valuing and advisory services as their professional hallmarks. They defined a land surveyor as:

one who has learned the art of admeasuring and delineating the surface of a country, is capable of dividing, allotting and arranging for enclosure, commons and wasteland, or dividing or allotting the interests of those holding as joint tenants ... versed in the knowledge of the various products of agriculture, their values and comparative advantages ... and in the relative uses, values, and mensuration of standing or fallen timber, having at the same time a perfect knowledge of all that appertains to the value, contracts, and arrangements of property in the character of land agent. (Thompson, 1968, 96)

Map-making was only one of a land surveyor's duties, and the Club later decided that a member did not need actually to have measured land. The Club foundered and the introduction of large-scale Ordnance Survey plans reduced the work of the private surveyor (Wallis, 1990, ix). The introduction of lithography, too, changed the practice of estate surveying: a Cornish surveyor Robert Symons, for example, advertised in 1844 that he intended to publish by subscription a lithographic map of the parish of Stithians and that landowners could order copies with their estates coloured in (F. Herbert, personal communication). The colonies and Empire also affected nineteenth-century surveying: many Scottish surveyors sought employment overseas (Webster, 1989, 88) and in 1843, George Warren of Norwich offered to teach land surveying to young emigrants.[1] A new phase in the development of the profession had begun, and the Institution of Surveyors (the Royal Institution of Chartered Surveyors since 1946), the professional body, was eventually founded in 1868.

The surveying profession, therefore, was slow to develop and official control of a surveyor's activities came very late: two centuries after Sweden (Baigent, 1990, 63) and one hundred years later than Ireland (Andrews, 1985, 100), whilst the *Act for Regulating Surveyors* was passed in 1683 in colonial Jamaica (Higman, 1988b, 20). At no time was a surveyor solely a map-maker and frequently an individual was not only a surveyor but had another source of income. A sample of surveyors, those who practised in Cambridgeshire before the Tithe Commutation Act, is examined in more detail.

SURVEYORS OF CAMBRIDGESHIRE'S ESTATES

Many estate surveyors practised in Cambridgeshire between about 1600 and 1836, and the names are known of nearly 200 of them. Some were men of national reputation who travelled long distances and drew many estate and other types of map, while others hardly moved outside the county boundary and were much less prolific.

The discussion in this and the following chapter is based on the careers of the men who drew estate maps of Cambridgeshire. The sample, therefore, is only as complete as the sample of estate maps, discussed in the preceding chapter. In addition, the surveyors of 18 % of the maps could not be identified, so there were certainly more men practising in the county than are examined here. From a number of printed and manuscript sources, brief biographies of the surveyors have been drawn up; these sources include Eden's *Dictionary of Land Surveyors* (1975 edition and its supplements; references in this text are to the forthcoming second edition), Venn (1922–54), the *Dictionary of National Biography*, surveying texts, the *Cambridge Chronicle*, published catalogues of estate maps in county record offices, and un-published catalogues in the Cambridgeshire County Record Office and Cambridge University Library (the General Catalogue of Printed Books, catalogues in the Map and Manuscripts departments, and the index to the Ely Probate Files). More detailed examination of the careers of three surveyors – Joseph Freeman and Alexander Watford and his son, Alexander – is based on the archives of Cambridge University and Clare, Emmanuel, Gonville and Caius, Jesus, Queens', St John's and Trinity colleges. As the search for material was mostly con-fined to sources which were available in Cambridge, the biographies are unavoidably incomplete, and the conclusions which have been drawn in these two chapters may be altered by future research.

The size of the body of surveyors who practised in Cambridgeshire seems to be fairly typi-cal for a moderately sized English county: Eden found 340 surveyors who worked in Norfolk over a longer time period, 1550–1850, and who did not necessarily draw estate maps (1973, 474). Twelve Cambridgeshire surveyors started their careers in the period to 1649, and eight in the second half of the seventeenth century; this closely compares with Pannett's 18 sur-veyors who practised in seventeenth-century Warwickshire (1985, 70). Fifty named surveyors worked in Essex before 1700, however, and 60 in Kent (Hull, 1987, 247). In the eighteenth century, the number of surveyors who worked in Cambridgeshire at some time began to grow: 27 from 1703 to 1751, 33 from 1752 to 1784, and 42 from 1785 to 1810. This increase continued in the early nineteenth century, with 62 new names appearing between 1811 and 1836. By comparison, there were fewer new surveyors in Warwickshire at this time: 127 between 1710 and 1840 (Pannett, 1985, 80). In Scotland, however, where the sur-veying profession was slower to develop, there were only 12 surveyors practising by 1745, though there was a rapid increase in the following two decades and 74 were employed by 1765 (Adams, 1975, 15). In 1810, there was one surveyor for every 18,000 people in Scotland. Even in Jamaica, the ratio was 1:12,000; the fortunes of surveyors closely fol-lowed the prosperity of the plantation system (Higman, 1988a). In Cambridgeshire, with a relatively dense and settled population, the situation was quite different, and from 1801 to 1831 the number of surveyors was about one per 2,800 people.

Fig. 4.1 shows how the number of Cambridgeshire surveyors increased at a roughly expo-nential rate from 1600. There was a slight growth in the 1650s when a number of surveyors started to practise, though they did not necessarily draw maps of Cambridgeshire estates in this decade. Despite Thompson's description of the stimulus to surveying which was caused by the Restoration (1968, 26), it did not cause surveyors with Cambridgeshire connections to begin their careers in the second half of the seventeenth century. The greater-than-average increase in the number of surveyors in the 1760s was similarly followed by a period when few new surveyors appeared (1770 to 1785). This lull may reflect a temporary saturation of the market, though with such a small sample it is difficult to do more than speculate. What is

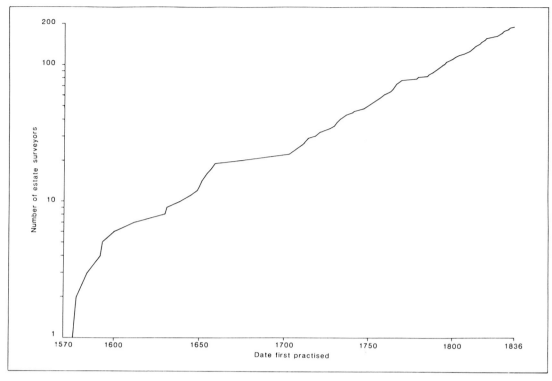

Fig. 4.1. Semi-logarithmic plot of the number of estate surveyors who practised in Cambridgeshire, by the date at which they started surveying.

clear, however, is the steady increase in the number of estate surveyors, which suggests that there were many social and economic stimuli to the development of their profession.

There are many examples of the varied composition of the group of estate surveyors who practised in Cambridgeshire, and this variety can be seen from their cartographic output. It was common for surveyors to produce only one or two maps: until 1811 between 50% and 60% of known surveyors fell into this category; thereafter the percentage increased to 75%. Conversely, only about one-quarter of the early nineteenth-century map-makers drew more than two maps, a decrease from an average of over 40% in the preceding two centuries. At all times, there was a number of men who were prolific. For example, Thomas Langdon mapped Gamlingay in Cambridgeshire in 1601/2 for Merton College, Oxford, and he drew at least 73 more estate maps for four other Oxford colleges (All Souls, New, Corpus Christi and Brasenose), and for the Charterhouse (including land at Castle Camps and Balsham in Cambridgeshire in 1617), Lady Ann Gresham and Sir Thomas Cecil (Eden, 1983b, 73–6). Christopher Saxton drew at least 25 estate maps and compiled 14 written surveys between 1587 and 1608 (Evans and Lawrence, 1979, 74–9) and at a similar time Ralph Treswell senior drew at least 18 (Schofield, 1987, 4). In the early eighteenth century, the Dougharty family of Worcester produced about 30 maps (Smith, 1967, 138), and Benjamin Fallowes, who mapped Great Abington for Maximilian Western in 1716/17 (GTA71701), drew 11 estate maps in Essex alone. Two of these were for William, another member of the Western family (Emmison, 1947). Fallowes also worked further west, in Monmouthshire, Herefordshire and Worcestershire, during his career (Eden F21). Two of the most prolific surveyors who worked in Cambridgeshire in the late eighteenth and early nineteenth centuries were Joseph Freeman and the younger Alexander Watford, who each drew at least 53 estate maps.

The general decrease in estate mapping was associated with an increase in production of other types of map. Until the mid-eighteenth century about 30% of surveyors had more diverse interests, while from 1752 the proportion was well over half. Surveyors drew drainage maps; an example is John Wing, who with his father Tycho mapped Thomas Gape's estate in Croydon, Cambridgeshire in 1747 (CRY74701–3) and was agent to the Duke of Bedford from 1750 to 1761 and between 1764 and 1780 (Eden W469; Taylor, 1966, no. 427).[2] Maps were drawn of parishes: Charles Evans did so, and he also mapped land in Newmarket and Swaffham Bulbeck for the Crown in 1756 (NEA75601–2 and SWB75601; Eden E104). Town maps were drawn, for instance by an employee of the Marquis of Granby, Thomas Warren junior, who mapped the Marquis' Cheveley estate in 1775 (CHG77501; Eden W123). Few of the Cambridgeshire surveyors became involved in the late eighteenth-century county surveys, unlike William Green who assisted William Yates in the survey of Lancashire and then in 1780 returned to his business as an estate surveyor (Harley, 1963, 121), or the estate surveyor William Crosley who carried out the topographical survey for a map of Surrey which was published in 1793 (Harley, 1966). William Elstobb, a Cambridgeshire estate surveyor (see CAR75401 and WLL75401), nearly became involved in completing the map of Cambridgeshire which was to be submitted for a Royal Society of Arts award but was unfinished at the death in 1770 of its author Charles Mason, Woodwardian Professor of Geology. Despite the efforts of Mason's widow, the map was never finished (Harley, 1964, 123). Other types of map were also drawn, such as road, river, navigation, parkland or inclosure. Surveyors' map-making activities have been taken from the evidence collected by Eden (forthcoming) and from published catalogues of estate maps; though the above figures of cartographic output are unavoidably incomplete, it is unlikely that further evidence would change the general picture of many small producers of estate maps throughout the period, and increasing numbers of surveyors who drew many different types of map.

RANGE OF PRACTICE

Surveyors worked over wide areas. They had to be mobile, as can be shown by examining the intra and inter-county activities of men who worked in Cambridgeshire, where they lived while they were drawing maps of Cambridgeshire estates in particular, and the pattern of surveyors' long-term movements.

Until the later eighteenth century, a majority of surveyors practised in relatively small areas: the Walkers (John, his son John and nephew Samuel) of Hanningfield in Essex, drew 29 maps and compiled six written surveys between them. A map of an estate at Foxcott near Andover in Hampshire is the only example of their work outside their native county, and this estate was surveyed for an Essex landowner (Edwards and Newton, 1984, 14). Land surveyors in Ireland, too, often confined their activities to a particular region and their spheres of influence extended no further than the hinterland of the market town in which they lived (Andrews, 1985, 241). Many Cambridgeshire surveyors only worked within the county boundary, especially before 1650 when 42% travelled very little; then mobility increased so that only about one-quarter confined their activities to Cambridgeshire in the late eighteenth century. In the early nineteenth century, however, nearly 60% of surveyors only worked within the county. This reflects a change in the type of practitioner, as will be seen in the following chapter.

Nevertheless, from the earliest days there were a number of men whose work covered larger areas. John Norden and Robert Treswell, for example, travelled large distances in their surveys of Crown lands. In 1611, Norden was granted the power and authority to travel into the ten most southerly counties of England to survey castles, forts, parks, lodges, impaled forests and chases, and to discover all the decays, ruins and needs for repair, for an annual pension of £50. Treswell was given similar authority for 21 counties north of the River Severn. They were given too much to do; to help, John Thorpe was granted three of Norden's and seven of Treswell's counties (Lawrence, 1985, 55). One-third of the surveyors who practised in Cambridgeshire before 1650 worked over a wide part of the country: for example, John Norden mapped Little Abington for John Spencer in 1603 (LLA60301), Ralph Agas surveyed Carlton cum Willingham (his map was the basis for a map which was drawn in 1767 for Thomas Brand, CAR76701), and Thomas Langdon mapped Gamlingay for Merton College, Oxford in 1601/2, and Balsham and Castle Camps for the Charterhouse in 1617 (GAM60201–16, BAL61701–6 and CAS61701–5) and he worked in at least another 12 counties in England. There were also surveyors who confined their activities to East Anglia or to counties which neighboured Cambridgeshire: Thomas Waterman, for example, who was probably responsible for a map of Ferdinand Parys' estate at Linton in 1600 (LIN60007; P. G. Eden, personal communication), was Rector of Great Ryburgh in Norfolk from 1576 to 1624 and he drew maps of Norfolk and Suffolk estates (Eden W135; Venn, I, 4, 346). William Hayward ventured further afield on rare occasions. He was the surveyor of an estate at Soham for the Earl of Holderness' trustees in 1626 (SOH62601–2) and lived at Cranwich in Norfolk in 1636; he mainly drew estate, drainage and town maps in East Anglia, Lincolnshire and London and regional maps of the southern fenland. In 1604, however, he surveyed at Morpeth in Northumberland, and in 1614 he mapped a mineral estate at Hartington, Derbyshire (Eden H250; Silvester, 1989; R. J. Silvester, personal communication).

In general, however, mobility increased as the surveying profession developed, and in Cambridgeshire about three-quarters of the surveyors practised in adjoining counties or further afield from 1650 to the early nineteenth century. Over one hundred possible examples can be given: Heber Lands, mentioned in the Introduction, is one, Benjamin Fallowes another. A spate of advertisements in the *Cambridge Chronicle*, which had a circulation throughout eastern England, provides further evidence for a willingness to travel. Messrs Heath and Dobson of London were prepared to go anywhere in Great Britain or Ireland in 1771, as was William Walton of Wisbech in 1777 (he mapped the Duke of Bedford's Thorney estate in 1767, THO76701). Messrs Allen and Codling of Kimbolton were prepared to travel up to 50 miles in 1778, Richard Annesley of Newark-upon-Trent would go anywhere in England in 1779, and so too would John Watte of Leverington, Cambridgeshire in 1780 (he drew a number of maps of Cambridgeshire estates: see LEV78201, UPW77401, WHR77501, WSM76901, WSP79201 and WSP79411). As a last example, in 1777 there was an advertisement from someone who wanted employment as a teacher, merchant or assistant to a surveyor and who had 'no objection to settle abroad'.[3] There is similar evidence for increasing mobility elsewhere in the country: in the early eighteenth century, Joseph Dougharty of Worcester drew maps of estates in his own county and also in Warwickshire, Gloucestershire and Essex (Smith, 1967, 146). In Norfolk, too, men with wider areas of work started to appear, such as James Corbridge, a Northumbrian, and Thomas Badeslade, a Kentish man who then moved to Nottingham (Eden, 1973, 480).

Within Cambridgeshire, most surveyors worked in the southern part of the county, as is reflected in the distribution of estate maps. About one-quarter of surveyors before 1752 only worked in the fenland north, but then the percentage declined to about 10% in the early nineteenth century. Very few surveyors drew maps in both the fenland and the south: 12 all together, or 6%. In many cases these men were simply mapping the dispersed estates of a single employer, such as Arthur Frogley, who mapped the Corporation of the Sons of the Clergy's land in Wisbech, West Wratting and Willingham between 1716 and 1719 (WEW71901–2, WLL71901–2 and WSM71601), or the John Lunds, father and son, who mapped estates in Ely, Isleham, Soham, Stow cum Quy, Tydd St Giles and Witchford for Frances Ingram, Viscountess Irwin in 1779 (EYT77901, ISL77901, SOH77901–2, STO77901, TYD77902 and WTF77901). Benjamin Hare was involved in the fenland drainage schemes and his map of Stonea in 1637 is endorsed by five of the associates of the 4th Earl of Bedford who agreed to accept the division of the land amongst them (WMB63701). Later, in 1652, he mapped Thorney for the 5th Earl of Bedford (THO65201). His map of Wimpole in the south for Thomas Chicheley in 1638 (WMP63801) may partly have arisen from his fenland work, as although Chicheley was not an Adventurer, he was probably known to them (Willmoth, 1985, 16).

While it has been shown that mobility increased amongst surveyors who worked in Cambridgeshire in the early modern period, the changing pattern of mobility can best be studied by examining where surveyors lived when they were mapping estates in the county. For some periods the sample is much reduced: until 1751 it is not known where about half of the surveyors were living. There is more information about surveyors in the late eighteenth century: the addresses of only 16% of those who first practised between 1752 and 1784 are unknown, and this figure is further reduced to 8% for those starting work between 1785 and 1810. Thereafter, however, the percentage rises again to 40%, so that all the analysis is based on minimum figures.

Overall, the majority of surveyors whose address is known did not live in Cambridgeshire while they were surveying it. In Essex and Kent few did so before 1700 (only 31% and a mere 12% of surveyors respectively were known to be based outside these two counties in the late sixteenth and seventeenth centuries) (Hull, 1987, 247); in Cambridgeshire, too, numbers of such men were lower at this time. By contrast, in most of the eighteenth century just over half of all of the surveyors lived elsewhere. Many lived in neighbouring counties: John Storer, who mapped Litlington for Sir Thomas Spencer Wilson in 1782, gave his address as Halstead, Essex (LIT78201–7), and he drew at least 16 maps of Essex estates from 1765 to 1796, including Hatfield Broad Oak and White Roothing for Sir Thomas in 1782 and 1784 (Emmison, 1964). Others came from further afield, such as Joseph Colbeck who lived at Marr in Yorkshire in 1732 and mapped Stow cum Quy for James Martin in 1737 (STO73701; Eden C319), or William Womack, who mapped the same estate for Martin's descendant, James Thomas Martin, in 1827, and came from Claines near Worcester (STO82701). Growing numbers lived in London: two (7% of contemporary surveyors of Cambridgeshire estates) from 1703 to 1751, three (9%) from 1752 to 1784, and then an increase to nine (21%) from 1785 to 1810 and ten (16%) from 1811 to 1836. From 1785, about one-quarter of estate maps were produced by London-based surveyors. This partly reflects the great growth of London at that time: the population doubled from half a million in 1700 (Harrison, 1984, 138) to 1,117,000 in 1801, and then doubled again to 2,239,000 by 1841 (Mitchell, 1988, 25). Eden, however, suggests that in Norfolk the growing numbers of surveyors resident in London was increasingly influential, as a number of London consultants found employment with larger estates, to some extent at the expense of local stewards and surveyors (1975, 124).

From the mid-eighteenth century, however, increasing numbers of surveyors lived in Cambridgeshire, and they accounted for a majority of the estate maps which were produced. Fig. 4.2 shows how the numbers grew, that these men were scattered throughout the county and that they did not necessarily map nearby parishes. At all periods there were men who mapped their own estates in their own parishes: Robert Millicent, for example, mapped his estate at Barham in Linton in 1600 (LIN60001–6), and Thomas Heckford, Vicar of Trumpington, probably drew the map which shows the effects of a fire there in 1780 (TRU78001). Heckford advertised his school at Trumpington in the *Cambridge Chronicle* in 1790, and the advertisement suggests that surveying may have been taught there.[4] The maps in Fig. 4.2 clearly show the increasing importance of Cambridge as a base for land surveyors; from 1785 over 10% of all the surveyors who practised in Cambridgeshire lived in the town and they were responsible for about one-half of the estate maps which were produced.

The ranges of practice of Joseph Freeman and both the senior and junior Alexander Watfords were excluded from Fig. 4.2 and are shown separately in Figs. 4.3–4.5. The patterns of mobility confirm the trends which have been discussed. All three of them were based in Cambridge and worked extensively both inside and outside the county. The year 1821 was a typically active one for the younger Alexander Watford. In mid-February he was in Bedfordshire,[5] he was surveying in Cambridge in mid-March and at the end of April,[6] he valued Queens' College's land at Burwell on 30 April,[7] on 21 May he valued land at Ware in Hertfordshire,[8] in June he went to value the tithes at Neatham, Hampshire (his first visit to

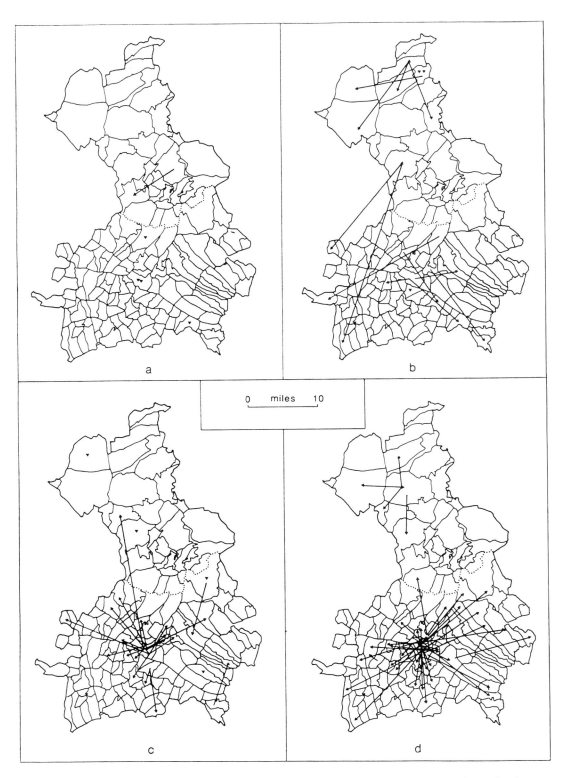

0   miles   10

a

b

c

d

Fig. 4.2. Range of practice within Cambridgeshire of surveyors who were resident in the county (a, To 1751; b, 1752–84; c, 1785–1810; d, 1811–36. Fenland parishes are north of the dotted line; upland parishes are to the south).

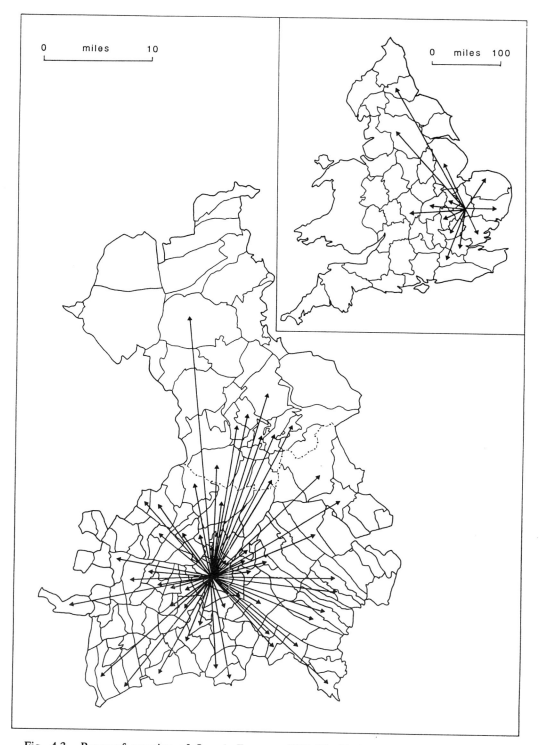

Fig. 4.3. Range of practice of Joseph Freeman 1768–99 (Fenland parishes are north of the broken line; upland parishes are to the south).

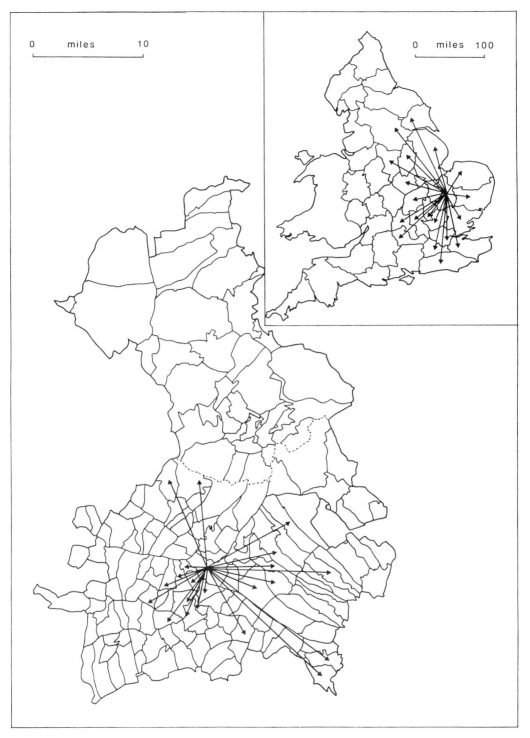

Fig. 4.4. Range of practice of Alexander Watford senior 1792–1801 (Fenland parishes are
north of the broken line; upland parishes are to the south).

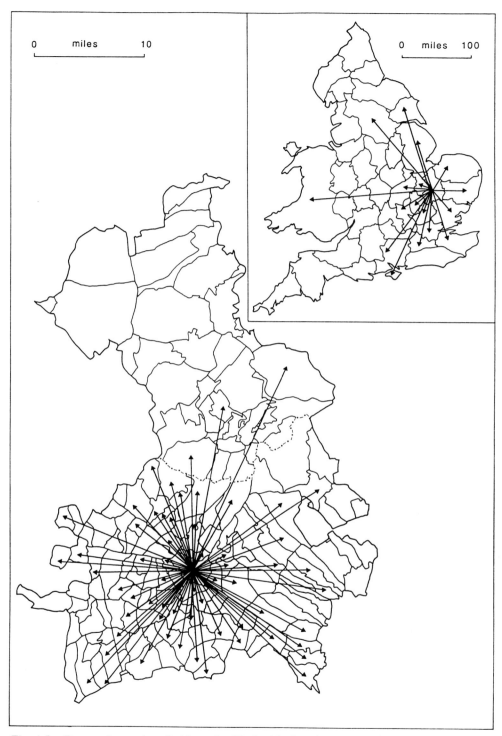

Fig. 4.5. Range of practice of Alexander Watford junior 1801–44 (Fenland parishes are north of the broken line; upland parishes are to the south).

this part of the country),[9] the following month he was at Capel in Suffolk and then at Ovington in Norfolk,[10] and by August he was back in Cambridgeshire and he went to Barrington.[11] He continued to travel in the winter months: in November he went to Wrestlingworth (Bedfordshire),[12] and on 18 December he went to Hitchin (Hertfordshire).[13] He also mapped Haddenham[14] and valued land at Harston[15] during the course of the year. In other years, too, he made many short visits within Cambridgeshire and to neighbouring counties, with occasional longer spells at more distant places.

The increasing mobility of surveyors also resulted from the permanent removal of their businesses. For example, John Matthews worked mostly within a 30-mile radius of his home at Mold near Wrexham in the early nineteenth century, and he moved his business twice: to Montgomeryshire in 1823 and then to Aberystwyth in 1828 (Thomas, 1985, 230). In Cambridgeshire, there were no removals of surveyors' practices before the eighteenth century. Then activity increased. In the early eighteenth century, nearly one-quarter of surveyors moved: John Grundy moved from Leicestershire to Spalding in 1731 (Hopper, 1980, 24), and in 1749 he mapped the estates of the 4th Duke of Bedford and 9th Earl of Lincoln in Thorney and Crowland, Lincolnshire (THO74901). Two surveyors moved into Cambridgeshire: Francis Warren[16] and William Elstobb (Eden E83; Taylor, 1966, no. 351). In the third quarter of the century, movement increased to about one-third of surveyors. Nine of these stayed in the same county and two moved into Cambridgeshire. These two were both clergymen, William Cole and Thomas Heckford, and map-making was very much a side-line for them (*DNB*, 4, 734–7; Venn, I, 1, 368 and II, 3, 320). Two surveyors moved within Cambridgeshire: Joseph Freeman moved within Cambridge in 1772 and again by 1788,[17] and John Watte moved from Leverington to Wisbech in 1783.[18] Movement was greatest between 1785 and 1810, when 45% of surveyors moved, and the pattern is shown in Fig. 4.6. Over half of the moves were within the same county and four of these were within Cambridgeshire: the elder Charles Wedge moved from Gazeley in Suffolk to Westley Bottom in Cambridgeshire in 1807 and then he moved within Cambridgeshire to Shudy Camps in 1817 (Eden W206), Thomas Norfolk moved from Soham to West Wratting between 1806 and 1825,[19] and the younger Alexander Watford twice moved within Cambridge. In 1808, he moved a few houses up Silver Street to the corner of Silver Street and Trumpington Street,[20] and then he moved across Cambridge to the house on the corner of Hills Road and Gonville Place in 1831.[21] Furthermore, in 1801 he had inherited his father's property in Free School Lane.[22] Besides Charles Wedge, three other surveyors moved into Cambridgeshire: William Custance, who later moved on to London (Eden C624), Alexander Watford senior from Bedford,[23] and Edward Gibbons (Eden G88). There were fewer removals after 1810: half were within the same county and Thomas Axford Melhuish moved within Cambridgeshire (Eden M293). Joseph Jackson and George Cuming moved into the county, though Cuming later returned to Northamptonshire (Eden C600 and J18), and Richard Grey Baker was at Earith in Huntingdonshire at some time (Eden B49) and in Sidney Street, Cambridge, in 1834.[24]

As the surveying profession developed, therefore, surveyors became more mobile: they travelled widely from one base and they increasingly frequently moved their businesses. Surveyors who practised in Cambridgeshire were no exception. Many surveyors came from

Fig. 4.6. Movement of surveyors' residences 1785–1810 (1, John Burcham; 2, George Cole; 3, William Custance; 4, Edward Driver; 5, John Dugmore; 6, Edward Gibbons; 7, Thomas Hogg; 8, Anthony Jackson; 9, Thomas Lovell; 10, George Morris; 11, John Newton; 12, Martin Nockolds; 13, Thomas Norfolk; 14, John Prickett; 15, Thomas Thorpe; 16, Alexander Watford senior; 17, Alexander Watford junior; 18, Charles Wedge; 19, William Womack).

outside the county, increasingly from London, to map Cambridgeshire estates, and those who lived in the county gravitated towards Cambridge. It is not possible, however, to discuss mobility without considering the relationship which a surveyor had with his employer.

SURVEYORS AND THEIR EMPLOYERS

Between 1600 and 1850, the relationship between surveyors and employers changed; surveyors were heavily dependent on patronage in the early days of the profession, but by the early nineteenth century they had become more independent. The changes can be seen by looking at patronage, the growth of self-supporting surveying businesses, and how surveyors were employed.

Patronage

Throughout the seventeenth and eighteenth centuries a majority of Cambridgeshire surveyors worked for only one employer, but as this figure partly reflects the many men already referred to who only produced one map it is insufficient evidence for patronage. Seventeen surveyors, however, travelled into more than one county for the same employer, who was therefore an important patron. John Norden, for example, mapped John Spencer's estates at Little Abington in 1603 (LLA60301) and in 1606 he mapped Spencer's Sussex estates (Steer, 1962). In Norfolk, Thomas Coke of Holkham Hall was an important employer of John Halsey from 1713 to 1736; he was a tenant from at least 1723 and he was regularly sent to survey Coke's properties outside the county (Eden, 1973, 476 and 479). Halsey, however, also worked for other employers: in 1731/2 he mapped the Duke of Bedford's estate at Thorney (THO73201). John Davis' map of Dry Drayton in 1740 (DRY74001) was one of several which he drew for the Duke between 1735 and 1743, mainly in Bedfordshire and Buckinghamshire. Davis was the tenant of the Duke's manor at Chenies, Buckinghamshire; from 1748 he was the steward for Chenies, Hitchin and Chesham, until he was succeeded by William Davis between 1785 and 1810.[25] Isaac Taylor's employment by Humphry Sturt took him to Dorset, Devon, Wiltshire, Middlesex and Essex as well as Cambridgeshire (where he drew DOD77001–2 and WMB77001).[26] Patronage continued to be important in the late eighteenth and early nineteenth centuries, when 21% of the fully qualified land surveyors who advertised in the *Cambridge Chronicle* between 1762 and 1836 were seeking a patron.

Elsewhere in the country, where there were more large landed estates, there is further evidence for patronage. Sir Thomas Tresham of Rushton, Northamptonshire, employed George Levens by 1585, who carried out much important survey work in connection with improvement of the estate and the purchase and sale of land. He also collected rents, kept the accounts, was secretary to Sir Thomas and tutor to his children (Finch, 1956, 185; Simon, 1966, 368). From 1607 to 1613, the younger Ralph Treswell surveyed the estates of the 9th Earl of Northumberland in Dorset, Middlesex, Sussex and Yorkshire (Startin, 1988, 8). William Senior was employed by four members of the Cavendish family (William and Charles, and their sons, both called William, who became the 2nd Earl of Devonshire and 1st Earl of Newcastle respectively) between 1609 and 1640, though there was a gap in his activities for the family from 1621 and 1626 when the existing estates had all been mapped and before new ones had been acquired (Fowkes and Potter, 1988, vii and xi). In the mid-eighteenth century, John Leslie worked for John, Earl of Hopetoun and other commissioners for annexing the Forfeited Estates for 20 years, and Leslie's son, Hamilton, followed him as an employee of the Earl (Adams, 1971, 9–11). Patronage was, therefore, important to the developing surveying profession, and the status of a surveyor who worked specifically for one or a few employers reflected the standing of his patron (Gunasena, 1982, 1) and in turn contributed to it.

Growing numbers of surveyors, however, worked for many employers: only one surveyor who practised in Cambridgeshire worked for more than five employers before the eighteenth century (Thomas Langdon), and Heber Lands was the only one to do so between 1703 and 1751. Thereafter numbers increased, and about one-fifth of the surveyors who started work between 1752 and 1810 worked for more than five employers; four of these worked for more than ten. For example, Joseph Freeman surveyed for at least eight Cambridge colleges, Cambridge University, and six private landowners. In Cambridgeshire alone, he surveyed estates for Mrs Bridget Southcoat (HIL77001), Benjamin Keene (LIN77901), the Duke of Bedford (WEW79402–3) and, probably, George Leonard Jenyns (FDI79601). He was also steward to the Charterhouse and St Thomas' Hospital, and was employed by the Earl of Hardwicke to copy portraits. Freeman was eager to ingratiate himself with such an influential local figure, and wrote to the Earl in 1788:

I am Steward to St Thomas's Hospital and the Governor of the Charter House for all their Estates in Essex Cambridgeshire Herts and Buckinghamshire a great many of the Tenants are respectable people particularly the Hanwells of Fulborn I wont Attempt to say that I could Influence them [to vote for Hardwicke] but when there is Occasion If youwill be pleased to signify your wishes you may depend on my best Endeavours and I flatter myself they may not Altogether prove unsuccessful.[27]

He also tried in this and the following year to secure a living for his son-in-law by using the Earl's patronage.[28] Similarly, the elder Alexander Watford worked for at least five colleges and the University, whilst his son was employed by at least eight colleges, the University and a number of other owners.

Many of these men also travelled widely for one or more of their employers. Joseph Freeman went to Yorkshire for Trinity College in 1769;[29] Alexander Watford senior went to Carmarthenshire for Queens' College in 1794[30] and in 1795 he went to Derbyshire in January and Yorkshire in November, both for St John's College.[31] In the early nineteenth century, Thomas James Tatham, a founder member of the Land Surveyors' Club in 1834, had an office in London. He mapped St Bartholomew's Hospital's estates in Cambridgeshire and Essex in the 1820s and 1830s (see BOT83301–5; Eden T34; Emmison, 1964).

The type of employer changed as demand increased from professional and business men, who invested in land, usually on a comparatively modest scale, partly for prestige reasons (Eden, 1975, 119). In 1812, Mr Shee of Southampton Row, London, announced in the *Cambridge Chronicle* that he was forming an establishment 'for extending the practice of Land Surveyors, Appraisers, and Auctioneers in the country parts of England and Wales, and for making them known to capitalists in the metropolis and throughout the empire'.[32] Changes in type of employer are discussed in further detail in Chapters 6 and 7.

Surveying businesses

The development of independent surveying businesses must have been partly a result of this changing demand. Many businesses were conducted as partnerships: two partnerships worked in Cambridgeshire in the late eighteenth century, and the number grew to 13 in the early nineteenth century. Thomas Lovell mapped Thomas Robinson's estate at Over in 1797 as 'clerk to Mr Jenkinson' (OVE79701). John Jenkinson had made Lovell a partner in his Huntingdon practice of 'Land and Building Surveyors and Auctioneers' by 1801, when they mapped Gamlingay Park for Downing College (GAM80101). In 1805, Lovell took over the entire business when his partner died:

Thomas Lovell, Land, Timber and Building Surveyor, and Auctioneer, Huntingdon, (late Partner with Mr Jenkinson, deceased), returns grateful thanks to his Friends and the Public in general, for favours received by his late Partner and himself, and takes the liberty of informing them, that he intends carrying on the above business on his own account, respectfully soliciting a continuance of their confidence and support.[33]

Then, in his turn, Lovell took his son into partnership in 1829 and he expanded his business as a land, timber and building surveyor, estate agent and auctioneer to sell household furniture and live and dead stock.[34]

A number of assistants were employed in surveying businesses, though the size of any one practice is difficult to determine. There were 24 advertisements for assistants in the *Cambridge Chronicle* from 1762 to 1836. John Watte, at Wisbech, for example, advertised for one on 31 March 1787:

LAND SURVEYING. WANTED immediately an Assistant in the above Business, who understands the field part of the same, and is master of planning and casting accurately, or can complete the rough draughts correctly. Such a person will meet with immediate employ by applying to J. Watte, Land and Tithe Surveyor, at Wisbech, in the isle of Ely.[35]

There were a further ten advertisements from men who wanted employment as assistants to surveyors, and evidence that another ten assistantships had occurred. Francis Marshall announced on 23 March 1793 that he was setting up on his own in Trumpington Street, Cambridge, after having been an apprentice to Joseph Freeman, and then two years later he was paid two guineas for helping Alexander Watford senior carry out a survey at Bottisham for Trinity College, Cambridge.[36] Marshall may have been connected with Freeman by the marriage in 1786 of the latter's daughter, Elizabeth, to William Marshall of Helions

Bumpstead, Essex (Venn, 1891, 96). At the same time, Freeman may have also had Nicholas King as an assistant: the cartouche of a 1791 map of Hockwold cum Wilton in Norfolk, in Freeman's style, was signed by King,[37] in the same year they compiled a terrier of land at March belonging to St John's College, Cambridge[38] and in 1792 a map of the College's estate at Melbourn in Freeman's style was accompanied by a terrier by King (MEB79201). Other surveyors also employed assistants without using the *Cambridge Chronicle* for an advertisement. George Salmon, who mapped Stetchworth in 1770 for John Fleming, had John Scott as his 'principal assistant' for 'several years' before 1772 (STN77001; Eden S10); William Newton was assistant to Robert Corby in 1818 before forming a partnership with Thomas Woodrow in 1823, and Newton mapped Henry Francis' estate in Wentworth in 1831 (WEO83101; Eden N75); and Daniel Mumford with his assistant John Doyley mapped James Johnson's estate in Castle Camps in 1794 and Doyley remained Mumford's assistant for another two years (CAS79401; Eden D298). Some assistants later became partners: John Croft was an assistant to John Grimsby Lenny in about 1828 (Eden C550), and then in 1833 they announced a partnership at 28 Angel Hill in Bury St Edmunds.[39] At about this time, Croft mapped James Drage Merest's estate at Soham (SOH83301).

Assistants carried out a variety of tasks. They helped in the survey itself: Alexander Watford junior mapped the Thriplow estate of St John's College in 1807, and on 12 January he charged seven guineas for as many days' work with a clerk 'in taking Lines thro*ugh* the Parish and laying each piece in its proper situation'.[40] Secondly, assistants plotted out maps in the office from measurements recorded in the field by a surveyor in a field book. In colonial Jamaica this division of labour was practised (Higman, 1988b, 59), while in England John Mackown, for example, advertised in 1766 that he wanted: 'immediately, A Person well acquainted with all the Hands necessary for Mapping; if he can Draw, will be more agreeable'.[41] Thirdly, assistants made fair copies of maps, reports, surveys and valuations. The map of the 3rd Earl of Hardwicke's seat at Wimpole, for example, has notes that it was 'Surveyed by Robert Withers', and 'Map*p*ed by B[radbury] Last, Whepstead [Suffolk]' (WMP81501). Alexander Watford's clerk helped him on three days around 27 April 1821 to examine land belonging to the University of Cambridge between Great St Mary's Street and St Michael's Church, and then the clerk spent another two days making a fair copy of the report and valuation. Watford charged two guineas a day for his services and one guinea a day for the clerk.[42] Similarly, William Newton advertised on 27 January 1826 for a clerk who 'is fully capable to survey and draw fair plans with neatness and dispatch'.[43] Finally, assistants were often employed in decorating maps. For example, in 1833 the following advertisement appeared in the *Cambridge Chronicle*:

TO WRITING MASTERS. AN ORNAMENTAL PENMAN is WANTED in a respectable Establishment in the county of Cambridge. He must also be a good Arithmetician – to be able to undertake Land~Surveying Practically, Mapping, &c. &c. – The most respectable reference is required. Letters addressed, (post~paid) to A.B., Mr. Wallis, Bookseller, Cambridge, will meet immediate attention.[44]

Similarly, the Suffolk surveyor John Johnson employed his artist son William to paint a cartouche in 1777 (Mason, 1990, 14). Map decoration did not always take place at the same stage of production of a fair copy. The map of Orwell which was drawn for Thomas

Chicheley by 1686 (ORW68601), for example, is finished and decorated with Chicheley's arms, but the penman did not write the title to the map in its cartouche. On the other hand, an early stage in the production of a map of Bisterne, Hampshire, in 1591 was to draw and decorate the compass rose; the topographical information was never completed (Harvey, 1988).

The number of assistants who were employed varied with the size of the practice. In Scotland, George Langlands made plans of the Inverary Estate in 1789, and from the styles of the finished work it has been suggested that he employed three or four draughtsmen (Fairhurst, 1968, 183). Similarly, Alexander Watford junior had a large business in Cambridge. Between 1822 and 1825 he surveyed and mapped all of the estates of Queens' College, Cambridge, and from a dispute concerning his charges for the atlas, it seems that he had at least three assistants. Two copies of the atlas were produced, one, on vellum, for the President, and a paper copy for the Bursar. On 16 January 1826, Watford submitted a statement of the various expenses involved in finishing the atlases, which shows a division of labour between his assistants. First, there was a 'Statement shewing the expense of the fair copy supposing that the College or Mr Watford has thought that the rough paper copy [the eventual Bursar's copy] would have been sufficient as a College Document', and Mr Merritt was paid £201 12s 0d. The second statement was to show 'what the excess the present fair copy has created under the supposition that the College would have had them committed to Vellum by Mr Smith or other ordinary Clerk'. Each plan would have been 'traced from the rough Copy, retraced on the Vellum inked & finished as the plain ones would have taken 6 days', and cost £100 16s 0d. Finally, there was an 'Estimate of the expense of the Ornamental Writing &c'. Mr Merritt would be paid 12 guineas for a title-page to the maps and two guineas for an index. James Richardson, Watford's nephew, would be paid six guineas for another title-page and one guinea for another index (presumably to the Bursar's paper copy), five guineas for the President's copy of the valuations of the estates, and two guineas for the Bursar's copy. Each of these assistants was employed by Watford on other occasions. In 1822, Mr Smith was employed for $20\frac{1}{4}$ days from 1 January in making a fair copy of Trinity College's Bursar's books at 10s 6d a day, on 30 April Watford charged one guinea a day for Mr Smith's ascertaining the College's corn rents at Barrington for four days and for making the schedule which took another 14 days, and on 16 May Smith took two days to make a fair copy of a valuation and report. Mr Merritt was paid for surveying, measuring and making a plan of Trinity College's buildings at Hitchin, and for helping to value them, on 4 May in the same year.[45] James Richardson was a messenger from Watford when he was about to start surveying St Nicholas Court in Kent, for Queens' College in 1823.[46]

Surveyors also employed local men to help in survey work. John Jackson, a tenant of the Duke of Bedford at Thorney, was paid £2 10s 9d for assisting Mr Ponton in his survey of that parish in 1751–2. Edward Lancaster, the local schoolteacher, was also paid for surveying at that time, and Abraham Quince was paid £1 5s 8d for leading the chain. In 1752–3, Vincent Wing produced a map of the whole parish (THO75301), and he paid £8 14s $11\frac{3}{4}$d to labourers for carrying the chain.[47] In 1809, William Custance, surveyor for Emmanuel College, paid five guineas to Mr Tinkler of Spalding for staking out and mapping the College's allotment at Pinchbeck in Lincolnshire.[48] Alexander Watford junior, too, employed local men: in his survey of Thriplow for St John's College in 1807, already referred to, he took his clerk with him but he also paid £2 18s 3d for chain leaders and expenses.[49] As a last example, Mr Giddens helped in a survey of roads at Longstowe for St John's College in 1824, and he was said to have been 'of more use as Assistant Surveyor than all the rest of the Parish for many years'.[50]

These surveying businesses carried out more than simply measuring and mapping land. Of the 53 advertisements of surveyors in the *Cambridge Chronicle* between 1762 and 1836, all said that they carried out surveys, all except one said that they surveyed land, 9% said that they surveyed buildings and one-quarter specified timber surveying. Only one-half of the advertisements actually mentioned map-making, just two offered to provide specimen plans and one stated that the practice would make maps for leases. Valuations and selling land, buildings and timber were the next most popular activity, and were mentioned by 40% of the advertisements. A few concerns said that they would manage estates, copy maps, carry out levelling, improve land, be involved in inclosure work or in farming activities. Carrying out repairs, lending money, or acting as an insurance agent was mentioned by one practice each. Other businesses, too, may have carried out these services but not mentioned them in their advertisements, and some advertisements may have exaggerated the surveyors' abilities, but they do indicate the range of work which was carried out.

The businesses changed at various times. Some diversified: John Watte first advertised as a land surveyor in 1778:

... he still continues the surveying business in all its branches, as, noblemen's and gentlemen's estates, surveyed and valued, with the timber standing thereon, and elegant maps given of the same if required. – He divides, encloses, &c. and gives the best mode of culture and quickest methods of improving of all kinds of waste lands, whether commons, meadows, fens, marshes, &c. &c. He takes levels and lays out rivers, drains, &c. either for navigation, or the conveyance of the water only, and points out the properest methods and outfalls for the drainage, both of fens and highlands, and gives schemes, plans, and estimates of the same founded upon the most experienced and approved methods – He surveys all kinds of works in the building way, and gives designs, and estimates for farm houses, &c.

Houses, lands, timber, &c bought and sold by commission, and all other country business in the land way, executed to any part, with the greatest care and expedition.[51]

His advertisement of 9 September 1780 announced similar services, then in 1783 he added another one:

Ready to be advanced, several sums of money on approved land security; also about 2000l by way of annuity for the life of the person advancing the same; or the most money will be given for annuities on single or joint lives of principals or nominees.[52]

Similarly, Richard Harwood, land surveyor and estate agent of Trumpington Street, Cambridge, announced in 1831 that he was adding the valuation of estates, tithes, timber, underwood and 'the various objects of Appraisement' to his three-year-old practice; and R. G. Baker advertised in 1834 that he intended to 'engage in THE SALE OF LANDED PROPERTY, HOUSES and TENEMENTS, also Bark, Timber, Underwood and Cropping'.[53] Other businesses contracted. For example, in 1830 Thomas Lovell sold his business as a printer, bookseller, stationer, bookbinder, music seller and dealer in patent medicines and concentrated on his work as a land, timber and building surveyor, estate agent and auctioneer.[54] The Drivers' business in the Old Kent Road in London was built up by

Samuel Driver, a market gardener, and was taken over in 1779 by his sons Abraham Purshouse and William (Barty-King, 1975; Eden D316, D323 and D324). In 1802, they sold off their nursery business and, like Lovell thirty years later, concentrated on the land surveying business.[55] Businesses were also bought out by other surveyors; for example, Richard and William Jacques took over from George Maxwell, William Drew succeeded Mr Pitt at Linton in 1812, and John Swan bought C. Wagstaff's business in Cambridge in 1825.[56]

How surveyors were employed

Surveyors were engaged in several ways. Some had carried out other work in the same area, such as William Newton of Norwich, who surveyed Wentworth in Cambridgeshire for the inclosure award of 1830 and in the following year mapped Henry Francis' estate there (WEO83101). Others were employed as a result of personal recommendations, and others advertised their skills.

Personal knowledge must have been important in many cases. In about 1656, Lady Sunderland was looking for a surveyor for Althorp in Northamptonshire to take charge of affairs there during her son's minority. She wrote to Sir Justinian Isham,

I am informed there is one Mr Gerard that was once your servant and that he behaved himself so well in your service that he gained a very good opinion from you, and I beseech you do me the favour to let me know first your thoughts of him, and if you believe he will be willing to take that employment.

Sir Justinian drafted a reply:

The person named by your ladyship I have good reason to know who finding him faithful to my Father his old master, entertained him somewhat myself and knowing him very honest was willing as much as I could to enable who I found very capable of whatever I put upon him; a good accountant, a good surveyor of land, of some judgement in the nature of it and used to the drawing of leases and the like, I well know him to be; of his knowledge of the mathematics and his late being at the East Indies I say little because not so pertinent to your Ladyship's purpose. (Isham, 1955, 110)

It was cheaper to employ men who lived near the estate to be mapped. Andrews calculated that in eighteenth-century Ireland, 10% was added to the cost of a survey of 200 acres if a surveyor had to travel ten miles to the land (1985, 238). It was not always easy to find a local man: Queens' College, Cambridge had some difficulty in finding a surveyor of their Carmarthenshire estates in 1775. The Reverend Henry Newcome, a former Fellow and Vicar of Gresford near Wrexham in Cheshire (Venn, I, 3, 246) was asked to advise; he asked a Mr Thomas of Chester, who in turn suggested asking Henry Leach of St Clears (Carmarthenshire). Leach wrote:

Mr Thomas of Chester having at the application of Revd Mr Newcome spoke to me to recommend a proper person to survey the Lands belonging to your College in the parish of Llanwinio & Trelech in Carmarthenshire now in lease to Mr Edwards of Rhydgorss. There are two persons whose names are Thomas Lewis & Henry John both who I have employed on the Like occasion and I think either is very Capable of

Surveying maping & Valuing and whenever I have the Honour of your directions I shall employ accordingly and as I Live within four or five miles of the place shall give every assistance in my power ...[57]

The maps, however, were eventually drawn by Charles Hassall in 1781,[58] a local man who later became known as a progressive farmer, land agent, secretary of agricultural societies and an authority on inclosure (Jones, 1943, 133–45; Howell, 1965, 133, 135 and 202). Employment of agents often helped in the search for local practitioners: Emmanuel College employed a firm of London agents, Messrs Nettleshipp, who often engaged men on the College's behalf, and frequently employed local practitioners, usually without much difficulty. For example, in 1806 Nettleshipps wrote:

This Farm [Hyde Farm, Balham, Surrey] should be accurately and carefully surveyed we used to employ Forster in some small things, but I found too much of the Quaker in him and could not make him so useful. Mr Whishaw we now employ on all matters, great and small. He is a man of great experience and perfectly to be relied on, we have constantly employed him for the last 10 years; and unless the College would wish to employ any other Person, I think, we had better let him regularly survey and report upon this Estate. His charges are Moderate.[59]

Similarly, in 1825 they employed Mr Wiggins, 'a land surveyor of very extensive practice and frequently referred to by us'.[60] Nettleshipps, too, used personal recommendations to suggest surveyors for their clients. They wrote of William Neale, when Emmanuel College queried his bill, that:

He is a very cleaver & most excellent man. When a Law Surveyor has much to do, for any Employer, he can of course afford to charge at a less rate than for a simple Business – I am quite sure he did the College justice in his exectring, whatever may be the charge. From our personal experience of him we have recommended him to many persons, who have been highly satisfied with him – He was originally recommended to us by the Sergt Best, whose property he managed greatly to his advantage.[61]

Sometimes, the advice of a Cambridge surveyor was asked. In 1811, Emmanuel College asked William Custance to employ someone to map its land at Sutton Coldfield. He asked H. S. O. Jacob, whom he thought lived there. The reply came back that Jacob had moved to Blackstone near Bewdley in Worcestershire two years previously, when he had entered into partnership with Mr Court with whom he had been an apprentice. He was willing to carry out the survey, however, and clearly had previously had dealings with Custance as he sent his 'respectful comp*liment*s to Mrs Custance and Family, and to Mr Simmons if he is still with you'.[62] Cambridgeshire surveyors were likewise asked by distant landowners to recommend someone: George Maxwell of Fletton, Huntingdonshire, was asked to suggest a surveyor of the Crown's property at Newmarket, and as a result Marion Welstead was given authority to survey on 25 October 1802.[63]

Some surveyors advertised their services: John Norden, for example, wrote a long theological tract to James I and concluded by offering either to continue his Elizabethan county surveys or to survey Crown land (Lawrence, 1985, 55). Others promoted their services in a more public arena. Charles Price and John Senex, for example, published a map of Great Britain in 1708, and above the scale they wrote: 'Estates Survey'd and all sorts of Measuring and Dyaling Perform'd by C. Price and I. Senex at their House in White's Ally in Coleman street London' (Shirley, 1988, 119). Trade cards were means of advertisement (Crawforth,

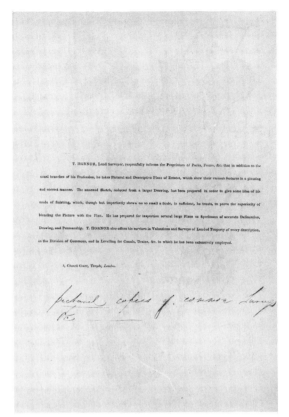

Plate 19. Advertisement of Thomas Hornor.

1985); Peter Chassereau's, for example, printed after his move to the Sign of the Gold Seal in Hanover Street, London shortly after 1745, claimed that: 'Estates in Land and Houses survey'd and plans thereof neatly drawn', 'timbers growing or squared measured' and 'sundials made and sold' (Mason, 1989, 4). Plate 19 shows one of the early nineteenth-century advertisements and specimen plans of Thomas Hornor, which he used to publicize his technique of 'panoramic chorometry' (Hyde, 1977).

Notices in local newspapers were a way of becoming known to the local community. The *Cambridge Chronicle and Journal and General Advertiser for the Counties of Cambridge, Huntingdon, Lincoln, Rutland, Bedford, Herts, Isle of Ely, &c* was first published in 1762 in competition with, and then in place of, the *Cambridge Journal and Weekly Flying Post*. Publicity was expensive; in the *Cambridge Journal* there was a charge of one shilling on every advertisement in 1712, by 1757 it had become 3 s 6 d but later local competition forced its reduction to three shillings if it were shorter than 24 lines (Cranfield, 1951, 15). The *Cambridge Chronicle*'s full title suggests that it had a wide distribution, but in fact its main influence was in Cambridgeshire and Huntingdonshire. It managed to attract a large number of advertisements, about 80 to 100 a week, and flourished as a result (Murphy, 1977, 19–20). For this book, notices from surveyors were sought in the issues from 1762 to 1836, as the paper was the major local vehicle for advertising.

Over the 74-year period, 68 surveyors advertised themselves, most of the notices were repeated for two to four weeks, and some surveyors advertised more than once over the years. About one-third gave addresses in Cambridgeshire: seven were seeking employment and only two of the remaining 12 did not map estates in the county at some time. London and Huntingdonshire were the main locations of the advertisers who did not live in the county, and accounted for about one-quarter of the advertisements each. Others came from neighbouring counties, especially Suffolk and Norfolk, and one came from Bath. Over one-third of these non-Cambridgeshire surveyors were looking for employment; of the rest, only four drew maps of Cambridgeshire estates.

Many of the advertisements have already been mentioned, especially those which were placed because of a change in ownership of the business, because different services were being offered or there was a need for an assistant. Others were printed because of a move into the area, such as John Bellingham's:

JOHN BELLINGHAM, Land~Surveyor, at St. Neots, Huntingdonshire, (lately from London) begs Leave to acquaint the Nobility and Gentry, &c. that they may have their Estates accurately surveyed and delineated, in the most exact and neatest Manner, with a Terrier to each Tenant's Farm, shewing the Quality of the different sorts of Land, with the Total Number of Acres, &c. and on the most reasonable Terms. N.B. He has been employed by many Persons of the first Distinction, and given great satisfaction.

Also, Timber measured either standing or taken down. Specimens of Plans may be seen by applying as above.[64]

Many advertisements, however, were simply to remind potential clients of a surveyor's existence. Simeon King, who mapped Babraham for St John's College in 1785 (BAB78501) and was also employed by Clare and Jesus colleges and the University, placed a typical notice in 1780:

SIMEON KING, LAND~SURVEYOR, at Histon near Cambridge, returns his sincere thanks to those gentlemen who have favoured him with their commands, and humbly begs leave to offer his services to any society or gentleman of the university, town or county, &c. as he has had the happiness of being employed and approved of by some of the heads of houses, as well as by several gentlemen of note there and elsewhere; so it will be his constant endeavour to merit future favours, and he flatters himself, that from many years experience in the repair of farms, the valuation of timber, the surveying of lands, planning, measuring, &c. he shall be able to give entire satisfaction to all who may be kind enough to honour him with their commands.[65]

Some surveyors advertised several times, such as John Watte. His first notice on 28 April 1770 was as a schoolmaster in Leverington, and then he advertised as a surveyor there on 30 May 1778 and on 9 September 1780. He announced his move to Wisbech on 23 August 1783, he was looking for an assistant on 31 March 1787 and he gave publicity to his *Report for the better Draining of the Middle Levels of the Fens* on 14 May 1791. Surveyors seem to have found advertisements a useful means of publicity.

Surveyors' relationships with their employers altered between 1600 and the mid-nineteenth century. Fewer men were solely dependent on one or two employers for their livelihood and increasing numbers formed surveying businesses with permanent assistants. These practices developed and changed; they were commissioned to carry out work both from local knowledge and recommendation, and from advertisements in local newspapers.

In the following chapter, discussion of surveyors' pay, their social status, the importance of additional occupations, and education of practitioners and their surveying techniques continues the description of the surveying profession in Cambridgeshire and beyond. At the same time, the relation of the changes amongst this group of people to other alterations in the economy and society of early modern Britain is further examined.

Chapter 5

ESTATE SURVEYORS: THEIR STATUS, TRAINING AND TECHNIQUES

This chapter continues the discussion of surveyors and their changing place in contemporary society. An examination of their pay, social status and the importance of additional occupations is followed by a description of the ways in which surveyors learned their skills and their surveying methods.

PAY AND STATUS

The social standing of a surveyor can be demonstrated in an examination of the amount he was paid and its relation to pay in other professions. Table 5.1 summarizes the charges which various surveyors made. It excludes annual and grand totals of payments which were made to surveyors like John Halsey (Eden, 1973, 476) or John Home (Adams, 1976, 26), as these figures are hard to compare with others.

Table 5.1. *Pay of surveyors*

Date	Surveyor	Area of practice	Charge	Employer	Source
c. 1580	Arthur Robins	England	10 s/day, 3 d/acre 4 d/acre if also describe land	–	Andrews, 1985, 35
c. 1590	Christopher Saxton	England	6 s 8 d/day	St Thomas' Hospital	Evans and Lawrence, 1979, 78
c. 1595	Thomas Langdon	England	2 s 6 d – 4 s/day	All Souls College, Oxford	Eden, 1983a, 73
1607	William Typper	Lincolnshire	8 s/day surveying drowned lands	Crown	Lawrence, 1985, 55

Date	Surveyor	Area of practice	Charge	Employer	Source
c. 1610	–	England	15 s/day in field 4 s/day drawing-up	Crown	Lawrence, 1985, 55
c.1610	Aaron Rathborne	Yorkshire	£1 2s/day	Crown	Lawrence, 1985, 55
1615– 22	John Norden John Norden jr	England	£1 6s/day 10 s/day	Duchy of Cornwall	Haslam, 1985, 61
1658	–	–	10 s/day	–	Atwell, 1658, 6
1689	Andrew Pellin	Cumberland	1 d/acre	Sir John Lowther	Tyson, 1986, 165
1714	Mr Matlock	Staffordshire	4 d/acre	Lord Dartmouth	Kettle, 1979, 84
c. 1720	John Dougharty sr	Worcestershire	3 d/acre	–	Smith, 1967, 150
1722	Edward Laurence	Essex, Lincolnshire, Yorkshire	6 d/acre inclosed land or 8 d/acre including assistance 9 d/acre open field land or 12 d/acre including assistance 3 d/acre if >100 a commons or 4 d/acre including assistance	Duchess of Buckingham	P. G. Eden, personal communication
1736	James Fish	Warwickshire	3 d/acre surveying 1 d/acre mapping & beautifying	–	Pannett, 1985, 74
1737	James Bermingham	Essex	6 d/acre	Guy's Hospital, London	Mason, 1990, 68
1741	James Bermingham	Essex	7 d/acre	Commissioners of Sewers	Mason, 1990, 68
1741	John Davis	Cambridgeshire	6 d/acre	Duke of Bedford	BRO R5/4498
c. 1745	John Dougharty jr	Worcestershire	6 d/acre	–	Smith, 1967, 150
1749	Edward Lancaster (schoolmaster)	Cambridgeshire	5 s/day $1\frac{1}{2}$ d/acre burnt land	Duke of Bedford	BRO R5/4007B
1757	William Fairbank jr	Lincolnshire	5 s/day	Parson Stacey	Hall, 1937, 215
1763	–	Ireland	3 d/acre	–	Andrews, 1985, 442
1764	James Dunthorn	Suffolk	6 d/acre	Queens' College, Cambridge	QCC Box 91

Table 5.1. *(cont.)*

Date	Surveyor	Area of practice	Charge	Employer	Source
1765	Thomas Yeoman (civil engineer)	Essex	£1/day	–	Mason, 1990, 24
1766	John Mackown	Cambridgeshire?	6 d/acre	–	*Gazetteer and New Daily Advertiser*, 1 Nov. 1766
1769	Joseph Freeman	Essex	7 d/acre, 15 s/day	Queens' College, Cambridge	QCC Box 92 Bill pd 9 Oct. 1769
1771	–	Ireland	4 d/acre	–	Andrews, 1985, 442
c. 1772	James Osborn	Norfolk	4 d/acre, 10 s 6 d/day	Small proprietors	Eden, 1973, 479
1777	Joseph Freeman	Cambridgeshire	2 d/acre tithes	Queens' College, Cambridge	QCC Box 92 Bill pd 20 Jan. 1778
1779	Simeon King	Cambridgeshire	5 s/day supervising repairs	University of Cambridge	CUA Min.VI.I. vol. 2, 37
1779	John Lund sr & jr	Cambridgeshire	8 d/acre	Viscountess Irwin	WRO Ra 1/4/ii
1780	Charles Hassall	Wales	4 d/acre	Queens' College, Cambridge	QCC Conclusions Book 1733–87, 111v
1782	William Fininley (schoolmaster)	Cambridgeshire	3 d/acre surveying cole for seed	Duke of Bedford	BRO R5/4009
1783	John Hand	Cambridgeshire	6 d/acre	Duke of Bedford	BRO R5/4250
1784	John Bodger	Huntingdonshire	4 d/acre inclosed land 3 d/acre fen, open field land 'lower than usual'	–	*Cambridge Chronicle*, 28 February 1784, 2
c. 1785	Matthew Hall	Essex	4 d/acre	–	Mason, 1990, 24
c. 1785	George Hutson	Essex	4 d/acre	–	Mason, 1990, 24
c. 1785	Isaac Johnson	Suffolk	6 d/acre	–	Mason, 1990, 24
1786	John Marquand	Cambridgeshire	1 guinea/day 5 s/day for clerk	Crown	PRO CRES 2/115

Date	Surveyor	Area of practice	Charge	Employer	Source
1789	Joseph Freeman	Huntingdonshire	1 guinea/day	Emmanuel College, Cambridge	ECC BUR.0.3c
c. 1790	–	–	£2 2s/day	Crown	Mason, 1990, 24
1794	Alexander Watford sr	Cambridgeshire	6 d/acre surveying 4 d/acre ocular survey & estimate, or 10% value	Trinity College, Cambridge	TCC Shelf 84, 19
1794	Alexander Watford sr	Norfolk	1 s/acre $1\frac{1}{2}$ guineas/day	University of Cambridge	CUA Geol.2/8(11)
1797	Alexander Watford sr	Cambridgeshire	1 s 6 d/acre	University of Cambridge	CUA CUR.34, 34
1798	Alexander Watford sr	Cambridgeshire	2 guineas/day	Queens' College, Cambridge	QCC Box 7 Bill pd 23 Mar. 1799
1798	Alexander Watford sr	Norfolk	2 d/acre tithes	Emmanuel College, Cambridge	ECC BUR.0.3d
c. 1800	Ordnance Survey	–	2 – 15 s/day	–	Seymour, 1980, 49
c. 1800	Inclosure surveyor	–	1 s 6 d/acre $1\frac{1}{2}$ guineas/day	–	Thompson, 1968, 36
1801	Joseph Truslove	Cambridgeshire	2 guineas/day	Queens' College, Cambridge	QCC Box 104 Bill pd 1 Apr. 1802
1801	Alexander Watford jr	Suffolk	1 guinea/day	Queens' College, Cambridge	QCC Box 104 Bill pd 3 Apr. 1802
1803	–	Ireland	8 d/acre	–	Andrews, 1985, 442
1804	Alexander Watford jr	Cambridgeshire	2 guineas/day	Frank Smythies	CRO 306/E10
1805	William Cole	Essex	6 d/acre	–	Mason, 1990, 24
1805	Inclosure surveyor	–	1 guinea/day	–	Stephenson, 1805, iii
1805	John Wiggins jr	Essex	7 – 10 d/acre	–	Mason, 1990, 24

Table 5.1. *(cont.)*

Date	Surveyor	Area of practice	Charge	Employer	Source
1810	T. Bartley	London	If >500 acres 1s/acre If <500 acres 1 guinea/6-hr day, 3 guineas/day drainage	–	*Cambridge Chronicle*, 13 July 1810, 2
1810	B. Hatton	Norfolk	If >800 acres 7 d/acre If <800 acres 8 d/acre If <400 acres 9 d/acre If <200 acres 10 d/acre If <100 acres 1 s/acre If <50 acres 1 guinea/day	–	*Norwich Mercury*, 6 Jan. 1810
1811	H.S.O. Jacob	Staffordshire	1 s/acre; not less because land scattered	Emmanuel College, Cambridge	ECC GBX 67 Letter of 4 Nov.
1811	William Wheatley	Huntingdonshire	If >200 acres 6 d/acre Smaller areas /acre or /day	–	*Cambridge Chronicle*, 30 August 1811, 3
1820	Alexander Watford jr	Norfolk	2 guineas/day, 2 s/acre	University of Cambridge	CUA VCV.42(2)
c. 1830	Charles Oakden	Cambridgeshire, Huntingdonshire	If >1500 acres & recently inclosed 6 d/acre If >500 acres & old inclosed 8 d/acre If >500 acres open field 9 d/acre If <200 acres & old inclosed 1 s/acre If survey & no map 6 d/acre	–	Plate 20
1830	Robert Corby	Norfolk	6 d/acre	Emmanuel College, Cambridge	ECC BUR.0.4d

Date	Surveyor	Area of practice	Charge	Employer	Source
1832	John King	Cambridgeshire	9 d/acre	John Hall	CUM Add.4403.287
1834	Thomas Jukes	Cambridgeshire	3 s/acre measuring & taking out balks	–	CRO P126/6/9
1834	Land Surveyors' Club	–	1 s 6 d/acre	–	Thompson, 1968, 97
1838	Alexander Watford jr	Cambridgeshire	1 s 6 d/acre 2 guineas/day for inclosure survey	–	I Vict. 1837–8, 8
1840	Alexander Watford jr	Cambridgeshire	2 s/acre old inclosures 1 s/acre heath	University of Cambridge	CUA VCV.58

Charges varied according to whether they included expenses and help in the field, and some surveyors were also paid an annual retainer, so interpretation of sums paid is not straightforward. For example, Edward Laurence, who surveyed land at Ickleton in Cambridgeshire in 1719 (ICK80301), entered into the following agreement with the Duchess of Buckingham on 8 May 1722 for surveying her estates in Essex, Lincolnshire and Yorkshire:

Articles of Agreement between Her Grace the Dutchess of Buckingham and Edward Laurence on Accountt of Surveying Measureing and Maping of Lordships &c.

1st For Every Lordship or Mannor of Inclosed Land Surveyed and Drawn into a Fair Draught with a Terrier of the Several Sorts of Lands belonging to Each Tenant, and also the yearly value of Each Parcel of Land to be Expressed in the said Terrier, and when the same is Compleated by being made up into Books or otherways to be Paid after the Rate of Sixpence for Every Acre, and According to the Usuall Custome the said Edward Laurence is to be Boarded so Long as he is Performing the said work, also to have his Expences Paid him to & From London and to have proper Assistance of a Man and a Boy to lead the Chain and Carry His Instruments in the Field. But if the said Edward Laurence is to be at his own Expence for the aforementioned Articles to be Paid after the Rate of Eight pence for Every Acre.

2d For Any Quantity of Common Field Land Surveyed Measured &c as above Mentioned, to be Paid after the Rate of Nine Pence for Every Acre; but if the said Edward Laurence is to be at His own Expences as above Mentioned, to be Paid after the Rate of Twelve pence for Every Acre.

3d For Any Quantity of Large Commons Exceeding an Hundred Acres or More to be as Accuratly Surveyed as the Abovementioned Lands (which ought to be so don in Case of its being Inclosed,) to be Paid after the Rate of three Pence for Every Acre but if the said Edward Laurence is to be at his own Expence in Performing the said work, to be Paid after the Rate of Four Pence for Every Acre.

4th For any Time the Said Edward Laurence shall spend in Measureing and Taking an Exact Account of the Number of the severall sorts of Timber Trees and Pollards &c and to make the same into a Terrier, Expressing the Quantity in the Hedge Rows as well as within the Inclosures; to be Paid after the Rate of Ten Shillings a Day but if the said Edward Laurence is to be at the Expence of Assistance &c as abovementioned, to be Paid after the Rate of Thirteen shillings a Day.

In the bill for the work, Laurence charged six pence an acre for surveying and mapping land in several manors, four pence an acre for surveying and drawing a rough draft of a farm and woodland, and three pence an acre for surveying and mapping common and moorland (P. G. Eden, personal communication). Thus any one surveyor sometimes paid for his own assistants and at other times did not, and his rates varied greatly.

The table does, however, show overall trends and characteristics of the ways surveyors were paid. Payment was made both by the day and by the acre, and earnings in general increased over the 250-year period. Movements of prices and wages over the period are plotted in Figs 3.5 and 3.6. They show that there was only slight inflation in the seventeenth century and the cost of surveys hardly rose either: Arthur Robins was charging ten shillings a day or three or four pence an acre in the late sixteenth century, George Atwell still recommended ten shillings a day in 1658 and John Dougharty surveyed for three pence an acre in the early eighteenth century. Then prices rose in the eighteenth century, and so did the costs of surveying. By 1750, surveyors were charging about six pence an acre, and in 1834 the Land Surveyors' Club recommended a charge of 1 s 6 d an acre, a three-fold increase. General prices, however, barely doubled over the same period (Phelps Brown and Hopkins, 1962, 195–6), which suggests that surveyors enjoyed an increased standard of living and status. By the early nineteenth century, there is evidence that some surveyors had hit hard times: Joseph Manning of Norwich advertised in 1828 that he carried out surveying and mapping at the shortest notice for half the usual prices,[1] and in 1837 James Wright of North Walsham, Norfolk, surveyed and drew tithe maps at half the usual cost.[2]

There was much variation: Thomas Langdon does not seem to have been well paid, though his work was of a high quality (see Plate 6). John Norden, on the other hand, was considerably better paid than the sum recommended in Atwell's surveying text. Similarly, Alexander Watford junior charged the University of Cambridge two shillings an acre in 1820, whilst ten years later Robert Corby only charged Emmanuel College six pence. The differences were caused by a number of factors.

Charges per acre depended partly on the type of land: Edward Lancaster only charged $1\frac{1}{2}$d per acre for surveying burnt land in 1749, and surveying titheable land was cheap at two pence an acre in 1777 and 1798. John Bodger in 1784 differentiated between open, inclosed and fen lands, and H. S. O. Jacob implied in 1811 that one shilling an acre was expensive, but the survey would be slow as the College's land was scattered in the open fields. In 1838, Alexander Watford junior charged two shillings an acre for surveying old inclosures, but only one shilling for heathland. Different types of survey could cost different amounts: Alexander Watford senior offered Trinity College, Cambridge a choice in 1794 between six pence an acre for a survey of its land at Shudy Camps, or four pence or 10 % of the value of the land for a less accurate and quicker 'ocular' survey and estimate. Some surveyors charged according to the area to be surveyed: B. Hatton advertised in the *Norwich Mercury* on 6 January 1810 that his charges were:

7 d per acre for estates larger than 800 acres,
8 d per acre for estates under 800 acres,
9 d per acre for estates under 400 acres,

CHARLES OAKDEN,

ꕮanꝺ ꕷurꔃepor,

WARESLEY, NEAR CAXTON, CAMBRIDGESHIRE.

——o✛o——

TERMS FOR SURVEYING AND MAPPING LORDSHIPS AND ESTATES.

Surveys under Acts of Inclosure faithfully and accurately executed, according to the directions of the Commissioners.

Parishes or Estates, inclosed within the last 30 years, and exceeding 1500 Acres, accurately measured and mapped, on a scale of 2, 3, 4, or 6 chains s. d. to the inch, at .... 0 6 per Acre.

Old inclosed Parishes or Estates, exceeding 500 Acres, 0 8 Ditto.

Parishes or Estates, in the open field state, and exceeding 500 Acres, ... 0 9 Ditto.

Old inclosed Estates, under 200 Acres, ... 1 0 Ditto.

The above charges include a neat Map, and every expense, when the Journey does not exceed 100 miles.

All Surveys requiring only the quantities, without a Map, 6d. per Acre.

Plans, on Vellum or Paper, of Gentlemen's Estates, Parishes, and Award Plans, neatly copied and reduced to any scale, at 1d. per Acre, exclusive of the Vellum or Paper.

THE GROUND PLANS AND ELEVATIONS OF BUILDINGS TAKEN OR COPIED.

Plans reduced to any scale, and inserted on Leases or Deeds, for Solicitors.

⁂ Apply as above directed, or to ....ck, and JOHN DAY, Melton-Mowbri

Plate 20. Advertisement of Charles Oakden.

10 d per acre for estates under 200 acres,
1 s per acre for estates under 100 acres and
1 guinea per day for estates under 50 acres (P. G. Eden, personal communication),

whilst his exact contemporary, T. Bartley of London, charged more: one shilling an acre for estates larger than 500 acres. These charges can be compared with those of Charles Oakden slightly later, attached to *A New Map Of the Country round Leicester, Melton Mowbray, and Loughborough* of 1830, which were intermediate between the two and suggest that provincial surveyors' prices had risen over the intervening two decades (see Plate 20).

111

Comparison of the charges of Hatton, Bartley and Oakden shows that at the same time different surveyors could command different fees. This partly reflected the area of the country in which they worked: Bartley was perhaps charging higher London prices in the early nineteenth century. Similarly, Irish surveyors were charging three pence an acre in 1763 at a time when their English colleagues could expect six pence, and Charles Hassall's four pence an acre in Carmarthenshire in 1780 was half the charge of the Lunds' survey in Cambridgeshire in the previous year. Charges also depended, however, on the skill and status of the man who was employed. Hassall became a leading figure in late eighteenth-century Welsh agriculture, but in 1780 he was near the beginning of his career (Jones, 1943, 142). A surveyor's charges could rise as he became more proficient: Joseph Freeman charged 15 shillings a day in 1769 and this rose to one guinea a day in 1789, at a time when general prices hardly rose at all. Alexander Watford senior's charges fluctuated, but in 1794 he was paid $1\frac{1}{2}$ guineas a day while in 1798 Queens' College paid him two guineas a day. His son, however, was only paid one guinea a day by the same college in 1801, though by 1804 he had become sufficiently well established to double this sum. By the 1820s, he was more expensive to employ than many of his contemporaries: two shillings an acre was four times as expensive as Robert Corby's six pence, and considerably more than John King's nine pence. This may indicate that Watford was a leading local figure in the surveying profession. Conversely, William Fininley's three pence an acre for surveying in 1782 was relatively low, but he was the schoolmaster at Thorney and surveying was very much a side-line.

The table does not show any evidence that particular employers used cheap or expensive men, though surveyors' charges were not merely taken for granted. It was necessary for a bill to be queried on occasion: on 18 April 1827, Queens' College appointed Thomas James Tatham of Bedford Place, London, and Alexander Watford appointed Martin Nockolds of Saffron Walden to arbitrate in a dispute over Watford's charge for his atlas of the College's estates.[3] Emmanuel College also showed concern over surveying costs, and in 1816 they wondered whether William Neale's bill for surveying at Balham in Surrey was reasonable.[4] Though cost rarely seems to have been the main factor in choice of a surveyor, it did sometimes form part of the recommendation, as when the Nettleshipps suggested that Emmanuel College should employ Francis Whishaw.[5] An exception was the advertisement by the Churchwardens and Overseers of the Poor of the Parish of Waltham Holy Cross, Essex, for a person to measure and map the parish in 1822. Twenty-seven men replied to the notice, and their charges ranged from three to 30 pence per acre. The four cheapest were short-listed, one of whom was appointed (A. S. Mason, personal communication).

To see what status these earnings brought, it is necessary to place them in context. Ten shillings a day in the mid-seventeenth century was ten times the pay of a labourer (Thompson, 1968, 21), a skilled stone-mason at Audley End in Essex could earn three shillings a day in the 1770s (Williams, 1966, 54), while the humblest labourer earned about eight shillings a week. Bread cost about four pence a loaf, ale one penny a pot, and a meal in a London tavern about 1 s 6 d (Porter, 1982, 13). A farm labourer's annual income was about £20, and the highest-paid artisan's about £105 (Mason, 1990, 25). In the early nineteenth century, a labourer's maximum weekly earnings were about 12 shillings a week at harvest time

(Hampson, 1934, 216), and a Cambridgeshire shepherd earned between £10 and £35 a year (Gooch, 1811, 285). Thus, a surveyor was considerably better off than these men. His earnings probably could not compete, however, with those of estate stewards. The latter's income was usually well up the scale of earnings of a professional gentleman: £100 a year in 1679 was adequate to maintain a gentleman's life-style (Hainsworth, 1987, 164); Hughes estimated that an eighteenth-century estate agent could match the income of a Regius Professor of Modern History at £400 (Hughes, 1949, 193), and an annual income of £550 in 1816 and £650 in 1821 was received by the estate steward at Holkham, Francis Blaikie (Parker, 1975, 135). This salary enabled him to accumulate £1,200-worth of land by 1832 (Wade Martins, 1980, 71). Though estate surveyors were probably less well off, many could still afford the standard of living of a gentleman. The Fillingham family of Syerston in Nottinghamshire could afford to buy a small estate in the eighteenth century (Holderness, 1978, 38). Essex surveyors at that time could earn about £156 per year and supplemented their income significantly through valuation and other work (Mason, 1990, 25), and in 1827 surveyors' earnings were superior to schoolmasters' and on a par with those of doctors and surgeons (Lindert and Williamson, 1983, 3).

Cambridgeshire surveyors, too, could enjoy a reasonable status: Joseph Truslove, for example, bought Fen Ditton Hall in 1821 (RCHM, 1972, 53). At 21 shillings a day, Joseph Freeman's maximum possible earnings were about £350, and he left goods worth £600 on his death in 1799.[6] His near-contemporary, the elder Alexander Watford, charged more per day and probably ranked rather higher. The difference in status with academics was illustrated in 1799. At a meeting of the Syndicate for the Hulse Estate of the University of Cambridge, it was proposed that a petition be made for the two trustees to the estate to proceed to the B.D. degree, whilst: 'It was observed <when this> at a previous Meeting on the Subject that Watford the Surveyor would be as well entitled & that the proper Reward would be a piece of Plate.'[7] On his death in 1801, Watford's estate was worth £1,000, more than Freeman's.[8] The younger Alexander Watford was even more comfortable. His maximum annual earnings were probably about £750. Even in 1828, his income was over £500, and this was despite an unfortunate accident which resulted from cellar-digging in Great St Mary's Street and 'produced a confinement of nearly three months'.[9] These figures compare very favourably with the £300-a-year stipend of the Vicar of Burwell in 1820 and 1830.[10] Watford became an influential local figure: in 1819, he was an arbitrator at the dissolution of the partnership of Edward and Thomas Tomson, stone and marble masons.[11] Later, in 1834, he was an overseer for the poor for his parish, St Andrew the Less.[12] He was considered acceptable company by men such as the Bursar of Queens' College, with whom he dined on 17 April 1836,[13] and on other occasions. He had few qualms in writing to national figures: in 1842, he presented a manuscript of his 'Collects of the Church of England rendered into Verse', set out with 'appropriate Psalm Tunes' chosen by Miss Calthrop of Isleham, to the Archbishop of Canterbury. The donation took place after Watford had suggested that each parish and chapel in the country could be supplied with a barrel-organ set with 12 tunes, at a cost of £30,500 which could be raised by 'the Committee to be formed by the Archbishop and Bishops', but the Archbishop had declared the manuscript's publication 'hopeless'.[14] Watford's estate was valued at £2,000 on his death in 1844,[15] his obituaries described him as an 'eminent surveyor',[16] and the advertisement for the auction of his goods in September 1844 gives further evidence of a considerable social standing as a professional gentleman:

The Dining and Drawing Rooms, which communicate, will comprise a nearly new handsome drab and crimson Brussels carpet, about 40 feet by 16 feet, two hearth~rugs to match; shield~back mahogany and rosewood chairs, loo table, set of capital sliding~frame dining tables, trio tables, large crimson morine window curtains, and muslin ditto and brass poles, Spanish mahogany sideboard, 7ft. 6in. long, sarcophagus cellaret, cheval fire~screen, two rosewood lounge chairs in claret leather, music~waggon, cabriole sofa, ladies' work~table, coffee~stand, what~not, candelabras, hand~screens, ornaments, &c. &c.

The notice goes on to describe the study, hall and bedroom furniture, the china, glass and kitchen requisites, and the out-door effects.[17]

Although incomes and status, therefore, did not match those of some colonial surveyors (Hughes, 1979, 71; Higman, 1988a), some English surveyors could enjoy a comfortable lifestyle. It was difficult, however, to become rich by measuring land alone (Mason, 1990, 24). Eden calculated that James Osborn would have to survey between 3,000 and 4,000 acres a year to maintain his standard of living, and this volume of work was not available locally (1973, 479). In 1806, Thomas Norfolk, who surveyed Swaffham Bulbeck and West Wratting in Cambridgeshire for various owners (SWB80001, SWB80101, WEW80901 and WEW81501), was declared bankrupt,[18] and when William Watson of Seaton Ross, Yorkshire died in 1857, his estate was valued at less than £100 (Harris, 1973, 157). To supplement their income, therefore, many surveyors had to have other occupations besides measuring and mapping land, and for some men these alternative employments were of prime importance.

ADDITIONAL OCCUPATIONS

There is abundant evidence that surveyors practised other occupations: over half of those who advertised in the *Cambridge Chronicle* had other forms of employment, as did nearly half of those who practised in Cambridgeshire. Before the middle of the eighteenth century, about one-third either supplemented their income or earned most of it in other ways; after 1750, the numbers who had other occupations grew. Advertisements in the *Belfast News Letter* from 1760 to 1840 show a similar trend (Lockhart, 1978, 103).

Some Elizabethan surveyors, such as Ralph Agas and Thomas Waterman, were clerics: they were rectors of Gressenhall and Great Ryburgh in Norfolk respectively (Eden A43 and W135). These men were highly educated: both Thomas Waterman and John Norden had been to Cambridge (Venn, I, 4, 346 and I, 3, 263), and Thomas Langdon was at New College, Oxford in about 1590 (Eden, 1983b, 72). For such men, map-making was part of their duties in the management of estate business in manorial courts (Eden, 1983a).

Educated men continued to draw maps and those surveyors who succeeded to high office could still draw the occasional estate map. Jonas Moore, for example, did so after he had finished his work connected with the fen drainage in 1659 and before he became Assistant

Surveyor (and, later, Surveyor-General) of the Ordnance in 1665 (Willmoth, 1990). About 15% of the Cambridgeshire surveyors were schoolteachers, mathematics teachers, authors of surveying manuals and members of learned societies. These occupations became common from the eighteenth century. Edward Laurence, surveyor of Ickleton in 1719 (see ICK80301), was a mathematics teacher, a member of the Spalding and Stamford Gentlemen's societies, and published a number of practical texts, including his *Young Surveyor's Guide* of 1716 and *The Duty of a Steward to his Lord*, 1727 (Eden L71; Taylor, 1966, 159 and 182; *DNB*, 11, 645–6). John Robertson surveyed the Charterhouse's land in Castle Camps in 1741 (CAS74101–2 and CAS74801). He signed himself 'F.R.S.' (CAS74101) and was clerk and librarian to the Royal Society from 1768 to 1776. From 1748 to 1755, he was assistant mathematics master at Christ's Hospital School, and then until 1766 he was first master at Portsmouth Naval Academy. He wrote astronomical and mathematical works, and his *Elements of Navigation* ran to seven editions (Eden R196; Taylor, 1966, no. 300; *DNB*, 16, 1299). In the early nineteenth century, a few academics drew estate maps: Robert Stockdale, Vice-Master and Bursar of Pembroke College, drew a map of land on Burwell Heath which was exchanged with the Jockey Club in 1817 (BUW81701; Venn, II, 6, 47), and the Master of Pembroke, Gilbert Ainslie, drew a map in 1824 of the College's allotment at West Wickham on inclosure (WEV82401).

Other Cambridgeshire surveyors were more humble schoolteachers: John Watte had a school at Leverington in the north of the county in 1770,[19] by which time he had already surveyed and mapped John Waddington's estate in Wisbech St Mary (WSM76901). He drew other estate maps in 1774 and 1775 (UPW77401 and WHR77501), and advertised as a surveyor in 1778.[20] Thomas Warren, who mapped Cheveley for the Marquis of Granby in 1775 (CHG77501), Audley End in Essex for Sir John Griffin Griffin in 1783 (Emmison, 1952), and Littleport for Edmund Tattersall in 1797 (LLP79701), was also a schoolmaster. In 1809, he won an award from the Society for the Encouragement of the Arts for designing an improved school slate (Eden W123). A final example of a Cambridgeshire surveyor and schoolmaster is William Chamberlain. He mapped John Fryer's estate in Chatteris in about 1836 (CHA83601). In February of that year, he was elected schoolmaster of Fringel's Charity School in March. He taught reading, writing and arithmetic to 100 pupils in winter and 50 in summer, he had an annual salary of £80, rent-free accommodation and $2\frac{1}{2}$ chaldrons of coals (Charity Commission, 1837, 309).

Cambridgeshire was not unusual in having schoolmasters who were also surveyors: Andrew Pellin, weaver and surveyor of Whitehaven in Cumberland, started a mathematical school there in 1697 (Tyson, 1986, 180). Henry Rathbone wrote to Lord Dartmouth's Sandwell agent in 1714 and mentioned a schoolteacher and surveyor in Lichfield, Staffordshire:

I have spoken to one Mr Matlock in our town who is a good surveyor and draws a map well. And if his lordship pleases he will do it for 4d. per acre and says that if he does not give his lordship entire satisfaction, he will have nothing for doing it. He keeps a great writing~school and would be glad to take the opportunity of surveying the estate a week before and in the Christmas holidays. (Kettle, 1979, 84)

Similarly, R. Wright had a boarding school at Pontefract in the West Riding of Yorkshire in 1743 and was also a practising surveyor (Sylvester, 1970, 252), and the schoolmaster in Goldsmith's *The Deserted Village* could survey:

> There in his noisy mansion, skilled to rule,
> The village master taught his little school; ...
> Lands he could measure, terms and tides presage,
> And even the story ran that he could gauge.
> (Goldsmith, 1770, lines 195–6 and 209–10)

Education was not the only indication that some surveyors were cultivated men: from the eighteenth century, some showed an interest in heraldry and antiquities. Thomas Browne, who mapped Potsgrove in Bedfordshire for the Duke of Bedford in 1731, described himself as a gentleman and Blanch Lyon Pursuivant of Arms[21] and he was later Garter King of Arms (*DNB*, 7, 72). The Welsh antiquary Lewis Morris earned his living as a surveyor and map-maker (Walters, 1988, 537), and William Cole was another well-known eighteenth-century antiquary. He moved to Waterbeach in Cambridgeshire in 1767 (Palmer, 1935, 8), and in the same year he copied the maps which had been made by Thomas Langdon in 1601/2 of Merton College's land in Gamlingay. The copies were made for his friend, Robert Masters, Rector of Landbeach, and they are decorated with the coats of arms of the College, Masters, Cole, Dr Stephen Apthorp (Cole's half-brother, whose family had owned land in the parish since the early seventeenth century (*DNB*, 4, 734; *VCH*, 5, 75)) and neighbouring landowners (GAM60201–16).[22] Surveyors sometimes included antiquities on their maps: John Brownrigg, an Irish estate surveyor, did so in the late eighteenth century (Andrews, 1986, 45). So too did Philip Crocker, son of Abraham, a schoolmaster at Ilminster, Somerset; Abraham later started a surveying business with his sons, and became estate steward at Stourhead where the landowner was Richard Colt Hoare. For his *Ancient History of Wiltshire*, Hoare employed Philip to carry out all the surveys. At about the same time, in 1805, Philip surveyed archaeological sites for the Sussex, Hampshire and Wiltshire sheets of the Ordnance Survey (Seymour, 1980, 64; Woodbridge, 1970, 198, 206 and 212). In Cambridgeshire, Alexander Watford junior became interested in local antiquities. In 1843, he dug up a Roman urn at Melbourn, which he presented to the Society of Antiquaries of London on 6 June 1844 (Society of Antiquaries of London, 1849, 46; Way, 1847, no. 84). He was interested in Roman roads (Babington, 1853, 29), and he was in correspondence with the Cambridge Antiquarian Society about a survey of them.[23]

Some surveyors earned or supplemented their income from agricultural activities, as owners or estate stewards. Five Cambridgeshire landowners mapped their own estates: for example, the Reverend Edward Serocold Pearce, M.A., J.P. drew a sketch of the land which he bought in 1834 on the inclosure of Hardwick (HAP83401; Venn, II, 5, 60). Others were smaller farmers and members of the rural professional classes (Barrell, 1972, 64), such as John Rain of Sunderland in the late eighteenth century (Miller, 1987, 417), Benjamin Fallowes (surveyor of GTA71701; Mason, 1990, 48) or Thomas Newitt of Chatteris. He mapped Thomas Grant's estate there in 1807 (CHA80701). Newitt seems to have had a reasonable income and he possessed his own maps: in his will, proved 20 April 1853, he bequeathed to his sons all his 'Goods Chattels Household Furniture Maps Books Pictures Silver Plate China [and] Earthenware ...'.[24] Estate stewards were closely involved in the agricultural production of the land in their charge, and from the mid-eighteenth century many had surveying skills (Chartres, 1989, 452; Mingay, 1967, 18). John Storer was land agent and surveyor to Sir Thomas Spencer Wilson from 1781 and mapped his land in Cambridgeshire in the following year (LIT78201–7; Mason, 1990, 78). Jeremiah Lagden was estate steward to several owners of Horseheath Hall in Cambridgeshire. In 1788, the owner was Stanlake Batson, for whom Lagden mapped the land at West Wickham (WEV78801; Parsons, 1948, 48). Members of the Wing family were estate stewards for the Dukes of Bedford at Thorney from 1750 to 1851. They carried out or supervised some map-making, but their main duties lay with the general running of the estate. They were successful, and in 1811 William Gooch praised the work of John (p.104): 'The perfection of fen husbandry is to be seen at Thorney, under the direction of Mr. Wing, whose management is so superior, that it is to be lamented his jurisdiction as superintendant of drainage and embanking, does not extend over the whole level of the fens.' Major estate surveys in the late eighteenth and early nineteenth centuries, however, tended to be carried out by specialist surveyors and cartographers; most estate stewards lacked the necessary expertise (Howell, 1986, 55).

The most noticeable development, though, was the growth of other land-related activities. The younger Alexander Watford's career was typical. Not only was he responsible for at least 125 maps between 1801 and 1844, but his office produced about the same number of valuations, and some terriers and surveys. He was surveyor and agent to many Cambridge colleges, he collected rents for them, supervised repairs and, in at least one case, managed their farms.[25] He proposed draining Coe Fen in 1824, though nothing came of the proposal.[26] In 1831, he announced his intention to become an 'Auctioneer for the Sale of Landed Property in general, also of Houses and Tenements',[27] and then, slightly later, he opened a register for letting property.[28] Some practitioners became property developers: William Custance, for instance, managed to acquire a potential building site on the inclosure of Chesterton in 1838 (*VCH*, 9, 8). Surveyors also became involved in the inclosure process: 34 surveyors of Cambridgeshire estates were employed as inclosure surveyors, and 26 as inclosure commissioners, and many were involved in more than one inclosure (Beresford, 1946, 132). Alexander Watford junior was an inclosure surveyor for at least 18 Cambridgeshire parishes, and commissioner for eight or more. He was also inclosure commissioner for more than ten parishes in neighbouring counties. As it was possible to earn between £3,000 and £4,000 per inclosure as a surveyor (Hull, 1955, 36), this must have been a major source of Watford's income.

Surveyors were also employed in a wide variety of other activities, which were only tenuously connected with estate mapping. Some, such as John Rocque, Joel Gascoyne and Thomas Badeslade, were also engravers and map-sellers (Varley, 1948; Ravenhill, 1972; Harris, 1979, 154–5). Some Cambridgeshire surveyors were printers and publishers, both of maps and of other items. John Bowles, who surveyed the Corporation of the Sons of the Clergy's estate at West Wratting in 1737 (WEW73701), was probably the London printer and publisher of that name (Eden B493; Tooley, 1987). Alexander Watford proposed publishing a plan of the town of Cambridge in 1822;[29] the project failed, but in 1828 he published his nephew James Richardson's circular map of the land 25 miles around Cambridge.[30]

Surveyors could have other technical skills, as engineers (Buchanan, 1989, 40; Robinson, 1962; Storrie, 1969), or as lesser craftsmen. George Skinner, who drew maps for Corpus Christi, King's and Queens' colleges in the mid-seventeenth century (GRT65401; GRT66601), was primarily a carpenter,[31] while Robert Grumbold, who drew maps for Queens' College in 1683 and 1692,[32] came from a Northamptonshire family of stone-masons (Airs, 1975, 149) and worked as such in at least eight Cambridge colleges and the University (Willis and Clark, 3, 1886, 533). He continued a family connection with Cambridge: two other members, Thomas and his son William, worked for Clare College from the 1630s (Wardale, 1899, 66; Willis and Clark, 1, 1886, 99), and Thomas also worked for King's College (Willis and Clark, 1, 1886, 513).

Several Dutch painters also worked as surveyors and cartographers (Dunthorne, 1988, 20), and the Cambridgeshire surveyor Joseph Freeman was also a portrait painter. He advertised his arrival in Cambridge in 1764 in the *Cambridge Chronicle*, and land surveying was not mentioned:

JOSEPH FREEMAN, coach~Painter, from London, Opposite the RED BULL Inn, in CAMBRIDGE; BEGS leave to inform the Nobility, Gentry and others, that he Paints, Gilds and Japans COACHES in the neatest and newest Fashion, on the most reasonable Terms.

He also paints Arms on Vellum, and all other Kinds of Heraldry, such as Escutcheons, Hatchments, &c.

He likewise copies Pictures faithfully, carefully cleans linen and mends all sorts of Paintings.

At the above Place may be had a variety of fine colours and Crayons ready prepared, and every other Article necessary to fine Painting.

N.B. Buys and sells all sorts of Paintings, Prints, &c.[33]

He kept this shop, in what is now Sidney Street, until 1772.[34] He was described by William Cole as 'an ingenious painter of Cambridge' (Nichols, 1812, 666), and as 'shy, diffident & reserved to a great degree', and 'from his appearance the least likely to prove a genius that you can meet with' (Owst, 1949, 80). He copied and repaired several portraits, and in this way earned at least £155 between 1764 and 1799. Among his clients were Emmanuel, Magdalene, Trinity, Queens' and Clare colleges, the University of Cambridge, the Earl of Hardwicke in 1784 and 1788,[35] and Thomas Hobson (Masters, 1790; Goodison, 1955 and 1985; Bushell, 1938, 62–3). He regarded himself primarily as a surveyor, however, as he wrote to the Earl of Hardwicke in 1788:

I will take very great Pains with it [a picture of Mr Yorke] to do that Justice to the Copy the Original deserves for it is a prodigious fine Picture, you will be kind enough to pardon me for saying that my principal reliance for support is acting in the Capacity of Land Steward Surveying Value*ing* buying and selling Estates which at times I have done for this 25 years; for this last 10 years have been much employ*ed* that way ...[36]

His brother, Charles, was a more humble painter, and sometimes it is unclear from account books which Freeman was being paid. Over the same period, Joseph earned at least £2,041 from land surveying and mapping, and he carried out very little portrait work in the 1790s. The notice of his death in the *Gentleman's Magazine* (69, I, 1799, 260) acknowledged his dual occupations: 'Suddenly, at his house near St. Peter's college, Cambridge, Mr. Freeman, landsurveyor and painter. He was well in the former part of the day, and went to church; at 9 o'clock he was taken ill, and died at 11.'

The list of possible additional occupations is seemingly endless. Landscape gardeners and nurserymen not uncommonly drew estate maps (Webster, 1989, 88); in Cambridgeshire, Edward E. and George Neale Driver came from a family with a longstanding connection with the nursery business (Barty-King, 1975), and William Emes was a landscape gardener (Eden E89). There was also a coroner, a high sheriff, a clerk, an astronomer, a money-lender, an architect, a stationer, an instrument-maker, a wine merchant, a dealer in patent medicines, an upholsterer, a cabinet-maker and a mayor amongst Cambridgeshire surveyors.

Land surveyors, therefore, were more than measurers and mappers. In some cases, surveying was an activity which was incidental to their main employment. For other men, it was necessary to take on additional tasks to supplement their income as a surveyor. There was much movement both into and out of the profession during any one individual's career: John Watte started out as a schoolmaster and then became a surveyor, whilst John Undy, surveyor to the Earl of Hopetoun in the late eighteenth century, later took out a 99-year lease for a nursery from the Earl (Adams, 1971, 13). The number of surveyors with other occupations increased in the seventeenth and eighteenth centuries, and the type of activity changed. Early on, surveyors were also lawyers and educated men who managed estates in similar ways to their medieval predecessors. By the eighteenth century, two main trends were emerging. First, the combination of surveying and teaching, and second, the growth of surveying businesses. These businesses carried out a wide variety of activities related to the land, and map-making was just one of the ways of generating an income.

TRAINING

Training was very important, for whatever the relative importance of surveying to an individual's income, he had to learn his skills. There were three main ways in which this was done: by studying surveying texts, by apprenticeship and at school.

Surveying texts

Didactic texts on estate management and surveying were not new in the sixteenth century; medieval works had been written, especially in the late thirteenth and early fourteenth centuries (Oschinsky, 1971, 56). After the introduction of printing, however, it became possible for texts to be more widely disseminated and their number grew with the rise of the surveying profession (Richeson, 1966). The present discussion is based on a reading of 33 surveying texts which were published between 1523 and 1827; they were selected from lists which have been published in Fussell (1947, 1950 and 1983), Grewe (1984) and Taylor (1954 and 1966).

Fig. 5.1 shows the pattern of publication of surveying and mathematical texts over 340 years. The coverage of the different sources varies greatly: Taylor (1954) includes works of all mathematical practitioners rather than just surveying texts, whilst Grewe aims to cover European publications. The comprehensiveness of Grewe's bibliography has not been examined, but the coincidence of the plots for texts published in English from his work and for the books which were read during the preparation of the present text suggests that the sample discussed here is not unrepresentative.

In the sixteenth century, as printed books became more available and literacy increased, there was a demand for the publication of practical works (Bennett, 1969, 109). Fig. 5.1 shows that the publication of surveying texts was part of a response to this growing demand: many were published in the early days of the profession, until about 1620. There was a decline during the Civil War, after which there was a great boom in publication of mathematical works; the proliferation of surveying manuals was smaller, but still notable (Harley, 1970, vi). By considering Fig. 5.2, it is possible to suggest a series of publication cycles. Leybourn's *Compleat Surveyor* was first published in 1653 and it continued to be influential until the last edition was published in 1722. Then in 1725 three works, by Wyld, Hammond and Wilson were published; they were all reprinted during the following decade and the seventh edition of Wyld was published in 1780. Few new texts were published while these three works remained in print, and then the third series started with works by Hutton, Burns and Talbot. Finally, the publication of Davis' *A Complete Treatise of Land Surveying* in 1798 marked the start of the fourth cycle which was continued with books by Beckett, Crocker and Sleeman.

The books were published in a variety of formats. In general, formats decreased and books became more portable. The first octavo publication was Holwell's *A Sure Guide to the Practical Surveyor* of 1678, and only one work after this, Wing's *Geodaetes Practicus Redivivus* of 1700, was published in folio. Three works (Martindale, 1682, Laurence, 1716 and Crocker, 1806) were published in a pocket-sized duodecimo. Martindale (1702, A2v) explained that previous publications had been 'too large for ordinary carrying in a Pocket' and were therefore: 'not so convenient for one that hath much occasion to be out of his own House; to say nothing of their price. I have therefore made my Book so little, that the price can neither much empty the Pocket, nor the Bulk over~fill it.' In four cases (Fitzherbert, Benese, Hutton and Ainslie), later editions were published in a smaller format, and one book, Digges' *Pantometria*, had its second edition published in a larger format. If it is assumed that the number of editions and years a work was available is some indication of its popularity, then it does not seem as if the works were designed to be carried about by surveyors, as the longest-running editions were not necessarily the smallest. Digges' *Tectonicon*, the last (17th) edition of which was published 146 years after the first, was a quarto, and Leybourn's *Compleat Surveyor* was a folio.

Many of the early texts were published in black-letter, the normal type until the mid-sixteenth century. In Elizabethan England, however, roman type became more popular; by

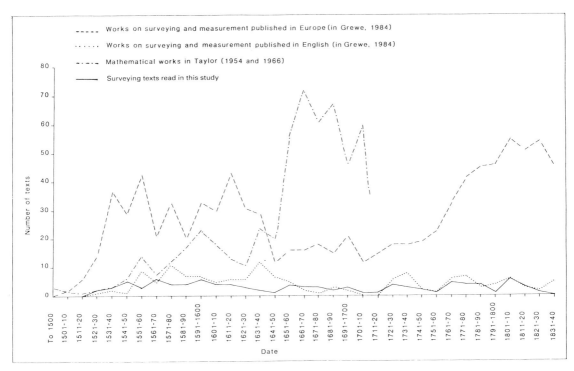

Fig. 5.1. Publication of mathematical and surveying texts 1500–1840.

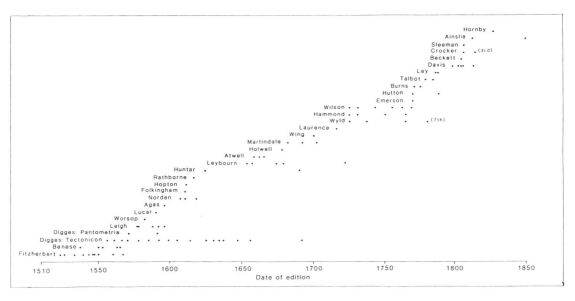

Fig. 5.2. Dates of editions of 33 surveying texts which were published between 1523 and 1849.

about 1580, black-letter was being abandoned in plays, Latin books and scientific and theological literature, though popular prose and ballads continued to be printed in it until well into the seventeenth century (McKerrow, 1927, 297). The first surveying texts to be printed in roman type were by Lucar (1590) and Agas (1596), though black-letter lingered on for Norden (1607), Folkingham (1610) and Hopton (1611), suggesting that the texts were considered as practical, popular literature. Norden's, indeed, was recommended to Crown and, later, Parliamentary surveyors (Lawrence, 1985, 55).

The cost of the texts would also suggest that they were aimed at practical surveyors. In 1598, the Stationers' Company tried to control book prices and ordained that most books should not cost more than one halfpenny per sheet, and book prices hardly rose between 1560 and 1635 despite the general inflation of the period. Leigh's *The Moste Profitable and Commendable Science of Surueying of Landes, Tenementes, and Hereditamentes* of 1577 cost six pence, and at 0.37 d per sheet fell well within this limit. Books with large numbers of illustrations and diagrams were exempt from control, and Digges' *Pantometria*, which was a grander work with a dedication, cost 1.16 d per sheet and was probably partly aimed at a different readership (Johnson, 1950). In 1716, Laurence's duodecimo text cost 3 s 6 d; Wyld's cost three shillings whilst Wilson's, which was published in 1725, the same year as Wyld, but again had a dedication, cost 5 s 6 d. Ley, in 1786, cost three shillings; Crocker, aimed at schools, cost 7 s 6 d in 1806. These prices were probably within a surveyor's means; Thomas Langdon was paid between 2 s 6 d and four shillings a day in the 1590s (Eden, 1983b, 73), and by 1795 the elder Alexander Watford was charging $1\frac{1}{2}$ guineas a day.[37]

A few of the later texts (Hutton, 1770, Burns, 1771, Davis, 1798 and Hornby, 1827) were published by subscription. This means of publication became increasingly popular in the eighteenth century among publishers of text books, sermons and collections of poetry, and so these surveying texts fit into this development. Subscription lists were attractive because they were a means by which schoolteachers and surveyors could advertise themselves (Robinson and Wallis, 1975a, ii–iii). For example, in 1765 an Irish grocer, James Ryan, subscribed to mathematical works and he drew a map in 1788 (Eden R318.8; R. V. Wallis, personal communication). Of the 631 subscribers to Hutton's *Treatise on Mensuration*, 18 % were schoolteachers, 3 % were mathematicians and 1 % were surveyors. Twelve surveyors (3 %) subscribed to Burns, in the company of nine teachers and five mathematicians. Davis' work had eight mathematicians (7 %) and two surveyors (2 %) as subscribers and only 3 % were teachers. Finally, 5 % of the subscribers to Hornby were teachers, 1 % were mathematicians and none said that he was a surveyor. From this it can be seen that although surveyors were part of the clientele, they were by no means the sole market for such works.

Texts were also sold by advertisement in local newspapers. The second edition of Talbot's *The Compleat Art of Land-Measuring* was advertised in the *Cambridge Chronicle* on 11 December 1784, and Ley's and Hutton's works were advertised on 9 June 1787 and 29 November 1788 respectively. On 12 August 1809, there was a notice of Crocker's *Elements of Land-Surveying*, and other works were also mentioned at various times.

Dedications to notable figures were common in late sixteenth and seventeenth-century publications (Bennett, 1965, 31–53; and 1970, 32), and surveying texts were no exception. Worsop's work was dedicated to Sir William Cecil, for example, and Norden's to Lord Robert Cecil. In 1653, Leybourn dedicated his *The Compleat Surveyor* to Edmund Wingate, because of 'Your knowledge in, and affection to the Sciences Mathematicall, as also the civill respect which You usually vouchsafe such as affect those Studies' (1653, A2r). Wingate was a Bedfordshire landowner, a J.P., an M.P. and a teacher, land surveyor and writer. His *Arithmetic* was one of the most popular of the times, and he was kind to newcomers such as Leybourn (Taylor, 1954, 205). This last example and later dedications suggest that personal contact with a patron helped to ensure the success of a work: Crocker's text of 1806 was dedicated to John Andrews Esq., a Devonshire landowner. Sleeman dedicated his *Practical Treatise* of 1806 to his pupil, John Rock Grosett Esq., and Ainslie's work was dedicated to the civil engineer John Rennie.

The aim of these works, therefore, was at a varied audience. Some authors were explicit: Worsop's was to be read by 'euery resonable man', and he hoped it would not 'come to the hands of learned Mathematicians' (1582, A2v and A3v). Lucar's, too, was aimed at a practical audience, though he did not want the market to be too restricted:

The phrase of my stile in this Lvcarsolace is deuised rather to profite you and others my friendes and louing countriemen, than to please the eares of the eloquent Rethoritian or curious schooleman: for as a lofty and long discourse that will make of a molehill a mountaine, and of an Emmet an Elephant, is a thing irkesome vnto them which desire plainnesse and couet breuitie ... my purpose in sending abroad this treatise is to profite Surueiors, Landmeaters, Landlords, Tenants, Buyers and Sellers of land, woods and trees, trauellers, gunners, men of warre, builders, and seamen. (1590, Aiiv)

Norden's *Svrveiors Dialogve* was intended for 'Landlords, Tenants, and Surueyors of Lands' (1610, *1r) and Atwell's work was for both the 'ingenious Scholar' and the 'honest countrey~farmer' (1658, *4r). Many mathematical teachers in the eighteenth century were self-taught from textbooks and periodicals (Hans, 1951, 185), and the geologist William Smith taught himself sufficient from books to become apprenticed to the surveyor Edward Webb of Stow-on-the-Wold (Boud, 1975, 83–4). The early nineteenth-century texts by Beckett, Crocker and Hornby were all aimed at schools; the poet John Clare owned Crocker's (Clare, 1951, 50). Surveyors were, at the very least, aware of these publications: William Fowler included a number of mathematical works in a cartouche to a seventeenth-century map, and among the books were the surveying manuals of Edmund Wingate and Aaron Rathborne (Phillips, 1979, 20). Fowler may have owned some texts; the inventory of his goods for probate in about 1664 includes 'Books & Instruments belonging to survey – £5' (Phillips, 1979, 17), though these books may have been note- or field books. Amongst Cambridgeshire surveyors, the cartouche to John Robertson's map of Castle Camps, illustrated in Plate 10, shows a volume which may be a surveying text. John Hammond of Sawston, Cambridgeshire, may also have owned some surveying manuals: he was a surveyor of roads, and the probate inventory of his possessions included 'some books'.[38]

Some of the authors of the texts were land surveyors: Agas claimed to describe techniques which he had learned 'by my reading and longe practise: (for I take thirty yeares to be a large stitch in a short age)' (1596, 1). John Wing had 26 years' experience (1700, Ar), Ley had been practising for 15 years and said that he had 'made use of every instrument commonly applied to the purpose of land measuring' (1786, 75), and Crocker's work was written after surveying for 30 years (1806, vi). Some authors took the opportunity to advertise their surveying practices in the front of their work: Edward Laurence wrote (1716, A4v),

Advertisement. Lordships Surveyed, and Maps drawn of the same. Timber Measured and Valued, with other Artificers Work; and Dialling in all its Parts, Performed by Edward Laurence.

He is to be heard of when in London at Mr Senex's at the Globe in Salisbury~Court.

N.B. In Winter, and at such Times as he is not Surveying, Gentlemen may have their Sons or Daughters Taught Accompts after a Natural, Easy and Concise Method, with the Use of the Globes and Maps, and all other useful Parts of the Mathematicks.

Hornby, too, advertised that estates were 'surveyed, planned, valued, &c. on the lowest terms', and that land surveying was 'taught in all its Branches' (1827, xvi). The combination of surveying with teaching was common: John Holwell, 'Philomath', emphasized the latter (1678, A4r): 'Arts and Sciences Mathematical, Professed and Taught by the Author ... at his House on the East side of Spittle~Fields, near the Red Lyon ... Likewise he doth Survey Land for any Person that hath occasion to imploy him, at a reasonable Rate.' Another author and teacher, George Atwell, had started his career as a surveyor. By 1624, he had settled in Cambridge and he offered his services there for 25 years as a teacher of mathematics, an instrument-maker, an astrologer and a surveyor (Feingold, 1984, 85). His *Faithfull Surveyour* was published in 1658 and dedicated to William Dillingham, Master of Emmanuel College. Atwell died in the same year and was buried in North Runcton Church near King's Lynn, where his gravestone lauded him as being 'De Studio et Praxi Mathematiccis non Ignobilis' (Bushell, 1938, 54). Burns, Talbot and Sleeman were also teachers. Some authors had other occupations: Richard de Benese was a Canon of the Augustinian Priory of Merton (Taylor, 1954, 312), and William Leybourn started his career as a printer and bookseller. His first surveying text, *Planometria*, was published in 1650 under the pseudonym of Oliver Wallinby. He became a teacher and a practical surveyor, and in 1666 he was one of the six men who surveyed London after the Great Fire (Kenney, 1950). Folkingham was also a publisher, and issued medical texts in the 1620s (Fussell, 1947, 22).

The surveying texts indicate the ways in which the surveying profession changed in the seventeenth and eighteenth centuries. The earliest work, Fitzherbert's, says nothing about measuring land or map-making. The first general introduction in English to geometrical survey and mensuration was Digges' *Tectonicon* of 1556, and Lucar was the first to show some concern for cartography. Rathborne's *The Svrveyor* was published in 1616, and this work was the first of a new style of publication, with an orderly presentation (Taylor, 1954, 343). It was also the last book to emphasize the legal aspects of a surveyor's work. Until the end of the seventeenth century, a number of miscellaneous tasks were described, such as dealing with tenants, collection of rents, presentation to livings (Fitzherbert, 1523), or how to extinguish a house fire (Atwell, 1658). From the texts of Wyld, Hammond and Wilson, all published in 1725, duties were more closely connected with the land: valuation, improvement, estate management, levelling, and how to measure timber. Late eighteenth-century texts, such as those by Hutton, Emerson, Burns, Talbot and Davis, typically for their times, mentioned the antiquity of the surveying profession.

Surveying manuals were therefore available and affordable to the seventeenth and eighteenth-century land surveyor, and in their various ways the texts all explained at least basic geometrical principles, surveying instruments and their use. There is some evidence that the texts were owned and used by surveyors, but it is likely that most surveyors learned their skills through other means.

Apprenticeship

Apprenticeship was an important means of professional education throughout the early modern period. Thomas Langdon, for example, was probably an assistant to Thomas Clerke in the late 1580s, and in 1615 and 1616 he had a pupil, Henry Wilcocke, who helped him to carry out surveys for Corpus Christi College, Oxford (Eden, 1983b, 72 and 75). Some early surveyors were trained by mathematicians: Thomas Digges, who completed his father Leonard's *Pantometria* in 1571, was a pupil of John Dee (McLean, 1972, 146), while Nicholas Lane was probably taught by the instrument-maker Elias Allen (Gunasena, 1982, 1). There is plenty of evidence of Cambridgeshire surveyors having served apprenticeships. For example, Thomas Utton, surveyor of land at Hardwick for Pembroke College, Cambridge in 1836 (HAP83601), practised with Henry Wyatt and was probably trained by him or his family (Eden U22). Others had apprentices to train: Mr Jenkinson of Huntingdon wanted an apprentice bookseller, binder and printer in 1771, but, 'if he has some Knowledge of Geometry, he may have an Opportunity of being practically instructed in Surveying of Land'.[39] A typical advertisement for an apprentice appeared in the *Cambridge Chronicle* on 22 September 1815:

LAND SURVEYING. A Gentleman in the above profession wishes for a youth of respectable connexions as an APPRENTICE. – He will be initiated into the rudiments of Geometry and Mathematics, if not already master thereof, and will be instructed in the theory and practice of Land Surveying, as well as the measuring and valuing of timber, and if necessary, in the business of an Auctioneer: and as the advertiser is the son of an eminent Surveyor in London, his apprentice will have the opportunity of learning an easy, quick, and experienced mode of doing business. As he will be treated in every respect as one of the family, it is requested no person but of respectability will apply.

A letter (post~paid) directed to A.B. Post~Office, St. Neots, Hunts, will meet with due attention, and if approved of, an interview will be appointed.[40]

In the eighteenth century, family practices developed, and many boys served apprenticeships with their fathers. At least ten of the 127 surveyors in Warwickshire between 1710 and 1840 practised with their fathers (Pannett, 1985, 80), and in Norfolk the emergent surveying businesses frequently employed sons and nephews to learn and carry out surveying and mapping (Eden, 1975, 126). The Fairbank family of Sheffield likewise kept the business in the family by training sons from generation to generation (Hall, 1932). Seven surveyors of Cambridgeshire estates were followed by their sons or close relatives: John Halsey

(THO73201), Tycho Wing (CRY74701–3), Thomas Warren (CHG77501 and LLP79701), William Walton (THO76701), Alexander Watford was followed by his son, Alexander, who was helped by his nephew, James Richardson, and John Prickett. Prickett was based in Highgate; he mapped Jacob John Whittington's estate in Guilden Morden in 1797 (GUI79701) and copied maps of the Charterhouse's Cambridgeshire estates (BAL61701–6 and CAS61701–5; Eden P333). Prickett's son, Joseph, was apprenticed to him for at least four years before he set up on his own. He intended to have a business at Eaton Socon in Bedfordshire, but in the end he moved to Bridge Street, St Ives.[41] Not all family firms themselves trained their offspring and successors: Robert Collier Driver, nephew of Edward and George Neale Driver, was apprenticed to James Marmont of Bristol in 1832 and became a partner in the Driver firm in 1837 (Barty-King, 1975, 84 and 105).

Apprenticeships were usually for a substantial length of time, and they could start when the pupil was young. In Norfolk, Thomas Coke of Holkham's surveyor, John Halsey, brought up his son as a surveyor and the boy made a field book when he was only ten years old (Eden, 1973, 477). A slightly older person wanted to start an apprenticeship in 1831:

TO ESTATE AGENTS & LAND SURVEYORS. A SITUATION is wanted for a YOUTH between 15 and 16 years of age, with a person in good practice, where a competent knowledge of land~valuing and land~surveying can be acquired.

Address, letters post~paid, to Mr. BUNN, Solicitor, Ipswich.[42]

A formal seven-year apprenticeship, a typical length of time, could cost about £30 to £40 in the early eighteenth century (Holmes, 1982, 21). A surveyor could still be an apprentice when he was in his early twenties: John Walker's son, John, was not allowed to participate in the draughtsmanship of the final version of estate maps of Essex until he was 21 or 22, and even then his work was not acknowledged. The younger John's name first appeared on a map in 1600 and he continued to qualify his name as 'junior' until 1616 even though there is no map with his father's draughtsmanship after 1601; his father died in 1626 (Edwards and Newton, 1984, 36). In 1805, it appeared a three-year apprenticeship at the age of 18 was not unusual:

Hitherto gentlemen have been under the necessity of putting their sons generally three years, and give a handsome premium, to learn the present mode of land surveying, &c., and that at the age of eighteen, which is a time when any person of only common ability and education might have taught himself, had there been a proper treatise on the subject, in as few weeks. (Stephenson, 1805, iii)

The Land Surveyors' Club, which was formed in 1834, required an apprenticeship of four years or service with one's father until the age of 24, though this rule was later relaxed and ten years' experience as a surveyor was sufficient for membership (Thompson, 1968, 96).

Schools

Finally, land surveying could be learned at school. Interest in a practical education began in the late seventeenth century (Cressy, 1975, 12); Whitehaven, Cumberland, is an early example, where the requirements of a growing port and an influential and interested local patron, Sir John Lowther, stimulated the demand for the teaching of such subjects (Robinson and Wallis, 1975b). Practical subjects were not widespread, however, until the eighteenth century. A few grammar schools taught surveying, such as Oundle which taught classics, geography, surveying, merchants' accounts and drawing to 45 boys (21 boarders) in 1792 (Vincent, 1969, 103), but it was at the private academies which developed in that century that subjects such as surveying were usually taught. For example, Mr Vaughan's Academy at Aspley Guise produced a map of that town in about 1778 (Hull, 1955, 33), and Henry Andrews opened a school which taught measuring of land at Royston in 1766 (Kingston, 1906, 213). It has been estimated that there were 4,500 mathematicians active between 1701 and 1760, and most of these taught, at least part-time (Wallis, 1976, iv–v). Many of these men were self-taught (Harding, 1972, 142): Charles Hutton was a coal miner's son (Porter, 1982, 66); he opened a school in Newcastle in 1760 and published his *Treatise on Mensuration* in 1770 (Howson, 1982, 59–63). By the mid-nineteenth century, surveying was fairly commonly taught at local schools; in *Adam Bede*, which was first published in 1859, the schoolmaster asks: 'But where's the use of all the time I've spent in teaching you writing and mapping and mensuration, if you're not to get for'ard in the world, and show folks there's some advantage in having a head on your shoulders, instead of a turnip?' (Eliot, 1859, 291).

A number of schools in the Cambridge region in the eighteenth century taught practical subjects (Black, 1972, 16), one of which was surveying. Twenty schools in Cambridgeshire advertised in the *Cambridge Chronicle* in the late eighteenth and early nineteenth centuries that they taught surveying. The location of these schools is shown in Fig. 5.3, and it can be seen that they were scattered over the county, with concentrations in Cambridge and Ely. At least 16 others announced that they taught subjects which may have included surveying. George Lodge, at Linton, taught: 'English, Latin, Greek, French, and Italian languages; writing in all the various hands; drawing, arithmetic, merchants' accounts after the Italian method, algebra, mensuration, surveying in theory and practice, navigation, geography, the Use of the globes, and every branch in the mathematics', for 15 guineas a year.[43] There were a further 54 schools outside Cambridgeshire which advertised in a similar fashion. Jeremiah Whitehead, at Donington (Lincolnshire) in 1774, for example, taught 'Land Surveying, and the delineating Plans, or Maps of Estates', and J. Storr announced in 1802 that he taught 'Practical Land Surveying' at his school in Thetford. In 1808 he held 'an exhibition of his pupils' performances of penmanship, drawing, mapping, &c. in a commodious room at the George Inn'.[44] Another 40 schools outside Cambridgeshire may have included surveying in their curriculum. Six schools taught land surveying as an extra, as at Prospect House Academy in Cambridge in

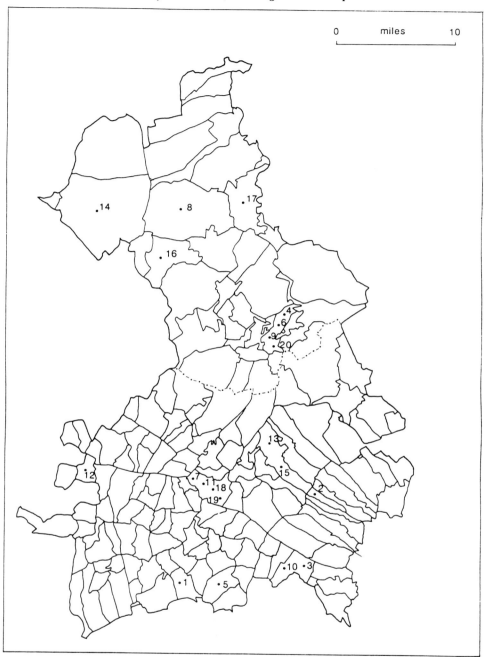

Fig. 5.3. Schools which advertised in the *Cambridge Chronicle* between 1762 and 1836 that they taught surveying (The schools advertised in the following years: 1, 1766–7; 2, 1777; 3, 1777–1802; 4, 1783–5; 5, 1788; 6, 1795–6; 7, 1798; 8, 1799; 9, 1804–37; 10, 1805–12; 11, 1807; 12, 1807; 13, 1807–17; 14, 1809; 15, 1809; 16, 1810; 17, 1823–5; 18, 1825–36; 19, 1826–36; 20, 1835. Fenland parishes are north of the broken line; upland parishes are to the south).

1825 for five shillings a quarter; lessons in the classics and drawing cost an extra guinea a quarter.[45]

The schools which advertised in the *Cambridge Chronicle* that they taught surveying fit into the general educational trends of the eighteenth century: about half were private boarding schools, there were ten academies and under 10% were grammar schools. Local schools were often dependent on particular individuals and were short-lived (O'Day, 1982, 29), and it seems as if the schools of the Cambridge region were no exception. Two-thirds only advertised once, and though they may have existed for a number of years, they probably closed when the master, or his successor, moved away or died. Five schools certainly lasted for more than ten years, and two, E. Lutt's at Ely and George Lodge's at Linton, for 25 or more. The cost of an education at one of these schools varied but was about 20 guineas a year: Jeremiah Slade's school at Fowlmere was cheap at £14 per annum with one guinea entrance, and Newton Bosworth's Cambridge establishment was the most expensive: 30 guineas a year with one guinea entrance.[46] Other schools in Cambridge were not necessarily more expensive, but general prices did tend to be higher from about 1810. The schools were not large: Campton Academy in Bedfordshire in 1807 could accommodate a maximum of 50 pupils, and it seems likely that this was a fairly large establishment.[47]

Apart from some surveying manuals which were aimed at schools, other school textbooks such as William Hawney's *Compleat Measurer* (1735) contained sections on land surveying. The poet John Clare talks about a variety of practical books aimed at schools and humble men (Tibble and Tibble, 1972). 'Who among the lower orders of youth', he asks, 'is ignorant of "The Young Man's best Companion" by Mr Fisher, Accountant, or the "Book of Wisdom", by Mr Fenning Philomath? They are almost as common as bibles and prayer-books in a cottage library', and in 1825 he received Charles Vyse's *Tutor's Guide* (Clare, 1951, 142 and 207). Both George Fisher's *Young Man's Best Companion* and Vyse's work contained sections on land surveying and were available in cheap duodecimo formats: the 29th edition of Fisher cost 3s 6d in 1806 while the 13th edition of Vyse sold for 4s 6d in 1807 (Peddie, 1914, 207 and 617).

It was, therefore, possible for surveyors to learn their skills in a number of ways, and the various methods could be combined if necessary. Learning by apprenticeship and example was probably the most usual method, but it became increasingly possible to learn the relevant skills at school or from visiting mathematical lecturers, and text books were always available. The content of the training can be seen from an examination of surveying techniques.

SURVEYING TECHNIQUES

A surveyor in the early nineteenth century had a much wider range of surveying instruments and techniques available to him than had his predecessor 250 years earlier, but many of the new instruments and ideas were not very useful for local land surveys.

Surveying texts give the theoretical background which was available to surveyors, and recommend the ways in which the theory was to be adopted in practical uses. One of the earliest

English texts, by Benese and first published in 1537, recommends the use of a waxed cord five perches long:

Meters of Lande, for the mooste parte do vse to mete lande with a pole made of woode, conteynynge in it the length onely of one perche. The whiche is a very tru and a perfyte way of metyng. But it is moche laborious & not spedefull to mete ther with a great quantyte of Lande in shorte tyme. And also it is very tedyous, to marke truely a great nombre of perches in metynge of them one after another. Therefore some men do vse (and best) for the more expidicion and spede, to mete with a corde or a lyne, conteynynge in it .v. perches in length ... But bycause a corde or a lyne by drawynge it vpon the grounde wyll somtyme shrynke, and ware shorter, yf it take wete, and somtyme streche longer by longe dryeng therfore it shalbe necessary, to sere it in hote waxe and rosyn, that it may kepe at all tymes his true length. (1550, bi–ii)

Other texts, too, such as Leigh's of 1577, recommend a rod or waxed 'line', together with a 'diall' or compass (1577, Oiir). The rod remained in use until the end of the nineteenth century:

A friend of mine (Mr W. C. Little, Assistant Commissioner to the Royal Commission on Agriculture) thus speaks of it to me: 'We always used a staff called a "gad" of 9 feet. It was nearly round, and tapered from the middle to each end. The measurer took hold in the middle, laid it nearly on the ground, rested the point very lightly, and turned it over. In this way a good hand would measure nearly as quickly as an ordinary person would walk'. Mr Little speaks of the country bordering on Norfolk and the Isle of Ely. But it was in use all over the country. (Pell, 1888, 276)

By 1590, a variant on the rod or waxed cord was being offered: the 'wier line', or chain (Lucar, 1590, 43; see Plate 21). Rathborne, in 1616, recommended a 'Decimall Chaine', with each perch divided into 100 parts or 'seconds' (1616, 131–2). This instrument was quickly replaced by Gunter's chain, in which a chain of 100 links was made 66 feet long, so that an acre was ten square chains (Leybourn, 1653, 46–9). The method is described by John Reid in *The Scots Gard'ner* (1683):

You may make first a supposed figure on a Paper before you begin, that thereon you may write your measures as you go along ... then let the two men with the chain begin at any angle: the foremost may have 10 small sticks to thrust in at every length of the chain, & let the hindermost man gather them up as he comes along, and when all up, given them to his assistant to being again, as before, calling that, one change ... when you come at the other end, compt how many changes, chaines, and link ... (quoted in Webster, 1989, 81)

Surveying by the chain and compass alone was recommended by several authors until well into the nineteenth century, and some even avoided any angle measurement (Harvey, 1987, 495). In 1771, Burns said that 'the Chain alone, for Expedition and Correctness, claims the Preference to any thing else in Surveying' (1771, iii). Davis described how to survey with the chain, helped only by the cross and offset staffs (1798); and in 1827, Hornby stated that '"Gunter's Chain" is the chief instrument used in surveying, for by it all the distances are measured in the field, except the short offsets' (1827, 45).

This recommended practice was adopted in some cases. Christopher Keighley, Receiver-General to the Earl of Salisbury, measured land at Bermondsey, Surrey, with a chain in 1626 (Stone, 1965, 312), and in the mid-seventeenth-century work in draining the fens, there are references to the use of a hemp line and chain, with assistants (Willmoth, 1985, 27). Joel Gascoyne surveyed the manor of Great Haseley in Oxfordshire in 1701, and Ravenhill suggests that the boundaries of the estate were surveyed with a chain, and the angles were taken by a circumferentor or semi-circle, a surveyor's compass (1973, 109). Similarly, James and Edmond Costello drew a map of Robert Longfield's estate in County Sligo in 1768, and to plot the boundary they 'Whipt it aboute with chain and Instrument [circumferentor]' (Longfield, 1977, 61). Theophilus Brookes' school at Buckden advertised in 1789 that it taught 'Land Surveying and planning by the easiest method possible, and by the chain only'.[48] Use of the chain involved two 'chain bearers': a leader with ten arrows which he placed in the ground every ten links, and a follower at the end of the chain who picked them up again. Almost the only references in surveyors' bills to their methods of survey are the charges for chain leaders: John Davis was paid £75 in 1741 for mapping the Duke of Bedford's Dry Drayton estate (DRY74001), and this sum included a payment to 'chain carriers'.[49] In 1798, Thomas Smith surveyed Great and Little Melton in Norfolk for Emmanuel College, and he paid the chain leader 2 s 6 d.[50] Use of the chain could result in inaccuracies: on 19 December 1823, Alexander Watford wrote on his report on Trinity College's farm at Barrington that,

I have been prevented delivering my Opinion and Calculations, relative to the Cropping, seed, and Tillage done by Mr John Pearce in the Farm at Barrington, and the probable compensation due to Mr William Pearce under the Covenants of the Lease, owing to a difference that arose between my Admeasurement and that of Mr Thorpe, as awarded. I have proved most satisfactorily that Mr Thorpe is correct, and that the difference was occasioned by my having made use of a Chain that was longer than the real Standard Measure.[51]

Two other instruments, the plane table and the theodolite, were used by estate surveyors, though to varying extents. The plane table was first described by Lucar in 1590 (p.10):

To measure lengthes, bredthes, heights, and depthes, and to draw the plat of a field, fort, campe, towne, cittie, lordship, shiers, or countries by the art taught in this booke, you shall prepare a geometricall table with all such necessarie things as appertaine to it. That is to say, a staffe or foote to beare the said table, a frame to hold fast down the paper which shall couer the same table, a ruler, a compasse, a square, a fine pointed coled or keeler, and a wyer line of two, three or foure pearches in length ...

In steed of a geometricall table you may vse if you please for any mensuration or plat a drumme, stoole, or any other superficies.

Lucar illustrated these instruments (see Plate 21); his mention of a drum as a substitute for a plane table is a reminder of the stimulus to cartography from rapid military surveys in the sixteenth century (Taylor, 1929, 209). An early English description of triangulation was given by Jean Rotz in a manuscript treatise presented to Henry VIII (Mason, 1985, 28), and mathematicians stressed the value of this technique and geometry. They were, however, in conflict with many surveyors who knew little mathematics and were accustomed to measure angles by ratios (Bennett, 1990). Authors of text books had to come to some degree of compromise between these two schools of thought and so use of the plane table was described, albeit reluctantly in some cases, especially for mapping small inclosures (Folkingham, 1610; Rathborne, 1616; Leybourn, 1653; Holwell, 1678; Martindale, 1682; Laurence, 1716; Wyld, 1725; Wilson, 1725; Hutton, 1770; Emerson, 1770; Sleeman, 1806 and Ainslie, 1812). The main advantages of the plane table were that it was easily portable and that a plot could be made in the field directly from observations. Thomas Langdon probably used a plane table (Woolgar, 1985, 137), and William Typper, who was commissioned to survey 'drowned lands' of the Crown in Lincolnshire, paid four shillings each to two 'table carriers' and two 'chayne leaders' (Lawrence, 1985, 55). Further evidence for use of the table comes from a map which was drawn in association with the drainage of the fens in the 1650s (Willmoth, 1985, 28); this map shows that by sticking pieces of paper together, it was possible to use the plane table to survey relatively large areas (Willmoth, 1990, 130). The title cartouche to a Staffordshire estate map by William Fowler in the mid-seventeenth century shows an alidade and a tripod for plane-tabling, a cross-staff, a measuring rod and a rod for measuring angles (Phillips, 1979, 20).

The title-page to Rathborne's *The Svrveyor* of 1616 illustrates the use of the plane table below the title, but demonstrates his preference for the theodolite (Plate 22). A surveyor is depicted demonstrating the use of the plane table to his friends, together with a demeaning Latin note 'Inertia strenua'; one of the criticisms of this instrument was that just by watching a practitioner, a man could think he would be sufficiently skilled to survey himself. Above the title, however, is illustrated use of the altazimuth theodolite by Artifex, the expert, treading on two fake surveyors, shown as fools and knaves with such features as lambs' ears (Bennett, 1990). In addition, figures are shown representing arithmetic on the left and geometry (which comes from the Greek, 'measuring the land') on the right. In the text itself, however, Rathborne, forced by demand, explains how to use the plane table and refers the reader to Digges' *Pantometria* (1571) for discussion of the more complicated theodolite. Agas was quite sure of his preference (1596, 3–4):

You shal first haue a plain table, faire spread, with white couer: which may peraduenture, in seeming promise vnto you many dainties, although vpon triall, it will hardely performe sufficient necessaries ... Twentie and fiue yeares past or there abouts I vsed the said table ... I considered her defectes, neglected the same, and tooke mee wholy to thee Theodolite, whereupon, I haue euer since practised, to the daily increase of my liking ... The table through her lightnes, and shrinking to the wether, is tottering, and vnsure, and oftentimes dangerous: euen by the heauy and grosse handling thereof.

Wilson, too, recommended the theodolite in inclement weather, despite his earlier statement (p.102), that the plane table was 'the most universally useful, of all the Instruments of Surveying':

It is the best way when the Weather is precarious or inclined to Moisture to work by the Theodolite, because with the plain Table, by which you may survey and protract all at once, the Sheet is in danger of being wetted and spoiled; and the Method by the Theodolite being performed, and the Angles and Distances brought into a Field~book, as already taught, the Work may be protracted at home, or in any convenient Place where you may be secured from the Injuries of the weather. (1731, 150)

Measurements taken by the theodolite were recorded in a field book and plotted out later in the office, often by a surveyor's assistants: James Osborn, for example, implied the existence of these two stages in his advertisement in the *Norwich Mercury* on 17 January 1767 that he had 'for some time since finished his surveys for this season and mostly done the Plans belonging to the same' (D. Cubitt, personal communication).

The theodolite was used by surveyors, especially for mapping large areas or when it was wet: Matthew Nelson used it in his surveys for Corpus Christi College, Oxford, unlike his colleague Thomas Langdon (Woolgar, 1985, 137). A draft map of land at Soham in 1656

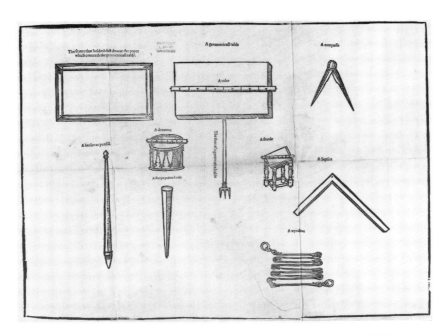

Plate 21. Surveying instruments in Lucar's *Lvcarsolace*, 1590, 10, including a 'geometricall', or plane, table at the top and a 'wyer line', or chain, at the bottom.

Plate 22. Title-page to Rathborne's *The Svrveyor*, 1616, showing a theodolite above the title and a plane table below the title.

(SOH65601) suggests that it has been plotted from readings recorded in a field book, taken with a theodolite. Other surveyors implied use of a theodolite, though perhaps for self-aggrandisement: the cartouche to John Robertson's map of Castle Camps in 1741 (CAS74101) shows a theodolite with a tripod to stand it on, a pair of dividers and an open field book (see Plate 10), and John Watte also drew a theodolite in the title cartouche of his map of Wisbech St Mary in 1769 (WSM76901). Theodolites were used in Ireland: on one of John Rocque's maps of the Irish estates of James, 20th Earl of Kildare, is a drawing of a surveyor entering into a notebook a reading which his assistants have measured with a chain, and the surveyor stands besides a theodolite (Horner, 1971, 62). However here and in the colonies, where relatively large areas were to be surveyed, circumferentors with magnetic compasses were often preferred to theodolites as there was then no need to rely on landmarks (Bennett, 1990). In England, though, the theodolite was often regarded as secondary to the plane table: it has been suggested that in the seventeenth-century fen drainage projects a theodolite was only used in tasks which had to be performed with some ceremony (Willmoth, 1990, 130). Even in the early nineteenth century the theodolite was not very common: John Brunton relied on a chain in his surveying for the London and Birmingham railway in about 1830 (Brunton, 1939, 35).

Despite Leonard Digges' description of an altazimuth theodolite in 1571 (1571, Iir; Johnston, Willmoth and Bennett, 1985, 6), and its appearance on the title-page to Rathborne's *The Svrveyor* of 1616, the theodolite in common use was a simple, azimuth, type for measuring in the horizontal plane (Bennett and Brown, 1982, 3–5). The more complex type developed slowly (Daumas, 1972, 21): in 1725, Hammond described the 'New Theodolite' and Ley recommended its use in 1786 (p.76). This new instrument was not quickly adopted: Hutton said in 1770 (p.484),

of all the absurd or false methods that by the use of what is called the new~improved theodolite is of the most dangerous consequence; for it is professedly adapted to the diminishing of all land by reducing it to an horizontal plain, even such as is wholly upon a regular declivity; by that means destroying sometimes a third or fourth of the true surface ... In short, let every gentleman, who would not have his real land reduced below its just quantity, beware of those surveyors who use this new~improved instrument.

Some sort of theodolite was in use in the early nineteenth century, however. In 1810, Mr De Bruyn of King's Lynn, Norfolk, wanted an assistant land surveyor who was 'competent to undertake extensive surveys during the absence of his principal. He must be well recommended for talent and industry, and understand the practical use of the theodolite, &c.'[52] Use of the theodolite was taught in schools: the Reverend J. Shillibeer, M.A., taught 'Landsurveying by the Theodolite, Mapping and Drawing' at his grammar school at Oundle in 1832.[53]

Other instruments were also used: cartouches to two maps by William Fowler in Shropshire and Derbyshire show surveyors at work using cross-staffs, back-staffs and quadrants (Phillips, 1980, 104), and the surveyor shown on the title-page of the atlas of Humphry Sturt's estates (which contains maps of Doddington and Wimblington, DOD77001–2 and WMB77001) is holding a cross-staff as well as a pair of dividers. A map of Boxworth, Cambridgeshire, in 1650, shows two geometrical squares which were also used to measure heights and distances (BOX65001 and Plate 23). Plate 24 shows an eighteenth-century way-wiser, which was used for measuring road distances. Many other instruments were described in surveying texts, but there is little evidence of their use. For example, George Atwell in 1658 described the Pandoron, and John Wing advocated the use of his Emperial Table in 1700. Some more sophisticated techniques, such as triangulation, were increasingly used. On a map by John Dougharty in 1731, for example, is an inset which illustrates the method of triangulation (Smith, 1967, 140).

Cost and availability of equipment affected the use of the various items. A chain was inexpensive; Thomas Badeslade was paid five shillings for one in 1719 by Robert Walpole for his survey of Houghton in Norfolk (Eden, 1973, 480), Humphry Repton bought one for 8 s 6 d in 1788 (Wallis, 1990, ix) and the London firm of W. and S. Jones sold them at prices ranging from 5 to 11 shillings, according to strength, in 1798 and for 10 s 6 d, 12 shillings and 16 s 6 d in 1850 (Catalogue, 1798, 5 and 1850, 7). A plane table and level could be bought for eight guineas in the 1740s (Wallis, 1990, ix); Messrs Jones were selling plane tables alone for between £3 13 s 6 d and five guineas in 1798 and from £5 15 s 6 d to eight guineas in 1850 (Catalogue, 1798, 5 and 1850, 7). The cost of theodolites was variable: Webster said that a good (probably altazimuth) instrument cost £50 in the eighteenth century, the equivalent of a surveyor's annual pay (1989, 87), and W. and S. Jones sold them at prices ranging from four to 30 guineas in 1798 (Catalogue, 1798, 4). Repton bought one and a level for £10 in 1788 (Wallis, 1990, ix), and in 1850 they could still be bought for as little as £5 15 s 6 d (Catalogue, 1850, 6). Messrs Jones also sold in 1798 circumferentors at a range of two to four guineas and perambulators for six to ten guineas; both of these instruments cost little more 50 years later (Catalogue, 1798, 5 and 1850, 6–7). For a surveyor to be fully equipped in 1800, he might have to pay £125 (Wallis, 1990, ix), and purchase of instruments could be a noteworthy event. James Utting, for example, announced in the *Norfolk Chronicle* on 24 March 1821 that he had bought a collection of instruments made purposely for him by the leading London firm of Troughton and Dolland (D. Cubitt, personal communication). Sometimes surveyors were helped by their employers, who either lent them or paid for their tools: Badeslade's chain was paid for by his employer. At a grander scale, the Admiralty lent Murdoch Mackenzie a theodolite, chain and plane table in 1751 (Webster, 1989, 87), and George Taylor, employed in Scotland by James Grant of Grant in 1770, was provided with a chain, theodolite, paper, lead pencils, chain bearers, a room for drawing in, coal, candles, bed, board and washing (P. G. Eden, personal communication).

Local knowledge remained very important. In 1740, John Davis surveyed Dry Drayton and asked two tenants to go over the fields with him and tell him every person's land.[54] Joseph Freeman was helped in his survey of land at Teversham belonging to Gonville and Caius College, Cambridge, by Mr Hancock who was paid £1 7 s 6 d for carrying the chain and showing the land at Lady Day 1773 (TEV77201–14).[55] Alexander Watford walked the bounds of Great and Little Eversden with a local inhabitant in his survey for Queens' College in 1801.[56] Sometimes locals played a more important role, as in Watford's survey of Over for Trinity College in 1823, when he wrote that,

Plate 23. Geometrical square on the estate map of Boxworth drawn by Matthew Hayward for Lady Ann Cutts, 1650 (shown rotated through 90°).

Plate 24. Eighteenth-century waywiser.

I clearly saw that this would take up considerable time, and \create/ unnecessary expense if I stopped at Over to ascertain all the quantities, piece by piece. I therefore gave my instructions to an intelligent Labourer, who attended me round the Lordship to collect the different kinds of land, and bring his statement to me at Cambridge. This being done I am enabled to make a Calculation of the Value of the entire tithes ... In order to get at the latter [the aggregate value from the stock, orchards and gardens] I have been compelled to estimate the quantity by the Eye of each separate Garden, and to put on them such value as I thought the nature of the produce and fruit trees would justify.[57]

Reliance on local knowledge had its disadvantages: the informant had to be trustworthy. It has been suggested, for example, that the County of Londonderry ended up much larger than had been intended when it was laid out in the early seventeenth century, because local opposition precluded the preparation of accurate plans. Indeed, on one occasion news of the murder of a surveyor in Donegal was suppressed in case a reconnaissance party from the City of London should take fright (P. C. D. Campbell, personal communication).

Surveying was partly a seasonal activity. In the summer months there was a potential damage to crops; Alexander Watford senior's survey of Shudy Camps for Trinity College was delayed from 21 May 1794 until after the harvest,[58] as was his son's survey of Hazelwood farm in Suffolk for Queens' College in 1801.[59] The weather was another hazard: after John Storer had completed the plan of Litlington in 1782 for Sir Thomas Spencer Wilson (LIT78207), he wrote to his employer: 'I have quite finished the Survey at Litlington, but not the Map and having an Opportunity to measure your other Farms at Canfield should therefore be glad of an Order to measure them, whilst the Weather is free from Snow, and then the whole mapping can be finished, if bad Weather should set in.'[60] Similarly, the elder Alexander Watford's survey of Eversden for Queens' College was difficult in February 1801 because the days were short and the weather was bad, but he persevered as it was essential to settle the fine for the renewal of the lease.[61] His son's survey of St Nicholas Court in Kent for Queens' in 1824 was also troublesome. It had been planned for the previous autumn, and Watford went early so as to be able to start as soon as the fields had been cleared of their crops, but then it was postponed until the following spring. Watford succeeded in April 1824, but he had to wait for the weather to improve before he could estimate how long it would take.[62] Sometimes the weather defeated a surveyor altogether: in 1795, Joseph Freeman reported that 'The Dam Heads and Cow Croft in Mr Sanxters Occupation [in Witcham], could not be Measured on Account of the Fens being covered with Water when the Survey was made. the Measurement is taken from a Field Book of the Fens' (WTC79501). Similarly, in December 1823 Alexander Watford junior had to delay his survey of Queens' Swaffham Prior estate 'because of the state of the fens'.[63]

Surveyors covered varying amounts of land in a day. In colonial Virginia, under what were probably the best possible conditions for contemporary land surveying, several hundreds of acres could be surveyed a day (Hughes, 1979, 68). Upper estimates for England are of 500 acres a day. Agas said that with a theodolite he could survey 400 to 500 acres daily, five times as much as he could with a plane table (1596, B3r), and in the early seventeenth-century surveys of Crown lands, 300 to 500 acres could be surveyed each day (Charlton, 1965, 292). Atwell suggested that 900 acres could be measured, plotted and cast up in three days, though 'Mr Wingate hath measured 1,000 on a day near Biggleswade in Bedfordshire' (1658, 7). Worsop was much more realistic (1582, 14r):

As I haue diuers times measured about CCCCC. acres in a day, so in some other dais, hauing had the like times, & help, and as faire weather, & taking as great or greater labour I could not ouercome xl. The formes & fashions of grounds are the chiefe causes why measures are either long or speedie in doing. Many grounds that lie long, & narrow, by an indenting, crooking, and winding brook side, cannot truly be measured, without great labour, & much expence of time.

This lower estimate seems much more probable: in Essex, surveyors probably measured about 20 acres in a day, and Thomas Archer's survey of 36 acres at Walthamstow was probably carried out in one day (Mason, 1990, 24 and 53). Eden suggests about 30 acres a day (1973, 479), and tithe surveyors managed about 50 acres daily (Thompson, 1968, 104). Figures for Cambridgeshire surveyors are also of this order: if Alexander Watford junior's charges of two shillings an acre for mapping are taken to be equivalent to two guineas a day for his general charges for surveying in Norfolk in 1820, then he surveyed about 20 acres a day.[64]

Despite, therefore, a proliferation of surveying texts which suggested a variety of methods, local land surveyors continued to use the simplest of instruments and techniques. The basic equipment of a surveyor was a chain and plane table, perhaps a circumferentor for measuring angles and possibly a simple theodolite. Surveying texts and instrument-makers sought to promote greater sophistication, but they only met with modest success (Bennett, 1987, 143). The estate surveyor of the early nineteenth century still relied on local knowledge, good weather and a number of assistants in the field and office to carry out his work.

CONCLUSION

As map-making became more widespread in early modern England, the characteristics of the map-producers changed. Surveyors who practised in Cambridgeshire illustrate the main trends. They increasingly became involved in producing other types of map, they became more mobile, less dependent on a single patron, formed surveying businesses and enjoyed a rising status. Surveying techniques improved, more through greater practice than through revolutionary developments, and apprenticeship remained an important means of education. Surveying texts became more common, and surveying was increasingly taught at school. At the same time, however, the spread of the ability to make maps led to increasing numbers of amateur surveyors who had a wide variety of alternative sources of income. These men produced a few maps of their own locality, for themselves or for a near neighbour.

These changes cannot be considered in isolation; they were part of wider social developments and were intimately connected with changes in the nature of the men who commissioned maps. The landowners and their influence on estate mapping are discussed in the next two chapters.

Chapter 6

LANDOWNERS AND THEIR INTERESTS

UPPER-CLASS CULTURE IN THE EARLY MODERN PERIOD

From the sixteenth century, the ruling classes in England increased in number and altered in character. As a system of military and physical control gave way to one of dominance through social and economic activities, a new kind of landlord emerged. His prestige depended on his wealth and the extent of his political influence: he bought a large estate and replaced his castle or fortified manor house with a 'country house' which was to be a visible centre of a new social order (Williams, 1973, 39; Williamson and Bellamy, 1987, 125). This increased importance of the land, both as a status symbol and as an economic unit, is reflected in the estate maps which were produced for both private and institutional owners and is central to the discussions in this and the following chapter.

Entrants to the land market in the sixteenth century included members of the expanding commercial and professional classes, such as London merchants, lawyers and financiers, who benefited from inflation at that time (Clemenson, 1982, 11). Sir William Courteen, for example, was a Fleming, an East India merchant of the City of London, a money-lender and bullion-smuggler; at one time he was a creditor to the Crown for nearly £40,000. He purchased an estate, reorganized his land in the Midlands and ended his life as a country squire (Wilson, 1965, 122). In 1635, he had his estate at Laxton in Nottinghamshire surveyed by Mark Pierce, and the resulting map is a typical example of a map which was used to show off land and status. It is ornamented with Sir William's coat of arms, drawings of contemporary agricultural activities, and a decorative title cartouche, scale bar and compass rose (see Plate 25).

Social changes continued in the seventeenth and eighteenth centuries. The abolition of the Court of Wards in 1660 led to the use of strict family settlement as a system of inheritance, and land was held in trust for future generations (Mingay, 1963, 32). Although the importance of strict settlement may have been exaggerated by some historians, there is little doubt that it encouraged a greater interest and respect for an estate (Beckett, 1984, 21; Habakkuk, 1940, 7 and 1979, 191). In the eighteenth century, new farming techniques were introduced (Beckett, 1986, 137), estates consolidated (Clay, 1985, 180), and leases and tenancies revised (Ashton, 1955, 37). As owners increasingly invested in business and finance, holdings in general became smaller and land became the conspicuous social investment of more varied forms of wealth (Anderson, 1969; Stone and Stone, 1984). Some of these changes were at

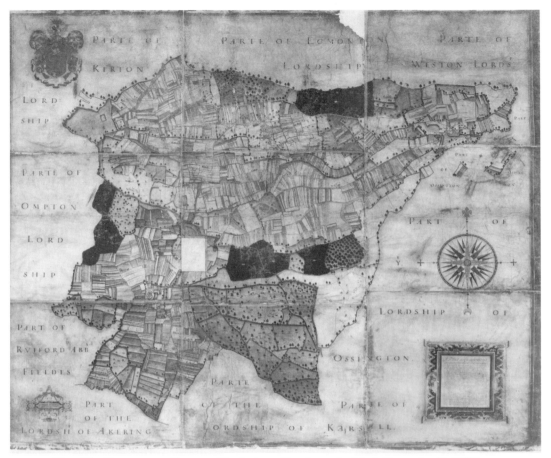

Plate 25. Estate map of Laxton, Nottinghamshire drawn by Mark Pierce for Sir William
Courteen, 1635.

the expense of lesser landowners, especially in the later eighteenth century (Beckett, 1984,
21), but it was still possible to buy an estate. For example, a tobacco merchant, James
Spedding, began trading in 1742 and by 1750 he had accumulated sufficient capital to buy
two small estates, one for £750 and the other for £1,600 (Beckett, 1978, 17). By the end of
the century, professional managers were employed, especially by absentee owners of large
estates (Scott, 1982, 41), and, as land values rose after about 1790, it was necessary to have
expensive surveys and to enter into negotiations with tenants in order to enable rents to keep
pace with inflation (Clay, 1968, 514).

Landownership, however, was not sufficient for entry into the aristocracy, who sought to
achieve dominance through a variety of political and cultural activities (Lears, 1985, 569).
Education, marriage and service in local and national government were important (Beckett,
1986, 92), and many country houses were built (Summerson, 1959). The emphasis in

chorographies on the pedigrees of county families (Simmons, 1978, 9), together with an interest in heraldry (Maclagan, 1956), show the significance of a family's history to members of the upper classes. Other antiquarian and historical interests were also increasingly popular (Hay, 1977; Mendyk, 1986; Piggott, 1956, 112). An interest in cartography was another acceptable pursuit.

To see how estate maps both affected and reflected these changes in seventeenth and eighteenth-century landownership, two main areas are now examined. First, the education of gentlemen in early modern England is discussed, together with their instruction and interest in science and surveying, and their awareness of maps. Then the men who commissioned maps of their Cambridgeshire estates are described, and the following chapter shows the part which estate maps played both in the management of their estates and in their standing within county society. The dissemination of the ideas and interests of landed society down the social scale and to other types of landowner will be seen throughout the discussion.

Gentlemen and their interest in mathematics

Ignorance was no longer regarded as gentlemanly by the early seventeenth century (Bennett, 1970, 230) and mathematics was one of the areas of knowledge in which the upper classes became interested. At the same time, universities increasingly began to cater for the needs of the ruling elite (Kearney, 1970, 23). The education which such men received, together with a growing fashion of book ownership (Girouard, 1980, 180) and virtuoso scientific interests (Houghton, 1942, 72), provides evidence for the landowning classes' awareness that there were, at the very least, recommended methods of estate surveying.

From the late sixteenth century, it was clear that if a gentleman were to maintain his position and engage in activities appropriate to his class, he needed some skill in practical mathematics (Turner, 1973, 51). For example, Henry Peacham, a notable contemporary who wrote educational works for gentlemen, stressed the importance of scientific instruction for estate management. In 1577, he recommended that geometry should be learned (p.77), for:

the use you shall have of Geometry will be in surveying your lands; affording your opinion in building anew or translation; working your mills as well for grinding corn as for throwing forth water from your lower grounds & bringing water far off for sundry uses; seeing the measure of timber, stones and the like (wherein gentlemen are many times egregiously abused and cheated by such as they trust); to contrive much with small charge and in less room!

Peacham and his son, also Henry, wrote other practical manuals on the necessary skills of a gentleman in mathematics, poetry, painting and heraldry. The younger Henry's *Compleat Gentleman* of 1622, for example, was originally written for the instruction of William Howard, the second son of Peacham's patron Thomas Howard, Earl of Arundel. The title-page of the book refers to noble and scientific pursuits: the figure of Nobility alludes to Peacham's patron and suggests the importance of heraldry to the upper classes, while the figure of Scientia and instruments of a gentleman's art show the importance of geometry in estate surveying, building and military activities, and a globe refers to a concern with cosmography (Corbett and Lightbown, 1979, 166–9).

Gresham College in London was founded in 1597 and became an important centre of scientific activity in the early seventeenth century (Smith, 1972, 41). Practical science was also taught at Oxford at that time: the Savilian chair of geometry was founded in 1619, and Henry Savile decreed that: 'It will, besides, be the business of the Geometry professor, at his own time, (as shall seem convenient to himself, with the consent of the University,) to teach and expound arithmetic of all kinds, both speculative and practical; land~surveying, or practical geometry; canonics or music, and mechanics' (Turner, 1986, 675). In early seventeenth-century Cambridge, however, mathematics had not yet become a fashionable subject: Thomas Hearne quoted John Wallis, a student at the time, as saying: 'For Mathematics, (at that time, with us) were scarce looked upon as Academical Studies, but rather Mechanical; as the business of Traders, Merchants, Seamen, Carpenters, Surveyors of Lands, or the like; and perhaps some Almanack~makers in London' (quoted in Costello, 1958, 103). The Royal Society was founded in 1662. It was independent of the government, so in order to survive, qualifications for Fellowship had to include wealth and influence as well as scientific merit (Hall, 1962, 195). The presence of the Society stimulated the formation of other similar bodies, such as the Dublin Philosophical Society, which was founded in 1683 (Andrews, 1980b, 231). Other informal societies which frequently met in coffee houses were formed after the Restoration (Armytage, 1960). By these and other means, interest in science continued to increase and was widespread among the educated classes by the end of the century (Smith, 1972, 173).

The popularity of science as a diversion continued to grow in the eighteenth century (Berman, 1975, 35). Most of the widely read periodicals regularly contained news of scientific discoveries, museums were established, lectures given and demonstrations held, and scientific instruments were designed specifically for teaching (Sambrook, 1986, 8). For example, the *Gentleman's Diary, or, The Mathematical Repository: ... Containing Many Useful and Entertaining Particulars Peculiarly Adapted to the Ingenious Gentleman Engaged in the Study and Practice of the Mathematics* was first published in 1740 as an annual calendar which contained much miscellaneous information, including calculations of future eclipses and mathematical questions and answers (Wallis, 1973, 301–2). Provincial scientific societies were started: the Spalding Gentlemen's Society was an early foundation, dating from 1710 (Evans, 1982, 162), and science could be linked with other gentlemanly interests such as antiquarianism (Mendyk, 1989, 238). It was possible to borrow scientific books from libraries: about 15% of the titles borrowed from the Bristol Library between 1773 and 1784 were scientific works, and 5% were mathematical (Kaufman, 1960). Eighteenth-century theorists about education listed suitable recreations for gentlemen, and these included gardening, botany, mathematical observations and surveying (Brauer, 1959, 93). Texts were published which were specifically aimed at landowners to help them manage their estates, for example Stone's *An Essay on Agriculture, With a View to Inform Gentlemen of Landed Property Whether their Estates are Managed to the Greatest Advantage* (1785). At both Oxford and Cambridge, mathematics remained largely outside the formal teaching and examination structure, though from 1760 readings of mathematical books at Christ Church,

Oxford, increased sharply (Quarrie, 1986, 505), and in the late eighteenth century university eminence was measured by the number of mathematical wranglers alone (Brooke, 1985, 157).

By the early nineteenth century, however, it was increasingly felt that there had been too much emphasis on aristocratic diversions and too little on serious studies and there was concern over the state of English science. The foundation of the Royal Institution in 1799 was in marked contrast to that of the Royal Society, where scientific research was part of the upper classes' cultural ideal. The Institution's aims were more entrepreneurial and professional, and it directed its early efforts primarily towards agricultural improvements. It relied on patronage in its first four decades, and it built the first lecture theatre in England specifically designed to hold scientific lectures (Berman, 1978, 2–28). The Cambridge Philosophical Society was founded in 1819 with similar practical and professional aims (Hall, 1969).

It can, therefore, be seen that there were increasing opportunities for gentlemen to develop scientific interests, and, in particular, land surveying could be learned. Further evidence for a knowledge of practical affairs of estate management comes from the contents of gentlemen's libraries.

Gentlemen's libraries

Gentlemen established libraries as printed books were produced in increasing numbers, sizes and formats in Renaissance England. The pattern of book ownership changed: institutional libraries which possessed relatively few expensive manuscripts declined in importance, especially after the Dissolution, while private collections started to be built up of the cheaper, printed, books. A result was that libraries came to be thought of as dynamic, ever-growing collections of a wide variety of works (Jayne, 1983, 29). Libraries in Cambridge also expanded in the sixteenth century (Oates, 1958, 215), though in the early Tudor period they contained few scientific works (Smith, 1974). In the seventeenth century, libraries continued to develop. In Oxford, first the colleges and then the Bodleian became interested in the systematic acquisition of books (Myers, 1958, 240). These libraries developed means of compact book storage as an alternative to the use of book chests, and their influence spread, via the elder sons of landowners who were attending the universities in increasing numbers, to country houses (Girouard, 1980, 166). Movable book presses of a good design did not appear until the Restoration, when scholarly books were collected and accommodated in elegant surroundings, and visiting scholars were frequently allowed access (Irwin, 1966, 208–11).

Many famous collections were compiled between 1660 and 1730 (Irwin, 1958, 12), and from the beginning of the eighteenth century, parochial libraries and literary and antiquarian societies gave the less fortunate members of the community a means for study (Douglas, 1951, 266). The lesser gentry became the principal patrons of circulating libraries which grew up (Mingay, 1976, 158). From 1732, country gentlemen and booksellers could obtain information about new books from monthly magazines such as the *Gentleman's Magazine* and book ownership continued to become more widespread (Pollard and Ehrman, 1965, 135). The earliest printed catalogue of a personal library was that of Evelyn Pierrepont, 1st Duke of Kingston, who died in 1726, and thereafter many more were published, especially in the late eighteenth and early nineteenth centuries (Taylor, 1986, 5). In Cambridge, books could be borrowed from the University Library. The Registrary in the early nineteenth century, Joseph Romilly, borrowed books for the Cotton family at Madingley Hall; Sir St Vincent Cotton (whose estates at Girton and Burwell were mapped in 1814 and 1821, GIR81403–4 and BUW82101) was an especially voracious reader (McKitterick, 1986, 22–3). The contents of these libraries varied, but many contained practical texts to assist in estate management: Lord Petre's did so in the early eighteenth century (Mason, 1990, 8), and those of the Glamorgan gentry at that time had works about law, estate management and farming as well as theology, classics, history and topography (Howell, 1986, 197).

A study of the contents of 35 libraries shows that surveying texts were owned; catalogues of these libraries were found from Holmes (1986), Jayne (1983), *List of Catalogues of English Book Sales 1676–1900 Now in the British Museum* (1915), Munby (1973) and Taylor (1986), and in the unpublished catalogue of the Founder's Library at the Fitzwilliam Museum in Cambridge, which contains the collection of Viscount Fitzwilliam.[1] The nature of the libraries varied widely. Some were the collection of an individual, such as that of Robert Devereux, 3rd Earl of Essex, who had 157 works at Essex House in London on his death in 1646. This was a comparatively large collection and, since Essex had been dispossessed of his inheritance when his father was executed in 1601, the books had been collected within a single generation. Most of the volumes listed in the inventory were religious and political writings; no surveying texts were mentioned, though they might have been in the libraries of his country estates, which were not included in the listing (Snow, 1966). Other collections were notable for their manuscripts. Sir Simonds D'Ewes, for example, High Sheriff of Suffolk and M.P. for Sudbury, had an 'outstanding' collection of manuscripts and charters. He was determined to establish himself as a gentleman: his father had bought an estate in Suffolk, and Simonds, who was born in 1602, went to Cambridge and then on to the Temple, and married the heiress of a wealthy Suffolk landowner. Typical of his time, he had an interest in the history of estates, family pedigrees and the law, but his library also contained practical works on horsemanship and husbandry, and *The Measuring of Land*, which is probably the work of either Benese or Digges (Watson, 1966). Other libraries were the collections of avid bibliophiles. Robert Harley, Earl of Oxford, built up a library, partly by buying the complete collections of other men, including D'Ewes. Edward Harley took over the management of the library when his father was confined to the Tower of London in 1715. By 1741, Edward had increased the size of the collection at least tenfold: the number of manuscripts and printed books had increased from 3,000 to 57,168 and there were now 350,000 pamphlets and 41,000 prints. He had bought books from two family libraries: Brampton Bryan in Herefordshire and Welbeck Abbey in Nottinghamshire, and he also collected antiquities, coins and medals (Wright, 1962). Thus, the presence of surveying texts in such a library was of little significance and they may or may not have been read and used.

Overall, at least 45% of the libraries contained surveying texts. This is a minimum figure as some of the collections were not completely catalogued and, notwithstanding the varied nature of the libraries, is evidence that the landowning classes were at least aware of the texts' existence. Likewise, 200 of the men who had their wills proved in the Vice-Chancellor's court of Cambridge University between 1535/6 and 1722 owned books (all but three had their wills proved before 1618), some had substantial libraries and others owned fewer than 20 volumes (Leedham-Green, 1986). Five owned surveying texts.

Only a small proportion of the texts which were discussed in Chapter 5 are found in these libraries, however. Digges' *Pantometria* was owned by at least five men: the Cambridge bookseller John Denys (Leedham-Green, 1, 1986, 333), Andrew Perne, Master of Peterhouse (Leedham-Green, 1, 1986, 463), Arthur, Earl of Anglesey (Bibliotheca Angleseiana, 1686, 34), Samuel Pepys (Latham, 1978, 52), and the Dukes of Devonshire (Catalogue, 1879), and possibly by Sir Simonds D'Ewes (Watson, 1966, 343). Pepys also owned Leybourn's *Compleat Surveyor* (Latham, 1978, 108), as did the Duke of Kingston (Catalogue, 1726, Ttiv) and Captain Samuel Sturmy (Kenney, 1947, 128). The most popular work among later owners was Wyld's *Practical Surveyor*. No fewer than six men possessed copies of this work. These included Robert Hoblyn, who was M.P. for Bristol from 1742 to 1754, elected F.R.S. in 1745, had an ancestral estate of Nanswhyden House, Cornwall and was a great book collector (Bibliotheca Hoblyniana, 1769, 169; *DNB*, 9, 944), Robert Child of Osterley Park, Middlesex (Catalogue, 1771, 100), the Suffolk antiquary Thomas Martin (Catalogue, 1772, 62; *DNB*, 12, 1,182), Charles Long of Hurt's Hall, Suffolk, whose estate at Castle Camps in Cambridgeshire was mapped in 1808 (CAS80801; Catalogue, 1813a, 31), Charles Townshend, 1st Lord Bayning (Catalogue, 1826, 10; *DNB*, 57, 120), and, finally, William Gooch, a student at Gonville and Caius College, who took Wyld's text with him on a voyage on the *Daedalus* in 1791 (Wordsworth, 1877, 328). Some men owned a single text, such as Sir William More of Loseley, Surrey, who owned 'Item a boke of land mesurying' in 1556 (Evans, 1855, 291), but it was more usual for a number of texts to be listed: Thomas Martin, for example, owned works by Fitzherbert, Benese, Leigh, two editions of Norden's *Svrveiors Dialogve*, Wyld and Laurence's *Young Surveyor's Guide*.

Science was, therefore, a common interest of a gentleman in early modern England. It was part of his education and there were opportunities for him to take part in scientific discussions with his peers. As it became fashionable to collect books and form libraries, scientific works, including surveying texts, were bought (though, of course, it is often not possible to say which books were actually read). These interests will be examined further when the interest of landowners in the management of their estates is discussed in the next chapter. To explain the commissioning of estate maps, however, it is also necessary to examine the extent to which landowners were aware of and possessed maps.

MAPS AND THE LANDOWNING CLASSES

England was no exception to the rest of Europe, where only a minute fraction of the population had seen a map by 1520 (Hale, 1971, 52). From then onwards, however, maps became increasingly common objects, as can be seen both from references to maps in literature and from map-ownership. Estate maps clearly form part of an increased cartographic awareness.

References to maps appear in English literature from the 1570s. Shakespeare mentions maps 11 times in his plays and four times in his poetry (Bartlett, 1894). He must have been aware of specific developments in map-making of the times; in *Twelfth Night* he refers to a map by Edward Wright which was printed in 1600 (Donno, 1985, 105): 'He does smile his face into more lines than are in the new map with the augmentation of the Indies' (III.ii.62–3). Similarly, John Donne refers to maps at least eight times in his poems (Combs and Sullens, 1940, 222).

The advantages of maps as decorative objects and status symbols were also stressed in the sixteenth century. For example, John Dee, wrote in 1570 (p.aiiij): 'Some, to beautify their Halls, Parlors, Chambers, Galeries, Studies, or Libraries with ... liketh, loveth, getteth, and useth, Maps, Charts, and Geographicall Globes.' Robert Burton, in his *Anatomy of Melancholy* of 1621, was more explicit about the pleasures and advantages of maps (pp.350–1):

But amongst all those Exercises, or recreations of the mind within doores, there is none so generall, so aptly to be applyed to all sorts of men, so fit and proper to expell Idlenesse and Melancholy, as that of studye. To read, walke and see Mappes, Pictures, Statues, old Coynes of severall sorts in a fayre Gallery ...

To some kind of men it is an extraordinary delight to study, to looke vpon a Geographicall mappe, and to behold, as it were, all the remote Provinces, Townes, Citties of the world, and never to goe forth of the limits of his study, to measure, by a Scale and Compasse, their extent, distance, examine their site, &c.

Estate maps were one type of map which could be hung in a study. In the early seventeenth century, Thomas Randolph, a steward's son (Hazlitt, 1, 1875, vii), was one of the first to say so in verse in his *Of that Inestimable Content He Enjoys in the Muses* (lines 123–5):

> Thou several artists dost employ to show
> The measure of thy lands, that thou mayest know
> How much of earth thou hast ...

Jonson's *Penshurst* has been likened to an estate map, with a few dryads and gods illuminated in to fill up blank patches, and described as a verbal equivalent of painted prospects of noblemen's seats (Hussey 1967, 21). Foster points out that landscape poetry developed as a genre from Sir John Denham's *Cooper's Hill* (1642) onwards. Denham was later Surveyor-General of the Works, and he stands on Cooper's Hill as a surveyor stands at his station. His 'wandring eye' moves as a surveyor swivels his eye and alidade on his theodolite or circumferentor, and as Denham's approach was adopted by others, the results have been likened to versified Ordnance Survey maps (Foster, 1974, 183, and 1975–6). Later, in the late eighteenth century, the picturesque movement encouraged other mentions of estate maps. Richard Payne Knight was more explicit in *The Landscape* (1795, lines 161–76):

'As you advance unto the palace gate,
'Each object should announce the owner's state;
'His vast possessions, and his wide domains;
'His waving woods, and rich unbounded plains.'
He, therefore, leads you many a tedious round,
To shew the extent of his employer's ground;
Climbs o'er the hills, and to the vales descends;
Then mounts again, through lawn that never ends.
But why not rather, at the porter's gate,
Hang up the map of all my lord's estate,
Than give his hungry visiters the pain
To wander o'er so many miles in vain?
For well we know this sacrifice is made,
Not to his taste, but to his vain parade;
And all it does, is but to shew combined
His wealth in land, and poverty in mind.

Thus, from literary evidence it seems that maps were known of by the late sixteenth century, and their advantages and uses as objects of decoration and display were soon realized. More tangibly, increasing ownership of maps shows an awareness of cartographic developments.

The library catalogues which were discussed in the previous section, together with other sources, show that maps were owned by landed society from the sixteenth century. Indeed, the catalogue of only one private library, that of Thomas Howard, Earl of Arundel in 1655, did not mention any maps. Similarly, over one-quarter of the book-lists in probate inventories of Tudor and Stuart Cambridge mentioned maps (Leedham-Green, 1986). Early map-owners did not necessarily possess books: Paulus Lauffenberger, a wealthy man of Strasbourg, died in 1542 and he owned no books but did have a map of the world (Chrisman, 1982, 70). English landowners of the mid-sixteenth century who owned maps included Sir William More, who in 1556 had maps of the world, France, England and Scotland on the walls of his closet, as well as a globe in the room (Evans, 1855, 285). Henry, Lord Stafford, a landed gentleman who had about 300 books by 1556, asked for maps of Venice, Antwerp, Milan and other cities from Mistress Burrell in St Paul's Churchyard in 1546 and 1547 (Anderson, 1966, 88). Maps were owned by university men: of the book-owners mentioned in Leedham-Green (1986), three owned either Ortelius' *Theatrum Orbis Terrarum* of 1570–90 or his *Epitome Theatri* of 1589–98, Andrew Perne owned 'Marcators mappe with a frame' and 'Mercatoris discriptio orbis', Perne also owned Saxton's *Atlas* of 1579–83, and John Nidd possessed Speed's octavo maps of England, Wales and Ireland (1620–46). In addition, two men owned globes, and four possessed surveying instruments. At St John's College there were probably two map-owners: in 'A note of the accomptes that remayne betwixt John Rawson [possibly of St John's College (Venn, I, 3, 426)] and John Jones [a bookbinder]', which were exhibited in the Vice-Chancellor's court of Cambridge University on 22 April 1597, Jones charged 'for colouringe Mr Shepphard [possibly Richard Shephard of St John's

College (Venn, I, 4, 60)] a map', and 'for colouringe 2 maps for Mr Crawshaw [probably either Thomas or William Crashawe, both of St John's College (Venn, I, 1, 413–14)]'.[2] In 1548, Queens' College, Cambridge made payments which were probably for maps, though a 'mappa' could possibly have been another wall-hanging: on 30 March they paid 'Will*ielm*o mone pro le pulley in quo mappa dependet in conclavi', and on 2 November they paid 'J skarlet bibliopole pro mappa [et] vna cu*m* Iunctura que pendet in conclavi'.[3]

Maps were bought and studied at universities in the seventeenth century. Many of the pupils of Samuel Blithe, Master of Clare College in Cambridge, bought books between 1658 and 1701. About 10% of the students, of all ranks, bought maps, atlases and globes. Mr Garneis, a Fellow Commoner, for example, bought between Lady Day and Midsummer 1672, 'Mercators mapps of the world large folio well coloured', 'Speeds epitome' and 'maps of England', and Mr Tob*ias* Harvey, another Fellow Commoner, bought 'Speeds mapps' and 'a mappe of England' in the quarter ending at Michaelmas 1679.[4] Poorer students also bought maps: Luke Bagwith, a pensioner, bought '6 mapps' on 19 August 1669, and frames for them on 24 August.[5] The atlases and maps were lent between students: in 1664, Samuel Blithe wrote: 'Atlas minor [Mercator-Hondius] with mapps in folio was lent to Bletsoe by Mingay, which booke Bletsoe carryed away with him into the countrey, soe I restored one of the same kinde new to Mingay, which must be allowed to me fro*m* Bletsoe. to be deducted out of his income.'[6] Students also owned globes: the bookseller Henry Dickinson supplied one man with a set of Moxon's globes between Michaelmas and Christmas 1673, and another set for Tallbut senior between Michaelmas and Christmas 1675.[7] Blithe himself owned a set; when he moved into a new room in 1663, he took with him 'A pare of Moxons Globes with leather covers' (Harrison, 1958, 13).[8] On 31 May 1681 Cambridge University Library, too, bought a globe from Moxon, together with an instruction book for it, and on 30 September they paid for a glass container for it (*'A Minority Interest'*, 1982, 11). Then, at the turn of the century, they paid J. Pindar 4 s 4 d for framing two maps.[9] Queens' College, Cambridge also owned maps in the late seventeenth century: in 1682 they paid for mending maps in the parlour, in 1687 and 1689 they bought maps for the parlour, and in 1690 they bought a map of Ireland.[10]

Among the private map-owners of the seventeenth century were Henry Percy, 9th Earl of Northumberland, who had a wainscot box with maps in his closet, a cupboard with mathematical instruments, one large and two small globes in his library, and two copies of Ortelius' *Theatre*, Saxton's *Atlas* and a book of maps of countries (Batho, 1960). Samuel Pepys was a discerning map collector and the present collection in Magdalene College, Cambridge contains 1,100 maps, charts and plans (Tyacke, 1984, 3). On 26 March 1664, for example, Pepys wrote in his diary: 'Dinner not being presently ready, I spent some time myself and showed them a map of Tanger, left this morning at my house by Creed, cut by our order, the Commissioners, new drawn by Jonas Moore – which is very pleasant and I purpose to have it finely set and hung up' (Latham and Matthews, 5, 1971, 98). Then, on 27 April 1666, he: 'bespoke some maps to hang in my new Roome (my boy's room), which will be very pretty. Home to dinner; and after dinner to the hanging up of maps and other things for the fitting of the room' (Latham and Matthews, 7, 1972, 111). Pepys' collection was meticulously indexed and stored, but his system was not infallible; on 19 September 1666 he was: 'mightily troubled, and even in my sleep, at my missing four or five of my biggest books – Speed's chronicle – and maps, and the two parts of Waggoner [Wagenaer's *Mariners Mirrour*], and a book of cards; which I suppose I have put up with too much care, that I have forgot where they are, for sure they are not stole' (Latham and Matthews, 7, 1972, 290). Among Cambridgeshire families, the probate inventory of Sir John Cutts of Childerley mentions in 1670: 'an old Mapp of the world' in the great parlour and 'six pictures one Mapp two Tables of the foundations of both Universities' at the 'staire head'; perhaps this second map was that of the family estate at Boxworth, mapped for Sir John's mother in 1650 (BOX65001; *VCH*, 9, 43).[11] Others owned surveying instruments; many of the splendid items found in museums today were never intended to be used but were bought by landowners to display as symbols of their status and interests (Bennett, 1990).

The study of the use of the globes was an occupation suitable for late seventeenth and early eighteenth-century gentlemen, and colouring maps was another pastime. Many of Blithe's pupils bought Blaeu's *Institutio Astronomica de Usu Globorum*, which was published in many editions in the seventeenth century and was a popular introduction to the use of the globes (Feingold, 1984, 193). This work was also owned by students at Christ Church, Oxford (Bill, 1988, 268). In his *Compleat Gentleman*, Henry Peacham said (1622, 65): 'I could wish you now and then, to exercise your Pen in Drawing, and imitating Cards and Mappes; as also your Pensill in washing and colouring small Tables of Countries and places, which at your leasure you may in one fortnight easily learne to doe', and he gave detailed instructions on drawing, limning (painting with watercolours) and making colours in his *Gentlemans Exercise* of 1612. It was necessary to be careful, however, and one author warned in 1666 that: 'For as much as Colouring Prints, and Maps, is of common use, and much Practised by the Gentry and Youths, who for want of knowledge therein, instead of making them better, quite spoyl them' (quoted in Clarke, 1981, 11). John Smith, too, described 'The whole Art and Mystery of Colouring Maps, and other Prints, in Water Colour' in the third edition of his *The Art of Painting in Oyl* which was published in 1702, and in subsequent editions:

Having, as yet, seen nothing published upon this Subject that is Authentick, I have thought fit for the sake of those that are inclined to Ingenuity, to set forth the way and manner of doing this Work, it being an excellent Recreation for those Gentry, and others, who delight in the Knowledge of Maps; who by being Coloured, and the several Divisions distinguished one from the other by Colours of different kinds, do give a better Idea of the Countries they describe, than they can possibly attain to uncoloured. (4th edition, 1705, 93)

Maps continued to be collected by the upper classes in the eighteenth century. Sir Robert Bernard had his estates in March, Cambridgeshire, mapped some time after he succeeded to them in 1766 (MAR76601–2), and a list of the maps which he owned at his death included atlases by Pitt, Janson, Sanson, d'Anville, Bowen and Kitchen, Speed, Collins, '3 large whole sheets of parchment Dutch Maps of Europe, the East, and the West Indies', 'Oliver's Map of the County of Essex, in 4 sheets' and 'A Roll of loose Maps, of British America, and a few County Maps of England'.[12] The nobility and gentry were the patrons of many eighteenth-century atlases. These volumes were dedicated to their patrons and reflect their interests (Harley, 1988c). The Duke of Bedford had a map-reading room in the ante-room to his library at Woburn in the early nineteenth century (*Woburn Abbey*, 1987, [26]). Map-ownership continued to grow within the universities. John Symonds, for example, proposed a set of rules which were accepted by Cambridge University in 1772 that the fees of noble-men, Fellow Commoners and their attendant private tutors should be devoted to remunerating the language masters and buying books and maps (Wordsworth, 1877, 150). Emmanuel, Jesus and Queens' colleges bought maps for their parlours,[13] and in 1762 Emmanuel College paid for the carriage of a set of globes and for covers for them.[14] The University Library's formal collection of maps was started in 1794 and cases were built for them; hitherto, maps had been placed on walls, and sometimes mounted on canvas and rollers (McKitterick, 1986, 309).

The ideas and interests of the ruling classes permeated society (Rosenthal, 1982, 42) and smaller landowners came to own maps. Jacobean household inventories of Bedfordshire do not mention any maps (Emmison, 1938), but by the early eighteenth century an awareness of cartography was developing. The Reverend John Crakanthorp, Rector of Fowlmere, Cambridgeshire, paid three shillings for two maps of Europe and Flanders in October 1709, for example (Brassley, Lambert and Saunders, 1988, 269). Similarly, Theophilus Lingard in 1744 had two pictures in the best parlour of his house in central Essex, 20 prints in frames on the staircase and two maps in the hall (Steer, 1969, 20). The *Gentleman's Magazine*, which was founded in 1731, advertised a wide array of maps at a price which most literate people could afford (Reitan, 1985, 54). So, too, did George Willdey: 'CHEAP useful instructive and diverting Ornaments for Halls, Rooms, Passages, &c. being 24 large Two~Sheet Maps for 8 d. each; 76 of one Sheet, at 4 d. each and a Three~Sheet Map of London at 1 s. each'.[15] By the end of the eighteenth century, even a worker in a cotton mill could own a map: William Chadwick, an employee at the mill at Quarry Bank, Styal, Cheshire, mortgaged his posses-sions on 28 October 1794, and besides the essential paraphernalia of pots, pans, cooking utensils, blankets and the like were three glass pictures and two maps.[16]

By the early nineteenth century, therefore, an awareness of maps had spread to all classes of society. In conjunction with an increased familiarity with mathematical skills, this led to improved methods of estate management and to greater uses for maps, as the detailed study of the landowners of Cambridgeshire shows.

THE LANDOWNERS WHO COMMISSIONED ESTATE MAPS OF CAMBRIDGESHIRE

Landownership in Cambridgeshire was distinctive; it has already been shown in Chapter 3 how, compared with other counties, there were relatively few large private owners and insti-tutional owners were unusually important. This section examines the men and institutions who commissioned maps of their Cambridgeshire estates, and shows who they were, where they lived and how many maps they had drawn.

The discussion in this survey is limited to the landowners who commissioned maps, and an increasing proportion of them did so. Of the 64 nobility and gentry families in 1673 (listed in

Carter, 1819), only three commissioned estate maps themselves and another three had estate maps which had been drawn for a previous generation. About 90% of the families, therefore, had no maps of their Cambridgeshire estates. By the time of the Lysons' *Britannia* (1808), the proportion had risen to 35% of 34 families (11 of these families commissioned estate maps during their ownership), and by 1860, 42% of the 36 families listed by Walford in that year had paid for estate maps at some time. The representativeness of the sample examined here therefore increases, and this partly reflects a wider knowledge and appreciation of maps.

The examination of landowners is based on evidence from the maps in Appendix 2 and from a number of other sources. Printed sources which were used include published catalogues of estate maps in county record offices, Venn (1922–54), Foster (1888–92), the *Dictionary of National Biography*, Burke's *Landed Gentry, Peerage and Baronetage, Dormant and Extinct Peerages* and *Extinct and Dormant Baronetcies*, the Cambridgeshire volumes of the *Victoria History of the Counties of England*, and published works on individual owners. The same unpublished catalogues were consulted as for the study of surveyors described in the previous chapters. The discussion and conclusions drawn in this and the following chapter reflect these sources, the estate papers of one private owner, the Dukes of Bedford, and of several collegiate owners (Clare, Emmanuel, Jesus, Queens' and St John's colleges). It is, however, likely that similar findings would be made in the study of other landowners.

Overall, there were 163 private and 38 institutional owners who commissioned maps of their Cambridgeshire estates. The graph in Fig. 6.1 shows that private owners accounted for an increasing proportion of the total number of owners, while it can be seen from the semi-logarithmic plot in Fig. 6.2 that the size of both groups of owners increased at more-or-less exponential, though different, rates. Six periods when the rate was fairly constant can be identified: to 1639, 1640–99, 1700–69, 1770–99, 1800–19 and 1820–36. These periods will be used in subsequent discussions.

Private landowners

The nature of private map-commissioning landowners changed between 1600 and 1836. Decreasing numbers were members of the peerage and baronetage: in the period to 1639, 45% of the private owners were listed in Burke's *Peerage and Baronetage*, and the proportion increased in the early eighteenth century to over half. By 1800, however, only 14% of owners were peers, and the figure further decreased to 7% in the period from 1820 to 1836. Likewise, the proportion of men who achieved national importance and were therefore included in the *Dictionary of National Biography* decreased, from 45% until 1639, to about one-third from 1640 to 1769, to 17% until the end of the eighteenth century, and then to only 11% and 2% in the periods between 1800 and 1819, and 1820 and 1836 respectively. Examples of members of the uppermost classes in English society who had their Cambridgeshire estates mapped include the Earls and Dukes of Bedford, who had their land at

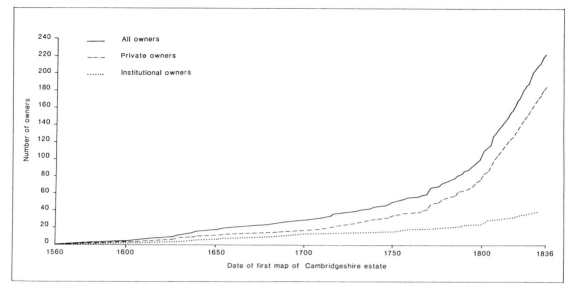

Fig. 6.1. Number of landowners who commissioned maps of their Cambridgeshire estates.

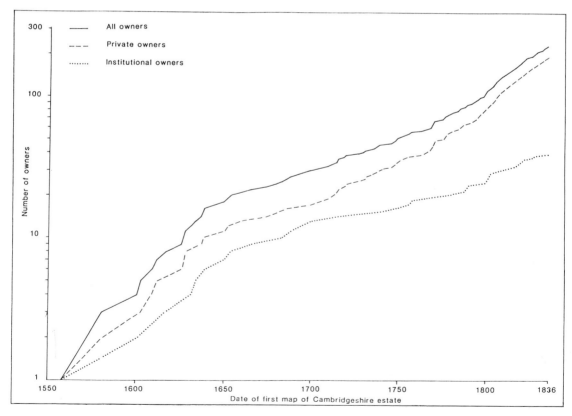

Fig. 6.2. Semi-logarithmic plot of the number of landowners who commissioned maps of their Cambridgeshire estates.

Thorney mapped several times between 1609 and 1822, and also had maps drawn of their estates at Dry Drayton, West Wratting and Whittlesey, Arthur Herbert, Earl of Torrington, whose land at Whittlesey was mapped in 1706 and 1710, Edward Harley, Earl of Oxford, who had his estates at Kingston and Wimpole mapped in 1720 and 1721 respectively, and William Ponsonby, 2nd Earl of Bessborough, lord of the manor of Wicken from 1764.

An increasing proportion of landowners was included in the *Landed Gentry*, however, though the maximum percentage reached was only 16% (from 1800 to 1819). James Martin, for example, was a banker in Lombard Street in London and came from a Worcestershire family. In 1725, he bought an estate at Stow cum Quy; he had it mapped in 1737 (STO73701), and he was M.P. for Cambridgeshire between 1741 and 1744 (*LG*, 1,717; Gerrit, 1955, 272). Other merchants and members of the professional classes also bought estates and entered landed society. Sir John Spencer was a London merchant who traded with Spain, Turkey and Venice and earned a large fortune (estimated at between £500,000 and £800,000 at his death in 1609/10). He was Lord Mayor of London in 1594–5, bought the Cambridgeshire manors of Great and Little Abington in 1599 and the manor of Fen Stanton in Huntingdonshire in 1600 (*VCH*, 9, 293). Despite his notorious parsimony, he had his Abington estates mapped in 1603 by John Norden, one of the foremost surveyors of the day, who also mapped his Sussex estates in 1606 (*DNB*, 53, 357; *VCH*, 6, 5; Steer, 1962, 1–2). Maximilian Western was the son of a wealthy London ironmonger to whom an estate in Great Abington was mortgaged in 1690. Maximilian then bought out the rights of the heirs of the former owner and developed the estate (*VCH*, 6, 5–6). Henry Slingsby, whose estate at Burrough Green was mapped in 1674 by William Palmer, later came under suspicion for his conduct as Master of the Mint and was heavily in debt when he died (*VCH*, 6, 142). A final example is Robert Jones, a director of the East India Company, who bought an estate at Babraham in 1770 and built a new hall there (*VCH*, 6, 22).

The clergy was a profession which was relatively well represented among Cambridgeshire's landowners: clerics accounted for on average over 6% of owners from 1700. The Reverend Samuel Knight bought an estate at Milton near Cambridge and also owned land at Willingham and Carlton cum Willingham. A former Fellow of Trinity College, Cambridge, he was Rector and Vicar of Fulham in Middlesex from 1751 to 1790 and Rector of Stanwick, Northamptonshire from 1757 to 1790 (Venn, I, 3, 29; *VCH*, 6, 146). The Reverend George Leonard Jenyns was Vicar of Swaffham Prior from 1787 to 1848 and owned an estate at Fen Ditton nearby (*LG*, 1,382; Venn, II, 3, 567). The Reverend Samuel Smith, Rector of Dry Drayton from 1808 to 1829 and again in 1831, was one of the two largest landowners there, and also inherited land in Toft from his father (Foster, II, 4, 1,319; *VCH*, 5, 129).

Some of the landowners held county offices: between 15% and 20% held offices in Cambridgeshire between 1640 and 1819, and from 8% to 16% held offices in other counties between 1700 and 1836. John Waddington, for example, had maps drawn between 1732 and 1775 of his estates in Benwick, March, Thorney, Wimblington and Wisbech St Mary, and was a J.P. and High Sheriff for Cambridgeshire in 1772 (Venn, I, 4, 307; Waddington, 1934, 119). Three years later, Daniel Swaine, a merchant of King's Lynn in Norfolk and owner of Leverington Hall, was High Sheriff, and he was also a J.P. (*VCH*, 4, 191).[17]

Charles Manners, 4th Duke of Rutland, owned and leased land in Cheveley, Newmarket and Swaffham Bulbeck. He was M.P. for Cambridge University between 1774 and 1779, Lord Lieutenant of Leicestershire from 1779 to 1787, and held various high offices including those of Privy Councillor, Lord Steward of the Household, Lord Privy Seal and Lord Lieutenant of Ireland (*PB*, 2,328; Venn, II, 3, 112; *DNB*, 36, 46). He was known as an 'amiable and extravagant peer, without any particular talent, except for conviviality' (Hore, 1899, 82). Later, in the nineteenth century, John Peter Allix of Swaffham Prior was High Sheriff in 1828, Deputy Lieutenant, J.P. and M.P. for Cambridgeshire between 1841 and 1847 (*LG*, 31; Venn, II, 1, 43). One of those who had a county office outside Cambridgeshire was Nicolson Calvert of Furneux Pelham and Hunsdon, Hertfordshire. He inherited his estate at Childerley in Cambridgeshire in 1802, was M.P. for Hertford from that year until 1826 and then represented the county in Parliament until 1834 (Warrand, 1907, 60).

Some landowners showed their influence and concern in the area where their lands lay by making charitable donations or by becoming trustees to charities. Benjamin Keene, for example, endowed a school at Castle Camps, as did the Honourable Thomas Windsor at Wendy in 1832 and Sir George William Leeds at Croxton in 1826 (County of Cambridge Local Education Committee, 1908, 40, 114, 126 and 127).

Many of these men had the typical gentlemanly interests of their times which were discussed at the beginning of this chapter. A fairly constant proportion, about one-third, received an education at either Oxford or Cambridge, and some owners were Fellows of either the Royal Society or the Society of Antiquaries. James Reynolds, the owner of an estate at Shudy Camps, for example, was admitted to Queens' College, Cambridge in 1702, and he held various legal offices, culminating in Lord Chief Baron of the Exchequer from 1730 to 1738 (*DNB*, 48, 45; Venn, I, 3, 444). Sir Robert Bernard matriculated at Oxford in 1758, and inherited the family estates at March in 1766 (*EDB*, 59; Foster, II, 1, 101). John Tharp was admitted as a Fellow Commoner to Trinity College, Cambridge in 1761, and became an entrepreneur in Jamaican estate management before buying Chippenham Park in 1791 and Badlingham Hall in the same parish in 1797 (*LG*, 2,487; Venn, II, 6, 146).[18] Among those with antiquarian interests was Philip Yorke, 2nd Earl of Hardwicke, whose Wimpole estate was mapped in 1790 (WMP79001). He matriculated at Corpus Christi College, Cambridge in 1747 and was awarded the degree of LL.D. in 1749. He became a Fellow of both the Royal Society in 1741, and the Society of Antiquaries in 1745, and he was a good classical scholar and trustee of the British Museum (*PB*, 1,246; Venn, I, 4, 491; *DNB*, 63, 351). Charles Long, too, was a Fellow of both societies and a trustee of the British Museum, a friend of George III and George IV, and he formed a gallery of paintings and sculptures; his estate at Castle Camps was mapped by John Bransby in 1808 (CAS80801; *DEP*, 331; *DNB*, 34, 99; *VCH*, 6, 40). The Reverend Edward Serocold Pearce was likewise a Fellow of the Society of Antiquaries; he drew a map of his own land in Hardwick in 1834 (HAP83401; *LG*, 2,287; Venn, II, 5, 60).

Besides an interest in science and agriculture, which will be discussed in the following chapter, other gentlemanly pursuits were sports, the countryside and gambling. Newmarket was a national centre for horse-racing, and a number of owners played a full part in its activities. The Master of the Horse in 1702 was the 6th Duke of Somerset; after the accession of

George I in 1703, Somerset devoted himself to the turf and built private studs at Newmarket and, later, at Petworth, Sussex. He bought his Cheveley estate in 1732, the seat and its grounds were mapped soon after (CHG73501) and over the next 13 years he became one of the major landowners in the county (Hore, 1899, 60–7). Jenison Shaftoe, similarly, built a house and stables at his estate at West Wratting for training racehorses. He committed suicide in 1771, and his brother, Robert, inherited the estate and had it mapped in the same year (WEW77101; *VCH*, 6, 192). Another racehorse owner was Thomas Panton, lord of the manor of Fen Ditton.[19] He inherited his interest in horses from his father, who had been Master of the Horse at Newmarket. Thomas also kept fox hounds (Venn, I, 3, 303; *DNB*, 43, 185). Sir St Vincent Cotton of Madingley Hall was a colourful character too. After his retirement from the Army in 1830, he enjoyed gambling, hunting, shooting, racing, cricketing and the world of pugilism. He dissipated his property at Madingley; he drove the London to Brighton coach until the railway became too competitive (Hore, 1899, 22; *PB*, 253; *DNB*, 12, 316). The 3rd Duke of Bedford was also a great gambler (Haas, 1960, 7).

As the idea of map-making spread, the number of lesser landowners who commissioned estate maps started to increase. William Finch, a Cambridge ironmonger who bought land at Little Shelford in 1745 and had it mapped in 1748, is an early example (*VCH*, 8, 222). By the end of the eighteenth century, a carpenter (James Doo of Linton)[20] and a speculative builder (Joseph Medworth of Wisbech) (*VCH*, 4, 246 and 262) were among those who commissioned estate maps. In the early nineteenth century, the range of occupations of smaller landowners broadened. There were seven farmers, such as Thomas Page of Grantchester,[21] Joseph Richardson of Warboys (Huntingdonshire) and then Chatteris, who owned land in Doddington,[22] and Henry Layton Blunt, farmer and grazier in Whittlesey.[23] The Beldam family of Royston were brewers and owned land in Bassingbourn (*VCH*, 8, 18), and William Frost of Brinkley was a schoolmaster at the charity school in March (*Gentleman's Magazine*, February 1819, 186; Charity Commission, 1837, 133). Besides the Mortlock family, who were substantial bankers (Clark-Kennedy, 1983), there were lesser tradesmen such as a carpenter (William Collin),[24] a lime merchant (Thomas Sumpter Headly),[25] a grocer (Robert Searle),[26] and a dairyman and wheelwright (James Carter).[27]

Length of ownership of the mapped estates

As time passed, growing numbers of estates were bought either by the owners who had them mapped or by their immediate ancestors. Thus until 1700, 16% of owners bought their estates themselves, and 72% of families had possessed their estates for many generations. The Parys family, for example, had owned land in Linton from the fourteenth century; Ferdinand Parys had the estate mapped in 1600 (LIN60007; *VCH*, 6, 85). Similarly, the Cutts family bought land at Childerley, Boxworth, Lolworth, Dry Drayton, Long Stanton and Swavesey in 1507; Sir John Cutts' widow, Ann, commissioned a map of Boxworth in 1650 (BOX65001; Parish, 1983, 24 and 28). Robert Peyton's estate at Wimblington, on the other hand, is an example of a relatively recent acquisition. His father, Sir John, had leased the manorial rights of the estate, and they were then granted to him outright in 1602. Robert inherited the estate in 1635 and sold it to the drainage adventurers in 1637, when an estate map was drawn (WMB63701; *EDB*, 412; Venn, I, 3, 354; *VCH*, 4, 112).

The pattern of estate acquisition changed, however, so that by the early nineteenth century 35% of owners had bought their estates, and only 46% of estates had been in the family's possession for a long time. Edward Harley, Earl of Oxford, for example, owned the Wimpole estate for only a few decades: the estate was bought by John Holles, Duke of Newcastle after 1707 and passed to Harley through Henrietta Cavendish Holles, whom he married in 1713. By 1739, however, he had to sell his estates to pay debts of £100,000 (*VCH*, 5, 265; *DNB*, 24, 394–5). Thomas Bromley, Lord Montfort of Horseheath, had similar difficulties. His grandfather, John Bromley, a Barbados sugar planter, bought the Horseheath estate between 1700 and 1705. Thomas inherited the estate in 1755 when his father Henry committed suicide. Both Henry and Thomas were extravagant; Henry employed William Kent to redesign the hall and gardens, and Thomas added an orangery. Financial difficulties ensued, which resulted in the furniture and paintings being sold in 1775 and the rest of the estate in 1777 (*DEP*, 76; *VCH*, 6, 71; Venn, II, 4, 445). The Reverend William Wilkieson bought his estate at Gamlingay in 1803, and had it mapped after 1806 (Venn, II, 6, 469; *VCH*, 5, 73). There were still some estates which had been in a family for a long time. Sarah Lonsdale bought Barham Manor at Linton in 1748 from the estate of her late husband, Robert Millicent, to pay his debts; his family had owned the land since the sixteenth century. She owned the estate until her death in 1807 (*VCH*, 6, 87). Similarly, the Reverend Dr William Foster's estate at Abington Pigotts had been in his wife's family since before 1430 (*VCH*, 8, 5). Sir John Maryon Wilson's estate at Litlington had also been in the family for generations: it was bought in 1666 by John Maryon, a clothier of Braintree; Sir John sold 464 acres in 1832 (*VCH*, 8, 58).

Where the landowners lived

The places of residence of the landowners provides further evidence for the patterns described above: an increasing proportion lived in Cambridgeshire, and similarly an increasing proportion did not own land outside the county. Thus smaller, local owners who commissioned maps of their estates grew in importance.

Apart from the early eighteenth century, landowners who were resident in Cambridgeshire were more numerous than those who had their principal seats elsewhere: until 1639, the proportion was 55%, it declined to 40% between 1700 and 1769, and rose thereafter to a maximum of 78% from 1820 to 1836. Thus, the Parys family was based in Cheshire in the fourteenth century; from the 1560s they usually lived at Pudding Norton in Norfolk, but by 1600 they lived at Linton (*VCH*, 6, 85). Roger Thornton, whose land at Soham was mapped in 1628–30, was the son and heir of John Thornton of Soham, and lived in Cambridge in

1588 and at Snailwell in 1625 (Venn, I, 4, 233). Sir Jacob Garrard Downing lived at Gamlingay Park in the mid-eighteenth century (French, 1978, 45). At the end of the century, Thomas Rumbold Hall lived at Hildersham (Venn, I, 2, 289),[28] and there are numerous examples of local residents by the early nineteenth century. For example, the Pembertons lived at Trumpington Hall (Venn, II, 5, 83; *LG*, 2,003; *VCH*, 8, 252), John Chester Pern lived at Little Abington (*VCH*, 8, 194),[29] and John Hemington lived at Denny Abbey (*VCH*, 8, 255). Some, however, did live elsewhere: Sir John Spencer lived at Crosby Place, Bishopsgate, in the early seventeenth century; he bought it in a dilapidated state and restored it to a sumptuous mansion (*DNB*, 53, 358), Arthur Herbert, Earl of Torrington, lived at Weybridge, Surrey, in the early eighteenth century (*DNB*, 26, 169–72), Thomas Brand lived at The Hoo, Kempston, Hertfordshire, in the mid-eighteenth century (*VCH*, 6, 150), Sir Thomas Spencer Wilson lived at Charlton House near Greenwich in the late eighteenth century (Venn, II, 6, 529) and at a similar time Wright Squire lived in Peterborough (*VCH*, 9, 333), Samuel Peach, a retired China merchant, lived at Idlicote, Warwickshire, in 1818 (*VCH*, 9, 246), and Christopher Anstey, who was a Fellow of King's College and a poet and who owned a substantial estate in Trumpington in the early nineteenth century, lived in Bath from 1770 (Venn, I, 1, 34; *DNB*, 2, 39).

Mapping activity

In general, the proportion of landowners who are known to have had only one estate mapped increased over time, which again reflects the growing number of smaller landowners who required estate maps to be drawn. Thus, until 1639, 36% of landowners had one estate mapped and the proportion increased to 48% in the early eighteenth century. From the 1770s, however, at least three-quarters of landowners probably commissioned only one map. John Robson, for example, had his land at Waterbeach mapped when he inherited it in 1680/1 (WAT68101; *VCH*, 9, 245), Mrs Bridget Southcoat's estate at Hildersham was mapped in 1770 (the estate passed to her when she married, in preference to her brother, who was insane) (HIL77001; *VCH*, 6, 62), and, in the early nineteenth century, Stokely Hutchinson, a farmer,[30] had a map drawn of his land in March (MAR83201). Some landowners, however, especially members of the aristocracy, had many maps drawn. The 4th Duke of Bedford, for example, had at least 43 maps drawn of his land in Cambridgeshire, Bedfordshire, Huntingdonshire, Middlesex, Devon and Cornwall between his inheritance of the estate in 1732 and his death in 1771, and his successor, the 5th Duke, had at least 36 maps drawn between 1771 and 1802 (*PB*, 226).[31]

Some estate maps were commissioned by more than one owner. These maps were almost always drawn for particular reasons, often to illustrate a boundary dispute, to show land to be exchanged or divided, or to show a joint inheritance. This type of map is discussed in more detail when reasons for commissioning estate maps are examined in the next chapter.

Institutional owners

Institutional owners were always less numerous than their private counterparts, but again a similar trend can be seen, with increasing numbers of local institutions. Most, however, also owned land elsewhere. In many ways, institutional owners were a more homogeneous group and detailed discussion of their characteristics belongs more appropriately to the next chapter, but a few general features are pointed out in this section.

The most notable institutional owners were the Cambridge colleges and Cambridge University, which together accounted for over 40% of the institutional owners; they all owned land outside the county. Other local institutions were the Bishopric and Dean and Chapter of Ely, the Bedford Level Corporation, and charities such as Hobson's Charity and Storey's Charity in Cambridge, Knight's and Watson's Charity in Burrough Green, and Whittlesey Charity. These bodies all started having maps drawn at the very end of the eighteenth or in the nineteenth century. The main institutions which were based outside the county were from London: the Charterhouse, Christ's Hospital, the Corporation of the Sons of the Clergy, the Crown, the Duchy of Lancaster, and St Bartholomew's and St Thomas' hospitals. Together with Merton College and Christ Church, Oxford, these were the institutions which had their estates mapped earliest: the Duchy of Lancaster in the sixteenth century, Merton College and the Charterhouse in the early seventeenth century, Christ's Hospital in the later seventeenth century, and the Corporation of the Sons of the Clergy and St Thomas' Hospital in the early eighteenth century.

Landownership in Cambridgeshire was therefore distinctive: there were relatively few large landed estates and many institutional owners. The characteristics of private landowners altered in a similar way to national developments: there were new entrants to the upper classes, the members of these classes pursued interests and occupations appropriate to their positions, and increasing numbers of smaller, local, landowners had their estates mapped as the idea of map-making spread. There were two main groups of institutional owners: those connected with the University, and large London-based organizations. The latter category tended to have its estates mapped earlier than the Cambridge colleges. The pattern of commissioning of estate maps reflects the interests and requirements of these two groups of owners. The next chapter, which examines first the practical and then the more ostentatious reasons for having maps drawn, shows this in detail.

Chapter 7

LANDOWNERS, THEIR ESTATES AND USES OF MAPS

PRACTICAL REASONS FOR COMMISSIONING ESTATE MAPS

In 1929, Marc Bloch warned that estate maps must be interpreted carefully, to discover why they were drawn and how this affects what they show (1929, 66); it is very rare to find explicit statements about why a map was commissioned and it has already been demonstrated in Chapter 3 that different types of map tend to have distinctive characteristics. Many estate maps were drawn for practical purposes, and they tend to be fairly plain; some are unsigned and some, with no scale statement or north point, are little more than sketch maps. To discover why the maps were drawn, it is first necessary to look at the increased interest by both private and institutional owners in the management of their estates in the seventeenth and eighteenth centuries.

Interest of private owners in their estates

Private owners' interest in their estates developed from the sixteenth century. At that time, many texts frowned upon gentlemen taking any day-to-day interest in farming (Charlton, 1965, 288). Soon, however, it came to be realized that it was advantageous for landowners to know something of the legal and agricultural aspects of estate management. In the early seventeenth century, Norden's *Svrveiors Dialogve* was 'very profitable for all men to peruse, but especially for all Gentlemen, or any other Farmar ...' (Norden, 1610, title-page). In 1609, Henry Percy, 9th Earl of Northumberland, imprisoned in the Tower of London for alleged involvement in the Gunpowder Plot, sold his land at Dullingham in Cambridgeshire. At the same time, he advised his son that he should be a diligent student of management and improvement of estates, that the first principle in estate management was: 'to understand your estate generally better than any of your officers', and,

I have so explained and laboured by books of surveyes, plots of manors and records that the fault will be your own if you understand them not in a very short time better than any servant you have. They are not so difficult now they are done, they are easy and yet cost me much time and expense to reduce them to order. (Startin, 1988, 9)

The result of employing the younger Ralph Treswell as surveyor was that instead of being a relatively poor nobleman, the Earl's income doubled and he became much more secure (Batho, 1957, 438–9). Sir Thomas Tresham of Rushton, Northamptonshire, also improved his financial position by taking a personal interest in all matters of estate management. He was always seeking means of improving his profits, he applied business methods and he closely supervised the servants who administered his estates. As a result, and because he employed a competent surveyor, George Levens, when Tresham died in 1605 his debts were comparatively small (Finch, 1956, 91). Robert Millicent, the owner of Barham Manor in Linton, was another contemporary who took an interest in his estate. He was diligent in asserting his feudal rights, and held up to four courts a year to control more strictly the tenants' transfer of property (*VCH*, 6, 87).

The Civil War and its aftermath encouraged practical efforts to improve the land (Mendyk, 1989, 138), when an owner's absence could lead him to make alternative arrangements. For example Katherine Knyvett, the wife of Thomas, an imprisoned Royalist, managed the family's estate at Ashwellthorpe in Norfolk: she dealt with leases of land, she supervised the setting of seed and the cutting of wood (Schofield, 1949, 38). Slightly later, when Sir Hugh Cholmley, Surveyor-General at Tangier from 1663 to 1674, went there in 1670, he arranged for careful estate accounts to be kept. Then in 1703, he employed Joseph Dickenson to map his estate at Crambe in the North Riding of Yorkshire (Cholmley, 1970, 8–10).

By the early eighteenth century, interest in estate management was becoming more widespread. John Holles, Duke of Newcastle, had a deep understanding of most aspects of estate management. When he enlarged his estates between 1700 and 1711 (an expansion which included buying the Wimpole and Arrington estate in Cambridgeshire), the land was carefully examined and there was some hard bargaining. His land agents had a list of 31 questions to answer which covered every aspect of the estate's value, natural resources, taxes and charges, the condition of the tenants' houses, rents, leases, arrears, and the capacity for improvement and inclosure. The Wimpole estate passed through his daughter, Henrietta, to Edward, Lord Harley, who took little interest in estate management (Davies, 1965, 43 and 46). During the later eighteenth century, expenditure on repairs and improvements increased in East Anglia, though much depended on accidents of inheritance, whether the owner was resident or absentee (and therefore less likely to plough back profits into the estate), and how an estate had been looked after in the past (Holderness, 1972). In Norfolk, Thomas Coke of Holkham, an innovative landlord, managed his extensive estates himself with the help of an accountant and assistant until 1816, when he appointed an agent, Francis Blaikie (Wade Martins, 1980, 51–2). At Wimpole, Cambridgeshire, in the 1790s, the 3rd Earl of Hardwicke, who was interested in new ideas in farming, tried to diversify the crops which were grown there and had extensive underground tiling drains constructed and open ditches dug (*VCH*, 5, 269). It was reported that the Earl's home farm even made a profit, which was very unusual as such farms rarely set examples of good practices; they were normally run at a loss and regarded merely as suppliers of fresh produce for the house (Beckett, 1989, 572). At this time, Sir Charles Cotton introduced to his estate at Madingley such improvements as hollow-draining and flattening the mole-infested common pastures (*VCH*, 9, 172). Charles Wale, whose estate at Little Shelford was mapped in 1813, had been sent to London in his youth to learn arithmetic (and fencing), and thus he knew something of estate management (Wale, 1883, 198). Henry John Adeane of Babraham, too, was interested in agriculture: he encouraged new methods and production from previously uncultivated land, and he stipulated a four-course rotation of crops and introduced Shorthorn cattle in about 1830. His estate was mapped in 1829 (BAB82901; *VCH*, 6, 26).

From the mid-eighteenth century, estates were increasingly organized along similar lines. As estate business grew in complexity and owners were absent from their properties for longer periods, it became ever more common to employ a professional steward or land agent and men like Thomas Coke, who managed his estate himself, became very rare (Beckett, 1986, 144). If an owner's land was scattered, he might employ a London solicitor as a chief or supervisory agent (Beckett, 1989, 591). Texts were produced, such as those by Richards (1730), Mordant (1761) and Marshall (1806), which outlined a steward's duties: when the stock of Ellen Feepound, a bankrupt bookseller, was valued in 1776, amongst the 100 books were two works on estate management (Feather, 1985, 125–9). Arthur Young described a model estate office: that of Sir Joseph Banks at Revesby. It was of two rooms, with a brick partition and an iron door as a safe-guard against fire. The furniture included map tables, a bookcase and a travelling bookcase, desks, measures and levels (Mingay, 1963, 173).

Several examples can be given of Cambridgeshire landowners who used land agents or stewards. Sir George Downing of East Hatley relied heavily on his agent. His grandfather, also Sir George, had bought the estate in 1661, and added to it until it was the largest one in the county. He was not noted for his generosity; Pepys said that he was 'so stingy a fellow I care not to see him'. Sir George's grandson inherited the property in 1711 (Beresford, 1925, 125; Sibley, 1873, 37), and he employed an attorney and steward, John Shipston. He died in 1737; thus deprived of practical advice on estate management, Sir George lost all interest in his duties as a landlord, he took no steps to keep the property in good repair and the estate fell into decline (French, 1978, 39). Samuel Shepheard, a London merchant and M.P. for Cambridgeshire (Darby, 1948b, 412; Jenkins, 1984, 11), employed Thomas Waddington, owner of an estate at Doddington (see DOD77002), as receiver of rents for Cambridgeshire from 1750. The Shepheard estates passed through the female line to Frances, who married Charles, 10th Viscount Irwin, in 1756 (*DEP*, 297); Waddington remained receiver until his death in 1770 and the Irwin estates were mapped in 1779 (EYT77901, ISL77901, SOH77901–2, STO77901, TYD77902 and WTF77901).[1] Sir Charles Cotton of Madingley was another local landowner who had an agent; in 1811 he was employing a Suffolk farmer (Gooch, 1811, 96).

The Russells, Dukes of Bedford, are an example of a Cambridgeshire landowning family who took an active interest in their property. Francis, the 4th Earl, succeeded to the estates in 1627. He reorganized the great estates around Tavistock in Devon and Woburn (Bedfordshire), he had plans for rebuilding on the land at Covent Garden, London, and he started draining the fens. He supervised everything himself, and his careful and progressive management brought prosperity to the estates and increased their income (Thomson, 1937, 27). William, the 5th Earl and 1st Duke, continued to be greatly concerned with the estates. He completed his father's projects for Covent Garden and Thorney in Cambridgeshire with vigour, and he had paid off the family's debts by the mid-1650s (Thomson, 1937, 79–81).

He largely rebuilt Thorney Abbey and spent much time there between 1663 and 1685 to superintend the drainage work (Bedford, 1897, 43).[2] To receive the rents, he appointed in 1660 Mr Collop, the son of one of the Duke's Dorset tenants. Collop was succeeded by a professional lawyer, Mr Fox, and then by Mr Middleton (Thomson, 1940, 208–9). The 3rd Duke was less satisfactory as a landlord: he was a gambler and nearly brought the family's fortunes to ruins. He took a personal interest in the house and land at Thorney, however, and may even have contemplated making it his principal residence. He paid many prolonged visits to the estate in 1728 and 1729 and spent especial care on the gardens (Haas, 1960, 7; Thomson, 1949, 186–7). Development of the Bloomsbury property in London in the early eighteenth century resulted in its income accounting for about one-third of the rental, and this enabled the 4th Duke to enlarge his Bedfordshire estate after 1732 (Clay, 1985, 191). The Duke was passionately interested in his estates and eager to follow up every agricultural improvement. On his succession in 1732, he appointed Mr Robert Butcher as agent-in-chief with an unprecedentedly high salary of £700 per annum, and Butcher arranged the estate papers into order (Thomson, 1940, 191 and 209–10). Francis, the 5th Duke, was on the Board of Agriculture in 1793, he had an experimental farm at Woburn where he held an annual exhibition of sheep shearing, and ploughing and other competitions (*DNB*, 49, 435). The 6th Duke, too, was interested in agriculture; in 1838 he was Governor of the newly founded Agricultural Society, and he was involved in the Bedford Level drainage scheme which was directed by Thomas Telford and John and Sir John Rennie (*DNB*, 49, 454–5).

Each of the Dukes' estates was looked after by an agent. In the early eighteenth century, there was mismanagement at Thorney by Platt Disbrowe, who was dismissed in 1741 because he showed false accounts and allowed too much land to be burnt over.[3] His successor, John Scribo, was equally unsatisfactory: in 1743, a list of 19 misdemeanours was submitted to the Duke.[4] The appointment of John Wing and his descendants as agents from 1750 marked a turning point. Indeed, John was such a success that from 1761 to 1764 he was sent to Hampshire to let the estates there which were mainly held in hand; unfortunately, his replacements at Thorney, John Lambe Davis and Gilbert Aislabie, proved unequal to the job.[5] John Wing was succeeded by his son, John, and then by his son, Tycho, who was known as 'King of the Fens' (Spring, 1963, 74). The estate was well managed; it has already been shown in Chapter 5 how Gooch praised the work of John Wing junior, and in 1833 Tycho Wing was told that: 'The Duke said "Wing has immortalized himself" and Mr Russell told me Lord Tavistock was so much pleased with the Tenantry – such Tenantry we have not always the opportunity of knowing what people say behind our back and as this is true genuine stuff I have <u>some</u> pleasure in letting you know it.'[6] Tycho Wing's accounts for 1830 show the breadth of his involvement. He bought surplices for the minister, he received rents, he paid the lock-keepers, he sent fish and game to Woburn, he was involved in the Huntingdon election campaign and provided transport for freeholders to go and vote, he paid the Duke's subscription to local charities, including Addenbrooke's Hospital, he paid the constable and schoolmaster, he bought new furnishings for the church, and he paid for repairs.[7]

Estate management therefore ranged from a motley collection of bailiffs, tenant farmers, part-time agents and others to a highly efficient organizational structure on estates such as those of the Dukes of Bedford. A competent steward or agent was never sufficient on his own, and demands on the landlord to make decisions increased through time. From about 1820, landlords had to be well versed in agricultural practices if they were to overcome the problems of the agricultural depression (Beckett, 1986, 155).

Interest of institutional owners in their estates

Institutional owners, too, became increasingly interested in their estates. From medieval times, the statutes of some Oxford colleges ordained that college officers should visit their estates and value the farm stock each year after the harvest: for example, Corpus Christi (Duncan, 1986, 574), Merton (Brodrick, 1885, 9) and New (Buxton and Williams, 1979, 11) colleges. In the sixteenth century, the estates of Queens' College, Cambridge were also supervised by annual progresses and visits. For instance, in September 1566 a college servant went to Abbotsley in Huntingdonshire, the following month the Senior Bursar went to Helions Bumpstead in Essex, in January 1566/7 he went to Eversden to collect rents, a Fellow went to Furneux Pelham in Hertfordshire and the Bursar and President visited Haslingfield and Eversden. In the February of the same year the Bursar and a carpenter went to Helions Bumpstead to select timber for felling to use in repairs in the College, in April the President went to Abbotsley to choose more timber for repairs and in May to Olmstead Hall in Castle Camps to supervise repairs, in June he and the Bursar visited Capel in Suffolk, two Fellows went to Furneux Pelham in July, and in August journeys were made to collect the rent at Eversden and to hold courts at Helions Bumpstead and Haverhill. In June 1579, five separate estates were visited in two progresses, and between June and September in the following year journeys were made to six estates (Twigg, 1987, 114). Similarly, King's College carried out surveys of its Norfolk estates between 1564 and 1587 (Corbett, 1897). Although these visits show a general interest in estates, they do not necessarily mean that anything more was done than to maintain the status quo.

More radical changes in estate management came from the need to increase revenues as inflation occurred in the sixteenth century. Changes in lease legislation made this possible: in 1571 and 1572, measures were passed in Parliament to limit the length of leases of agricultural property to three lives or 21 years, and of urban property to 40 years. The 1576 Corn Rent Act stated that one-third of the rent of property from the colleges at Oxford, Cambridge, Winchester and Eton had to be paid either in kind, or in cash at the current market value of wheat and malt. This was a form of index-linking and receipts rose accordingly (Aylmer, 1986, 534–5). The Crown became interested in its property in the early seventeenth century, when the poverty of James I stimulated surveys of its lands (Wilson, 1965, 30). The surveys showed that there was much inefficient management and the need for rents to be increased fourfold (Madge, 1938, 55–6). The Warden of New College, Oxford, between 1659 and 1675 took an interest in his College's estates and he improved the management of the timber resources (Eland, 1935, 81). He was not universally successful, however: by the time of his death, the College had still not recovered any of the customary rents or tithes from its estate at

Hornchurch in Essex, the leaseholders were still enriching themselves at the College's expense, and the bailiff was still unsatisfactory (McIntosh, 1987, 181). Other colleges were less concerned about their land: St Catharine's College, Cambridge, for example, ignored the advice of its surveyor at Over in 1707 that manorial courts be resumed to maintain the College's rights, and no action seems to have been taken (*VCH*, 9, 350).

In general, however, institutional interest in land further increased in the eighteenth century. Emmanuel College paid one shilling in 1731 for a copy of Edward Laurence's *A Dissertation on Estates upon Lives and Years, Whether in Lay or Church-Hands*, which gave details on how to value land, and suggests that the College was interested in so doing.[8] Some large estates such as those of the London hospitals (St Bartholomew's and St Thomas' had land in Cambridgeshire) were effectively controlled and let on leases at full economic rents (Mingay, 1963, 61). St Bartholomew's Hospital appointed its first professional surveyor in 1748; it had already had a rent collector from the seventeenth century (Kerling, 1974a, 26 and 1974b, 302). It was not until the 1770s, however, that colleges in both Oxford and Cambridge started to commission surveys of their land (Dunbabin, 1986, 284). St John's College, Cambridge, for example, had surveys carried out from this time (Howard, 1935, 150). Professional surveyors were usually employed, but Dr James Wood, the Senior Bursar from 1789 to 1795, carried out some detailed surveys of the college's Kentish estates: he reported on the value of the land, its acreage, the state of repairs, and made recommendations about leases and tenants.[9]

This growing concern of institutions in their land from the 1770s was not always kindly regarded by their tenants. Queens' College, for example, decided in 1775 to have its Carmarthenshire estates surveyed and mapped. The tenant, the antiquary David Edwardes (Howell, 1986, 202), was very suspicious and a long correspondence ensued. On 11 August 1775, he wrote to Robert Plumptre, President of Queens', that,

I am afraid you have been led into an opinion by some designing person, that the lands are of infinite more value than what they will appear to be upon inspection, otherwise why should Doctor Plumtre be more particular in his Enquiry's at this time than any of his Predecessors have been for near a Century past, I have lived in a friendly regard with your society these 36 years, and thank God my honour and Character will bear the strictest Scrutiny. I was favoured with my last lease in your Headship, without being put to much difficulty.[10]

Plumptre replied on 21 February 1776:

It gives me concern likewise that you will still consider our Resolution to know particularly what we Lease to you, and have it properly described before we make another <to> Lease <to you> as a reflection on your Character. It \is not/ founded in any suspicions of that, nor \any/ <no>thing to do with it. <Necessity and> The proper regard to the just rights of the Body, & our Duty <to the present Body of> \respecting/ <to> our Successors in it have obliged us to the part we have taken in the business between us and you and every other Gentleman would \(I am persuaded)/ in the like circumstances act in the like manner. It may likewise prove beneficial to your family, as the inquiry we have now set on foot must be made some time or other, and the longer it is delayed the less likelihood there will be of an amicable issue to it.[11]

Eventually all was settled; in 1781 Edwardes' son John was admitted as a pensioner to the College and he became a Fellow there in 1787 (Venn, II, 2, 389).

Colleges were not deterred by these complaints and surveys continued to be carried out. In 1796, Clare College had a sufficient number of maps of its estates to need to make a decision on where to keep them: the treasury was decided upon, but then in the following year the maps were moved to the library.[12] King's College had its land surveyed to obtain accurate measurements in statute acres and to replace earlier figures, in customary measures, which were based on information from tenants (Eden, 1973, 477). Visits by college officers to their estates continued: from 1816 to 1820, for example, the newly elected Master of St John's College visited the college's estates. He found many buildings seriously in need of repair, and expenditure on buildings rose considerably after 1822.[13]

It was not, however, until the system of letting land on beneficial leases had been replaced by letting land at rack-rent, that colleges and other institutions could hope to derive a realistic income from their estates and were tempted to become more than mere rent collectors. Beneficial leases were for a number of years with a low annual rent and high entry or renewal fine, whereas land let at rack-rent was much more sensitive to market fluctuations. For example, the Bishops of Ely let the impropriate rectory at Harston on a beneficial lease with the same rent from the 1530s to the 1850s (*VCH*, 8, 183). The timing of the changeover varied from college to college: St John's College started to extend the practice of letting at rack-rent in the 1770s and St Catharine's College introduced rack-rents at about that time (Howard, 1935, 115; Jones, 1936, 230). In 1785, Queens' College decided to let its estate at Oakington at rack-rent,[14] and in 1818, the advantages of letting at rack-rent were set out.[15] Continuing interest in such matters in 1823 is shown by the levy of a fine for returning Francis Baily's *Tables for the Purchasing and Renewing of Leases* late to the College library.[16] The first rack-rent at Gonville and Caius College was set in 1816 and the last beneficial agricultural lease ran out in 1881 (Gross, 1912, ix–x), and at Clare College the substitution occurred under the mastership of William Webb from 1815 to 1856. He was a keen agriculturalist and took a great interest in the management of the college's estates (Forbes, 1928, 159).

As with private landowners, institutions also increasingly employed professional agents. Until the later eighteenth century, either Fellows or local men collected rents: Mr Power of Ely, for example, collected rents for Clare College in Ely, Littleport and Downham in 1726.[17] A Fellow of Emmanuel College, Edward Banyer, received the rents for the College's estate in Ash, Kent, in 1723.[18] In 1762, Queens' College drew up instructions for its bailiff at Helions Bumpstead in Essex. He was to: note the type and quantity of timber which he assigned for repairs, the uses to which it was to be put and the tenants to whom it was to be allocated; record the number of trees felled for sale, the quantity of timber therein and to whom it was sold; bring his accounts to the yearly audit; ensure that purchasers of under-woods felled their timber by a fixed time, leave six of the best trees marked by the bailiff and pay for the wood at the next audit, with a penalty of £10 if they did not meet these conditions; make sure the fences were well made and kept, that there was no waste of the woods and that the College was informed of any wrongdoers. Bailiffs on all estates were to make out a rental and note the defaulters.[19] Distant estates of colleges were often the first to be managed by professional agents. Trinity College, for example, employed the Teal family of Leeds as agent to its northern estates in the eighteenth and nineteenth centuries.[20] In 1776, St John's College agreed:

to appoint Mr Baxby Agent for the College to prevent or put a stop to abuses & to take care that the College may not suffer by neglect of their Tenants in Yorkshire & some neighbouring counties; & that he order maps & surveys to be made where they may be wanting; & send to us once a year an account of the condition of the Buildings & a particular one of the state of Husbandry in each farm; & that Mr Baxby have for his trouble a salary of Thirty Pounds per annum to commence from the First of May last, & to continue during the pleasure of the College.[21]

By the late eighteenth century, estates which were closer to Cambridgeshire were managed by agents: in 1785, Joseph Freeman was the agent for Jesus College at Tempsford, Bedfordshire,[22] and colleges employed agents in London. Emmanuel College, for example, employed the Nettleshipp partnership in the early nineteenth century.[23] It was necessary to change the agent from time to time; on 20 November 1821, the Fellows of St John's College decided to do so:

The Bursar having represented the disordered & difficult circumstances of many of the College Manours arising partly from the recent inclosures of parishes within the Manours, partly from former inattention to the correct keeping of the court rolls & in a great measure from a want of an active & personal superintendance of the courts – Agreed to transfer to Mr Pemberton \the business/ hitherto entrusted to Mr Ingle.[24]

The increased interest taken by colleges in their estates can be seen from their expenditure on them. Fig. 7.1 shows that the fortunes of different colleges varied. St John's College, for example, had relatively healthy finances, with overall deficits only occurring in occasional years from 1812. Clare College's situation was more mercurial, and it was hard-hit by the depressed agriculture of the 1820s. Queens' and Jesus colleges, on the other hand, were far less affluent. Queens' College only made an overall surplus of more than £1,000 on one occasion between 1700 and 1840, and Jesus College's maximum surplus over the same period was under £400. There were several periods in both colleges when there was an overall deficit, which approached £2,000 on several occasions at Queens' College. Indeed, Queens' frequently had to keep fellowships vacant so that the income which would normally go to Fellows could be used to pay off debts or to pay for repairs.[25] The balances given in Fig. 7.1 have been adjusted for inflation by comparing them with prices in 1700.

In this general picture of diversity, however, expenditure on surveying and estates increased in all the colleges which were studied in detail. Fig. 7.2 shows that Emmanuel and Jesus colleges were relatively early spenders of money on their estates; the very high figure for Jesus College in 1736 was probably caused by surveys connected with the purchase of college livings.[26] Emmanuel College's relative expenditure was highest from 1803 to about 1810; Jesus College spent more in the following decade. Queens' College, on the other hand, hardly spent any money on its estates until the middle of the eighteenth century. It was more active in the 1770s, but its period of maximum expenditure was in the 1820s, when the percentage expenditure on estates was particularly high for the colleges examined here. Partial payment for an atlas of the College's estates in 1828 (£457 of a total bill of £757), accounted for over 21% of the total expenditure of the College in that year.[27] St John's College spent most between 1788 and 1813, though as expenditure never exceeded 5% of the total College

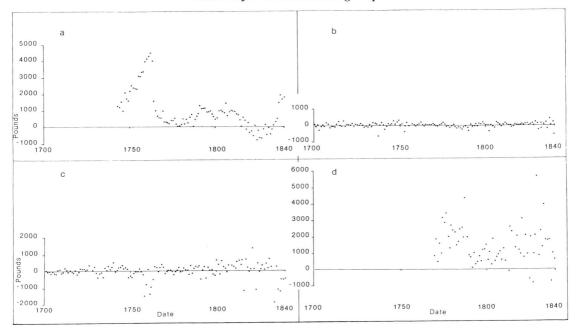

Fig. 7.1. Balance of income over expenditure in Clare, Jesus, Queens' and St John's colleges, Cambridge, corrected to prices in 1700 (a, Clare College; b, Jesus College; c, Queens' College; d, St John's College).

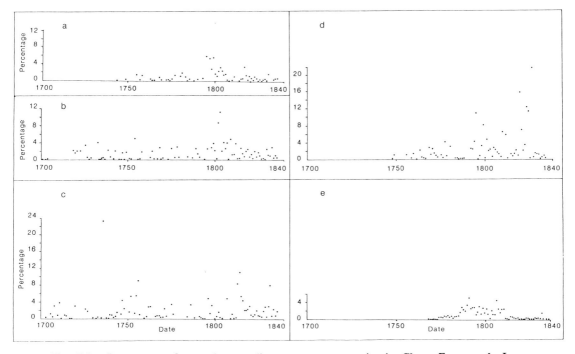

Fig. 7.2. Percentage of annual expenditure spent on surveying in Clare, Emmanuel, Jesus, Queens' and St John's colleges, Cambridge (a, Clare College; b, Emmanuel College; c, Jesus College; d, Queens' College; e, St John's College).

costs of any one year, it was relatively unimportant compared with colleges such as Queens'. The graph only shows expenditure from 1770, and money was probably laid out on estates before then. The figures for Clare College date from 1740; the College followed St John's, and maximum expenditure occurred between 1795 and 1807. It can therefore be seen that expenditure on estates was not closely linked with the overall prosperity of a college: relatively high expenditure on estates by Clare and St John's colleges occurred during periods of affluence, Jesus College was fairly affluent during the period of high expenditure on estates in the early nineteenth century but was not necessarily so successful in the eighteenth-century periods of estate outlay, and the maximum outgoings of Queens' College happened immediately after a year of a deficit of over £1,000.

Institutions therefore came to take greater interest in their estates and to spend larger proportions of their income on them. At the same time, they delegated much of the responsibility for the day-to-day management of their land to professional agents and surveyors. Improvements developed slowly and unevenly: New College, Oxford, for example, was for 43 years unaware of 12 acres which had been allotted to it on the inclosure of Kirkby Green, Lincolnshire, in 1799 (Dunbabin, 1986, 277).

Practical uses for estate maps

Of the maps listed in the carto-bibliography in Appendix 2, nearly one-third were drawn for a specific practical use. By the end of the eighteenth century, maps were regarded as potentially helpful documents. For example, on 8 July 1791 Sarah Lonsdale bequeathed the map of her estate at Linton (LIN78501) to Pembroke College under certain conditions:

shall and do upon my Decease deliver to the Master Fellows and Scholars of the College or Hall of Mary Valence commonly called Pembroke Hall in the University of Cambridge the Plan or Map that I have of my Manor Messuages Lands Tenements Tithes and Hereditaments in Linton or Elsewhere in the County of Cambridge Upon Condition that they do engage to permit the Executors of my said Will or any other Person or Persons who shall be thereby interested in any Part of my said Estate or any of their Agents at any Time or Times to inspect the said Plan or Map as Occasion may require.[28]

Functional estate maps were especially common in the early nineteenth century, when they accounted for over half of institutional owners' maps but fewer of the maps which were drawn for private owners (not more than 40%). The pattern of increased production of various tools of estate management – maps, terriers, valuations and surveys – is first examined, and then the specific practical uses of maps are looked at in greater detail.

The graphs in Fig. 7.3 show the increase in production of maps, terriers, valuations and surveys for one private landowning family, the Dukes of Bedford, and four Cambridge colleges: Emmanuel, Jesus, Queens' and St John's. Interpretation once again depends upon estimated survival of documents, which is varied. The survival rate for maps has been discussed in Chapter 3. Survival for terriers ranges from 99% in St John's College to 57% in Emmanuel, for valuations the range is from 93% (St John's) to 63% (Queens'), and between

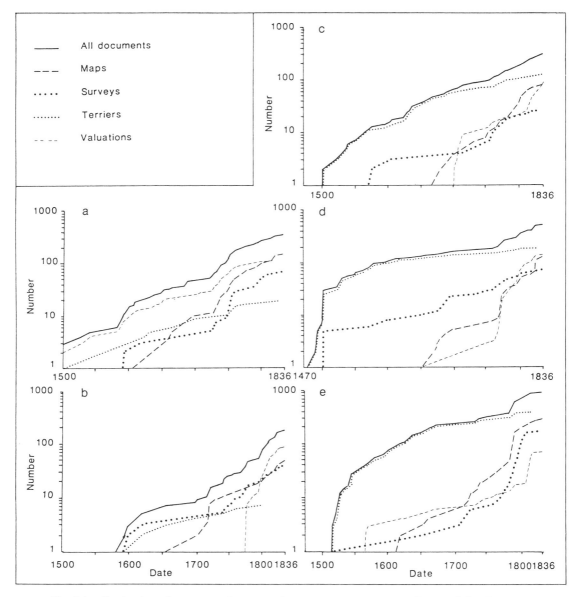

Fig. 7.3. Production of maps, terriers, valuations and surveys by the Dukes of Bedford and Emmanuel, Jesus, Queens' and St John's colleges, Cambridge (a, Dukes of Bedford; b, Emmanuel College; c, Jesus College; d, Queens' College; e, St John's College).

169

97% and 26% of surveys survive (from St John's and Emmanuel colleges respectively). If, however, consideration is limited to documents for which there is independent documentary evidence of their existence, the survival rate for terriers ranges from 67% in St John's and Jesus colleges to 0% in Emmanuel, between 64% and 44% of valuations remain (for Emmanuel and Jesus colleges respectively) and the survival of surveys varies from 53% in Jesus College to 8% in Emmanuel. Surveys, therefore, seem to have the lowest chances of survival; apart from Emmanuel College, terriers are most likely to survive, followed by maps and valuations. The overall survival rate for all four types of document depends upon the institution: for St John's College it was 94%, for Jesus 86%, for Queens' 70% and for Emmanuel 55%. Again, if examination is confined to those documents for which there is independent documentary evidence of their existence, the percentages fall and variation decreases, to 57% (Jesus), 50% (St John's), 46% (Queens') and 36% (Emmanuel).

All the graphs show a gradual increase in production of maps, terriers, valuations and surveys, with a greater rate of increase from some time in the eighteenth century. The rate of increase and relative importance of the various tools of estate management differ between the owners. The Dukes of Bedford started having maps drawn relatively early, in 1607; production of all items increased rapidly from the accession of the 4th Duke in 1732, though terriers were relatively unimportant. For Jesus, Queens' and St John's colleges, by contrast, terriers were much more numerous; it was suggested above that the survival rate for terriers in Emmanuel College is probably very low. Emmanuel College started having many of its estates mapped relatively early in the 1720s; Queens' and St John's colleges were later, in the 1770s and 1790s respectively, though St John's had started commissioning more maps in the earlier part of the eighteenth century. In Jesus College, the increase was much more gradual. The production of valuations, which grew most rapidly for the Dukes of Bedford between 1725 and 1760, followed a different pattern for the colleges, with a later period of great increase. Queens' and Emmanuel colleges show the most abrupt starts, in the 1760s and 1770s respectively; for Jesus and St John's colleges, the most rapid growth was in the 1810s. Surveys were produced for the Bedford estates in increasing numbers from 1726; they became more common among the colleges in the eighteenth century, too, especially in the later eighteenth century for St John's College. Thus, in general the colleges show a later development in production of tools of estate management than the Dukes of Bedford, and terriers were more important. There was, however, much variation within similar types of owner, and between similar owners in different locations. A number of Oxford colleges, for example, had their estates mapped in the late sixteenth or early seventeenth centuries, and this was unparalleled in their Cambridge counterparts (Eden, 1983b). Therefore, conclusions have been drawn with caution.

The location of a college's estate did not seem to affect whether it was valued, surveyed or mapped relatively early or late, though in general land in Cambridgeshire was examined early. These local estates also account for the greatest proportion of the activity, but this is probably because they were the most numerous. Emmanuel College is an exception: its Staffordshire and Norfolk estates were recorded in the seventeenth century, land in London, Kent, Essex, Suffolk and Cambridgeshire in the early eighteenth century, and its estates in Huntingdonshire, Lincolnshire, Northamptonshire and Somerset in the late eighteenth century. This pattern does not reflect the dates of acquisition of estates. Nor was Cambridgeshire dominant: most of the maps were drawn of London property, and the valuations were mainly of urban properties in Cambridgeshire, Surrey and London. None of the colleges had their Cambridgeshire estates mapped first: the earliest estate map for Jesus College was of its London property, for St John's the first map was of land in Essex, and Emmanuel and Queens' colleges started having estate maps drawn when they had their Norfolk estates mapped.

Maps, therefore, were just one of the tools of estate management. Land was surveyed for a number of reasons: when land was about to or had just changed hands, to determine a boundary, when an estate was to be let, or when land was to be improved or inclosed. As a result, maps, terriers, valuations or surveys were produced, in a variety of combinations. For example, the title-page to the atlas of Humphry Sturt's estates (see DOD77001–2 and WMB77001) depicts the surveyor sitting with volumes at his feet labelled title-deeds, maps, leases and terriers. On some occasions, maps were felt to be too expensive: an entry in the Conclusions Book for St John's College on 17 August 1817 reads: 'Agreed that Mr Lake be employed to procure for the College a survey & admeasurement of the Parish of Headcorne [Kent] – & a map if it can be had upon reasonable terms \Oct 18th N.B. On Enquiry the Map is too expensive/.'[29] Trinity College contemplated following the example of Queens' College and employing Alexander Watford to make an atlas of its southern estates. On 15 December 1826, however, the Senior Bursar noted: 'Mr Watford's estimate for new plans of our southern estates. Having this before me, I dare not advise the board to employ him – much as it seems to me desirable to have such plans in our possession.' On 6 February in the following year, he confirmed that the plans were 'Too expensive'.[30]

Many estate maps were drawn when land was bought or inherited or when settlements changed. An advertisement in the *Daily Post* on 1 July 1732 suggests that a map might be useful at such a time:

WHEREAS the Map or Survey of the Manor of Broughton in the County of Oxon, late the Estate of William Goodenough, Esq; deceased, was by him lodged in some Friend's Hands unknown to his Family: This is to desire the Person in whose Hands the same is, to give Notice to Robert Goodenough, at Mr. Barkley's, an Apothecary, in King~street, St. Anne's, Soho, and it will be acknowledged as a Favour, and all Charges will be paid. (D. Hodson, personal communication)

For example, the Corporation of the Sons of the Clergy had their estates at West Wratting and Willingham mapped in 1719, shortly after their acquisition (WEW71901–2 and WLL71901–2; Cox, 1978, 57). In 1791, St John's College had a map drawn of its newly purchased estate at St Clement's in Cambridge.[31] Estates were also mapped when they were inherited. Henry Clinton, 7th Earl of Lincoln, ingratiated himself with Arthur, Earl of Torrington and inherited Torrington's estates on his death in 1716. In 1706 and 1710, Torrington had his estates at Whittlesey mapped by Val. Deepup and Thomas Boyce (WHR70601 and WHR71001); then, in about 1716, Clinton had his bequest mapped, again by Thomas Boyce (WHR71601; *DNB*, 26, 169–72; *PB*, 1,961). Similarly, Emmanuel College was left land at Ash in Kent by George Thorp in 1719. Under the terms of his will, this stock of money, with all the writings belonging to the said estate & the Register & account book aforesaid & map of the Lands before~mentioned be placed in a convenient Chest to be provided for that purpose out of the rent & profits aforesaid to be called Cista De Chequer: with three locks & keys, of different forms, the one key to be kept by the Master of Emanuel College another by him, that keeps the accounts aforesaid & the third by the president or other person to be nominated by the master & fellows of Emanuel College.[32]

In 1721, 1s 6d was spent on a frame for the map.[33] William Woodham had his estate at Shepreth mapped when he inherited it and inclosed some land in 1764 (SHE76401; *VCH*, 5, 257), and the map of the Marquis of Granby's estate at Cheveley in 1775 was probably drawn in connection with the docking of the entail of the estates in that year (CHG77501).[34]

Estates were mapped when land was to be sold. For example, Sir Thomas Chicheley's land at Orwell was probably mapped in 1686, on its sale to Sir John Cutler. Cutler was a wealthy and avaricious London merchant, who was Master Warden of the Grocers' Company in 1652–3 and 1685–6, and then assistant to Chicheley when he was Master in the following year (ORW68601; *DNB*, 13, 364; *VCH*, 5, 243). Sir Clement Trafford's estate at Tydd St Giles was part of his property which was not settled in trust for his wife and issue. When matrimonial difficulties arose, the unsettled properties were conveyed to trustees for sale, and the Tydd St Giles land was mapped at about this time (TYD77901; *VCH*, 4, 228). Similarly, the map of General Sparrow's estate at March was drawn in 1805, probably after his death in that year (MAR80501), and Lawrence Banyer's estates in the fenland (Leverington, Tydd St Giles, Upwell and Wisbech St Mary) were probably mapped just before they were advertised for sale in the *Cambridge Chronicle* in 1811 (LEV81101, TYD81101, UPW81101 and WSM81101).[35] Many early nineteenth-century maps were drawn on particulars of sale; over one-third of maps which were drawn for private owners between 1827 and 1836 fell into this category. For example, maps were drawn when Sarah Rayner sold her land at Soham, Swaffham Prior and Wicken in 1825 (SOH82501, SWP82501 and WIC82501; Knowles, 1902, 38). Similarly, maps were included in the particulars of sale of the land belonging to Henry Peyto, 16th Lord Willoughby de Broke, in Steeple Morden (Cambridgeshire) and in Hertfordshire in 1828 (STM82801; *VCH*, 8, 113; *PB*, 2,839).

Many estate maps arose out of disputes over property. The Duchy of Lancaster early recognized such a use: in 1528, it ordered the Abbot of Derby, the Vicar of Bakewell and two other men to go to Over Haddon in Derbyshire and to put into writing 'by a cart or platt the meres and boundes' (Yates, 1964, 121). Nearly one-third of the late sixteenth-century estate maps by Christopher Saxton were connected with disputes over land, boundary or water rights (Evans and Lawrence, 1979). The Earls of Devonshire employed William Senior to map and survey their estates in the early seventeenth century, and his work was almost solely concerned with establishing ownership, boundaries, the precise extent of land, field names and, occasionally, land use (Fowkes and Potter, 1988, vii). In the early nineteenth century, estates in the Western Isles were mapped for similar reasons (Caird, 1989).

There are abundant examples of maps drawn in connection with property disputes among both private and institutional owners in Cambridgeshire; many of the joint commissions of estate maps arose from these controversies. In 1628–30, for example, two maps were drawn of land in dispute in Soham between Roger Thornton and Robert and Edward Ramsay, trustees for Sir John Ramsay, Viscount Haddington and Earl of Holderness (SOH63001–2; Lysons, 254). The Dean and Chapter of Ely were engaged in lawsuits about rights of common at Sutton at about the time that their estate there was mapped in 1639 (SUT63901; *VCH*, 4, 160), and the map of Stapleford which was drawn in 1740–1 arose from the division of the heath there between them and Francis, 2nd Earl Godolphin (STL74101; *VCH*, 8, 233). In 1777, Benjamin Keene and Thomas Wolfe were involved in a boundary dispute at Linton, and a map was drawn of the relevant piece of land (LIN77701). The map of the Waldegrave estates in Whittlesey which was drawn about 1786 was connected with chancery proceedings. Lord Waldegrave had left his three daughters fairly well provided for when he died in 1763, but their fortunes had dwindled during their long minorities. The husbands of two of the sisters, Charlotte Maria and Horatia, tried in chancery to retrieve part of the inheritance, and the map was drawn as a result (WHR78601; Biddulph, 1938, 153). St John's College had a map drawn of its land in Cranwell in Lincolnshire in 1811 because of a boundary dispute,[36] and in 1826 Emmanuel College employed Alexander Watford to survey land in dispute in Great Gransden, Huntingdonshire.[37] These maps often show little more than the boundary under discussion, and various devices are used to highlight particular features: in a map of Capel St Mary, Suffolk, which was drawn for Queens' College in 1751, the responsibility for fences was shown by colour.[38]

The renewal of leases led to much survey work, and from the eighteenth century it became increasingly common for new surveys and valuations to be carried out on each renewal. Edward Hubbard, of Emmanuel College, recommended this in 1721:

I wish Colleges themselves had not contributed (as they have greatly) to the Undervaluing their own Estates; who, when a Fine is to be set for Renewing a Lease, never perhaps so much as once take the pains to calculate the real Worth of such Renewals, but only turn to their Books to see *what* the Fine for that Estate was set at, Seven Years before. So that if Fines have ever been set too low, that is too much looked upon as a good Reason why they should always be as low.[39]

As farm prices and rents rose from the 1760s, the number of surveys increased too (Howell, 1986, 84). Maps were not necessarily drawn in every case: in 1802, for example, John Clark inspected the Carmarthenshire lands belonging to the Bishop of St Davids, and he said that: 'To have made an actual measurement of these extensive Estates would have been a wanton expenditure of money to little purpose' (Evans, 1977, 52).

Maps were used in growing numbers, however: overall, about two-thirds of the maps drawn for Queens' College and one-third of those drawn for Clare and St John's colleges were associated with the renewal of leases. In early eighteenth-century Norfolk, the Holkham estates were in the hands of guardians during Thomas Coke's minority from 1707 to 1718, and it was ordained that former rents should not be used as a guide in the renewal of leases, so surveys and valuations were carried out and many estate maps from that time survive today (Parker, 1975, 7). There are many examples in college archives from the late eighteenth century of decisions to have an estate mapped before the lease was renewed, and a general decision was taken by Gonville and Caius College on 10 May 1776: 'Agreed that the College Estates to which Fines are to be set next Michaelmas be mapped & valued & so every Year.'[40] St John's College found it useful for the map of its estate at Fen Drayton in 1792 to distinguish between land let under beneficial lease and at rack-rent (FDY79201). St Bartholomew's Hospital, London, had a similar policy too. The Minutes of the Board of Governors for 12 December 1792 record that:

Mr Waltham [the Hospital's agent and surveyor] attended and made his report of Bottisham Farm &c in Cambridgeshire, the letting of which he recommended to be postponed for the present and in the meantime It Was Ordered that Mr Waltham do procure \a Plan/ of the whole parish to be made as until that is done it will be impossible to ascertain its value.[41]

The map was made by Francis Marshall the following year (BOT79301). By the early nineteenth century, solicitors were finding maps invaluable. For example, when an estate near Llanelli in Wales was being purchased at about this time, the solicitor who was involved wrote,

The old Deeds do not appear to contain even the names of the Farms ... and the Modern Deeds are equally defective ... are you possessed of any Maps or admeasurements? If not I do not see how the necessity for having a Plan or admeasurement prepared can be obviated, as it can hardly be expected that a future Purchaser ... would be satisfied with the general description inserted either in the Contract or the Mortgage. (Evans, 1977, 52)

The London Company of Drapers also used maps: in 1817, it found that,

the maps and surveys [of its estates in Ulster] of which the Company are in possession are not always to be relied upon for accuracy as to quantity; and that, since the last survey was made, much land, which was then in a state of mountain, and bringing but little profit, has been brought into a state of cultivation.

The Company recognized the necessity of surveying, mapping and valuing its Irish estate by 1818 so that arrangements could be drawn up with new tenants by 1819 (Curl, 1979, 25 and 32). In the following year, the Fishmongers' Company decided to resurvey its estates in Ulster, to standardize all measures, and to draw up plans before leases were renewed (Curl, 1981, 53–9).

Maps came to be drawn on the leases themselves, and therefore acquired a legal status. An early example is a map of the Rose Garden estate in Cambridge of Clare College, which was drawn on a lease of 1634.[42] In the early eighteenth century, a map on a lease was still rare, but could be useful under certain circumstances. When a lease of part of the Leveson-Gower estates at Lilleshall in Shropshire was renewed in 1725, a map was attached which showed the exact area of the farm. The map was necessary because the farm had been substantially enlarged since the last renewal, and was now laid out in a comparatively compact and orderly manner at the centre of the estate (Wordie, 1982, 163). Maps on leases were much more common in the early nineteenth century, partly because increasing numbers of maps were available on which these plans could be based. The advertisement by Charles Oakden in Plate 20, for example, says: 'Plans reduced to any scale, and inserted on Leases or Deeds, for Solicitors.' Amongst Cambridgeshire estate maps, plans were included on a lease of land at Landbeach in 1808, which belonged to Wort's Charity (LAB80801–2), on land at Fordham let by the Bishop of Ely in 1821 and 1826 (FOR82101–2 and FOR82601–1) and on land at Trumpington let by Martha Humphreys in 1829 (TRU82902). Maps were also used on other legal documents, such as deeds of exchange. For example, in 1801 John Tharp and the

Reverend Hill exchanged land between Chippenham and Snailwell parishes, and a map was included on the deed (CHP80101).

Development or improvement of an estate often resulted in maps being drawn. The Duchy of Lancaster commissioned many surveys in the second half of the sixteenth century as a useful preliminary to estate improvement; the Elizabethan map of Soham may have been drawn for such a reason (SOH55801; Somerville, 1953, 319). Another very early map, which was probably produced in the same decade, was of an estate at Calstock, Cornwall. Ravenhill (1984, 173) suggests that it was drawn as a result of structural changes on Sir Richard Edgcumbe's estate, especially the creation of a deer park. Mineral exploitation in late seventeenth-century Warwickshire led to the commissioning of estate maps; these maps were usually plain, as artistic embellishment was expensive and superfluous (Pannett, 1985, 70). The surveys which George Withiell carried out for the Luttrell family in Somerset at about the same time show a similar awareness of the use of maps as an aid to rural land management, the collection and fixing of rents, the valuation of the estate, the planning of improvements and thereby increasing the income from the land (Harley and Stuart, 1982, 48).

In Cambridgeshire, too, many examples can be given of maps drawn in connection with estate improvement. The Downing estates in Croydon, East Hatley and Tadlow, for instance, had a chequered history. It has already been shown how Sir George let the land fall into ruin in the early eighteenth century. When his heir, Sir Jacob Garrard Downing, inherited the estate in 1750, one of his first acts was to commission a 28-sheet atlas from Joseph Cole. Downing took a great pride in his land and slowly rehabilitated the estate. On his death in 1764, however, his widow challenged Sir George Downing's will which left the estate to found a college in Cambridge if there were no surviving heir. The dispute remained in chancery for many years and the property fell into disrepair once again. Downing College was eventually founded in 1800 and the land was surveyed shortly afterwards in 1802 and again in 1814 (French, 1978; Henderson, 1982, 22). The only maps which were drawn, however, were of the remains of Gamlingay Park; the house there had been demolished in 1776 (GAM80101 and GAM80301; RCHM, 1968, 110). The Crown, too, had problems with ill-managed estates; to try to improve revenues, G. A. Selwyn was asked in 1786 to present an account of all lands leased from the Crown, and he compiled a report and produced a map of land at Newmarket and Swaffham Bulbeck which was to be relet to the Duke of Rutland and Countess of Aylesford (NEA78601–2 and SWB78601; Madge, 1938, 279). The Corporation of the Sons of the Clergy, on the other hand, had taken an interest in its estates from earlier in the eighteenth century; then in 1809 and 1811 the Treasurer visited the land in Essex and Cambridgeshire, and maps were drawn in connection with these inspections (TYD81102–3, UPW81102–4, WEL81101, WSM81102–5 and WSP81101; Pearce, 1928, 121).

Specific improvements caused maps to be drawn. For example, a map of Chippenham was drawn in 1816 to accompany an estimate of the cost of repairing walls to the park, and in 1829 two maps were drawn to show the buildings which had been destroyed by fire at nearby Badlingham Hall (CHP81601; CHP82901–2). Similarly, William Hyde Laughton had a map drawn to assist in repairing his house in Snailwell in 1820 (SNA82001). Plans could also be associated with more wholesale rebuilding: a survey and map of an estate in mid-Argyll in

1792 were drawn to plan the reorganization of the farm's fields and buildings (Fairhurst, 1968, 185). Many maps were drawn in association with drainage schemes, though the majority of drainage maps cover larger areas than a single estate and so are not included here. A few estate maps, however, were connected with drainage. A map of the Duke of Bedford's estate at Thorney was drawn in about 1750 to show recommended changes in the distribution of drainage engines (THO75001), and in 1823, the Eau Brink Commissioners of Appeal ordered maps to be drawn of the land belonging to Francis, Henry and Isaac Ibberson and Isaac Sanders in Benwick, and to Henry Layton Blunt, Thomas Roslyn and John Waddelow in Whittlesey (BEN82301 and WHR82301).

Inclosure, however, was probably the most influential stimulus to estate map production in the early nineteenth century. It has already been shown in Chapter 3 how parliamentary inclosure was relatively late in Cambridgeshire, and reasons for this, such as agricultural conditions and the type of landowner and land tenure, were suggested. The major period of activity was between 1800 and 1826, when 45% of parishes were inclosed, and 86% of the maps which were drawn were of these parishes. About one-fifth of the maps which were drawn of Clare College's estates in Cambridgeshire were to show land allotted on inclosure, for example, and the 1806 inclosure award for Impington was used to draw maps to show the allotments to Christ's College, Uriah Taylor, the Dean and Chapter of Ely, William Collin and Elizabeth Drage (IMP80601–5). As a result of inclosure, much land was exchanged, and so more maps were drawn. The Reverend Thomas Briggs and John Spring exchanged land on the inclosure of Little Gransden in 1822 (LLG82201), and in 1827 a map was drawn to show land exchanged between the Earl of Hardwicke and New College, Oxford, after inclosure of Steeple Morden (STM82701). Landowners in Warwickshire, too, commissioned maps of their newly inclosed estates or had copies drawn of the award map (Pannett, 1985, 78).

The production of estate maps resulted from a multitude of other factors. In 1813, Joseph Beevers mapped the land of St Thomas' Hospital in Cherry Hinton, Comberton and Fulbourn for fire insurance purposes (CHE81301, COM81301 and FUL81301), and land belonging to Storey's Charity in Impington was mapped in about 1828 for the same reason (IMP82801). In 1825, Queens' College was asked for a sketch of the College buildings by the Guardian Assurance Office: 'I am to suggest that the sketch with which you favored the Office, not being sufficiently distinctive of the Communications in the Buildings, it will be essentially useful to that end, if you will have the goodness to request your Surveyor to supply a Compleat Ground Plan exhibiting the same.'[43] Bankruptcy proceedings also led to estate maps being drawn. In 1825, John Sculthorpe of Elm was declared bankrupt, and the map of his estate at Elm was probably drawn at this time (ELM82501).[44]

Landowners, therefore, became increasingly interested in the management and development of their estates. They became aware of recommended practices, they visited the land themselves and they employed professional agents to supervise the daily running of the farms. Maps were one of the growing number of documents which were produced to help in estate management, and they were most frequently drawn when land changed hands, to settle boundary disputes, for legal reasons and to help in improvements on the estate. Chapter 3 showed that some of these maps were very plain as there was no need for elaborate ornamentation. Others, however, were more decorative, and the production of such maps must have been influenced by additional factors.

ESTATE MAPS AS STATUS SYMBOLS

For the upper classes, land was of central importance, and owners used it to show their social standing and authority. This use of property was carried out in a number of ways. Trees, for example, confirmed the power of property: the pattern of their planting affected the impression which a parkland gave, and strict settlement often protected them as part of an estate's capital (Daniels, 1988, 44–5). Paintings of estates enabled an owner to demonstrate the extent of his land and his position as a pillar of a stable community in which little changed. Thus, peaceful rural and sporting scenes were common, and new agricultural developments were not included (Coombs, 1978, 14; Cosgrove, 1984, 233; Prince, 1988). Maps could be used in similar ways: enlarged drawings of manor houses helped an owner to stress his authority and legal power in a rural community and coats of arms expressed his right to land and to the social rank of an aristocrat (Harley, 1983, 37). This book was introduced by the example of the maps of the Chippenham estate of the Earl of Orford; Cheveley provides another illustration of this point. The estate was painted by Jan Siberechts in 1681 when it was owned by the Jermyn family and was frequently visited by the royal family when they were staying at Newmarket Palace, and the picture shows sporting scenes (Harris, 1979, 71; Hore, 1899, 26). The 6th Duke of Somerset bought the estate in the early eighteenth century, and in 1750 it passed to John Manners, Marquis of Granby on his marriage to Lady Frances Seymour, Somerset's daughter, on 3 September (*PB*, 2,328). Manners took an interest in the turf and hunting (Manners, 1899, 408), and his son Charles (the future 4th Duke of Rutland) had his Cheveley estate mapped by Thomas Warren in 1775 (CHG77501). The map shows the 'Kings Chair', an ornamental seat for watching horse-racing (Bodger, 1787).

In some cases, owners went to great lengths to have ornamental maps produced and had decoration pasted on, such as the border to a map of Aspley Guise in Bedfordshire. The map was drawn in about 1745, the border is probably of a seventeenth-century Flemish engraving, and inset on the map is a drawing of the manor house and farmyard with an eighteenth-century Flemish border attached (Fowler, 1928, 21). George King's map of land in Essex belonging to the Charterhouse in 1613 is drawn on a printed proforma.[45] Similarly, Sir George William Leeds' map of Croxton in 1823 has the scale, compasses and some of the lettering pasted on (CRX82301), and the map of land at Whittlesey belonging to Christ's Hospital in 1683/4 uses a pre-printed coat of arms (WHR68401).

Surveying texts gradually became more explicit about the ways in which estate maps should be decorated. Folkingham, in 1610, was one of the first authors to mention including a coat of arms (p.58): 'Under this Title may also be rainged the Lordes~Coate with Crest and Mantells.' In 1653, Leybourn gave more detailed instruction on:

177

How to draw a perfect draught of a whole Mannor, and to furnish it with all necessary varieties, also to trick and beautifie the same: in which, (as in a Map) the Lord of the Mannor may at any time (by inspection only) see the symetry, scituation and content of any parcell of his Land. (p.274)

He described the topographical information which should be shown, how it should be coloured and how to draw the compass rose and scale. Then,

draw the Coat of Arms belonging to the Lord of the Mannor, with Mantle, Helme, Crest, and Supporters; or in a Compartment, but be sure you blazon the Coat in its true Colours. These things being well performed, your plot will be a neat Ornament for the Lord of the Mannor to hang in his Study, or other private place, so that at pleasure he may see his Land before him, and the quantity of all or every parcell thereof without any further trouble. (Leybourn, 1653, 274–5)

Plate 26 shows Leybourn's exemplar of an estate map, with its heraldry, title cartouche, scale surmounted by dividers, compass rose, church and perspective view of the manor house. In 1678, Holwell (p.154) gave a similar recommendation; by the eighteenth century, Wyld was suggesting that a vignette of the manor house should be placed in the border of the map:

But if you would express a Gentleman's Seat, or Manor~house, 'tis best done in some Corner of the Draught, or in a Plan by itself, annexed to that of the Estate to which it belongs. And the House must be drawn in Perspective (as you will be shewed hereafter) and if the Gardens, Walks and Avenues to the House are expressed, it must be in the same Manner; and where there are Trees, they must be shadowed on the light side.
    If you will take the Pains, you may, in one of the upper Corners of the Plan, draw the Mansion~House, &c. in the other the Lord's Coat of Arms, with Mantle, Helm, Crest, and Supporters, or in a Compartment, blazoning the Coat in its true Colours: In one of the Corners at the Bottom, you may describe a Circle, with the 32 Points of the Mariners Compass, according to the Situation of the Ground, with a Flower~de~luce at the North Part thereof, always allowing for the Variation of the Needle: And, in the other Corner, make a Scale equal to that by which the Plot was laid down, adorning it with Compasses, Squares, Ovals, &c. (1764, 133)

Burns, in 1771, stressed the importance of showing the owner's house at the edge of the map (p.215):

Return the Ground Plot (only) of all Edifices, Buildings, &c. except you have Orders to shew the Elevation of some beautiful Edifice, such as the Manor House, Hall, &c. which should not appear in the identical Place where the same stands, but in some vacant Corner or Place of the Map laid down from as large a Scale as that Vacancy will admit of; for if erected, or drawn upon the Foundation or Ground Plot, according to its real Size, that is to say, projected from the same Scale, the Beauty of the Edifice will be rendered thereby almost inconspicuous; and if it be drawn or laid down (where its real Foundation is) from a larger Scale, the adjoining Gardens, Folds, Closes, &c. will consequently be concealed or covered thereby, which induce me to recommend Vacancies to represent the Elevation of Buildings in.

He then proceeded to describe the information which a map should contain, and how the plan should be coloured. Then he gave instructions on how to add the coat of arms, and finally he reiterated Leybourn's statement about how the map will be used:

in the Map, make Choice of a Compartment, or Vacancy therein, at the Top, if possible, to draw the Coat of Arms belonging to the Gentleman that owns the Estate, with Shield, Crest, and Supporters; the Shield should be drawn so that it may contain the Title, Township, and Country, or any thing else that is proper to denote the Situation thereof ...
    Now, if the whole be well performed, the Map will be a neat Ornament to hang up in the Owner's Study, or wherever else he shall chuse, so that at Pleasure he may see his whole Estate in his Chamber, and likewise

Maps as status symbols

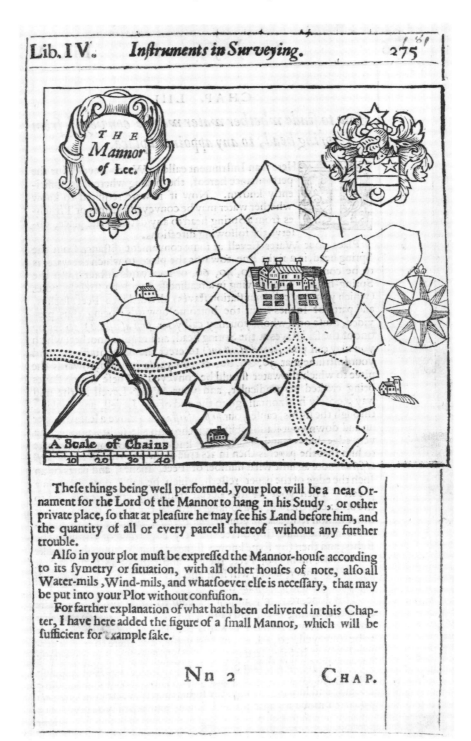

These things being well performed, your plot will be a neat Ornament for the Lord of the Mannor to hang in his Study, or other private place, so that at pleaſure he may ſee his Land before him, and the quantity of all or every parcell thereof without any further trouble.

Alſo in your plot muſt be expreſſed the Mannor-houſe according to its ſymetry or ſituation, with all other houſes of note, alſo all Water-mils, Wind-mils, and whatſoever elſe is neceſſary, that may be put into your Plot without confuſion.

For farther explanation of what hath been delivered in this Chapter, I have here added the figure of a ſmall Mannor, which will be ſufficient for example ſake.

Nn 2   CHAP.

Plate 26. Exemplar of an estate map (Leybourn, *Compleat Surveyor*, 1653, 275).

the particular Quantity of each and every Inclosure therein, without any Manner of Trouble, but rather a Pleasure. (Burns, 1771, 240–1)

Authors of surveying texts were therefore aware that estate maps should be attractive objects; early works were less concerned with this aspect of a map, but later writers devoted more space to it and included exemplars of finished maps.

Maps which were to be hung on walls or placed on library shelves were often the most ornamented; indeed, Welu (1987, 160) has shown that sixteenth-century Dutch wall maps had some of the most elaborate cartouches. The surveying texts imply that decorative estate maps were rarely hung in estate offices and so were not used for day-to-day estate management. Sir John Griffin Griffin of Audley End in Essex (1719–97), for instance, kept in his dressing room the map which was made to show the prospects and possibilities for rounding out his property (Clay, 1985, 181). The eighteenth-century maps of Rampton and Wicken in Cambridgeshire (RAM75401 and WIC77001) are still on the rollers which were used to hang them up, and the practice of keeping estate maps in the house continued into the nineteenth century. For example, in 1991 the map of the Reverend Dr William Foster's estates in Abington Pigotts, Litlington and Steeple Morden which was drawn in 1804 was still hanging in a bookcase specially adapted for it in the early nineteenth century (ABI80401; see Plate 27), opposite another bookcase altered so that the map of Cambridgeshire by R. G. Baker (1821) could hang from it. Owners often had volumes in their library bound in fine bindings, and volumes of estate maps could be similarly bound. Crichel House is one of Dorset's great eighteenth-century mansions and it was inherited by Humphry Sturt in 1765 (Delderfield, 1970, 57). In that year, he employed Isaac Taylor to survey and map his estates. To the resulting atlas were added maps of Sturt's estates in Cambridgeshire (DOD77001–2 and WMB77001), Essex and Middlesex, and the whole was splendidly bound in red morocco leather with gold tooling. In the mid-1770s, Sturt enlarged the house so that it 'has the appearance of a mansion of a prince more than that of a country gentleman', including a new library; he also landscaped the park and removed the village to form a New Town in nearby Witchampton (Hutchins, 3, 1868, 127; RCHM, 1975, 41–4, Tipping, 1925, 774). The estate atlas must have been a fitting volume for such a seat.

In the century from about 1550 to 1650, persons of royal, noble or gentle birth became interested in emblematic devices. Emblematic title-pages to books began to appear, and the reader could be edified by the message which it conveyed, he could savour the erudition and enjoy the allusions and the means of presentation. The symbolism was closely related to the contents of the book (Corbett and Lightbown, 1979, 35), and the title-page to Rathborne's *The Svrveyor* of 1616 was discussed in Chapter 5. Emblematic devices have been identified on estate maps. A map of Ticehurst and Etchingham in Sussex in 1612 by William Gier has a cartouche with a *putto* leaning on a skull and blowing bubbles towards a flaming urn and a winged hour glass. Marchant (1986) has traced this motif to a Flemish engraving of 1594; the skull was a common *memento mori* as was the *putto* with the hour glass, the smoking urn and bubble-blowing were symbols for the brevity of life. The design was placed on a cartouche to a bird's-eye view of the manor house. It is possible that Gier was presenting the pride and joy of the owner in his manor and gardens and simultaneously drawing attention to the

Plate 27.   Estate map of Abington Pigotts, Litlington and Steeple Morden drawn by H. I. Fox
for Reverend Dr William Foster, 1804, in a bookcase specially adapted for it in the early
nineteenth century.

transience and futility of earthly possessions. The 1650 map of Boxworth has an emblematic device (BOX65001; see Plate 3). It can be described and interpreted as follows (H. Marchant, personal communication). Above the title cartouche is the motto 'Honi soit qui mal y pense' (Shamed be he who thinks evil of it), and over the motto is a closed pair of gates, surmounted by a ship with three masts, each in the form of a cross. Each mast carries a pennant resembling an animal head, with a single eye in the middle of each. Below the title is a second motto 'Prudentis est in consilio fortunam semper alabere' (The prudent one in his plans always assists Fortune). The single eye was an Egyptian symbol for divinity, the ship may have been a symbol for the Church, the gates may have been those to Lady Cutts' estate. The emblem and mottoes together, therefore, read as a wish to ward off ill-will towards the property and to protect it, by ensuring that it is under God's all-seeing eye. The rest of this map is also decorative, with trees and deer on the boundaries to the estate. However this emblem is interpreted, it demonstrates that owners could show their standing by an awareness of contemporary interests in symbolism.

The right to heraldic devices symbolized the right to possess land (Clarke, 1988, 457). The last part of Henry Peacham's *The Gentlemans Exercise* of 1612 was: 'a Discourse tending to the Blazon of Armes, with a more Philosophicall and particular examination of the causes of Colours and their participation, with the light, according to the Opinions as well of Ancient as later Writers' (p.129). It has been shown in Chapter 3 how coats of arms were included on many Cambridgeshire estate maps, especially those which were drawn for private owners in the early eighteenth century. One of the clearest examples of the use of estate maps and heraldry to display social standing and authority is the 1754 map of John Leman's estate at Rampton (RAM75401). In 1753, Lucy Alie, a member of the Leman family, died and left her estates in Cambridgeshire, Hertfordshire, Huntingdonshire and Middlesex to her estate steward, John Granger, on condition that he took the name and arms of Leman (Correct, Brief and Interesting Account, 1840; *VCH Hertfordshire*, 2, 359). He did so by Act of Parliament (27 George II Cap. 1), and in 1754 his estate at Rampton was mapped by Henry Fensham. The map is very colourful, it has a decorative title cartouche (Plate 9) and Plate 28 shows the new owner's coat of arms and crest. The pomegranates are the Granger arms, and the dolphin, owls and crest of a pelican in his piety are of the Leman family. Thus, this map helped to stress Leman's rights to land and to an elevated social rank. His main seat was at Warboys in Huntingdonshire, and he merited a monument in the parish church on his death in 1781 (see Plate 29). The map of Rampton contrasts with a map of Warboys which was made in the following year to divide land between John Leman and two descendants of the ancient Leman family, Elizabeth and John Newnham. This map was drawn for a practical purpose, and so although it is attractive and has a decorative title cartouche, it is not as lavishly ornamented as the Rampton map and has no coat of arms.[46] The 1659 map of Badlingham Hall in Chippenham similarly shows the owner's control over the land. It was drawn shortly after John Clarke acquired the estate in 1657;[47] an enlarged drawing of the manor house with a milkmaid in the foreground demonstrates his authority over his tenants (see Plate 17a), and the Lord is on the heath surveying his estate and showing his control over it (see Plate 30). Interpretation of the coat of arms on the map, however, is less straightforward. The title to the map is very rubbed, but the date is clear and John Clarke has been confirmed as the

Plate 28. John Leman's coat of arms on the estate map of Rampton drawn by Henry Fensham, 1754.

Plate 29. The monument to John Leman in Warboys Church, Huntingdonshire.

Plate 30. John Clarke looking over his estate at Badlingham Hall, Chippenham, on the estate map drawn by William Covell, 1659.

owner. The College of Arms has been unable to identify the coat, so it seems as if Clarke made an unofficial assumption of the heraldic device, in order to elevate his status and to stress his rank among his peers (T. Woodcock, Somerset Herald, personal communication). Heraldry still conveyed power at the end of the eighteenth century: Humphry Repton suggested in 1791 that milestones with the owner's coat should be placed on the approach road to Tatton Park in Cheshire to convey the greatness of his property (Clemenson, 1982, 77). By the early nineteenth century, however, coats of arms were less frequently used status symbols. In 1812, Ainslie described how to embellish a plan, but he did not mention adding a coat of arms (p.248):

When a land~surveyor has finished a plan of a nobleman or gentleman's estate, in as elegant a style of drawing as he is capable of, if the scale he has adopted is large, he will upon his plan have several blank corners; one of which should be filled up with a neat wrote title, another with a table of contents; he should also, on any convenient place, insert a scale, and on another blank space a compass; and if there is any other blank corner remaining, it may be filled up with a view of the mansion~house ... or an old ruin of a castle, or any particular building, if there are any on the property ... If neatly drawn, and like the building, it is a fine embellishment to a plan.

On paintings, too, coats of arms became less common. John Sell Cotman (1782–1842) was regarded as old-fashioned in working for personal friends and patrons and inserting a patron's coat of arms into a drawing (Clarke, 1981, 134).

Some institutional owners also commissioned decorative maps. The atlas of Queens' College's estates, which has already been referred to, was requested from Alexander Watford on 12 January 1822.[48] The copy for the Master or President had a decorative title-page and the College's arms facing it, and there was an inferior paper copy for the Bursar.[49] Although, as has been seen, the atlas was very expensive and its existence may have caused Trinity College to consider commissioning a similar work in 1826,[50] the atlas was probably produced more for domestic appreciation and less for ostentatious display. In any case, such an atlas was an exception, and most institutional owners commissioned maps for more immediately practical purposes.

It is therefore clear that, especially for private owners, estate maps were more than working documents. They could be highly decorated, and, as one of the forms of display which were available to owners, ornamented estate maps were used to enhance an owner's standing in contemporary society.

THE SURVEYORS EMPLOYED

For whatever reason an estate map was commissioned, a surveyor had to be engaged to produce it. The relationship between a surveyor and his employer was discussed in some detail in Chapter 4; this section examines their interaction from the landowner's point of view.

Although landowners often employed men who were local to the area, or at least who had worked for them elsewhere, this was not necessarily the case. In late seventeenth-century

Ireland, for example, Lord Kerry sought a surveyor for his estates in Kerry. While he was in Dublin, he engaged Henry Pratt who practised in the city. As the survey was expected to last two months, the cost of travel from Dublin would have been a small additional price to pay for metropolitan standards of professionalism (Andrews, 1980a, 6).

In Cambridgeshire, however, private landowners tended to employ men from the Cambridge region to map their Cambridgeshire estates, and they increasingly engaged men from within the county. None of the Cambridgeshire owners were therefore patrons of just one surveyor at a time. Thus, in the years until 1639, 9% of private owners employed Cambridgeshire men, whereas between 1820 and 1836 the proportion rose to 53%. In some cases, men were employed who worked near an estate of a landowner in another part of the country. For example, Ferdinand Parys, who had an estate at Pudding Norton in Norfolk, employed Thomas Waterman of Great Ryburgh, a nearby parish, to survey his Linton estate in 1600 (LIN60007; *VCH*, 6, 85; Eden W135). Humphry Sturt employed Isaac Taylor of Ross, Herefordshire, who had just completed a map of Dorset (Rodger, 1972, 5), to survey his estates in Dorset, Devon and Wiltshire in 1765, and sent him to map his Cambridgeshire estates in 1770 (DOD77001–2 and WMB77001). Sir Thomas Spencer Wilson employed John Storer of Halstead in Essex to map his Litlington estate in 1782 (LIT78201–7), and his land at Hatfield Broad Oak and White Roothing in Essex in 1782 and 1784 respectively (Emmison, 1964). Edward Roger Pratt's estate at Cottenham was mapped in 1802 by John Burcham of Holt, Norfolk (COU80201), and Pratt's seat was at Ryston Hall near Downham Market (Eden B708; Venn, II, 5, 182). Similarly, James Thomas Martin of Overbury Park, Worcestershire, employed William Womack of Claines near Worcester to map his land at Stow cum Quy in 1827 (STO82701; *LG*, 1,719); William Wilshere of The Frythe, Hertford, employed John Willding of Willian to map his land at Foxton for an atlas of his estates in 1830 (FOX83002; Foster, II, 4, 1,580); and James Drage Merest and the surveyor who mapped his land in Soham in 1833, John Croft, both lived in Bury St Edmunds (SOH83301; Venn, II, 4, 393). The question remains, however, of why John Fleming, who had land in Cambridgeshire and Hampshire, employed George Salmon of Warwickshire to map Stetchworth in 1770 (STN77001; Eden S10; *VCH*, 6, 172). Occasionally the surveyor lived in the same parish as the landowner's estate: John Chester Pern's land at West Wratting was mapped in 1809 by a local, Thomas Norfolk (WEW80901).[51] Likewise, Henry Tasker, Vicar of Soham, employed William Warren of the same parish in 1832 (SOH83201; Eden W126; Venn, II, 6, 112).

The Dukes of Bedford employed 72 surveyors in the years between the early seventeenth century and 1836; 89% of these men worked for the Duke in only one county, and only John Davis and Humphry Smith worked in as many as three counties. Sixty-four per cent of the surveyors drew maps; 32 men drew only one map for the Duke, and eight drew more than five maps each. Thomas Evans was the most prolific: he drew 33 maps of the 5th and 6th Dukes' Bedfordshire estates between 1795 and 1827; this figure includes two sets of 19 plans of woodland.[52] Professional surveyors such as Benjamin Hare, Vincent and Tycho Wing and John Halsey were employed to map the Bedford estate at Thorney in Cambridgeshire. Local men were also involved in survey work, such as Alexander Hughes, clerk to John Wing,[53] in 1756 (THO75601–3); a tenant, Thomas Bellamy, in 1786;[54] and the schoolmasters Edward Lancaster in 1749, 1751 and 1753,[55] Walter Maitland in 1754[56] and William Fininley in 1782.[57]

Institutional owners employed similar numbers of surveyors to the Dukes of Bedford from the sixteenth to early nineteenth centuries. In the Cambridge colleges, for example, over the whole period, Queens' College employed 48 surveyors, Emmanuel College employed 50 and Clare and Jesus colleges both employed 61. St John's College, however, a larger institution, employed 133. As with private owners, institutions also tended to employ men who lived near their estates, though some of their surveyors travelled long distances. Gonville and Caius College, for example, may have employed John Crippen of Canterbury, Kent, to survey its estates in Essex in 1731 because in the previous year the Master, Thomas Gooch, had become a Canon at Canterbury Cathedral (Mason, 1990, 38). Overall, over 80% of the surveyors who were employed by Emmanuel and Queens' colleges lived in the locality of the estate to be mapped, the proportion of local surveyors who worked for Jesus College was 79% and for St John's College 74%. Only for Clare College were local men relatively unimportant, though the proportion was still 59%. For all of the colleges, fewest local men were employed in the late eighteenth and early nineteenth centuries, between about 1780 and 1820; they became more predominant again thereafter. Most of these local men were only employed by a college on one occasion: the lowest proportion was for Clare College, for whom three-quarters of the local surveyors were only employed once; the maximum proportion was 83% for Jesus and Queens' colleges. Conversely, however, most of the surveyors who travelled for colleges outside Cambridgeshire and its neighbouring counties were employed by them for a number of years, frequently over five. Fewer than half of the surveyors who were employed by colleges drew maps for them: St John's and Queens' colleges engaged the highest proportion of map-makers (50% and 45% respectively); 22% of the surveyors employed by Emmanuel College drew maps, 18% of those employed by Jesus College and only 15% of those employed by Clare College. Most of the surveyors were employed to carry out valuations and surveys; they also managed woods, collected rents, supervised repairs, were bailiffs of estates and found suitable tenants.

To a large extent, colleges all employed the same men, and they tended to have one main surveyor and map-maker at any one time. Clare College, for example, employed Simeon King between 1783 and 1788, Joseph Freeman from 1790 to 1798, Joseph Truslove from 1800 to 1806, William Custance from 1807 to 1816, Edward Gibbons from 1808 to 1820 and Alexander Watford junior from 1817 to 1843. Similar progressions are found in the other colleges: at Emmanuel, Joseph Freeman was employed between 1773 and 1797, then the elder Alexander Watford took over from 1798 to 1801, and he was superseded by William Custance from 1802 to 1820. Joseph Freeman worked for Queens' College between 1768 and 1787, the elder Alexander Watford was employed between 1792 and 1801, then Joseph Truslove worked for the College from 1801 to 1816 and finally the younger Alexander Watford was the main surveyor until 1839 (he first worked for the College in 1801, but he did not carry out much work before 1821). Jesus and St John's colleges both employed John Smith in the mid-eighteenth century: Jesus College employed him in 1766 and 1767, and then engaged Joseph Freeman from 1770 to 1796. The elder Alexander Watford, Joseph Truslove and the younger Alexander Watford followed him. St John's College employed John Smith for longer, between 1760 and 1776; Joseph Freeman was employed between 1770 and 1798, and Simeon King was also employed on many occasions at this time. The elder Alexander Watford worked for the College between 1792 and 1801, Joseph Truslove was employed between 1797 and 1816 and the younger Alexander Watford from 1806 to 1812. The amount each college paid each surveyor varied greatly. Joseph Freeman earned at least £1,445 16s 8d from St John's College, £469 18s 9d from Clare College, and only £130 3s 6d, £772 19s 11d and £52 2s 0d from Queens', Emmanuel and Jesus colleges respectively. The elder Alexander Watford earned £2,005 3s 8d from St John's College, the highest sum paid to any surveyor by any of the colleges studied here. Queens' College paid him £555 17s 11½d, Emmanuel paid him £221 9s 4d and Jesus only spent £48 12s 2d on his services. His son's main collegiate employer was Queens' College, who paid him £1,885 6s 6d. Clare College also employed Alexander Watford junior on several occasions and paid him £483 19s 9½d; he only earned, however, £133 4s 2½d and £125 8s 1d from Jesus and St John's colleges in turn. Colleges, therefore, tended to employ a few surveyors to carry out most of their work, and they were helped by many surveyors from the locality of their estates.

It is rare to find examples of instructions from employers to their surveyors, and often a surveyor can only have been given general directions. A few surviving sets, however, suggest that, in some cases at least, a surveyor was given very precise and detailed instructions. For example, the Scottish Earl of Hopetoun had his estates surveyed in 1746; he gave his surveyor, James Jamieson, very detailed instructions, which suggests both that Jamieson was not a skilled professional surveyor and that Hopetoun was familiar with methods of estate survey (Adams, 1971, 7). Later in the century in Essex, a letter from George de Horne to his surveyor Samuel Hervey in 1771 says:

The surveyor is desired drawing out the map in the table casting up the number of acres to make two columns at the top of which putting their proper titles. One the contents of the land belonging to each field, the other the contents of the improvable arable land exclusive of the fences ponds etc. To get the proper and most usual name of every field of the tenant and sett down the names to note which part of the land or part of a field is copyhold and how much. Colour all the parishes all different so that by a view of the mapp may be seen in what parish each is in or if any lies in two the exact bounds of each parish.

I would not choose to have the map on a large scale but as compact as the accuracy of delineating every curve in the hedge rows and roads and giving the exact and true form of each field will admit – and in each hedge row or anywhere else if any to note the timbers or trees like for timber therein and I hope that it will be done not only in a very accurate but a neat manner. (Mason, 1990, 10–11)

In 1803, John Blackadder received a specification for plans of North Uist and Skye in the Hebrides:

On your plans, you will mark all the High Roads, the course of Rivers and Burns and you will shade and represent the Hills, and to a nearness mark their height, and distinguish the Grounds into Arable, infield, outfield, green pasture, hill pasture, moor, moss and woodlands, but you need not take notice of Patches or pieces less than an acre. You will show the farms and grazings as they are occupied at present, and the Marches [boundaries] as they ought to be on a new and better arrangement, and generally mark such things as are usually marked on the plan of an estate ... (Caird, 1989, 62)

All landowners, therefore, employed surveyors to do more than make maps for them. Many local men were engaged on a few occasions; large institutional owners, such as the Cambridge colleges, tended to be more influential patrons than private owners who had land in Cambridgeshire.

CONCLUSION

From the Dissolution to the Tithe Commutation Act, therefore, English landowners became increasingly aware of the importance of land, both as a source of income and as a status symbol, and of developments in science and cartography. These two features combined to encourage the production of estate maps. Landownership in Cambridgeshire was distinctive: there were relatively few large landed estates, and institutional owners were unusually prevalent. This affected the type of estate map which was produced. Both types of owner took a growing interest in their land and commissioned maps for a wide variety of practical purposes, especially when land changed hands, to settle disputes, when land was to be let and to assist with development of an estate. At the same time, estate maps were sometimes very elaborately decorated, and, for private owners in particular, they were used as symbols of power and social standing. Both types of owner had similar relationships with their estate surveyors, and the discussions in this and the previous chapter show clearly how the interaction between them contributed to the spread of map-making in early modern England.

ESTATE MAP DESCRIPTION FORM

County   **Parish**   **Reference**

Title

Surveyor

Scale
    As on map
    Representative fraction
Date On map/external evidence/estimate
Size Within frame/ whole sheet/drawing
    Vertical (in.)   Horizontal (in.)
Orientation
Manuscript/copy/lithograph/engraving/photograph/photocopy/printed/
tracing/
Material Parchment/paper/
    Coloured/black and white

Extent Grid ref.   Farm/church/
    Total area   Given/estimated

Features
    Names farm/field/owners/tenants/neighbours/roads/features/
    Buildings plan/perspective

    Fields open/clcsed/all strips/owner's strips
    Common meadow waste heath fen wood trees:
    State of cultivation colour/shading/words
    Acreages dimensions responsibility for boundaries hedges fences
    Road footpath gate stile milestone turnpike verge
    Watercourse direction of flow pond bridge
    Park garden orchard yard cross fishpond earthwork moat

Decoration
    Border
    Title cartouche   Location
    Scale   Location
    Compass points/rose   No. points   Location
    Table tenants/field names/acreages/land use/   Location
    Figures animal/human   Location
    Heraldry   Location
    Colours:

Terrier On map/accompanying/missing

Notes on map

Notes

CARTO-BIBLIOGRAPHY OF CAMBRIDGESHIRE ESTATE MAPS
temp. ELIZABETH I – 1836

FORM OF THE CARTO-BIBLIOGRAPHY

Arrangement

Parish, Date, Map code, Location

Parish. The entries are arranged alphabetically by parish, and in chronological order within the parishes. Maps of a parish of uncertain date are listed before dated maps. Each map which was drawn on a separate sheet has been treated as a separate map unless the sheets interlock to make up a whole map. If a series of maps has been split, cross-references are given to locate the companions to any one sheet.

Date. The range of dates over which a map was drawn is stated: e.g. 1780–1. In all cases, the year has been taken as beginning on 1 January; for maps which were drawn before 1752 and between 1 January and 24 March, the two dates are separated by a slash: e.g. 1601/2. Dates are transcribed as they appear on the map. If there is no date and it is stated in accompanying documents, it is given in square brackets. If the date has been estimated from information on the map, the names of neighbouring owners, the style of the map, documentary evidence, or is suggested in a repository's catalogue with no evidence for its deduction, it is given as *circa* in square brackets. Dates which have been estimated from the names of neighbouring owners must be used with great caution, as these people may not in fact have been the current owners of adjacent land when a map was drawn.

Map code. Each map is identified by a code, for example BAB78502. See pp.xxi–xxiv for further details.

Location. Abbreviations of repositories are given on pp.xix–xx.

Physical description

Title. The title is copied exactly from the map, using the conventions of transcription which have been set out above. If there is no title, a description of the map is given in square brackets. Any omissions are indicated by '...'

Statements of responsibility. Persons responsible for the production of the map are named, and their full names are given if possible. Surveyors are named first, then other persons in alphabetical order of their role (e.g. draughtsman, lithographer, printer). Names are given in square brackets when they are not stated on the map.

Scale. First, the representative fraction is given from any statement of the scale in the title. Second, the scale is given as it appears on the map: 'scale bar 1–0–10 chains (= 3 in.)' indicates a scale bar extending from one chain on the left side of zero to ten chains on the right side, the whole measuring three inches. Measurements are made to the nearest $\frac{1}{16}$ in. Finally, the scale is given as a representative fraction, to four significant figures, from the scale bar or other separate scale statement. If the scale is only stated in words, the representative fraction is given to five significant figures. If only one representative fraction is given and there are two or more statements of the scale, the fraction applies to them all. Measurements are statutory unless stated otherwise. If there is no statement of the scale, an estimate has been made by comparing measurements between significant features on the map with the measurements on the 1:10,560 Ordnance Survey map, and is stated as a representative fraction to three significant figures.

Size. Measurements are made to the nearest $\frac{1}{16}$ in., and are stated as vertical x horizontal.
(i)   measured within the border of the map,
(ii)   size of the whole sheet,
(iii)   size of the drawing.

Orientation. Real orientation of the top of the map is given; if the compass is incorrectly placed, this is indicated in a note.

Material. For manuscript maps:
(i)   indicates a map based directly on an original survey,
(ii)   indicates a copy of a primary map with unrevised topographical content,
(iii)   indicates a copy with revised topographical content; date of copy is stated,
(iv)   indicates a map copied from a base map to show different landownership; date of copy is stated.
   These conventions follow those devised by Hodson (1978).

For other maps, it is stated whether it is printed, a lithograph, a photograph, a photocopy or a photostat; the material of the map is noted ('parchment' is used in its general term describing animal skin); and whether the map is coloured or black and white.

Geographical information

Extent. The grid reference of the owner's house or some other notable feature is given, followed by a description of the area in words. Estimated acreages are given to the nearest acre (to two significant figures), preceded by *circa*.

Geographical content. Types of name on the map are given (furlong names are not mentioned), types of buildings and their present names, and features. Boundaries are not mentioned except for parish and county boundaries when a map shows land on both sides of such a boundary.

Decorative information

Type of border, location of title with a brief description of its cartouche, position of the scale on the map, and means of showing orientation with its location are all noted. Tables and their contents, heraldic devices, decoration of the map with vignettes, human figures and animals, and other devices are described. The use of colour is also mentioned.

Notes

Notes on the map are transcribed. The presence is mentioned of accompanying documents, or of suggestions that they once existed. Copies of the map are described, and the location is given of photographic reproductions. Evidence is cited for suggesting a date, title, surveyor or owner if any is not stated on the map.

For bibliographical references, see the Bibliography. Abbreviated references to the Bibliography are given on pp.xix–xx.

CAMBRIDGESHIRE ESTATE MAPS
temp. Elizabeth I – 1836

A

Abington Pigotts – 1804 – ABI80401 – PRI
A Plan of Estates in the County of Cambridge the Property of The Revd Dr William Foster Situate in the Parishes of Abington Littlington & Steeple Morden Comprising the whole of the Parish of Abington with the Manor of Ovesdale and Berry Farm within the Parishes of Littlington and Steeple Mordon. Surveyed by H.I. Fox 1804.
Surveyor: H.I. Fox; **Scale bar** 1–0–10 chains (= 2 3/4in.), 1:3,168; **Size:** (i) 87 x 47 7/8in.; **Top** is NE; Manuscript(i), parchment, coloured.
Manor Farm, TL304447, and 1,405a.1r.35p. in Abington Pigotts, Litlington and Steeple Morden parishes bounded by Hertfordshire in S, Shingay Parish in N, Bassingbourn Parish in E and Guilden Morden Parish in W.
Names of fields and roads. Buildings shown in plan form and include The Bury, Tythe, Malting and Church farms, Down Hall, cottages, mill house and tower mill. Open fields showing all strips; closes; wood, trees and avenue of trees; waste and rough ground; meadow, common and pasture; roads and watercourses; garden and its layout; orchard; clunch and clay pits; gates; fences and hedges; ponds; bridges; moats; boundary between Abington Pigotts and Litlington parishes.
Border of 1 broad band with 1 narrow band on inside; title top left in a cartouche of decorative line-work; scale beneath title; compass middle right showing 32 points. Grass and trees coloured green, buildings coloured red, water coloured blue, fields coloured blue, orange, yellow, red and purple.
Note along road from Royston to Baldock: 'Boundary of the Parish of Littlington as Perambulated by the Parishoners of the adjacent Parish of Tharfield'. Accompanying terriers give acreages of arable, meadow, wood and cottages: 'A Terrier of the Parish of Abington', and, 'A Terrier of the Parish of Littlington And Lands Belonging to the Berry Farm within the Parish of Steeple Morden'. Copy of map, signed 'Richard Allerton deli*neavi*t', measures 13 3/4 x 22 1/4in., is at 1:13,450 and has top as ESE. Title centre top in a rococo cartouche with a lion, compass top right showing 8 points. Arable coloured in brown stripes, owner's strips coloured red. Buildings in Litlington village not shown. Bottom left: 'Note. The different tints in the Parish of Abington, shew the separate farms, as now held by Messrs Dickerson. North. Flitten. Thurley and Pearman The Nos 1.2.3 & 4 in North's farm are in the Parish of Little Morden The Nos 74 & 75 called New Ditch and at present attatched to the farm of Down Hall. are in the Parish of Littlington'. Centre bottom: 'Note. In the Parish of Littlington, the three great Divisions or Fields, are also distinguished by a separate tint That the Lands distinguished by the letters D.E.F.G.K.L M are half year or Lammas grounds That, these distinguished by the letters H.Q.R.S T belonging to the Berry Farm are in the Parish of Great Morden'. Richard Allerton practised between 1817 and 1845 [Eden A86]. Reduced positive photostats of original map at BL 1640.(29), CUL Maps.aa.53(1).92.1–2 and

CRO TR868/P1–6. Map drawn soon after Foster's wife, Mary, inherited estate in 1802 [*VCH*, 8, 5].

Arrington – [1828] – ARR82801 – COL C43.C32.3
VI Wragg's Farm.
Surveyor: [Robert Withers]; **Scale:** 1:9,504; **Size:** (i) 8 7/16 x 10 3/4in.; **Top** is N; Manuscript(iii), paper, coloured.
Wragg's Farm, TL327507, and 305a.2r.23p. in E of parish bounded by Croydon Parish in W and road from Royston to Huntingdon in E, and including 5a.0r.36p. in W of Wimpole Parish.
Names of roads and neighbouring owners. Farm buildings, cottages, church and mill shown in plan form. Closed fields; trees; state of cultivation shown by colour; roads and turnpike; watercourses and bridge; hedges and fences; boundary between Wimpole and Arrington parishes.
Border of 1 broad band with 1 narrow band on inside; title bottom left; compass top right showing 8 points. Roads and arable coloured brown, buildings coloured red and grey, grass coloured green, water coloured blue.
Accompanying terrier gives field names, acreages and tenant. Map is in volume: 'Survey of Estates belonging to the Right Honourable Philip Earl of Hardwicke. K.G. Situate in the Parishes of Wimpole and Arrington in the County of Cambridge. By Robert Withers. 1815. Reviewed and adjusted. 1828'. On following page: 'Note. All the Maps in the following Survey are upon a Scale of Twelve Chains to an Inch', 1:9,504. At end is abstract of survey [3,816a.1r.18p. in total]. See also ARR82802–4 and WMP82801–11.

Arrington – [1828] – ARR82802 – COL C43.C32.3
VII Haydon's Farm.
Surveyor: [Robert Withers]; **Scale:** 1:9,504; **Size:** (i) 8 3/8 x 10 11/16in.; **Top** is N; Manuscript(iii), paper, coloured.
Arrington Church, TL325503, and 340a.1r.0p. belonging to farm E of church, bounded by Croydon Parish in W.
Names of roads and neighbouring owners. Farm buildings, cottages, church and 'Hardwicke Arms Inn' shown in plan form. Closed fields; trees; state of cultivation shown by colour; roads; watercourses and ponds; hedges and fences; bridge; yard; clunch pit identified on terrier.
Border of 1 broad band with 1 narrow band on inside; title bottom left; compass top right showing 4 points. Roads and arable coloured brown, grass coloured green, water coloured blue, buildings coloured red or grey.
In volume which gives owner, surveyor, date and scale; see ARR82801 for details. Accompanying terrier gives field names, acreages and tenant. See also ARR82803–4 and WMP82801–11.

Arrington – [1828] – ARR82803 – COL C43.C32.3
VIII Hardwick Arms Inn and Farm.
Surveyor: [Robert Withers]; **Scale:** 1:9,504; **Size:** (i) 8 3/8 x 10 11/16in.; **Top** is N; Manuscript(iii), paper, coloured.
'Hardwicke Arms Inn', TL328503, and 107a.1r.36p. in Arrington and Wimpole parishes bounded by Wimpole Park in E.
Names of roads and neighbouring owners. 'Hardwick Arms' and farm buildings shown in plan form. Closed fields; spinney and trees; state of cultivation shown by

colour; roads and turnpike; watercourses and bridge; hedges and fences; garden and meadow identified on terrier.

Border of 1 broad band with 1 narrow band on inside; title top right. Roads and arable coloured brown, grass coloured green, water coloured blue, buildings coloured red or grey.

In volume which gives owner, surveyor, date and scale; see ARR82801 for details. Accompanying terrier gives field names, acreages and tenant. See also ARR82802,4 and WMP82801–11.

Arrington – [1828] – ARR82804 – COL C43.C32.3
X Letter. L. Arrington Bridge Farm.
Surveyor: [Robert Withers]; **Scale:** 1:9,504; **Size:** (i) 8 3/8 x 5 1/4in.; **Top** is N; Manuscript(iii), paper, coloured.

Arrington Bridge Farm, TL332487, and 76a.0r.6p. bounded by Wendy Parish in S and Croydon Parish in W.

Names of roads. Farm buildings shown in plan form. Closed fields; state of cultivation shown by colour; roads, turnpike and 'Intended Road'; watercourses; Arrington Bridge; hedges and fences; meadow identified on terrier.

Border at top, bottom and left of 1 broad band with 1 narrow band on inside; title at top; compass bottom right showing 4 points. Arable and roads coloured brown, pasture coloured green, water coloured blue, buildings coloured red or grey.

On left of sheet which also contains WMP82807. In volume which gives owner, surveyor, date and scale; see ARR82801 for details. Accompanying terrier gives field names, acreages and tenant. See also ARR82802–3 and WMP82801–11.

Arrington – [c. 1834] – ARR83401 – CUL MS Plans R.a.7
Map of the Parish of Arrington Cambridgeshire the Property of The Right Honourable Charles Philip Earl of Hardwicke From a corrected Survey by Robert Withers, in the Year 1828.
Surveyor: Robert Withers; **Scale bar** 5–0–30 chains (= 8 3/4in.), 1:3,168; **Size:** (i) 73 1/4 x 39in.; **Top** is NW; Manuscript(iv), paper mounted on cloth, coloured.

Church Farm, TL326503, and c. 1,400a. in whole parish.

Names of neighbouring parishes. Arrington Church shown in perspective, other buildings shown in plan form and include Wragg's and Church farms, Hardwicke Arms, vicarage, mill, farm buildings and buildings no longer extant E of road from Royston to Caxton. Closed fields; wood and trees; waste; roads, milestones and footpaths; watercourses; ponds and decoy pond; fences; responsibility for boundaries; part of Wimpole Park; chalk pit.

Border of 1 narrow band; title top left; scale middle left. Roads coloured brown, buildings coloured red, water coloured blue.

Numbers on plots suggest map originally accompanied by a terrier. Photograph in CRO. Map drawn after Charles Philip Yorke, 4th Earl of Hardwicke, inherited estate in 1834 [PB, 1,246].

Ashley cum Silverley – [c. 1835–48] – ASH83501 – SRO 1429/8
Plan of the Estate in the Parishes of Lidgate & Ashley belonging to T.J. Ireland Esqr.
Surveyor: T[homas] A[xford] Melhuish; **Scale** of 3 Chains in an Inch, 1:2,376, Scale bar 0–20 chains (= 6

5/8in.), 1:2,391; **Size:** (i) 69 3/8 x 47 1/8in.; **Top** is NNW; Manuscript(i), paper mounted on cloth, coloured.

35a.3r.10p. in E of Ashley Parish in TL7161 bounded by road to Dalham in N, and 380a.2r.18p. in Lidgate Parish [Suffolk].

Names of allotments, roads and neighbouring owners. Lidgate Hall, parsonage, cottages, farms and blacksmith's shop [identified on table] shown in plan form, Lidgate Church shown in perspective. Closed fields showing owner's land; meadow; acreages; roads; watercourses and direction of flow; 'Cropley Park'; division of farms; 'The Old Fence', 'The New Fence' and 'The Grass Links' in Ashley Parish.

Border of 1 narrow band; title centre left; scale under title; compass centre right showing 4 plain points, 2nd compass under the plots in Ashley Parish. Table top left giving tenants, field names, acreages, inclosures and allotments. Roads coloured yellow, water coloured blue, meadow coloured green, fields outlined in yellow, brown and green.

Under table: 'Note – The red Lines are the boundaries of each Allotment & the Numbers in each Field will correspond with the Award & the Corn Rent Schedule The Fields with the Yellow border are in the Parish of Ashley'. Surveyor's 1st names were Thomas Axford [Eden M293]. In bundle of maps of Suffolk estates of Thomas James Ireland dated 1835, 1840 and 1848.

B

Babraham – 1785 – BAB78501 – SJC MPS 225
Plan of the Lands at Babraham in the County of Cambr*idge* belonging to St Johns the Evangelist's coll*ege* Cambridge. Being a true copy of the Plan, particular Estimate and Valuation as taken by Messrs Ellis & King. 1785.
Surveyors: James Ellis, Simeon King; **Scale bar** 0–20 chains (= 3 3/4in.), 1:4,224; **Size:** (i) 22 1/8 x 10 9/16in.; **Top** is NE; Manuscript(i), parchment, coloured.

78a.3r.26p. E of village, bounded by road running NE of village to Six Mile Bottom in E and crossed by road from Cambridge to Little Abington in S; clunch pit is at TL517508.

Names of tenants, fields and roads. Public house, lodge and barn shown in plan form. Open fields; closes and new inclosures; Babraham Heath; plantation; 3 thorn bushes; acreages; roads and footpaths; watercourses; gardens; hedges; rick yard; clunch pit.

Border of 1 broad and 1 narrow band; title top right; scale middle right; compass top right showing 4 points. Table at bottom giving field names, land use, acreages and land value. Roads and trees coloured brown, water coloured blue, closes and hedges coloured green.

Later pencil note: 'Mr Pemberton thinks Mr Adeane wishes to take Coll*ege* Land up to this Road'. Christopher Pemberton was a solicitor in Cambridge [Jackson, 1990, 313]. Memoranda middle right give key to pieces belonging to Robert Jones' grandson and heir Robert Jones Adeane [VCH, 6, 22] to show changes lately made, College land planted by Mr Adeane, boundaries destroyed by alterations and internal lines ploughed up. Note on table that: 'Surveyed by James Ellis on behalf of the Executors of the late Robt Jones Esqr and Simeon King on behalf of the Masters and Fellows, of St Johns College Cambridge ...' Photograph at 1:6,670 at CRO TR869/P1.

Babraham – 1829 – BAB82901 – PRI

Plan of the Babraham Estate in the County of Cambridge the Property of Henry John Adeane Esqr. 1829.

Scale bar 0–20 chains (= 6 5/8in.), 1:2,391; **Size:** (i) 67 1/8 x 63in.; **Top** is NW; Manuscript(i), parchment, coloured.

Babraham Hall, TL511505, and 2,425a.0r.19p. bounded by roads from Chesterford to Newmarket in NE and from Cambridge to Linton in SE, Stapleford Parish in N and Sawston and Pampisford parishes in W, and including 51a.3r.16p. in N of Little Abington Parish.

Names of farms, fields and roads. Buildings shown in plan form and include Babraham Church, Babraham Hall, farm buildings, lodge and icehouse. Closed fields; wood, plantations, spinney, groves and trees; 'The Nursery'; common and meadow; sheep walk; parsley beds; acreages; roads, footpaths and milestones; park, gardens and orchard; watercourses, ponds, 'Roman ponds', moat, sluice and bridge; rick yard; gravel pits; limekiln; fences, hedges and gates; responsibility for boundaries; boundary with Little Abington Parish.

Border of 1 broad band with 1 narrow band on inside; title top left; scale bottom right; compass below title showing 16 points. Roads coloured brown, water coloured blue, parish boundary coloured red.

Numbers on plots suggest map originally accompanied by a terrier. Positive photostat in 6 sheets at 1:3,520 at CUL Maps.bb.53(1).95.58–64.

Balsham – 1617 – BAL61701 – GLC ACC.1876/MP2/3a

The description of the Manor of Balsham in the County of Cambridge being parcell of the possessions of the hospitall of King Iames founded in the Charterhouse in the countye of Middlesex at the humble peticion and at the proper costes and charges of Thomas Sutton esquier, made in September Anno domini 1617. by Thomas Langdon.

Surveyor: Thomas Langdon; **Scale bar** 20–0–160 perches (= 3in.), 1:11,880; **Size:** (i) 15 7/8 x 22 15/16in.; **Top** is NE; Manuscript(i), parchment, coloured.

Balsham Church, TL589509, and 4,308a.0r.36p. in whole parish.

Names of fields, roads and neighbouring owners. Church, farms and 2 windmills shown in perspective. Open fields showing direction of strips; closes; meadow; 'Balsham woode'; heath and common heath; acreages of some plots; roads and footpaths; tenure of some plots.

Border of 1/4in.-wide decorated blue and brown band; title top left in a strapwork cartouche with green leaves, red, blue and yellow flowers, yellow, blue, red and pink fruit and a red ribbon; 3-dimensional brown scale bar bottom right surmounted by brown dividers in a similar cartouche with blue vases and red flames; compass rose centre bottom showing 16 yellow, blue and purple points with a red and green border. Fields coloured in brown stripes or coloured green, wood coloured green, roads coloured yellow, buildings have red roofs, heath outlined in yellow, parish boundaries coloured pink, brown and yellow.

Copy drawn by John Prickett in 1791 at GLC ACC.1876/MP2/2 measures 15 15/16 x 22 7/8in. Border of 1 broad band with 1 narrow band on inside, title in a yellow oval cartouche with red and blue flowers and green leaves, scale bar has no cartouche, compass showing 16 points above scale. Pencil notes on copy. See also BAL61702–6.

Balsham – [1617] – BAL61702 – GLC ACC.1876/MP2/3b

The description of Balsham woode, the youle, Turnow Meadow, Cossey Den, Part of Gatherow fielde and other Lands adjoyning being in the parish of Balsham and in the county of Cambridge; made and ratified as is before expressed.

Surveyor: [Thomas Langdon]; **Scale bar** 0–60 perches (= 2 7/8in.), 1:4,132; **Size:** (i) 16 1/8 x 22 5/8in.; **Top** is NNE; Manuscript(i), parchment, coloured.

c. 780a. in SE of parish extending W of road from Balsham to Linton and bounded by West Wickham Parish in E and Linton Parish in S.

Names of fields, owners, tenants, roads and neighbouring owners. Windmill shown in perspective. Open fields showing all strips; closes; meadow; 'Balsham woode' and trees; 'Lamas grounde'; acreages; roads; hedges and 'Goodwines hedg'; tenure.

Border of 5/16in.-wide band with a blue and brown geometrical pattern; title top right in a cartouche with red, green, yellow and blue strapwork; 3-dimensional yellow scale bar bottom right surmounted by blue dividers with green, red and orange ribbons; compass rose on left showing 16 purple and yellow points in a blue, red and green border. Trees coloured green, fields outlined in green or brown, wood and roads outlined in yellow.

'Mr Henidg' written on 1 plot in red. Title has faded and map is damaged on left. Copy drawn by John Prickett in 1791 at GLC ACC.1876/MP2/2 measures 16 1/16 x 23 1/8in. Border of 1 broad band with 1 narrow band on inside, no title cartouche, compass shows 16 points. Pencil notes on copy. Surveyor and date given on BAL61701, see also BAL61703–6.

Balsham – 1617 – BAL61703 – GLC ACC.1876/MP2/3c

The description of parte of Broade fielde, parte of Gatherow fielde, Hildersham Denne Top of Downe fielde, lieinge togeather in the parish of Balsham in the countye of Cambridge made in September Anno domini 1617.

Surveyor: [Thomas Langdon]; **Scale bar** 0–40 perches (= 1 15/16in.), 1:4,088; **Size:** (i) 16 1/4 x 23 3/16in.; **Top** is NE; Manuscript(i), parchment, coloured.

c. 880a. SE of village W of BAL61702, bounded by Hildersham and Linton parishes in S.

Names of fields, roads, owners and tenants. Open fields showing all strips; acreages; roads and footpaths; tenure; hedge.

Border of 5/16in.-wide brown band with a geometrical pattern; title top right in a cartouche with red, yellow and blue strapwork; scale bottom right surmounted by blue dividers with red, yellow and blue strapwork, green leaves, yellow fruit and a red ribbon; compass rose top left showing 16 green, yellow and purple points in a red and blue border. Strips outlined in brown, roads coloured yellow, 2 balks and hedge coloured green.

'Mr Henidg' written on some areas in red. Copy drawn by John Prickett in 1791 at GLC ACC.1876/MP2/2 measures 16 3/16 x 23in. Border of 1 broad band with 1 narrow band on inside, no cartouche to title, scale bar is undecorated, compass shows 16 points. Surveyor given on BAL61701, see also BAL61702,4–6.

Balsham – 1617 – BAL61704 – GLC ACC.1876/MP2/3d

The description of A parte of Diche fielde Porteway fielde and Broade fielde in the parishe of Balsham in the Countie of Cambridge being parcell of the possessions of the governors of the hospitall of Kinge Iames founded in the Charterhouse in the countie of Midlesex at the humble peticion and at the proper costes & charges of of [sic.] Thomas Sutton esquier, made in September Anno domini 1617. by Tho. Langdon.

Surveyor: Thomas Langdon; **Scale bar** 0–60 perches (= 3in.), 1:3,960; **Size:** (i) 16 1/4 x 23 5/16in.; **Top** is NE; Manuscript(i), parchment, coloured.

c. 900a. N of BAL61703 bounded by West Wratting Parish in N and heath in W.

Names of fields, roads, owners, tenants and neighbouring owners. Open fields showing all strips; closes; heath; acreages; roads and footpaths; tenure; hedges.

Border of 5/16in.-wide band with a blue and brown geometrical pattern; title top left in a cartouche with pink, red, yellow, green and blue strapwork, green leaves and blue, yellow and pink fruit and flowers; 3-dimensional yellow scale bar bottom left; compass rose centre top showing 16 purple, yellow and green points with a red and blue border. Roads outlined in yellow, strips outlined in brown, closes outlined in green.

'Mr Henidg' written on some plots in red. Copy drawn by John Prickett in 1791 at GLC ACC.1876/MP2/2 measures 16 3/16 x 23 3/8in. Border of 1 broad band with 1 narrow band on inside, title in an uncoloured cartouche of leaves, scale bar is uncoloured, compass shows 16 points. Ink notes on copy. See also BAL61701-3,5-6.

B a l s h a m – [1617] – BAL61705 – GLC ACC.1876/MP2/3e
['Cotlow Fielde' and 'Beneathe Down' in Balsham, owned by the Charterhouse.]

Surveyor: [Thomas Langdon]; **Scale bar** 0–65 perches (= 3 1/8in.), 1:4,118; **Size:** (i) 16 9/16 x 23 1/4in.; **Top** is NE; Manuscript(i), parchment, coloured.

c. 690a. in far W of parish W of BAL61703, bounded by heath in W and Little Abington Parish in S.

Names of fields, roads and neighbouring owners. Open fields showing all strips; acreages; roads; tenure; 'Crunnes hole'; balks.

Border of 1/4in.-wide band with a blue and brown geometrical pattern; 3-dimensional yellow scale bar on left surmounted by blue dividers; compass rose top right showing 16 purple, yellow and green points in a red and blue border. Table on left giving tenants, acreages and tenure in a cartouche with yellow, blue, red and pink strapwork, green leaves and pink, yellow and orange fruit and flowers. Roads outlined in yellow, strips outlined in brown, balks coloured green.

'Mr Henidg' written on some plots in red. Copy drawn by John Prickett in 1791 at GLC ACC.1876/MP2/2 measures 16 5/16 x 23 1/8in. Border of 1 broad band with 1 narrow band on inside, compass shows 16 points, scale bar is uncoloured, no cartouche to table. Surveyor and date given on BAL61701, see also BAL61702-4,6.

B a l s h a m – [1617] – BAL61706 – GLC ACC.1876/MP2/3f
[Land in Balsham village, owned by the Charterhouse.]

Surveyor: [Thomas Langdon]; **Scale bar** 0–60 perches (= 2 15/16in.), 1:4,044; **Size:** (i) 16 1/4 x 23in.; **Top** is NE; Manuscript(i), parchment, coloured.

Balsham Church, TL589509, and c. 820a. in village bounded by West Wratting Parish in N, West Wickham Parish in E and 'The Way from Newmarket to Balsham' in W.

Names of fields, roads, owners, tenants and neighbouring owners. Houses, parsonage, church and windmill shown in perspective. Open fields showing all strips; closes; trees; acreages; roads; tenure; hedges and fences; site of the manor house.

Border of 5/16in.-wide band with a blue and brown geometrical pattern; 3-dimensional scale bar bottom left with blue edges; compass rose centre bottom showing 16 green, yellow and pink points in a red and blue border. Table top left giving tenants, acreages, closes and tenure, in a cartouche with red, blue and yellow strapwork and green and blue leaves and flowers. Roads outlined in yellow, closes outlined in green or yellow, hedges coloured green, strips coloured brown, houses have red roofs, church has a blue roof, parish boundary coloured red.

'Tho Teversham' written on some plots in red. Ink notes. Map has faded. Copy drawn by John Prickett in 1790 at GLC ACC.1876/MP2/2 measures 15 13/16 x 23 1/8in. Border of 1 broad band with 1 narrow band on inside, compass shows 16 points. Ink notes on copy. Prickett could not copy all the words on Langdon's map because of fading. Date and surveyor given on BAL61701, see also BAL61702-5.

Balsham – [1791] – BAL79101 – GLC ACC.1876/MP2/2
Balsham Dennis Taylor.

Surveyor: [Thomas Langdon]; **Draughtsman:** [John Prickett]; **Scale bar** 0–15 chains (= 3in.), 1:3,960; **Size:** (i) 5 7/8 x 8 7/16in.; **Top** is ESE; Manuscript(iv), paper, coloured.

3a.3r.0p. at TL582508, bounded by a road in N.

Names of former tenants. Houses shown in perspective. Closes; acreages; roads and gates; fences and hedge; former tenure.

Border of 1 narrow band; title at top; scale on right; compass top left showing 4 points. Road coloured brown, fields and hedge coloured green, buildings have red roofs.

Ink numbers on plots and notes of neighbours in 1791. Probably drawn by John Prickett and based on Thomas Langdon's maps of the Charterhouse estate in Balsham, BAL61701-6.

Balsham – 1825 – BAL82501 – GLC ACC.1876/MP2/2
Copy of a Plan made from the Inclosure. Award of the Estates belonging to The Revd Henry Allen Lagden in the Parish of Balsham, in the County of Cambridge distinguishing the Lands and Premises now belonging to the said Henry Allen Lagden 1825.

Surveyor: [Edward Gibbons]; **Scale bar** 0–30 chains (= 6 11/16in.), 1:3,553; **Size:** (i) 17 3/8 x 58 1/4in.; **Top** is NNE; Manuscript(iii), paper mounted on cloth, coloured.

Balsham Church, TL589509, and 655a.0r.5p. scattered throughout parish.

Names of farms, roads, owners and neighbouring owners. Gunner's Hall and Worsted ['Balsham'] Lodge shown in plan form, church shown in perspective. Closed fields; acreages; roads; tenure.

Border at top and sides of 1 broad band with 1 narrow band on inside; title bottom left; scale centre bottom; compass centre top showing 8 points. Roads coloured brown, buildings coloured red, land coloured brown, blue, yellow, green, and yellow with a deeper yellow edge.

Pencil notes, ink note after title: 'and those sold, with the Dates of such Sales'. Numbers on fields refer to inclosure award. Accompanying terrier gives colour of the land, shows to whom land was sold, date of sale, land tax, acreage and land tenure. Edward Gibbons was inclosure surveyor for Balsham.

Balsham – [1829] – BAL82901 – GLC ACC.1876/MP2/2
Balsham Plan of Mr Watson's Copyhold. –
Scale: 1:2,490; **Size:** (ii) 8 x 6 3/8in.; **Top** is N; Manuscript(i), paper, uncoloured.
2a.1r.15p. N of village street and 1a.3r.22p. E of a lane.
Names of owner, former owners, neighbouring owners and roads. Buildings shown in plan form. Closed fields; acreages; roads.
Title top right; 'North' written at top of plots. Table bottom left giving acreages.
Date on dorse. Land probably owned by the Charterhouse.

Balsham – [1831] – BAL83101 – GLC ACC.1876/MP2/7
A Plan of the Allotments now Occupied by the Poor of Balsham in the County of Cambridge the Property of the Right Honourable the Governors of the Charterhouse Containing with Allotments Fences and Roads – 21A.2R.0P.
Scale: 1:3,170; **Size:** (i) 22 1/4 x 17 3/4in.; **Top** is WNW; Manuscript(i), paper, coloured.
Building in TL5850, and 21a.2r.0p. in SE of parish SE of village.
Building shown in plan form. Closed fields; trees; roads.
Border of 2 broad bands with 1 narrower band in-between; title at top; compass in centre showing 4 points. Table on left giving tenants. Roads coloured brown.
Pencil notes. Date on dorse.

Balsham – [1833] – BAL83301 – GLC ACC.1876/MP2/2
Plan Of The Green Youl. With A Sketch of Balsham Hall Farm. The Property Of The Right Honourable The Governors Of The Charter House.
Scale: 1:3,250; **Size:** (i) 15 1/4 x 12 1/4in.; **Top** is S; Manuscript(i), paper, coloured.
Yole Farm, TL578496, and c. 160a. bounded by road to Linton in W and Balsham Wood in E.
Names of farm, roads and neighbouring owners. Farm buildings shown in plan form. Closed fields; trees drawn as conifers; roads and footpaths; gates and stiles; watercourses and ponds; gardens; pit; well; hedges; dimensions of 'Green Youl'.
Border of 1 broad band with 1 narrow band on inside; title at bottom; compass middle right showing 4 points. Roads coloured yellow, trees, hedges and grass coloured green, buildings coloured red, water coloured blue.
Notes top right of: 'Distance From Well On Green Youl To The Various Allotments', and, 'Extreme Distance From Well On Green Youl To Bounds Of Farm'. Date on dorse.

Balsham – [1834] – BAL83401 – GLC ACC.1876/MP2/8
Balsham Cambridgeshire. Lands, belonging to the Governors of the Charter~house as set out in the Map of the Commissioners of Inclosure, with two small Parcels, since purchased.
Surveyor: [Edward Gibbons]; **Draughtsmen:** [William] Newton, [Miles] Berry; **Scale bar** 11–0–40 statute chains (= 8 1/2in.), 1:4,752; **Size:** (i) 20 1/4 x 57 1/4in.; **Top** is NE; Manuscript(iv), paper, coloured.
Farm at TL586508, and 1,288a.3r.37p. scattered throughout parish.
Names of fields and roads. Farm buildings shown in plan form. Closed fields showing owner's land; acreages; roads

and footpaths; meadow; heath; responsibility for boundaries; gravel pit; reasons for allotments.
Border of 1 broad band with 1 narrow band on inside; title centre bottom; scale bottom left; compass top right showing 8 points. Table below title giving acreages. Roads coloured brown, old inclosures coloured green, heath outlined in green.
Numbers on fields refer to table and inclosure award. Note below table: 'N:B: This Mark signifies that the Fences belong to those Pieces in which the Mark is made. The Old Inclosures are coloured Green'. Pencil notes on table altering acreages as given in the notes on dorse of map: 'Note. This Plan contains all the Lands allotted or awarded (or Purchases or Exchanges) to the Governors on the Balsham Inclosure – and the old Inclosures stated in the Award to belong to them – also No. 51 the site of a Cottage & Garden purchased 1833 – and No. 10 Land purchased 1834. making a total of 1288-3-37'. Also notes of land in Fulbourn Parish always let with the Balsham estate, land given in exchange in 1832, deficiencies from the 1836 plan by Alexander Watford and a note of this acreage [see BAL83601], and plots which Alexander Watford thinks do not belong to the Charterhouse. Also a note: 'Rough Draft from which Mr Watford's Plan of Balsham was made 1834'. Edward Gibbons was inclosure surveyor for Balsham, draughtsmen's 1st names were William and Miles [Eden N74 and B292.5].

Balsham – 1836 – BAL83601 – GLC ACC.1876/MP2/9
Estate belonging to the Governors of the Charter House In The Parish of Balsham In The County of Cambridge 1836.
Surveyor: Alexander Watford [jr]; **Scale bar** 0–40 chains (= 6 5/8in.), 1:4,782; **Size:** (i) 27 1/4 x 62 7/8in.; **Top** is NE; Manuscript(i), paper mounted on cloth, coloured.
Balsham Church, TL589509, and 1,289a.1r.11p. in W of parish around Dotterel Hall ['Dotterel Farm'] and S of village around Wood Farm, and 7a.3r.7p. in far E of Fulbourn Parish.
Names of fields and roads. Farm buildings shown in plan form, church and windmill shown in perspective. Closed fields showing owner's land; wood; state of cultivation shown by colour; acreages; roads; gardens; ponds; fences; responsibility for boundaries.
Border of 1 broad band with 1 narrow band on inside; title centre bottom; scale under title; compass centre top showing 8 points. Tables bottom left, centre and right giving acreages and land use for each farm, and acreages of gardens. Roads and arable coloured brown, pasture and wood coloured green, some buildings coloured red, water coloured blue, roads outlined in red/brown.
Pencil notes.

Barrington – [c. 1740–50] – BAP74001 – TCC Box 35 Barrington 420
['Plan of the fruit trees in the orchard'.]
Size: (ii) 6 1/2 x 8 1/8in.; **Top** is N; Manuscript(i), paper, uncoloured.
Orchard, bounded by a watercourse and pond in N, parsonage land in E, lane in W and barn in S.
Names of trees. Barn shown in plan form. Roads; watercourses and pond; trees, including 'Golden Pear Main', 'Kentish Pippin', 'Spencer Pippin', 'Girton Pippin', 'French Pippin', 'Golden Runnet' [Reinette], 'Brewers

End', 'Non Pareil', 'Rosemary Pippin', 'Golden Pippin', 'Landore', pear.

'North Side' written at top of plan.

On p.13 of volume with entries dating between 1740 and 1750. On cover of book: 'Barrington Family Names Small Tythes'. Title at end. Land probably owned by Trinity College, Cambridge.

Barrington – [1798] – BAP79801 – TCC Great Chest 1

[Map of Barrington, showing land owned by Trinity College, Cambridge.]

Surveyor: [Alexander Watford sr]; **Scale:** 1:1,440; **Size:** (ii) 115 x 77 5/8in.; **Top** is W; Manuscript(i), paper mounted on cloth, coloured.

Barrington Church, TL397499, and c. 2,300a. in whole parish.

Buildings, including church, shown in plan form. Open fields showing all strips; trees; roads and gates; watercourses; ponds; bridges; hedges and fences; crosses; balks.

Buildings coloured brown, trees, village green and some strips [possibly those belonging to Trinity College] coloured green, water coloured blue, areas [possibly furlongs] outlined in yellow and pink.

Pencil notes, possibly giving survey lines. TCC Box 35 Barrington 447, missing in 1988, was a terrier which may have accompanied map. Alexander Watford sr was paid £100 for a map of Barrington in 1798 [TCC 30,15].

Barrington – 1800 – BAP80001 – TCC Box 35 Barrington 448

Map of the Parish of Barrington in the County of Cambridge As allotted and divided by the Commissioners under an Act of Parliament passed in the Year of the Reign of his Majesty King George the 3rd Thos Thorpe Surveyor 1800.

Surveyor: Thomas Thorpe; **Scale bar** 0–30 chains (= 3 1/2in.), 1:6,789; **Size:** (i) 24 1/2 x 38in.; **Top** is NNE; Manuscript(iii), paper mounted on cloth, coloured.

Barrington Church, TL397499, and c. 2,300a. in whole parish.

Names of owners, tenants and neighbouring owners. Buildings shown in plan form, church shown in perspective. Closed fields; trees; acreages of some areas; roads and footpaths; watercourses and ponds; responsibility for boundaries; village green; tenure; mill; 'Quarry or Chalk Pit'; land exchanged.

Border of 1 narrow band, sometimes obscured by green ribbon which edges map; title top right in a cartouche with a *putto* holding the title with a blue carpet underneath; scale bottom left with a ribbon, and part of scale bar coloured blue; compass bottom right showing 8 blue and uncoloured points. Water coloured blue, Trinity College rectory lands coloured blue, vicarage lands coloured red, Prime's Farm coloured yellow, Rayner's Farm coloured green, Jepps' Farm coloured brown.

Pencil notes. Numbers on fields refer to inclosure award. At back of volume which contains a copy of the award, Commissioners' account, schedule of old inclosures, particulars of old inclosures, index to copyhold allotments, copy of act, 'Schedule of the Allotments in the Parish of Barrington, chargeable with a Corn Rent in lieu of Tythes with the Amount of such Corn Rent in Money, and Bushels of Wheat, as Collected from the Award,' and, 'Summary of the Allotments, and Old Inclosures chargeable with a Corn Rent, in lieu of Tythes, with the amount of such Corn Rent, with which each Proprietor is charged, in Money, and

Bushels of Wheat'. On dorse of map: 'Barrington Map Belonging to the Master Fellows & Scholars of Trinity College Cambridge Corn Rent <R> Newling S. Pearce'.

Barrington – [1817] – BAP81701 – TCC Box 35 Barrington 458b

['Hooper's Farm', Barrington, owned by Trinity College, Cambridge.]

Surveyor: [Alexander Watford jr]; **Scale:** 1:349; **Size:** (ii) 8 15/16 x 14 3/8in.; Manuscript(i), paper, uncoloured.

c. 1a. in Barrington Parish.

Names of buildings, areas and neighbouring owners. Buildings shown in plan form and include 'Dove Cot', house, 'Barley Barn', 'Granery', 'Hay Barn', 'Cow House', stable, pigsty, 'Little Barn', 'Cart Lodge', 'Wheat Barn'. Closed fields; dimensions of areas; gates; orchards; 'addition to Barn'.

Accompanies: 'Watford's Report of Barrington Hoopers May 4th 1817', at TCC Box 35 Barrington 458a. Surveyor's 1st name was Alexander [Eden W141.1].

Barton – 1796 – BAR79601 – CLC ACC.1985/5

Plan of a Farm in the County of Cambridge belonging to Clare Hall Surveyed in the Year 1796.

Surveyor: [Joseph Freeman?]; **Scale bar** 5–0–15 chains (= 3 3/8in.), 1:4,693; **Size:** (i) 27 7/16 x 24 15/16in.; **Top** is N; Manuscript(i), parchment, coloured.

Barton Church, TL408558, farm to NW and 84a.0r.27p. bounded by Comberton Parish in W, Grantchester Parish in E and Bourn Brook in S.

Names of fields, roads, balks and neighbouring owners. Farm buildings, cottages and church shown in plan form. Open fields showing owner's strips; closes; common; meadow; state of cultivation by colour; roads and footpaths; watercourses, 'The Ford', 'Lords Bridge' and footbridge; spring; balks; hedges; number of lands between strips; 'Hobbersons' and 'Mill' hills shown as mounds.

Border of 1 broad band with 1 narrow band on inside; title middle right; scale under title; compass centre top showing 4 points. Table top right giving field names and acreages. Balks, hedges and closes coloured green, water coloured blue, arable strips and roads coloured brown, farm buildings coloured red.

Note under table: 'In Whitwell field the old Terrier calls 22a.3r. of Land – It is now Intermixed with Whitwell farm, and cannot be found'. Copy dated 1797 in pencil on dorse, cut from a lease, measures 30 3/16 x 24 3/4in. Hills coloured green, arable coloured yellow; individual strips not shown. At CLC Safe B:34/2 is a valuation of the estate which was taken in the 1790s, and at CLC Safe C:5/4 f.200v is a valuation by Alexander Watford sr taken in 1797. Map is in similar style to others drawn for Clare College, probably by Joseph Freeman.

Barton – [c. 1803] – BAR80301 – PCC

Survey of Lands at Barton Exchanged under the Grandchester & Coton Inclosure Act. belonging to the Society of Pembroke College.

Surveyor: William Custance; **Scale** 3 Chains in an Inch, 1:2,376; **Size:** (i) 17 1/2 x 22 1/2in.; **Top** is WNW; Manuscript(i), paper, coloured.

3a.2r.28p. in TL4054, TL4154 and TL4155, bounded by road from Cambridge to Wimpole in NW.

Names of fields and neighbouring owners. Closed fields showing owner's land; acreages; hedges; roads; balks.

Border of 1 broad and 1 narrow band; title bottom left; scale in centre; compass in centre showing 4 points. Table bottom right giving acreages and furlongs. Road coloured brown.

Inclosure award for Grantchester and Coton was drawn up in 1803.

Barton – [1803] – BAR80302 – CUA CUR.34.36
The General Plan of Payne's Farm Yard.
Surveyor: [Charles Humfrey]; **Scale:** 1:647; **Size:** (i) 5 13/16 x 6 7/8in.; **Top** is S; Manuscript(i), paper, coloured.

2a.2r.0p. at University Farm, TL408557.
Names of areas. Farm buildings shown in plan form and include dovecote, chaff barn, pigsties, oat barn, wheat barn, 'Cart Hovel', 'Cow=house', stables, barley barn, straw house, 'Granery' and farmhouse. Closes; roads; hedges; moat; churchyard; straw, cow and stack yards; garden and orchard. All of features except for hedges are identified on table.

Border of 1 narrow band; title beneath map; compass top right showing 4 points. Table beneath title giving key to areas and buildings to be demolished. Buildings coloured grey, water coloured blue, yards coloured yellow, grass coloured green, buildings to be demolished coloured red.

Note on dorse: 'Barton Farm. Valuation by Watford in 1797 who then made the Quantity of Land 277A.1R.35P In 1823. Mr Watford made it only 249.1.13. Mr Harwood went over all the Land < > measured every Piece in 1829; & according to his Survey (very accurately particularized in a large Book) the Farm contains only 239A.2R.26P Statute Measure. In Watfords *could* In only be computed Measure but it is difficult to reconcile the difference they make in the Quantity between the years 1797 & 1723 [sic.] W[illiam] C[hristmas]'. Note refers to Alexander Watford sr and jr [Eden W141 and W141.1] and Richard Harwood [Eden H188]. Accompanied by: 'Report. on the State of the Buildings at Payne's Farm at Barton' by Charles Humfrey [CUA CUR.34.26], and, 'An Estimate of the Dilapidations of a Farm House and Out~Buildings, situate at Barton in Cambridgeshire; belonging to The University of Cambridge, and occupied by Mr Payne 5 Aug 1803' [CUA D.XV.66].

Barton – [1805] – BAR80501 – CUA D.P.I.1(i)
['Payne's Farm', Barton, owned by the University of Cambridge.]
Surveyor: [Charles Humfrey]; **Scale bar** 0–120 feet (= 7 1/2in.), 1:192; **Size:** (i) 18 11/16 x 26 3/8in.; **Top** is S; Manuscript(i), paper, coloured.

Barton Church, TL408558, and c. 2a. bounded by church in SW and moat in NE.
Names of buildings. Buildings shown in plan form and include brew house, dairy, wash house, 'Fowl House', servants' hall, kitchen, East and West parlours, beer cellar, ale cellar, 'granery', tool house, straw house, barns, stables, 'cow house', 'Pidgeon House', 'Cutting House', 'chaff house' and 'Cart Hovel'. Watercourses; garden and orchard; 'hogsties'; churchyard, rick yards; stairs to cellars; posts to 'Cart Hovel'.

Border of 1 narrow band; scale in centre. Water coloured blue, walls coloured pink, yellow and blue.

Note bottom right: 'The Yellow Tints shews the Timber Sills The Red do the under pining & Brick Foundations The Blue shews the Buildings that are to be taken down Likewise were Ground Sills and under pining is wanted'.

Accompanying documents signed by Charles Humfrey in 1805 give changes to be made to the building.

Barton – 1829 – BAR82901 – CUA D.P.I.2
A Plan of the Inclosed Property of the Lordship Farm, lying in the Parish of Barton, Cambs. Belonging to the University of Cambridge. Also, of Two Closes, in the Parish of Grantchester.
Surveyor: R[ichard] Harwood; **Scale:** Three Chains to an Inch, Scale bar 0–18 chains (= 5 15/16in.), 1:2,376; **Size:** (i) 21 1/2 x 33 3/4in.; **Top** is W; Manuscript(i), paper, coloured.

Barton Church, TL408558, and 66a.3r.36p. E of road from Haslingfield to Barton, including 21a.3r.27p. in W of Grantchester Parish.
Names of neighbouring owners. Farm buildings and church shown in plan form. Closed fields showing owner's land; pightle; common; wood; hedges; roads; gates; watercourses and ponds.

Border of 1 broad band with 2 narrow bands on inside; title top right in a rococo cartouche; scale middle right; compass middle top showing 8 points. Table on left giving field names, acreages and land use. Roads coloured brown, fields outlined in green, water coloured blue, buildings coloured red, yards coloured yellow.

Surveyor's 1st name was Richard [Eden H188].

Barton – 1834 – BAR83401 – SCC XVIII/8
Males Farm Homestall Barton held by. Mr Wilson Holben.
Surveyor: [William Gray]; **Scale** one inch to twenty feet, 1:240; **Size:** (i) 11 1/8 x 14 3/8in.; Manuscript(i), paper, uncoloured.

c. 2r. in Barton Parish.
Names of farm and features. 'House converted into cottage tenements', wheat, barley and 'Heidle' barns, 'Cow house' and 'Grenery' shown in plan form. Dimensions of areas; gate; fence, 'hedge fence' and 'Tale fence'.

Border of 1 narrow band; title in centre; scale at top.

Accompanies: 'Valuation of Buildings and fences Males Homestall Barton held – by Mr Wilson Holben'. At end of valuation: 'Measured & Valued by me Nov: 4 – 1834 William Gray'. Land owned by St Catharine's College, Cambridge.

Bassingbourn – [c. 1806] – BAS80601 – CRO R56/20/35/1
Sketch of Mr Josh Beldam's Allotment at Bassingborne.
Surveyor: [Thomas Thorpe]; **Scale:** 6 Chains to an Inch, 1:4,752; **Size:** (ii) 26 3/4 x 14 3/4in.; **Top** is N; Manuscript(ii), tracing paper, uncoloured.

c. 170a. on W edge of parish N and S of Ashwell Street; junction of Ashwell Street and Ermine Street ['London Road'] is at TL349432.
Names of roads, owners and neighbouring owners. Closed fields showing owner's land; lengths of plots in chains; roads.

Title middle right; scale in centre; compass middle left showing 4 points.

Based on map surveyed by Thomas Thorpe which accompanied 1806 inclosure award.

Bassingbourn – [c. 1806] – BAS80602 – CRO R56/20/35/1

Sketch of the Allotments to Messrs Jos Beldam Senr Jos Beldam Junr & John Beldam in the Parish of Bassingborne, exclusive of the Allotment to the Workhouse Farm.
Surveyor: [Thomas Thorpe]; **Scale:** 1:7,520; **Size:** (ii) 18 5/8 x 15 1/8in.; **Top** is N; Manuscript(ii), tracing paper, uncoloured.

c. 1,100a. SW of TL335440, junction of main road in village ['Bassingborn Causeway'] and 'North Road' running S, crossed by Ashwell Street and bounded in S by road to Baldock.

Names of some owners, neighbouring owners and roads. Closed fields showing owners' land; 'The marsh'.

Title top right; compass top left showing 4 points.

2nd abbreviated title middle right. Based on map surveyed by Thomas Thorpe which accompanied 1806 inclosure award.

Bassingbourn – [c. 1806] – BAS80603 – GCC XLIII.22

['Sketch of Caius College Bassingbourne Allotments'.]
Surveyor: [Thomas Thorpe]; **Scale:** 1:2,360; **Size:** (ii) 16 7/16 x 20 3/4in.; **Top** is S; Manuscript(iv), paper, uncoloured.

Bassingbourn Church, TL331441, and 55a.3r.28p. bounded by Litlington Parish in W.

Names of roads and neighbouring owners. Church, mill and cottage shown in plan form. Closed fields; acreages; responsibility for boundaries; roads; watercourses; bridge.

Title on dorse. Based on map surveyed by Thomas Thorpe which accompanied 1806 inclosure award.

Bassingbourn – [1810] – BAS81001 – CRO R56/20/36/1

['Waste Land alloted to the said Thomas Nash and demised by this present Indenture to the said William Elbourn containing 7 square poles and 3 quarters'.]
Scale bar 100–0–5 feet (= 6in.), 1:210; **Size:** (i) 6 3/4 x 5 5/8in.; **Top** is SE; Manuscript(i), parchment, coloured.

Plot of waste land, TL332434, which measures 7 3/4 poles and is bounded by road running from W of Bassingbourn to Ashwell Street ['Water Lane Road'] in W, and by private roads in N, E and S.

Names of fields, roads and neighbouring owners. Closed field; waste; length of boundaries; roads.

Border of 2 parallel red lines; 'title' in centre of plot; scale at bottom; cardinal points stated in border.

Pencil note of a barn. Drawn on indenture dated 1810: 'Mr Thos. Nash to Mr Wllm Elbourn Lease of Waste Ground at Bassingbourn', for 21 years. Title on dorse.

Bassingbourn – [c. 1816–38] – BAS81601 – CRO 124/P68

[Land at Bassingbourn, owned by Hale Wortham Esq.]
Scale of chains, 6 in an Inch, 1:4,752, Scale bar 0–20 [chains] (= 3 5/16in.), 1:4,782; **Size:** (i) 16 3/8 x 32 3/8in.; **Top** is N; Manuscript(i), parchment, coloured.

Manor Farm, TL331440, and 306a.2r.23p. N of road from Litlington to Kneesworth extending into NW of Wendy Parish.

Names of roads and neighbouring owners. Manor Farm, cottages and outbuildings shown in plan form. Closed fields showing owner's land; pightle; trees and bushes; roads and watercourses; moat, earthworks [Site of John o'

Gaunt's house]; fen, rick yard, spinney and dovecote identified on table.

Border of 1 broad band with 1 narrow band on each side; scale bottom left; compass middle left showing 16 points alternately coloured pink and decorated with dots, and shaded grey. Table top left giving field names and acreages. Roads coloured yellow, Manor Farm coloured pink, moat coloured white.

Numbers on plots refer to another reference table as well as to that on map; do not refer to inclosure award. Map drawn after inclosure in 1806, many of surrounding owners are unchanged and LSA81602, at bottom of the sheet, was drawn c. 1816–38 and shows the estates of three of the Hatton sisters. Hale Wortham was married to another Hatton sister, Mary [VCH, 8, 15].

Benwick – [c. 1771] – BEN77101 – CRO 283/P

A Survey of an Estate lying in the Hamlet of Benwick in the Isle of Ely Belonging to John Waddington Esq.
Scale bar 0–20 chains (= 3 5/16in.), 1:4,782; **Size:** (i) 19 7/8 x 13 5/16in.; **Top** is NNW; Manuscript(i), paper, coloured.

White Fen Farm, TL356924, and 472a.2r.12p. in White Fen bounded by River Nene in E and S, and drain running N from White Fen pumping station in W.

Names of river, drains and neighbouring owners. Farm, farm buildings and 3 windmills shown in perspective. Closes; acreages of land in N of map; roads and watercourses.

Border of 1 broad band with 1 narrow band on either side; title bottom right in a rococo cartouche; scale beneath title; compass top right showing 4 points. Table top left giving field numbers and acreages. Water and buildings coloured grey.

Probably drawn soon after John Waddington inherited estate in 1771 [Waddington, 1934, 119].

Benwick – 1823 – BEN82301 – CRO 515/P

Survey of Messrs Ibberson's Farms made in pursuance of an Order of the Eau Brink Commissioners of Appeal by Joseph Jackson, Land Surveyor, March. 1823.
Surveyor: Joseph Jackson; **Scale:** 4 Chains to an Inch, 1:3,168; **Size:** (ii) 29 7/8 x 42in.; **Top** is NNE; Manuscript(i), paper mounted on cloth, uncoloured.

Puddock Bridge, TL871880, and 831a.3r.12p. in Benwick Mere in S of parish, bounded by Huntingdonshire in W, S and E and Benwick Turf Fen in N.

Names of river, roads, owners and neighbouring owners. Farms and farm buildings including Stanley Hall and Betty's Nose Farm shown in plan form, 4 windmills shown in perspective. Closes; trees; acreages; roads and watercourses; gates and toll gate; bridges and fences; bank.

Title bottom left; scale middle bottom; compass top right showing 4 plain points. Table bottom left giving owners and acreages.

Numbers on fields suggest map originally accompanied by a terrier. Pencil calculations. Owners were Francis, Isaac and Henry Ibberson, and Isaac Sanders.

Bottisham – 1759 – BOT75901 – LBH Hc 19/7/45

A Survey of the Freehold and Leasehold Estates at Bottisham in the County of Cambridge belonging to the Worshipfull the Governors of St Bartholomew's Hospital London taken Octr 1759 by Edmd Dipper, Jos: Hickman junr.

Surveyors: Edmund Dipper, Joseph Hickman jr; **A Scale** of 40 Poles to one Inch, Scale bar 1–0–20 poles (= 5 1/8in.), 1:7,920; **Size:** (i) 40 7/8 x 32 5/8in.; **Top** is NNW; Manuscript(i), parchment, coloured.

Bottisham Church, TL545604, and 407a.3r.15p. centred around village and extending along roads from Cambridge to Newmarket and from Six Mile Bottom to Lode.

Names of fields, tenants, neighbouring owners, roads and some farms. Buildings shown in plan form and include Bottisham Hall, Anglesey Abbey, Hare Park House, farm buildings, buildings in Lode Hamlet and stables; Bottisham, Little Swaffham and Wilbraham churches shown in perspective. Owner's land in open fields; closes; pightles; common; glebe; meadow; fen and waste; wood and trees; state of cultivation shown by colour; acreages; roads, footpaths and milestones; watercourses; parks, gardens; 'King's hedge'.

Border of 1 broad and 1 narrow band; title top left, decorated by a double line at bottom; scale middle bottom; compass rose middle top showing 4 yellow and red points. Table bottom left giving tenants, fields and acreages. Roads coloured brown, wood coloured yellow, pasture coloured green, buildings outlined in red, fields outlined in yellow, fen outlined in blue.

Note right of table: 'N.B. The Arable Land is stained with a Yellow bordering, The Pasture Land with a Green. The Fenn Ground with a blue. The Red Figures refer to the Table'. Positive photostat at CUL Maps R.b.11.

Bottisham – [1793] – BOT79301 – LBH Hc 19/6B/1

A Map of the Parish of Bottisham in the County of Cambridge and also a Farm in the Occupation of Mr Newman belonging to the Right Honourable the Governors of Saint Bartholomews Hospitall to whom this Map is humbly Inscribed by their obedient Servant Francis Marshall Surveyor.

Surveyor: Francis Marshall; **Scale bar** 0–50 chains (= 5 5/8in.), 1:7,040; **Size:** (i) 25 3/8 x 62 1/2in.; **Top** is NNE; Manuscript(i), paper mounted on cloth, coloured.

Bottisham Hall, TL549617, and 594a.2r.5p. in parish.

Names of fields, roads and neighbouring owners. Buildings shown in plan form and include Bottisham Hall and Church, Anglesey Abbey, 'The Rose', houses and farm buildings. Open fields showing owner's strips; closes; pightles; common; wood and trees; waste and fen; vineyards; clay, gravel, sand and turf pits; watercourses; 'Whiteland Spring', springs and pond; bridges; roads and footpaths; gates; park; gardens; orchard; hedges and 2 bushes; fishponds and moats; 'Mill dam'; farmyard.

Border of 1 narrow and 1 broad band; title centre top with a cartouche of fish and flowers intertwined; scale bottom right; compass top right showing 4 points. Tables at top giving farm and parish acreages, acreages of open-field land, inclosures and buildings for each farm, land use, and whether land is titheable. Above title is a vignette of the church in perspective surrounded by trees. Animals. Roads coloured brown, buildings coloured red, water coloured blue, trees and grass coloured green, heath outlined in blue, arable strips coloured brown, fields outlined in yellow, red and brown.

The Governors of St Bartholomew's Hospital commissioned the map on 12 December 1792 in order to value the estate before letting it; on 24 July 1793 they were told that the plan was not yet complete, and they asked Mr Marshall to finish it as soon as possible [LBH Ha 1/15 pp.240,

269]. Photograph in 12 sheets at 1:7,543 at CUL Atlas.5.97.211. Copy at 1:15,000 in CRO.

Bottisham – [Early 19th century] – BOT80001 – NRO D.S.391

Bottisham.

Scale: 1:5,070; **Size:** (i) 5 3/4 x 10 11/16in.; **Top** is NNE; Manuscript(i), paper mounted on cloth, coloured.

c. 57a. in 2 plots in TL5460 and TL5560 E of church, and extending along road to Newmarket.

Names of roads, buildings and neighbouring owners. Houses and public house shown in plan form. Closed fields; roads including turnpike; watercourses.

Border of 1 narrow band; title on right; compass top left showing 4 points. Fields coloured yellow, water coloured blue, roads coloured brown.

Note that this is 'Lot 7'. Top right of sheet; see also OVE80001 and RAM80001. A neighbouring owner on OVE80001 had an estate mapped in 1797 and died in 1828, so map drawn in early 19th century.

Bottisham – 1802 – BOT80201 – TCC Box 28 Bottisham 18

Plan of an Estate, situate at Bottisham in the County of Cambridge belonging to the Society of Trinity College in the University of Cambridge. 1802.

Scale bar 0–20 chains (= 3 1/4in.), 1:4,874; **Size:** (i) 15 1/4 x 41 1/2in.; **Top** is N; Manuscript(i), parchment, coloured.

478a.2r.25p. in TL5361 and TL5460, bounded by road to Newmarket in N and Stow cum Quy Parish in SW.

Names of roads and neighbouring owners. Buildings shown in plan form. Closed fields showing owner's land and 1 plot belonging to St Bartholomew's Hospital, London; state of cultivation probably shown by colour; acreages; roads; watercourses; hedges; garden identified on table.

Border of 1 narrow band; title top left in a cartouche of green and yellow lines; scale bottom left; compass top right showing 8 points. Table centre bottom giving acreages and allotments. Roads coloured brown, buildings coloured red, fields coloured green or yellow.

Bottisham – 1814 – BOT81401 – DCC Map Cabinet Drawer 4 E14

Estate belonging to Downing College in the Parish of Bottisham in the County of Cambridge 1814.

Scale: 12 Chains to One Inch, 1:9,504; **Size:** (i) 15 1/4 x 38 7/8in.; **Top** is NE; Manuscript(i), paper, coloured.

Bottisham Church, TL546605, and 467a.3r.7p. in NE of village, in Bottisham Fen in N and in NE and SW of parish.

Names of roads, parishes and neighbouring owners. Houses shown in plan form, church shown in perspective. Closed fields showing owner's land; fen; acreages; roads and watercourses.

Border of 1 narrow band; title on left; scale under title; compass centre top showing 4 points. Buildings coloured red, roads coloured brown, water coloured blue.

Numbers on some plots suggest map originally accompanied by a terrier.

Bottisham – [1814] – BOT81402 – TCC Box 28 Bottisham 27d

[Land at Bottisham, owned by St Bartholomew's Hospital, London.]

Scale: 1:5,010; **Size:** (iii) 1 3/8 x 2in.; **Top** is N; Manuscript(i), paper, uncoloured.

1a.3r.25p. at TL548602, bounded by road from Bottisham in N.

Buildings shown in plan form. Closed fields; acreages; roads; watercourses.

Note underneath map of owners of plots. Numbers on plots refer to inclosure award. Calculations on map. Accompanying documents dated 1814 relate to boundaries of property and proposals to lease it. See also BOT81403.

Bottisham – [1814] – BOT81403 – TCC Box 28 Bottisham 27d
[Land at Bottisham, owned by St Bartholomew's Hospital, London.]
Scale: 1:480; **Size:** (ii) 8 13/16 x 7 1/4in.; **Top** is N; Manuscript(i), paper, uncoloured.

c. 1r. at TL548602, bounded by road from Bottisham in N.

Names of neighbouring owners. Buildings shown in plan form. Close; road; dimensions of area.

Calculations on dorse. Probably enlarged drawing of plot numbered 89a on BOT81402. Accompanying documents dated 1814 relate to boundaries of the property and proposals to lease it.

Bottisham – 1833 – BOT83301 – LBH Hc 19/7/47
The Bottisham Estate Cambridgeshire 1833.
Surveyor: T[homas] J[ames] Tatham; **Scale bar** 5–0–15 chains (= 5in.), 1:3,168; **Size:** (i) 48 3/4 x 26 7/8in.; **Top** is NNW; Manuscript(i), paper mounted on cloth, coloured.

Long Meadow Farm, TL544628, and 349a.0r.5p. centred around farm, bounded by droveways in W and E, and road from Cambridge to Swaffham in SE.

Names of farms, fields, roads and neighbouring owners. Farm buildings shown in plan form. Closed fields; wood including 'The Holms' and trees; 'coarseground' and 'moor'; acreages; roads and footpaths; watercourses and ditches; gardens and orchards; gates; hedges.

Border of 1 narrow band; title top right; scale middle bottom; compass middle left showing 8 points. Table middle right giving acreages of fields. Fields and roads coloured brown, hedges and trees coloured green, water coloured blue.

Numbers on plots suggest map originally accompanied by a terrier. 4 insets: see BOT83302-5. At LBH EO 3/5 is an inexact copy: 'The Bottisham Estate'. In volume: 'Maps of the Landed Estates belonging to the Governors of St Bartholomews Hospital situate in the several counties of Cambridge, Essex, Hants, Hertford, Hereford, Kent, Lincoln, Middlesex, Northampton, Oxford, Somerset, and Warwick. Taken from the Original Surveys in possession of the Hospital. By Messrs Tatham & Son 1848'. Copy has a scale bar 5–0–25 chains (= 3 3/8in.), 1:7,040, and measures 13 x 19 3/4in. Top is NE. Names of neighbouring owners and Long Meadow Farm. Buildings shown in plan form. Closed fields; wood and trees; hedges; state of cultivation shown by colour; roads and footpaths; ditches and watercourses; gates; gardens and orchards. Border of 1 broad and 1 narrow band; title at bottom; scale beneath title; compass centre top showing 8 points. Table on right giving acreages. Arable coloured brown, grass and trees coloured green, buildings coloured red and grey, water coloured blue. Terrier on next page. Surveyor's 1st names

were Thomas James [Eden T34]. Positive photostat of original map at CUL Maps.R.b.12.

Bottisham – 1833 – BOT83302 – LBH Hc 19/7/47
Brands Garden and Close.
Surveyor: T[homas] J[ames] Tatham; **Scale bar** 1–0–4 chains (= 3 3/8in.), 1:1,173; **Size:** (i) 5 3/4 x 7 1/4in.; **Top** is SE; Manuscript(i), paper mounted on cloth, coloured.

4r.1p., probably in TL5460, bounded in SW by 'Bottisham Street'.

Names of roads and neighbouring owners. Farm buildings shown in plan form. Closed field; wood; acreages; roads and footpaths; watercourses and pond; garden; hedges.

Border imitating the edge of a sheet of paper; title middle top; scale middle bottom; compass bottom left showing 4 points. Roads and fields coloured brown, hedges and garden coloured green, water coloured blue.

Numbers on plots suggest map originally accompanied by a terrier. Map is an inset at bottom left of BOT83301. At LBH EO 3/5 is an inexact copy, made in 1848, showing a fence and no footpath, house coloured red, terrier on next page; see BOT83301 for details. Surveyor's 1st names were Thomas James [Eden T34]. Positive photostat of original map at CUL Maps R.b.12.

Bottisham – 1833 – BOT83303 – LBH Hc 19/7/47
Garden at Bottisham Lode.
Surveyor: T[homas] J[ames] Tatham; **Scale bar** 0–3 chains (= 4 1/16in.), 1:585; **Size:** (i) 5 7/8 x 5 3/4in.; **Top** is NE; Manuscript(i), paper mounted on cloth, coloured.

16p. in NW corner of TL5362, bounded in NE by 'Bottisham Lode Street'.

Names of roads and neighbouring owners. Acreage; roads; garden.

Border imitating the edge of a sheet of paper; title at top; scale middle bottom; compass top right showing 4 points. Garden coloured green, road and path coloured brown.

Numbers on plots suggest map originally accompanied by a terrier. Map is an inset at middle right to BOT83301. At LBH EO 3/5 is an inexact copy, drawn in 1848, at bottom right of sheet and shows a fence, terrier on next page; see BOT83301 for details. Surveyor's 1st names were Thomas James [Eden T34]. Positive photostat of original map at CUL Maps R.b.12.

Bottisham – 1833 – BOT83304 – LBH Hc 19/7/47
Premises in the Village.
Surveyor: T[homas] J[ames] Tatham; **Scale bar** 0–100 feet (= 1 1/2in.), 1:800; **Size:** (i) 6 1/8 x 5 3/4in.; **Top** is NNW; Manuscript(i), paper mounted on cloth, coloured.

1r.22p. in TL5460, bounded by 'Bottisham Street' in NE and land owned by Peterhouse in SW.

Names of roads and neighbouring owners. Farmhouse and outbuildings shown in plan form. Acreages; roads and watercourses; garden; fences.

Border imitating the edge of a sheet of paper; title middle top with a decorative line beneath; scale middle bottom; compass at left showing 4 points. Water coloured blue, garden coloured green, roads coloured brown, farmhouse coloured red.

Numbers on plots suggest map originally accompanied by a terrier. Map is an inset at bottom right to BOT83301.

At LBH EO 3/5 is an inexact copy, drawn in 1848, at top left of sheet, terrier on next page; see BOT83301 for details. Surveyor's 1st names were Thomas James [Eden T34]. Positive photostat of original map at CUL Maps R.b.12.

Bottisham – 1833 – BOT83305 – LBH Hc 19/7/47
Quy Fen.
Surveyor: T[homas] J[ames] Tatham; **Scale bar** 0–8 chains (= 2in.), 1:3,168; **Size:** (i) 8 5/8 x 7 3/8in.; **Top** is NW; Manuscript(i), paper mounted on cloth, coloured.
26a.1r.29p., probably in W of TL5362, bounded in NW by 'Quy Mill Street'.
Names of neighbouring owners. Closed fields; acreages; roads and watercourses.
Border imitating the edge of a sheet of paper; title middle top; scale bottom right; compass middle right showing 4 points. Water coloured blue, fields coloured green and brown.
Numbers on plots suggest map originally accompanied by a terrier. Map is an inset at top left to BOT83301. At LBH EO 3/5 is an inexact copy, drawn in 1848, at top right of sheet, fields coloured green, roads coloured brown, terrier on next page; see BOT83301 for details. Surveyor's 1st names were Thomas James [Eden T34]. Positive photostat of original map at CUL Maps R.b.12.

Bourn – 1791 – BOU79101 – SJC MPS 6
A Map of the Parsonage Farm at Bourn in the County of Cambridge; Surveyed in the Year 1791.
Surveyor: [Joseph Freeman?]; **Scale bar** 0–20 chains (= 2 1/2in.), 1:6,336; **Size:** (i) 25 7/8 x 21 5/16in.; **Top** is NW; Manuscript(i), parchment, coloured.
'Parsonage Farm', probably Manor Farm at TL325566, and 218a.3r.39p. bounded by Caldecote Parish in E and Bourn Brook in S, and extending along Riddy Lane ['Wood Way'] in SW and along Broadway as far as common in N.
Names of fields, roads and neighbouring owners. Farm buildings, cottages and dovecote shown in plan form, post mill shown in perspective. Open fields showing owner's strips; closes; common and meadow; wood and trees; roads and watercourses; hedges; bridges; ponds; 'Old Hop garden'.
Border of 1 broad and 1 narrow band; title top right in a rococo cartouche; scale middle top; compass middle left showing 4 points. Table on right giving acreages of each plot and number of ridges in open fields, decorated with a floral strand at bottom. Trees and pasture coloured green, buildings coloured red, roads coloured brown, strips may have been coloured but the colour has now faded.
Note at bottom starts: 'Note There are 6 Acres of Tumbrell [fodder?] or Lott Grass, not specified in this Map; it being Measured and set out by a Pole every year: – They abutt as follows ...' In similar style to that of Joseph Freeman, who worked for St John's College in the 1790s. Land leased by St John's College from Christ's College [VCH, 5, 10]. Photograph at 1:8,739 at CRO TR869/P2.

Bourn – 1795 – BOU79501 – CCC
Parsonage Farm at Bourn in the County of Cambridge 1795.
Surveyor: [John Dugmore]; **Scale bar** 0–40 chains (= 2 1/2in.), 1:12,670; **Size:** (i) 23 1/4 x 16 1/2in.; **Top** is N; Manuscript(i), parchment, coloured.
'Parsonage Farm', probably Manor Farm at TL325566, and 218a.3r.39p. in whole parish bounded by Caldecote

Parish in E and roads from Huntingdon to London in SW and from Cambridge to St Neot's in N.
Names of fields, neighbouring owners and roads. Farm buildings shown in plan form, post mill shown in perspective. Open fields showing owner's strips; closes; common; wood and trees; meadow and stocking; acreages; roads and watercourses; bridges; hedge.
Border of 1 narrow band; title top left; scale at bottom; compass above scale showing 4 points. Buildings coloured red, fields outlined in red, blue, green and yellow, water coloured blue.
Accompanying terrier gives names of areas and acreages. Note beneath terrier starts: 'Note There are Six Acres of Tumbrell [fodder?] or Lott Grass not specified in this Plan, it being measured and set out by a Pole every year. They abutt as follows: ...' Map is in volume of maps by Dugmore; his 1st name was John [Eden D344]. Land owned by Christ's College, Cambridge.

Bourn – [Early 19th century] – BOU80001 – CCC PL25
Bourne.
Scale 12 Chains Per Inch, 1:9,504; **Size:** (i) 20 7/8 x 29 1/2in.; **Top** is NW; Manuscript(i), paper, coloured.
Bourn Church, TL325563, and c. 4,000a. in whole parish, bounded by Caldecote Parish in E, Longstowe and Caxton parishes in W, Kingston Parish in S and road to St Neot's in N.
Names of farms, fields and roads. Cottages and farm buildings shown in plan form, church and 2 post mills shown in perspective. Open fields showing owner's strips; closes and pightles; common and meadow; wood and trees; acreages; roads and footpaths; watercourses and bridges.
Border of 1 narrow band; title top left; scale bottom left across middle of compass which shows 8 plain points. Fields outlined in yellow and red.
Numbers on plots suggest map originally accompanied by a terrier. Far E corner of sheet torn off. Shows land owned by Christ's College, Cambridge, and drawn in early 19th century before 1820 inclosure award.

Bourn – [1813] – BOU81301 – CLC Safe B:38/9
[Allotment in Bourn to Clare College, Cambridge.]
Surveyor: [William Farr]; **Scale:** 1:3,420; **Size:** (iii) 4 x 4 3/4in.; **Top** is E; Manuscript(iii), paper, uncoloured.
9a.1r.2p. in NW of TL3457, bounded by Caldecote Parish in S, road to Bourn in N and tributary to Bourn Brook ['Westward Dean'] in W.
Names of tenants and neighbouring owners. Closed fields; acreages; entrances.
Accompanying letter from William Farr of Kingston School to the Master of Clare College [John Torkington; VCH, 3, 346], 22 January 1813: 'Sir, By Mr Radford I understand that you request the Plan of the Allotment in Bourn Field with the Division lines that seperates one Occupier from the other, which is as in the following Plan'. After plan, Farr describes entrances to property.

Bourn – [c. 1820] – BOU82001 – BLM Add.36230 f.234
[Land at Bourn allotted to John Butler on inclosure.]
Surveyor: [William Custance]; **Scale:** 1:4,700; **Size:** (i) 4 1/2 x 3 15/16in.; **Top** is N; Manuscript(ii), tracing paper mounted on paper, uncoloured.
7a.1r.0p. in TL3256, E of road from Bourn to Childerley.
Name of owner. Farm buildings shown in plan form. Closed fields showing owner's land; acreages; roads.
Border of 1 narrow band.

Note at bottom: 'Copied from Bourn Inclosure Plan'. Numbers on plots refer to 1820 inclosure award; William Custance surveyed map which accompanied award. Shows land gained by exchange with Philip Yorke, 3rd Earl of Hardwicke.

Bourn – 1826 – BOU82601 – CCC Maps and Plans 19

A Map and Survey of the Rectory and Parish of Bourn In the County of Cambridge, in which are exhibited the Glebe Lands and Estates yielding Tythes to The Master, Fellows and Scholars of Christ's College in the University of Cambridge and also thes [sic.] Estates held by Copy of Court Roll of their Manor of Bourn in Bourn.
Surveyor: [William Custance]; **Draughtsman:** S[amuel] K[empson] Simmons; **Scale bar** 1–0–25 chains (= 3 1/4in.), 1:6,336; **Size:** (i) 35 x 45 15/16in.; **Top** is WNW; Manuscript(i), parchment mounted on cloth, coloured.
Bourn Church, TL325563, and c. 4,000a. in whole parish bounded by Caldecote Parish in E, Longstowe and Caxton parishes in W, Kingston Parish in S and road from Cambridge to St Neot's in N.
Names of farms, fields, hills and roads. Buildings shown in plan form and include church, Bourn Hall, farm buildings, cottages, and Caldecote and Caxton mills. Closed fields; common; wood and trees; hedges; acreages; state of cultivation shown by colour; roads, including turnpike; footpaths; watercourses and ponds; bridges; gardens and orchards; 'Kingston Stones'; 'Stub Cross'; 'New Cross'; 'Drayton Gap'; gravel pit.
Border 5/8in. wide of 4 bands, middle 2 have alternately coloured and uncoloured squares; title at top in a cartouche with drapery; scale on left in compass which shows 8 points. In the title cartouche is Christ's College's coat of arms. Top left: 'The Village of Bourn from Howard Dole No 363' showing Bourn Hall, farmers, sheep, a dog and trees. Fields coloured brown and green, buildings coloured red, water coloured blue, acreages of copyhold land given in red.
Note: 'From the Inclosure Survey By S. K. Simmons Received 1826'. Accompanying terrier at CCC Drawer 119. William Custance surveyed map which accompanied 1820 inclosure award.

Boxworth – 1650 – BOX65001 – HRO LR23/367

The Plott, or Description of Boxworth in Cambridgeshire, beinge parte of the demeanes of the Lady Ann Cutts, wherein there is to be observed, that the Arable growndes are shaddowed with a Lande, or Arable Coulour, and stripte with the same, to represent the ridges, and marked with Figures, directing to the Feilde=booke wherein theire seuerall Quantities are sett downe, and in whose occupacon they are; The Rectorie Land (for Destinction sake) in euery Furlonge, is prickt out, and drawen in greene the two seuerall numbers in euery peece, the one, as 1:2:3 &c sheweth how many landes, or Ridges there bee, the other hath a relacon to the Feilde=booke; the Meadowes and pastures are saddowed about with grasse Greene and as if were filled with Mowls hills The High wayes or hauens are likewise under a Greene and likewise the woods, both pastures, meadowes, and and [sic.] woodes are marked with letters hauinge relacon to the Booke. The Compasse or Seacart sheweth how every parcell of lande whether arable, Meadow, pasture, or woode is buttalled and bownded. The Compasses, and Scale shewes nothing of consequence only how many pooles or perches are represented in the plott, in an Intch which are so accordinge to the statute in that case made 16 and 1/2 feete in euery pole or perch finished the Twenty fiyth of Apriell anno Domini 1650 per Mattheu. Haywarde.
Surveyor: Matthew Haywarde; **Scale:** 1:4,950; **Size:** (i) 54 x 36 1/8in.; **Top** is N; Manuscript(i), parchment, coloured.
Boxworth Church, TL348645, and c. 2,600a. in whole parish except for S of Bird's Pasture Farm in far S, with 6a. in NW of Childerley Parish.
Names of fields, balks, roads, neighbouring parishes and neighbouring owners. Manor house, cottages, farm buildings, Boxworth and Knapwell churches and post mill shown in perspective. Open fields showing direction of strips; closes; 'Boxworth Meadow' and pasture; wood and trees; waste; 'The Downes in Common to all the Tenants'; pasture land shown by 'mowls hills'; acreages of some strips; roads and gates; watercourses and ponds; Childerley Park adjoining map; 'white pitts'; hedges and fences.
Border 1/2in. wide of a central yellow band with 1 broad black band on either side; title bottom right in a square cartouche with an emblematic device with a ship at top, leaves around, a wall on left and right, 'Honi Soit Qui Maly Pense' above and 'Prudentis est in Concilio Fortunam Semper alabere' below, and coloured red, yellow and green; yellow dividers beneath title with a red top but no scale bar; compass rose middle right showing 32 red and yellow points and location of pole star. Geometrical squares with yellow and black edges in top right and left corners. Deer shown in Childerley Park, and some trees at an enlarged scale. Trees also shown in land in Knapwell Parish, flowers under dividers. Balks coloured green, roads coloured yellow, arable coloured in brown stripes and outlined in brown, pasture shown by blue 'mowls hills', buildings coloured red, trees and water coloured blue.
Pencil notes. Bottom left and right of map are missing. Numbers and letters on furlongs and pasture closes. Related survey at CRO P15/28/1: 'Boxworth Booke of Survey taken the 26th day of Apriell Anno Domini 1650', which shows that the extent of the estate was 2,494a.1r.36p. and gives land use. Photograph at 1:9,000 at CRO TR373/P1.

Brinkley – 1817 – BRI81701 – CRO L62/1

A Plan of an Estate Situated in the Parish of Brinkley in the County of Cambridgeshire the Property of William Frost Esqr Taken 1817 By Jno Golding.
Surveyor: John Golding; **Scale:** 1:7,490; **Size:** (i) 28 7/8 x 17 1/2in.; **Top** is WNW; Manuscript(i), parchment, coloured.
Brinkley Hall, TL631549, and c. 1,000a. in NW of parish bounded by Carlton cum Willingham Parish in W and Westley Waterless Parish in N, and extending as far SE as village centre.
Names of roads, parishes and neighbouring owners. Brinkley Hall shown in perspective, church and a few buildings S of church shown in plan form. Closed fields showing owner's land; wood and trees; acreages; roads; hedges; clunch pit.
Border of 2 narrow red lines; title top right in a cartouche of 2 red lines decorated with yellow dots inside; compass middle right showing 8 points coloured yellow and red. Some plots coloured blue, others coloured brown or outlined in yellow, buildings coloured red.
Numbers on fields suggest map originally accompanied by a terrier.

Burrough Green – [c. 1634–9] – BUR63401 – SCC I/3

[Land in Burrough Green and Dullingham in 'Grove' and 'Underwood' fields NW of Burrough Green village, owned by St Catharine's College, Cambridge.]

Scale: 1:5,610; **Size:** (ii) 8 1/8 x 12 7/8in.; **Top** is S; Manuscript(ii), paper, uncoloured.

Land N and S of 'Grove~Field Way', bounded by 'Westley Town Land' in S.

Names of fields, roads, tenants and neighbouring owners. Cottages shown in perspective. Open fields showing owner's strips; acreages; roads.

Compass rose centre bottom showing 4 points.

Accompanied by copies made in 1725–6 of terriers drawn up in 1634 and 1639. Map is probably also a copy made in 1725–6 of an original drawn between 1634 and 1639. See also BUR63402–4.

Burrough Green – [c. 1634–9] – BUR63402 – SCC I/3

[Land in 'Chalk~Pitt~Field' in Burrough Green and Dullingham NW of Burrough Green village, owned by St Catharine's College, Cambridge.]

Scale: 1:4,480; **Size:** (ii) 8 1/4 x 12 7/8in.; **Top** is S; Manuscript(ii), paper, uncoloured.

Land bounded by 'Chalk~pitt Way' in N and 'Westley Hall Mead' in S.

Names of field, roads, tenants and neighbouring owners. Open field showing owner's strips; acreages; roads; 'Shoot Butts'; 'Dead man's Bushes'; 'Westley Hall Mead'.

Compass rose centre bottom showing 4 points.

Accompanied by copies made in 1725–6 of terriers drawn up in 1634 and 1639. Map is probably also a copy made in 1725–6 of an original drawn between 1634 and 1639. See also BUR63401,3–4.

Burrough Green – [c. 1634–9] – BUR63403 – SCC I/3

[Land in 'Rad~Field' in Burrough Green, owned by St Catharine's College, Cambridge.]

Scale: 1:3,380; **Size:** (iii) 4 1/2 x 6in.; **Top** is S; Manuscript(ii), paper, uncoloured.

6a.0r.9p. in 'Rad~Field' in E of parish, bounded by Out Wood in E.

Names of neighbouring owners. Closed fields; Out Wood; state of cultivation given in words; acreages.

Compass rose centre bottom showing 4 points.

Pencil notes. Accompanied by copies made in 1725–6 of terriers drawn up in 1634 and 1639. Map is probably also a copy made in 1725–6 of an original drawn between 1634 and 1639. See also BUR63401–2,4.

Burrough Green – [c. 1634–9] – BUR63404 – SCC I/3

[Land in Burrough Green, owned by St Catharine's College, Cambridge.]

Scale: 1:4,610; **Size:** (iii) 5 1/2 x 5 3/4in.; Manuscript(ii), paper, uncoloured.

2a.0r.25p. bounded by roads on left and right.

Names of neighbouring owners. Open fields showing owner's strips; acreages; roads.

Accompanied by copies made in 1725–6 of terriers drawn up in 1634 and 1639. Map is probably also a copy made in 1725–6 of an original drawn between 1634 and 1639. See also BUR63401–3.

Burrough Green – 1674 – BUR67401 – CRO 101/P1

A descripti{on of} the Mannor of Burrough cum {Bret}tons in the County of Cambridge belonging to Henry Slingsby Esqr with other lands & Tenement in Brinkley Westley & Dullingham thereunto apperteyning.

Surveyor: [William?] Palmer; **Scale bar** {0–40}–100 perches (= 2 7/8in.), 1:3,960; **Size:** (i) 25 3/8 x 95 11/16in.; **Top** is SSW; Manuscript(i), parchment, coloured.

Burrough Green Hall, TL636555, and c. 2,700a. in whole parish, and 23 plots in Westley Waterless, Dullingham and Brinkley parishes.

Names of fields, roads, owners, tenants and neighbouring owners. Church, hall, parsonage, mill, cottages and post mill shown in perspective. Open fields showing all strips in blocks for each occupier; closes; common and meadow; waste and heath; Park, 'Brettons', Out and 'Hundred' woods, Sparrows' Grove, trees; state of cultivation given in words on most plots; acreages; tenure; roads and watercourses; gardens and orchards; moats; Sipsey Bridge.

Border of 2 broad brown bands, each with a narrow yellow band on either side; title top left in a rectangular cartouche of 2 brown lines; scale bottom left coloured yellow, green and brown; large compass rose top left with 8 brown and yellow points, smaller rose bottom right with 8 red and green points. Plots outlined in yellow, brown and green, hall coloured red.

Pencil notes. Some holes in parchment. 24 insets top and bottom of strips in neighbouring parishes. Each has orientation, acreages and names of neighbouring owners and tenants and is surrounded in a border of 1 broad yellow band with 1 narrow brown band on either side. Surveyor might possibly be the man who drew FOR65601–7 and SOH65601–12.

Burrough Green – 1796 – BUR79601 – PCC

Estate in the Parish of Bor*ough* Green in the County of Cambridge belonging to the Master & Fellows of Pembroke Hall, Cambridge Surveyed 1796.

Scale bar 0–10 chains (= 3 1/4in.), 1:2,437; **Size:** (i) 14 7/8 x 11 13/16in.; **Top** is NW; Manuscript(i), parchment, coloured.

Burrough Green Church, TL635555, and 26a.0r.33p. E of it and road to Great Bradley bounded by Dullingham Parish in N, and 1 close in SE of parish S of Padloe End.

Names of fields, roads and neighbouring owners. Farm buildings and school shown in plan form, church shown in perspective. Closes of owner's land; acreages; hedges; roads and watercourses.

Border of 1 narrow band; title top left; scale bottom left; compass centre top showing 4 plain points, incorrectly giving top as N. Table top right giving field numbers and acreages. Roads coloured brown.

Pencil notes of land use and variant acreages.

Burrough Green – 1796 – BUR79602 – PTC Treasury Burrough Green C35

Estate in the Parish of Bor*ough* Green in the County of Cambridge belonging to the Master and Fellows of Peterhouse College, Cambridge Surveyed 1796.

Surveyor: [Joseph Freeman?]; **Scale** of Ten Chains, Scale bar 0–10 chains (= 3 5/16in.), 1:2,391; **Size:** (i) 14 1/2 x 11 7/8in.; **Top** is N; Manuscript(i), parchment, coloured.

23a.1r.27p. S of village bounded by road from Burrough Green to Thurlow in W.

Names of fields, roads and neighbouring owners. Closed fields; trees; acreages; roads.

Border of 1 narrow band; title top left; scale under title; compass at bottom showing 4 points. Table top right giving acreages. Roads coloured brown.

Pencil notes correcting acreages. In style of Joseph Freeman.

Burrough Green – 1814 – BUR81401 – PCC
Farm at Borough Green.
Surveyor: J[ames] Charville; **Scale:** 1:980; **Size:** (ii) 9 1/4 x 14 1/2in.; **Top** is N; Manuscript(i), parchment, uncoloured.

Farm at TL638555, and 55a.0r.14p. E of road to Great Bradley bounded by Dullingham Parish in N, and 1 close in SE of parish S of Padloe End.

Names of roads and neighbouring owners. Farm buildings and cottages shown in plan form. Closes of owner's land; acreages; roads and footpaths; gates.

Title at top.

Note on left of acreages and 2a.2r.28p. added to map. The neighbouring owners, footpaths, gates, road names and note of land added are all in a different hand from that of the title, date, surveyor's signature and a sketch, bottom right, of 7a.2r.10p. Surveyor's 1st name was probably James; he was the schoolmaster in 1821 [Charity Commission, 1837, 131–2]. Land owned by Pembroke College, Cambridge.

Burrough Green – [c. 1820] – BUR82001 – CRO P17/25/47
Dr Cages Charity.
Surveyor: [C[harles] Wedge [jr]]; **Scale:** Six Chains to an Inch, 1:4,752; **Size:** (ii) 12 1/2 x 7 7/8in.; **Top** is NW; Manuscript(i), paper as endpaper to volume, uncoloured.

Blacksmith's shop in Burrough Green End, TL625561, and 11a.3r.7p. in NW of parish in 2 plots: 'Sheldrake's' at corner of roads from Newmarket to Brinkley and from Burrough Green to Westley Waterless, and 1 plot with smithy further W at Burrough End.

Names of fields and neighbouring owners. Blacksmith's shop shown in plan form, windmill and Westley Waterless Church shown in perspective. Closed fields showing owner's land; acreages; roads; hedges.

Title middle top; scale middle bottom; compass top right showing N with a feathered tail.

Map is front endpaper of: 'Account of Borough Green Charities', with C[harles] Wedge's name inscribed. Account was started in 1820 and gives history of charity, copy of trust deed, details of land, tenure and accounts. Wedge's 1st name was Charles [Eden W206.1]. See also BUR82002.

Burrough Green – [c. 1820] – BUR82002 – CRO P17/25/47
Dr Knight's Charity.
Surveyor: [C[harles] Wedge [jr]]; **Scale:** 6 Chains to an Inch, 1:4,752; **Size:** (ii) 12 7/16 x 7 7/8in.; **Top** is SE; Manuscript(i), paper as back endpaper to volume, uncoloured.

Burrough Green Church, TL635555, and 48a.1r.15p. E of it and road from Dullingham to Great Bradley ['Newmarket to Thurlow'], and extending N to boundary with Dullingham Parish. In addition, 1 plot to SE bounded by road and brook, and 1 plot called 'Watson's Charity' N of road from Westley Waterless to Burrough Green and W of school land.

Names of fields, roads, owners and neighbouring owners. 'School House' and other buildings shown in plan form, church shown in perspective. Closed fields showing owner's land; wood and trees; pasture; acreages; roads; watercourses and pond.

Title top left; scale middle right; compass in centre showing N with a feathered tail.

Map is back endpaper of: 'Account of Borough Green Charities', with C[harles] Wedge's name inscribed. See BUR82001 for details of Account and surveyor.

Burrough Green – 1833 – BUR83301 – PCC
Estate in the Parish of Boroughgreen in the County of Cambridge belonging to the Master & Fellows of Pembroke Hall Cambridge. Surveyed 1833 By Alexr Watford.
Surveyor: Alexander Watford [jr]; **Scale bar** 0–[10] chains (= 3 5/8in.), 1:2,185; **Size:** (i) 23 1/8 x 15 7/16in.; **Top** is N; Manuscript(i), parchment, coloured.

Farm at TL638555, and 30a.0r.13p. bounded by roads from Burrough Green to Dullingham in NW and to Dullingham Ley in E, and 1 close in SE of parish S of Padloe End.

Names of fields, roads and neighbouring owners. Farm buildings shown in plan form. Closed fields showing owner's land; wood; waste; state of cultivation shown by colour; acreages; roads; watercourses; land received in exchange from Dullingham Parish; part of village green 'taken in by the Tenant' identified on table.

Border of 1 broad band with 2 narrow bands on inside; title top left with decorative line-work; scale under title; compass top right showing 8 points. Table on left giving description of land, acreages and reasons why land received or exchanged on inclosure. Pasture coloured green, arable coloured in brown stripes, roads coloured yellow.

Pencil notes of tenants in 1848.

Burwell – 1806 – BUW80601 – PRO MR 509
A Map of the Demesne and Copyhold Lands of the Manor of Burwell Ramseys in the Parish of Burwell in the County of Cambridge belonging to the King's Most Excellent Majesty.
Surveyor: William Custance; **Scale** of half a Mile, Scale bar 1–0–40 chains (= 6 3/4in.), 1:4,811; **Size:** (i) 62 3/8 x 47 3/8in.; **Top** is NW; Manuscript(i), parchment, coloured.

Burwell Church, TL589661, and 956a.2r.2p. in whole parish except for Adventurers Fen in NW.

Names of fields, droves and neighbouring owners. Houses, church and 'Weighing House' shown in plan form, 2 post mills shown in perspective. Open fields showing owner's strips; 'Town Land'; 'Lammas Ground'; 'Encroachments'; state of cultivation shown by colour; roads and footpaths; bridleways and 'The Flat'; milestones; gates; watercourses and bridges; ponds, including 'Wa[r]braham Hole'; stone pit; churchyard; 'Seite of the Tower'; Devil's Ditch and gaps; 'The turn of the Lands'.

Border of 1 broad band with 1 narrow band on inside; title top right; scale bottom left; compass middle right showing 8 points. Table bottom right giving tenants, field names, 'Content by estimation' and 'Content by Statute Measure'. Roads coloured brown, pasture coloured green, arable coloured red, buildings coloured red.

Land in far S of parish in Newmarket Heath shown as inset centre bottom. Note centre top added later: '171 0 7

Sold to T{he Tr}ustees of The Jockey Club Feb: 1819[?] Vide Sale Book: 6–p:170'.

Burwell – 1816 – BUW81601 – PRO MPEE 80
Plan of an Estate situate at Burwell in the County of Cambridge belonging to The King's most excellent Majesty.
Scale bar 0–24 chains (= 4in.), 1:4,752; **Size:** (i) 27 7/16 x 35 1/16in.; **Top** is NE; Manuscript(i), parchment, coloured.
Junction of roads from Swaffham Prior to Fordham and from Exning to Burwell at TL588667, and 712a.3r.1p. in whole parish except for SE.
Names of fen, droves, tenants and neighbouring owners. Farm buildings shown in plan form. Closed fields showing owner's land; fen; 'Church Land'; acreages; roads and footpaths; watercourses and bridges; hedges.
Border of 1 broad band with 1 narrow band on inside; title top left; scale centre bottom; compass in centre showing 4 points with a decorated N. Table bottom right giving field names, acreages, land use and tenants. Roads coloured brown, water coloured blue, buildings coloured red, hedges coloured green, fen outlined in blue.

Burwell – 1817 – BUW81701 – PCC Burwell C13
Burwell Heath.
Surveyor: Robert Stockdale; **Scale:** 1:2,540; **Size:** (ii) 7 5/16 x 9in.; Manuscript(i), paper, uncoloured.
35a.3r.37p. in 'Burwell Heath'.
Names of fields. Closed fields showing owner's land; acreages; Beacon Course [racecourse].
Title at top.
Later note on 1 field: 'This piece was given to the Jockey Club in exchange for 14 Acres of arable June 1817* *But the Master has given me 17.2.20 as the measure Custance approved of the Exchange. G[ilbert] A[inslie] 1826'. Note refers to William Custance [Eden C624]. Later note on dorse: 'Note. This is by Robert Stockdale the then Treasurer. June 1817 G[ilbert] A[inslie] 1834'. Land owned by Pembroke College, Cambridge; Gilbert Ainslie was a Fellow of the College from 1815, and Master from 1828 to 1870 [Venn, II, 1, 20].

Burwell – [Post 1818] – BUW81801 – CRO R57/15c/1(c)
Tracing from Burwell Award Map re Alfred Dawson's copyholds.
Surveyor: [Samuel Kempson Simmons]; **Scale:** 1:4,860; **Size:** (ii) 9 11/16 x 7 5/8in.; **Top** is W; Manuscript(iv), tracing paper on paper, uncoloured.
12a.2r.3p. at TL588665 in W of village, W of the 'Cartway' and E of 'Low Road'.
Names of roads, owners, tenants and neighbouring owners. Closed fields showing owner's land; acreages; tenure; roads; kiln.
Title middle top.
Tracing from map by Samuel Kempson Simmons which accompanied 1818 inclosure award; names changed since that time.

Burwell – [c. 1821–63] – BUW82101 – PRO CRES 2/107
[Land at Burwell, owned by the Crown and by Sir St Vincent Cotton 6th Bart.]
Scale: 1:4,760; **Size:** (ii) 10 x 16 3/8in.; **Top** is NE; Manuscript(ii), paper, uncoloured.
c. 320a. in TL5965 and S of TL5966, bounded by Exning Parish [Suffolk] in S and road to Exning in N.

Names of owners, tenants and roads. Closed fields; acreages; roads; tenure.
Compass top left showing 4 points.
Drawn between 1821, date of watermark of the paper, and 1863, when Sir St Vincent Cotton died [*DNB*, 12, 316].

Burwell – [1825] – BUW82501 – QCC 355 A21, B21
Estate at Burwell In The County of Cambridge.
Surveyor: [Alexander Watford jr]; **Scale bar** 0–25 chains (= 4 3/16in.), 1:4,728; **Size:** (i) 15 7/8 x 38 1/2in.; **Top** is NW; Manuscript(ii), paper, coloured.
Farm in village in TL5867, and 48a.2r.13p. in E of parish from Hallard's Fen in W to Ness Farm in E.
Names of fields, roads and neighbouring owners. Homestead and cottages shown in plan form. Closed fields showing owner's land; state of cultivation shown by colour; acreages; hedges; roads and footpaths; watercourses; 'Springhead'; orchards.
Border on top and 2 sides of 1 broad band with 1 narrow band on either side; title at top; scale top right; compass in centre showing 4 points. Table above scale giving field names, acreages, land use and allotments. Roads coloured brown, water coloured blue, fields coloured yellow and green.
Under scale: 'Note. The Situation of the Pieces of Land in Burwell is sketched in, with respect to the Distance from one piece to the other; and may therefore be inaccurate as to the real Distance, when measured on the Ground'. Above homestead is enlarged sketch of it, which measures 4 1/2 x 2in.: 'Buildings on Scale of two Chains to the Inch', 1:1,584. Vertical dimension is measured to bottom of drawing. Map at top of sheet, which also contains maps of Chesterton [CHF82501], Dullingham [DUL82501] and Swaffham Prior [SWP82502], and in volume drawn in 1825: 'Plans of the Several Estates in England and Wales belonging to the President and Fellows of the College of St Margaret and St Bernard commonly called Queen's College in the University of Cambridge Delineated from Authentic Documents in the possession of the said President and Fellows and from actual Surveys taken By their most obedient and obliged Servant Alexr Watford'. Title page drawn by James Richardson [Watford's nephew]. This is the Bursar's copy; 2nd, finer, copy [the Master's copy] at QCC 355 B21 measures 14 7/8 x 36 5/8in., is drawn on parchment and has a scale bar 0–20 chains (= 3 1/4in.), 1:4,874. Border 7/16in. wide of a central blue band with 1 broad band on either side, title has gothic lettering, compass on left shows 8 points. Table has a border imitating a scroll of paper and red lines. Fields coloured in brown and yellow stripes and have green borders, roads have red/brown edges. Written by the buildings is 'given to School'. Positive photostat of this copy at BL 1640.(28) at 1:10,560.

C

Caldecote – [1788] – CAL78801 – CLC Safe B:39/8
[Copy of map of land in Caldecote, owned by Clare College, Cambridge.]
Surveyor: [Joseph Freeman?]; **Scale:** 1:4,420; **Size:** (ii) 20 3/4 x 36 5/8in.; **Top** is W; Manuscript(ii), paper mounted on cloth, coloured.
Caldecote Church, TL348563, and 268a.2r.39p. scattered throughout parish.
Names of fields, roads and neighbouring owners. Church, houses and farm buildings shown in plan form.

Open fields showing owner's strips; closes; trees; roads; hedges; balks.

Table bottom left giving tenants, field names and acreages. Land let to Radford coloured yellow, land leased by Sole coloured red, balks, trees and old inclosures coloured green.

Note under table of initials of neighbours: 'C.C. Christ College Sole Occupier with black Ink T.T. Thomas Towney Radford [occupier] with Red T.C. Thomas Cocksedge Note where the Lands are marked out and numbered or not coloured they belong to the Revd T. Gregory'. Pencil notes. Late 18th-century copy of map probably drawn in 1788; copy of a reference to the map, dated 1788, is at CLC Safe B:38/9. Map in style of Joseph Freeman, who drew a series of maps for Clare College in late 1780s and 1790s.

Carlton cum Willingham – 1612 – CAR61201 – CUL MS Plans R.b.19

The viewe and Forme of the mannors of Weston Colvyle & Carlton parva, and of the demesne lands nowe occupied with the sceyte of the sayd mannors & other fearms thervn belonging: Together with all and all manner, landes, tenenmentes, meaddowes, pastures, feadinges, wooddes, underwooddes, and other thapurtennaintes, beyng parcell of the hereditamentes of the Honorable Mr Samson Leonard Esqe being sittuate lying, extending or being, within the townes, parishes, hamlettes and fyldes, of Weston Collvile, Carlton parva, & Carlton Magna Willingame, Brinckeley, & West Wratton, or in either of them in the County of Cambridge, euen as the sayd landes tenementes & hereditamentes, ben layed linated & occupied to & with the sayd mannors & messuages and to & with euery of them seuerally, vewed, seene, pervsed and measured by the pole or perch contayning in length. xvj. foot & a halfe, at the appoyntement of the sayd Mr Samson Leonard and also by the Information & confession of Robte Holeum baylyff & Lamberte Abbut, Gyles Samon, Thomas Tye, Willm Haigh, Gylberte Webb, & many others the tennantes in June & July in the tenth yeare of his Majesties Raygne of Ingland, 1612.
Surveyor: William Norton; **Scale bar** 0–16 [chains] (= 2 7/8in.), 1:4,408; **Size:** (i) 37 1/2 x 117in.; **Top** is SW; Manuscript(i), parchment, coloured.
Weston Colville ['Weston Colvyle'] Church, TL617532, and c. 1,100a. in Weston Colville and Carlton cum Willingham parishes.
Names of farms, fields, tenants, neighbouring owners and roads. Buildings shown in perspective and include Carlton Hall, Weston Colville and Carlton churches, parsonage, 'Willingam chapple', farms, barns and outbuildings, cottages and windmill. Open fields showing all of owner's strips and some others; glebe; common and pasture; wood, trees and tree near 'Carlton Hall'; 'Wesson grene' and 'Little grene'; waste; state of cultivation shown by colour; acreages; tenure; roads and footpaths; ponds and moat; 'glachman gate'; pound; 'the pulpit'; 'the lyme kill'; 'bowell hill'; 'shrub'; 'West Wratten shrub' and 'Wratten lowe shrub' adjoining map.
Border of 5/8in.-wide blue band; title bottom left; scale middle left surmounted by green and brown dividers with a red top; compass rose top left coloured red, green, blue and yellow and showing 16 points, ink compass rose on far right showing 4 points. Parish boundaries shown in red, common, pasture and heathland coloured green, roads and arable belonging to certain farms or tenants coloured brown, cottages coloured blue with red roofs.

Note middle bottom: 'Noate that in the Common Fylde is set downe these letters Followinge, that nowe doe occupye the landes, other the surnames of the men, or other wise the name of the farmes. viz: for Collvills fearme is set downe – coll: for Abbut fearme is set downe – moyns. for Hocum fearme is set downe – lever for Samon fearme is set downe – mad: for Cooper fearme is set downe – Coper: And for all the Rest by ther sur mames [sic.]'. Under this note: 'Per me Willm Norton superuisor: huius maneri:'. Right of these notes is inset: 'All other the lands belonging to dobido fearme lyeth in the comon fylds of Willinghame'; this is land lying NW of St Matthew's Chapel at Willingham Green, and W of road to Brinkley Chapel, TL625539. Note far right by heath: 'These ronndells doe dovle out the heaths'. Ink notes. Facsimile at CUL MS Plans 533. Photograph in CRO.

Carlton cum Willingham – 1754 – CAR75401 – CRO L3/33

A Map of some Lands belonging to The Revrd Mr Samu: Knight lying in The Parish of Carlton with Willingham near Burrow Green in The County of Cambridge Surveyed 1754 by Wm Elstobb Jnr.
Surveyor: William Elstobb jr; **Scale bar** 1–0–15 Gunter's chains (= 6 7/16in.), 1:1,969; **Size:** (i) 14 3/4 x 18 9/16in.; **Top** is NNE; Manuscript(i), paper mounted on paper, coloured.
Site of home close, TL626540, and 29a.3r.20p. in NW of parish mainly SE of Willingham Green, extending N and S of Brook Lane and crossing River Stour.
Names of fields, roads and neighbouring owners. Farm and cottages shown in plan form. Open fields showing owner's strips; closes; common and trees; state of cultivation shown by colour; acreages; roads and footpaths; watercourses, pond and 'Rayners bridge'; gates; hedges; yard.
Border of 1 narrow and 1 broad band; title top right in a coloured cartouche of branches and leaves, flowers, grapes and birds; scale middle bottom with scale bar coloured yellow and black; compass rose middle top showing 16 red, yellow and green points. Table on right giving acreages of plots. Willingham Green, trees and pasture coloured green, arable and roads coloured brown, water coloured blue, buildings coloured red and grey.

Carlton cum Willingham – 1767 – CAR76701 – CRO R54/21/1

A Plan of the Manors of Carleton cum Willingham, in the County of Cambridge; And of Bradley, in the County of Suffolk; belonging to Thomas Brand Esqr Taken in the Year 1767.
Surveyors: Ralph Agas, Thomas Jefferys; **Scale** of 4 chains to an Inch, Scale bar 0–20 chains or 1 Quarter of a mile (= 4 15/16in.), 1:3,168; **Size:** (i) 59 x 145 5/8in.; **Top** is NNE; Manuscript(iii), paper mounted on loosely-woven cloth, coloured.
Lopham Hall, TL647521, and 1,310a.1r.16p. in parish and 978a.0r.28p. in Great Bradley Parish [Suffolk], with some strips in Weston Colville and Brinkley parishes.
Names of farms, fields, roads and some neighbouring owners. Carlton Church, Willingham Chapel and post mill in Great Bradley Parish shown in perspective, farms and cottages in Carlton, Little Carlton Green, Willingham Green and Great Bradley, 'Hunts Hall barn' and church in Great Bradley, Carlton Rectory, Carlton, 'Loppham's' and Great Bradley halls shown in plan form. Open fields

showing owner's strips and all strips in some fields; 'penns', closes, milking close and pightles; common; wood including Park, Duddock, Breed and Fennel woods in Great Bradley; trees; acreages; roads and footpaths; watercourses; gardens and orchards; earthworks and moats; fences and hedges; hop ground; ponds and springs; Sipsey Bridge in Great Bradley; pound in Great Bradley; chalk pit in Carlton; 'Bradley Hill' shown by hachures.

Border of 1 broad and 1 narrow band; title top left; scale middle top in a rococo cartouche; compass above scale showing 8 points. Tables giving tenants, field names, acreages of open and inclosed land and colour of plots for each farm; those for Great Bradley Parish are on right, those for Carlton Parish are at bottom left. Colour used to differentiate between land owned by various farms, trees coloured green, water coloured blue/green, buildings coloured red.

Note under title: 'The Estate and Manor of Carleton was copied from an ancient Survey taken by Rodolphus Agas in Queen Elizabeth's Time, into which are inserted several new Pieces since purchased: The whole revised on the Spot in the Year, 1767. At the same Time the Estate at Bradley was surveyed by Thomas Jefferys'.

Carlton cum Willingham – [1829] – CAR82901 – HERO D/EHmT89
Land belonging to John Hall Esqre in the Parish of Carlton with Willingham in the County of Cambridge, Sold to The Right Honble Thomas Lord Dacre.
Scale: 1:2,150; **Size:** (i) 11 1/2 x 19 5/16in.; **Top** is NNE; Manuscript(i), parchment, coloured.
42a.2r.16p. bounded by Brinkley Parish in NW and road from Brinkley to Weston Colville in E.
Names of neighbouring owners. Cottage shown in plan form. Closed fields; acreages; road; tenure.
Border 3/16in. wide with a decorative pattern; title top left; compass top right showing 8 points. Land outlined in red, road coloured brown.
Notes on plots of allotments under the Brinkley and Carlton inclosure acts, including: 'The Land intended to be Conveyed to Lord Dacre being Land Awarded to Richard Frost under the Carlton Inclosure Act containing 42A.2R.16P.' Note at bottom: 'NB. The Lands intended to be conveyed are shaded round with this Colour [red line]'. Map is on lease endorsed: 'Dated 4th day of April 1829 John Hall Esqre to Lord Dacre Appointment and Release of Freehold and Covenant to surrender Copyhold Lands at Carlton in Cambs'.

Castle Camps – 1617 – CAS61701 – GLC ACC.1876/MP2/2
The Description of Weste Fielde, Gidding Fielde, Langley Wood, and Diverse other Groundes thereunto near adjoyninge lieing in Castle Campes in the Countye of Cambridge being parcell of the possessions of the Governors of the Hospitall of King James founded in the Charter House in the Countie of Middlesex at the humble peticion and at the proper Costes and Charges of Thomas Sutton Esqr made in October Anno Domini 1618, by Thomas Langdon; And Ratified at a Courte of Survey there holden on Wednesday the viiith Daye of the same Month uppon the Oathe of Willm Freeman, Edwarde Freeman Tho Simson, Alexander Dodd Augustine Veisey, Willm Laggerd, Ro Maskall Senr Ro Osborne Ric Flacke Ric Stubbing, Jo Cowle, Simon Wakefield, Millt Minor, Ro Parker, Tho Lettice.

Surveyor: Thomas Langdon; **Draughtsman:** J[ohn] Prickett; **Scale bar** 0–60 perches (= 3in.), 1:3,960; **Size:** (i) 16 1/2 x 23 1/8in.; **Top** is NE; Manuscript(ii), parchment, coloured.
Camps Hall, TL615432, and c. 720a. in E of parish bounded by Ashdon Parish [Essex] in SW and Camps End in S, and extending N of road from Ashdon to Camps Hall.
Names of fields, owners and tenants. Cottages shown in perspective. Open fields showing all strips; closes; 'Pig's Pightle'; Langley and 'Willeysey' woods; meadow; acreages; roads and 'Olde Streete'; watercourses; tenure; hedges; yard; limekiln.
Border of 1 broad band with 1 narrow band on inside; title bottom left in a cartouche with a shell at top and leaves; scale centre bottom; compass to left of scale showing 8 points. Table top right, which gives 'A Note of the Contents of Acres of the Demeanes of Castle Camps', 1,592a.1r.24p., and field names, acreages, tenants and tenure. Roads outlined in yellow, wood and trees coloured green, strips outlined in brown, closes outlined in blue/green.
Pencil and ink notes, red numbers referring to terrier to CAS80002. 8 October was a Wednesday in 1617 [Old Style], not 1618 as in the title. Map was 'Redrawn, August 1790 By J Prickett'. Prickett's 1st name was John [Eden P333]. Original map, now lost, was probably GLC ACC.1876/MP2/22a. See also CAS61702–5.

Castle Camps – 1617 – CAS61702 – GLC ACC.1876/MP2/22b
The description of certaine of the hall groundes in the tenur of Iohn Whitney gent and diuerse other groundes vnto the same neare adioyning lieing in the parishe of Castle Camps and in the Countie of Cambridg being parcell of the possessions of the gouernours of the hospitall of Kinge Iames &c. made in octob: 1617.
Surveyor: [Thomas Langdon]; **Scale bar** 0–60 perches (= 2 15/16in.), 1:4,044; **Size:** (i) 16 5/16 x 23 5/16in.; **Top** is W; Manuscript(i), parchment, coloured.
Castle Camps Church, TL625425, and c. 920a. bounded by Castle Farm in S and road running W of Camps Hall in W.
Names of fields, roads, owners and tenants. Shudy and Castle Camps churches, windmill, Camps Castle, Camps Hall and farm buildings shown in perspective. Open fields showing all strips; closes; 'Frakenow woode' and trees; meadow; acreages; roads and watercourses; hedges and fences; tenure; 'The Okes'; barn yards; 'Conigree' [rabbit warren].
Border of 5/16in.-wide band with a blue and brown geometrical pattern; title middle right in a cartouche with pink, yellow, blue and green strapwork, green leaves and orange and blue fruit and flowers; 3-dimensional blue scale bar under title surmounted by yellow dividers; compass rose bottom left showing 16 purple, orange and yellow points in a red and blue border. Table top left, which gives: 'The contentes of the freeholde and copieholde groundes in Campes', 922a.0r.24p., and tenants, acreages and tenure. Table in a cartouche with pink, blue and yellow strapwork, green leaves, blue flowers and orange and pink fruit. Roads outlined in yellow, closes outlined in green, some areas coloured green, strips outlined in brown, water coloured blue, hedges coloured green, buildings have red roofs, churches have blue roofs.
Pencil notes. Copy drawn by John Prickett in 1791 at GLC ACC.1876/MP2/2 measures 16 1/2 x 22 3/4in.

Border of 1 broad band with 1 narrow band on inside, title on a scroll hanging from a tree coloured yellow and green on green grass, compass shows 16 points. Ink and pencil notes, red numbers referring to terrier to CAS80005. See also CAS61701,3–5, surveyed by Thomas Langdon.

Castle Camps – 1617 – CAS61703 – GLC ACC.1876/MP2/2

The Description of Haverell End with diverse and Sundry Grounds unto the same neare adjoyning lieing in the Parish of Castle Campes in the County of Cambridg belonging to the Governors of the Hospitall of King James founded in the Charter House in the Countye of Middlesex at the humble peticion and at the proper Costs and Charges of Thomas Sutton Esquier. Made in October Anno Domini 1617 by Thomas Langdon.

Surveyor: Thomas Langdon; **Draughtsman:** J[ohn] Prickett; **Scale bar** 0–60 perches (= 2 7/8in.), 1:4,132; **Size:** (i) 16 11/16 x 23 1/8in.; **Top** is ESE; Manuscript(ii), parchment, coloured.

Castle Camps Church, TL625425, and c. 960a. in village bounded by Shudy Camps Parish in N, Castle Farm in S and Helions Bumpstead Parish [Essex] in E.

Names of fields, owners and tenants. Church, Camps Castle, tower near the castle and cottages shown in perspective. Open fields showing all strips; closes; 'Bigs Grove' and 'Goodwoode'; acreages; roads and gates; gardens; fences and hedges; tenure; former orchard; moat.

Border of 1 broad band with 1 narrow band on inside; title top right; scale middle left; compass centre top showing 16 points. Table top left giving cottages, tenants and acreages. Roads outlined in yellow, wood coloured green, closes outlined in green, strips outlined in brown, buildings have red roofs, parish boundary coloured red and yellow.

Pencil notes, red numbers referring to terrier to CAS80004. Map was 'Accurately Redelineated A.D. 1791. By J. Prickett'. Prickett's 1st name was John [Eden P333]. Original map, now lost, was probably GLC ACC.1876/MP2/22c. See also CAS61701–2,4–5.

Castle Camps – [1617] – CAS61704 – GLC ACC.1876/MP2/2

[Land in 'Further Stone Field', owned by the Charterhouse.]

Surveyor: [Thomas Langdon]; **Draughtsman:** J[ohn] Prickett; **Scale:** 1:4,490; **Size:** (i) 16 1/2 x 23 1/8in.; **Top** is W; Manuscript(ii), parchment, coloured.

c. 840a. in NW of parish.

Names of fields, owners and tenants. Open fields showing owner's strips; closes; 'Westow Woode'; meadow; acreages; roads and watercourses; hedges; tenure.

Border of 1 broad band with 1 narrow band on inside; cartouche on left with no title written in and decorated with blue and brown leaves; compass top right showing 8 points. Roads outlined in yellow, strips outlined in brown, wood and hedges coloured green, closes outlined in blue/green, water coloured blue.

Pencil notes, red numbers referring to terrier to CAS80006; this map does not extend as far SE as CAS80006. Map was 'Redrawn Septr 1790. By J Prickett'. Prickett's 1st name was John [Eden P333]. Original map, now lost, was probably GLC ACC.1876/MP2/22d. See also CAS61701–3,5, surveyed by Thomas Langdon.

Castle Camps – 1617 – CAS61705 – GLC ACC.1876/MP2/22e

The descrription [sic.] of Campes Castle in the Countie of Cambridg togeather with the groundes thereunto belonging lieinge on the southeaste & southeweste partes towwardes Olmsted, and Bartelow being parcell of the possessions of the governours of the hospitall of kinge Iames founded in the Charterhouse in the countie of Middlesex at the humble peticion and at the proper costes and charges of Thomas Sutton esquier, made in october Anno domini 1617. at the measure of xvj foote and an halfe to the pole & according to the proportion of xxtie perches to an ynche by Thomas Langdon.

Surveyor: Thomas Langdon; **Scale:** 1:3,960, Scale bar 0–60 perches (= 2 15/16in.), 1:4,044; **Size:** (i) 16 5/16 x 23 5/16in.; **Top** is NNE; Manuscript(i), parchment, coloured.

Camps Castle, TL626424, and c. 780a. to S bounded by Olmstead Green in S and Helions Bumpstead Parish [Essex] in E, and mostly E of road from Camps Hall to Camps End.

Names of fields, roads, owners, tenants and neighbouring owners. Camps Castle and cottages shown in perspective. Open fields showing all strips; closes; 'Willeysey Wood' and trees; 'Olmested Greene'; acreages; roads; gardens; hedges and fences; tenure; 'The conigree' [rabbit warren]; 'Barne yarde'; 'olde orchard'; earthworks round castle.

Border of 5/16in.-wide band with a blue and brown geometrical pattern; title middle right in a cartouche with yellow, blue and pink strapwork, green leaves, yellow and pink fruit and flowers and a red ribbon; 3-dimensional yellow scale bar centre bottom surmounted by blue and grey dividers; compass rose top left showing 16 purple, yellow and green points with red and blue edges. Roads outlined in yellow, hedges and trees coloured green, strips outlined in brown, closes outlined in green, buildings have red roofs.

Bottom right: 'Note that the leete extendeth it selfe from Olmested green southward aboute 4 furlonges, and eastward aboute one furlonge vnto the boundes of Bumstead Helions in the Countye of Essex. Note also that Olmsted. payeth tiethes to Bumsted both & to the Kinge and Lord at Campes'. Note further right: 'Mascalls tenement payeinge yearelye to Camps castle xd of which the halfe is in the tenure of wade the other halfe in the tenure of Iames Reynoldes esquier. and they pay either of them vd per annum. & was sometimes petittes'. Copy at GLC ACC.1876/MP2/2, drawn by John Prickett in 1791 measures 16 1/2 x 23in. Border of 1 broad band with 1 narrow band on inside, no title cartouche, compass shows 16 points. Pencil notes, red numbers referring to terrier to CAS80003. Also a copy of the SW of this map bounded by 'Skillettes Field' in E, 'Willeysey Wood' in NW and Ashdon Parish in W: 'A Plan of the South West Corner of { } Lands near Campes Castle in the Coun{ty of} Cambridge Belonging to the Rt Honble the Governors of the Charter House Accurately Copied in May 1791 by J. Prickett from an Old Plan made in AD 1617', measuring 7 15/16 x 13 5/8in. Scale bar bottom right: 0–30 poles (= 1 1/2in.), 1:3,960. See also CAS61701–4.

Castle Camps – 1741 – CAS74101 – GLC ACC.1876/MP2/23a

A Map of the Leasehold Estates in the Parish of Castle~Camps in Cambridgeshire, belonging to the Governours of the Hospital of King Iames, founded in Charter~House in the County of Middlesex, at the humble

Petition, and only Costs & Charges of Thomas Sutton Esqr Surveyed in Sepr & Octr 1741. by Iohn Robertson F.R.S.

Surveyor: John Robertson; **A Scale** of 1/2 a Mile. or 160 Perches, Scale bar 0–160 perches (= 6 5/8in.), 1:4,782; **Size:** (i) 28 3/4 x 38 13/16in.; **Top** is SW; Manuscript(i), parchment, coloured.

Castle Camps Church, TL625425, and 1,636a.0r.2p. in whole parish.

Names of fields and roads. Church, Camps Hall, Castle and Moat farms and farm buildings shown in plan form, windmill shown in perspective. Open fields showing owner's strips; closes; pightles; Langley and 'Willesey' woods, groves and trees; meadow and pasture; state of cultivation shown by colour; acreages; roads and footpaths; gates; gardens and orchards; pond; moats; 'Brick Ground'; fences; Camps Green.

Border of 1 narrow band with 1 broad band on inside; title bottom right in a cartouche of a tombstone with a theodolite and tripod, open field book, pair of dividers, pen, map and closed book [surveying text?] above and latitude and longitude below: 'Castle~Camps. Lat 52° 05'N. Long 00° 20'E. à London'; scale above title; compass top left showing 4 red, grey and blue points and magnetic N. Table top right giving field names and acreages, including acreages of lanes. Roads coloured brown, buildings coloured red, water coloured blue, hedges and trees coloured yellow, arable coloured in brown stripes, land outlined in blue, red, yellow and grey.

Left of table is a note of tenants' names and colours in which their land is outlined. Pencil notes. At GLC ACC.1876/MP2/23b is a copy, with 'Reduced November 1752 by Thos Panton' at end of title. Border of 1 broad green band with 1 uncoloured band inside; title top right in a plain green cartouche with blue and yellow rectangles inside, scale bar of 1–0–10 chains (= 1 9/16in.), 1:5,576, table at bottom. At GLC ACC.1876/MP2/29 is a reference to a map by Robert Arber in 1838. At front: 'A Comparison of the Maps in respect of Quantity of Land in the Parish of Castle Camps in the County of Cambridge between a Map made for The Governors of Charterhouse in the year 1742 by John Robertson F.R.S. and another made by Robert Arber in 1827. And also its being Remeasured and Corrected in the year 1838 by Robert Arber aforesaid'. Robertson's map shows 2,700a.0r.1p., Arber's 1827 map shows 2,699a.2r.10p. and the 1838 map shows 2,701a.2r.15p.

Castle Camps – 1741 – CAS74102 – CRO R51/7/10
Tracing from Robertsons Map 1741 & 2.

Surveyor: [John] Robertson; **Scale:** 1:4,270; **Size:** (ii) 5 1/4 x 7 3/4in.; **Top** is N; Manuscript(ii), paper, uncoloured.

16a.0r.14p. in TL6143, NW of parish E of Camps Hall, bounded by 'Westhoe Field' in E, demesne land in W and 'Lord's Wood' in S.

Names of fields. Closed fields showing all land; common; wood and trees; acreages.

Title at top. Table on right giving tenants and acreages.

Note bottom left saying that the draughtsman is unsure which is the field owned by the Charterhouse. Drawn to identify 'Payns Lay'. Plan is in an extract from the Minute Books of the Charterhouse. Original map was by John Robertson [CAS74101]. See also CAS74801 and CAS82701.

Castle Camps – [c. 1748] – CAS74801 – CRO R51/7/10
Tracing taken from Plan at Charter House Judith Reynolds was admitted to this property, Robertsons survey 1741 and 1742.

Surveyor: [John] Robertson; **Scale:** 1:4,750; **Size:** (iii) 3 3/4 x 5in.; **Top** is NE; Manuscript(iii), paper, uncoloured.

'Tredget's Farm' in NE of TL6241, and 18a.0r.28p. in 'Park Field' along road from Castle Camps to Olmstead Green.

Names of farm, fields and tenants. Farm and outbuildings shown in plan form. Closed fields showing owner's land; acreages; roads.

Title at top.

Note at bottom that: 'The Tenement was suffered to go into ruins = the Pond and foundation spot is still useable'. Land owned by the Charterhouse. Plan in an extract from the Minute Books of the Charterhouse, which says that Judith Reynolds was admitted in 1748 and she died in 1761. Map based on survey by John Robertson [CAS74101]. See also CAS74102 and CAS82701.

Castle Camps – 1771 – CAS77101 – QCC 328
A Survey of Holmsted Hall Farm in the Parish of Hellions Bumpstead and Countys of Essex and Cambridge belonging to Queens College in the University of Cambridge.

Surveyor: Joseph Freeman; **Scale bar** 0–100 Statute Perches (= 6 1/4in.), 1:3,168; **Size:** (i) 22 1/4 x 28 15/16in.; **Top** is NE; Manuscript(i), parchment, coloured.

Olmstead Hall, TL626406, and 286a.0r.24p. in S of Castle Camps Parish bounded by Great Bendysh Wood in SE.

Names of fields and neighbouring owners. Houses and barns shown in perspective. Closed fields showing owner's land; numbers and species of trees, identifying ash, pollards, elm and oak; wood, 'Bendish' and 'Sleepers' woods and groves; land quality; state of cultivation shown by colour; acreages; roads and footpaths; gates; moats and ponds; 'Back yard'; orchard.

Border of 1 narrow band; title bottom right in a rococo cartouche coloured purple, pink, gold and green; scale at bottom coloured yellow and black; compass top left showing 16 decorated uncoloured points. Table top right giving field names, acreages and land use. Trees coloured green, roads coloured brown, fields have yellow stripes, wood coloured green, blue and brown, meadow coloured blue, plots outlined and coloured blue, moats and water coloured purple, houses have red roofs, barns have yellow roofs.

Note bottom right: 'NB The Woods crossed with Red Ink are proposed to be grubed up at Lady day 1800'.

Castle Camps – [1773] – CAS77301 – QCC 328
A Plan of the Several Farms in the Countys of Essex Cambridge and Suffolk in the Parishes of Hellions Bumpsted, Haverhill &c. Belonging to Queens College Cambridge taken by J Freeman Cambridge.

Surveyor: J[oseph] Freeman; **Scale:** 1:11,800; **Size:** (i) 22 x 29 3/4in.; **Top** is NNW; Manuscript(i), parchment, coloured.

Haverhill Church, TL671455, and c. 3,700a. extending from Olmstead Hall in Castle Camps Parish in W to Haverhill Parish [Suffolk] in N and E, and 2 areas in Birdbrook and Stambourne parishes [Essex].

Names of farms, neighbouring owners and parishes. Buildings shown in perspective and include Haverhill Church and Olmstead Hall, Draper's, 'Horsham Hall',

Copy, 'Lancelets', Moon Hall, 'Motts' and 'Stanbron' farms. Closed fields showing owner's land; common; wood and trees; hedges; roads; gates; moats; watercourses.

Border of 1 narrow band; title top right in a rococo cartouche coloured red, purple and gold; compass top left showing 16 decorated purple points. Roads coloured brown, buildings have red roofs, trees coloured green, water coloured blue, each farm's land coloured a different colour: orange, green, pink, yellow, blue, purple, red and turquoise.

Note bottom left of the colours of the different farms' land. Pencil notes. At QCC Box 92 is Joseph Freeman's bill for this map, dated 7 May 1773.

Castle Camps – [c. 1792–5] – CAS79201 – GLC ACC.1876/MP2/24

Camps plan of late Challis's *Per* Owen Swan.

Surveyor: Owen Swan; **Scale:** 1:2,070; **Size:** (i) 28 3/4 x 48 1/16in.; **Top** is SW; Manuscript(i), paper, uncoloured.

Site of Shudy Camps Church, TL621444, and land in Castle and Shudy Camps parishes mostly N of road from Linton to Helions Bumpstead and S of Shudy Camps Church.

Names of fields, roads, tenants and neighbouring owners. Barns shown in plan form, cottages shown in perspective. Open fields showing owner's strips; closes; common, meadow and pasture; acreages; roads and watercourses; gardens; hedges; clay pit; boundary between Castle Camps and Shudy Camps parishes.

Border of 1 broad band with 1 narrow band on inside; title top left.

Notes of tenure and rents and 'This hedge broke up'. Note bottom right of land in 'Post Field' and to whom it was let, note at top describing the land. The land in Camps Rows is repeated as an inset top left at 1:3,540, with land outlined in brown. Later ink notes, and later note on dorse: 'Mr Nockolds Walden with a Book'. Red numbers and letters refer to estate documents. Date suggested in handlist in GLC, one note refers to 1795. Land owned by the Charterhouse.

Castle Camps – 1794 – CAS79401 – ERO D/DHt P27

A Plan of Perry Appleton Charlwood and Green House Farms situate in the Parishes of Helion Bumsted and Castle Camps In the Counties of Essex and Cambridge Belonging to Jas Johnson Esqr Surveyed by D Mumford & J Doyle 1794.

Surveyors: D[aniel] Mumford, J[ohn] Doyle[y]; **Scale bar** 1–0–27 chains (= 3 11/16in.), 1:6,014; **Size:** (i) 15 1/8 x 17 5/16in.; **Top** is NNE; Manuscript(i), parchment mounted on paper, coloured.

Greenhouse Farm, TL632411, and 376a.3r.29p. in W of Castle Camps Parish and E of Helions Bumpstead Parish [Essex], and strips in 'Westley's Common' in Castle Camps Parish E of road from Helions Bumpstead to Linton.

Names of farms, fields and neighbouring owners. Farm buildings and cottages shown in plan form. Closed fields showing owner's land; strips in 'Westley's Common'; common; trees and grove; state of cultivation shown by colour; roads and gates; watercourses, ponds; gardens and orchards; meadow; hedges and fences; moats.

Border of 1 narrow band with 1 broad band on inside; title top right in a grey rectangular cartouche with decorated corners; yellow scale bar bottom right; compass top left showing 8 points. Table on left giving field names,

acreages, land use and parishes. Water coloured blue, roads coloured yellow, buildings coloured red, hedges coloured green, fields coloured green or yellow.

Pencil and ink notes. Mumford's 1st name was Daniel [Eden M517]; John Doyley was his assistant 1794–6 [Eden D298].

Castle Camps – [Early 19th century] – CAS80001 – GLC ACC.1876/MP2/42

A Sketch of Part of the Charter House Farm at Castle Camps in the County of Cambridge.

Scale bar 0–20 chains (= 3 5/16in.), 1:4,782; **Size:** (i) 24 1/2 x 36in.; **Top** is NE; Manuscript(i), paper, coloured.

Castle Farm, TL626424, and c. 1,500a. to E and NW.

Names of fields. Castle Farm, Moat Farm and Camps Hall shown in plan form. Open fields showing owner's strips; closes; meadow; state of cultivation given in words; roads; moats; 'Brick Kiln Yard'.

Border of 1 broad band with 1 narrow band on inside; title bottom left; scale centre bottom; compass top left showing 4 points. Land outlined in yellow, blue, brown and red.

Note left of scale: 'Lands coloured Yellow are in Occupation of Mr Leonard Lands coloured Brown are in Occupation of Mr French Lands coloured Blue are in Occupation of Mr Britton Lands coloured Red are in Occupation of Mr Pavitt. Lands not coloured are in Ocupation of Mr Collier'. Handlist in GLC suggests map drawn in 1st half of 19th century.

Castle Camps – [c. 1800] – CAS80002 – GLC ACC.1876/MP2/2

[Land in Castle Camps, owned by the Charterhouse.] No 1.

Surveyor: [John Prickett?]; **Scale bar** 0–100 perches (= 4 15/16in.), 1:4,010; **Size:** (i) 16 3/4 x 24 3/8in.; **Top** is NE; Manuscript(i), parchment, uncoloured.

c. 620a. in E of parish bounded by Ashdon Parish [Essex] in SW and Camps End in S, and extending N of road from Ashdon to Camps Hall.

Names of fields, roads, tenants and neighbouring owners. Farm buildings shown in plan form. Open fields showing owner's strips; closes; Langley and 'Willesey' woods; 'Lammas Ground', meadow and pasture; acreages; roads; hedges and fences; tenure.

Border of 1 broad band with 1 narrow band on inside; plan number top left; scale bottom left.

Accompanying terrier on paper gives acreages and tenure. Pencil notes and ink notes, including a compass bottom left and an 'Arch'. See also CAS80003–6. Names of neighbouring owners suggest these maps drawn c. 1800. They are in a similar style to the copies of CAS61701–5 by John Prickett in 1790–1.

Castle Camps – [c. 1800] – CAS80003 – GLC ACC.1876/MP2/2

[Land in Castle Camps, owned by the Charterhouse.] No. 2.

Surveyor: [John Prickett?]; **Scale bar** 0–60 perches (= 2 15/16in.), 1:4,044; **Size:** (i) 16 7/8 x 24 3/8in.; **Orientation:** Top is N; Manuscript(i), parchment, uncoloured.

c. 760a. S of Camps Castle, TL626424, bounded by Olmstead Green in S and Helions Bumpstead Parish [Essex] in E, and mostly E of road from Camps Hall to Camps End.

Names of fields and tenants. Farm buildings shown in plan form. Closed fields; Olmstead Green; acreages; roads; tenure; hedges; moat, earthworks of castle.

Border of 1 broad band with 1 narrow band on inside; plan number top left; scale bottom right.

Accompanying terrier on paper gives acreages and tenure. Pencil notes of tenure, references to tithe map and pencil compass top right. See also CAS80002,4–6. Names of neighbouring owners suggest these maps drawn c. 1800. They are in a similar style to the copies of CAS61701–5 by John Prickett in 1790–1.

Castle Camps – [c. 1800] – CAS80004 – GLC ACC.1876/MP2/2

[Land in Castle Camps, owned by the Charterhouse.] No. 3.

Surveyor: [John Prickett?]; **Scale bar** 0–60 perches (= 3in.), 1:3,960; **Size:** (i) 17 x 24 5/8in.; **Top** is E; Manuscript(i), parchment, uncoloured.

c. 860a. in village N of Castle Farm, TL626424, bounded by Shudy Camps Parish in N and Helions Bumpstead Parish [Essex] in E.

Names of fields and tenants. Castle Farm and Moat Farm shown in plan form. Closed fields; pasture; acreages; roads; hedges; tenure; yards; 'Hop Ground'; earthworks of castle.

Border of 1 broad band with 1 narrow band on inside; plan number top left; scale bottom right.

Accompanying terrier on paper gives acreages and tenure. Pencil notes. See also CAS80002–3,5–6. Names of neighbouring owners suggest these maps drawn c. 1800. They are in a similar style to the copies of CAS61701–5 by John Prickett in 1790–1.

Castle Camps – [c. 1800] – CAS80005 – GLC ACC.1876/MP2/2

[Land in Castle Camps, owned by the Charterhouse.] No 4.

Surveyor: [John Prickett?]; **Scale bar** 0–60 perches (= 3in.), 1:3,960; **Size:** (i) 17 x 24 1/2in.; **Top** is W; Manuscript(i), parchment, uncoloured.

Camps Hall, TL614432, and c. 840a. N of Castle Farm and E of road running W of Camps Hall.

Names of fields and tenants. Camps Hall and cottages shown in plan form, windmill shown in perspective. Closed fields; a few of owner's strips in open fields; meadow and pasture; acreages; roads; hedges; yards; tenure; 'Brick Kiln Yard'.

Border of 1 broad band with 1 narrow band on inside; plan number top left; scale bottom right.

Accompanying terrier on paper gives acreages and tenure. Pencil notes. See also CAS80002–4,6. Names of neighbouring owners suggest these maps drawn c. 1800. They are in a similar style to the copies of CAS61701–5 by John Prickett in 1790–1.

Castle Camps – [c. 1800] – CAS80006 – GLC ACC.1876/MP2/2

[Land in Castle Camps, owned by the Charterhouse.] No 5.

Surveyor: [John Prickett?]; **Scale bar** 0–120 perches (= 6in.), 1:3,960; **Size:** (i) 17 x 24 7/16in.; **Top** is W; Manuscript(i), parchment, uncoloured.

c. 710a. in NW of parish.

Names of fields and tenants. Farm buildings shown in plan form. Open fields showing owner's strips; closes;

grove; pasture; acreages; roads and watercourses; tenure; hedges.

Border of 1 broad band with 1 narrow band on inside; plan number top left; scale bottom right.

Accompanying terrier on paper gives acreages and tenure. Pencil notes. See also CAS80002–5. Names of neighbouring owners suggest these maps drawn c. 1800. They are in a similar style to the copies of CAS61701–5 by John Prickett in 1790–1.

Castle Camps – 1808 – CAS80801 – GLC ACC.1876/MP2/2

Westoe~Lodge in Cambridgeshire the Property of The Rt Honble Charles Long. Surveyed Sep: 26° 1808. by J Bransby.

Surveyor: J[ohn] Bransby; **Draughtsman:** J[ohn] Newton; **Scale bar** 0–70 [poles] (= 4 3/8in.), 1:3,168; **Size:** (i) 13 1/2 x 19 3/8in.; **Top** is N; Manuscript(i), paper, uncoloured.

Site of Westoe Lodge, TL597443, and 62a.2r.28p. to N bounded by road from Linton to Castle Camps in N and Bartlow Parish in W, with a few strips in E of Bartlow Parish.

Names of fields and roads. Farm buildings shown in plan form. Closes, a few strips in Bartlow Parish; groves; meadow; 'wilderness'; acreages; roads; yards; pond; 'gravel~pit Piece'; gardens.

Border of 1 narrow band; title middle left in a square border of 1 narrow band; scale top right; compass above scale showing 4 plain points. Table bottom right in a border of 1 narrow band giving field names and acreages for open and inclosed land.

Surveyor's and draughtsman's 1st names were John [Eden B538 and N69]. Copy at CRO 495/P1 at 1:3,203 with no border.

Castle Camps – 1810 – CAS81001 – GLC ACC.1876/MP2/2

A Survey and plan of Land Belonging to Benj Keene Esqr. Lying at Westoe in the Parish of Castle Camps Near Linton in the County of Cambridge 1810.

Surveyor: Robert Arber; **Scale:** This plan is laid down by a Scale of Two Chains in One inch, 1:1,584; **Size:** (ii) 17 1/8 x 24 1/16in.; **Top** is SSE; Manuscript(i), paper, coloured.

Site of Westoe Lodge, TL597443, and 8a.1r.29p. bounded by road from Castle Camps to Ashdon in N and Bartlow Parish in E.

Names of fields and neighbouring owners. Farm buildings shown in plan form. Closes; wood and trees; 'The Paddoc'; roads and footpaths; gates; gardens and their layout; hedges and fences; ponds; yards.

Title centre top in an oval cartouche of 1 narrow band with 1 broad band on inside; scale at bottom; compass left of title showing 4 points with a feathered tail. Table bottom right giving field names and acreages of lands 'Purchased by Benj Keene Esqr of the Charterhouse 1810'. Fields coloured green and brown, water coloured blue.

2 copies at GLC ACC.1876/MP2/2: the 1st measures 12 7/8 x 17 5/16in., has top as S, gives names of neighbouring owners, does not show all the fields, has neither title nor scale and has a compass top right showing 8 points. Land coloured green, orange and red. 2nd copy is a rough preliminary sketch with survey lines and is uncoloured except for the grove and hedges which are green. At CRO 495/P2 is a 3rd copy, which measures 16 x 24 7/16in.

Castle Camps – [1825] – CAS82501 – QCC 355 A7, B7
Holmstead Hall Farm at Bumpstead Helions In The
County of Essex.
Surveyor: [Alexander Watford jr]; **Scale bar** 0–20
chains (= 5in.), 1:3,168; **Size:** (i) 25 1/4 x 38 1/2in.;
Top is NE; Manuscript(ii), paper, coloured.
Olmstead Hall, TL626406, and 287a.3r.22p. in S of
Castle Camps Parish.
Names of farm, fields, roads and neighbouring owners.
Farm buildings and cottages shown in plan form. Closed
fields showing owner's land; woods, including part of
'Bendish Wood', 'Long Valley', 'Bush Pasture' and 'Wood
Field' groves; trees; meadow; state of cultivation shown by
colour; acreages; hedges; roads, gates; watercourses; pond;
moat; pightle; garden; orchards.
Border of 1 broad band with 1 narrow band on either side;
title top left; scale centre bottom; compass bottom right
showing 8 points. Table on right giving field names,
acreages and land use. Fields coloured green and yellow,
roads coloured brown, water coloured blue, wood coloured
green.
On right is inset of: 'Holmsted Hall Farm Homestead on
scale of two Chains to the Inch', 1:1,584, measuring 3 x
4in. and its top is NE. At top is inset of: 'No. 31 In the occupation of W.P. Johnson Esqr on scale of two Chains to
the Inch', 1:1,584, measuring 3 1/2 x 2in. In volume
drawn in 1825: 'Plans of the Several Estates in England and
Wales belonging to the President and Fellows of the
College of St Margaret and St Bernard commonly called
Queen's College in the University of Cambridge Delineated
from Authentic Documents in the possession of the said
President and Fellows and from actual Surveys taken By
their most obedient and obliged Servant Alexr Watford'.
Title page drawn by James Richardson [Watford's nephew].
This is the Bursar's copy; 2nd, finer, copy [the Master's
copy] at QCC 355 B7 measures 24 7/8 x 36 5/8in., top
points N and is on parchment. Garden shown in more detail. Border 7/16in. wide of a blue central band and 1 broad
band on either side, scale bottom left, compass top left.
Table has red lines. Fields coloured in brown and yellow
stripes, roads coloured brown with a red/brown outline.
Inset of no. 31: 'No 31 on Scale of two Chains to an Inch'.
Photograph of this copy at ERO T/M 138 at 1:5,069, and
positive photostat at BL 2355.(15) at 1:10,560.

Castle Camps – [c. 1827] – CAS82701 – CRO R51/7/10
The following is a tracing from Arbors Map 1827.
Surveyor: [Robert] Arber; **Scale:** 1:5,300; **Size:** (iii)
5 3/8 x 4 5/8in.; **Top** is SE; Manuscript(ii), paper,
uncoloured.
c. 50a. in TL6143, NW of Camps Hall and S of road from
Castle Camps to Linton.
Names of fields, roads and owners. Farm buildings
shown in plan form. Closed fields showing owner's land;
state of cultivation given in words; roads; Camps Hall
Park.
Title at top; pencil note middle left giving compass with
4 points.
Note at bottom: 'Great and Little Weshoe [sic.] Fields are
in the possession of William Clayden of Westhoe Lodge
The property of Cane Esqre William Clayden lives at
Linton'. Pencil numbers on fields. Land owned by the
Charterhouse. Plan is in an extract from the Minute Books
of the Charterhouse and is a tracing from a map by Robert
Arber at GLC ACC.1876/MP2/25a. See also CAS74102
and CAS74801.

Castle Camps – [1831] – CAS83101 – GLC
ACC.1876/MP2/26b–d
A Plan of the Allotments now Occupied by the Poor of
Castle Camps in the County of Cambridge the Property of
the Right Honourable the Governors of the Charterhouse
Containing with Allotments fences and Roads 12A.0R.8P.
Scale: 1:1,170; **Size:** (i) 22 3/8 x 17 5/8in.; **Top** is S;
Manuscript(i), paper, coloured.
12a.0r.8p. E of road to Castle Camps.
Names of roads. Cottage shown in plan form. Closed
fields; roads; gates.
Border of 4 narrow bands; title at top; compass in centre
showing 4 points. Roads coloured brown.
Note on left of occupiers. Copies at c and d have title
crossed out and are dated 1831.

Castle Camps – 1833 – CAS83301 – GLC
ACC.1876/MP2/26e
Plan of six acres of land granted as additional cottage
gardens to the labourers of Castle Camps 1833. By the
Right Honourable the Governors of the Charter House.
Scale: 1:1,620; **Size:** (i) 10 x 8in.; **Top** is S;
Manuscript(i), paper mounted on paper, coloured.
6a.0r.0p. S of village street.
Names of roads. 'Anderson's' shown in plan form.
Closed fields; roads and gates; hedges.
Border of 1 broad band with 1 narrow band on either side;
title at bottom; compass on right showing 4 points. Table
top left giving acreages. Roads coloured brown, hedges
and land coloured green, building coloured red.
On dorse: '1833 Castle Camps Allotments of part of
Rectors Glebe'.

Caxton – 1749/50 – CAX75001 – BLO R.M.S.
C17:17(22)
An Actual Survey of the Manor of Caxton in the County
of Cambridge wherein is Measured & Described The Wood
Land, Inclosed Land, Common, Ley~Ground &c. belonging
to Thomas Gape Esqr Lord of the said Manor taken Anno
Domini 1749.1750 by T Wing.
Surveyor: T[ycho] Wing [sr]; **Scale bar** 1–0–27
chains (= 7in.), 1:3,168; **Size:** (i) 35 7/8 x 59in.; **Top** is
W; Manuscript(i), parchment, uncoloured.
Caxton Hall, TL302583, and c. 2,300a. in parish crossing Ermine Street, and bounded by Eltisley Parish in W and
Bourn Parish in S.
Names of fields and roads. Farm buildings and cottages
shown in plan form. Open fields showing all strips;
closes; common, meadow and pasture; wood and trees;
waste; roads and footpaths; milestones; watercourses;
ponds and 'Cow Pond'; gardens and orchards; moats;
hedges and fences; 'Great sand pitt close', 'Brickhill
close'; green; bridge.
Border of 1 broad band with 1 narrow band on inside; title top left in a baroque cartouche; scale bottom left with
baroque decoration; compass middle top with baroque
decoration showing 2 points, incorrectly giving top as E.
Beneath title: 'Note the Particulars of the Common Field
Lands are in a Field Book or Terrier thereof belonging to
this Survey'. Pencil notes. Terrier missing in 1988.
Surveyor's 1st name was Tycho [Eden W471]. Positive
photostat at CUL Maps R.b.10.

Caxton – [c. 1772] – CAX77201 – GCC XV.25

Survey of Part of the Manor of Swanesley in Caxton in the County of Cambridge Belonging to Gonvill and Caius College Cambridge.

Surveyor: [Joseph Freeman?]; **Draughtsman:** [Mr Gee?]; **Scale:** 1:5,520; **Size:** (ii) 12 1/2 x 8in.; **Top** is E; Manuscript(ii), paper, coloured.

Caxton Gibbet, TL296606, and 131a.1r.34p. S of road from St Neot's to Cambridge bounded by road to Caxton and London in W, and 1 plot in village near church.

Names of fields and roads. Buildings shown in perspective and include church, manor house and barns. Closes; 'Swanesley~hill'; hedges; roads and gates; gibbet; 'Esqr Gapes Wood' adjoining map; acreages given on table.

Roads coloured brown, arable coloured in yellow stripes, trees and hedges coloured green, buildings have red roofs.

Title on facing page. Table beneath title giving field names and acreages. Joseph Freeman was paid for surveying and mapping Teversham in the half year ending at Lady Day 1773, and Mr Gee was paid for transcribing the survey in the half year ending at Michaelmas 1777 [GCC Bursar's Book 1758–75 and 1775–91]. These entries probably refer to TEV77201–14, in same volume as this map, which may thus have been surveyed and copied at similar times.

Caxton – [1786] – CAX78601 – HERO D/EAmP1

Farm at Caxton in the County of Cambridge.

Surveyor: [Luke Pope]; **Scale bar** 100 links–0–25 chains (= 8 5/8in.), 1:2,387; **Size:** (i) 23 13/16 x 27 1/4in.; **Top** is NW; Manuscript(i), parchment, coloured.

Caxton Church, TL300578, farm to W and 90a.1r.3p. to N, bounded by road from London to Huntingdon in E and Great Gransden Parish [Huntingdonshire] and Eltisley Parish in W.

Names of fields, roads and neighbouring owners. Farm buildings and cottages shown in plan form, church shown in perspective. Closes; trees; waste; state of cultivation shown by colour; acreages; roads and footpaths; watercourses and ponds; fences; gardens.

Border of 1 broad band with 1 narrow band on inside; title centre top; scale bottom left; compass in centre showing 4 points. Buildings coloured red, roads coloured yellow, arable coloured in yellow stripes, pasture outlined in green, trees coloured green, water coloured blue.

Pencil grid on map. Accompanying terrier gives acreages, land use and values, including those for open-field lands not shown on the map. Estate is of 256a.3r.34p. in total. Map is in volume: 'Surveys and Plans of the Estates of Robert Hucks, Esqr. of Aldenham in the County of Hertford'. Title page decorated with fruit, flowers and leaves coloured red, blue, purple, yellow, pink and gold, and has Hucks' coat of arms at bottom and a face at top. Bottom right: 'Surveyed and Planed by Luke Pope Charlotte Street Mary le Bone 1786'.

Caxton – [c. 1835] – CAX83501 – CRO R56/20/11/1

[Land at Caxton allotted to Dean and Canons of Windsor on inclosure.]

Surveyor: [John King]; **Scale:** 1:5,080; **Size:** (ii) 20 x 42 5/8in.; **Top** is W; Manuscript(ii), tracing paper, coloured.

Red Lion Farm, TL305581, and c. 1,100a. S of Crow Dean bounded by Bourn Parish in E, N of Crow Dean bounded by Knapwell and Elsworth parishes in N, and W of Ermine Street as far as churchyard, and bounded by Longstowe Parish in S.

Names of farm, some fields, owner, tenants, neighbouring owners, roads and parishes. Red Lion Farm, other buildings and church shown in plan form. Closed fields showing owner's land; common; acreages; tenure; roads and footpaths; watercourses; gates; garden; ponds; stone pit; responsibility for boundaries.

Compass top right showing 4 points with a decorated N. Roads coloured brown, water coloured blue, some plots coloured green.

Based on map by John King which accompanied 1835 inclosure award.

Chatteris – [Early 18th century] – CHA70001 – CCO Maps Chatteris 1

[Holwood Farm, Chatteris, owned by Christ Church, Oxford.]

Scale: 1:2,260; **Size:** (ii) 17 1/4 x 15 3/4in.; **Top** is E; Manuscript(i), parchment, uncoloured.

c. 420a. in Chatteris Fen in S of parish around Holwood Farm, TL384790, bounded by Colne Fen in S and Sutton Fen in E.

Names of features. Buildings shown in perspective and include: 'a barne Built by the Tennant', 'A house Built by the Tennant' and 'One Barne'. Closed fields showing owner's land; state of cultivation given in words; crops including grass, oats, ley, willows and 'wilton'; roads and footpaths; gates; 'Woods Planted by the Tannents'; 2 dunghills; 'A flour[?] Mill built by the tennant'.

Map is an irregular shape and cut from a lease. Handlist in CCO suggests a date of early 18th century.

Chatteris – [Late 18th century] – CHA77501 – EDR CC.10124

The Plan of Chatteris Fenn.

Scale: 1:12,500; **Size:** (ii) 9 1/8 x 15 1/8in.; **Top** is SW; Manuscript(i), parchment, uncoloured.

295a.1r.0p. in E of parish bounded by Byall Fen in NE and Langwood Fen in S.

Names of river and neighbouring land. House shown in perspective. Closed fields; acreages; 'Forty Foot Bank River'.

Title bottom left; cardinal points stated at edge of map.

Cut from a lease. Some plots outlined in black and labelled 'B', others labelled '1'. Land owned by Bishop of Ely.

Chatteris – 1780 – CHA78001 – CCO Maps Chatteris 2

A True Survey and Plan of the Farm belonging to Christ Church College in Oxford lying in the Parish of Chatteris within the Isle of Ely in the County of Cambridge called the Holwoods Farm with the contents of every separate Piece in Acres Roods & Perches also the Length of every Dike in poles & Quarters in Long Measure for the knowledge of Diking.

Surveyor: John Smith; **Scale:** 1:8,680; **Size:** (ii) 16 x 12 3/4in.; **Top** is SE; Manuscript(i), paper mounted on paper, uncoloured.

Holwood Farm, TL384790, and 419a.3r.3p. in S of parish bounded by Colne Fen in S and Sutton Fen in E.

Names of farm, fields, owner, tenants, neighbouring owners, roads and watercourses. Farm buildings shown in plan form. Closed fields showing owner's land; state of cultivation given in words; dimensions of areas; roads including turnpike; gates; watercourses; 'The old west water'; bridges.

Title at top; cardinal points stated at edge of map. Table on right giving acreages of fields.

Note: 'NB There is 2832 poles & 1/2 Long Measure in the Dikes'; note of dykes not belonging to farm; pencil notes of crops.

Chatteris – [1798] – CHA79801 – CCO Cambs.Chatteris 24

Plan of Hallwood Farm to which the Lease refers.

Scale bar 0–20 chains (= 5in.), 1:3,168; **Size:** (i) 23 7/8 x 29 1/4in.; **Top** is N; Manuscript(i), parchment, coloured.

Holwood Farm, TL384790, and 422a.0r.3p. in S of parish bounded by Colne Fen in S and Sutton Fen in E.

Names of neighbouring owners. Farm buildings shown in plan form, post mill shown in perspective. Closed fields showing owner's land; trees and hedges; roads and watercourses; osier holts.

Border of 1 narrow band; title top left; scale at bottom; compass above scale showing 4 points. Table bottom right giving field names and acreages. Land outlined in yellow, water coloured blue.

On lease dated 1798: 'Trustees for the Senior Masters of Christ Church Oxford to Messrs Skeels and Fryer Lease of a Farm at Chatteris', for 14 years.

Chatteris – [c. 1800] – CHA80001 – CCO Maps Chatteris 3

Hallwood Farm.

Scale bar 4–0–20 [chains] (= 6in.), 1:3,168; **Size:** (i) 21 7/8 x 31 13/16in.; **Top** is N; Manuscript(ii), tracing paper mounted on paper, coloured.

Holwood Farm, TL384790, and 422a.0r.5p. in S of parish bounded by Colne Fen in S and Sutton Fen in E.

Names of neighbouring owners. Farm buildings shown in plan form, post mill shown in perspective. Closed fields showing owner's land; roads; paddocks.

Border of 1 narrow band; title top left; scale bottom left; compass at top showing 4 points. Table bottom right giving field names and acreages. Land outlined in red, buildings coloured red, roads coloured brown.

Copy of map drawn after CHA79801, some neighbouring owners are the same, others have changed, one name crossed out on later map. Land owned by Christ Church, Oxford.

Chatteris – 1807 – CHA80701 – PRO J90/945

Survey and Map, of Mr Thos Grant's Farm, Chatteris~Ferry : with some Adjacent Lands Annexed.

Surveyor: Thomas Newitt; **Scale bar** 0–12 chains (= 2 15/16in.), 1:3,235; **Size:** (ii) 26 x 23 3/4in.; **Top** is E; Manuscript(i), paper, coloured.

'Dolvers Corner', TL388834, and 111a.0r.14p. to S bounded by road from Chatteris to Somersham in W and Ferry Burrows and Old Halves in E.

Names of fields, roads and neighbouring owners. Farm buildings shown in plan form. Closed fields; roads; 'Chatteris Toll'; 'Dolvers Corner'; 'Stocking Gate'; 'Somersham School Land'; garden identified on table.

Title at top; yellow scale bar bottom left surmounted by green and yellow dividers. Table bottom right in a plain yellow cartouche giving acreages and lengths of roads. Roads coloured yellow, land coloured red, 1 strip coloured green, land belonging to 'Waddington Esqr' [Thomas?; Waddington, 1934, 143] coloured brown.

Later pencil additions of gates, and survey lines with their dimensions. Ink notes of field names and manors, and 'Dolvers as they were before the late Inclosure' written on 1 plot.

Chatteris – [c. 1836] – CHA83601 – WM DIV.19

A Map of an Estate belonging to I. Fryer Esq. situate in the Parish of Chatteris in the Isle of Ely and County of Cambridge.

Surveyor: W[illiam] Chamberlain; **Scale:** Four chains to an inch, Scale bar 1–0–25 chains (= 6 1/2in.), 1:3,168; **Size:** (i) 37 7/8 x 24 5/8in.; **Top** is NW; Manuscript(i), paper, coloured.

178a.2r.28 1/4p. in NE of parish bounded by Turf Fen and Doddington Parish in N and Sixteen Foot Drain in SE.

Names of neighbouring owners. Farm buildings shown in plan form, windmill shown in perspective. Closed fields showing owner's land; trees; state of cultivation shown by colour; acreages; roads and gates; watercourses, drains and bridges; hedges; fences; responsibility for boundaries; pond; 'Stack' and 'Barn' yards; bank and 'stamp' [gravel; Reaney, 1943, 262].

Border 1/2in. wide of 1 grey band with 1 blue band on inside; title on left in a cartouche of 2 bands with gold lettering; scale centre bottom; compass centre top showing 4 points with feathers for N point. Table on right giving acreages and land use. 'Stamp' and road coloured green, bank coloured brown, water coloured blue, buildings coloured red, arable coloured in grey stripes.

John Fryer sr died in 1826 and left his estate to his nephews John, Daniel and Thomas [CRO EPR CW 1826 WR C52:251]; Daniel and Thomas are neighbouring owners. Date of map suggested in handlist in WM. Surveyor's 1st name was probably William [CRO P116/6/2].

Cherry Hinton – [1733] – CHE73301 – GLC H1/ST/E107/3

['The Survey of an Estate belonging to the Honble The Governors of Stt Thomases Hospital in the Borough of Southwork. Taken in December 1733, Lying in the parish of Cherry Hinton near Cambridge']. Heath Field.

Surveyor: [John Tracy]; [**Scale bar** 10 links–0–11 chains (= 6in.)], 1:1,584; **Size:** (ii) 19 3/8 x 28 1/2in.; **Top** is W; Manuscript(i), paper, coloured.

50a.3r.20p. probably in TL4855 and TL4955, bounded by 'From a Heath Babraham Way' in E, Worts' Causeway ['Haverel Way'] in S and 'Tutton Way' in W, with road to Fulbourn in N.

Names of fields and roads. Closes; roads.

Border of 1 narrow band on left and right of map; orientation given by cardinal points. Fields outlined in green.

Note in centre: 'To Wall Gate'. In volume, accompanied by terrier: 'To the Honble Governors of Stt Thomas's Hospital. In the Borrough of South=work An Account of the Several Lands lieing and being in Cambridgeshire In the parish of Cherry Hinton near Cambridge In the Occupacon of Walter Serocole Esqr & others'. Terrier gives field names, tenants' names, acreages 'as Lett at \or the nominal or reputed measure/' [added in ink], acreages 'Short Pole of 15:foot', acreages 'Middle Pole 16:foot:1/2:', description of boundaries and furlong names. At end of terrier is title of survey, surveyor, scale and note: 'NB: The Single Lines Shaded with Green are <ls> Margins of Grass (commonly called Bauks or Sheep Walks). And the double Lines with Green between them are Land covered with Bushes. And the Blew Cular is Water, Ponds, Motes, &

Ditches, &c. And the Square pieces in No 38: Is a Pound'. Later ink notes correcting spelling and: 'The names of the Lands or furlongs were so uncertain that they are not put downe'. See also CHE73302–4.

Cherry Hinton – [1733] – CHE73302 – GLC H1/ST/E107/3

[Land in 'Quarry Field', Cherry Hinton, owned by St Thomas' Hospital, London.]
Surveyor: [John Tracy]; **Scale:** 1:1,584; **Size:** (ii) 19 3/8 x 28 1/2in.; **Top** is W; Manuscript(i), paper, coloured.
31a.0r.8p. W of CHE73301, probably in TL4855, bounded by Church Lane in N, Worts' Causeway ['Haverel Way'] in S, 'Tutton Way' in E and Limekiln Hill in W.
Names of fields and roads. 'Vickridg House' shown in perspective. Closes; common, 'Cherry Hinton Green'; roads and watercourses; pound.
Border of 1 narrow band on left and right; orientation given by cardinal points. Fields outlined in green, water coloured blue.
In volume. See CHE73301 for details of accompanying terrier which gives surveyor, date and scale. See also CHE73303–4.

Cherry Hinton – [1733] – CHE73303 – GLC H1/ST/E107/3

[Land in 'Fendon' and 'Youngton' fields, Cherry Hinton, owned by St Thomas' Hospital, London.]
Surveyor: [John Tracy]; **Scale:** 1:1,584; **Size:** (ii) 19 3/8 x 28 1/2in.; **Top** is W; Manuscript(i), paper, coloured.
67a.3r.38p., probably in TL4755, bounded by 'Ford Way to Church Lane' in N, 'Three Hill Way to Cambridge' in W, Worts' Causeway ['Haverel Way'] in S, and Limekiln Hill ['To Qarrey Way'] in E.
Names of fields and roads. Closes; roads.
Border of 1 narrow band on left and right; orientation given by cardinal points. Balks coloured green.
In volume. See CHE73301 for details of accompanying terrier which gives surveyor, date and scale. See also CHE73302,4.

Cherry Hinton – [1733] – CHE73304 – GLC H1/ST/E107/3

[Land in 'Youngton' and 'Church' fields and 'Gallow Marsh Leys', Cherry Hinton, owned by St Thomas' Hospital, London.]
Surveyor: [John Tracy]; **Scale:** 1:1,584; **Size:** (ii) 19 3/8 x 28 1/2in.; **Top** is W; Manuscript(i), paper, coloured.
19a.2r.16p., probably in TL4756 and TL4856.
Names of fields. Closes; watercourses.
Orientation given by cardinal points. Fields outlined in green, water coloured blue.
In volume. See CHE73301 for details of accompanying terrier which gives surveyor, date and scale. See also CHE73302–3.

Cherry Hinton – 1812 – CHE81201 – GCC Drawer 1 Map 1 (Cherry Hinton)

Plan of the Estates, at Cherry Hinton in the County of Cambridge, belonging to the Master Fellows and Scholars of Gonville and Caius College in the University of Cambridge. Made AD 1812, By Alexdr Watford.

Surveyor: Alexander Watford [jr]; **Scale bar** 0–20 chains (= 3 5/16in.), 1:4,782; **Size:** (i) 11 1/4 x 18 1/16in.; **Top** is N; Manuscript(i), parchment, coloured.
76a.1r.12p., probably in TL4755, bounded by roads from Linton to Cambridge in W and from Great Shelford to Cambridge in E, crossed E–W by road to Trumpington.
Names of fields, roads, some tenants and neighbouring owners. Farm buildings and cottages shown in plan form. Closed fields showing owner's land; acreages; roads; hedges; tenure of some plots and reasons for allotments; orchards and pightle identified on table.
Border of 1 broad band with 1 narrow band on inside; title centre top; scale bottom right; compass bottom left showing 8 points. Table centre bottom giving field names, acreages and tenure. Hedges coloured green, roads coloured yellow, buildings coloured red.
Numbers on some plots refer to inclosure award. Pencil notes and pencil grid on map.

Cherry Hinton – [1813] – CHE81301 – GLC H1/ST/E22/1

Farm Yard and Buildings at Netherhall in Hinton.
Surveyor: [J[oseph] Beevers]; **Scale:** 1:392; **Size:** (ii) 12 1/8 x 7 3/8in.; Manuscript(i), paper, uncoloured.
c. 2r. at Netherhall Farm, TL475551.
Names of buildings. Buildings shown in plan form and include house, kitchen, 'cart lodge', 'cattle sheds', 'Cutting House', 'Chaff House', stable, barn, 'Cow lodge'. Dimensions of areas; farmyard.
Title in centre of farm. Table at top giving buildings, height of walls, building materials and valuation.
On dorse: 'Please to insure, for 7 years, in the Name of Abel Chapman Esq. Treasurer of St Thomas's Hospital, £1500 on a farm House & Buildings, in the Parish of Cherry Hinton, near Cambridge, in the possession of Thos Sumpter Headly. J Beevers Jany 5, 1813'. At front of policy book for property insured at the Hand in Hand Fire Office. See also COM81301, which gives surveyor's 1st name, and FUL81301.

Cherry Hinton – 1830 – CHE83001 – CUL MS Plans 378g

Plan of the Estate purchased of Joseph Barron, 1830.
Surveyor: [Alexander Watford jr]; **Draughtsman:** E[dward] Serocold Pearce; **Scale:** 1:4,800; **Size:** (iii) 2 1/4 x 4 1/4in.; **Top** is NE; Manuscript(iv), paper mounted on paper, coloured.
12a.3r.19p. in centre of TL4857, bounded by Rosemary Lane in NW, Church End in NE and Coldham's Lane in SW.
Names of fields and tenant. Closed fields; roads and footpaths.
Title top left; compass bottom right showing 4 points. Table in middle giving tenants, field names and acreages. Cuffed hands indicate directions of roads. Freehold land coloured red, land belonging to Netherhall coloured blue, rectory land coloured purple.
Inset at bottom showing: 'Actual subdivision of estate on enclosure, boundaries copied from award plan, rest measured by E.S.P.' Shows state of cultivation by colour, and garden. Same size and orientation as main map. Map and inset were copied by E. Serocold Pearce from that by Alexander Watford which accompanied 1810 inclosure award; Pearce's 1st name was Edward [Venn, II, 5, 60].

Cherry Hinton – 1831 – CHE83101 – CUL MS Plans y.1(29)

Land at Cherry Hinton Cambridgeshire the property of the late Mr T.S. Headly. May 1831.

Draughtsman: [Elliot Smith]; **Scale:** 1:7,960; **Size:** (ii) 20 7/8 x 28 3/4in.; **Top** is W; Manuscript(i), paper, coloured.

204a.0r.13p. extending from Queen Edith's Way in S to N of Coldham's Lane, including crossroads at TL486562 between roads from Fulbourn to Great Shelford and from Cambridge to Cherry Hinton.

Names of tenants. Houses shown in plan form. Closed fields showing Headly's land; common; roads and footpaths; watercourses; gardens and orchard identified on table.

Title middle top. Table on left giving tenants, field names, acreages and tenure. Roads shown in grey, buildings coloured black.

Drawn for fire insurance purposes, in volume from Elliot Smith and Sons, Auctioneers and Estate Agents. Thomas Sumpter Headly died in 1831 [*Cambridge Chronicle*, 6 May 1831].

Chesterton – 1790 – CHF79001 – SJC D31.34

Plan of the Buildings &c belonging to Morris's Farm, of which Farm the within is a Terrier.

Surveyor: [Joseph Freeman]; **Scale:** 1:356; **Size:** (i) 14 1/2 x 10 1/8in.; Manuscript(i), parchment, uncoloured.

3r.38p. in 'Cambridge Field', bounded by a street at top.

Names of areas. Buildings shown in plan form and include cottages, 'cellar or wash house', 'chaff house', 'cow house', barn, stables, barley and wheat barns, granary, cart shed, dovecote, 'corn and hay cases'. Dimensions of areas; roads; garden; yards.

Border of 2 narrow bands; title bottom right. Table on right giving buildings, their building materials and state of repair.

Note bottom left: 'the Dimensions are expressed in Feet and Inches'. Accompanies terrier by Joseph Freeman: 'A Terrier of the Land in Cambridge Field, called Morrises Farm, belonging to St Johns the Evangelists' College, now in the occupation of William Banks'.

Chesterton – 1790 – CHF79002 – SJC MPS 7

Plan of a Farm at Chesterton in the County of Cambridge belonging to St. John the Evangelist's College. Mrs Lydia Banks Lessee - 1790.

Surveyor: Joseph Freeman; **Scale:** 1:1,930; **Size:** (i) 14 1/8 x 21 13/16in.; **Top** is N; Manuscript(i), parchment, coloured.

48a.0r.20p. E of TL443594, junction of roads from Cambridge to Huntingdon and to Histon, extending as far S as River Cam, and E along road to Ely as far as Arbury ['Meer Way'].

Names of fields, roads and neighbouring owners. Open fields showing owner's strips; 'Parishes' and 'Kettles' meadows and 'The Folly' [meadow]; roads and footpaths; watercourses and bridge.

Border of 1 broad and 1 narrow band; title middle bottom; compass in centre showing 4 points with a decorated N. Table middle top giving acreages of each plot. Strips coloured yellow, meadow outlined in green, pasture coloured green.

Accompanying terrier at SJC D31.52. Photograph at CRO TR869/P15.

Chesterton – 1790 – CHF79003 – CLC ACC.1985/5

A Plan of the Lands in Cambridge and Chesterton Fields belonging to the Master and Fellows of Clare Hall. 1790.

Surveyor: [Joseph Freeman?]; **Scale bar** 1–0–20 chains (= 2 5/8in.), 1:6,336; **Size:** (i) 28 x 19 9/16in.; Top is NE; Manuscript(iii), paper, coloured.

Junction of roads from Cambridge to Huntingdon and to Histon, TL443594, and 22a.0r.33p. in W of Chesterton Parish and 31a.3r.32p. in West fields of Cambridge.

Names of fields, roads, watercourses and neighbouring owners. Farmhouse in Mount Pleasant, tenement NE of St Peter's Churchyard and 'The House in the Field' shown in plan form. Open fields showing owner's strips; closes; state of cultivation shown by colour; roads and footpaths; watercourses; balks; hedges; meadow adjoining map.

Border of 1 broad band with 1 narrow band on inside with corners with rococo decoration, fruit and flowers; title top left in a cartouche of flowers and leaves with a bow on top; scale bottom left; compass in centre showing 4 points. Table on right giving acreages. Water coloured blue, buildings coloured red, arable strips coloured grey, grass and balks coloured green.

Note under table: 'The parts Colored Yellow, are Arable, and the parts colored Green are pasture. The Numbers 53 and 54 are Leys and the Number 55 is an Inclosure called Hows Close'. Note on table of 3r.8p., 'Additions since the plan was made'. On dorse: 'Cambridge & Chesterton Castle End Farm'. This is probably the map referred to in a valuation by Joseph Freeman made in 1795 with a note: 'Mr Freeman was misinformed for there are Buildings, & there are more Acres. Vide his Map of the Estate. J[ohn] Torkington' [CLC Safe B:44/2]. John Torkington was Master of Clare College 1781–1815 [Venn, II, 6, 210].

Chesterton – 1793 – CHF79301 – SJC MPS 8

Plan of Lands, at Chesterton, belonging to St Johns the Evangelists College Cambridge. Surveyed in 1793 Robert Johnson Lessee.

Surveyor: [Joseph Freeman?]; **Scale:** 1:1,070; **Size:** (i) 12 9/16 x 22 1/8in.; **Top** is N; Manuscript(i), parchment, coloured.

6a.2r.38p. in TL4459, bounded by road from Cambridge to Huntingdon in W and River Cam in S.

Names of fields, owner, tenants, neighbouring owners and roads. Open fields showing owner's strips; trees and hedges; arable indicated by words; balks; roads and footpaths; watercourses.

Border of 1 broad and 1 narrow band; title middle left; compass top left showing 4 points. Table at bottom giving acreages of strips, and number of ridges which each plot contains. Roads coloured brown, balks and trees coloured green, water coloured blue.

Note right of table: 'Edwd Benson Esqr is the present Lord of the Manor'. Land shown is identical to that on CHF79401. In style of Joseph Freeman, who surveyed for the College in the 1790s.

Chesterton – 1794 – CHF79401 – SJC MPS 9, 10

Plan of Certain Lands lying in the Open Fields of Chesterton. belonging to St Johns the Evangelists College in the University of Cambridge.

Surveyor: [Joseph Freeman?]; **Scale:** 1:1,070; **Size:** (i) 13 7/16 x 20 9/16in.; **Top** is N; Manuscript(i), parchment, coloured.

6a.2r.38p. in TL4459, bounded by road from Cambridge to Huntingdon ['Hows Causey'] in N and River Cam in S.

Names of fields, owner, neighbouring owners and road. Open fields showing owner's strips; trees and hedges; arable strips indicated by words; balks; roads and footpaths; watercourses.

Border of 1 band; title middle bottom; compass middle right showing 4 points. Table bottom left giving acreages and number of ridges in each strip. Strips coloured brown.

Land shown is identical to that on CHE79301. 2nd copy at SJC MPS 10 is identical except that it measures 15 3/16 x 20 1/4in. and has compass middle top. Maps are in style of Joseph Freeman, who surveyed for the College in the 1790s.

Chesterton – 1794 – CHF79402 – CLC ACC.1985/5
Plan of a Farm at Chesterton, in the County of Cambridge. belonging to Clare Hall. Surveyed in the Year 1794. John Johnson Lessee.
Surveyor: [Joseph Freeman]; **Scale bar** 10–0–20 chains (= 3 3/4in.), 1:6,336; **Size:** (i) 24 1/4 x 27 9/16in.; **Top** is N; Manuscript(i), parchment, coloured.
Houses in Chesterton village at TL462598, and 97a.1r.10p. bounded by Milton Parish in NE, road from Huntingdon to Cambridge in NW and 'Chesterton Fen' in S.
Names of fields, roads, balks and neighbouring owners. Houses in village and mill shown in plan form. Open fields showing owner's strips; closes; meadow; trees; state of cultivation shown by colour; roads and watercourses; number of lands between strips; hedges and 'Kings Hedge'; balks.
Border of 1 broad band with 1 narrow band on inside; title top right; scale bottom left; compass centre top showing 4 points. Table on left giving field names, acreages and land use. Roads and arable strips coloured brown, hedges and pasture coloured green, water coloured blue, buildings coloured red.
Under scale: 'Note. The present Lord of the Manor is Edwd Benson Esqr. There are no Buildings whatever belonging to this Farm'. Rough copy on paper mounted on cloth, whole sheet measures 21 3/8 x 29 3/8in. and has no title. Accompanies valuation made in May 1794 by Joseph Freeman [CLC Safe B:44/3].

Chesterton – 1804 – CHF80401 – SJC MPS 11
A Plan of Lands in Chesterton Parish belonging to Saint John's College in the University of Cambridge.
Scale: 1:4,610; **Size:** (i) 13 3/4 x 23 1/8in.; **Top** is NW; Manuscript(i), parchment, coloured.
8a.2r.11p. bounded by roads to Milton in SE and to Huntingdon in NW; junction of roads from Cambridge to Huntingdon and to Histon is at TL443594.
Names of fields, owner, tenants, neighbouring owners and roads. Open fields showing owner's strips; trees; roads and footpaths; watercourses; 'Procession Balk'.
Border of 1 band; title at top. Table on right giving land use and acreages. Roads coloured brown, water coloured blue, strips coloured red, balks coloured green.
Faded pencil notes. Accompanying terrier, SJC MPS 12.

Chesterton – 1816 – CHF81601 – TCC Box 22 Chesterton 85
Plan of the Impropriate Homestead and Premises situate at Chesterton and belonging to the Master Fellows and Scholars of Trinity College in the University of Cambridge Taken January 9th 1816.
Surveyor: [Alexander Watford jr]; **Scale:** 1:1,710;

Size: (iii) 6 x 7 3/4in.; **Top** is N?; Manuscript(i), paper, coloured.
c. 3a. E of church, probably in TL4659.
Names of areas and roads. Buildings shown in plan form and include farm, 'Old Tower', kitchen, shed, 'Wheat Barn', 'Cow House', cottages, 'Little Barly Barn', 'Cart Shed', 'Great Barley Barn', pigsties, calf pens, stables and 'Old Malting'. Closed fields; acreage of farmyard; roads and gates; gardens; 'Orchard & Drying Ground'; walls; farm, 'Hay', 'Stack', 'Cow', 'Hog', 'Wood' and 'Back' yards.
Title at top. Road coloured brown, buildings coloured red, water coloured blue, some yards coloured green or yellow.
At beginning of: 'Terrier & Valuation of the Impropriate Glebe Land', signed by Alexander Watford.

Chesterton – [1825] – CHF82501 – QCC 355 A21, B21
Estate at Chesterton In the County of Cambridge.
Surveyor: [Alexander Watford jr]; **Scale bar** 0–10 chains (= 3 5/16in.), 1:2,391; **Size:** (i) 6 1/2 x 4in.; **Top** is N; Manuscript(ii), paper, coloured.
1a.2r.7p. in a close bounded by a road in N and W.
Names of field and neighbouring owner. Closed field; state of cultivation shown by colour; acreage; hedges; road.
Border at top, bottom and left of 2 narrow bands, border on right of 1 broad band with 1 narrow band on either side; title at top; scale at bottom; compass on left showing 4 points. Field coloured green, road coloured brown.
On right of sheet, which also contains maps of Burwell [BUW82501], Dullingham [DUL82501] and Swaffham Prior [SWP82502], and in volume drawn in 1825: 'Plans of the Several Estates in England and Wales belonging to the President and Fellows of the College of St Margaret and St Bernard commonly called Queen's College in the University of Cambridge Delineated from Authentic Documents in the possession of the said President and Fellows and from actual Surveys taken By their most obedient and obliged Servant Alexr Watford'. Title page drawn by James Richardson [Watford's nephew]. This is the Bursar's copy; 2nd, finer, copy [the Master's copy] at QCC 355 B21 measures 6 3/8 x 4 3/8in., is drawn on parchment and has a scale bar 0–9 chains (= 3in.), 1:2,376. Border imitates a scroll of paper, title has gothic lettering, road has red/brown edges. Top right of sheet and with a note: 'Sold'. Positive photostat of this copy at BL 1640.(28), at 1:5,200.

Chesterton – 1836 – CHF83601 – CUL MS Plans 312
Plan of a Pasture Close at Chesterton, the Property of Miss Benson being the Intended Site for the Chesterton Union Poorhouse.
Surveyor: R[ichard?] H[arwood?]; **Scale bar** 0–5 chains (= 5in.), 1:792; **Size:** (i) 14 5/8 x 12 1/4in.; **Top** is W; Manuscript(i), paper mounted on paper, coloured.
Site of Chesterton Infirmary, TL461600, and 4a.0r.7p. bounded by Mill Lane in E.
Names of field, roads, neighbouring owners and tenants. Closed field with wood at edge; acreage; roads and footpaths; fences.
Border of 1 broad and 1 narrow band; title top left; scale middle bottom. Roads coloured brown, pasture coloured green.
Surveyor was possibly Richard Harwood [Eden H188], Miss Benson's 1st name was Mary [CUM Add.5720 f.48].

Cheveley – [c. 1735] – CHG73501 – WLT Accession 1332 Duke of Somerset Papers Box 51

[Cheveley Park, owned by 6th Duke of Somerset.]

Scale bar 10–0–160 feet (= 5 1/4in.), 1:389; **Size:** (ii) 20 1/4 x 37in.; **Orientation:** Top is SW; Manuscript(i), paper, coloured.

Cheveley Park, TL672608, and c. 13a. bounded by 'The Lane to Cheveley' in S.

Names of areas. Buildings shown in plan form and include 'Terras Room', 'Terras Bedchamber', 'Great Dining Room', 'Withdrawing Room', 'Lady's Bed=Chamber', 'Little' and 'Great' parlours, 'Little drawing Room', 'Maids Room', 'Servants Hall', still houses, 'Stone Room', pantries, 'New Kitchen', 'Old Kitchen', 'Stewards Room', 'Drying Room', laundry, scullery, 'Little house', 'Well house', brew house, 'Bakehouse', 'Chase House', office, oat barn, wheat barn, pea barn, stables, 'Great Stable', 'Carters Stable', 2 'hay houses', coach houses, 'cart lodge', 'Hog Sty', 'bolting' house, 2 'Cheese Houses', 'Broom House', 'Porters Lodge', 'Partridge House', 'Pidgeon House', 'Gardeners Room'. Dimensions of areas; trees; roads; park; garden and 'Old Kitchen Garden'; 'Old Orchard'; 'Terrase Walk'; steps; pond and its depth, 'Horse pond' and 'An Old Pond that wont hold Water Which is began upon to be filled vp with Brick Rubbish, &c'; foundations and 'The New foundations – length 521 feet, from Z to Z built by Sir Germain [Jermyn] Davers'; yard, 'Wood Yard' and 'Great Court Yard'; walls and park wall; iron gates.

Scale centre bottom; compass showing 4 red and green points in centre of scale. Foundations and edge of 'Horse pond' coloured red, water coloured pale green and hatched with brown, walls of buildings, edge of terrace walk and steps coloured grey or brown.

Notes along walls in W: 'This line from A to B represents the Park wall; & was taken from Mr Nash's Draught, which is to Near the Great house by 60 foot', and, 'These Red lines denotes the old foundations of the late Kitchen Garden & orchard Walls'. Owner was Charles Seymour, 6th Duke of Somerset [Hore, 1899, 64], date suggested by A. P. Baggs [personal communication].

Cheveley – 1775 – CHG77501 – CRO 101/P/2

A Survey of the Estate lying in the Parishes of Cheveley and Little Woodditton in the County of Cambridgeshire belonging to The Right Honble the Marquis of Granby. Taken in the Year 1775 by Thos Warren Bury St Edmunds.

Surveyor: Thomas Warren [jr]; **Scale bar** 0–60 perches (= 3 3/4in.), 1:3,168; **Size:** (i) 67 7/8 x 50 1/4in.; **Top** is SE; Manuscript(i), parchment, coloured.

Cheveley Park, TL672608, and c. 4,300a. in whole parish except for far S and in E half of Woodditton Parish as far W as Little Ditton.

Names of fields, buildings, parishes, tenants and neighbouring owners. Barn, stables and brick kiln shown in plan form, farms, warren house, almshouses, well, post mill, White Hart Inn, cottages and Saxon Hall shown in perspective, Cheveley Park shown in exaggerated perspective. Open fields showing owner's strips; closes; common; Derisley Wood, 'Saxon Grove' and trees; heath and waste; acreages; roads and footpaths; watercourses; gates including gates to Cheveley Park; stiles; park, gardens including layout of garden at Cheveley Park, orchards; Castle Hill earthworks shown as a mound; wells; pits; ponds including duck pond; kennel; 'The Kings Chair'

shown in perspective on heath [an ornamental seat for watching horse-racing; Bodger, 1787]; pound.

Border of 1 broad green band outlined in brown; title bottom right in a cartouche decorated with flowers and leaves; scale middle right in a square cartouche of a similar style; compass middle top showing 16 points coloured red with a decorated centre. Land outlined in red, yellow, blue, green or brown to show the tenants, boundary between Cheveley and Woodditton parishes coloured red, roads and trees coloured green.

Pencil notes of acreages and extensions to map. Explanation left of title giving key to letters and colours showing occupiers of the land. 3 insets top left and on right extending map to SE. Accompanying terrier at CRO R54/10/7(c). Surveyor was Thomas Warren jr [Eden W123].

Childerley – [c. 1802] – CHI80201 – CUL MS Plans 552

A Plan of the Mannor and Parish of Childerley in the County of Cambridge being the Estate of Nicolson Calvert Esqr.

Scale bar 30–0 chains (= 3 7/8in.), 1:6,132; **Size:** (i) 21 3/4 x 14 3/4in.; **Top** is NE; Manuscript(i), parchment, coloured.

Childerley Hall, TL356617, and c. 1,100a. in whole parish.

Names of fields, tenants and neighbouring owners. Farm buildings, houses, dovecote, cottage and stable shown in plan form. Closed fields; wood and trees; pasture; state of cultivation given in words on most plots; park and orchard; ponds and fishponds; bowling green; use of barns; 'brick clamps' [stacks].

Border of 1 broad band with 1 narrow band on either side; title middle left; scale middle bottom; compass above title showing 4 points with an ornamented N and points coloured red and yellow. Fields outlined in blue, green, brown, yellow and red, buildings coloured red, trees coloured brown, water coloured grey.

Drawn before CHI81701, possibly when Calvert inherited the estate in 1802 [LG, 346].

Childerley – 1817 – CHI81701 – CUL MS Plans 313

Plan of Childerley Farm. The Property of N. Calvert Esqr. 1817.

Draughtsman: W[illiam] Buckland; **Scale bar** 0–30 chains (= 3 1/16in.), 1:7,758; **Size:** (i) 20 1/4 x 16 7/8in.; **Top** is NE; Manuscript(iii), paper mounted on paper, coloured.

Childerley Hall, TL356617, and 1,058a.0r.0p. in whole parish.

Names of some neighbouring owners. Farm buildings and cottages shown in plan form. Closed fields; common; wood, plantations and trees; state of cultivation shown by colour; roads and footpaths; watercourses; gates; moat; fishponds; gardens and orchards identified on table.

Border of 1 broad band; title top left; scale middle bottom; compass top right showing 8 points. Table on right giving field names, acreages, state of cultivation, land under plantations and land tended by 'Starve Goose Farm'. Arable coloured red, pasture and wood coloured green, water and buildings coloured black.

Pencil notes, crops marked in pencil and include barley, wheat, fallow, seeds, oats and beans. Note bottom right: 'Copied by W. Buckland Surveyor, Dunstable Beds 1817'. Draughtsman's 1st name was William [Eden B676], owner's 1st name was Nicolson [see CHI80201].

Childerley – 1827 – CHI82701 – CUL MS Plans.b.23
  Childerley. 1827.
  Scale bar 0–30 chains (= 3 3/4in.), 1:6,336; **Size:** (ii) 25 1/4 x 31 3/8in.; **Top** is W; Manuscript(i), paper mounted on cloth, coloured.
  Childerley Hall, TL356617, 1,058a.0r.0p. in whole parish and a small acreage [less than 10a.] in E of Boxworth Parish.
  Names of parishes, neighbouring owner and roads. Hall and farm buildings shown in plan form. Closed fields showing owner's land; trees, groves and plantations; state of cultivation shown by colour; boundary between Boxworth and Childerley parishes; roads; watercourses and pond; park, orchard, yard, sheep walk and gardens identified on table.
  Title centre top; scale centre bottom; compass top right showing 4 points, incorrectly giving top as N. Tables on right and at bottom giving field names, acreages and land use. Buildings coloured red, roads coloured brown, water coloured blue, woods and pasture coloured green, arable coloured pink.
  Pencil notes of acreages and land use. Dissected into sections before mounting. Owner was Nicolson Calvert [*LG*, 346].

Chippenham – 1659 – CHP65901 – SPA
  A true and perfect Survey of the Mannor of Badlingham hall in Chippenham in the County of Cambridge with all the Lands, Meadows, Pastures, Heath, Grounds & Feedings thereunto belonging. being the Estate of John Clarke Esqr and also of all such Lands & Tenements as are holden of the said Mannor as the same are Particularly distinguished from the demeasne Lands by the several coulers above mentioned & sett downe at the end of every particular Tennants name. made and taken in the year of Or Lord 1659. By Will. Covell.
  Surveyor: William Covell; **Scale bar** 0–8 [chains] (= 5 1/2in.), 1:1,152; **Size:** (i) 23 1/2 x 48in.; **Top** is NNE; Manuscript(i), parchment, coloured.
  Badlingham Hall, TL678708, and c. 170a. in N of parish bounded by roads to Barton Mills in NE and to Newmarket in E, and Lee Brook ['Dam Breeds'] in SW.
  Names of fields. Buildings shown in perspective and include cottages and barns, Badlingham Hall shown in exaggerated perspective. Open fields showing owner's and tenants' strips; closes; common; meadow and pasture; wood and trees; heath and waste; roads and footpaths; gates; watercourses; gardens; moat; hedges.
  Border 1in. wide with blue, red and green pattern; title bottom right in a cartouche with red, blue and yellow strapwork; scale bottom left surmounted by gold dividers and surrounded by red and blue strapwork; compass middle top showing 16 red points with a gold N. Table middle right giving tenants and colour of strips. Coat of arms shown top left.[1] Rabbits and sheep drawn on heath, milkmaid milking a cow near hall, whole scene watched by Lord of the Manor on heath. Grass coloured green, roads coloured brown, trees coloured green, water coloured blue, strips coloured purple, blue, red, yellow and brown.
  Numbers on plots suggest map originally accompanied by a terrier. Title and table are very faded; title taken from a transcription attached to the map. Positive and negative photostats at 1:1,690 at CUL Maps.bb.53(1).96.27–30.

Chippenham – 1712 – CHP71201 – CRO R58/16/1
  A Survey of part of the Mannor or Lordship of Chippenham in the parish of Chippenham in the County of Cambridge belonging to the Right Honourable Edward Earl of Orford Viscount Barflevr and Baron of Shingay &c. By Heber Lands 1712. No. 1.
  Surveyor: Heber Lands; **Scale bar** 80–0–10 statute poles (= 5 1/2in.), 1:3,240; **Size:** (ii) 22 7/8 x 30 3/16in.; **Top** is NNW; Manuscript(i), parchment, coloured.
  c. 440a. in NW of parish bounded by road from Fordham to Chippenham in W and Lee Brook in E, and crossed by road from Fordham to Freckenham in N. Roads from Chippenham to Fordham and to Isleham to cross at TL662701.
  Names of fields, roads and tenants. Post mill shown in perspective, farm buildings shown in plan form. Open fields showing all strips; common; acreages; roads and footpaths; watercourses; pound; fences.
  Title bottom right in a baroque cartouche coloured green, blue and red; scale bottom left surrounded by a border with a green edge imitating the edge of a sheet of paper; compass rose middle right showing 4 red and green points. Coat of arms of Edward Russell, Earl of Orford, middle left in a green, red and blue cartouche. Roads coloured brown, water coloured blue, common coloured yellow, strips outlined in green.
  Note at bottom: 'This Joynes to No 2 on the North side of Fordham Road'. Positive and negative photostats at 1:4,387 at CUL Maps.bb.53(1).95.16. See also CHP71202-8.

Chippenham – 1712 – CHP71202 – CRO R58/16/1
  A Survey of part of the Mannor or Lordship of Chippenham in the parish of Chippenham in the County of Cambridge belonging to the Right Honourable Edward Earl of Orford Viscount Barfleur and Baron of Shingay &c. By Heber Lands 1712. No. 2.
  Surveyor: Heber Lands; **Scale bar** 80–0–10 statute poles (= 5 9/16in.), 1:3,204; **Size:** (ii) 23 x 30 3/8in.; **Top** is NW; Manuscript(i), parchment, coloured.
  Chippenham Church, TL663698, and c. 800a. in village W of Vicarage Lane ['New Street'] and in W of parish, bounded by Fordham and Snailwell parishes in N and W, road from Chippenham to Fordham in E and Chippenham Park in S.
  Names of fields, tenants and roads. Some houses in village shown in plan form. Open fields showing all strips; closes; common; wood and trees; waste and Chippenham Fen; state of cultivation given in words; acreages; roads and footpaths; gates; watercourses.
  Title bottom left in a green, red and blue baroque cartouche; scale middle top surrounded by a border with a green edge imitating the edge of a sheet of paper; compass rose top right showing 4 green and red points in a green border. Coat of arms of Edward Russell, Earl of Orford, top left in a green and red cartouche. Roads coloured brown, marsh and common coloured yellow, fields outlined in green, boundary of park coloured red.
  Note at bottom: 'This Joynes to No 1 on the South side of Fordham Road'. Positive and negative photostats at 1:4,387 at CUL Maps.bb.53(1).95.17. See also CHP71201,3-8.

---

[1] The College of Arms has not managed to attribute the coat of arms to John Clarke, or to any other person.

Chippenham – 1712 – CHP71203 – CRO R58/16/1

A Survey of part of the Mannor or Lordship of Chippenham in the parish of Chippenham in the County of Cambridge belonging to the Right Honourable Edward Earl of Orford Viscount Barflevr and Baron of Shingay &c. By Heber Lands 1712. No. 3.

Surveyor: Heber Lands; **Scale bar** 80–0–10 statute poles (= 5 1/2in.), 1:3,240; **Size:** (ii) 23 x 30in.; **Top** is NW; Manuscript(i), parchment, coloured.

Chippenham Hall, TL664693, and c. 690a. in Chippenham Park and village extending as far N as junction of roads to Isleham and Fordham, and as far E as Lee Brook.

Names of fields, tenants and roads. Hall buildings shown in plan form; houses, barns, church, school, dovecote and lodges shown in perspective. Open fields showing all strips; common; wood and layout of trees in park; acreages; roads and footpaths; gates including detailed drawing of main gate to park; watercourses; park; kitchen garden, layout of formal garden; ponds; drying yard; 2 benches in park shown on hills drawn as mounds.

Title bottom left in a red, green/brown and blue baroque cartouche; scale bottom right with a blue and green border imitating the edge of a sheet of paper; compass rose top right showing 4 green and red points with a decorated green border. Coat of arms of Edward Russell, Earl of Orford, top left in a green and blue cartouche. Deer in park. Water coloured green/blue, common and paths in garden coloured yellow, roads coloured brown, fields outlined in green, trees coloured green, houses and cottages coloured brown, park outlined in red.

Note at bottom: 'This Joynes to No 2 at the South side of Snailwell Road'. Positive and negative photostats at 1:4,387 at CUL Maps.bb.53(1).95.18. See also CHP71201–2,4–8.

Chippenham – 1712 – CHP71204 – CRO R58/16/1

A Survey of part of the Mannor or Lordship of Chippenham in the parish of Chippenham in the County of Cambridge belonging to the Right Honourable Edward Earl of Orford Viscount Barflevr and Baron of Shingay &c. By Heber Lands 1712. No. 4.

Surveyor: Heber Lands; **Scale bar** 80–0–10 statute poles (= 5 1/2in.), 1:3,240; **Size:** (ii) 22 15/16 x 30 5/16in.; **Top** is SE; Manuscript(i), parchment, coloured.

c. 300a. W of Chippenham Park in TL6468 and TL6568, bounded by Snailwell Parish in W and common marsh in N, and 1 field S of road to Snailwell.

Names of fields, tenants and roads. Open fields showing all strips; common; acreages; roads and footpaths; gates.

Title middle right in a green, blue and red baroque cartouche; scale bottom right with a border imitating the edge of a sheet of paper with a green edge and red back; compass rose top right showing 4 green and red points in a green/brown border. Coat of arms of Edward Russell, Earl of Orford, middle left in a green cartouche. Roads coloured brown, balks coloured green, strips outlined in green, park outlined in red, common coloured yellow.

Note bottom right: 'This Joynes to No 3 of West side of Chippenham Hall park'. Positive and negative photostats at 1:4,387 at CUL Maps.bb.53(1).95.19. See also CHP71201–3,5–8.

Chippenham – 1712 – CHP71205 – CRO R58/16/1

A Survey of part of the Mannor or Lordship of Chippenham in the parish of Chippenham in the County of

Cambridge belonging to the Right Honourable Edward Earl of Orford Viscount Barflevr and Baron of Shingay &c. By Heber Lands 1712. No. 5.

Surveyor: Heber Lands; **Scale bar** 80–0–10 statute poles (= 5 9/16in.), 1:3,204; **Size:** (ii) 23 x 30 1/4in.; **Top** is SE; Manuscript(i), parchment, coloured.

Farm ['the new farme'] at TL679680, and c. 330a. SE of Chippenham Park bounded by Kennett Parish in E, and roads to Newmarket ['road from Norwich towards London'] in S and to Moulton in W.

Names of farm, fields, tenants and roads. Farm buildings shown in perspective and include 1 building [a dovecote?]. Open fields showing all strips; common; trees; waste and heath; acreages; roads, footpaths and bridleway; gates; pond.

Title bottom right in a red, yellow, blue and green/brown baroque cartouche; scale top left surrounded by a border imitating the edge of a sheet of paper with a green edge and red back; compass rose middle right showing 4 green and red points in a green border. Coat of arms of Edward Russell, Earl of Orford, middle left in a green and red cartouche. Roads and buildings coloured brown, strips outlined in green, farms coloured red, trees coloured green, common and heath coloured yellow.

Note bottom right: 'This Joynes to No 3 at Moulton Gate & at No 3 Jules Common'. Positive and negative photostats at 1:4,387 at CUL Maps.bb.53(1).95.20. See also CHP71201–4,6–8.

Chippenham – 1712 – CHP71206 – CRO R58/16/1

A Survey of part of the Mannor or Lordship of Chippenham in the parish of Chippenham in the County of Cambridge belonging to the Right Honourable Edward Earl of Orford Viscount Barflevr and Baron of Shingay &c. By Heber Lands 1712. No. 6.

Surveyor: Heber Lands; **Scale bar** 80–0–10 statute poles (= 5 9/16in.), 1:3,204; **Size:** (ii) 23 1/8 x 35in.; **Top** is ENE; Manuscript(i), parchment, coloured.

c. 420a. in TL6667, bounded by Chippenham Park in N, roads to Newmarket ['road from Norwich towards London'] in S and W, and to Moulton in E.

Names of fields, tenants and roads. Open fields showing all strips; common; waste and heath; acreages; roads and gates; watercourses and bridges over Lee Brook.

Title bottom right in a red, green and blue baroque cartouche; scale middle top with a border imitating the edge of a sheet of paper with a green edge and yellow back; compass rose bottom left showing 4 green and red points in a green and red border. Coat of arms of Edward Russell, Earl of Orford, top left in a green and red cartouche. Roads coloured brown, strips outlined in green, heath coloured yellow, park outlined in red.

Note at bottom: 'This Joynes to No 5 on the West side of Moulton Road and this Joynes to No 3 on the South side of Chippenham Park'. Positive and negative photostats at 1:4,387 at CUL Maps.bb.53(1).95.21. See also CHP71201–5,7–8.

Chippenham – 1712 – CHP71207 – CRO R58/16/1

A Survey of part of the Mannor or Lordship of Chippenham in the parish of Chippenham in the County of Cambridge belonging to the Right Honourable Edward Earl of Orford Viscount Barflevr and Baron of Shingay &c. By Heber Lands 1712. No. 7.

Surveyor: Heber Lands; **Scale bar** 80–0–10 statute

poles (= 5 9/16in.), 1:3,204; **Size:** (ii) 22 7/8 x 30 1/8in.; **Top** is WSW; Manuscript(i), parchment, coloured.

c. 300a. in TL6567 and TL6667 W and S of Chippenham Park, extending as far as Snailwell Parish in W and road to Newmarket ['road from Norwich towards London'] in S.

Names of fields, tenants and roads. Open fields showing all strips; trees; waste; acreages; roads; watercourses and bridges over Lee Brook; pond.

Title middle bottom in a blue, red and green baroque cartouche; scale top right with a border imitating the edge of a sheet of paper with a green edge and red back; very ornate compass rose top left with crowns in each of the 4 red and green points with a red and green border. Coat of arms of Edward Russell, Earl of Orford, bottom left in a green, blue and yellow cartouche. Roads coloured brown, water coloured blue/green, waste coloured yellow, fields and trees coloured green, park outlined in red.

Note bottom left: 'This Joynes to the West side No 6 and the South side of No 4'. Positive and negative photostats at 1:4,387 at CUL Maps.bb.53(1).95.22. See also CHP71201–6,8.

Chippenham – 1712 – CHP71208 – CRO R58/16/1
A Survey of part of the Mannor or Lordship of Chippenham in the parish of Chippenham in the County of Cambridge belonging to the Right Honourable Edward Earl of Orford Viscount Barflevr and Baron of Shingay &c. By Heber Lands 1712. No. 8.

Surveyor: Heber Lands; **Scale bar** 80–0–10 statute poles (= 5 9/16in.), 1:3,204; **Size:** (ii) 22 3/4 x 29 11/16in.; **Top** is SE; Manuscript(i), parchment, coloured.

583a.2r.0p. in TL6766 and TL6866, bounded by roads from Norwich to London in N and from Bury St Edmunds in S, Snailwell Parish in W and Kennett Parish in E.

Names of fields and roads. Wood and trees; waste and heath; acreages; roads; some hills shown as mounds; 'Lyme Kills'.

Title bottom right in a green and blue baroque cartouche; scale top right with a border imitating the edge of a sheet of paper with a green edge and blue back; compass rose top left showing 4 green and red points in a green border. Coat of arms of Edward Russell, Earl of Orford, middle left in a green and blue cartouche. Shepherd, dog and sheep on heath. Roads coloured brown, heath coloured green and brown and outlined in green.

Note at bottom: 'This Joynes to the South side of No 5 No 6 No'[7?]. Positive and negative photostats at 1:4,387 at CUL Maps.bb.53(1).95.23. See also CHP71201–7.

Chippenham – 1801 – CHP80101 – CRO R55/7/45/159
A Plan of certain Lands, the property of Iohn Tharp Esqr. in the parishes of Chippenham, and Snailwell in the County of Cambridgeshire. July 1801.

Scale: 4 Chains to an Inch, 1:3,168; **Size:** (i) 10 1/4 x 22 3/8in.; **Top** is W; Manuscript(i), parchment, coloured.

2a.0r.31p. SE of junction of track from Chippenham to Snailwell ['Portway Road'] with parish boundary, TL652681, and extending along parish boundary with Snailwell as far as county boundary with Suffolk in SE.

Names of owners, neighbouring owners and roads. Closed fields in Chippenham Parish, open fields in Snailwell Parish; waste; glebe; roads; dimensions of plots to be exchanged between parishes; boundary stones; hedges.

Border of 1 narrow band; title top right; scale top left; compass middle top showing 8 points with a decorated N.

Table bottom left giving acreages, land to be exchanged and a key to the colours used. Parish boundary coloured green, new straight boundary coloured red, roads coloured brown, glebe outlined in yellow.

On deed: 'John Tharp Esqr and The Revd Mr Hill: Deed of Exchange'. Shows land of John Tharp sr [Venn, II, 6, 146]. Conveyancer was Josh Rushton.

Chippenham – [1814] – CHP81401 – CRO R55/7/7/258
[Plan of John Tharp jr's farm at Chippenham, leased to Edward Palmer.]

Scale: 1:8,620; **Size:** (ii) 20 1/2 x 19 3/4in.; **Top** is N; Manuscript(i), parchment, coloured.

Manor Farm, TL662700, and 828a.3r.28p. in W of parish NW of village, bounded by roads to Fordham in N, from Newmarket to Bury St Edmunds and Exning Parish [Suffolk] in S, and former road running due S from Park in E.

Names of roads. Farm buildings and mill shown in plan form. Closed fields showing owner's land; wood in far S of heath, trees; heath; acreages; roads and footpaths; watercourses.

Table on right giving acreages, land use and crop rotations for each field. Pasture and heath coloured blue/green, roads coloured brown.

Accompanies: 'Lease to Edward Palmer of a Farm at Chippenham in Cambridgeshire, belonging to John Tharp'. Date taken from lease. Owner was John Tharp jr [LG, 2,487].

Chippenham – [1816] – CHP81601 – CRO R55/7/109/17(b)
['Park walls'.]

Surveyor: George Tappen; **Scale:** 1:11,400; **Size:** (ii) 10 x 7 3/4in.; **Top** is NW; Manuscript(i), paper, uncoloured.

c. 370a. in Chippenham Park; NW lodges to park are at TL664696.

Names of nearby features. Rough sketch of hall in plan form. Paddock; roads; gates; park; walls and fence; nearby swamp.

Title on dorse.

Accompanies an estimate of cost of repairing walls of the park in 1816 and an agreement to carry out the work, at CRO R55/7/109/17(a): 'Chippenham Park the Estate of the late John Tharp Esq'. John Tharp sr died in 1804 and estate passed to his son, John jr. In 1815, John jr was declared a lunatic and administration of estate passed to his uncle, John, who died in 1851 [CRO Handlist to Tharp papers].

Chippenham – 1829 – CHP82901 – CRO R55/7/10/8
Plan of the Farm Buildings, Stacks, &c, destroyed by fire, at Badlingham Septr 21st 1829.

Draughtsman: [James Overton?]; **Scale:** 1:1,440; **Size:** (ii) 8 7/8 x 7 3/16in.; **Top** is E; Manuscript(i), paper, coloured.

Badlingham Hall farmyard, TL678709, c. 7a., extending from River Kennett in E to road to Chippenham in W, and bounded by roads to Freckenham in N and to house in S.

Names of buildings and roads. Buildings shown in plan form and include barns, stable, 'cow house', 'waggon lodge', 'bullock lodges', coach house, harness house, lean-to and stacks. Dimensions of stacks; crops shown by colour; roads and watercourses; yard; bridge; pump; 'Thrashing machine'.

Title middle right with decorative lettering, in a circular cartouche of 1 broad and 1 narrow band; compass middle top showing 4 points with a decorated N and feathered tail. Water coloured blue, roads coloured brown, buildings coloured grey, stacks coloured to show crop type: wheat coloured blue, barley coloured pink, oats coloured yellow, peas coloured brown, hay coloured green.

In notebook: 'Shorthand Writing. James Overton'. Owner was John Tharp jr; estate was administered by his uncle, John, who died in 1851 [CRO Handlist to Tharp papers]. See also CHP82902.

Chippenham – [1829] – CHP82902 – CRO R55/7/10/8
Plan of Stack yard.
Draughtsman: [James Overton?]; **Scale:** 1:928; **Size:** (ii) 10 9/16 x 5 5/16in.; **Top** is W; Manuscript(i), paper, coloured.
Badlingham Hall stackyard, TL678709, c. 2a., bounded by roads to Chippenham in W, to Freckenham in N, to Badlingham Hall in S and road dividing stackyard and farmyard in E.
Names of roads, buildings and stacks. 'Sparke's Cottage' and 'waggon lodges' shown in plan form. Dimensions of areas; crops in each stack; roads; gates; yard.
Title at top. Stacks coloured to show crop type: wheat coloured yellow, peas coloured brown, hay coloured blue, barley and straw coloured grey, oats coloured dark yellow.
Drawn after fire in 1829. Stack with thatched roof in which fire started is noted. Note beneath title describing each stack and which stacks have common roofs. Pencil notes of dimensions of stack; pencil notes of scales on dorse. Map is a loose sheet to accompany a notebook: 'Shorthand Writing. James Overton'. Owner was John Tharp jr; estate was administered by his uncle, John, who died in 1851 [CRO Handlist to Tharp papers]. See also CHP82901, drawn in 1829.

Comberton – [1723] – COM72301 – GLC H1/ST/E107/2
The West Field.
Surveyor: [James Gould]; **A Scale** of Chains each 4 Pole, Scale bar 1–0–20 chains (= 5 3/8in.), 1:3,094; **Size:** (ii) 20 x 27 1/4in.; **Top** is N; Manuscript(i), parchment, coloured.
Birdlines Manor Farm, TL382558, and 41a.1r.15p. to S and W.
Names of fields, roads and neighbouring owners. Manor house and barns shown in plan form. Open fields showing owner's strips; closes; 'Midsummer pasture'; acreages; roads; gardens and orchards; common adjoining map.
Title top left; scale middle right; compass rose in centre showing 32 plain points. Fields outlined in yellow and coloured green, manor house coloured red, roads coloured grey.
Pencil notes. Accompanying terrier on paper describing the land, its use, boundaries and acreages: 'A terrar of the arable lands, meadowes, and pasture ground, of the Mannor of Burdelynes; in the Parish of Cumberton, in the County of Cambridge: belonging to the Worshipfull the Governours of St Thomas's Hospitall in the Borough of Southwark. The survey made by James Gould Anno: Domini 1723'. At end of terrier is total acreage of land covered, and pencil notes. See also COM72302–4.

Comberton – [1723] – COM72302 – GLC H1/ST/E107/2
The Stallow~Field.

Surveyor: [James Gould]; **A Scale** of Chaines each 4 Pole, Scale bar 1–0–20 chains (= 5 3/8in.), 1:3,094; **Size:** (ii) 27 1/8 x 20 1/16in.; **Top** is N; Manuscript(i), parchment, coloured.
54a.2r.25p. bounded by road to Cambridge in N and Bourn Brook in S, with 'Clay Pitt hill' in NE.
Names of fields, roads and neighbouring owners. Open fields showing owner's strips; closes; meadow and leys; acreages; roads; 'watering place'; ditches; 'Leek beds'; 'stallow hole'; 'Midsummer Ground' identified on terrier.
Title top left; scale bottom left; compass rose middle left showing 32 points. Fields outlined in yellow and green, some fields coloured green.
Pencil notes. See COM72301 for details of accompanying terrier which gives owner, surveyor and date. See also COM72303–4.

Comberton – [1723] – COM72303 – GLC H1/ST/E107/2
The Harborough~Field.
Surveyor: [James Gould]; **A Scale** of Chaines each 4 Pole, Scale bar 1–0–20 chains (= 5 3/8in.), 1:3,094; **Size:** (ii) 20 x 27 1/8in.; **Top** is W; Manuscript(i), parchment, coloured.
66a.0r.30p. N of road from Barton and bounded by 'The North Brook' in N.
Names of fields, roads and neighbouring owners. Open fields showing owner's strips; acreages; roads; ditches; hedges; meadow; bridges.
Title at top; scale bottom right; compass rose in centre showing 32 points. Fields outlined in yellow and green, some fields coloured green.
Pencil notes. See COM72301 for details of accompanying terrier which gives owner, surveyor and date. See also COM72302,4.

Comberton – [1723] – COM72304 – GLC H1/ST/E107/2
The North Field.
Surveyor: [James Gould]; **A Scale** of Chaines each 4 Pole, Scale bar 1–0–20 chains (= 5 3/8in.), 1:3,094; **Size:** (ii) 19 7/8 x 27 1/8in.; **Top** is N; Manuscript(i), parchment, coloured.
29a.1r.30p. in far N of parish in TL3858, TL3958, TL3859 and TL3959, bounded by road to St Neot's in N and 'The North Brook' in SW.
Names of fields, roads and neighbouring owners. Open fields showing owner's strips; acreages; roads; 'Clements Well'.
Title top left; scale bottom left; compass rose centre top showing 32 points. Fields outlined in yellow and green, some fields coloured green.
Pencil notes. See COM72301 for details of accompanying terrier which gives owner, surveyor and date. See also COM72302–3.

Comberton – 1794 – COM79401 – SJC MPS 15
Plan of a small Farm at Comberton in the County of Cambridge. belonging to St Johns the Evangelists College in the University of Cambridge. Surveyed in 1794 Sarah Holder Lessee.
Surveyor: [Joseph Freeman?]; **Scale bar** 5–0–20 chains (= 3 1/8in.), 1:6,336; **Size:** (i) 12 5/16 x 21 15/16in.; **Top** is N; Manuscript(i), parchment, coloured.
5a.3r.25p. in TL3856, bounded by 'North Brook' in N and Tit Brook ['The Brook'] in S.
Names of fields, owner, tenants, neighbouring owners and watercourses. Houses and barns shown in plan form.

Open fields showing owner's strips; closes; hedges; state of cultivation shown by colour; roads and watercourses.

Border of 1 broad and 1 narrow band; title middle left; scale bottom left; compass top left showing 4 points. Table on right giving acreages and number of ridges in each strip. Water coloured blue, grass coloured green, houses coloured red, strips and roads coloured brown.

In style of Joseph Freeman, who surveyed for the College in the 1790s.

Comberton – [c. 1813] – COM81301 – GLC H1/ST/E22/1

Birdlines Farm at Comberton in the County of Cambridge.

Surveyor: Joseph Beevers; **Scale:** 1:521; **Size:** (ii) 11 7/8 x 7 5/16in.; **Top** is N; Manuscript(i), paper, uncoloured.

Birdlines Farm, TL382558, and c.1a of land surrounding it.

Names of farm and buildings. Buildings shown in plan form and include 'Dwelling House', barns for barley, oats, 'pease', beans and wheat, 'Cowhouse and Calf pens', dovecote, stable, 'Chaff~house', 'Pigs Cote', 'Strawhouse' and site of new 'Cowhouse'. Dimensions of areas; farmyard.

Title at top; orientation given by cardinal points. Table at bottom giving buildings, building materials and valuation.

Note beneath table: 'In the above estimate for Insurance I have not mentioned the Wheatcase & Hay Shed nor Cart house which are such poor buildings that 25£ in the gross would cover the value of them all – but in truth the Tenant will want a Cowhouse which I should propose to build at A. The House also is too large by almost half & the walls at ab are drawn away 6 inches or more at the top. I should therefore recommend to take down all on the East side of the dotted line ab & apply the materials to other repairs – the rest of the house is in tolerable good preservation & under all circumstances, I should think 700 or 750£ the utmost would be necessary to insure for'. On dorse: 'Plans in Gt Parndon & Roydon', addressed to 'Mr Josp Beevers'. In policy book for property insured at the Hand in Hand Fire Office. Probably drawn by Joseph Beevers in 1813, when he drew CHE81301 and probably FUL81301. Land owned by St Thomas' Hospital, London.

Comberton – [1830] – COM83001 – CUL Maps.PSQ.18.85

['Plan ... of an Excellent House, with large Garden and Orchard, and fine old pasture close, ... in ... Comberton'.]

Auctioneer: Randall and Son; **Lithographer:** W[illiam] Metcalfe; **Scale:** 1:449; **Size:** (i) 5 1/4 x 10 7/8in.; **Top** is N; Lithograph, paper, uncoloured.

School ['house'] at TL382563, and 5a.0r.18p. N of crossroads in centre of village.

Names of field, road and neighbouring owners. House shown in plan form. Closed pasture field; trees; state of cultivation given in words; acreages; gates; pond; orchard identified on particulars of sale.

Border of 1 broad and 1 narrow band.

Accompanies: 'Plan, Particulars and Conditions of Sale, of an Excellent House, with large Garden and Orchard, and fine old pasture close, in the pleasant village of Comberton, near Cambridge; ... To be sold by Auction ... on Tuesday, the 4th day of May, 1830 ...' Land occupied by Miss Sole. Lithographer's 1st name was William [CRO EPR CW 1825 WR C52:178].

Coton – [1801] – COT80101 – SJC MPS 285

A Plan of the Property of St Johns College in the University of Cambridge As allotted by the Commissioners appointed in an Act of Parliament for dividing and inclosing the Common and Open Fields of Grandchester and Coton in the County of Cambridge.

Scale bar 0–15 chains (= 5in.), 1:2,376; **Size:** (i) 15 7/8 x 20 3/8in.; **Top** is W; Manuscript(i), parchment, coloured.

Coton Church, TL409589, and 60a.1r.18p. bounded by Whitwell Parish in W and road to St Neot's in N, and 1a.2r.6p. in Barton Parish.

Names of neighbouring owners and roads. Farm buildings and 'college barn' shown in plan form, Coton Church shown in perspective. Closed fields showing owner's land; hedges; acreages; roads.

Border of 2 narrow bands; title top left; scale in centre. Table in centre giving acreages. Roads coloured brown, land outlined in green.

Note below scale: 'NB The Barn marked No. 5 in Lane leading to Mr Jno Angers Junr belongs to College'. Ink notes and additions to acreages in Coton and Barton parishes. Date on dorse.

Coton – [1825] – COT82501 – QCC 355 A18, B18

Estate at Coton, and in the Hamlet of Whitwell together with an Allotment In The Parish of St Giles In The County of Cambridge.

Surveyor: [Alexander Watford jr]; **Scale bar** 0–30 chains (= 5 5/8in.), 1:4,224; **Size:** (i) 25 1/2 x 21 3/8in.; **Top** is NE; Manuscript(ii), paper, coloured.

Coton Church, TL409589, and 33a.0r.25p. bounded by Madingley Parish in N, in E of Whitwell hamlet bounded by Coton village street, and 1 plot in far W of St Giles' Parish, Cambridge.

Names of roads and neighbouring owners. Houses and cottages shown in plan form, church shown in perspective. Closed fields showing owner's land; state of cultivation shown by colour; acreages; hedges; roads, turnpikes and footpaths.

Border on right, top and bottom of 1 broad band with 1 narrow band on either side, border on left of 2 narrow bands; title at top; scale at bottom; compass in centre showing 4 points. Table bottom right giving field names, acreages, land use and allotments. Roads coloured brown, fields coloured yellow and green.

On right is an enlarged plan, measuring 2 x 5in., of the homestead: 'Buildings on Scale of two Chains to the Inch', 1:1,584. On right of sheet, which also contains a map of West Wickham [WEV82501], and in volume drawn in 1825: 'Plans of the Several Estates in England and Wales belonging to the President and Fellows of the College of St Margaret and St Bernard commonly called Queen's College in the University of Cambridge Delineated from Authentic Documents in the possession of the said President and Fellows and from actual Surveys taken By their most obedient and obliged Servant Alexr Watford'. Title page drawn by James Richardson [Watford's nephew]. This is the Bursar's copy; 2nd, finer, copy [the Master's copy] at QCC 355 B18 measures 24 5/8 x 18 1/16in. and is drawn on parchment. Top points NW. Border 7/16in. wide of a central blue band with 1 broad band on either side, title has gothic lettering, scale centre bottom, compass on right shows 8 points. Table above scale has a border imitating a sheet of paper and red lines. Fields coloured in yellow and brown stripes with green edges, roads have red/brown edges.

Cottenham – [1631] – COU63101 – CCC Cottenham O7

A Plattforme of the exact measure in length in bredth of that peece of the Burdleyes called the Reede bushe.

Surveyor: [Richard Graves]; **Scale bar** 0–5 [chains] (= 1 5/8in.), 1:2,437; **Size:** (ii) 17 7/8 x 6 3/4in.; Manuscript(i), paper, uncoloured.

c. 7a. in 2 plots in 'Reedebushe' and 1 plot in 'Burdlaryes Crease', probably in NW of parish near boundary with Rampton Parish.

Names of butts and bounds. Watercourses; dimensions of plots.

Title at top; scale at bottom.

At end of a terrier, in which the copyholds and rents were collected by Richard Graves: 'A true and perfect Terre or groundplatt plainlie settinge forth and shewinge all the demeanes of lands Pastures, inclosures Meadowes Marrishes and Fermings severallie appertaininge and belonginge unto the Mannor of Burdleyes otherwise Harlstons in Cottenham within the Countie of Cambridge, and of every of their severall abuttals ... by the direction <and> decree appointment and legall comannd and order of \the right worshippfull/ Thomas Bainbrigge Docter in Divinitie & Master of Christs Colledge in \the Universitie of/ Cambridgge and likewise of the worshipfull Fellowes and Schollars of the same Colledge the seaven and twentieth day of October in Anno Regnis Carolus septimo et Anno Domini juxta computatione Ecclesiae Anglicane millesimo septentesimo tricesimo primo'.

Cottenham – 1791 – COU79101 – SJC MPS 18

A Map of certain Lands at Cottenham; belonging to St Johns College Cambridge.

Surveyor: Joseph Freeman; **Scale bar** 0–20 chains (= 3 1/4in.), 1:4,874; **Size:** (i) 13 7/8 x 10 1/8in.; **Top** is N; Manuscript(i), parchment, coloured.

2a.3r.6p. in village in TL4467 and TL4567, and strips to N in Smithy Fen and to S in 'Dunstall Field'.

Names of fields, owner and neighbouring owners. Cottage shown in plan form, post mill shown in perspective. Open fields showing owner's strips; closes; trees; state of cultivation shown by colour; acreages; roads and footpaths.

Border of 1 broad and 1 narrow band; title in middle; scale beneath title. House coloured red, roads coloured brown, strips coloured green and brown.

Terrier on right dated 1793 and giving acreages, land use and common rights. Later note on dorse: 'Cottenham Late Wilson Lessee 1791 now Smith'.

Cottenham – 1791 – COU79102 – SJC MPS 16

A Map of certain Lands at Cottenham, belonging to St Johns College. Cambridge. 1791 Alice Watson Lessee.

Surveyor: Joseph Freeman; **Scale:** 1:2,890; **Size:** (ii) 13 x 16 1/4in.; **Top** is W; Manuscript(i), parchment, coloured.

1a.3r.24p. in TL4467 and TL4567, and 2 strips to N in Smithey Fen.

Names of fields, owner, tenants, neighbouring owners and fen. Buildings shown in plan form and include house, 2 'cowhouses', barley barn, stable and 'hogstye'. Open fields showing owner's strips; closes; hedges; state of cultivation shown by colour; roads.

Border of 2 narrow bands with 1 broad band on inside; title top left. Grass coloured green, buildings coloured red.

On right: 'Note of common rights', signed 1794. Bottom right: 'Map of the Buildings' at 1:358, also showing the yard. Right of this inset is a description of the buildings, contents of house and nature of the walls and roof. Accompanying terrier, SJC D31.39, has a map of the farm buildings on dorse at 1:240.

Cottenham – 1791 – COU79103 – SJC MPS 17

Plan of a Farm at Cottenham in the County of Cambridge; belonging to St. Johns College in the University of Cambridge. Surveyed in the Year 1791.

Surveyor: [Joseph Freeman?]; **Scale bar** 10–0–20 chains (= 3 11/16in.), 1:6,443; **Size:** (i) 25 x 20 1/4in.; **Top** is NNE; Manuscript(i), parchment, coloured.

Cottenham Green, TL448671, and 59a.1r.6p. to S and W bounded by Histon Parish and road to Histon ['Cambridge Way'] in E, with strips E of 'Cambridge Way' in Dunstal Field, to NE in Church Field, and to NW in Smithy Fen.

Names of fields, roads, neighbouring owners or tenants. Farm buildings NE of green shown in plan form. Open fields showing owner's strips; closes and pightle; meadow in Smithy Fen; roads and footpaths; watercourses; ponds; bridge; hedges; gates.

Border of 1 broad and 1 narrow band; title bottom right in a cartouche with leafy decoration and a bow on top; scale beneath title; compass middle top showing 8 points. Table on left giving field names and acreages of strips and inclosures. Grass and trees coloured green, strips coloured yellow, houses coloured red, roads coloured yellow.

Note top right: 'The Meadowing in Smithy Fen lies about 2 Miles North West from the Town of Cottenham'. Note on dorse: 'Plan of Mr Hall's Farm at Cottenham 1791 Manr Jaques'. In style of Joseph Freeman, who worked for the College in the 1790s. Photograph at 1:9,051 at CRO TR869/P16.

Cottenham – [1797] – COU79701 – SJC MPS 19, 20

Plan of a Farm at Cottenham. Late Dowsings.

Surveyor: [Joseph Freeman?]; **Scale:** 1:4,870; **Size:** (i) 24 7/8 x 18 7/8in.; **Top** is N; Manuscript(i), parchment, coloured.

2a.3r.6p. in village in TL4467 and TL4567, and strips S and N in Smithy Fen.

Names of fields, owner, tenants, neighbouring owners and roads. Houses shown in plan form. Open fields showing owner's strips; closes and pightle; state of cultivation shown by colour; roads and footpaths; watercourses and bridge.

Border of 1 broad and 1 narrow band; title on right; compass in centre showing 4 plain points. Table on left giving field names, acreages and number of ridges in each strip. Buildings coloured red, strips coloured yellow and green.

Note bottom right: 'There is appurtenant to the House on this Farm, an Acre of Grass in the Shifting Lotts and about half an Acre in Chaff Fen. – Also Right of Commonage for 7 Cows & 15 sheep. for Horses without Stint'. On dorse: 'Plan of W Halls farm at Cottenham 1797'. Farm owned by St John's College, Cambridge. In style of Joseph Freeman, who worked for the College in the 1790s. Copy at SJC MPS 20 measures 25 7/8 x 18 5/8in.

226

Cottenham – 1802 – COU80201 – CRO R61/5/1

Plan of an Estate belonging to Edward Roger Pratt Esqr at Cottenham Cambridge*shire*. Surveyed by John Burcham. Holt. 1802.

Surveyor: John Burcham; **Scale** 6 [chains] in an inch, 1:4,752; **Size**: (i) 45 x 26 3/4in.; **Top** is NNE; Manuscript(i), paper mounted on cloth, coloured.

Cottenham Church, TL455687, and strips scattered among c. 7,200a. in Smithy Fen, and Church, Dunstal ['Dunstall'], Further Farm ['Foxal or Farther Field and Farm'] and Two Mill fields, bounded by Histon common in E, Westwick Parish in S, The Holme in W and River Ouse in N.

Names of fields, roads and neighbouring owners. Farm buildings shown in plan form, church shown in perspective. Open fields showing owner's strips; closes; trees; fen; roads and watercourses; hedges.

Border of 1 broad and 1 narrow band; title middle right; compass in centre showing 4 points with scale written between W and E. Field boundaries and strips in different fields shown in different colours: pink, green, yellow, orange or blue, buildings coloured grey.

Numbers on plots suggest map originally accompanied by a terrier. Pencil notes, including sketch of a post mill.

Cottenham – [c. 1803–29] – COU80301 – CUA D.P.III.1.a–c

C Cottenham estate.

Scale: 1:4,760; **Size**: (i) 10 1/4 x 21 7/8in.; **Top** is N; Printed, paper mounted on cloth, uncoloured.

Pond at TL448671, and 105a.1r.24p. to N and E and E of village, bounded by Back Lane in NW, Town's End in W and Histon and Landbeach parishes in S.

Names of roads, parishes and neighbouring owners. Buildings shaded and shown in plan form. Fields; acreages; roads and watercourses; responsibility for boundaries.

Border of 1 narrow band; title in middle; compass middle top showing 8 points.

At bottom of sheet entitled at bottom: 'Plan of the estates in Cambridge, Over, Cottenham and Rampton Belonging to Hobsons Charity'. Sheet has a border of 1 broad and 1 narrow band. Probably drawn after 1803, the date of death of William Linton's father Salmon [a copyholder on RAM80301; *VCH*, 9, 109], and before 1829, when the Gaol shown on the map of the Cambridge estate ceased to be used. 2 unmounted paper copies. See also OVE80301 and RAM80301.

Coveney – 1783 – COV78301 – QCC 328

['Contents of some Inclosed Lands in the Parish of Coveney and Isle of Ely in the County of Cambridge belonging to Queens College'.]

Surveyor: [Joseph Freeman]; **Scale**: 1:2,350; **Size**: (i) 9 7/16 x 15 7/8in.; **Top** is N; Manuscript(i), paper, coloured.

Coveney Church, TL489821, and 23a.3r.12p. to S and W.

Names of farms and neighbouring owners. Church and houses shown in perspective. Closed fields showing owner's land; tree by church; acreages; roads and gates.

Border of 1 narrow band. Table top left giving field names, acreages, land use and value. Land coloured green.

Note beneath table: 'Observations. These Lands appear to have been neglected they are very Poor but may be greatly Improved by Draining and Manure; if a Lease of 21 Years was granted I would advise there being let as here

valued for the first seven Years to encourage the Tenant to Improve, the rest of the Term at 20 Shillings an Acre, viz £21 4S 6D at the expiration of Seven Years. Valued by Joseph Freeman in the Month of May 1783. Fen Land in the Occupation of Waterlow 7S *per* acre'. Pencil notes and notes of responsibility for boundaries. Title to map and surveyor are taken from table and note beneath it.

Coveney – 1817 – COV81701 – QCC Box 20

Sketch of Lands in Lease to Waddelow.

Surveyor: Alexander Watford [jr]; **Scale**: 1:6,720; **Size**: (i) 4 3/4 x 9 3/8in.; **Top** is SW; Manuscript(i), paper, uncoloured.

30a. in TL4983, bounded by Downham Parish in NE, drains in SW and SE and 'Downham Hill Drove' in NW.

Names of fields and roads. Closed fields showing owner's land; acreages; drains; droves.

Border of 1 narrow red band on left and right, and 2 narrow red bands at top and bottom; title at top.

Note on left about valuation, pencil note of value of land. Map is on: 'Valuation of an Estate at Coveney in the Isle of Ely, belonging to the President and Fellows of Queen's College, in the University of Cambridge. Dated 2d January – 1817', by Alexander Watford. See also COV81702.

Coveney – 1817 – COV81702 – QCC Box 20

Sketch of Lands, in Lease to Messrs Charles & Richard Clay.

Surveyor: Alexander Watford [jr]; **Scale**: 1:4,720; **Size**: (iii) 2 5/8 x 4 1/8in.; Manuscript(i), paper, uncoloured.

23a.3r.2p. in Coveney Parish.

Names of tenants. Closed fields; acreages; roads.

Title at top. Table on left giving tenants, acreages and value.

Note at bottom about valuation, pencil notes of values. Map is on a valuation [see COV81701].

Coveney – [1825] – COV82501 – QCC 355 A19, B19

Estate at Coveney In The Isle of Ely and County of Cambridge.

Surveyor: [Alexander Watford jr]; **Scale bar** 0–20 chains (= 6 11/16in.), 1:2,369; **Size**: (i) 25 1/2 x 21 7/16in.; **Top** is N; Manuscript(ii), paper, coloured.

Coveney Church, TL489822, and 60a.2r.35p. to SW, and in E of parish bounded by Downham Parish in E.

Names of fields, tenants, roads and neighbouring owners. Church shown in perspective, 2 buildings shown in plan form in the churchyard. Closed fields showing owner's land; meadow; state of cultivation shown by colour; acreages; hedges and fences; roads and gates; drains; bridges.

Border of 1 broad band with 1 narrow band on either side; title top left; scale bottom right; compass in centre showing 4 points. Table at bottom giving tenants, field names, acreages and land use. Fields coloured yellow and green, roads coloured brown, water coloured blue.

Under table: 'Note. The Lands in Coveney are not in their relative situations exactly on the Plan; the distance from one part of the Estate to the other is so great, that the connexion is only attempted to be shewn'. On right of opening, on left is a map of Pampisford [PAM82501]. In volume drawn in 1825: 'Plans of the Several Estates in England and Wales belonging to the President and Fellows of the College of St Margaret and St Bernard commonly called Queen's College in the University of Cambridge Delineated from Authentic Documents in the possession of the said President and Fellows and from actual Surveys taken By their most obedient and obliged Servant Alexr Watford'. Title page drawn by James Richardson [Watford's nephew]. This is the Bursar's copy; 2nd, finer, copy [the Master's copy] at QCC 355 B19 measures 24 7/16 x 18 3/16in., is drawn on parchment, has top pointing NE and has a scale bar 0–15 chains (= 5in.), 1:2,376. Border 3/8in. wide of a central blue band with 1 broad band on either side, title in middle, scale at bottom has gothic lettering, compass on left shows 8 points. Table bottom right has red lines. Fields coloured in yellow and brown stripes and have green edges, roads have red/brown edges.

Coveney – 1829 – COV82901 – PCC
Plan of an Estate in the Parish of Coveney In the Isle of Ely. and County of Cambridge. belonging to the Master and Fellows of Pembroke Hall, in the University of Cambridge. made A.D. 1829, by Alexr Watford.
Surveyor: Alexander Watford [jr]; **Scale bar** 0–15 chains (= 5in.), 1:2,376; **Size:** (i) 24 1/4 x 15 3/4in.; **Top** is WNW; Manuscript(i), parchment, coloured.
Coveney Church, TL489822, and 45a.0r.15p. bounded by roads to Wardy Hill in W and to Hale Fen ['Coveney Green Way'] in S and E.
Names of fields, roads, drains and neighbouring owners. Houses and 'The Cross Keys' shown in plan form, church shown in perspective. Closed fields showing owner's land; grove; state of cultivation shown by colour; acreages; hedges; roads; watercourses and ponds.
Border of 2 narrow bands; title top left; scale beneath title; compass centre top with 4 points incorrectly giving top as NNW, and a corrected compass added in pencil bottom right showing top is WNW. Table at bottom giving field names, acreages and land use. Water coloured blue, roads coloured brown, fields coloured green or outlined in yellow.
Note under table: 'NB. The exterior Ditches of the Twenty Acres Fen are not measured'. Copy on paper measures 19 5/8 x 15 1/2in., with a note: Scale 3 Chains to the Inch, 1:2,376, pencil additions and alterations to the school, houses and areas of land. 2nd copy, accompanied by a valuation, at PCC LE p.119 [COV82902].

Coveney – [1829] – COV82902 – PCC LE p.119
[Estate in Coveney, owned by Pembroke College, Cambridge.]
Surveyor: [Alexander Watford jr]; **Scale:** 1:2,390; **Size:** (iii) 6 5/8 x 5in.; **Top** is NW; Manuscript(ii), paper, uncoloured.
Coveney Church, TL499822, and 45a.0r.15p. N of village.
Names of neighbouring owners. Houses shown in plan form, church shown in perspective. Closed fields; acreages; roads; pond.
Compass centre right showing 4 points.
Accompanies: 'Valuation of the Farm at Coveney', by Alexander Watford in 1829. Note of value in 1843. Copy of COV82901.

Croxton – [1823] – CRX82301 – HRO 112/3(x50)
['Plan of the Croxton Estate belonging to Sir George Wm Leeds Bart 1823'.]

Scale bar 0–30 chains (= 2 7/16in.), 1:9,748; **Size:** (i) 15 7/8 x 13 7/8in.; **Top** is NNE; Manuscript(i), paper mounted on paper, coloured.
Croxton Hall, TL252593, and c. 2,100a. in whole parish.
Names of farms and roads. Croxton Hall, rectory, cottages, farm buildings, kennel, brick kiln, 'Black[?]. Smith Shop' and lodge shown in plan form, church and post mill shown in perspective. Closed fields; glebe; wood and trees; acreages; roads and footpaths; watercourses and ponds; hedges and fences; responsibility for boundaries; park, gardens and aviary; 'Allotment for glebe'.
Border of 1 broad band with 1 narrow band on inside; scale bottom right surrounded by a cartouche; compass above scale showing 8 points. Roads coloured brown, buildings coloured red, park and wood coloured green, parish boundary coloured blue.
Title on cover to map, date has been altered to 1826. Pencil notes. Some of the lettering of neighbouring parishes, scale and compass have been mounted on the paper separately from the main map. Numbers on plots suggest map originally accompanied by a terrier. Positive and negative photostats at CUL Maps.bb.53(1).93.118.

Croydon cum Clopton – 1747 – CRY74701 – CRO L88/13
A Survey of Croydon Wyld Farm in the Lordship of Croydon & County of Cambridge belonging to Thomas Gape Esq. Lord of the Manor taken Anno Domini 1747. By T. & I. Wing Surveyors.
Surveyors: T[ycho] Wing [sr], J[ohn] Wing; **Draughtsman:** T[ycho] Wing [sr]; **A Scale** of XVI Gunters Chains, Scale bar 1–0–16 chains (= 4 1/4in.), 1:3,168; **Size:** (i) 15 11/16 x 26 7/8in.; **Top** is W; Manuscript(i), parchment, coloured.
'Croydon Wilds Farm', TL304515, and c. 460a. in NW of parish bounded by East Hatley Parish in N and W, Arrington Parish in E and land belonging to Manor ['Middle'] Farm in S.
Names of fields and parishes. Farm buildings shown in plan form. Open fields showing all strips; closes; trees; meadow; waste and sheep walk; pasture shown by symbol depicting tufts of grass; acreages; roads and footpaths; gates; orchard; earthworks around farm; moat; hedges; responsibility for boundaries; pond; yards; bank shown by hachures.
Border of 1 broad and 1 narrow band; title top right; scale bottom right; compass middle top showing 8 plain points with a decorated N. Farm buildings coloured red.
Pencil notes. Surveyors' 1st names were John and Tycho [Eden W469 and W471].

Croydon cum Clopton – 1747 – CRY74702 – CRO L88/15
A Survey of the Lower Farm and Glebe Land in the Lordship of Croydon and County of Cambridge belonging to Thomas Gape Esq. Lord of the Manor And Impropriator. Taken A.D. 1747. By T. & I. Wing Surveyors.
Surveyors: T[ycho] Wing [sr], J[ohn] Wing; **Draughtsman:** T[ycho] Wing [sr]; **A Scale** of XVI Gunters Chains, Scale bar 1–0–16 chains (= 4 1/4in.), 1:3,168; **Size:** (i) 12 5/8 x 22 15/16in.; **Top** is WNW; Manuscript(i), parchment, coloured.
Croydon Church, TL315496, farm to S and c. 320a. extending as far S as River Cam and boundary with Shingay Parish.

Names of farms, fields, roads and neighbouring owners. Church, vicarage, houses SW of village, farm belonging to Sir George Downing, and farm buildings, houses and barns belonging to 'Lower Farm' shown in plan form. Open fields showing all strips; closes; glebe; wood and trees; pasture shown by symbol depicting tufts of grass; acreages; roads; River Cam and Shingay Bridge; gates; moats; hedges; responsibility for boundaries; yards.

Border of 1 broad and 1 narrow band; title middle bottom; scale bottom left; compass top right showing 8 points with a decorated N. Church, vicarage and farm buildings coloured red, other houses coloured brown, moat coloured blue.

Note under title: 'The tops of the Fences are placed in those Grounds to which they belong'. Pencil note of land lying fallow. Surveyors' 1st names were John and Tycho [Eden W469 and W471].

Croydon cum Clopton – 1747 – CRY74703 – CRO L88/14

A Survey of the Middle Farm in the Lordship of Croydon and County of Cambridge belonging to Thomas Gape Esquire Lord of the Manor. Taken A.D. 1747. By T. & I. Wing Surveyors.

Surveyors: T[ycho] Wing [sr], J[ohn] Wing; **Draughtsman:** T[ycho] Wing [sr]; **A Scale** of Twenty Gunter's Chains, or 1/4 of a Mile, Scale bar 1–0–20 chains (= 5 3/16in.), 1:3,206; **Size:** (i) 15 13/16 x 26 15/16in.; **Top** is WSW; Manuscript(i), parchment, coloured.

Manor ['Middle'] Farm, TL311498, and c. 540a. bounded by roads to East Hatley in W and to Tadlow in S, Arrington Parish in NE and 'Croydon Wilds Farm' in N, and extending 1 field E of farmhouse.

Names of fields, roads and neighbouring owners. Farm buildings and houses in SW of village shown in plan form. Open fields showing all strips; closes; wood and trees; sheep walk; pasture land shown by symbol depicting tufts of grass; acreages; roads; gates; garden; moat; hedges; responsibility for boundaries; yard; bank shown by hachures.

Border of 1 broad and 1 narrow band; title middle bottom; scale bottom left; compass middle right showing 8 points with a decorated N. Farm buildings coloured red, houses coloured brown.

Pencil notes. Surveyors' 1st names were John and Tycho [Eden W469 and W471].

Croydon cum Clopton – 1750 – CRY75001 – DCC

A Survey. of Arnolds Dairy, in the Parish of Croydon, and County of Cambridge The Estate of the Honble Sir Jacob Garrard Downing Bart By Jos. Cole 1750.

Surveyor: Joseph Cole; **Scale bar** 10–0–70 perches (= 4 15/16in.), 1:3,208; **Size:** (i) 20 3/4 x 14in.; **Top** is N; Manuscript(i), parchment, coloured.

Farm in TL3248 [possibly Valley Farm, TL322487], and 109a.3r.3p. SE of village bounded by Wendy Parish in S and Arrington Parish in E.

Names of fields, roads, river and neighbouring owners. Farm buildings shown in plan form. Closed fields showing owner's land; 'Long grove' and trees; 'mead'; 'Great Marsh'; hedges; roads and gates; watercourses and ponds; acreages given on table.

Border of 1 broad band with 1 narrow band on inside; title top right in a rococo cartouche with flowers and leaves coloured gold, red, green and purple; yellow scale bar bottom right; compass rose centre right showing 8 red, blue, green and yellow points. Table bottom left giving field

names and acreages. Above table is a perspective drawing of the farmhouse. River coloured blue, trees coloured green, fields outlined in green, buildings coloured red, ponds coloured blue, roads coloured yellow.

Numbers on edge of map refer to adjacent sheets. This is number 1 in a volume of maps of the Downing estate. See also CRY75002–11, EAS75001–8 and TAD75001–9.

Croydon cum Clopton – 1750 – CRY75002 – DCC

A Survey. of Adam's Dairy in the Parish of Croydon, and County of Cambridge The Estate of the Honble Sir Jacob Garrard Downing Bart By Jos. Cole 1750.

Surveyor: Joseph Cole; **Scale bar** 10–0–70 perches (= 5in.), 1:3,168; **Size:** (i) 20 3/4 x 14in.; **Top** is N; Manuscript(i), parchment, coloured.

102a.2r.10p. in TL3147 and TL3148 W of CRY75001, bounded by Wendy Parish in S and extending N of road to Royston.

Names of fields, river, roads and neighbouring owners. Farm buildings shown in plan form, Wendy Church shown in perspective. Closed fields showing owner's land; pightle; trees; meadow and pasture; hedges and fence; roads and gates; watercourses and ponds; area which might be an orchard; acreages given on table.

Border of 1 broad band with 1 narrow band on inside; title top left in a rococo cartouche with leaves and flowers and coloured purple, red, green and gold; yellow scale bar bottom right; compass rose top right showing 8 red, blue, yellow and green points. Table bottom left giving field names and acreages. Centre top is a perspective drawing of the farmhouse. Fields outlined in green, trees coloured green, water coloured blue, roads coloured yellow, buildings coloured red.

Numbers on edge of map refer to adjacent sheets. This is number 2 in a volume of maps of the Downing estate. See also CRY75001,3–11, EAS75001–8 and TAD75001–9.

Croydon cum Clopton – 1750 – CRY75003 – DCC

A Survey. of Porters Church Farm in the Parish of Croydon, and County of Cambridge of the Honble Sir Jacob Garrard Downing Bart By Jos. Cole 1750.

Surveyor: Joseph Cole; **Scale bar** 10–0–70 perches (= 5in.), 1:3,168; **Size:** (i) 20 3/4 x 14 1/16in.; **Top** is N; Manuscript(i), parchment, coloured.

Croydon Church, TL315496, and 201a.0r.27p. N of CRY75001 and S of church, bounded by Arrington Parish in E and S.

Names of parishes, fields, roads and neighbouring owners. Farm buildings and vicarage shown in plan form, church shown in perspective. Closed fields showing owner's land; wood and trees; meadow; glebe; state of cultivation shown by colour; hedges; roads and footpaths; gates; watercourses; spring; ponds; orchards; bath; balks; moats; acreages given on table.

Border of 1 broad band with 1 narrow band on inside; title top right in a rococo cartouche with leaves and flowers and coloured purple, red, green and gold; yellow scale bar centre bottom; compass rose top left showing 8 red, blue, yellow and green points. Table middle left giving field names, acreages and land use. Above table is a perspective drawing of the farmhouse. Farm buildings coloured red, water coloured blue, trees and hedges coloured green, fields outlined in green, arable coloured in yellow stripes, roads coloured yellow.

Note below table: 'NB These two Orchards, enclosed by a Homestall &c belonging to Thos Gape Esqr are a Seperate

Old Rent of 20s per Annum.', with a drawing of the orchards which are enclosed by moats. Numbers on edge of map refer to adjacent sheets. This is number 3 in a volume of maps of the Downing estate. See also CRY75001–2,4–11, EAS75001–8 and TAD75001–9.

Croydon cum Clopton – 1750 – CRY75004 – DCC

A Survey. of Porters Mill Dairy, in the Parish of Croydon, and County of Cambridge The Estate of Sir Jacob Garrard Downing Bart By Jos. Cole 1750.

Surveyor: Joseph Cole; **Scale bar** 10–0–80 perches (= 5 5/8in.), 1:3,168; **Size:** (i) 20 11/16 x 14in.; **Top** is N; Manuscript(i), parchment, coloured.

99a.1r.31p. in TL3148, bounded by CRY75002 in E; road to Royston runs E–W through farm.

Names of fields, roads and neighbouring owners. Farm buildings shown in plan form. Closed fields showing owner's land; hedges showing hedgerow trees; roads; gates; ponds; feature which may be an orchard; feature which may be a footpath; acreages given on table.

Border of 1 broad band with 1 narrow band on inside; title top left in a rococo cartouche with drapery, leaves and flowers and coloured purple, red, green and gold; yellow scale bar bottom right; compass rose top right showing 8 red, blue, yellow and green points. Table bottom left giving field names and acreages. Middle right is a perspective drawing of the farmhouse. Roads coloured yellow, fields outlined in green, buildings coloured red, water coloured blue, hedges coloured green.

Numbers on edge of map refer to adjacent sheets. This is number 4 in a volume of maps of the Downing estate. See also CRY75001–3,5–11, EAS75001–8 and TAD75001–9.

Croydon cum Clopton – 1750 – CRY75005 – DCC

A Survey. of Normans Dairy, in the Parish of Croydon, in the County of Cambridge. The Estate of Sir Jacob Garrard Downing Bart By Jos: Cole 1750.

Surveyor: Joseph Cole; **Scale bar** 10–0–80 perches (= 5 5/8in.), 1:3,168; **Size:** (i) 20 11/16 x 14in.; **Top** is NNE; Manuscript(i), parchment, coloured.

134a.1r.7p. in TL3148, bounded by CRY75004 in SE, 'Road from Clapton to Croydon' in N and 'Croydon Lane' in E.

Names of fields, roads and neighbouring owners. Farm buildings shown in plan form. Closed fields showing owner's land; 'The Grove' and trees; hedges; roads and gates; ponds; 'Chalybeat Spring'; acreages given on table.

Border of 1 broad band with 1 narrow band on inside; title top left in a cartouche of red drapery with a gold top; yellow scale bar bottom left; compass rose centre right with 8 red, blue, yellow and green points. Table bottom right giving field names and acreages. Beneath title is a perspective drawing of the farmhouse. Fields outlined in green, hedges and trees coloured green, water coloured blue, buildings coloured red, roads coloured yellow.

Numbers on edge of map refer to adjacent sheets. Pencil notes at top. This is number 5 in a volume of maps of the Downing estate. See also CRY75001–4,6–11, EAS75001–8 and TAD75001–9.

Croydon cum Clopton – 1750 – CRY75006 – DCC

A Survey of Pettits Dairy, in the Parish of Croydon, and County of Cambridge The Estate of Sir Iacob Garrard Downing Bart By Jos. Cole 1750.

Surveyor: Joseph Cole; **Scale bar** 10–0–80 perches (= 5 5/8in.), 1:3,168; **Size:** (i) 20 3/4 x 14 1/16in.; **Top** is NW; Manuscript(i), parchment, coloured.

157a.3r.27p. in TL2947, bounded by Shingay Parish in S and CRY75004 and CRY75005 in E.

Names of fields, parishes and neighbouring owners. Farm buildings shown in plan form. Closed fields showing owner's land; wood, Rowses ['Rousers'] and Gilrays ['Iilrags'] woods and trees; meadow; hedges; gates; watercourses and ponds; acreages given on table.

Border of 1 broad band with 1 narrow band on inside; title top right in a rococo cartouche with leaves and flowers and coloured purple, green, red and gold; yellow scale bar bottom right; compass rose middle left showing 8 red, blue, yellow and green points. Table bottom left giving field names and acreages. Bottom right is a perspective drawing of the farmhouse. Fields outlined in green, wood coloured green, water coloured blue, buildings coloured red.

Pencil notes at top. Numbers on edge of map refer to adjacent sheets. This is number 6 in a volume of maps of the Downing estate. See also CRY75001–5,7–11, EAS75001–8 and TAD75001–9.

Croydon cum Clopton – 1750 – CRY75007 – DCC

A Survey of Simpson's Dairy, in the Parish of Croydon, and County of Cambridge The Estate of Sir Jacob Garrard Downing Bart By Jos. Cole 1750.

Surveyor: Joseph Cole; **Scale bar** 10–0–80 perches (= 5 1/2in.), 1:3,240; **Size:** (i) 20 13/16 x 13 7/8in.; **Top** is N; Manuscript(i), parchment, coloured.

120a.1r.3p., probably in TL2947, bounded by Shingay Parish in S and CRY75006 in E.

Names of fields. Farm buildings shown in plan form. Wood, 'Simpsons Wood' and trees; meadow; hedges; gates; watercourses and ponds; 'Hill Ground'; feature which may be an orchard; acreages given on table.

Border of 1 broad band with 1 narrow band on inside; title top right in a rococo cartouche with purple drapery, green leaves, red flowers and gold ornament; yellow scale bar bottom right; compass rose top left showing 8 red, blue, yellow and green points. Table middle left giving field names and acreages. Bottom left is a perspective drawing of the farmhouse. Fields outlined in green, wood coloured green, water coloured blue, buildings coloured red.

Pencil notes at top. Numbers on edge of map refer to adjacent sheets. This is number 7 in a volume of maps of the Downing estate. See also CRY75001–6,8–11, EAS75001–8 and TAD75001–9.

Croydon cum Clopton – 1750 – CRY75008 – DCC

A Survey. of Salt's Dairy, in the Parish of Croydon, In the County of Cambridge The Estate of Sir Iacob Garrard Downing Bart By Jos. Cole 1750.

Surveyor: Joseph Cole; **Scale bar** 10–0–80 perches (= 5 9/16in.), 1:3,204; **Size:** (i) 20 3/4 x 14 1/6in.; **Top** is N; Manuscript(i), parchment, coloured.

119a.3r.7p. in TL2947, bounded by Shingay Parish in S and CRY75007 in E.

Names of fields and parishes. Farm buildings shown in plan form. Closed fields showing owner's land; meadow; hedges showing hedgerow trees; gates; watercourses and ponds; acreages given on table.

Border of 1 broad band with 1 narrow band on inside; title top left in a cartouche of red drapery and a gold top; yellow scale bar bottom right; compass rose centre right showing 8 red, blue, yellow and green points. Table bottom left giving field names and acreages. Above table is a perspective drawing of the farmhouse. Fields outlined in green, water coloured blue, buildings coloured red.

Pencil notes at top. Numbers on edge of map refer to adjacent sheets. This is number 8 in a volume of maps of the Downing estate. See also CRY75001–7,9–11, EAS75001–8 and TAD75001–9.

Croydon cum Clopton – 1750 – CRY75009 – DCC

A Survey of Wiltshires Farm, in the Parish of Croydon, and County of Cambridge The Estate of Sir Jacob Garrard Downing Bart By Jos. Cole 1750.

Surveyor: Joseph Cole; **Scale bar** 10–0–80 perches (= 5 5/8in.), 1:3,168; **Size:** (i) 20 13/16 x 14 1/16in.; **Top** is W; Manuscript(i), parchment, coloured.

153a.1r.34p., probably in TL2949, bounded by East Hatley Parish in N, and CRY75007 and CRY75008 in S.

Names of fields. Farm buildings shown in plan form. Closed fields showing owner's land; trees; state of cultivation shown by colour; hedges; gates; ponds; balks; acreages given on table.

Border of 1 broad band with 1 narrow band on inside; title top left in a rococo cartouche coloured gold, red, purple and green; yellow scale bar bottom left; compass rose top right showing 8 red, blue, yellow and green points. Table bottom right giving field names, acreages and land use. At bottom is a perspective drawing of the farmhouse. Fields outlined in green, arable coloured in yellow stripes, buildings coloured red, water coloured blue.

Note on 1 plot: 'Part of Hatley Parish'. Pencil notes at top. Numbers on edge of map refer to adjacent sheets. This is number 9 in a volume of maps of the Downing estate. See also CRY75001–8,10–11, EAS75001–8 and TAD75001–9.

Croydon cum Clopton – 1750 – CRY75010 – DCC

A Survey of Hubbards Farm, in the Parish of Croydon, in the County of Cambridge, The Estate of Sir Iacob Garrard Downing Bart By Jos. Cole. 1750.

Surveyor: Joseph Cole; **Scale bar** 10–0–80 perches (= 5 5/8in.), 1:3,168; **Size:** (i) 20 3/4 x 14in.; **Top** is W; Manuscript(i), parchment, coloured.

246a.0r.31p., probably in TL2949, bounded by road from Royston to Hatley in E, East Hatley Parish in N and CRY75009 in W.

Names of fields, roads and neighbouring owner. Farm buildings shown in plan form. Closed fields showing owner's land; state of cultivation shown by colour; hedges showing hedgerow trees; roads and gates; ponds; balks; acreages given on table.

Border of 1 broad band with 1 narrow band on inside; title top left in a rococo cartouche with leaves and flowers and coloured red, green, purple and gold; yellow scale bar bottom right; compass rose bottom left showing 8 red, blue, green and yellow points. Table top right giving field names, acreages and land use. Centre top is a perspective drawing of the farmhouse. Roads coloured yellow, fields outlined in green, arable coloured with yellow stripes, hedges and trees coloured green, water coloured blue, buildings coloured red.

Numbers on edge of map refer to adjacent sheets. This is number 10 in a volume of maps of the Downing estate. See also CRY75001–9,11, EAS75001–8 and TAD75001–9.

Croydon cum Clopton – 1750 – CRY75011 – DCC

A Survey. of Clapton Dairy, in the Parish of Croydon, & County of Cambridge The Estate of Sir Jacob Garrard Downing Bt By Jos. Cole 1750.

Surveyor: Joseph Cole; **Scale bar** 10–0–80 perches (= 5 5/8in.), 1:3,168; **Size:** (i) 20 11/16 x 14in.; **Top** is ENE; Manuscript(i), parchment, coloured.

247a.1r.24p. in TL3047 and TL3048, extending N of 'Road to Croydon' and bounded by CRY75005 in E, CRY75007 in W, CRY75006 in S and CRY75010 in N.

Names of fields, roads and neighbouring owner. Farm buildings shown in plan form. Closed fields showing owner's land; wood, 'Great Grove', spinney and trees; hedges; roads and gates; moats; ponds and oval-shaped watercourse in 'Canal Close' [probably the former channel from Bury Manor moat to Clopton water mill, at site of former village of Clopton [*VCH*, 8, 38]]; acreages given on table.

Border of 1 broad and 1 narrow band; title top right in a cartouche with drapery, leaves and flowers coloured green, purple, pink and gold; yellow scale bar bottom right; compass rose top left showing 8 red, blue, yellow and green points. Table bottom left giving field names and acreages. Centre top is a perspective drawing of the farmhouse. Fields outlined in green, wood and trees coloured green, water coloured blue, buildings coloured red, roads coloured yellow.

Numbers on edge of map refer to adjacent sheets. This is number 11 in a volume of maps of the Downing estate. See also CRY75001–10, EAS75001–8 and TAD75001–9.

D

Doddington – 1770 – DOD77001 – PRI

An Estate In the Parish of Doddington In the Isle of Ely &c And County of Cambridge Surveyed &c, 1770.

Surveyor: [Isaac Taylor]; **A Scale** of 40 Chains or 1/2 a Mile, Scale bar 0–40 chains (= 3 7/16in.), 1:9,216; **Size:** (i) 13 1/4 x 18 1/4in.; **Top** is N; Manuscript(i), parchment, coloured.

Doddington Church, TL400906, and 1,497a.2r.3p. W of village bounded by Ransonmoor Drove in W, Chatteris Parish in S and Flood's ['Middle'] Drain in N.

Names of fields, former and neighbouring owners and roads. Buildings shown in plan form and include church, cottages, farms buildings and parsonage, blacksmith's shop, dovecote and granary identified on table, 'Town Windmill' [post mill] shown in perspective. Open fields showing owner's strips; closes; wood, 'Appleborough Coppice' and trees; fen; state of cultivation given in words; tenure of some plots; roads and turnpike; watercourses and drains; gates and stiles; ponds and sheep-washing pond; gravel pit; hedges and fences; orchards; yards; gardens identified on table.

Border 3/8in. wide of 1 blue band with 1 uncoloured band and 1 band alternately coloured blue and uncoloured on inside, forming grid to map of rectangles which measure 1 3/8 x 2 1/8in.; title middle right in a rococo cartouche with flowers; scale bottom left; compass top right showing 8 points which extend all over map. Tables top left and on dorse giving tenants, former owner, field names, acreages, land use and grid-references to this map, to DOD77002 and to WMB77001. Church and farm coloured red, water coloured blue.

'Query' written by tenants and former owners of some plots. Later ink note on left under table: 'No 96 is since found to belong to Mr Orme Sturt & Hervey', later ink note on 1 plot: 'claimed by Mr Brown'. Map and tables are pp.194–6 of a volume bound in red leather with gold tooling: 'Map's Of Estates in The Counties of Dorset, Devon, & Wilts. Belonging to Humpry, Sturt, Esqr; Surveyed In the Year's 1765, 1766, 1767. And the Drawings Compleated, In January, 1770. by Isaac Taylor. Of Ross, Herefordshire.' Humphry Sturt inherited estate in 1765 [Pevsner, 1972, 298]. Positive photostats at BL 1640.(21), CRO 382/P2. See also DOD77002 and WMB77001.

Doddington – [1770] – DOD77002 – PRI
Fen Lands In the Parish of Doddington & County of Cambridge.
Surveyor: [Isaac Taylor]; **A Scale** of 20 Chains Or 1/4 of a Mile, Scale bar 0–20 chains (= 1 15/16in.), 1:8,175; **Size:** 12 7/8 x 8in.; **Top** is W; Manuscript(i), parchment, coloured.
Junction of Forty Foot Drain with Chatteris Parish, TL377885, and 329a.1r.21p. in Beezling and Dyke Moor fens, bounded by Forty Foot Drain in S, 'Dikamoor Drove' in N, Chatteris Parish in E and Benwick Parish in W.
Names of fens, fields, droves and former and neighbouring owners. Site of 'Old Windmill'. Closes; fen; roads and droves; gates; watercourses, drains and 'Old River'; 'Nine Swarths'; 'Beeslin Barr's'; Turf Fen ['Turfing Common'] adjoining map.
Border 1/4in. wide of 1 broad blue band with 1 broad and 1 narrow uncoloured band on inside; title bottom left in a rectangular cartouche with a border 1/8in. wide of 1 broad blue band with 1 narrow uncoloured band on inside; scale above title; compass top right showing 16 points which extend all over map. Water coloured blue.
Note on 1 plot: 'Mr G Waddington claimed, 10 Acres here, which was denied, by his late Son Mr Thos W'. On p.198 of a volume which gives owner and surveyor; see DOD77001 for details. Tables on DOD77001 include this map, which was probably drawn at same time. Positive photostats at BL 1640.(22), CRO 382/P3. See also WMB77001.

Doddington – [1803] – DOD80301 – CUL
Maps.PSQ.18.79
[Beezling Fen, Doddington.]
Surveyor: William Custance; **Auctioneer:** John Custance; **Engraver:** F. Hodson; **Scale:** 36 Chains to an Inch, 1:28,512; **Size:** (i) 4 3/8 x 7 1/4in.; **Top** is NW; Engraved, paper, uncoloured.
c. 1,000a. in TL3688, TL3689 and TL3789 in S of parish, bounded by Dykemoor Drove in N, Forty Foot Drain in S and road from Chatteris to Doddington in E.
Names of fields, droves and drains. Open fields showing owner's strips; roads and watercourses.
Border of 1 broad and 1 narrow band; scale middle bottom; compass top right showing 4 plain points.
Accompanies: 'Particular of A Valuable Estate, at Doddington and Wimblington, In the Isle of Ely; which will be sold by Auction ... August, 1803'. Particulars of sale give details of acreages, tenure, land use and date. See also DOD80302–3.

Doddington – [1803] – DOD80302 – CUL
Maps.PSQ.18.79
['Park', 'Mill' and 'Clay' fields, Doddington.]
Surveyor: William Custance; **Engraver:** F. Hodson; **Scale:** 9 Chains to an Inch, 1:7,128; **Size:** (i) 4 7/8 x 7 1/4in.; **Top** is N; Engraved, paper, uncoloured.
46a.3r.26p. S of junction of road from Wimblington to Doddington with Old Chapel Lane, TL413918, bounded by road from Wimblington to Doddington in W and ponds in SW.
Names of fields and neighbouring owners. Post mill shown in perspective. Open fields showing owner's strips; glebe; roads and watercourses; 'Wair ponds'.
Border of 1 broad and 1 narrow band; scale bottom right; compass middle top showing 4 points.
Accompanies particulars of sale which give date; see DOD80301 for details. See also DOD80303.

Doddington – [1803] – DOD80303 – CUL
Maps.PSQ.18.79
A Map of Doddington Estate.
Surveyor: William Custance; **Auctioneer:** John Custance; **Engraver:** F. Hodson; **Scale:** 36 Chains to an Inch, 1:28,512; **Size:** (i) 5 1/4 x 8 3/8in.; **Top** is NW; Engraved, paper, uncoloured.
Doddington Church, TL400906, and 1,500a. in village bounded by Forty Foot ['Forty Feet'] Drain in S, Coneywood Fen in N and Wimblington Parish in E.
Names of fields and roads. Houses shown in plan form. Open fields showing owner's strips; closes; roads and footpaths; watercourses; bank shown by hachures.
Border of 1 broad and 1 narrow band; title top left; scale bottom left; compass top right showing 4 plain points.
Accompanies particulars of sale which give date; see DOD80301 for details. See also DOD80302.

Doddington – 1820 – DOD82001 – CRO 515/P
Mr Joseph Richardson's Farm in Tick Fen containing 241a.0r.3p. including Ditches and 1/2 the Drove. Surveyed 22nd May 1820. J.J.
Surveyor: J[oseph] J[ackson?]; **Scale:** 1:3,370; **Size:** (ii) 47 x 37 3/8in.; **Top** is N; Manuscript(i), paper, uncoloured.
Puddock Bridge, TL351880, and 244a.3r.10p. in West Moor and Tick Fen, and in St Ives, Warboys and Ramsey parishes in Huntingdonshire, mostly S of Forty Foot River and bounded by boundary between Ramsey and St Ives parishes in W and boundary between Doddington and Chatteris parishes in E.
Names of parishes, rivers and bridge. Farm buildings and cottages shown in plan form and include Morley's Farm, Tick Fen Farm, Tick Farm and Purrant's Farm, 5 windmills shown in perspective. Closes; trees and Lambe's Plantation; acreages; roads and watercourses; gates; bridges; fences and hedges; bank; St Bennett's Cross ['Boundary Stone']; lock and sluice.
Title middle bottom.
Numbers on plots suggest map originally accompanied by a terrier. Lot numbers on fields. Survey lines marked in pencil. Some pencil calculations. Surveyor was probably Joseph Jackson [Eden J18]. Positive photostat at 1:8,940 at BL 1640.(21).

Downham – 1793 – DOW79301 – CLC ACC.1985/5

No. 1 Plan of Lands in the Parish of Downham in the Isle of Ely; belonging to Clare Hall Cambridge. Surveyed in the Year 1793.

Surveyor: [Joseph Freeman?]; **Scale bar** 10–0–30 chains (= 5in.), 1:6,336; **Size:** (i) 18 15/16 x 24 1/2in.; **Top** is N; Manuscript(i), parchment, coloured.

Downham Church, TL527842, and 19a.2r.12p. to S crossed by road to Ely, and a few strips W of church.

Names of fields, roads, droves and neighbouring owners. Farm buildings and church shown in plan form, 2 windmills shown in perspective. Open fields showing owner's strips; closes; trees; state of cultivation shown by colour; roads and droves; hedges; balks; number of lands between strips.

Border of 1 broad and 1 narrow band; title in centre; scale bottom right; compass top right showing 4 points. Table bottom left giving field names and acreages. Droves, hedges, balks and grass coloured green, roads and arable coloured brown, buildings coloured red.

Pencil notes on table. Copy, cut from a lease, measures 14 1/2 x 24 5/8in. and has no border at bottom. Title on right. In similar style to others drawn for Clare College in the 1790s, probably by Joseph Freeman. See also DOW79302.

Downham – 1793 – DOW79302 – CLC ACC.1985/5

No 11 Plan of Lands in the Parish of Downham in the Isle of Ely; Belonging to Clare~Hall Cambridge. Surveyed in 1793.

Surveyor: [Joseph Freeman?]; **Scale bar** 10–0–70 chains (= 4in.), 1:15,840; **Size:** (i) 19 x 24 1/2in.; **Top** is N; Manuscript(i), parchment, coloured.

Downham Church, TL527842, and 85a.2r.8p. to N in Fodder Fen and North Fen, to NW in Westmoor Fen, and 2 plots to SW in West Fen.

Names of fens, droves, drains and neighbouring owners. Church shown in perspective, barn adjoining map shown in plan form. Closes; fen; common; state of cultivation shown by colour; drains and bridge; droves.

Border of 1 broad band with 1 narrow band on inside; title top left; scale bottom right; compass in centre showing 4 points. Tables bottom left showing land let to James Eagle and top right showing land let to William Knights, giving field names and acreages and also referring to land on DOW79301. Arable coloured in brown stripes, pasture coloured green.

Rough copy on paper mounted on cloth, whole sheet measures 17 1/8 x 21 1/8in. and has pencil notes. In similar style to others drawn for Clare College in the 1790s, probably by Joseph Freeman. See also DOW79301.

Downham – [c. 1794] – DOW79401 – EDR CC.10117

['Map & Proposed Division of Downham Park Lease~hold into 7 Lots on Leases for 21 yrs'.]

Scale: 1:3,060; **Size:** (ii) 24 1/2 x 18 3/4in.; **Top** is N; Manuscript(i), paper, coloured.

Downham Church, TL527842, and c. 500a. to N bounded by 'Commissioners Drain' in N and crossed by Grunty Fen Drain.

Names of droves and drains. Church, house and windmill shown in perspective. Closed fields; state of cultivation given in words; gates; droves; dykes and drains; bridges; hedge; ownership of fences and of a dyke.

Cardinal points stated at edge of map. Lots outlined in yellow, orange, brown and blue.

Lot numbers on map. Red ink notes of field names, land use and acreages 'exempt'. Pencil notes. Title on dorse, date written on dorse in pencil. Land owned by Bishop of Ely.

Downham – [Early 19th century] – DOW80001 – CRO 283/P

Plan of an Estate lying partly in Littleport Fen, and partly in the Hundred Feet Wash, in the Parish of Downham, in the Isle, the Property of the Revd Jonathan Townley.

Scale bar 0–30 chains (= 3 3/4in.), 1:6,336; **Size:** (i) 18 3/8 x 22 1/4in.; **Top** is NW; Manuscript(i), parchment, coloured.

339a.2r.24p., probably in TL4988 and TL5088, bounded by Old Bedford River in NW and crossed by New Bedford River in SE.

Names of rivers and neighbouring owners. Farm buildings, cottage and 4 windmills shown in perspective. Closes; wood and trees; acreages; roads and watercourses; gates; banks shown by hachures and include Cradge Bank ['The Scradge']; 'delph'.

Border of 1 broad band with 1 broad yellow band inside; title top left in a brown rectangular cartouche; brown scale bar bottom left; compass below title showing 4 green points with a yellow N. Table bottom right giving field numbers and acreages. Field boundaries coloured blue, red and yellow, trees coloured green.

Dry Drayton – 1740 – DRY74001 – CUL MS Plans 269

A Plan of part of an Estate in the Parish of Dry Drayton, in the County of Cambridge copied from His Grace the Duke of Bedford's Plan. Surveyed and Delineated by John Davis Gent.

Surveyor: John Davis; **Draughtsman:** Henry Sayer; **Scale bar** 10–0–80 perches (= 7 7/16in.), 1:2,396; **Size:** (i) 17 3/8 x 17 1/8in.; **Top** is NW; Manuscript(ii), paper mounted on cloth, coloured.

c. 88a. in village, SW of TL380619, corner of Scotland Road ['Upper Street'] and road to Madingley ['Church Lane'].

Names of fields and roads. Church, houses and farm buildings shown in plan form. Open fields showing all strips; closes and kitchen closes; wood; avenue of trees; roads and footpaths; watercourses and pond; hedges.

Border of 1 broad and 1 narrow band; title middle top; scale middle bottom; compass top left showing 4 points with a feathered tail. Colour used to distinguish some strips, buildings coloured red, trees coloured green, water coloured blue, roads coloured brown.

Numbers on plots suggest map originally accompanied by a terrier. Note after title: 'Copied by Hy Sayer, 1842'. Land owned by John Russell, 4th Duke of Bedford.

Dry Drayton – 1816 – DRY81601 – CRO R65/5/370

[Dry Drayton Manor.]

Surveyor: Richard Catten[?]; **Scale bar** 0–40 chains of 22 yards (= 3 3/8in.), 1:9,528; **Size:** (i) 21 1/2 x 15 5/8in.; **Top** is N; Manuscript(i), paper mounted on cloth, coloured.

Manor House, TL378621, and 1,831a.1r.10p. in whole parish.

Names of neighbouring owners and parishes. Church, manor house, houses, cottages, barns and outbuildings shown in plan form, windmill shown in perspective.

Closed fields; trees; acreages; roads and watercourses; hedges; ponds.

Border of 1 narrow band; scale at bottom. Table on right giving tenants and acreages. Water coloured blue, land coloured to show occupation by different tenants.

Numbers on plots suggest map originally accompanied by a terrier. Ink and pencil notes of crops in 1817 and 1818, which include fallow, oats, peas, pasture, wheat, seeds and beans; notes of alterations to be made to map, and pencil calculations. This is a draft map. Surveyor's name is difficult to read. Land owned by Rev. Samuel Smith [VCH, 9, 75].

Dullingham – 1786 – DUL78601 – QCC Box 126
['Queens' College Grove', Dullingham.]
  Surveyor: Benjamin Arber; **Scale bar** 0–25 poles (= 2 9/16in.), 1:1,932; **Size:** (iii) 2 3/4 x 3 1/2in.; Manuscript(i), paper, coloured.
  6a.28p. in Dullingham Parish.
  Names of gates. Closed field; 'Gate into Woods' and 'Gate to Mr Chapman's'.
  Scale at bottom. Red dotted line around boundary.
  Sketch map on letter from Benjamin Arber at Burwell to Robert Plumptre, Master of Queens' College, Cambridge, 20 May 1786, about surveying and valuing the grove.

Dullingham – [1797] – DUL79701 – CLC ACC.1985/5
[Land in Dullingham, owned by Clare College, Cambridge.]
  Surveyor: [Joseph Freeman?]; **Scale bar** 5–0–25 chains (= 3 3/4in.), 1:6,336; **Size:** (ii) 21 1/8 x 46 1/8in.; **Top** is N; Manuscript(ii), paper mounted on cloth, coloured.
  Dullingham Church, TL631578, and 327a.1r.38p. in strips scattered throughout parish.
  Names of fields, roads and neighbouring owners. Cottages, church, mill and 'Publick House' shown in plan form. Open fields showing owner's strips; closes; meadow and 'Lammas Meadow'; state of cultivation shown by colour; roads and watercourses; plantation; hedges; balks; chalk pits; 'Pen'; green.
  Scale centre bottom; compass in centre showing 4 points. Table top right giving field names, acreages and land use. Arable coloured in brown stripes, pasture and hedges coloured green.
  Bottom right: 'A Ground Plan of the Buildings', which measures 5 15/16 x 11 3/8in. within a border of 1 narrow band, at 1:367. Plan shows the house, barn, stable, 'Cow house', 'Wood house', 'Barley Shop', 'Malting Kiln', 'Kiln House & Malt Shop' and dovecote. Copy, cut from a lease dated 1798, at CLC Safe B:49/2, measures 16 1/4 x 24 5/8in. and is at 1:12,230. 'Publick House' now called an 'Alehouse' and heath is shown. Border of 1 broad band with 1 narrow band on inside, compass points at centre top. Ground plan of the buildings top left, measures 4 15/16 x 6 1/16in., at 1:496. Inset has a border of 2 narrow bands and is uncoloured. Original of these maps was probably one of the series drawn for Clare College in the 1790s, probably by Joseph Freeman. Valuation of the estate by Joseph Freeman in 1797 at CLC Safe B:49/3.

Dullingham – [1825] – DUL82501 – QCC 355 A21, B21
  Estate at Dullingham In the County of Cambridge.

Surveyor: [Alexander Watford jr]; **Scale bar** 0–10 chains (= 3 5/16in.), 1:2,391; **Size:** (i) 6 3/16 x 4 5/8in.; Manuscript(ii), paper, coloured.
  4a.2r.29p. in Dullingham Parish.
  Names of field and neighbouring owner. 'College Grove'; state of cultivation shown by colour; acreages; hedges.
  Border on top, bottom and right of 2 narrow bands, border on left of 1 broad band with 1 narrow band on either side; title at top; scale at bottom. Grove coloured green.
  On left of sheet, which also contains maps of Burwell [BUW82501], Chesterton [CHF82501] and Swaffham Prior [SWP82502], and in volume drawn in 1825: 'Plans of the Several Estates in England and Wales belonging to the President and Fellows of the College of St Margaret and St Bernard commonly called Queen's College in the University of Cambridge Delineated from Authentic Documents in the possession of the said President and Fellows and from actual Surveys taken By their most obedient and obliged Servant Alexr Watford'. Title page drawn by James Richardson [Watford's nephew]. This is the Bursar's copy; 2nd, finer, copy [the Master's copy] at QCC 355 B21 measures 7 1/8 x 4 13/16in., is drawn on parchment and has a scale bar 0–10 chains (= 3 3/8in.), 1:2,347. Border imitates a scroll of paper, title has gothic lettering. Positive photostat of this copy at 1:5,200 at BL 1640.(28).

Duxford St John – 1826 – DUX82601 – GCC Drawer 1
Map 1 (Duxford)
  Plan of an Estate in the Parishes of Duxford St Iohn and Duxford St Peter in the County of Cambridge. belonging to The Master Fellows & Scholars of Gonville & Caius College.
  Surveyor: John King; **Scale bar** 0–20 chains (= 3 5/16in.), 1:4,782; **Size:** (i) 23 5/8 x 31 3/16in.; **Top** is NNW; Manuscript(i), parchment, coloured.
  St John's Church, TL478462, and 419a.2r.9p. to W and E and 1 plot in W of parish, bounded by Ickleton Parish in S and road from London to Newmarket in N.
  Names of roads and neighbouring owners. Cottages and mill shown in plan form, St John's and St Peter's churches shown in perspective. Closed fields showing owner's land; waste; state of cultivation shown by colour; acreages of some plots; hedges; roads, turnpike and footpaths; watercourses and bridges; names of those to whom tithes should be paid.
  Border of 1 broad and 1 narrow band; title top right; scale centre bottom; compass centre left showing 8 points. Table bottom right giving field names and acreages. Water coloured blue, roads coloured yellow, arable coloured in brown stripes, buildings coloured red, hedges and pasture coloured green.

Duxford St John – [1830] – DUX83001 – C U L
Maps.PSQ.18.84
  Plan of a Farm lying in The Parishes of Duxford St. John, and St. Peter, in the County of Cambridge The Property of the late Revd James Hitch, and Miss Hitch.
  Auctioneer: Elliot Smith; **Lithographer:** W[illiam] Metcalfe; **Scale bar** 0–40 chains (= 2 1/4in.), 1:14,080; **Size:** (i) 7 3/4 x 8 7/8in.; **Top** is NE; Lithograph, paper, uncoloured.
  318a.0r.38p. SW of village along both sides of road to Ickleton and along 'Duxford Street'; roads from

Whittlesford to Ickleton and to Duxford ['Occupation Road' to 'Duxford Street'] meet at TL477457.

Names of farm, fields, owners and roads. Closed fields; glebe; common; tenure; roads.

Border of 1 broad and 1 narrow band; title top left, underlined; scale beneath title. Table bottom right giving acreages and lot numbers.

Accompanies: 'Plan, Particulars & Conditions of Sale, of valuable Freehold and Copyhold Land, Farm~House, &c. desirably situated at Duxford, Cambridgeshire. To be sold by auction ... January, 1830'. Particulars of sale give quit rent, date and indicate that farm has a house, garden, orchard and pasture. Lithographer's 1st name was William [CRO EPR CW 1825 WR C52:178]; Miss Hitch's 1st name was Alicia [*VCH*, 6, 209].

E

East Hatley – 1750 – EAS75001 – DCC

A Survey. of Feaks's Dairy In the Parish of East Hatley In the County of Cambridge The Estate of Sir Jacob Garrard Downing Bt Surveyed by Jos. Cole. 1750.

Surveyor: Joseph Cole; **Scale bar** 10–0–80 perches (= 5 5/8in.), 1:3,168; **Size:** (i) 20 11/16 x 14in.; **Top** is E; Manuscript(i), parchment, coloured.

157a.3r.32p. in TL2849, bounded in S by CRY75009 and CRY75010 in Croydon Parish and in W by TAD75007 in Tadlow Parish.

Names of fields. Farm buildings shown in plan form. Closed fields showing owner's land; pightle; trees; meadow; hedges; gates; ponds; acreages given on table.

Border of 1 broad band with 1 narrow band on inside; title top left in a rococo cartouche with leaves and coloured red, purple, green, blue and gold; yellow scale bar bottom right; compass rose top right showing 8 red, blue, yellow and green points. Table bottom left giving field names and acreages. Above table is a perspective drawing of the farmhouse. Fields outlined in green, water coloured blue, buildings coloured red.

Pencil notes. Numbers on edge of map refer to adjacent sheets. This is number 21 in a volume of maps of the Downing estate. See also CRY75001–11, EAS75002–8 and TAD75001–9.

East Hatley – 1750 – EAS75002 – DCC

A Survey. of Manor House Farm, in the Parish of East Hatley, and County of Cambridge The Estate of Sir Jacob Garrard Downing Bt Surveyed By Jos. Cole, 1750.

Surveyor: Joseph Cole; **Scale bar** 10–0–80 perches (= 5 5/8in.), 1:3,168; **Size:** (i) 20 13/16 x 14in.; **Top** is NNW; Manuscript(i), parchment, coloured.

Farm at TL285504, and 194a.0r.22p. bounded by Hatley St George Parish in N and E and EAS75001 in S.

Names of fields and parishes. Farm and parsonage shown in plan form, church shown in perspective. Closed fields showing owner's land; Buff ['Hatley'] Wood and trees; state of cultivation shown by colour; hedges; roads and gates; watercourses, moats and ponds; orchards; balks; acreages given on table.

Border of 1 broad band with 1 narrow band on inside; title top left in a rococo cartouche with leaves and flowers and coloured green, blue, red, purple and gold; yellow scale bar bottom left; compass rose top right showing 8 red, blue, yellow and green points. Table bottom right giving field names, acreages and land use. Left of table is a

perspective drawing of the farmhouse. Fields outlined in green, arable coloured in yellow stripes, water coloured blue, roads coloured yellow, buildings coloured red, trees and hedges coloured green.

Numbers on edge of map refer to adjacent sheets. This is number 22 in a volume of maps of the Downing estate. See also CRY75001–11, EAS75001,3–8 and TAD75001–9.

East Hatley – 1750 – EAS75003 – DCC

A Survey. of Lewis Flints Farm In the Parish of East Hatley In the County of Cambridge The Estate of The Honble Sir Iacob Garrard Downing Bat By Jos. Cole 1750.

Surveyor: Joseph Cole; **Scale bar** 10–0–80 perches (= 5 5/8in.), 1:3,168; **Size:** (i) 20 13/16 x 14in.; **Top** is N; Manuscript(i), parchment, coloured.

155a.2r.16p. in TL2950, bounded by Hatley St George Parish in NW and EAS75002 in W.

Names of fields and parishes. Farm buildings shown in plan form. Closed fields showing owner's land; pightles; trees; pasture; state of cultivation shown by colour; hedges; gates; apple, pear and cherry orchards [no trees are shown in cherry orchard]; balks; ponds; acreages given on table.

Border of 1 broad band with 1 narrow band on inside; title top left in a cartouche of a vine coloured brown, blue and green; yellow scale bar bottom left; compass rose top right showing 8 red, blue, yellow and green points. Table bottom right giving field names, land use and acreages of fields and lanes. Centre top is a perspective drawing of the farmhouse. Fields outlined in green, arable coloured in yellow stripes, buildings coloured red, water coloured blue, trees coloured green.

Numbers on edge of map refer to adjacent sheets. This is number 23 in a volume of maps of the Downing estate. See also CRY75001–11, EAS75001–2,4–8 and TAD75001–9.

East Hatley – 1750 – EAS75004 – DCC

A Survey. of Holbens Farm In the Parishes of East Hatley & Croydon In the County of Cambridge. The Estate of Sir Iacob Garrard Downing Bt By Jos. Cole 1750.

Surveyor: Joseph Cole; **Scale bar** 10–0–80 perches (= 5 5/8in.), 1:3,168; **Size:** (i) 20 3/4 x 14in.; **Top** is W; Manuscript(i), parchment, coloured.

Holbeins Farm, TL296505, and 213a.0r.38p. bounded by road from Croydon to East Hatley in E and EAS75003 in N.

Names of fields, road bounding map and neighbouring owner. Farm buildings shown in plan form. Closed fields showing owner's land; trees; state of cultivation shown by colour; hedges; gates; meadow; 'pyghtle'; ponds; balks; boundary between East Hatley and Croydon parishes not shown; acreages given on table.

Border of 1 broad band with 1 narrow band on inside; title top left in a rococo cartouche with flowers and coloured purple, pink, green, yellow, blue and red; yellow scale bar at bottom; compass rose middle right showing 8 red, blue, green and yellow points. Table top right giving field names, acreages and land use. Centre top is a perspective drawing of the farmhouse. Buildings coloured red, water coloured blue, trees coloured green, fields outlined in green, arable coloured in yellow stripes.

Pencil notes. Numbers on edge of map refer to adjacent sheets. This is number 24 in a volume of maps of the Downing estate. See also CRY75001–11, EAS75001–3,5–8 and TAD75001–9.

East Hatley – 1750 – EAS75005 – DCC

A Survey. of Flints, and Streets, Farms In the Parish of East Hatley In the County of Cambridge The Estate of Sir Iacob Garrard Downing Bt Surveyed by Jos. Cole 1750.

Surveyor: Joseph Cole; **Scale bar** 10–0–80 perches (= 5 5/8in.), 1:3,168; **Size:** (i) 20 13/16 x 13 15/16in.; **Top** is N; Manuscript(i), parchment, coloured.

135a.1r.4p. in TL2950, bounded by Hatley St George Parish in NW, EAS75004 in S and EAS75003 in W.

Names of fields and parishes. Farm buildings shown in plan form. Closed fields showing owner's land; pasture; trees; state of cultivation shown by colour; hedges; gates; ponds; balks; feature which may be a footpath; acreages given on table.

Border of 1 broad band with 1 narrow band on inside; title top left in a rococo cartouche with a vine and coloured green, purple, blue, pink and gold; yellow scale bar at bottom; compass rose middle left showing 8 red, blue, yellow and green points. Tables top right and bottom left giving field names, acreages and land use for each farm. Underneath each table is a perspective drawing of the respective farmhouse. Fields outlined in green, arable coloured in yellow stripes, buildings coloured red, hedges coloured green, water coloured blue.

Numbers on edge of map refer to adjacent sheets. These are numbers 25 and 26 in a volume of maps of the Downing estate. See also CRY75001–11, EAS75001–4,6–8 and TAD75001–9.

East Hatley – 1750 – EAS75006 – DCC

A Survey. of Teats Farm, in the Parish of East Hatley In the County of Cambridge The Estate of The Honble Sir Iacob Garrard Downing Bart Surveyed By Jos. Cole. 1750.

Surveyor: Joseph Cole; **Scale bar** 10–0–80 perches (= 5 11/16in.), 1:3,133; **Size:** (i) 20 3/4 x 13 15/16in.; **Top** is N; Manuscript(i), parchment, coloured.

103a.0r.24p. in TL2950, bounded by EAS75005 in W.

Names of fields, lane and neighbouring owners. Farm buildings shown in plan form. Closed fields showing owner's land; state of cultivation shown by colour; hedges showing hedgerow trees; gates; ponds; 'Croydon Lane'; balks; acreages given on table.

Border of 1 broad band with 1 narrow band on inside; title top left in a rococo cartouche coloured gold, purple, pink, red, blue and green; yellow scale bar at bottom; compass rose bottom right showing 8 red, blue, yellow and green points. Table bottom left giving field names, acreages and land use. Centre top is a perspective drawing of the farmhouse. Fields outlined in green, arable coloured in yellow stripes, buildings coloured red, water coloured blue, hedges coloured green.

Numbers on edge of map refer to adjacent sheets. This is number 27 in a volume of maps of the Downing estate. See also CRY75001–11, EAS75001–5,7–8 and TAD75001–9.

East Hatley – 1750 – EAS75007 – DCC

A Survey. of Abbotts Farm In the Parish of East Hatley In the County of Cambridge. The Estate of Sir Iacob Garrard Downing Brt By Jos. Cole 1750.

Surveyor: Joseph Cole; **Scale bar** 10–0–80 perches (= 5 11/16in.), 1:3,133; **Size:** (i) 20 3/4 x 14in.; **Top** is N; Manuscript(i), parchment, coloured.

162a.2r.23p. in TL2952, bounded by Great Gransden and Longstowe parishes in N, Hatley St George Parish in NW and EAS75006 in S.

Names of fields, lanes, parishes and tree. Farm buildings shown in plan form. Closed fields showing owner's land; spinney; trees and 'Farseen Oak'; area of rough ground; state of cultivation shown by colour; hedges showing hedgerow trees; gates; ponds; balks; acreages given on table.

Border of 1 broad band with 1 narrow band on inside; title top left in a rococo cartouche coloured purple, gold, red, pink and green; yellow scale bar bottom left; compass rose centre bottom showing 8 red, blue, green and yellow points. Table bottom right giving field names, acreages and land use. Underneath title is a perspective drawing of the farmhouse. Fields outlined in green, arable coloured in yellow stripes, buildings coloured red, water coloured blue, hedges and trees coloured green, roads coloured yellow.

Numbers on edge of map refer to adjacent sheets. This is number 28 in a volume of maps of the Downing estate. See also CRY75001–11, EAS75001–6,8 and TAD75001–9.

East Hatley – 1750 – EAS75008 – DCC

A Survey. of Grey's Farm In the Parish of East Hatley In the County of Cambridge The Estate of The Honble Sir Iacob Garrard Downing Bt Surveyed by Jos Cole 1750.

Surveyor: Joseph Cole; **Scale bar** 10–0–80 perches (= 5 5/8in.), 1:3,168; **Size:** (i) 20 3/4 x 14in.; **Top** is NW; Manuscript(i), parchment, coloured.

110a.0r.10p. in TL3052, bounded by Longstowe Parish in NE, 'Croydon Lane and Road to Cambridge' in S and EAS75007 in W.

Names of fields, roads and common adjoining map. Farm buildings shown in plan form. Closed fields showing owner's land; state of cultivation shown by colour; hedges showing hedgerow trees; roads and gates; ponds; acreages given on table.

Border of 1 broad band with 1 narrow band on inside; title top left in a rococo cartouche coloured purple, blue, pink, green, red and gold and with a bird above; yellow scale bar centre bottom; compass rose above scale showing 8 red, blue, yellow and green points. Table top right giving field names, acreages and land use. Bottom left is a perspective drawing of the farmhouse. Fields outlined in green, arable coloured in yellow stripes, roads coloured yellow, water coloured blue, buildings coloured red, hedges coloured green.

Numbers on edge of map refer to adjacent sheets. This is number 29 in a volume of maps of the Downing estate. See also CRY75001–11, EAS75001–7 and TAD75001–9.

Elm – [Late 18th century] – ELM77501 – EDR CC.10123 ['Gresemere'.]

Scale: 1:13,500; **Size:** (ii) 15 5/8 x 12 15/16in.; **Top** is N; Manuscript(i), paper, coloured.

Farm at TF417010 in Gray's Moor, and c. 2,300a. bounded by Long Drove in N and by Twenty Foot River in S from Hobb's Lot Farms ['Hobbs House'] in W to Tilney Hirne ['Tilney Hurn Corner'] in E, and land in Wisbech St Mary Parish W of 'Black Dicke'.

Names of watercourses, droves and neighbouring owners. 'Hobbs House', Graysmoor ['Gresemere'] Farm and cottages shown in perspective. Closed fields; acreages; roads and droves; watercourses and drains; March Chain Bridge; 'Waldersea Bank'.

Compass on right showing 4 points. 'Gresemere Farm' coloured grey.

Title on dorse. Land owned by Bishop of Ely.

Elm – 1818 – ELM81801 – EDR CC.10114

Plan of the Lands of the late Reverend Charles Percival belonging to the Manor of Waltersea in the Parish of Elm held by Lease for Lives from the Right Reverend Lord Bishop of Ely.

Scale: 1:14,000; **Size:** (ii) 15 1/4 x 19 1/2in.; **Top** is N; Manuscript(i), paper, uncoloured.

Hobbs Lots ['Hobbs house'], TF395011, and 705a.2r.20p. in SW of parish bounded by Twenty Foot River in S, Long Drove in N and 'Gold Dyke alias Crooked Bank' in NE.

Names of fields, droves and drains. 'Hobbs house' and cottages shown in plan form, windmill shown in perspective. Closed fields; drains and dykes; banks; March Chain Bridge; 'Cherry Tree Corner'; 'Birch Holts'.

Title at top. Table bottom right giving field names, acreages and to whom land was sold.

Ink notes of leases and corrections to table.

Elm – [c. 1825] – ELM82501 – WM 9/19

Plan of Mr John Sculthorpes Estates at Elm in the Isle of Ely in the County of Cambridge and Emneth in the County of Norfolk.

Scale: 9 Chains to an Inch, 1:7,128; **Size:** (ii) 19 x 23 1/2in.; **Top** is W; Manuscript(i), paper, coloured.

Elm Church, TF470069, and 325a.2r.7p. to W and S in Laddus Fen, and 22p. in Emneth Parish [Norfolk].

Names of fields, fen and roads. Houses shown in plan form, church and windmill shown in perspective. Closed fields showing owner's land; roads; watercourses, sluice and bridge.

Title centre top; scale bottom right; compass top right showing 4 plain points. Table bottom left giving acreages, former owners and key to colours. Land coloured to show former owners: blue, red, yellow, light and dark brown, light and dark green.

Pencil notes. Drawn in early 19th century, possibly in connection with bankruptcy of John Sculthorpe, announced in *Cambridge Chronicle* on 21 January 1825.

Eltisley – 1814 – ELT81401 – JCC Eltisley

Plan of an Estate in the County of Cambridge Belonging to the Master Fellows and Scholars of Jesus College in the University of Cambridge made in 1814 by Alexr Watford.

Surveyor: Alexander Watford [jr]; **Scale bar** 0–30 chains (= 5in.), 1:4,752; **Size:** (i) 33 1/4 x 25 1/16in.; **Top** is N; Manuscript(i), parchment, coloured.

Eltisley Church, TL268597, and 163a.0r.2p. in whole parish bounded by Croxton Parish in W, Yelling Parish [Huntingdonshire] in NW, Papworth Everard Parish in NE, Caxton Parish in E and Great Gransden Parish [Huntingdonshire] in S.

Names of neighbouring owners, roads and farm. Rectory Farm and cottages shown in plan form, church shown in perspective. Open fields showing owner's strips; closes; common; acreages; division of fields; roads and footpaths; gates; watercourses; toll bar and turnpike; ponds and moat; fences; village green; site of Papley Grove.

Border of 1 broad band with 1 narrow band on each side; title top left; scale under title; compass on right showing 8 points. Table at bottom giving field names and acreages. Direction to Cambridge shown by cuffed hand. Roads coloured brown, buildings coloured red, strips coloured yellow, grass coloured green, water coloured blue.

Pencil notes and note: 'NB. There are 201 Pieces of Open Field Land and 4 Old Inclosures'.

Eltisley – 1816 – ELT81601 – ECC 12.C.17

A Sketch of the Strip of Land in Eltisley belonging to Emmanuel College.

Scale: 1:2,330; **Size:** (i) 15 5/8 x 9 1/4in.; **Top** is N; Manuscript(i), paper, coloured.

3r.22p. in NE of parish in TL2861, bounded by Papworth Everard Parish in E.

Names of parishes. Acreages.

Border of 1 narrow band; title middle left; compass top right showing 4 points. Table bottom right giving acreages. Boundary with Papworth Everard Parish coloured red.

At bottom: 'Explanation. The red line is the boundary of Papworth. The land between the red line and the Dotted one, is in contemplation whether it should be given in exchange for land to Mr Cheere or not'. Cheere's 1st names were Charles Madryll [*VCH*, 5, 50].

Ely St Mary – [c. 1650] – EYM65001 – CLC Safe B:56/4

[St John's Hospital, Ely, owned by Clare College, Cambridge.]

Scale: 1:1,010; **Size:** (ii) 7 3/4 x 10 1/2in.; **Top** is N; Manuscript(i), paper, uncoloured.

St John's Hospital, TL535802, and 7a.2r.17p. bounded by close in W, West End in N and road to Cambridge in E.

Names of roads, areas and buildings. Buildings shown in plan form and include 'Chappell', 'Chappell without any roofe', cloisters, hall, 'a little parlour', 'a cellar for beer', 'a large square kitchen', 'a large parlour now used for a deary', 'horse house', 'brew house & bath house', wash house and 'a large room not much used'. Roads; garden; orchards; walls and material with which they are built; 'The entrance from the street into the Area or Court'.

Entrance is stippled; doors between rooms are indicated by dotted red lines; buildings outlined in pencil.

Notes bottom left of rooms on 1st floor: 'The short lines of red pricks shew the doores from one entrance to another'; 'the Chappell ground may be conveniently added to the garden'. Probably drawn before a farmhouse was built in 2nd half of 17th century [*VCH*, 4, 31].

Ely St Mary – [Late 18th century] – EYM77501 – CRO R65/16

A Plan of Barton Farm in Ely.

Scale: 1:2,000; **Size:** (i) 56 1/4 x 31 1/2in.; **Top** is NE; Manuscript(i), paper, uncoloured.

Barton Farm, TL539798, and 298a.3r.0p. to S and E, mostly E of road to Witchford and bounded by Cawdle Fen in E, including 49a.1r.27p. at Witchford Brook.

Names of fields, roads and neighbouring owners. Farm buildings shown in plan form. Closed fields; common; trees; hedges; responsibility for boundaries; roads and footpaths; gates and stiles; 'Gristle Hill'; gallows; oval hatched features [pits?]; 'Cherry Grounds', orchard and gardens identified on table.

Border of 1 narrow uncoloured band with 1 broad uncoloured band on inside, separated by red line; title in centre surrounded by 2 narrow red lines; compass centre right showing 4 points. Table top left giving tenants, land use and acreages both including and within the fences.

Plots outlined in yellow, red, green and blue, trees coloured green.

Inset at bottom of 49a.1r.27p. at Witchford Brook. Later ink notes on table. Owned by Bishop of Ely. Drawn in late 18th century, before a tenant died in 1794.

Ely St Mary – 1792 – EYM79201 – CLC ACC.1985/5

A Plan of a Farm at Ely called St. Johns Farm; belonging to the Revnd; the Master and Fellows of Clare Hall, in the University of Cambridge. Surveyed in the Year 1792.

Surveyor: [Joseph Freeman?]; **Scale bar** 10–0–40 chains (= 3 1/16in.), 1:12,930; **Size:** (i) 25 1/16 x 20 9/16in.; **Top** is N; Manuscript(i), parchment, coloured.

Farm at TL535802, and 79a.1r.17p. scattered throughout parish.

Names of fields, roads, headlands and neighbouring owners. Farm buildings shown in plan form. Open fields showing owner's strips; closes; trees; state of cultivation shown by colour; roads; garden; hedges; meadow adjoining map.

Border of 1 broad band with 1 narrow band on inside; title top left in a rococo cartouche with fishing nets and rods underneath; scale under title; compass top right showing 4 points. Table on right giving field names and acreages. Above title is a vignette of the farm buildings. Roads and arable strips coloured brown, pasture and hedges coloured green.

Pencil notes. Note beneath scale: 'The Buildings on this Farm, are A Dwelling house, built with Stone and tiled; consisting of three Rooms on a floor. A Back~house containing two Rooms on a Floor. A Dove house, built with stone and tiled. A Barn built part with Brick and part boarded, having a Cowlodge at the east end; and a Stable with Rack, manger and chaffhouse at the west end. A Brick barn with a Midsty, and a Cart lodge on the North side, Thatched. A Barn, called the Hospital barn, situate on the North side of the Road; boarded and thatched containing two Midstys'. Copy cut from a 1797 lease measures 30 7/8 x 12 15/16in. and is at 1:9,052. Some strips have later been outlined in red and blue. Table bottom left and on right. Pencil notes, top left: 'Note. There are two other pieces belonging to this Farm, One situate in Padnell Fen and the other in North Fen, not measured, on Account of their being Covered with Water at the time this Survey was made'. These plots are not shown on original map. In style of Joseph Freeman, who valued the estate in March and April 1792 [CLC Safe B:56/4].

Ely St Mary – [c. 1798] – EYM79801 – CLC ACC.1985/5

No. 1. 2. 12. and 20, and 11,

Surveyor: [Joseph Freeman?]; **Scale bar** 10–0–100 feet (= 3 5/8in.), 1:364; **Size:** (ii) 14 7/8 x 17 1/8in.; **Top** is NW; Manuscript(i), paper, coloured.

c. 2a. at TL532802, bounded by West End in NE and road to Witchford in SW.

Names of roads, areas and neighbouring owners. Buildings shown in plan form and include houses, 'Turf house', 'Cow lodges', barn and stable. Roads; dimensions of areas; yard; gardens.

Title top left; scale bottom left. Some walls coloured blue.

One of a set of plans of tenements belonging to Clare College, Cambridge, and probably accompanies the valuation by Joseph Freeman of the tenements on 26 April

1798 [CLC Safe B:56/11]. See also EYM79802–6 and EYT79801–3.

Ely St Mary – [c. 1798] – EYM79802 – CLC ACC.1985/5

No. 3. 4. 7. 16. and A.

Surveyor: [Joseph Freeman?]; **Scale bar** 10–0–50 feet (= 6in.), 1:120; **Size:** (ii) 14 3/4 x 18 1/4in.; **Top** is NW; Manuscript(i), paper, coloured.

c. 20p. at TL542803, bounded by 'Bishops Garden' in S, Market ['Jail'] Street in N and crossed by 'Butchery Lane'.

Names of roads, areas and neighbouring owners. Buildings shown in plan form and include houses, 'Turf house' and 'Cart house'. Roads; dimensions of areas; yard; gardens.

Title top left; scale in centre. Some walls coloured blue.

Plan is one of a set; see EYM79801 for owner, surveyor and date. See also EYM79803–6 and EYT79801–3.

Ely St Mary – [c. 1798] – EYM79803 – CLC ACC.1985/5

No. 5. 13. 15. and 25.

Surveyor: [Joseph Freeman?]; **Scale bar** 10–0–100 feet (= 3 5/8in.), 1:364; **Size:** (ii) 14 13/16 x 17 5/16in.; **Top** is N; Manuscript(i), paper, coloured.

c. 2r. at TL539804, bounded by St Mary's Street in S.

Names of areas, roads and neighbouring owners. Buildings shown in plan form and include houses and wheelwright's shop. Roads; dimensions of areas; yard; gardens.

Title top left; scale bottom right. Some walls coloured blue.

Plan is one of a set; see EYM79801 for owner, surveyor and date. See also EYM79802,4–6 and EYT79801–3.

Ely St Mary – [c. 1798] – EYM79804 – CLC ACC.1985/5

No. 6 and 23.

Surveyor: [Joseph Freeman?]; **Scale bar** 10–0–50 feet (= 6in.), 1:120; **Size:** (ii) 14 7/8 x 18 1/4in.; **Top** is N; Manuscript(i), paper, coloured.

c. 10p. at TL537802, bounded by St Mary's Street in S and road in E; no. 23 is a garden to W.

Names of areas, roads and neighbouring owners. Tenements shown in plan form. Roads; dimensions of areas; yard; garden.

Title top left; scale bottom right. Some walls coloured blue.

Plan is one of a set; see EYM79801 for owner, surveyor and date. See also EYM79802–3,5–6 and EYT79801–3.

Ely St Mary – [c. 1798] – EYM79805 – CLC ACC.1985/5

No. 8.

Surveyor: [Joseph Freeman?]; **Scale bar** 10–0–100 feet (= 3 5/8in.), 1:364; **Size:** (ii) 17 15/16 x 14 13/16in.; **Top** is NE; Manuscript(i), paper, coloured.

c. 3r. at TL534802, bounded by West End in SW.

Names of areas, roads and neighbouring owners. Buildings shown in plan form and include barn, stable, lodge and dovecote. Trees; roads; dimensions of areas; yards; orchard.

Title top right; scale at bottom. Some walls coloured blue, trees coloured green.

Plan is one of a set; see EYM79801 for owner, surveyor and date. See also EYM79802–4,6 and EYT79801–3.

Ely St Mary – [c. 1798] – EYM79806 – C L C ACC.1985/5
No. 9. 24. and 26.
Surveyor: [Joseph Freeman?]; **Scale bar** 10–0–100 feet (= 3 5/8in.), 1:364; **Size:** (ii) 14 7/8 x 17 7/8in.; **Top** is W; Manuscript(i), paper, coloured.
c. 1a. at TL534803, bounded by 'Gift Lane' in N.
Names of areas, roads and neighbouring owners. Tenements shown in plan form. Roads; dimensions of areas; gardens.
Title top left; scale bottom right. Some walls coloured blue.
Plan is one of a set; see EMY79801 for owner, surveyor and date. See also EYM79802–5 and EYT79801–3.

Ely St Mary – [1826] – EYM82601 – CRO 132/T421
['Lucerne Piece adjoining Downham Lane in Ely let to Mr Edward Ingram 1826 to be planted with fruit trees'.]
Scale: 1:257; **Size:** (ii) 8 13/16 x 7 3/8in.; **Top** is NW or SE; Manuscript(i), paper, uncoloured.
c. 2r. in TL5380 bounded by Egremont Street ['Downham Lane'].
Names of neighbouring owners. 'Mr Cropley's' house, barn and lodge, and 'B. Ingram's' house shown in perspective. Closed field; roads and gates; wall; orchard.
Note on dorse describing piece and conditions of lease and giving date and title.

Ely St Mary – 1827 – EYM82701 – CUL MS Plans 133
Plan of Cawdwell Fen. Braham Farm and three Glebe Pastures in Ely Cambridgeshire.
Scale bar 0–30 chains (= 5in.), 1:4,752; **Size:** (i) 33 3/4 x 24 1/8in.; **Top** is N; Manuscript(i), paper, coloured.
Braham Farm, TL533774, and c. 760a. in SE of parish bounded by Station Road, Ely [road from Ely to Soham] in N, Thetford Parish in S and Cawdle ['Cawdwell'] Fen Drove in W.
Names of fen, fields, roads and neighbouring owners. Houses and farm buildings shown in plan form. Closed fields; wood and trees; waste; state of cultivation shown by colour; roads and footpaths; watercourses and ponds; garden and orchard.
Border of 1 broad and 1 narrow band; title top left; scale bottom right; compass middle right showing 4 points with feathered N and S. Buildings shown in red or grey, arable and roads coloured brown, pasture coloured green, river coloured blue.
Numbers on fields suggest map originally accompanied by a terrier. 6 small insets on left of land nearby probably owned or leased by farm; pencil sketches around insets.

Ely Trinity – 1779 – EYT77901 – WRO CR114/2/vi
Stuntney Map.
Surveyors: [John] Lund [sr and jr]; **A Scale** of four Chains in One Inch, Scale bar 0–21 chains (= 5 1/4in.), 1:3,168; **Size:** (i) 23 3/16 x 15 1/16in.; **Top** is N; Manuscript(i), paper, coloured.
c. 140a. S of Stuntney village bounded by Soham Parish in SW.
Names of roads and neighbouring owners. Closes; trees; roads and gates.

Border of 1 broad band; title on left; scale centre bottom of sheet; compass in centre of sheet showing 4 points. Trees coloured green, roads coloured brown, fields outlined in red, green, yellow and brown.
Numbers on plots suggest map originally accompanied by a terrier. On left of sheet which also contains WTF77901 and entitled centre top: 'A Map of the Estates of the Right Honourable Lady Viscountess Irwin at Stuntney and Whichford in the Isle of Ely and County of Cambridge. Surveyed by Messrs Lund's in 1779'. Surveyors' 1st names were John [Eden L294 and L294.1].

Ely Trinity – [c. 1784] – EYT78401 – CRO 283/P
A Survey of the Manor of New Barns in the Parish of Trinity in Ely Cambridgeshire.
Scale: 1:3,600; **Size:** (i) 32 1/2 x 23 3/4in.; **Top** is NE; Manuscript(i), paper mounted on cloth, uncoloured.
Newbarns House, TL550818, and 694a.1r.16p. bounded by Kettlesworth Drove in N, Clayway Drove in E, road to King's Lynn in W and Springhead and Deacon's ['Lower'] lanes in S.
Names of fields and roads. House, cottages and windmill shown in perspective, farm buildings, ice house and brick kilns shown in plan form. Closed fields; common; hedges and fences; 'Dogkennel' and 'Rookery' woods, plantations, trees; paddocks; roads and turnpike; gates and stiles; ponds and fishponds; 'Rosley Hill'; gardens; 'Cherry Ground'.
Border of 1 narrow band with 1 broad band on inside; title top left in a cartouche of 1 narrow band with 1 broad band on inside; compass top right showing 16 points. Table middle right giving field names, acreages and land use.
Pencil notes. Later notes above table: 'This Map belongs to HR Evans Ely', and in red ink: 'The Red numbers are taken from the Tithe Commutation Map'. Drawn c. 1784 when farm leased by Bishop of Ely to Richard Tattersall [Manning, 1988 and 1989].

Ely Trinity – [c. 1798] – EYT79801 – C L C ACC.1985/5
No. 10. 18. and 21.
Surveyor: [Joseph Freeman?]; **Scale bar** 10–0–100 feet (= 3 5/8in.), 1:364; **Size:** (ii) 18 1/4 x 14 7/8in.; **Top** is NE; Manuscript(i), paper, coloured.
c. 1a. at TL542807, bounded by Nutholt ['Nuthole'] Lane in NE and Market ['Jail'] Street in SW.
Names of areas, roads and neighbouring owners. Buildings shown in plan form and include houses, 'hot House', stable, 'cart lodge' and 'cow lodges'. Roads; dimensions of areas; yards; gardens.
Title on left; scale at bottom. Some walls coloured blue.
One of a set of plans of tenements belonging to Clare College, Cambridge, and probably accompanies the valuation by Joseph Freeman of the tenements on 26 April 1798 [CLC Safe B:56/11]. See also EYM79801–6 and EYT79802–3.

Ely Trinity – [c. 1798] – EYT79802 – C L C ACC.1985/5
No. 17 and 19.
Surveyor: [Joseph Freeman?]; **Scale bar** 10–0–100 feet (= 3 11/16in.), 1:358; **Size:** (ii) 14 3/4 x 17 5/8in.; **Top** is SE; Manuscript(i), paper, coloured.

c. 1a. bounded by Broad Street in NW; no. 17 is at
TL543800 and no. 19 is at TL543798.

Names of areas, roads and neighbouring owners.
Tenements shown in plan form. Roads; dimensions of
areas; yard; gardens.

Title top left; scale bottom left. Some walls coloured
blue.

Plan is one of a set; see EYT79801 for owner, surveyor
and date. See also EYM79801–6 and EYT79803.

Ely Trinity – [c. 1798] – EYT79803 – C L C
ACC.1985/5
No. 22. and B.

Surveyor: [Joseph Freeman?]; **Scale bar** 10–0–100
feet (= 3 5/8in.), 1:364; **Size:** (ii) 14 3/4 x 16 3/4in.;
Top is SE; Manuscript(i), paper, coloured.

c. 2r. at TL544798, bounded by 'Navigable Cut' in SE.

Names of areas and neighbouring owners. Buildings
shown in plan form and include stable, drying shed and
work shops. Tree; 'Navigable Cut'; dimensions of areas;
yards; 'Read fence'; garden.

Title top left; scale bottom right. Water and some walls
coloured blue.

Pencil notes. Plan is one of a set; see EYT79801 for
owner, surveyor and date. See also EYM79801–6 and
EYT79802.

Ely Trinity – 1807 – EYT80701 – EDR CC.12396
A Plan of Northney Grange Farm. 1807.

Scale: 1:3,840; **Size:** (i) 23 5/8 x 17 1/8in.; **Top** is
NE; Manuscript(i), parchment, coloured.

Nornea Farm, TL574780, and 372a.0r.1p. bounded by
Soham Parish in SE.

Names of neighbouring land. Farm buildings and mill
shown in plan form. Closed fields; trees; acreages; roads
and gates; watercourses and bridge.

Border of 1 broad band with 1 narrow band on inside; title top left in a rectangular cartouche of 2 narrow bands;
compass top right showing 4 points. Table bottom right
giving acreages and whether land is exempt or to be taxed.
Water coloured blue, trees coloured green, red lines.

Pencil and ink notes. Land owned by Dean and Chapter
of Ely.

F

Fen Ditton – [Ante 1731/2] – FDI73201 – YAS DD5/28
A Map of Part of Ditton ...

Scale bar 0–70 poles (= 4 1/4in.), 1:3,261; **Size:** (i)
21 3/4 x 32 1/2in.; **Top** is ESE; Manuscript(i), parchment,
coloured.

Ditton Hall, TL482603, and c. 840a. bounded by River
Cam in W, Teversham Parish in E and 'The Boults' in S.

Names of fields and roads. Buildings shown in plan form
and include Ditton Hall, church, mill, farm buildings and
'Boulin house'. Open fields showing all strips; closes;
fen; trees; hedges; roads; footpaths; gates; stiles; watercourses; ponds; orchard; holts and 'Town Holt'; 'cony
warren'; 'Loden-Well'.

Border of 2 narrow bands; title top left in a 1/4in.-wide
rectangular cartouche with a leaf pattern; black and white
scale bar bottom right; compass rose centre top showing 8
red and blue points with a yellow, blue and black fleur-de-
lys. Table at bottom giving tenants, field names and
acreages: '... Tenants of the several Houses Close

Ozier~Holts &c in the Parish of Ditton the red Letters and
Figures referring to those in the Map.' Roads coloured
yellow, buildings coloured red, water coloured blue, fields
outlined in green, common land coloured green, gates
coloured red.

Writing very feint. Probably drawn when owner was Sir
William Willys, 6th Bart [succeeded 1726, died 1732; *EDB*,
572]. The Rector, John Davis, was probably a tenant to
land on FDI73203 and died in 1731/2 [Venn, I, 2, 16]. See
also FDI73202–4. Photographs at CRO TR626/P1; terrier
c. 1735 at CRO R85/85.

Fen Ditton – [Ante 1731/2] – FDI73202 – YAS DD5/28
A Second [Part] of Ditton [Parish] ... Qui Water.

Scale: 1:3,300; **Size:** (i) 24 1/4 x 28 1/8in.; **Top** is
NNE; Manuscript(i), parchment, coloured.

Quy Mill, TL509599, and c. 790a. bounded by Stow cum
Quy Parish in E, Horningsea Parish in N and Teversham
Parish in S.

Names of fields and roads. Quy Mill shown in perspective. Open fields showing all strips; marsh; hedges; roads;
footpaths; gates; stiles; watercourses.

Border of 2 narrow bands; title top right in an oval
baroque cartouche 1/2in. wide; compass rose bottom left
showing 8 red and blue points with a yellow, blue and black
fleur-de-lys. Table bottom right giving tenants, field
names and acreages: 'A Table ...' Roads coloured yellow,
buildings coloured red, water coloured blue, fields outlined
in green, common land coloured green, gates coloured red.

Writing very feint. See FDI73201 for details of date and
owner. See also FDI73203–4. Photographs at CRO
TR626/P1; terrier c. 1735 at CRO R85/85.

Fen Ditton – [Ante 1731/2] – FDI73203 – YAS DD5/28
A Third Part of Ditton Parish being the Low Fenn.

Scale: 1:3,351; **Size:** (i) 18 5/8 x 33 15/16in.; **Top**
is E; Manuscript(i), parchment, coloured.

Honey Hill, TL503605, and c. 510a. bounded by
Horningsea Parish in W and N and Stow cum Quy Parish in
E, and including 4a.2r.24p. in Horningsea Parish.

Names of tenants and roads. Almshouses in Horningsea
Parish and cottages shown in plan form. Closed fields; fen;
acreages; banks; roads; gates; watercourse; ditches.

Border of 1 broad band with 1 narrow band on either side;
title centre top in a baroque cartouche; compass rose centre
bottom showing 8 red and blue points with a yellow, blue
and black fleur-de-lys. Table bottom right giving field
names and acreages: 'The whole Contents of Ditton Parish
Land and parts adjoining.'

At top of sheet containing FDI73204 (gives scale). See
FDI73201 for details of date and owner. See also
FDI73202. Photographs at CRO TR626/P1; terrier c. 1735
at CRO R85/85.

Fen Ditton – [Ante 1731/2] – FDI73204 – YAS DD5/28
A Fourth Part of Ditton Parish.

Scale bar 10–0–100 poles (= 6 1/2in.), 1:3,351;
Size: (i) 15 x 33 5/8in.; **Top** is ESE; Manuscript(i),
parchment, coloured.

Biggin Farm, TL487617, and c. 320a. in Fen Ditton and
Horningsea parishes bounded by Milton and Chesterton
parishes in W and Horningsea Parish in E.

Names of fields, roads and tenants. Farm buildings,
cottages and 'Red House' shown in plan form, windmill
shown in perspective. Open fields showing all strips;

closes; common; meadow; fen; trees; acreages; hedges; roads; footpaths; gates; watercourse; 'The Old Orchard'; 'The Hu[ ]e'; boundary between Fen Ditton and Horningsea parishes.

Border of 1 broad band with 1 narrow band on either side; title in centre in a baroque cartouche; black and white scale bar right of title; compass rose bottom right showing 8 red and blue points with a yellow, blue and black fleur-de-lys. Table on left giving tenants, field names and acreages: 'These Furlongs are in the Second Map', 'A Continuation of Ditton Parish Land.'

At bottom of sheet containing FDI73203. See FDI73201 for details of date and owner. See also FDI73202. Photographs at CRO TR626/P1; terrier c. 1735 at CRO R85/85.

Fen Ditton – 1796 – FDI79601 – CUL MS Plans R.b.9

Plan of an Estate at Fen Ditton in the County of Cambridge. The Property of The Revd Mr Jenyns Surveyed in 1796.

Surveyor: [Joseph Freeman?]; **Scale bar** 5–0–20 chains (= 4 3/16in.), 1:4,728; **Size:** (ii) 35 3/4 x 54 3/4in.; **Top** is N; Manuscript(i), paper mounted on cloth, coloured.

'Tabrams House', TL487492, and 421a.1r.2p. bounded by Horningsea Parish in N, road to Horningsea in W and Quy Water in E.

Names of fields, roads and neighbouring owners. Houses, farm buildings and Quy Mill shown in plan form. Open fields showing owner's strips; closes; common; trees; waste, marsh and sheep walk; meadow; state of cultivation shown by colour; roads and footpaths; Fleam Dyke ['High Ditch']; watercourses; hedges and fences; pond; gardens; 'Windmill hill'.

Title bottom right in an oval rococo cartouche; scale middle bottom; compass top right showing 4 points. Table on right giving tenants, field names, acreages and land use. Buildings coloured red, roads and strips in open fields coloured brown, water coloured blue, grass coloured green, and land let to Mr Bond coloured yellow.

3 insets top left showing holdings of common land. Owner's 1st names were George Leonard [LG, 1,382]. In style of Joseph Freeman.

Fen Ditton – [1809] – FDI80901 – B L O Johnson.b.62(5), CRO 65/04, L42/1, L75/10, CUL Maps.PSQ.18.457

Fen Ditton. Lot 13.

Auctioneer: John Swan; **Engraver:** F. Hodson; **Scale:** 1:9,748; **Size:** (ii) 8 3/4 x 11 1/8in.; **Top** is N; Engraved, paper, uncoloured.

Ditton Hall, TL481602, and 209a.0r.23p. bounded by River Cam in NW, Barnwell Parish in W and road to Newmarket in S.

Names of parishes and neighbouring owners. Ditton Hall, cottage and blacksmith's shop shown in plan form. Closed fields showing owner's land; roads and footpaths; watercourses and ponds; garden and orchard identified on particulars of sale.

Title at top; compass middle right showing 4 points.

Accompanies: 'Particulars and conditions of sale of a ... freehold And small part Copyhold Estate situate in the several parishes of Barnwell, Fen Ditton, Horningsea, Teversham, Histon and Waterbeach, in the County of Cambridge ... will be sold by auction ... November, 1809'.

On dorse: 'Particulars of the late Mr Panton's Estate at Barnwell'. Particulars of sale give lot number, present occupant, state of cultivation, land tax, tithes and common rights. Scale given on map of land in Barnwell Parish, Cambridge. This is Plate 9. Mr Panton's 1st name was Thomas [Venn, I, 3, 303]. See also FDI80902–4, HIS80901 and HRN80901–6.

Fen Ditton – [1809] – FDI80902 – B L O Johnson.b.62(5), CRO 65/04, L42/1, L75/10, CUL Maps.PSQ.18.457

Fen Ditton and Horningsea. Lots 15 and 16.

Auctioneer: John Swan; **Engraver:** F. Hodson; **Scale:** 1:9,748; **Size:** (ii) 9 3/8 x 14in.; **Top** is N; Engraved, paper, coloured.

Quy Mill, TL509599, and 180a.3r.10p. in plots in N of parish bounded by Stow cum Quy Parish in E and Horningsea Parish in W, in SW of parish between High Street and road to Newmarket, 2 plots N of High Street, and 1 plot at Honey Hill in Horningsea Parish.

Names of parishes and neighbouring owners. Farmhouse, farm buildings and Quy Mill shown in plan form. Closed fields showing owner's land; roads and watercourses.

Title middle top; compass top left showing 4 points. Boundary between Horningsea and Fen Ditton parishes shown in yellow.

Accompanies particulars of sale of Thomas Panton's estate in 1809; see FDI80901 for details. This is Plate 10. See also FDI80903–4, HIS80901 and HRN80901–6.

Fen Ditton – [1809] – FDI80903 – B L O Johnson.b.62(5), CRO 65/04, L42/1, L75/10, CUL Maps.PSQ.18.457

Fen Ditton. Lots 14, 27, 28, 29, 30, 31, 32, 33 and 34.

Auctioneer: John Swan; **Engraver:** F. Hodson; **Scale:** 1:9,748; **Size:** (ii) 11 x 8 7/8in.; **Top** is N; Engraved, paper, uncoloured.

Plough Inn, TL481606, and 140a.3r.0p. bounded by Field Lane in N, road to Horningsea in E, River Cam in W and High Street in S; and land further E to S of High Street bounded by Teversham Parish in S.

Names of neighbouring owners. Farm buildings, cottages, 'Plough Public House' and blacksmith's shop shown in plan form. Closed fields showing owner's land; roads and footpaths; watercourses; gardens.

Title middle top; compass middle right showing 4 points.

Accompanies particulars of sale of Thomas Panton's estate in 1809; see FDI80901 for details. This is Plate 11. See also FDI80902,4, HIS80901 and HRN80901–6.

Fen Ditton – [1809] – FDI80904 – B L O Johnson.b.62(5), CRO 65/04, L42/1, L75/10, CUL Maps.PSQ.18.457

Fen Ditton. Lots 16, 17, 18, 19, 20, 21, 22, 23, 24 and 25.

Auctioneer: John Swan; **Engraver:** F. Hodson; **Scale:** 1:9,748; **Size:** (ii) 8 5/8 x 11 1/8in.; **Top** is N; Engraved, paper, uncoloured.

102a.2r.21p. in TL4759 and TL4859, bounded by Barnwell Parish in W, Teversham Parish in E and road from Cambridge to Newmarket in N.

Names of parishes and neighbouring owners. 'Globe Public House' and outbuildings shown in plan form.

Closed fields showing owner's land; roads and footpaths; watercourses including mill-stream; toll bar on road from Cambridge to Newmarket; garden, yard and site of water corn mill identified on particulars of sale.

Title centre top; compass below title showing 4 points.

Accompanies particulars of sale of Thomas Panton's estate in 1809; see FDI80901 for details. This is Plate 12. See also FDI80902-3, HIS80901 and HRN80901-6.

Fen Drayton – 1792 – FDY79201 – SJC MPS 222

A Plan of Lands in the Parish of Fen Drayton; belonging to St. Johns the Evangelists College, in the University of Cambridge. Rt Daintree Lessee Surveyed in 1792.

Surveyor: [Joseph Freeman]; **Scale:** 1:4,820; **Size:** (ii) 22 1/4 x 28 1/4in.; **Top** is NE; Manuscript(i), parchment, coloured.

Fen Drayton Church, TL339681, and 70a.2r.26p. in strips scattered in whole parish except for N, though extending to River Ouse in far NE. Also 5 strips in N of Conington Parish.

Names of fields, parishes, roads and neighbouring owners. Church shown in plan form. Open fields showing owner's strips; closes; meadow; roads; watercourses and ditches; 'Meadow gates' and gates; hedges; bridges; site of mill.

Border on left and bottom of 1 broad and 1 narrow band; title top left. Table on right giving field names and acreages for land with a renewable lease and with an 'increase at rack rent'. Strips coloured red and blue, river coloured blue.

Cut from a lease. Ink note of land in Bassingbourn Parish. Accompanying terriers surveyed by Joseph Freeman at SJC D31.41 and D31.42. Photograph at 1:7,670 at CRO TR869/P17.

Fordham – [1656] – FOR65601 – CRO

['Comonable houses Cottages Yards Gardens Orchards Tofts Crofts meadows pastures meares mearegoundes Fengrounds Lakes Hoults Groves hempegrounds and Arable Lands in Fordham Soham and Barway And all Wasts Moores Fennes Comons Intercomons therto belonging being within the precincts of the Lordship or Manor of Soham in the County of Cambridge being parcel of the Duchie of Lancaster and part of the possessions of Thos Chichelie Esqre together with the Adventurers grounds being within the same precincts'.] A. [Mill and land to S.]

Surveyor: [William Palmer]; **The Scale** of Perches 20 to one inch, Scale bar 0–80 perches (= 4in.), 1:3,960; **Size:** (ii) 20 x 14 7/8in.; **Top** is E; Manuscript(ii), tracing paper, coloured.

Fordham Mill, TL631703, and c. 190a. bounded by mill-stream in E and Water Lane in N, and crossed by Market Street in W.

Names of fields, owners, tenants and roads. Houses and mill shown in perspective. Open fields showing all strips; closes; acreages; roads and footpaths; watercourses and bridge.

Yellow and pink scale bar bottom left; compass rose top left showing 8 yellow, blue and brown points. Fields outlined in green, yellow, pink and blue, water coloured blue, coloured lettering.

In volume of tracings of maps of the manor of Soham; title, surveyor and date given on front flyleaf, and note: 'Copied by W.A.G. 1860'. See also FOR65602-7 and SOH65602-12.

Fordham – [1656] – FOR65602 – CRO

B. [N of Water Lane in Fordham village.]

Surveyor: [William Palmer]; **Scale:** 1:3,960; **Size:** (ii) 20 x 14 7/8in.; **Top** is SE; Manuscript(ii), tracing paper, coloured.

c. 380a. in TL6270, bounded by River Snail in E, Market Street in W and Water Lane in S, and crossed by Carter ['Counter'] Street in N.

Names of fields, owners and tenants. Cottages shown in perspective. Closes; acreages; roads and footpaths; watercourses.

Compass bottom left showing 2 points with a yellow decorated N with a crown and 'Robert H. Peck' in ribbon at bottom of N. Fields outlined in green, yellow, pink and blue, water coloured blue, coloured lettering.

In volume of tracings made in 1860; title, surveyor, date and copyist given on front flyleaf [see FOR65601, which gives scale]. See also FOR65603-7 and SOH65602-12.

Fordham – [1656] – FOR65603 – CRO

C. [NW of Fordham village in 'Fordham Hales'.]

Surveyor: [William Palmer]; **Scale:** 1:3,960; **Size:** (ii) 20 x 14 7/8in.; **Top** is S; Manuscript(ii), tracing paper, coloured.

c. 260a. in TL6171, crossed by road to Wicken.

Names of fields, roads, owners and tenants. Open fields showing all strips; closes; acreages; roads and watercourses.

Compass top right showing 2 points with a yellow decorated N with a crown and 'Robert H. Peck' in ribbon at bottom of N. Fields outlined in green, yellow, pink and blue, water coloured blue, coloured lettering.

In volume of tracings made in 1860; title, surveyor, date and copyist given on front flyleaf [see FOR65601, which gives scale]. See also FOR65602,4-7 and SOH65602-12.

Fordham – [1656] – FOR65604 – CRO

E. [W of Fordham village.]

Surveyor: [William Palmer]; **Scale:** 1:3,960; **Size:** (ii) 20 x 14 7/8in.; **Top** is SE; Manuscript(ii), tracing paper, coloured.

c. 300a. in TL6271, crossed by Market Street and road to Wicken.

Names of fields, roads, owners and tenants. Open fields showing all strips; acreages; roads and footpaths.

Compass rose top left showing 8 yellow, blue and brown points. Fields outlined in green, yellow, pink and blue, coloured lettering.

In volume of tracings made in 1860; title, surveyor, date and copyist given on front flyleaf [see FOR65601, which gives scale]. See also FOR65602-3,5-7 and SOH65602-12.

Fordham – [1656] – FOR65605 – CRO

F. [SW of Fordham village.]

Surveyor: [William Palmer]; **Scale:** 1:3,960; **Size:** (ii) 20 x 14 7/8in.; **Top** is SW; Manuscript(ii), tracing paper, coloured.

c. 350a. in W of TL6270 SW of village, crossed by Market Street and road to Burwell.

Names of fields, roads, owners and tenants. Open fields showing all strips; closes; meadow; acreages; roads and footpaths.

Compass top left showing 2 plain points. Fields outlined in green, yellow, pink and blue, coloured lettering.

In volume of tracings made in 1860; title, surveyor, date and copyist given on front flyleaf [see FOR65601, which gives scale]. See also FOR65602–4,6–7 and SOH65602–12.

Fordham – [1656] – FOR65606 – CRO
G. [NW of Fordham village.]
Surveyor: [William Palmer]; **Scale:** 1:3,960; **Size:** (ii) 20 x 14 7/8in.; **Top** is SE; Manuscript(ii), tracing paper, coloured.
c. 320a. in TL6171, bounded by Soham Parish in W and road to Wicken in S.
Names of fields, roads, owners and tenants. Open fields showing all strips; closes; acreages; roads and footpaths.
Compass centre top showing 2 plain points. Fields outlined in green, yellow, pink and blue, coloured lettering.
In volume of tracings made in 1860; title, surveyor, date and copyist given on front flyleaf [see FOR65601, which gives scale]. See also FOR65602–5,7 and SOH65602–12.

Fordham – [1656] – FOR65607 – CRO
H. [Far W of Fordham Parish.]
Surveyor: [William Palmer]; **Scale:** 1:3,960; **Size:** (ii) 20 x 14 7/8in.; **Top** is SW; Manuscript(ii), tracing paper, coloured.
c. 300a. in TL6060 in far W of parish, bounded by Burwell Parish in S and Wicken Parish in E.
Names of fields, roads, owners and tenants. Open fields showing all strips; acreages; roads and footpaths; watercourses.
Compass top left showing 2 plain points. Fields outlined in green, yellow, pink and blue, water coloured blue, coloured lettering.
In volume of tracings made in 1860; title, surveyor, date and copyist given on front flyleaf [see FOR65601, which gives scale]. See also FOR65602–6 and SOH65602–12.

Fordham – 1795 – FOR79501 – SJC MPS 25
A Plan of the Manor of Bassingbourn, at Fordham; in the County of Cambridge. belonging to St. Johns the Evangelists College, in the University of Cambridge. Surveyed in the Year. 1795.
Surveyor: [Joseph Freeman?]; **Scale bar** 5–0–20 chains (= 3 1/4in.), 1:6,092; **Size:** (i) 26 1/8 x 30 3/16in.; **Top** is W; Manuscript(i), parchment, coloured.
Fordham Church, TL633707, and 195a.3r.29p. in strips scattered throughout parish except for far W and N.
Names of fields, roads and neighbouring owners. Church, buildings in village, 'Mr Noble's' house and barns shown in plan form. Open fields showing owner's strips; closes; pasture closes indicated by symbol representing tufts of grass; roads and footpaths; watercourses; hedges; site of mill; 'windmill bridge'; sand pits; common, meadow and fen adjoining map.
Border of 1 broad and 1 narrow band; title bottom right with decorative lettering; scale beneath title; compass top left showing 4 points. Table on left giving field names, acreages and state of cultivation for open and inclosed land. Arable coloured brown, pasture coloured green, buildings coloured red, hedges coloured green.
In style of Joseph Freeman, who surveyed for the College in the 1790s. Photograph at 1:8,562 at CRO TR869/P18.

Fordham – [c. 1809] – FOR80901 – CRO R55/28/16/1
Plan of a Freehold Estate, called The Block Farm, situated in the Parish of Fordham, and County of Cambridge the Property of [Francis Glossop?]
Surveyor: Thomas Hogg; **Scale bar** 1–0–20 chains (= 5 1/4in.), 1:3,168; **Size:** (i) 24 7/8 x 31 3/4in.; **Top** is NNE; Manuscript(i), paper, coloured.
Block Farm, TL601709, and 205a.2r.0p. in W of parish bounded by Soham Parish in N and Burwell Parish in S and W.
Names of neighbouring fields and owners. Farm buildings and cottage shown in plan form. Closed fields showing owner's land; state of cultivation shown by colour; roads; 'New River'; gates; dam and site of pumping engine; osiers and pightle identified on table.
Border of 1 broad band with 2 narrow bands on either side; title top left with decorative lettering; scale middle bottom; compass middle left showing 4 plain points with a decorated N. Table bottom right giving field names and acreages. Water coloured blue, farm coloured pink, arable coloured brown, pasture coloured green.
Pencil note of road or path and addition to table of acreages. Hogg's practice was at 34 Castle Street, Holborn from 1807 to 1809 and possibly until 1814 [Eden H433]; map gives this address and was probably drawn in 1809, when parish was inclosed and farm allotted to Francis Glossop; inclosure award is dated 1820.

Fordham – 1809 – FOR80902 – SJC MPS 289
Plan (As Copied from the Award Map of the Parish) of Fordham, Cambs; – The Estate of the Master, Fellows, & Scholars of St John's College, In the University of Cambridge.
Surveyor: [Alexander Watford jr]; **Scale bar** 5–0–20 chains (= 4 1/8in.), 1:4,800; **Size:** (i) 20 x 14 11/16in.; **Top** is NE; Manuscript(iv), paper mounted on cloth, coloured.
190a.3r.1p. N of TL634707, junction of roads from Fordham to Isleham, Soham and Mildenhall, and land W of road to Isleham.
Names of neighbouring owners and roads. Cottages shown in plan form. Closed fields showing owner's land; trees and hedges; acreages of some plots; roads and footpaths; right of way; watercourses; responsibility for boundaries.
Border of 2 narrow bands with decorated corners; title top right; scale bottom right; compass top left showing 4 points. Table bottom left giving acreages and tenure. Roads coloured brown, buildings coloured red, water coloured blue, old inclosures coloured blue/green, old inclosures purchased from Rev. J.B. Isaacson coloured yellow.
Alexander Watford was inclosure surveyor for Fordham.

Fordham – [1821] – FOR82101 – TCC Box 23 Fordham 16a–b
[Fordham rectory lands leased by Bishop of Ely to William Dunn Gardner.]
Scale: 1:4,510; **Size:** (i) 17 3/16 x 16 3/8in.; **Top** is ESE; Manuscript(i), parchment, coloured.
Fordham Church, TL623707, and 232a.3r.15p. to N, bounded by roads to Isleham in W and to Mildenhall in SE.
Names of roads and neighbouring owners. Church shown in perspective. Closed fields showing owner's land; acreages; roads; hedges.

Border of 2 red lines. Roads coloured brown, land coloured green.

On lease: 'Dated 6th January 1821 Fordham Rectory Lands A. The Right Revd Bowyer Edwd Lord Bishop of Ely to Wllm Dunn Gardner Esqre Lease for three Lives'. Counterpart lease, TCC Box 23 Fordham 16b, has a compass top right showing 4 plain points with a feathered tail.

Fordham – [1821] – FOR82102 – TCC Box 23 Fordham 17a–b

[Fordham rectory lands leased by Bishop of Ely to William Dunn Gardner.]

Scale: 1:5,080; **Size:** (i) 8 7/8 x 13 5/8in.; **Top** is WNW; Manuscript(i), parchment, coloured.

129a.1r.25p. in TL6367, bounded by Snailwell Parish in E, Exning Parish [Suffolk] in S and road to Newmarket in W.

Names of roads and neighbouring owners. Closed fields showing owner's land; acreages; roads and watercourses; hedges; 'Allotment for Stone and Gravel'; 'Bayleys Pen received of St Johns College'.

Border of 2 red lines; compass centre top showing 4 plain points with a feathered tail. Roads coloured brown, water coloured blue, fields coloured yellow, hedges coloured green.

On lease: 'Dated 6th January 1821 Fordham Rectory Lands B The Right Revd Bowyer Edwd Lord Bishop of Ely to Willm Dunn Gardner Esqre Lease for three Lives'. Counterpart lease, TCC Box 23 Fordham 17b, colours fields green.

Fordham – [1826] – FOR82601 – TCC Box 23 Fordham 20a–b

[Fordham rectory land leased by Bishop of Ely to William Dunn Gardner.]

Scale: 1:4,510; **Size:** (i) 17 5/8 x 16 11/16in.; **Top** is ESE; Manuscript(i), parchment, coloured.

Fordham Church, TL633707, and 232a.3r.15p. to N, bounded by roads to Isleham in W and to Mildenhall in SE.

Names of roads and neighbouring owners. Church shown in perspective. Closed fields showing owner's land; acreages; roads; hedges.

Border of 2 red lines; compass top right showing 4 plain points. Land coloured blue.

On lease: 'Dated 25th April 1826 Fordham Rectory Lands A The Rt Revd Bowyer Edward Lord Bishop of Ely to Willm Dunn Gardner Esqr Lease for Three Lives'. Counterpart lease at TCC Box 23 Fordham 20b.

Fordham – [1826] – FOR82602 – TCC Box 23 Fordham 21a–b

[Fordham rectory land leased by Bishop of Ely to William Dunn Gardner.]

Scale: 1:5,080; **Size:** (i) 9 1/2 x 13 1/8in.; **Top** is WNW; Manuscript(i), parchment, coloured.

129a.1r.25p. in TL6367, bounded by Snailwell Parish in E, Exning Parish [Suffolk] in S and road to Newmarket in W.

Names of roads and neighbouring owners. Closed fields showing owner's land; acreages; roads and watercourses; hedges; 'Allotment for stone and gravel'; 'Bayleys Penn received of St Johns College'.

Border of 2 red lines; compass top left showing 4 plain points with a feathered tail. Roads coloured brown, water coloured blue, land coloured yellow.

On lease: 'Dated 25th April 1826 Fordham Rectory Lands B. The Right Reverend Bowyer Edward Lord Bishop of Ely to Wm Dunn Gardner Esqre Lease for Three Lives'. Counterpart lease at TCC Box 23 Fordham 21b.

Foxton – [c. 1795] – FOX79501 – CLC Safe B:58/1

Lands at Foxton Clare Hall.

Surveyor: [Joseph Freeman?]; **Scale:** 1:1,700; **Size:** (ii) 12 x 14 1/2in.; **Top** is E?; Manuscript(i), paper, uncoloured.

Foxton Church, TL412483, and 4a.3r.21p. bounded by Shepreth ['Shepherds'] Brook in W.

Names of fields and neighbouring owners. Church shown in plan form. Closed fields; acreages; roads and watercourses.

Title bottom left.

Ink notes on right. Survey lines marked. May accompany valuation by Joseph Freeman dated 1795 in same bundle of documents.

Foxton – [1830] – FOX83001 – EDR CC.12328

Foxton.

Surveyor: [Joseph Jackson]; **Scale:** 1:5,210; **Size:** (ii) 8 1/2 x 12 1/2in.; **Top** is NE; Manuscript(ii), paper, uncoloured.

Foxton Church, TL412483, and 19a.0r.5p. to S.

Names of roads and owners. Farm and church shown in plan form. Closed fields; acreages; roads and turnpike; footpaths; responsibility for boundaries; reasons for allotments.

Title top right; compass bottom left showing 8 points.

Red ink notes to footpaths: 'foot Way Stopped up'. Copied from map by Joseph Jackson which accompanied 1830 inclosure award, shows land allotted to Dean and Chapter of Ely. Numbers on plots refer to inclosure award. Tracing of this copy shows neighbouring owners.

Foxton – [1830] – FOX83002 – HERO 61068

Foxton, Cambs.

Surveyor: [J[ohn] Wilding]; **Scale:** Six Chains to an Inch, 1:4,752; **Size:** (i) 4 1/4 x 5 1/2in.; **Top** is N; Manuscript(i), paper, coloured.

7a.1r.8p. in S of parish, bounded by road from Fowlmere to Foxton in E and Fowlmere Parish in W.

Names of roads and neighbouring owners. Closed fields; state of cultivation shown by colour; acreages; roads and watercourses.

Border of 1 broad band with 1 narrow band on inside; title at top; scale at bottom of whole sheet. Fields outlined in green and coloured in brown stripes, water coloured blue, roads coloured brown with a red edge.

Top right of p.10 of volume: 'Maps of the Estates of Wm Wilshere Esq in Herts, Beds, Cambs & Essex 1830 J. Willding, Surveyor &c, Willian'. Summary of tenants and acreages at back of volume. Surveyor's 1st name was John [HERO].

Fulbourn – [1813] – FUL81301 – GLC H1/ST/E22/1

Farm Yard & Buildings on The Hospital Farm at Fulbourn.

Surveyor: [J[oseph] Beevers]; **Scale:** 1:296; **Size:** (ii) 14 3/4 x 12 1/8in.; Manuscript(i), paper, uncoloured.

c. 1r. in Fulbourn Parish.

Names of buildings. Buildings shown in plan form and include house, barn, stable, 'cart lodge', granary, 'Waggon shed', cottage, 2 lean-tos, 'Brew House', 'Wash House', kitchen and privy. Dimensions of areas; farmyard.

Title in centre of farm. Table top left giving buildings, heights of walls, building materials.

Pencil notes on table of insurance values. Pencil note on left: 'To be insured at 2000£'. Accompanied by CHE81301, which is signed and attached to front of policy book for property insured at the Hand in Hand Fire Office. See also COM81301, which gives surveyor's 1st name. Land owned by St Thomas' Hospital, London.

Fulbourn – [Post 1814] – FUL81401 – C R O R51/19/24/26

Plan of 10 Cottages & gardens at Fulbourn.
Scale bar 0–35 feet (= 3 3/16in.), 1:132; **Size:** (ii) 17 3/4 x 15 3/4in.; **Top** is E; Manuscript(i), paper, uncoloured.

c. 2r. in NW of village NW of church, TL515565, bounded by northern road to Cherry Hinton in W and Fen Drove Way in NE.

Names of buildings and neighbouring owners. Cottages, bath house, privy and pigsties shown in plan form. Closed field; roads; dimensions of plots; site of oven.

Title middle bottom; scale left of title; compass bottom left showing 4 points.

Draft map, pencil notes give instructions for drawing fair copy. Drawn after 1814 inclosure award.

Fulbourn – [1825] – FUL82501 – QCC 355 A15, B15

Estate at Fulbourn In The County of Cambridge.
Surveyor: [Alexander Watford jr]; **Scale bar** 0–30 chains (= 5in.), 1:4,752; **Size:** (i) 25 3/8 x 18 15/16in.; **Top** is NNW; Manuscript(ii), paper, coloured.

Queens' College Farm, TL521563, and 228a.3r.38p. in NE of parish NE of church, bounded by New Cut ['Public Drain'] in E and Little Wilbraham River in N.

Names of farm, fields, roads and neighbouring owners. Church shown in perspective, farm buildings shown in plan form. Closed fields showing owner's land; allotment on common and fen; wood and trees; hedges; acreages; roads and watercourses; garden, yard and pightle identified on table.

Border of 1 broad band with 1 narrow band on either side; title top left; scale bottom right; compass above scale showing 8 points. Table top left giving field names, acreages and land use. Roads coloured brown, water coloured blue, fields coloured yellow and green, farm buildings coloured red.

Pencil notes. On right of sheet, which also contains a map of Great Eversden [GTE82501], and in volume drawn in 1825: 'Plans of the Several Estates in England and Wales belonging to the President and Fellows of the College of St Margaret and St Bernard commonly called Queen's College in the University of Cambridge Delineated from Authentic Documents in the possession of the said President and Fellows and from actual Surveys taken By their most obedient and obliged Servant Alexr Watford'. Title page drawn by James Richardson [Watford's nephew]. This is the Bursar's copy; 2nd, finer, copy [the Master's copy] at QCC 355 B15 measures 24 1/2 x 18 1/4in. and is drawn on parchment. Top points N. Border 7/16in. wide of a central blue band with 1 broad band on either side, title has gothic lettering, scale at bottom, compass on left. Table bottom right and has red lines. Fields coloured green or with brown and yellow stripes, roads have red/brown edges. Positive

photostat of this copy at 1:8,000 at BL 1640.(27). Positive and negative photostats of QCC 355 A15 at CUL Maps.bb.53(1).95.72 at 1:5,431 measure 22 1/8 x 16 5/8in.

Fulbourn – 1831 – FUL83101 – CUL Maps.PSQ.18.88

Plan of a farm at Fulbourn, Cambs: containing fifty~six Acres and a half; For sale by Auction, by E. Smith & Son, 1831.
Auctioneer: Elliot Smith; **Lithographer:** W[illiam] Metcalfe; **Scale:** 1:4,000; **Size:** (i) 7 7/16 x 12 11/16in.; **Top** is W; Lithograph, paper, coloured.

Barnsbury House ['Barnsbury Farm'], TL516566, and 56a.2r.0p. in NW of village N of Fulbourn Old Drift ['To Frog End'] and mostly E of Fen Drove Way ['Private Road'].

Names of neighbouring owners. Farm buildings shown in plan form, particulars of sale identify 2 barns, stable and 'cow lodge'. Closed fields; hedges; tenure; state of cultivation shown by colour and given in words; roads and footpaths; watercourses; responsibility for boundaries; garden identified on particulars of sale.

Border of 1 broad and 1 narrow band; title middle top; compass middle right showing 4 plain points. Roads coloured brown, water coloured blue, arable coloured red/brown, pasture coloured green.

Accompanies: 'Particulars and Conditions of Sale of a desirable small farm situate at Fulbourn, Cambridgeshire; which will be sold by auction ... December, 1831'. Lithographer's 1st name was William [CRO EPR CW 1825 WR C52:178].

G

Gamlingay – 1601/2 – GAM60201 – MCO 6.17.1

The description of the mannor of the Mertonage and the Mannor of Avenelles togeather with the freeholde and copyholde grovndes belonginge vnto the saide mannors or holden there on lieinge and beinge in the parishe of Gamlingay in in [sic.] the Countye of Cambridge drawne and made in the monethe of marche Anno domini 1601 Anno Eliz. xliiijo. which mannors are parcell of the possessions of the warden and schollers of the house or colledge of schollers of Merton in the vniversity of Oxford: Measured after xvj foote and an halfe to the pole and according to the proportion of xlviij perches to an ynche. Note that herein is sett downe in generall the proportion of the whole parishe (excepte the mannor of woodberry) and also the largeste grovndes as comons meadowes enclosures and the furlonges in the fieldes balkes and hades and highe wayes the severall landes are more perticulerly expressed in the plattes folllowinge [sic.].
Surveyor: [Thomas Langdon]; **Scale:** 1:9,504, Scale bar 0–200 perches (= 4 1/4in.), 1:9,318; **Size:** (i) 16 1/8 x 24 5/8in.; **Top** is N; Manuscript(i), paper, coloured.

Gamlingay Church, TL242521, and 3,255a. in all of parish except for far W.

Names of fields, meadows, woods and roads. Houses, farms, church, post mill and 'Mr St George's' house [John St George; *VCH*, 5, 107] shown in perspective. Open fields showing all strips; closes; common; meadow; wood and trees; heath; state of cultivation shown by colour; roads and footpaths; watercourses; bridges, with the bridge on 'Hatley waye' shown in perspective with 2 arches; fences; milestone ['The stone'].

Border of 1 broad brown band 5/16in. wide; title top left in a cartouche of orange, yellow, green and blue strapwork with coloured flowers, fruit [oranges, pears and grapes] and leaves; 3-dimensional blue and brown scale bar bottom left surmounted by yellow dividers and with a blue and brown ribbon; cardinal points stated in border. Fields coloured brown, balks and trees coloured green, houses have red roofs, water coloured blue/green, roads and fences coloured brown.

Numbers on plots suggest map originally accompanied by a terrier. At MCO 6.19.1–15 are copies by William Cole in 1767 ['by W.C. A:M:*Rector* of B*letchley* in Co:Bu*ckingham*'], with an uncoloured copy of no. 12 at front and a note: 'Ellen x Barker'. Note at back of acreages and on back cover: 'Mr Charles Roope to The Revd Robert Marsters [sic.]'. Maps use same colours as original but are more highly decorated with coats of arms and shields of Merton College, Robert Masters [Rector of Landbeach for whom copies were made], and neighbouring owners. William Cole describes these copies at BLM Add.5823 ff.147–52. 1st map is at 1:9,748 and measures 16 1/4 x 24 5/8in. On right are arms of Merton College with those of Mr Masters beneath. A set of copies by Charles Oakden in December 1827 is at MCO 6.18.1–15. At front is a note of acreages of the manors, and: 'A Note of Certain Lands appertaining unto the said Manors but which are not in their possession but either usurped by others or not used at all' [5a.0r.24p.]. 1st map measures 16 3/8 x 24 3/4in., shows buildings in plan form and colours grass and trees green, strips brown and water blue. There is no title or scale. Positive and negative photostats of original at CUL Maps.bb.53(1).96.3 and positive photostat at CRO TR274/P1, all at 1:11,310. See also GAM60202–16, surveyor given on GAM60203.

Gamlingay – [1601/2] – GAM60202 – MCO 6.17.2
[Land NW of Gamlingay Wood, owned by Merton College, Oxford.]
Surveyor: T[homas] Langdon; **Scale bar** 0–40 perches (= 3 3/8in.), 1:2,347; **Size:** (i) 18 1/8 x 24 7/16in.; **Top** is W; Manuscript(i), paper, coloured.

c. 250a. NW of crossroads in centre of village, TL238524, bounded by Tetworth Parish [Huntingdonshire] in NW and common land in W.

Names of fields, owners, tenants of manor land, woods and some features. Houses and farm buildings shown in perspective. Open fields showing all strips; closes; common; wood; tenure; state of cultivation shown by colour; acreages; roads and footpaths; 'spittle pitte'; 'Crosse tree'.

Border of 5/16in.-wide brown band; 3-dimensional green and brown scale bar middle bottom surmounted by brown dividers; cardinal points stated in border. Fields coloured brown, trees and balks coloured green, closes outlined in yellow, green and blue, Merton land written on in red, houses have red roofs.

Top right in a cartouche with a brown border and blue, green, brown and red strapwork: 'Note that in theis descriptions the haire colored lines doe represente the landes in the fielde that are arable and the greene lines doe represente the leaes balkes hades and meadows all which are sett ovt in the same forme nomber and proportion of measure as they are fovnde to contei*en* on which are also written the names of the tenauntes or holders thereof together with the contentes of acres of the seuerall percelles. wherein it is to be noted that when as ijo names are found written on one

parcell the former is the name of the owner the latter is the name of the farmor in whose occupation it is. And whereas there is on the perticuler landes A twofolde contente the former of them is sett downe according to the comon estimation and the other is theire contente according to the statute measure. vidz xvj foote & an halfe to the pole'. Numbers on fields suggest map originally accompanied by a terrier. Copy drawn by William Cole in 1767 at MCO 6.19.2 measures 18 x 24 7/16in. Top left is a shield with arms of Walter de Merton and on right is a large tree with flowers underneath, and hanging from the branches another shield with arms of Robert Masters. Copy drawn by Charles Oakden in 1827 at MCO 6.18.2 measures 17 7/8 x 24 5/8in. Buildings shown in plan form, grass coloured green, strips coloured brown, buildings coloured red. There is no title or scale. Positive and negative photostats of original at CUL Maps.bb.53(1).96.4 and positive photostat at CRO TR274/P1, all at 1:2,880. See also GAM60201 [gives date], GAM60203 [gives Langdon's 1st name] and GAM60204–16.

Gamlingay – 1601/2 – GAM60203 – MCO 6.17.3
The description of certaine woode grovndes landes meadowes pastur and lea grovndes lieinge and being in the parishe of Gamlingay in the countye of Cambridge, beinge parcell of the possessions of the warden and schollers of the howse or colledge of schollers of Merton in the vniversitie of Oxforde. Made in Marche An*n*o *domini* 1601 Anno Eliz. xliiijo by Thomas Langdon.
Surveyor: Thomas Langdon; **Scale bar** 0–40 perches (= 3 3/8in.), 1:2,347; **Size:** (i) 17 7/8 x 25in.; **Top** is W; Manuscript(i), paper, coloured.

c. 360a. in TL2453, in fields N and S of Gamlingay ['Mertonage', 'Avenelles' and 'Sugley'] Wood. Names of fields, roads, owners and tenants; occupiers of individual strips not named. Open fields showing all strips; common; wood and trees; tenure; state of cultivation shown by colour; acreages, except for land belonging to Waresley Parish [Huntingdonshire]; roads; 'Holie well'.

Border of 5/16in.-wide brown band; title top right surrounded by a floral strapwork cartouche with fruit and coloured orange, green, blue and brown; 3-dimensional yellow/brown scale bar bottom left surmounted by brown dividers; cardinal points stated in border. Trees coloured brown, wood outlined in blue and yellow, strips coloured brown, balks and roads outlined in green.

Numbers on fields suggest map originally accompanied by a terrier. Copy drawn by William Cole in 1767 at MCO 6.19.3 measures 18 1/8 x 24 1/2in. Shields top left with Merton College arms, on right with Robert Masters' arms and bottom left with arms of Avenelles and the Babington family, the last hanging off branches of a tree. Copy drawn by Charles Oakden in 1827 at MCO 6.18.3 measures 18 3/16 x 24 3/4in. Grass and trees coloured green, strips coloured brown. There is no title or scale. Positive and negative photostats of original at CUL Maps.bb.53(1).96.5 and positive photostat at CRO TR274/P1, all at 1:2,880. See also GAM60201–2,4–16.

Gamlingay – [1601/2] – GAM60204 – MCO 6.17.4
[Land in NW of 'Easte Fielde', Gamlingay, owned by Merton College, Oxford.]
Surveyor: [Thomas Langdon]; **Scala** perticarum xvj ped*um* & dj., Scale bar 0–40 perches (= 3 3/8in.), 1:2,347;

Size: (i) 17 7/8 x 24 3/8in.; **Top** is W; Manuscript(i), paper, coloured.

c. 330a. in TL2553, in 'Easte Fielde' SE of Gamlingay ['Avenelles'] Wood and N of road to Little Gransden ['Cambridge Waye'].

Names of fields, roads, woods, owners and tenants. Open fields showing all strips; closes; common; wood and trees; waste; tenure; state of cultivation shown by colour; acreages except for land belonging to Waresley Parish [Huntingdonshire]; roads; 'Waresley crosse'; 'Procession waye' marks county boundary with Huntingdonshire; 'Greenway Bushe' and 'Harborowe bushe'.

Border of 5/16in.-wide brown band; brown scale bar middle top surmounted by uncoloured dividers and surrounded by blue, orange, green, yellow, red and brown strapwork; cardinal points stated in border. Strips coloured brown, balks, lanes and wood coloured green, Merton land coloured red, closes coloured blue or yellow.

Numbers on fields suggest map originally accompanied by a terrier. Copy drawn by William Cole in 1767 at MCO 6.19.4 measures 18 x 24 1/2in. Top left are arms of Merton College and Robert Masters. Copy drawn by Charles Oakden in 1827 at MCO 6.18.4 measures 17 3/4 x 25 1/16in. Grass and trees coloured green, strips coloured brown. There is no title or scale. Positive and negative photostats of original at CUL Maps.bb.53(1).96.6 and positive photostat at CRO TR274/P1, all at 1:2,880. Date and surveyor given on GAM60203. See also GAM60201–2,5–16.

Gamlingay – [1601/2] – GAM60205 – MCO 6.17.5
[Land in NE of 'Easte Fielde', Gamlingay, owned by Merton College, Oxford.]

Surveyor: [Thomas Langdon]; **Scale bar** 0–40 perches (= 3 3/8in.), 1:2,347; **Size:** (i) 18 x 23 5/8in.; **Top** is W; Manuscript(i), paper, coloured.

c. 280a. in TL2552 and TL2553 in NE corner of parish, bounded by road to Little Gransden ['Cambridge Waye'] in S, Little Gransden Parish in E and Huntingdonshire in W.

Names of fields, roads, owners and tenants. Open fields showing all strips; trees; tenure; state of cultivation shown by colour; acreages except for land owned by Waresley Parish [Huntingdonshire]; roads; 'Procession Waye' marks county boundary with Huntingdonshire.

Border of 5/16in.-wide brown band; 3-dimensional brown scale bar middle bottom; cardinal points stated in border. Trees and balks coloured green, strips coloured brown, Merton land written on in red.

Numbers on fields suggest map originally accompanied by a terrier. Copy drawn by William Cole in 1767 at MCO 6.19.5 measures 18 1/8 x 23 5/8in. On right are arms of Robert Masters and bottom left are arms of Merton College. Copy drawn by Charles Oakden in 1827 at MCO 6.18.5 measures 18 1/4 x 23 5/8in. Grass and trees coloured green, strips coloured brown. There is no title or scale. Positive and negative photostats of original at CUL Maps.bb.53(1).96.7 and positive photostat at CRO TR274/P1, all at 1:2,880. Date and surveyor given on GAM60203. See also GAM60201–2,4,6–16.

Gamlingay – [1601/2] – GAM60206 – MCO 6.17.6
[Land in E of 'Middle Fielde', Gamlingay, owned by Merton College, Oxford.]

Surveyor: [Thomas Langdon]; **Scale bar** 0–40 perches (= 3 3/8in.), 1:2,347; **Size:** (i) 17 3/4 x 23 3/4in.; **Top** is W; Manuscript(i), paper, coloured.

c. 260a. in TL2652 in E of parish, bounded by road to Little Gransden ['Cambridge Waye'] in N, Millbridge Brook in S and East Hatley Parish in E.

Names of fields, roads, owners and tenants. Open fields showing all strips; closes; common; trees; tenure; state of cultivation shown by colour; acreages; roads and watercourses; 'Gransden crosse', 'Gamlingay crosse'; 'Procession waye' marks boundary with East Hatley Parish; 'Cambridge waye bushe'.

Border of 5/16in.-wide brown band; 3-dimensional brown scale bar bottom left with a red background, surmounted by dividers and in a strapwork cartouche with blue, green, red and brown fruit and leaves; cardinal points stated in border. Trees, balks and roads coloured green, strips coloured brown, water coloured blue, 'Clare Hall' close coloured green/blue, Merton land written on in red.

Numbers on fields suggest map originally accompanied by a terrier. Copy drawn by William Cole in 1767 at MCO 6.19.6 measures 17 3/4 x 23 7/8in. Top right is a tree and Robert Masters' arms and on left are arms of Walter de Merton impaled with See of Rochester. Copy drawn by Charles Oakden in 1827 at MCO 6.18.6 measures 17 13/16 x 23 5/8in. There is no title or scale. Positive and negative photostats of original at CUL Maps.bb.53(1).96.8 and positive photostat at CRO TR274/P1, all at 1:2,880. Date and surveyor given on GAM60203. See also GAM60201–2,4–5,7–16.

Gamlingay – [1601/2] – GAM60207 – MCO 6.17.7
[Land in centre of 'Middle Fielde', Gamlingay, owned by Merton College, Oxford.]

Surveyor: [Thomas Langdon]; **Scale bar** 0–40 perches (= 3 3/8in.), 1:2,347; **Size:** (i) 17 13/16 x 23 1/4in.; **Top** is W; Manuscript(i), paper, coloured.

c. 280a. in TL2452 and TL2552 in E of parish, bounded by roads to Little Gransden ['Cambridge Waye'] in N and to Hatley St George ['Hatley Waye'] in S, and crossing Millbridge Brook.

Names of fields, roads, owners and tenants. Open fields showing all strips; closes and pightles; trees; meadow; tenure; state of cultivation shown by colour; acreages; roads and watercourses; 'Cambridge waye bushe'; 'Bennett hill Bushe'; 'Cambridge crosse'; 'Preston grave'.

Border of 5/16in.-wide brown band; 3-dimensional brown scale bar middle bottom; cardinal points stated in border. Trees and balks coloured green, strips coloured brown, water coloured blue, closes coloured blue, yellow and green.

Numbers on fields suggest map originally accompanied by a terrier. Copy drawn by William Cole in 1767 at MCO 6.19.7 measures 17 15/16 x 23 1/8in., with scale coloured blue. Top right are Robert Masters' arms and on left are Merton College arms. Copy drawn by Charles Oakden in 1827 at MCO 6.18.7 measures 17 11/16 x 23 1/4in. There is no title or scale. Positive and negative photostats of original at CUL Maps.bb.53(1).96.9 and positive photostat at CRO TR274/P1, all at 1:2,880. Date and surveyor given on GAM60203. See also GAM60201–2,4–6,8–16.

Gamlingay – [1601/2] – GAM60208 – MCO 6.17.8
[Land in Gamlingay in W part of 'Middle Fielde' and E part of village, owned by Merton College, Oxford.]

Surveyor: [Thomas Langdon]; **Scale bar** 0–40 perches (= 3 3/8in.), 1:2,347; **Size:** (i) 17 1/2 x 22 3/4in.; **Top** is W; Manuscript(i), paper, coloured.

Brook End ['Brooke'] Farm, TL248522, and c. 230a. E of village, bounded by Station Road ['Hatley Waye'] in S.

Names of farms, fields, roads, owners and tenants. Houses and 'Brooke Farme' shown in perspective. Open fields showing all strips; closes; tenure of manor land; state of cultivation shown by colour; acreages; 'Hatley way bush'; roads; watercourses including 'Gamlingay Head'.

Border of 5/16in.-wide brown band; 3-dimensional brown scale bar bottom right surmounted by dividers and in a green and blue scroll; cardinal points stated in border. Trees and balks coloured green, strips coloured brown, closes coloured yellow, green and blue, water coloured blue, houses have red roofs.

Note top right in a cartouche coloured red, blue and brown describing a cottage whose details could not be fitted on map: 'Edwarde Mann A cotage copyhold of Merton 0.0.17'. Numbers on fields suggest map originally accompanied by a terrier. Copy drawn by William Cole in 1767 at MCO 6.19.8 measures 17 5/8 x 22 5/8in. Bottom right are 2 trees with shields of Clare Hall, William Cole and Dr Stephen Apthorp [Cole's half-brother; *DNB*, 4, 734] hanging between them, and top left is a tree with a staff and arms of Merton College and Robert Masters. Copy drawn by Charles Oakden in 1827 at MCO 6.18.8 measures 17 3/8 x 22 1/2in. Buildings shown in plan form. There is no title or scale. Positive and negative photostats of original at CUL Maps.bb.53(1).96.10 and positive photostat at CRO TR274/P1, all at 1:2,947. Date and surveyor given on GAM60203. See also GAM60201-2,4-7,9-16.

Gamlingay – [1601/2] – GAM60209 – MCO 6.17.9
[Land in Gamlingay village, owned by Merton College, Oxford.]

Surveyor: [Thomas Langdon]; **Scale bar** 0–40 perches (= 3 3/8in.), 1:2,347; **Size:** (i) 17 9/16 x 21 7/8in.; **Top** is W; Manuscript(i), paper, coloured.

Gamlingay Church, TL241523, and c. 170a. in village extending from Green End in W to Dutter End in E.

Names of closes, roads, some features, owners and tenants. Buildings shown in perspective and include church, farm and stables, 'tieth barn', cottages and 'a cotage decayed'. Closes, including 1 with 2 claims to it; trees; state of cultivation shown by colour; acreages; tenure; roads and footpaths; gates; watercourses; fences; 'spitle pitt'; 'Stone Bridge' shown in perspective; hayrick.

Border of 5/16in.-wide brown band; scale bottom left surmounted by brown dividers and in a strapwork cartouche with a red background and fruit and flowers coloured green, blue, brown and red; cardinal points stated in border. Table top left giving tenants, in a similar cartouche coloured orange, brown, green, blue and red. Human figure on Mertonage land near Millbridge Brook. Roads coloured brown, hedges coloured green, closes coloured blue, green and yellow, houses have red roofs, water coloured blue.

Numbers on fields suggest map originally accompanied by a terrier. Copy drawn by William Cole in 1767 at MCO 6.19.9 measures 17 3/4 x 21 11/16in. Top right is a shield with arms of See of Rochester impaled with those of Merton and a staff, and on left is a shield with Robert Masters' arms. Copy drawn by Charles Oakden in 1827 at MCO 6.18.9 measures 17 3/4 x 22 3/8in. Buildings shown in plan form, pit coloured blue. Table bottom left.

Positive and negative photostats of original at CUL Maps.bb.53(1).96.11 and positive photostat at CRO TR274/P1, all at 1:2,880. Date and surveyor given on GAM60203. See also GAM60201-2,4-8,10-16.

Gamlingay – [1601/2] – GAM60210 – MCO 6.17.10
[Land SW of Gamlingay village in 'Weste Meadowe', owned by Merton College, Oxford.]

Surveyor: [Thomas Langdon]; **Scale bar** 0–40 perches (= 3 3/8in.), 1:2,347; **Size:** (i) 16 5/8 x 24 1/8in.; **Top** is W; Manuscript(i), paper, coloured.

Mill Bridge, TL238515, and c. 260a. SW of village, bounded by Cow Lane and Everton Road in N, Potton Parish [Bedfordshire] in S and Little Heath ['Litle Heathe'] in W.

Names of fields, meadow, roads, some features, owners and tenants. House, barn and post mill shown in perspective. Open fields showing all strips; closes; wood and trees; waste; tenure of manor land; state of cultivation shown by colour; acreages; roads and footpaths; gates; watercourses; 'Milne Bridge'; 'The stone'; 'Monkes burge'.

Border of 5/16in.-wide brown band; brown scale bar bottom left surmounted by dividers and in a strapwork cartouche with orange, green, blue and brown fruit and flowers; cardinal points stated in border. Strips coloured blue and brown, roads coloured brown, trees and balks coloured green, closes coloured green, blue and yellow, water coloured blue, houses have red roofs.

Numbers on fields suggest map originally accompanied by a terrier. Copy drawn by William Cole in 1767 at MCO 6.19.10 measures 16 3/4 x 24in. Top right are 2 trees with shields with Clare Hall's, Mrs [Catherine; *PB*, 33] Brudenell's and Mr Abraham Jacob's arms, middle top is shield with Merton arms and mitre, bottom right is a tree and shield with Robert Masters' arms. Copy drawn by Charles Oakden in 1827 at MCO 6.18.10 measures 16 11/16 x 24 1/16in. Buildings shown in plan form. There is no title or scale. Positive and negative photostats of original at CUL Maps.bb.53(1).96.12 and positive photostat at CRO TR274/P1, all at 1:2,880. Date and surveyor given on GAM60203. See also GAM60201-2,4-9,11-16.

Gamlingay – [1601/2] – GAM60211 – MCO 6.17.11
[Land in W of 'Southe Fielde', Gamlingay, owned by Merton College, Oxford.]

Surveyor: [Thomas Langdon]; **Scale bar** 0–40 perches (= 3 1/4in.), 1:2,437; **Size:** (i) 17 3/4 x 24 1/4in.; **Top** is W; Manuscript(i), paper, coloured.

Martin Barrow ['Stone'] Bridge, TL243521, and c. 320a. to SW and S of village, bounded by Gamlingay Road ['Potton Way'] in W and boundary with Potton Parish [Bedfordshire] in S.

Names of fields, roads, owners and tenants. Cottages, barns, post mill, Mill Bridge and 'Stone Bridge' shown in perspective. Open fields showing all strips; closes including disputed land; trees; tenure of some strips; state of cultivation shown by colour; acreages; roads and footpaths; watercourses; 'Mill Hill' shown in perspective as a mound; 'Procession waye' marks boundary with Potton Parish.

Border of 5/16in.-wide brown band; scale middle top surmounted by dividers and in a strapwork cartouche with fruit and flowers, coloured green, orange, blue and brown; cardinal points stated in border. Strips coloured brown, trees and balks coloured green, closes coloured blue, houses have red roofs, Merton land coloured red.

248

Numbers on fields suggest map originally accompanied by a terrier. Copy drawn by William Cole in 1767 at MCO 6.19.11 measures 17 7/8 x 24 1/4in. Around scale bar are arms of Merton and Robert Masters. Copy drawn by Charles Oakden in 1827 at MCO 6.18.11 measures 17 7/8 x 24 5/16in. Buildings shown in plan form. There is no title or scale. Positive and negative photostats of original at CUL Maps.bb.53(1).96.13 and positive photostat at CRO TR274/P1, all at 1:2,947. Date and surveyor given on GAM60203. See also GAM60201–2,4–10,12–16.

Gamlingay – [1601/2] – GAM60212 – MCO 6.17.12
[Land in W of 'Southe Fielde', Gamlingay, owned by Merton College, Oxford.]
Surveyor: [Thomas Langdon]; **Scala** perticarum xvj pedum et dj ad per[t]icam, Scale bar 0–40 perches (= 3 3/8in.), 1:2,347; **Size:** (i) 17 1/16 x 23 3/4in.; **Top** is W; Manuscript(i), paper, coloured.
c. 290a. in TL2451 S of road to Hatley St George ['Hatley Waye'], bounded by Potton Parish [Bedfordshire] in S and 'Hole Brooke' in W.
Names of fields, roads, headlands, owners and tenants. Open fields showing all strips; common; 'towne meade'; trees; tenure; state of cultivation shown by colour; acreages; roads and footpaths; watercourses and pond; 'Gilberte crosse'; 'Stone hill bushe'.
Border of 5/16in.-wide brown band; 3-dimensional brown scale bar bottom right surmounted by blue and brown dividers; cardinal points stated in border. Balks coloured green, strips coloured brown, meadow coloured blue.
Note top right about tenancy of 1 strip: 'Thomas Park one that betwen Mrs Bendn in the tennure of Edw. malin and the land of John Chesham'. Numbers on fields suggest map originally accompanied by a terrier. Copy drawn by William Cole in 1767 at MCO 6.19.12 measures 17 1/16 x 23 5/8in. Bottom right are arms of Merton and Robert Masters. Copy drawn by Charles Oakden in 1827 at MCO 6.18.12 measures 18 5/8 x 25 7/8in. There is no title or scale. Positive and negative photostats of original at CUL Maps.bb.53(1).96.14 and positive photostat at CRO TR274/P1, all at 1:2,880. Date and surveyor given on GAM60203. See also GAM60201–2,4–11,13–16.

Gamlingay – [1601/2] – GAM60213 – MCO 6.17.13
[Land in middle E of 'Southe Fielde', Gamlingay, owned by Merton College, Oxford.]
Surveyor: Thomas Langdon; **Scale bar** 0–40 perches (= 3 3/8in.), 1:2,347; **Size:** (i) 17 5/8 x 23in.; **Top** is W; Manuscript(i), paper, coloured.
c. 110a. in TL2551, bounded by road to Hatley St George ['Hatley Waye'] in N, Potton Parish [Bedfordshire] in S and 'Hole Brooke' in E.
Names of fields, roads, owners and tenants. Open fields showing all strips; trees; state of cultivation shown by colour; tenure; acreages; roads and watercourses; 'Chapell Stile'; 'Prestons grave'; 'Procession waye' marks boundary with Potton Parish.
Border of 5/16in.-wide brown band; brown scale bar bottom left surmounted by dividers in a very ornate strapwork cartouche with fruit and flowers and coloured blue, brown, green and orange; cardinal points stated in border. Table top right giving tenants, in a strapwork cartouche coloured brown, red, blue and green. Balks, roads and trees coloured green, strips coloured brown.

Note above table in the same cartouche: 'Memorandum that this <presentment> Survey was presented at the severall Courtes holden for the Mannours of Martinage and Avenells the Five & twentyth daie of September one thousand six hundred & fouer <before> holden by Humffrey Winch Esquier Stuard by the Jurors of both the mannours whose names are herein under written in the preseuce of the colledge officers Christophorus Dale Vicecustos, Nathanael Brent bursarius in progressu, Tho. Langdon surveyer. Jurors of the Martinage: ... Jurors of the Avenells: ...'
Numbers on fields suggest map originally accompanied by a terrier. Copy drawn by William Cole in 1767 at MCO 6.19.13 measures 17 11/16 x 23in. Table extends down entire right side of sheet. On left are arms of Merton College and Robert Masters. Copy drawn by Charles Oakden in 1827 at MCO 6.18.13 measures 17 1/4 x 24 3/8in. There is no title or scale. Positive and negative photostats of original at CUL Maps.bb.53(1).96.15 and positive photostat at CRO TR274/P1, all at 1:2,947. Date of survey given on GAM60203. See also GAM60201–2,4–12,14–16.

Gamlingay – 1601/2 – GAM60214 – MCO 6.17.14
The description of diverse landes meadowes pasture and lea grovndes lieinge and beinge in the fieldes of Gamlingay in the county of Cambridge beinge parcell of the possessions of the warden and schollers of the howse or colledge of schollers of Merton in the vniversitie of Oxforde drawne in the moneth of March Anno domini 1601. Anno Eliz. &c xliiijo. by the measure of xvj foote and an halfe to the pole and according to the proportion of xij perches to an ynche by Tho. Langdon.
Surveyor: Thomas Langdon; **Scale:** 1:2,376, Scale bar 0–40 perches (= 3 3/8in.), 1:2,347; **Size:** (i) 17 3/8 x 22/9/16in.; **Top** is W; Manuscript(i), paper, coloured.
c. 300a. in TL2651 in SE corner of parish, bounded Hatley St George Parish ['Hungrye Hatley'] in E and Millbridge Brook in N.
Names of fields, roads, owners and tenants. 'Mr St George his howse' [John St George; VCH, 5, 107] shown in perspective. Open fields showing all strips; trees; tenure; state of cultivation shown by colour; acreages; roads and footpaths; watercourses; 'Milne Hill' shown in perspective; cross at parish boundary with Hatley St George; 'Procession waye' marks parish boundary; some land owned by Hatley St George Parish.
Border of 5/16in.-wide brown band; title top right in a strapwork cartouche with fruit and flowers and coloured orange, blue, green and brown; 3-dimensional scale bar bottom left surmounted by dividers and all coloured brown; cardinal points stated in border. Balks and trees coloured green; strips coloured brown, Hatley St George ['Hungrie Hatley'] outlined in yellow, houses have red roofs, Merton land noted in red.
Beneath title: 'Note that all those landes which in this platte or in the others are written whollye with redde letters are the demeane landes belonginge vnto the same howse as parcell of the manor comonly called the Mertonage, or of theire mannor of Avenelles, and those which are written partely with redde letters and partely with blacke are copiholdes belongeinge vnto the same mannors and those which are written with blake only are the landes of the freeholders there'. Notes about land ownership on furlongs. Numbers on fields suggest map originally accompanied by a terrier. Copy drawn by William Cole in

1767 at MCO 6.19.14 measures 17 1/2 x 22 7/16in. Bottom right are 2 trees with John St George's and John Burgoyne's arms [VCH, 5, 74] between them, bottom left is a shield with arms of Sawtry Abbey [Huntingdonshire] and top left are arms of Merton and Robert Masters. Copy drawn by Charles Oakden in 1827 at MCO 6.18.14 measures 17 7/16 x 22 1/2in. Buildings shown in plan form. There is no title or scale. Positive and negative photostats of original at CUL Maps.bb.53(1).96.16 and positive photostat at CRO TR274/P1, all at 1:2,880. See also GAM60201-13,15-16.

Gamlingay – [1601/2] – GAM60215 – MCO 6.17.15
[Land in E part of 'Southe Fielde', Gamlingay, owned by Merton College, Oxford.]
   Surveyor: [Thomas Langdon?]; **Scale:** 1:3,130; **Size:** (ii) 22 1/4 x 32 7/8in.; **Top** is E; Manuscript(i), paper, coloured.
   c. 180a. in TL2651 in E of parish, bounded by Millbridge Brook in N and Hatley St George Parish in E.
   Names of fields, owners, tenants and some features. Buildings shown in perspective and include 'Mr St Georg his house' [John St George; VCH, 5, 107], buildings and church of 'Gamlingaye towne' at bottom of map, and 'the brickkyll'. Open fields showing approximate position of strips; closes; common; wood and trees; 'Broad Lease'; roads; watercourses; 'The drinking place'; state of cultivation shown by colour; 'Gransden crosse', 'The stone crosse'; 'The Wyndmill Hill'; 'Procession balk' marks boundary with Hatley St George Parish; fence; gate.
   Houses have red roofs, roads, strips, fence and 'Porte Woodes' coloured brown, water coloured blue, grass coloured green, 'brickkyll' coloured red, Gamlingay Parish outlined in red, 'Gransden feilde' outlined in yellow.
   Note at top: 'Mr St George his pasture lately inclosed'. Note on dorse: 'The plot of Broad lease & the rest in controversy betwene the towne of Gamblingay & St George Hatly for common & tyth. adiudged to Gamblingay at a trial in the country at midsomer 1601 and as on that in Kings bench termino Michaelis. 1601'. Much cruder drawing of NE corner of GAM60214, drawn inaccurately with straight lines. Copy drawn by William Cole in 1767 at MCO 6.19.15 measures 21 1/4 x 29 7/8in. Bottom right are Merton arms and middle bottom are Robert Masters' arms. Copy drawn by Charles Oakden in 1827 at MCO 6.18.15 measures 21 x 28 7/8in. Positive and negative photostats of original at CUL Maps.bb.53(1).96.17 and positive photostat at CRO TR274/P2, all at 1:2,100. Surveyor may be Thomas Langdon, who drew GAM60201-14,16.

Gamlingay – [1601/2] – GAM60216 – MCO 6.17
   Gamlingay in com: Cantabrig: A note of the contentes of acres there accordinge to the measure of xvj foote and an halfe to the pole.
   Surveyor: [Thomas Langdon]
   Table of acreages.
   Copy of this table drawn by William Cole in 1767 at MCO 6.19. Positive and negative photostats of original at CUL Maps.bb.53(1).96.18 and positive photostat at CRO TR274/P1. Date and surveyor given on GAM60203. See also GAM60201-2,4-15.

Gamlingay – 1752 – GAM75201 – DCC
   A Survey of Adams's, Easy's, & Littleworth Farms, in the Parish of Gamlinghay, and County of Cambridge The

Estate of The Honble Sir Iacob Garrard Downing Bart By Jos: Cole 1752.
   Surveyor: Joseph Cole; **Scale bar** 10–0–70 perches (= 5in.), 1:3,168; **Size:** (i) 14 7/8 x 20 3/4in.; **Top** is N; Manuscript(i), parchment, coloured.
   Gamlingay Church, TL241523, and 107a.3r.32p. to W.
   Names of fields, roads, features and neighbouring owners. Farm buildings shown in plan form, church and 2 post mills shown in perspective. Closed fields showing owner's land; trees; state of cultivation shown by colour; acreages; hedges; roads and gates; watercourses; pond; bridge; 'Folly'; '50 Mile Stone'; balks; feature which may be an orchard.
   Border of 1 broad band with 1 narrow band on inside; title bottom right in a rococo cartouche with trees and flowers and coloured purple, red, blue, green and yellow; yellow scale bar beneath title; compass rose bottom left showing 8 red, blue, yellow and green points. Centre top, middle right and middle bottom are perspective drawings of the farmhouses. Roads coloured yellow, fields outlined in green, arable coloured in yellow stripes, trees and hedges coloured green, water coloured blue, farm buildings coloured red.
   Accompanied by: 'A Terrar and Particular of Adams's Farm in the Parish of Gamlinghay and County of Cambridge the Estate of The honourable Sir Jacob Garrard Downing Bart By Jos: Cole 1752'. Terrier gives names of fields and furlongs, buttings and boundings, the number of lands and pieces, and acreages. The other 2 farms may also have been accompanied by terriers. Map and GUI75101 are at end of a volume of maps of the Downing estate, CRY75001-11, EAS75001-8 and TAD75001-9.

Gamlingay – 1793 – GAM79301 – CLC ACC.1985/5
   Plan of a Farm at Gamlingay; in the County of Cambridge. belonging to the Revd the Master & Fellows, of Clare Hall; Cambridge. Surveyed in the Year 1793 Woodham Lessee.
   Surveyor: [Joseph Freeman?]; **Scale bar** 5–0–15 chains (= 2 1/2in.), 1:6,336; **Size:** (i) 24 13/16 x 23 1/2in.; **Top** is E; Manuscript(i), parchment, coloured.
   Farm in TL2351, N of road from Potton to St Ives and S of Stock's Lane, and 111a.2r.20p. scattered throughout parish bounded by Waresley Parish [Huntingdonshire] in N and Potton Parish [Bedfordshire] in S.
   Names of fields, balks, roads and neighbouring owners. Farm buildings shown in plan form. Open fields showing owner's strips; closes; meadow and common; trees; state of cultivation shown by colour; roads and watercourses; balks; sand pit; hedges; 'Meadow Bank'.
   Border of 1 broad band with 1 narrow band on inside; title bottom left; scale in centre; compass top left showing 8 points. Table on left giving field names and acreages. Roads and arable strips coloured brown, pasture, balks and hedges coloured green, water coloured blue.
   Rough copy on paper mounted on cloth; whole sheet measures 18 3/8 x 22 1/8in. Compass bottom right shows 4 points and top as N, summary table top left. Grass coloured blue. Endorsed with later ink note: 'Gamlingay College Farm 1793'. In style of Joseph Freeman, who valued the farm in 1791 [CLC Safe B:60/11].

Gamlingay – 1794 – GAM79401 – CLC ACC.1985/5
   Plan of a Farm, at Gamlingay, in the County of

Cambridge. belonging to Clare~Hall in the University of Cambridge. Surveyed in the Year 1794.

Surveyor: [Joseph Freeman]; **Scale bar** 5–0–20 chains (= 3 1/8in.), 1:6,336; **Size:** (i) 28 1/16 x 24 1/4in.; **Top** is N; Manuscript(i), parchment, coloured.

Blythe Farm, TL238521, and 111a.3r.0p. scattered throughout parish.

Names of fields, roads and neighbouring owners. Farm buildings, cottages and mill shown in plan form. Open fields showing owner's strips; closes; trees; meadow; state of cultivation shown by colour; roads and gates; watercourses; hedges; balks; number of lands between each strip; 'Dammocks Grave'; pits including gravel pit.

Border of 1 broad band with 1 narrow band on inside; title centre left; scale in centre; compass top right showing 8 points. Table bottom right giving field names and acreages. Roads and arable strips coloured brown, buildings coloured red, hedges, balks and lanes coloured green, water coloured blue.

Ink note after title: 'Paine Lessee'. Paine's 1st name was James [*VCH*, 5, 77]. Later ink note on dorse: 'Dr Blithe's 1794'. Blithe benefaction accounts [CLC Safe A:3/3] record that [Joseph] Freeman was paid £5 18s in the half-year from Michaelmas 1796 to Lady Day 1797 for 'surveying & mapping Gamlingay'.

Gamlingay – 1801 – GAM80101 – DCC

Plan of an Estate late the Property of S*i*r Geo. Downing, Bart. at Gamlingay, in the County of Cambridge. 1801.

Surveyors: [John] Jenkinson, [Thomas] Lovell; **Scale:** 1:1,680; **Size:** (i) 29 1/4 x 34 7/16in.; **Top** is NE; Manuscript(i), paper mounted on paper, coloured.

Site of Gamlingay Park, TL226518, and 233a.3r.22p. surrounding it bounded by Gamlingay Heath in SW.

Names of features. Cottages shown in perspective. Wood and trees; roads and footpaths; park; fences; gardens; watercourses, ponds and 'The large Pond'; 'Labyrinth'; 'Full Moon' and 'Half Moon' [gates]; walls of house.

Border of 1 narrow yellow band; title top left; compass on right showing 4 points. Bottom left is Downing family coat of arms. Top right: 'South View of the Hall', demolished in 1776 [RCHM, 1, 110]. Water and paths outlined in blue, walls outlined in red, trees coloured green, land coloured yellow and green.

Note on left: 'This Labyrinth was inclosed by a Brick Wall; The Paths were 10 Feet wide and gravelled, with Hornbeam Hedges on each Side Ten Feet high'. Note of surveyors bottom right in an oval cartouche: 'Jenkinson and Lovell, Land and Building Surveyors and Auctioneers, Huntingdon'. Surveyors' 1st names were John and Thomas respectively [Eden J86 and L267]. Features marked on map by letters, with notes in margins: 'At E. a famous Figure of the Roman Gladiator', 'At O. an Obelisk', 'At S. two Pyramids', 'At U. a Figure of Mercury', 'At V. Fame on a Pedestal', 'At W. a beautiful Figure of Diana', 'At Y. a Gothic Gate', 'At Z. an Urn'. Acreage taken from GAM80301. Park owned by Downing College, Cambridge.

Gamlingay – 1803 – GAM80301 – DCC Map Cabinet Drawer 4 E7

Plan of Gamlingay Park 1803.

Scale: 1:2,020; **Size:** (i) 21 7/8 x 26 1/2in.; **Top** is E; Manuscript(i), paper mounted on cloth, uncoloured.

233a.3r.22p. at TL226518.

Farm buildings shown in plan form, 1 building [a monument] shown in perspective. Acreages; roads and watercourses; bridge; park; outlines of paths and ponds; gothic gate; sites of urn and statue of Diana.

Border of 1 narrow band; title top right.

Park owned by Downing College, Cambridge. Sites of urn and statue of Diana taken from GAM80101.

Gamlingay – [c. 1806–28] – GAM80601 – CRO L99/13

Woodbury, in the County of Cambridge.

Scale bar 0–21 chains (= 2in.), 1:8,316; **Size:** (i) 13 1/16 x 21 5/8in.; **Top** is N; Manuscript(i), parchment, coloured.

Woodbury Hall, TL209521, and c. 1,100a. in far W of parish, bounded by Tetworth Parish [Huntingdonshire] in N, Everton Parish [Bedfordshire] in S, Tempsford Parish [Bedfordshire] in W and road from Waresley to Everton in E. In addition, some small areas in Tempsford and Everton parishes.

Names of fields and neighbouring owners. Woodbury Hall, Woodbury Hall Farm, Woodbury Low Farm and farm buildings shown in plan form. Closes; wood including White Wood; trees; state of cultivation shown by colour; roads and watercourses; gates and stiles; park; Story moats; bridges and ponds.

Border of 1 broad and 1 narrow band; title top left in cartouche of blue leaves; scale bottom left; compass bottom right showing 8 points. Roads and arable coloured brown, pasture and wood coloured green, water coloured blue, buildings and boundary of manor coloured red.

Numbers on plots suggest map originally accompanied by a terrier. Pencil notes of areas sold c. 1842. Land owned by William Wilkieson, who built Woodbury Hall between 1803 and 1806 [*VCH*, 5, 73]. Map drawn after hall was built and before 1828, when a neighbouring owner died.

Gamlingay – 1807 – GAM80701 – MCO

A Plan of the Old inclosures and part of the Open field Lands of the several Estates in the Parish of Gamlingay in the County of Cambridge belonging to Merton College, Oxford. Octr 10th 1807.

Scale bar 0–30 chains (= 4 15/16in.), 1:4,812; **Size:** (i) 30 1/2 x 26 3/4in.; **Top** is N; Manuscript(i), paper, coloured.

Gamlingay Church, TL241523, and 567a.3r.21p. in plots to S, around Mill Hill, in N of parish W of Fuller's Hill Farm and E of road to Waresley, in W of village in Green End, and in far W of parish S and E of White Wood and N and W of Gamlingay Great Heath.

Names of fields and woods. Buildings shown in plan form and include church, cottages, barns and public house. Open fields showing owner's strips; closes and pightle; common; 'Avenell's' and 'Mertonage' woods; trees; hedges and fences; roads and footpaths; watercourses; gardens; yards; meadow.

Border of 1 broad and 1 narrow band; title middle bottom with a cartouche of a ship on the sea underneath clouds and a castle on top of clouds; scale bottom right; compass in centre showing 8 points, with points extending over whole map. Tables on left and right giving tenants, field names and acreages. Roads coloured yellow, fields coloured brown, buildings coloured red.

Pencil notes, probably of tenants.

Gamlingay – 1835 – GAM83501 – CRO L4/27a

Plan of Land situate in the Parish of Gamlingay Belonging to Mr James Carter.

Surveyor: Charles Oakden; **Scale:** 2 Chains to an Inch, 1:1,584; **Size:** (i) 18 5/8 x 10 1/16in.; **Top** is NNE; Manuscript(i), paper, uncoloured.

10a.3r.19p. including a pond at TL252519, and land to N to E of village, bounded by Millbridge Brook in N.

Names of neighbouring owners. Coach house shown in plan form. Closes; meadow; acreages; roads; hedges; pond.

Border of 1 narrow band; title middle top; scale middle bottom; compass middle left showing 8 plain points with a decorated N. Table bottom right giving field names and acreages.

Girton – [c. 1814] – GIR81401 – CLC Safe B:58/2

Plan of the Parish of Girton as allotted under the Act of Inclosure of \18th/ of George III – 1808.

Surveyor: [Samuel Kempson Simmons]; **Scale:** 1:3,220; **Size:** (iii) 1 5/8 x 2in.; **Top** is SW; Manuscript(ii), paper, uncoloured.

1a.1r.32p. SW of TL421618.

Closed fields; roads.

Title at top.

Numbers on plots refer to inclosure award. Above map are notes of acreages of land allotted to Clare Hall, below are acreages of land allotted to neighbouring owners. Sketch based on map by Samuel Kempson Simmons which accompanied 1814 inclosure award, shows land allotted to Clare College, Cambridge.

Girton – [c. 1814] – GIR81402 – CLC Safe B:58/3

['Girton Lands Award'.]

Surveyor: [Samuel Kempson Simmons]; **Scale:** 1:21,600; **Size:** (ii) 5 1/4 x 6 3/4in.; **Top** is SW; Manuscript(ii), tracing paper, uncoloured.

c. 220a. NE of Girton Corner, TL427607.

Names of roads and neighbouring owners. Closed fields; roads; responsibility for boundaries.

Numbers on some plots refer to inclosure award. Title on dorse. Attached to a piece of paper with a watermark of 1829. Based on map by Samuel Kempson Simmons which accompanied 1814 inclosure award, shows land allotted to Clare College, Cambridge.

Girton – [Post 1814] – GIR81403 – CRO 124/P47

Plan of an estate in the parishes of Girton and Histon lying North of the Huntingdon Turnpike Road, and belonging to Sir St Vincent Cotton Bart.

Surveyor: Alexander Watford [jr]; **Scale bar** 5–0–20 chains (= 4 1/8in.), 1:4,800; **Size:** (i) 43 9/16 x 58 5/16in.; **Top** is NNE; Manuscript(i), paper mounted on cloth, coloured.

Girton Church, TL423623, and 778a.3r.39p. in N of parish bounded by Oakington Parish in W, Impington Parish in E and road from Huntingdon to Cambridge in S, and extending into S of Histon Parish as far as road to Oakington.

Names of parishes, roads and neighbouring owners. Church, farm buildings and 'White Horse' public house shown in plan form. Closed fields showing owner's land; wood and trees including a few coniferous trees in wood S of road to Oakington; roads including turnpike road; watercourses; gates; bridges and ponds; responsibility for

boundaries; gardens, orchards and pound identified on table.

Border of 1 broad band, 1 broad blue band and 2 narrow bands; title top right with ornamental lettering; scale beneath title; compass top left showing 8 points. Table at bottom giving tenants, state of cultivation, descriptions of land and acreages. Roads coloured brown, water coloured blue, houses and boundary between Histon and Girton parishes coloured pink.

Pencil notes dividing land into lots. Drawn after 1814 inclosure award. See also GIR81404.

Girton – [Post 1814] – GIR81404 – CRO 124/P48

[Land in Girton and Histon parishes, owned by Sir St Vincent Cotton Bart.]

Surveyor: [Alexander Watford jr?]; **Scale:** 1:4,800; **Size:** (i) 32 1/2 x 59 3/4in.; **Top** is NNE; Manuscript(i), paper mounted on cloth, coloured.

Girton Church, TL423623, and 778a.3r.39p. in N of parish bounded by Oakington Parish in W, Impington Parish in E and road from Huntingdon to Cambridge in S, and extending into S of Histon Parish as far as road to Oakington.

Church, farm buildings and 'White Horse' public house shown in plan form. Closed fields showing owner's land; acreages of some fields; roads including turnpike; watercourses; gates; responsibility for boundaries; bridges and ponds; gardens, orchards and pound identified on table on GIR81403.

Border of 1 broad band with 1 narrow band on either side. Roads coloured brown, water coloured blue, boundary between Girton and Histon parishes coloured red.

Pencil notes filling in details. Numbers on plots refer to table on GIR81403 by Alexander Watford, of which this map may be a draft. Drawn after 1814 inclosure award.

Grantchester – [1654] – GRT65401 – CRC XXXVI no. 13

A True plot of all The Parsonage Land in Grancester feild: performed By George: Skinner.

Surveyor: George Skinner; **A Scale** of Chaines: viz Gunters Chaine: 66 foot long, Scale bar 1–0–10 chains (= 5 1/2in.), 1:1,584; **Size:** (i) 19 x 33 5/8in.; **Top** is N; Manuscript(i), paper mounted on cloth, uncoloured.

Strips scattered throughout parish.

Names of fields. Open fields showing owner's strips; meadow; roads; watercourses; balks; dimensions of strips.

Border of 1 broad band; title centre top surmounted by dividers; scale beneath title; cardinal points stated at edge.

Date written on cloth backing map. Living owned by Corpus Christi College, Cambridge. Positive photostat at 1:2,681 at CUL Maps.bb.53(1).95.85.

Grantchester – 1666 – GRT66601 – KCC

Skinner's map of Granchester. The Field Book of Granchester 1666 is a Terrier to the Field Land in this Map.

Surveyor: [George] Skinner; **Scale:** 16 poles or fower Chains in one inch: or 400 links Gunters Chaine: 100 Links in 4 Pole, A Scale of Chains: fower Poles to the Chaine, Scale bar 0–20 [chains] (= 5in.), 1:3,168; **Size:** (ii) 38 1/4 x 52 1/4in.; Manuscript(i), paper mounted on cloth which is mounted on paper, coloured.

c. 600a. scattered throughout parish.

Names of roads. Houses and mills shown in perspective; most of village not shown. Open fields showing owner's strips; closes; common; wood and trees; waste; meadow; acreages; roads and footpaths; watercourses; footbridge; crosses; yards; number of lands and their dimensions.

Title top right surmounted by dividers; scale bottom left surmounted by dividers; compass points with scale. Land belonging to King's College coloured red, water coloured blue [now faded].

Accompanied by a terrier at KCC F63, with a copy at F64. Map is in 4 sheets. See also GRT65401, which gives surveyor's 1st name. Positive photostat at 1:3,054 at CUL Maps.aa.53.91.1–4.

Grantchester – [Early 18th century] – GRT70001 – TH Newnham Croft
This is the Survey of Newnham Croft.
Scale: 1:1,590; **Size:** (ii) 10 5/8 x 8 1/4in.; **Top** is N; Manuscript(i), paper, uncoloured.
c. 1a. in TL4457, bounded by River Cam in W.
Names of neighbouring owners. Owner's land; dimensions of area; verges; crosses; 'The perambulation balk'.
Title at bottom; 'North' stated at top.
Land owned by Trinity Hall, Cambridge.

Grantchester – 1795 – GRT79501 – TCC Box 20 Grantchester 24a
A Plan of the Property belonging to the Master Fellows and Scholars of Trinity College situated in the Parish of Granchester in the County of Cambridge taken in the Year 1795 by A Watford.
Surveyor: A[lexander] Watford [sr]; **Scale bar** 0–20 chains (= 5in.), 1:3,168; **Size:** (i) 20 3/4 x 14 13/16in.; **Top** is WNW; Manuscript(i), parchment, coloured.
18a.3r.26p. in strips scattered throughout parish, Grantchester Church, which is not shown, is at TL434555.
Names of furlongs and neighbouring owners. Open fields showing owner's strips; trees; 'Broad Meadow'; leys and green; state of cultivation shown by colour; roads and 'Port Way'; watercourses; balks; hedges; gravel pit identified on table.
Border 3/16in. wide of bands coloured grey, uncoloured, brown and dark blue from outside to inside; title top left in a rococo cartouche coloured green, yellow and grey; scale in centre; compass on right showing 4 points. Table bottom left giving acreages, number of lands and furlongs. Fields outlined in green or yellow, water coloured blue, balks coloured green.
Pencil notes. Surveyor's 1st name was Alexander [Eden W141].

Grantchester – 1795 – GRT79502 – TCC Box 20 Grantchester 24b
A Plan of the Property belonging to the Master, Fellows, and Scholars, of Trinity College. situated in the Parish of Granchester, in the County of Cambridgeshire. taken from a Survey made in the Year 1795. by A. Watford.
Surveyor: A[lexander] Watford [sr]; **Scale** of Three Chains to an Inch, 1:2,376, Scale bar 0–10 chains (= 3 5/16in.), 1:2,391; **Size:** (i) 11 3/16 x 15in.; **Top** is W; Manuscript(ii), parchment, coloured.
18a.3r.26p. in strips scattered throughout parish; Grantchester Church, which is not shown, is at TL434555.
Names of furlongs and neighbouring owners. Open fields showing owner's strips; 'Broad Meadow'; state of cultivation probably shown by colour; roads and 'Port Way'; watercourses; hedges; balks; gravel pit.

Border of 1 broad band with 2 narrow bands on inside; title on right in a cartouche of flowers and leaves coloured green, purple, yellow and pink; scale bottom left with a scale bar alternately coloured blue and left uncoloured; compass above title showing 4 points. Table bottom right giving acreages, number of lands and furlongs. Fields outlined in purple or green, balks coloured yellow, water coloured blue.

Strips all drawn as insets rather than in correct relation to each other. Surveyor's 1st name was Alexander [Eden W141].

Grantchester – 1804 – GRT80401 – MCO
Plan of the Leasehold and Copyhold Estates held of the Manor of Merton Hall situate in Cambridge, Grantchester and Chesterton, in the County of Cambridge.
Surveyor: W[illiam] Custance; **Scale:** 6 Chains to an Inch, 1:4,752; **Size:** (i) 16 7/8 x 21 3/8in.; **Top** is N; Manuscript(i), paper, coloured.
203a.1r.26p. in Grantchester Parish in W of TL4356 W of road to Cambridge, and at TL436548 bounded by River Cam in N, mill-stream in W and Byron's Pool in S; in Cambridge in TL4258 and TL4259 bounded by Coton Parish in W and Trinity Conduit Head and road to Madingley in N, and in TL4458, bounded by Northampton Street in NW, Magdalene Street in NE and River Cam in SE.
Names of neighbouring owners. Buildings shown in plan form and include houses, mill, 'The Bell' [public house] and 'The Slaughter House'. Closed fields showing owner's land; waste; roads, footpaths and public bridleway; watercourses; millpool; bridge; orchards; hedges; gardens; tenure; 'Toll bar' on Castle Hill.
Border of 1 narrow band; title at bottom surrounded by decorative line-work; compass centre left showing 8 points. Table top right giving tenants and acreages. Roads coloured brown, water coloured blue, buildings coloured red.
Surveyor's 1st name was William [Eden C624].

Grantchester – [1806] – GRT80601 – CRO R57/1/2
Plan of the within conveyed Close of Pasture.
Scale bar 0–3 chains (= 3in.), 1:792; **Size:** (i) 6 5/8 x 7 3/8in.; **Top** is N; Manuscript(i), parchment, uncoloured.
3r.1p. in TL4355 in village.
Names of roads and neighbouring owners. Close; roads and hedges.
Border of 1 broad and 1 narrow band; title middle top in a diamond-shaped cartouche with decorated corners; scale middle bottom; compass on right showing 4 points. Table on left giving field names and acreages.
Accompanies a release dated 1806: 'Mr Thomas Page and Wife to Mr Richard Harraden and this Trustee: Appointment and Release of a Close of Pasture in Grantchester with Covenant to Produce foods'.

Graveley – 1766 – GRV76601 – JCC Graveley Rectory 2 Bundle C
The Lands or Three Grounds called Stow Groves.
Surveyor: John Smith; **Scale:** 1:89; **Size:** (ii) 16 3/8 x 13 1/8in.; **Top** is E; Manuscript(i), paper, uncoloured.
29a.10r.0p. in Graveley Parish.
Closed fields showing owner's land; grove, numbers and type of shrub timbers: ash, oak, elm and pollards; land

quality and 'This part the best land'; state of cultivation given in words; acreages; grass and pasture; fences.

Title at top; orientation given by cardinal points. Table on right giving field names and acreages; valuation of land at bottom.

Note at top after title of lessees and rents. Land owned by Jesus College, Cambridge.

Graveley – [1807] – GRV80701 – JCC Graveley

Plan of an Estate situate in the Parish of Graveley, in the County of Huntingdon; belonging to the Master, Fellows and Scholars of Jesus College in the University of Cambridge.

Surveyor: [Joseph Truslove]; **Scale:** 1:4,990; **Size:** (i) 22 3/4 x 20 3/8in.; **Top** is N; Manuscript(i), parchment, coloured.

Farm at TL251640 and 244a.2r.14p. mostly N and E of church, bounded by Papworth St Agnes Parish in NE, and plot S of church bounded by Yelling Parish [Huntingdonshire] in S.

Names of neighbouring owners, fields and roads. Farm buildings and cottages shown in plan form, church shown in perspective. Closed fields of owner's land; acreages; hedges; roads and watercourses; 'Allotment for Royalty'.

Border of 2 narrow bands; title top left; compass centre bottom showing 4 points with a feathered tail. Table bottom right giving field names and acreages. Roads coloured brown, water coloured blue.

Joseph Truslove was paid £4 16s 9d for surveying the 'Royalty estate' at Graveley in 1807 [JCC A/C.1.9]. Estate was in Cambridgeshire.

Great Abington – 1716/17 – GTA71701 – B L 1640.(15), CUL Maps.bb.53(1).93.63–6

An Exact Map. Containing 636 acres 2 Roods 6 pole of the Mannor Farm of Abington Hall In the parish of Great Abington in the County of Cambridge Belonging to Maximilian Western of London Esqr now in his own occupation Surveyed & Drawn Febru; 7th: 1716.

Surveyor: Benjamin Fallowes; **Scale bar** 22–0–1 [chains] (= 5 13/16in.), 1:3,134; **Size:** (i) 39 3/4 x 29in.; **Top** is SSW; Positive and negative photostat, paper, uncoloured, 4+4 sheets.

Abington Hall Farm, TL531488, and 636a.2r.6p. in NE corner of parish bounded by Hildersham Parish in E and Pampisford Parish in W.

Names of fields, roads, woods and neighbouring owners. Farm buildings, stables and outbuildings shown in perspective. Open fields showing owner's strips; closes; common; wood, trees and 'Abington Grove'; meadow; acreages; roads, footpaths and gates; watercourses; garden; orchard; pond.

Border of leaf-like ornament; title middle right surrounded by a leafy cartouche; scale bar beneath title surmounted by dividers with a floral pattern in pivot; compass rose top left showing 8 points. Surveyor mentioned between title and scale bar in a circular cartouche. Western's coat of arms top right.

Note beneath scale: 'From the Hall Door thorow the walnut tree walk to Abington Grove is 1 mile 2 *quarters* 1 fur*long* 3 pole'. Scale bar incorrectly says that it shows poles rather than chains. Manuscript original owned by Mrs Alice Mortlock of Great Abington in 1930s; not found in 1988. Copy at BL 1640.(15) is a positive photostat in 1 sheet mounted on cloth.

Great Abington – 1818 – GTA81801 – C U L Maps.bb.53(1).93.73–4

Plan of Farms at Great Abington in the County of Cambridge belonging to the Exe*cute*rs of John Mortlock Esqr in the Respective Occupations of Mr J. Ward and Mr Jno Lyles made in 1818 by Alexr Watford.

Surveyor: Alexander Watford [jr]; **Scale:** 1:4,920; **Size:** (i) 21 1/8 x 32 1/8in.; **Top** is W; Positive and negative photostat, paper, uncoloured, 2+2 sheets.

Newhouse Farm, TL528482, and 1,215a.0r.20p. in S of parish including Abington Park ['The Park'] Farm, bounded by Hinxton and Pampisford parishes in W, Great Chesterford Parish [Essex] in S, Hildersham Parish in E, and road from Linton to Pampisford and Newhouse Farm in N.

Names of farms, fields, owners and neighbouring owners. Farm buildings and cottages shown in plan form. Closed fields; common; wood and trees; state of cultivation given in words which identify land to be planted with sainfoin now and in future; tenure; acreages; turnpike roads and toll bar; footpaths; park; gardens; 'The great ditch' shown by shading.

Probably a border [original is in a wooden frame]; title top left with ornamental line-work; compass top right showing 4 points, incorrectly giving top as N. Table on right giving tenants, field names, acreages and land use.

Estate owned by John Mortlock, who died in 1816 and left his property to his 2nd and 4th sons, Thomas and Frederick Cheetham [*VCH*, 6, 6]. Manuscript original owned by Mrs Alice Mortlock, Great Abington, in 1937; not found in 1988.

Great Abington – [1818] – GTA81802 – C R O 509/T159

Plan of the respective shifts referred to by this Lease.

Scale: 1:9,810; **Size:** (i) 9 1/4 x 9 11/16in.; **Top** is S; Manuscript(i), parchment, coloured.

Newhouse Farm, TL524482, and 657a.2r.23p. mostly S of road from Linton to Pampisford, bounded by roads from Newmarket to Great Chesterford in W and running S from Great Abington in E.

Names of roads. Newhouse Farm and farm buildings shown in plan form. Closed fields showing owner's land; wood and trees; state of cultivation shown by colour; acreages; roads including turnpike; gates; hedges and fences; responsibility for boundaries.

Border of 1 broad band with 1 narrow band on either side; title at top. Table at bottom giving field names and acreages. Roads coloured brown, arable coloured yellow, pasture coloured green, buildings coloured red.

Notes of land to be planted with sainfoin in crop rotation. Later ink notes giving occupier, tenure and altered acreages for some plots. Pencil notes of neighbouring owners. Alterations possibly marked in 1834, see GTA83403. Numbers on plots refer to accompanying lease: 'Thomas Mortlock Esq to Mr John Lyles: Counterpart of Lease, 1818'. Land owned by Thomas and Frederick Cheetham Mortlock [*VCH*, 6, 6].

Great Abington – 1819 – GTA81901 – CRO 509/T160

[Abington Lodge, Great Abington, owned by Thomas and Frederick Cheetham Mortlock.]

Scale: 1:5,910; **Size:** (i) 11 1/2 x 8 3/4in.; **Top** is S; Manuscript(i), parchment, coloured.

Abington Lodge, TL534489, and 31a.0r.7p. mostly W of road running S through village and crossed by road from Great Abington to Linton in S, and bounded by River Granta in N.

Names of tenant and roads. Abington Lodge, cottages and outbuildings shown in plan form. Closed fields showing owner's land; meadow; state of cultivation shown by colour; acreages; roads and watercourses; site of gravel pit.

Border of 2 red lines. Table top left giving field names and acreages. Arable coloured brown, pasture coloured green, buildings coloured red.

Notes of land exchanged, notes of rent on dorse, pencil note of acreage of 1 plot. Accompanies lease: 'Thomas Mortlock Esquire to Mrs Frances Holt: Lease of Lands at Great Abington commencing Michaelmas 1818'. Land owned by Thomas and Frederick Cheetham Mortlock [VCH, 6, 6].

Great Abington – [c. 1834] – GTA83401 – C R O 509/T169
[Abington Hall, Great Abington, owned by Thomas Mortlock.]
Scale: 1:1,920; **Size:** (ii) 14 7/8 x 8 7/8in.; **Top** is S; Manuscript(i), paper, uncoloured.
Abington Hall, TL527488, and c. 53a. in Great and Little Abington parishes bounded by Pampisford Parish in W, grove in S and road from Cambridge to Linton in N, and extending just E of Abington Hall.
Names of fields, roads and river. Abington Hall shown in plan form. Closed fields showing owner's land; wood; waste; meadow; state of cultivation given in words; acreages; crops, including seeds, fallow, turnips, wheat and 'cinque foil'; roads and footpaths; watercourses; 'pleasure ground'; lawn; ponds.
Later ink notes on dorse referring to acreages. Probably drawn at same time as GTA83402; letters on map possibly refer to lease which accompanies GTA83402.

Great Abington – [1834] – GTA83402 – C R O 509/T169
[Abington Hall Farm, Great Abington, owned by Thomas Mortlock.]
Scale: 1:5,080; **Size:** (ii) 7 3/8 x 9in.; **Top** is S; Manuscript(i), paper, uncoloured.
Abington Hall Farm, TL531487, and c. 200a. to S and W, extending W of road running to Abington Hall from road from Pampisford to Linton, and bounded by grove in S.
Name of farm. Closed fields showing owner's land; wood and trees; state of cultivation given in words; acreages; crops to be planted, including barley, oats, wheat, seeds and tares; roads; gates; gardens.
Notes of 1847 adding numbers and crops to fields. Notes on dorse. Accompanies lease: 'Thomas Mortlock Esqre to Messrs John & Thos Lyles; Lease of the Hall Farm in the parishes of Great and Little Abington for 4 years from Michaelmas Old Style 1834'.

Great Abington – [1834] – GTA83403 – C R O 509/T168
[Newhouse Farm, Great Abington, owned by Thomas Mortlock.]
Scale: 1:9,810; **Size:** (i) 11 7/16 x 10 1/2in.; **Top** is W; Manuscript(iv), tracing paper, coloured.

Newhouse Farm, TL524482, and 657a.2r.23p. mostly S of road from Linton to Pampisford, bounded by roads from Newmarket to Great Chesterford in W and running S from Great Abington in E.

Names of roads. Farm and outbuildings shown in plan form. Closed fields showing owner's land; wood and trees; state of cultivation shown by colour; acreages; roads including turnpike; hedges; responsibility for boundaries.

Border of 1 narrow band; compass top left showing 4 plain points. Table top right giving field names and acreages; table at bottom summarizing acreages. Roads coloured brown, buildings coloured red, grass coloured green.

Notes of land to be laid down to grass and to be planted with sainfoin in crop rotation. Notes of acreages in red and pencil notes. Numbers on plots refer to accompanying lease: 'Thomas Mortlock Esqre to Mr. John Lyles: Counterpart Lease of a Farm at Great Abington in the County of Cambridge for 8 years from Michaelmas Old Style 1834'. Incorporates pencil additions to GTA81802.

Great Eversden – 1801 – GTE80101 – QCC 328
Part of Old Enclosures & Lammas Grounds belonging to Eversden Lordship in the occupation of Rycroft.
Surveyors: [Alexander Watford sr and jr]; **Scale** 3 Chains = 1 Inch, 1:2,376; **Size:** (i) 25 x 31 7/8in.; **Top** is N; Manuscript(i), paper, uncoloured.
Manor Farm, TL360536, and land scattered throughout parish.
Names of fields, roads and neighbouring owners. Farm buildings, barns and cottages shown in plan form, church shown in perspective. Closed fields showing owner's land; wood and trees; waste and meadow; roads; watercourses and bridges; 'Bell Pitt'; moat; areas of plots.
Border of 1 narrow band; title top left; scale beneath title.
Numbers on plots suggest map originally accompanied by a terrier. Pencil notes. 5 insets: on left of land in 'Mill Field', at top of 'Chicken Pasture', and on right of 'Bassingbourn Doles', 'Mr Butlers Homestead' and 'Star Goose (Middle Field)'. Alexander Watford sr started surveying estate for Queens' College in February 1801; survey was finished in December by his son, Alexander jr [QCC Box 104].

Great Eversden – [1801] – GTE80102 – QCC 328
[Land in 'Brook' and 'Middle' fields, Great Eversden, owned by Queens' College, Cambridge.]
Surveyors: [Alexander Watford sr and jr]; **Scale:** 1:1,100; **Size:** (ii) 13 1/2 x 18 7/8in.; Manuscript(i), paper, uncoloured.
c. 10a. S of boundary with Toft Parish.
Names of fields, roads, areas and neighbouring owners. Open fields showing owner's strips; areas of plots; roads and footpaths; watercourses; balks; clay pit.
Land in 'Middle Field' has a border of 1 narrow band.
Numbers on plots suggest map originally accompanied by a terrier. Plots are at different orientations. Alexander Watford sr started surveying estate for Queens' College in February 1801; survey was finished in December by his son, Alexander jr [QCC Box 104]. See also GTE80103–5.

Great Eversden – [1801] – GTE80103 – QCC 328
[Land in 'Brook' and 'Mill' fields, Great Eversden, owned by Queens' College, Cambridge.]

Surveyors: [Alexander Watford sr and jr]; **Scale:** 1:1,080; **Size:** (ii) 13 1/8 x 18 13/16in.; Manuscript(i), paper, uncoloured.

Land in centre of parish S of road to Cambridge.

Names of fields and neighbouring owners. Open fields showing owner's strips; areas of plots; roads; watercourses; balks; 'Wood Pightle'; common and wood adjoining map.

Numbers on plots suggest map originally accompanied by a terrier. Pencil notes and calculations. Plots are at different orientations. See GTE80102 for surveyors and date; see also GTE80104–5.

Great Eversden – [1801] – GTE80104 – QCC 328

[Land in 'Middle Field', Great Eversden, owned by Queens' College, Cambridge.]

Surveyors: [Alexander Watford sr and jr]; **Scale:** 1:1,090; **Size:** (ii) 15 7/8 x 19in.; Manuscript(i), paper, uncoloured.

Land in N of parish S of Claypit Hill, bounded by Wimpole Parish in SW.

Names of fields, roads and neighbouring owners. Open fields showing owner's strips; areas of plots; roads; balks.

Numbers on plots suggest map originally accompanied by a terrier. Plots are at different orientations. See GTE80102 for surveyors and date; see also GTE80103,5.

Great Eversden – [1801] – GTE80105 – QCC 328

[Land in 'Brook' and 'Mill' fields, Great Eversden, owned by Queens' College, Cambridge.]

Surveyors: [Alexander Watford sr and jr]; **Scale:** 1:1,070; **Size:** (ii) 26 7/8 x 18 7/8in.; Manuscript(i), paper, uncoloured.

Land in centre of parish.

Names of fields, roads and neighbouring owners. Open fields showing owner's strips; areas of plots; roads; stream and ditches; marsh; balks.

Numbers on plots suggest map originally accompanied by a terrier. Plots are at different orientations. See GTE80102 for surveyors and date; see also GTE80103–4.

Great Eversden – [1825] – GTE82501 – QCC 355 A15, B15

Estate at Great and Little Eversden In The County of Cambridge.

Surveyor: [Alexander Watford jr]; **Scale bar** 0–30 chains (= 3 3/4in.), 1:6,336; **Size:** (i) 25 3/8 x 20 1/2in.; **Top** is NW; Manuscript(ii), paper, coloured.

Great Eversden Church, TL367533, and 372a.3r.9p. in centre of parish and in N of Little Eversden Parish.

Names of parishes and neighbouring owners. Manor Farm, Great Eversden, Manor House, Little Eversden and Great and Little Eversden churches shown in plan form. Closed fields showing owner's land; wood; acreages; hedges; roads; watercourses, bridges and moats; orchard, pightle, spinney and yards identified on table.

Border of 1 broad band with 1 narrow band on either side; title top left; scale middle bottom; compass at bottom showing 8 points. Table bottom left giving tenants, field names, acreages and land use. Roads coloured brown, fields coloured yellow, water coloured blue, buildings coloured red.

Numbers on plots suggest map originally accompanied by a terrier. On left of sheet, which also contains a map of Fulbourn [FUL82501], and in volume drawn in 1825:

'Plans of the Several Estates in England and Wales belonging to the President and Fellows of the College of St Margaret and St Bernard commonly called Queen's College in the University of Cambridge Delineated from Authentic Documents in the possession of the said President and Fellows and from actual Surveys taken By their most obedient and obliged Servant Alexr Watford'. Title page drawn by James Richardson [Watford's nephew]. This is the Bursar's copy; 2nd, finer, copy [the Master's copy] at QCC 355 B15 measures 24 3/4 x 18 1/4in. and is on parchment. Scale bar 0–40 chains (= 5in.), 1:6,336. Border 7/16in. wide of a central blue band with 1 broad band on either side, title top right and has gothic lettering, compass in centre. Table gives acreages of some fields and has red lines. Fields either coloured green or have yellow and brown stripes, roads have red/brown edges. Some red numbers on fields. Positive photostat of this copy at 1:10,560 at BL 1640.(27).

Great Eversden – [1829] – GTE82901 – CRO 296/B109

['Plan of Mansion House, Barns, Stables, Outhouses Buildings & fences situate at Eversden Cambridgeshire held by Lease by the Earl of Hardwicke of Queens College Cambridge. taken Feby 26th 1829'.]

Surveyors: [unidentified] Cockett, [unidentified] Nash; **Scale:** 1:440; **Size:** (ii) 7 1/4 x 4 1/4in.; Manuscript(i), paper, uncoloured.

c. 27p., probably in TL5653, in W of village.

Description of areas; ground floor of house and outbuildings, which include 'gig house', dairy, cellar, brew house and stable, shown in plan form. Dimensions of areas; yards.

Above plan is a scale drawing of front elevation of house. On opposite page is a rough draft of plan. In notebook dated 1829 containing details of repairs to be made.

Great Eversden – 1836 – GTE83601 – QCC 352

Plan of an Estate situate at Great Eversden & Little Eversden in the County of Cambridge the Property of Mr George Dobson.

Surveyor: C[harles] Oakden; **Scale bar** 5–0–15 chains (= 10in.), 1:1,584; **Size:** (i) 29 9/16 x 51in.; **Top** is NW; Manuscript(i), paper mounted on cloth, coloured.

Manor Farm, Great Eversden, TL361538, and 162a.0r.9p. to NE bounded by Bourn Brook; and, at bottom of sheet, land in Great and Little Eversden parishes N of Great Eversden Church, bounded by Bourn Brook in N.

Names of neighbouring owners. Manor Farm, Great Eversden Church and farm buildings shown in plan form. Closed fields showing owner's land; state of cultivation shown by colour on map at bottom of sheet; acreages; responsibility for boundaries; hedges; roads; watercourses.

Border of 1 narrow band; title bottom left; scale beneath title; compass in centre of map at bottom of sheet showing 4 points. Table on right giving land use and acreages. Water coloured blue, 1 boundary coloured brown on main map, arable coloured brown and pasture coloured green on map at bottom of sheet.

Pencil notes. Map at bottom of sheet has a separate scale bar on left, 10–0–50 chains (= 7 1/2in.), 1:6,336. Manor Farm, Great Eversden, owned by Queens' College, Cambridge. Surveyor's 1st name was Charles [Eden O1].

Great Shelford – [c. 1773] – GTS77301 – G C C XXXVIII.Map 1

A Plan Of A Farm in the Parish of Great Shelford and County of Cambridge Belonging to Gonvil and Cajus College Cambridge.

Surveyor: [Joseph Freeman?]; **Scale bar** 0–160 statute perches (= 4 15/16in.), 1:6,416; **Size:** (i) 19 1/4 x 27 1/8in.; **Top** is N; Manuscript(i), parchment, coloured.

Great Shelford Church, TL458518, and 252a.2r.26p. mostly to N and E, bounded by Trumpington Parish in N and Hauxton Parish in W.

Names of roads and neighbouring owners. Hauxton and Great Shelford churches shown in perspective. Open fields showing owner's strips; closes; meadow; acreages; roads and hedges; watercourses; 'Sheep Moor' and common meadow adjoining map.

Border of 1 narrow band; title top right in a rococo cartouche; yellow scale bar on left; cardinal points stated at edge of map. Table above scale bar giving tenants, acreages and land use. Water coloured blue, roads coloured brown, trees coloured green, arable coloured brown, Mr Thomas Northfield's land coloured green.

At bottom: 'Note, the Figures at the Ends of the dotted lines denotes the distance from Each Piece, for instance 980 is 9 Chains & 80 Links the Measured distance between the Ends of those Pieces'. Note top left: 'Lands in the Occupation of Thos Northfield are coloured Green'. Ink alterations to acreages and to orientation. At 'South' is written 'East according to the Terrier'. Accompanied by a terrier attached to right of sheet. Joseph Freeman was paid in the half year ending at Lady Day 1774 for mapping Shelford [GCC Bursar's Book 1758–75]. See also GTS77302.

Great Shelford – [c. 1773] – GTS77302 – G C C XXXVIII.Map 2

[Land SW of Great Shelford Church, owned by Gonville and Caius College, Cambridge.]

Surveyor: [Joseph Freeman?]; **Scale:** 1:2,280; **Size:** (iii) 13 x 7 1/2in.; **Top** is N; Manuscript(i), parchment, coloured.

53a.0r.39p. in TL4551, bounded by River Cam in W.

Names of fields and owners. Closes; hedges showing hedgerow trees; acreages; watercourses; park; 'Hunch' [mound?].

Water coloured blue, fields outlined in green.

Top right: 'Note, those Numbers marked here correspond with those Numbers marked in the Fields on the Map'. Notes on fields of landownership, acreages and areas claimed by Gonville and Caius College. Pencil notes. Left of terrier which accompanies GTS77301 and was probably surveyed at a similar time; Joseph Freeman was paid in the half year ending at Lady Day 1774 for mapping Shelford [GCC Bursar's Book 1758–75].

Great Shelford – [c. 1791] – GTS79101 – SJC MPS 221

[Granhams Farm, Great Shelford, owned by St John's College, Cambridge.]

Surveyor: [Joseph Freeman?]; **Scale bar** 0–30 chains (= 3 11/16in.), 1:6,443; **Size:** (i) 27 7/8 x 25 1/2in.; **Top** is NNE; Manuscript(i), parchment, coloured.

Granhams Farm, TL463531, and 213a.2r.18p. in strips scattered throughout parish.

Names of fields, roads and neighbouring owners. Granhams Farm, Great Shelford Church and buildings in village shown in plan form. Open fields showing owner's strips; closes; common; trees; heath; meadow; roads; watercourses and 'Cow pond'; bridge; Nine Wells Springs; moat; clunch pit.

Border of 1 broad and 1 narrow band; scale bottom right; compass middle left showing 4 plain points with a decorated N. Table top left giving field names and acreages for open and inclosed land. Water coloured grey, strips and roads coloured brown, trees, grass and meadow coloured green.

Cut from a lease; map drawn before 1793, when a neighbouring owner died, and possibly in connection with renewal of lease of farm in 1791 [SJC C5.3, 27]. In style of Joseph Freeman, who surveyed for the College in the 1790s. Copies at SJC MPS 207A and B. Photograph at 1:8,640 at CRO TR869/P26.

Great Shelford – [c. 1828] – GTS82801 – CUL MS Plans y.1(23)

Plan of Gt Shelford Flour & Oil Mills and Premises.

Draughtsman: [Elliot Smith]; **Scale:** An Inch to 20 ft, 1:240; **Size:** (ii) 14 1/2 x 21in.; **Top** is E; Manuscript(i), paper, uncoloured.

Mills at TL458515, and c. 1a. in SW of village bounded by River Cam.

Names of tenants. Buildings shown in plan form and include stables, shed and cottages. Roads and watercourses; bridge; furnaces, copper and 'Bath stove'; roofing types.

Title middle left; scale beneath title.

Note above title: 'No. 57994 and 57995'. Note below title: 'The Flour mill works 4 pair of stones Oats are not shelled therein No Kiln adjoining or communicating Only a small Bath Stove in the Counting House marked △ The Mill is used only for Grinding Flour'. Similar notes about Oil Mill. Drawn for fire insurance purposes, in volume from Elliot Smith and Sons, Auctioneers and Estate Agents; most maps in volume drawn c. 1828.

Great Shelford – [c. 1835] – GTS83501 – G C C XXXVIII.40

Estate of Caius College at Great Shelford.

Surveyor: G[eorge] Cuming; **Scale bar** 0–30 chains (= 3 5/16in.), 1:7,173; **Size:** (i) 10 15/16 x 18 1/4in.; **Top** is N; Manuscript(i), paper, coloured.

386a.0r.28p. scattered throughout parish bounded by Cherry Hinton Parish in N, Trumpington Parish in NW and Stapleford Parish in E; Great Shelford Church, which is not shown, is at TL458518.

Names of roads and neighbouring owners. Closed fields; acreages; responsibility for boundaries; roads; footpaths; milestone; watercourses.

Border of 1 broad band with 1 narrow band on inside; title top left; scale bottom left in a grey rectangular border; compass top right showing 4 points. Roads coloured brown, land outlined in green.

Later ink notes of buildings in plan form. Pencil notes. Note on dorse: 'Map of Shelford Farm Alexr Watford Esqr Land Surveyor Cambridge only single sheet'. Paper has a watermark of 1831, map probably drawn by Cuming at same time as his map which accompanied 1835 inclosure award.

Great Shelford – [1835] – GTS83502 – JCC Great Shelford 6

Jesus College Impropriators in Lieu of Glebe Lands and

Common Rights Great Shelford.

Surveyor: [George Cuming]; **Scale:** 1:8,720; **Size:** (ii) 10 15/16 x 8 7/8in.; **Top** is NW; Manuscript(ii), tracing paper, uncoloured.

45a.1r.26p. in NE of TL4551, bounded by River Cam in SW and road to Cambridge in E.

Names of owner, fields and roads. Cottages shown in plan form. Closed fields; meadows; acreages; roads and watercourses; 'Warts [Worts'] corner'.

Title at top; compass on right showing 4 points.

Tracing of part of map by George Cuming which accompanied 1835 inclosure award.

Great Shelford – 1835 – GTS83503 – GCC Drawer 1 Map 3

The Estate belonging to Caius College Cambridge at Great Shelford Cambridgeshire 1835.

Scale bar 0–40 chains (= 4 7/16in.), 1:7,139; **Size:** (i) 25 15/16 x 24 7/8in.; **Top** is NNE; Manuscript(i), parchment, coloured.

Great Shelford Church, TL458518, and 403a.0r.1p. in whole parish, except for 13p. in Little Shelford Parish.

Names of fields, roads and neighbouring owners. Church, 'King's Mills' and cottages shown in plan form. Closed fields showing owner's land; state of cultivation shown by colour; acreages of arable [all acreages given in table]; roads; watercourses and 'The Nine Wells' [springs]; gravel and clunch pits; responsibility for boundaries; gardens and orchards identified on table.

Border of 1 broad band with 1 narrow band on either side; title top left; scale under title; compass centre left showing 16 points. Table bottom right giving tenants, field names, acreages and reasons for allotments. Water coloured blue, roads coloured brown, fields coloured green or brown, buildings coloured red.

Pencil notes and grid.

Great Wilbraham – [c. 1801] – GTW80101 – JCC Great Wilbraham

Master & Fellows of <Christ> Jesus College Farm at Gt Wilbraham.

Scale: 1:1,750; **Size:** (ii) 9 3/4 x 8 1/4in.; **Top** is NE; Manuscript(i), paper, uncoloured.

88a.3r.10p. in Great Wilbraham Parish.

Names of neighbouring owners. Closed fields showing owner's land; state of cultivation given in words; acreages and dimensions of plots; ditches; roads.

Title at top; cardinal points added later in red pencil.

Copy in JCC measures 4 1/2 x 2 7/8in. and is on a sheet measuring 7 x 4 1/2in., gives responsibility for boundaries but not orientation. Date is given in catalogue in JCC; map probably drawn soon after 1801 inclosure award.

Guilden Morden – 1751 – GUI75101 – DCC

A Survey. of Moreden Hall Farm, & also of late Pain's, in the Parish of Gilded Moreden, and County of Cambridge The Estate and Lordship, of the Honble Sir Iacob Garrard Downing Bart By Jos. Cole 1751.

Surveyor: Joseph Cole; **Scale bar** 10–0–80 perches (= 5 11/16in.), 1:3,133; **Size:** (i) 20 13/16 x 13 7/8in.; **Top** is NNE; Manuscript(i), parchment, coloured.

Morden Hall ['Moreden Hall Farm'], TL285439, and 782a.3r.37p. to N bounded by Steeple Morden Parish ['Little Morden Parish'] in E.

Names of fields, roads, parishes and neighbouring owners. Farm buildings and cottages shown in plan form, church shown in perspective. Closed fields showing owner's land; pightles; trees and grove; acreages; hedges; roads and gates; watercourses, ponds and moat; gardens and orchards.

Border of 1 broad band with 1 narrow band on inside; title top left in a rococo cartouche with leaves and flowers and coloured gold, pink, blue, green and red; scale bar bottom right with a yellow outline; compass rose at bottom showing 8 red, blue, yellow and green points. Bottom right is a perspective drawing of Morden Hall, bottom left is a perspective drawing of 'Pain's Farm'. Fields outlined in yellow, green and red, water coloured blue, buildings coloured red, trees coloured green, roads coloured brown.

Top right is inset of land in Tadlow Bridge Field, Shingay Parish. Under inset is a note of colours in which each farm is depicted. Accompanied by 2 terriers: 'A Terrar and Particular of Moreden Hall Farm in the Parish of Gilded Moreden in the County of Cambridge the Estate and Lordship of the Honourable Sir Jacob Garrard Downing Bart, by Jos. Cole', and: 'A Terrar and Particular of late Pains Farm in the Parish of Gilded Moreden and County of Cambridge Surveyed 1751 by Jos: Cole'. Both terriers give names of fields and furlongs, the bounds of each area, number of lands and statute acreages, and have notes of lands in 'Manor of Shingey, and Tyth free'. Terrier of Moreden Hall Farm also has a note of a right of way. Map, terriers and GAM75201 are at end of a volume of maps of the Downing estate, CRY75001–11, EAS75001–8 and TAD75001–9.

Guilden Morden – 1797 – GUI79701 – CUL MS Plans 273

A Survey of Moreden Hall Farm and also of late Pains in the Parish of Gilded Moreden in the County of Cambridge.

Surveyor: J[ohn] Prickett; **Scale bar** 10–0–80 poles (= 5 5/8in.), 1:3,168; **Size:** (i) 20 5/16 x 13 13/16in.; **Top** is NNE; Manuscript(i), parchment, coloured.

Morden Hall, TL435440, and c. 330a. in E of parish, bounded by Tadlow Parish in N and Steeple Morden Parish in E.

Names of fields, roads, owners and neighbouring owners. Church shown in exaggerated perspective, cottage and farm buildings shown in plan form. Open fields showing owner's strips; closes and pightle; wood and trees; acreages; roads and watercourses; gates; gardens; orchard; 2 moats; ponds.

Border of 1 broad and 1 narrow band; title top left; scale bottom right; compass bottom left showing 8 points. Colour used to distinguish between different farms: Hall Farm land has green border, Ellis' farm has brown border and Pain's farm has yellow border; roads coloured brown, buildings coloured red, trees coloured green, water coloured blue.

2 insets: top right, land to N in Tadlow Bridge Field, Shingay Parish, containing 1r.9p. belonging to Hall Farm and 1a.0r.17p. belonging to Ellis' farm. Bottom left, 1a.3r.15p. in a farmyard and close belonging to Hall Farm in 'Towns~end furlong' to S. Estate owned by Jacob John Whittington [VCH, 8, 99]. Surveyor's 1st name was John [Eden P333]. Photograph in CRO.

H

Haddenham – [1773] – HAD77301 – QCC 328

A Plan of the Delphs in the Parish of Haddenham and County of Cambridge Belonging to Queens College Cambridge.

Surveyor: [J[oseph] Freeman]; **Scale bar** 0–90 perches (= 3 3/8in.), 1:5,280; **Size:** (i) 7 5/8 x 8 1/16in.; **Top** is N; Manuscript(i), parchment, coloured.

88a.1r.15p. in TL4173, bounded by River Great Ouse in W, Gall Fen ['Gaul Fenn'] in NE and 'Ewel Fenn' in SE.

Names of areas, fens and neighbouring owners. Building in Ewell Fen shown in perspective. Closed fields showing owner's land; acreages; watercourses.

Border of 1 narrow band; title top left; scale bottom left. Tables top right and bottom right of whole sheet giving tenants and acreages. River coloured blue, fields outlined in blue with yellow strips, red numbers refer to table.

Bottom left of a sheet entitled: 'A Plan of a Farm called Haslewoods in the Parish of Haverhill [Suffolk] allso Haven Wood in the Parish of Bumpsted Hellions [Essex], Both Belonging to Queens College Cambridge taken by J. Freeman, Cambr*idge*, 1773'. Surveyor and date of Haddenham map are assumed to be those of main map on sheet. Freeman's 1st name was Joseph [Eden F209].

Haddenham – [1818] – HAD81801 – CLC ACC.1985/5

['Sketch of Lands at Haddenham 1818 To the Master & Fellows of Clare Hall'.]

Surveyor: [Alexander Watford jr]; **Scale:** 1:3,510; **Size:** (i) 15 x 18 13/16in.; **Top** is N; Manuscript(i), paper, coloured.

Haddenham Church, TL463755, and 5a.0r.30p. E of Hilrow, bounded by road from Hilrow to Wilburton in S, Wentworth Parish in N and Wilburton Parish in E.

Names of roads and neighbouring owners. Church shown in perspective, built-up area in village shown in plan form. Open fields showing owner's strips; closes; acreages; roads and footpaths; watercourses; hedges.

Border of 2 narrow bands. Roads coloured brown, 'way' coloured green, buildings coloured red, fields outlined in yellow, strips coloured yellow with brown edges, old inclosures outlined in blue, water coloured blue.

Title and date on dorse. Surveyor was Alexander Watford, who drew up accompanying terrier on 27 March 1818 [CLC Safe A:18/11].

Haddenham – 1821 – HAD82101 – QCC 328

Plan of an Estate at Haddenham in the Isle of Ely and County of Cambridge Belonging to the President & Fellows of Queen's College in the University of Cambridge made AD 1821.

Surveyor: [Alexander Watford jr?]; **Scale bar** 0–15 chains (= 5in.), 1:2,376; **Size:** (i) 20 1/2 x 15 7/8in.; **Top** is N; Manuscript(i), paper, coloured.

Flat Bridge Farm ['Flat Ferry House'], TL418730, and 89a.2r.2p. to N and W in Upper Delphs and Ewell Fen.

Names of farms, fields and neighbouring owners. 'Flat Ferry House' and another building shown in plan form. Closed fields showing owner's land; Upper Delphs and common; state of cultivation shown by colour; acreages; responsibility for boundaries; roads and gates; watercourses and 'Drain to Mill'; bank; osier holt; pump.

Border of 1 broad band with 1 narrow band on each side; title top right; scale beneath title; compass at top showing

4 plain points. Table at bottom giving field names, acreages and tenants. Water coloured blue, pasture coloured green, arable coloured in yellow stripes, buildings coloured red.

Pencil notes on table: 'John Fortington's occupation', and, 'T & W Sutton lessees'. In style of Alexander Watford jr, who was employed by the College in 1821.

Haddenham – [1825] – HAD82501 – QCC 355 A23, B23

Estate at Haddenham In The Isle of Ely And County of Cambridge.

Surveyor: [Alexander Watford jr]; **Scale bar** 0–20 chains (= 6 11/16in.), 1:2,369; **Size:** (i) 25 5/16 x 19 1/8in.; **Top** is N; Manuscript(ii), paper, coloured.

Flat Bridge Farm ['Flat Ferry House'], TL418730, and 89a.2r.2p. in W of parish bounded by Upper Delphs in W and Ewell Fen in E.

Names of fields, roads and neighbouring owners. 'Flat Ferry House' shown in plan form. Closed fields showing owner's land; land quality; state of cultivation shown by colour; acreages; hedges; roads and gates; bank; osier holt; bridge or weir; pump; drains and 'drain to mill'.

Border to top, bottom and left of 1 broad band with 1 narrow band on either side; title top left; scale at bottom; compass top right showing 4 points. Table bottom left giving tenants, field names, acreages and land use. Pasture coloured green, arable coloured with yellow stripes, roads coloured brown, water coloured blue.

On left of sheet, which also contains a map of Furneux Pelham [Hertfordshire], and in volume drawn in 1825: 'Plans of the Several Estates in England and Wales belonging to the President and Fellows of the College of St Margaret and St Bernard commonly called Queen's College in the University of Cambridge Delineated from Authentic Documents in the possession of the said President and Fellows and from actual Surveys taken By their most obedient and obliged Servant Alexr Watford'. Title page drawn by James Richardson [Watford's nephew]. This is the Bursar's copy; 2nd, finer, copy [the Master's copy] at QCC 355 B23 measures 24 11/16 x 18 3/8in., is drawn on parchment and top points NNW. Pump not shown. Border 7/16in. wide of a central blue band with 1 narrow band on either side, title top right and has gothic lettering, scale bottom right, no compass. Table at bottom and has red lines. Fields have yellow and brown stripes, roads have red/brown edges. On right of sheet. Positive photostat of this copy at 1:5,200 at BL 2865.(9).

Haddenham – 1827 – HAD82701 – GCC Drawer 3 Map 1

High Land Parts of Estates in the Parish of Haddenham and Hamlet of Hilrow. in the Isle of Ely. together with certain Lands in the Parishes of Sutton and Wentworth in the said Isle belonging to the Master and Fellows of Gonville and Caius College in the University of Cambridge as ascertained in 1827. By Alexr Watford.

Surveyor: Alexander Watford [jr]; **Draughtsman:** James Richardson; **Scale bar** 0–40 chains (= 6 5/8in.), 1:4,782; **Size:** (i) 39 1/8 x 31 9/16in.; **Top** is N; Manuscript(iii), parchment, coloured.

Haddenham Church, TL464756, and 171a.0r.14p. mostly N of village, bounded by North Fen in W and Wilburton Parish in E, in W of Wentworth Parish S of road from Sutton to Ely, and in E of Sutton Parish.

Names of fields, fen, roads and neighbouring owners. Farm buildings shown in plan form, church shown in perspective. Open fields showing owner's strips; closes; fen and meadow; acreages; roads and 'Toll Bar'; watercourses and ponds; hedges and fences; balks; glebe; 'Mill Yard'; 'Gallons', 'Clay' and 'Sutton' hills.

Border 3/8in. wide with a central broad blue band; title top left; scale bar centre bottom alternately coloured blue and uncoloured; compass centre top showing 8 points. Table top right giving tenants, field names and acreages. Roads coloured yellow and outlined in brown, buildings coloured red, balks coloured green, water coloured blue, fields outlined in blue and pink, strips coloured yellow, pink and blue.

Note bottom right: 'The Terriers upon which this Survey has been founded are numbered in red Ink and the quantities of the separate Lands from Mr Waudby's Plan inserted in pencil the aggregate could only appear on the face of this reduced Plan'. These terriers [GCC XIX.1 and 2], by W. Waudby in 1801, give content of land, owner and occupier. No map by Waudby has been found; his 1st name may have been William [see MAR80501]. Pencil notes. Positive photostat at 1:4,608 at CRO TR836/P1, and at 1:10,560 at BL 1640.(26).

Hardwick – 1831 – HAP83101 – PCC Hardwick I1

Plan of Arable, Pasture, & Woodland, lying in Hardwicke, Cambridgeshire, Part belonging to the Master of Pembroke College, Cambridge; and Part belonging to the Masters of Pembroke, St Peter's and Jesus Colleges, as Lords of the Manor of Hardwicke, in trust for Pembroke College Chapel.

Surveyor: R[ichard] Harwood; **Scale bar** 0–10 chains (= 3 5/16in.), 1:2,391; **Size:** (i) 15 1/8 x 25 3/8in.; **Top** is NW; Manuscript(i), parchment, coloured.

15a.3r.10p. in SE of TL3558 in SW of parish, bounded by Caldecote Parish in W, Toft Parish in S and Hardwick Wood in SE.

Names of fields, owners and neighbouring owners. Closed fields showing owner's land; wood and 'Brushwood'; pasture; state of cultivation shown by colour; acreages; hedges; roads and 'Right of way'; gates.

Border 1/4in. wide with 1 broad band and 2 narrow bands; title top right; scale middle bottom; compass bottom left showing 8 points. Table on right giving field names, tenants, acreages, land use, description of land and boundaries. Fields outlined in green except for 2 outlined in red, and coloured green or in yellow stripes.

Inset bottom left of 26p. 'alloted under Toft Inclosure to the Lords of the Manor of Hardwicke for their proportion of the Right of Soil of the Common in the Intercommon; ...' Surveyor's 1st name was Richard [Eden H188].

Hardwick – 1834 – HAP83401 – PCC Hardwick I3

Sketch of Mr Pearces Old Inclosures in Hardwick.

Draughtsman: E[dward] S[erocold] Pearce; **Scale:** 1:5,000; **Size:** (ii) 8 7/8 x 7in.; **Top** is N; Manuscript(i), paper, coloured.

Hardwick Church, TL372586, and c. 110a. S of village green.

Names of fields, houses and neighbouring owners. Houses and church shown in plan form. Closed fields and pightle; roads; 'pea spinney'; 'Rickyard'; feature which may be a pond.

Title on right; compass top left showing 4 plain points. Freehold land coloured red, copyhold land coloured blue.

Note under title: 'The Freehold is coloured Red The Copyhold [is coloured] Blue'. Note at bottom: 'This Sketch was made by the Revd E.S. Pearce'. Note on dorse: 'Sketch of Inclosures purchased in Hardwick by Revd Edwd Serocold Pearce May 30 1834 with an Account of the Settling of the Copyhold Lands'. Accompanies: 'Minute concerning the Fines paid by Mr Royston's heir and by the Revd Edward Serocold Pearce, who has recently purchased Mr Royston's Estate at Hardwick'. Minute describes land and gives acreages and land use. Royston's 1st name was William [VCH, 5, 101].

Hardwick – 1836 – HAP83601 – PCC Hardwick I6

[Land in Hardwick, owned by Pembroke College, Cambridge.]

Surveyor: Thomas Utton; **Scale bar** 0–20 chains (= 3 5/16in.), 1:4,782; **Size:** (i) 26 1/4 x 25 7/8in.; **Top** is NE; Manuscript(ii), tracing paper, coloured.

Plan of whole parish to show 37a.2r.2p. in TL3558 in SW of parish, bounded by Caldecote Parish in W and Toft Parish in S.

Names of roads, some closes and owners. Buildings in village near church shown in plan form. Closed fields; woods; acreages; roads, their width and 'Public Bridle Road'; 'Footway'.

Border of 1 broad and 1 narrow band; scale bottom left; compass top left showing 8 points. Roads coloured brown, 'Village of Hardwick' written in blue.

Note bottom left: 'If the Lords of the Manor take Mr Pearce's Wood there will be to pay for 9a.1r.32p. If the Lords of the Manor do not take Mr Pearce's Wood there will be to pay for 5a.2r.32p.' Pearce's 1st names were Edward Serocold [see HAP83401]. Numbers on fields refer to inclosure award.

Harlton – 1816 – HAQ81601 – TCC Box 27 Harlton 51

Sketch & Valuation of Estate at Harlton belonging to the Master Fellows & Scholars of Trinity College in Lease to John Whitechurch 4th June 1816.

Surveyor: Alexander Watford [jr]; **Scale:** 1:2,340; **Size:** (iii) 10 1/4 x 7in.; **Top** is SW; Manuscript(i), paper, uncoloured.

19a.2r.19p. either in TL3751 and TL3752, or in TL3853, bounded by road from Arrington to Cambridge in NW.

Names of roads and neighbouring owners. Closed field; acreage; turnpike road; responsibility for boundaries.

Title at top. Direction to Cambridge shown by cuffed hands.

Note under acreage: 'Value of Allotment 25l:10s:0d'; note along boundary: 'This fence to make'.

Harlton – 1824 – HAQ82401 – GHL 277

Plan of Harlton Manor Farm in the Parishes of Harlton, Haslingfield, and Little Eversden, in the County of Cambridge; belonging to the Governors of Christ's Hospital – London. Also of the Copyhold Estates, held under them as Lords of the Manor of Harlton aforesaid.

Surveyor: James Trumper; **Scale bar** 0–36 chains (= 6in.), 1:4,752; **Size:** (i) 25 1/4 x 45 1/2in.; **Top** is NW; Manuscript(i), paper mounted on cloth, coloured.

Harlton Church, TL387525, and 759a.3r.22p. to W and mostly SE of road from Arrington to Cambridge, 1 plot in SE of Little Eversden Parish and 2 plots in W of Haslingfield Parish.

Names of roads, tenants and neighbouring owners. Manor Farm, cottages and public house shown in plan form, church shown in perspective. Closed fields showing owner's land; wood, deciduous and fir trees; meadow; common; state of cultivation shown by colour; roads and turnpike; footpaths; watercourses; ponds; bridges; gardens and orchards; earthworks and moats; hedges; 'Orwell Maypole'; boundaries between Harlton, Haslingfield and Little Eversden parishes.

Border 1/2in. wide of a central broad purple band with 1 narrow black band between broader uncoloured bands on either side; title top left; scale centre bottom; compass bottom left showing 8 points. Table on right giving tenants, field names, acreages and land use. Roads coloured brown, trees coloured green, buildings coloured red, arable coloured in brown stripes, pasture coloured green, water coloured blue, copyhold land outlined in yellow.

Pencil notes.

Harlton – [1825] – HAQ82501 – QCC 355 A17, B17
Estate at Harlton In the County of Cambridge.
Surveyor: [Alexander Watford jr]; **Scale bar** 0–20 chains (= 3 5/16in.), 1:4,782; **Size:** (i) 9 5/16 x 12 3/8in.; **Top** is NW; Manuscript(ii), paper, coloured.
32a.0r.9p. in TL3651 in NW of parish, bounded by road from Royston to Cambridge ['Arrington Turnpike Road'] in SE, Little Eversden Parish in NE and Orwell Parish in W.
Names of allotments, roads and neighbouring owners. Closed fields showing owner's land; state of cultivation shown by colour; acreages; hedges; roads and turnpike; tenure; 'Orwell May Pole'.
Border of 1 broad band with 1 narrow band on either side; title top left; scale at bottom; compass top right showing 4 points. Table bottom left giving allotments, acreages, land use and tenure. Fields coloured yellow, roads coloured brown.
Pencil notes and reasons for allotments. Above map of Haslingfield, HAS82501, and in volume drawn in 1825: 'Plans of the Several Estates in England and Wales belonging to the President and Fellows of the College of St Margaret and St Bernard commonly called Queen's College in the University of Cambridge Delineated from Authentic Documents in the possession of the said President and Fellows and from actual Surveys taken By their most obedient and obliged Servant Alexr Watford'. Title page drawn by James Richardson [Watford's nephew]. This is the Bursar's copy; 2nd, finer, copy [the Master's copy] at QCC 355 B17, measures 9 1/2 x 11in. and is drawn on parchment. Border 3/8in. wide and imitates a scroll of paper, title top right and has some gothic lettering, compass shows 8 points and is in a plain style. Table has red lines. Fields coloured in yellow and brown stripes and have green edges, roads have red/brown edges. Pencil alterations to acreages.

Harlton – 1829 – HAQ82901 – CUL Maps.PSQ.18.82
Plan of a valuable freehold & copyhold estate, at Harlton, Cambridgeshire; which will be sold by auction by Elliot Smith ... July, 1829. By direction of the Executors of the late Mr John Whitechurch.
Surveyor: [Joseph] Truslove; **Auctioneer:** Elliot Smith; **Lithographer:** W[illiam] Metcalfe; **Scale:** 1:9,600; **Size:** (i) 9 9/16 x 13 9/16in.; **Top** is NW; Lithograph, paper, uncoloured.

Farm at TL387523, and 274a.2r.10p. bounded by Little Eversden Parish in W, Barrington Parish in S and road from Harlton to Comberton in E.
Names of roads and neighbouring owners. Farm buildings shown in plan form, particulars of sale identify farmhouse, barn, granary, dovecote, stable, 'piggeries', 'hen house' and 'chaff house'. Closed fields; trees; tenure; acreages of land for sale; roads; watercourses and 'Foxe's Bridge'; gardens and orchards; responsibility for boundaries.
Border of 1 broad and 1 narrow band; title bottom left.
Accompanies: 'Plan, Particulars and Conditions of Sale, of desirable freehold & copyhold estates, situate at Harlton, Cambridgeshire, which will be sold by auction ... July, 1829'. Particulars of sale give details of tenure, acreages, occupants, taxes and rents. Surveyor's 1st name was Joseph [Eden T266], lithographer's 1st name was William [CRO EPR CW 1825 WR C52:178].

Harston – 1801 – HAR80101 – EDR CC.10108
Plan of the Impropriate Estate within the Parish of Harston in the County of Cambridge 1801.
Scale: 1:5,200; **Size:** (ii) 18 x 31 13/16in.; **Top** is ESE; Manuscript(i), paper, coloured.
Farm at TL426505, and 204a.0r.36p. in plots S of village bounded by roads to Newton in NE and to Royston in NW, and in NW of parish bounded by Haslingfield Parish in W.
Names of roads and neighbouring owners. Hatched area shows location of farm buildings. Closed fields; acreages; roads and watercourses; responsibility for boundaries.
Border of 1 broad grey band; title bottom left; compass top left showing 4 points. Table centre bottom giving acreages. Some road directions shown by cuffed hands. Roads coloured brown, water coloured grey.
Torn in half and centre is damaged. Land owned by Bishop of Ely.

Harston – 1813 – HAR81301 – JCC Harston 4
Plan of the Impropriate Farm at Harston in the County of Cambridge. Taken in 1813.
Surveyor: A[lexander] Watford [jr]; **Scale bar** 0–25 chains (= 2 3/4in.), 1:7,200; **Size:** (i) 18 1/8 x 10 13/16in.; **Top** is N; Manuscript(i), parchment, coloured.
Farm at TL425506, and 206a.0r.17p. scattered in N of parish bounded by Hauxton Parish in E and River Cam in W, and around junction of roads from Haslingfield to Newton and from London to Cambridge.
Names of neighbouring owners and roads. Buildings shown in plan form and include farm buildings and cottages. Closed fields showing owner's land; hedges and fences; state of cultivation shown by colour; acreages; roads, footpaths and bridleway; watercourses and bridge.
Border of 1 broad band with 1 narrow band on each side; title top right; scale bottom left; compass at top showing 4 points. Table on left giving acreages. Roads coloured brown, water coloured blue, 2 fields of grass coloured green.
Accompanies: 'Valuation & report by John Wiggins. March 1814'. Farm leased by Jesus College, Cambridge from Bishop of Ely. Surveyor's 1st name was Alexander [Eden W141.1].

Haslingfield – 1777 – HAS77701 – QCC 328

A Survey of the Inclosed Pasture in the Parish of Haslingfield in the County Cambridge [sic.] belonging to Queens College.

Surveyor: Joseph Freeman; **A Scale** of Chains & Links, Scale bar 1–0–10 chains (= 3 5/8in.), 1:2,403; **Size:** (i) 13 3/8 x 25 1/4in.; **Top** is W?; Manuscript(i), parchment, coloured.

Haslingfield Church, TL403521, and 24a.3r.15p. to S bounded by 'Burnt Mill' and River Cam in SE.

Names of fields, roads and neighbouring owners. Church, farmhouses and barns shown in perspective. Closed fields showing owner's land; wood and trees; state of cultivation shown by colour and shading; fences; roads and gates; watercourses; bridge; 'Burnt Mill'; gardens, orchards and yards identified on table; common adjoining map.

Border of 1 narrow band; title at bottom; scale bottom right. Table on right giving farms, field names and acreages. Houses have red roofs, barns have yellow roofs, water coloured blue, trees coloured green, roads coloured brown, plots outlined in blue and red.

Note bottom left: 'NB those pieces of pasture & the Homestall belonging to Sterns farm are coloured round the edges with Red'.

Haslingfield – [1796] – HAS79601 – QCC 366

[8 closes at Haslingfield, owned by Queens' College, Cambridge.]

Scale: 1:1,580; **Size:** (i) 14 9/16 x 8 5/8in.; Manuscript(i), paper, coloured.

17a.3r.17p. scattered throughout parish.

Names of fields and neighbouring owners. Farm buildings shown in plan form. Closes; trees; state of cultivation shown by colour; acreages; roads; watercourses and pond; hedges and fences.

Border of 1 narrow red band. Water coloured blue, roads coloured brown, grass coloured green.

Closes shown in individual maps on p.13 of: 'A Terrier Of an Estate in the occupation of Edwd Prime situate in the Parish of Haslingfield in the County of Cambridge Belonging to the Master Fellows and Scholars of Queens College in the University of Cambridge 1796'.

Haslingfield – [Post 1820] – HAS82001 – C R O 124/P54

[Haslingfield Parish showing land owned by Queens' College, Cambridge.]

Scale: 1:3,920; **Size:** (ii) 41 1/2 x 35 3/8in.; **Top** is NNE; Manuscript(i), paper mounted on cloth, coloured.

Spring Hall Farm, TL404542, and c. 2,600a. in whole parish.

Buildings in village including Haslingfield Hall, farms and mill shown in plan form, church shown in perspective. Closed fields showing owner's land; roads; River Cam; moat and ponds.

Compass bottom right showing 8 points. Roads coloured brown, water coloured blue, land belonging to Queens' College coloured green.

Pencil notes of acreages, land use and references to a terrier. Numbers on fields also suggest map originally accompanied by a terrier. Drawn after 1820 inclosure award.

Haslingfield – [1825] – HAS82501 – QCC 355 A17, B17

Estate at Haslingfield In the County of Cambridge.

Surveyor: [Alexander Watford jr]; **Scale bar** 0–30 chains (= 5in.), 1:4,752; **Size:** (i) 25 5/16 x 38 1/4in.; **Top** is W; Manuscript(ii), paper, coloured.

Haslingfield Church, TL403521, and 409a.2r.30p. in whole parish.

Names of fields, tenants, owners and roads. Farm buildings shown in plan form, church shown in perspective. Closed fields showing owner's land; wood; 'Cow Common'; state of cultivation shown by colour; acreages; hedges; roads; watercourses, Bourn Brook and River Cam; pond; bridges; 'Allotment for Gravel'; garden.

Border of 1 broad band with 1 narrow band on either side; title top left; scale at bottom; compass above scale showing 4 points. Table bottom left giving tenants, field names, acreages, land use and allotments. Water coloured blue, fields coloured green and yellow, roads coloured brown, wood coloured green, buildings coloured red.

Note on 1 plot of land received in exchange. Pencil notes. Beneath map of Harlton, HAQ82501, and in volume drawn in 1825: 'Plans of the Several Estates in England and Wales belonging to the President and Fellows of the College of St Margaret and St Bernard commonly called Queen's College in the University of Cambridge Delineated from Authentic Documents in the possession of the said President and Fellows and from actual Surveys taken By their most obedient and obliged Servant Alexr Watford'. Title page drawn by James Richardson [Watford's nephew]. This is the Bursar's copy; 2nd, finer, copy [the Master's copy] at QCC 355 B17 measures 24 7/16 x 36 5/8in., is drawn on parchment and has a scale bar of 0–40 chains (= 6 5/8in.), 1:4,782. Haslingfield Church not shown. Border 3/8in. wide of a central blue band with 1 broad band on either side, title has gothic lettering, scale bottom right, compass bottom left shows 8 points. Table centre bottom and has red lines. Fields coloured in brown and yellow stripes, roads have red/brown edges, buildings coloured grey.

Hauxton – [c. 1801] – HAU80101 – EDR CC.12329

Hauxton.

Surveyor: [Thomas Thorpe?]; **Scale:** 1:2,350; **Size:** (ii) 12 3/4 x 16in.; **Top** is N; Manuscript(ii), paper, uncoloured.

46a.1r.16p., in 1 plot E of 'Main Road', and in 1 plot, probably in TL4451, bounded by road to Little Shelford in S.

Names of roads. Closed fields; acreages; roads and watercourses; responsibility for boundaries; reasons for allotments.

Title top right; compass centre right showing 4 points.

Probably copied from map by Thomas Thorpe which accompanied 1801 inclosure award, shows land allotted to Dean and Chapter of Ely. Later ink note on dorse: 'Hauxton Rectory'.

Hauxton – [c. 1801] – HAU80102 – EDR CC.12330

Hauxton.

Surveyor: [Thomas Thorpe?]; **Scale:** 1:2,190; **Size:** (ii) 11 1/16 x 15 1/8in.; Top is N; Manuscript(ii), paper, uncoloured.

Hauxton Mill, TL432528, and 7a.1r.23p. E of river.

Name of owner. Mill buildings shown in plan form.
Closed fields; acreages; roads and watercourses.
Title top right; compass bottom left showing 4 points.
Note on 1 plot: 'Dean & Chapter or Garden indispute'.
Later ink note on dorse: 'Hauxton Mills'. Probably copied
from map by Thomas Thorpe which accompanied 1801 in-
closure award, shows land allotted to Dean and Chapter of
Ely.

Hauxton – 1815 – HAU81501 – EDC 6/1/2/4
Sketch from a map of the late Mr Gillam's Estate at
Haukston Mills.
Surveyor: P.Y.; **Scale**: 1:1,790; **Size**: (ii) 18 5/8 x
15 5/16in.; **Top** is NW; Manuscript(ii), tracing paper,
uncoloured.
Hauxton Mill, TL432527, and c. 130a. to W.
Mill buildings shown in plan form. Closed fields; roads
and watercourses; bridges; plantation.
Title at top.
Land owned by Dean and Chapter of Ely.

Hildersham – 1770 – HIL77001 – NRO Petre Estate 22
Plan of Hildersham Wood belonging to Mrs Southcoat
Taken by J. Freeman Cambridge 1770.
Surveyor: J[oseph] Freeman; **Scale bar** 0–40
perches (= 2 1/2in.), 1:3,168; **Size**: (i) 6 5/8 x 12 5/8in.;
Top is S; Manuscript(i), parchment, coloured.
21a.0r.1p. in S of parish in TL5345, bounded by
'Chesterford Park' in S, Catley ['Catlige'] Park in E and
'Great Abington Common' in W.
Names of wood and neighbouring owners. Wood;
acreages; roads.
Border of 1 narrow band; title on left in a yellow rococo
cartouche; yellow and black scale bar bottom left; compass
bottom right showing 8 points. Trees coloured green and
brown, roads coloured brown.
Surveyor's 1st name was Joseph [Eden F209]. Mrs
Southcoat's 1st name was Bridget [VCH, 6, 62].

Hildersham – 1795 – HIL79501 – CUL MS Plans R.c.20
Plan of the Parish of Hildersham in the County of
Cambridge 1795.
Scale bar 5–0–10 chains (= 3 7/8in.), 1:3,066; **Size**:
(i) 57 1/2 x 26 5/16in.; **Top** is N; Manuscript(i),
parchment, coloured.
Site of 'The mansion house of Hall Esq', TL546486, and
1,499a.2r.20p. in whole parish.
Names of fields, owners and tenants. Hildersham Hall,
church, cottages, farms and farm buildings shown in plan
form. Open fields showing all strips; closes; common;
wood and trees; waste; meadow; acreages; roads and
watercourses; hedges.
Border of 1 broad and 1 narrow band; title bottom right
with decorative line-work; scale beneath title; compass
bottom left showing 4 points. Table on right giving
acreages of land owned by Thomas Rumbold Hall.
Common field land coloured brown, inclosures and trees
coloured green, buildings coloured red.
Pencil notes. Inset to S: 'This part is a continuation of
the parish & placed here for want of length in parchment'.
Estate owned by Thomas Rumbold Hall [VCH, 6, 63].
Photograph in CRO.

Hildersham – [Post 1801] – HIL80101 – C R O
R59/5/10/3
Hildersham Mill and House.
Scale bar 0–80 feet (= 5in.), 1:192; **Size**: (i) 17 1/8 x
8 3/4in.; **Top** is S; Manuscript(i), paper, coloured.
Hildersham Mill, TL548482, and c. 13p. surrounding it.
Names of buildings. Stable, 'hog stye', mill, kitchen,
parlour and wash house shown in plan form. Roads and
watercourses; garden.
Border of 1 narrow band; title at top; scale at bottom;
orientation given by 'North' written at bottom. Water
coloured blue, buildings outlined in yellow, some parts of
buildings coloured red.
On other half of sheet is a plan of barns and stables with
same scale and orientation. On dorse are pencil sketches of
a plan drawing of a house. Paper has a watermark of 1801;
William Emson was the miller from that year [CRO
334/010].

Hildersham – [c. 1815–29] – HIL81501 – CRO 124/P57
[Hildersham Hall, owned by John or Mary Burgoyne.]
Scale: 3 chain scale [to 1 inch], 1:2,376; **Size**: (ii) 94
1/4 x 34 1/8in.; **Top** is NNE; Manuscript(i), paper,
coloured.
Hildersham Hall, TL542483, and strips scattered
throughout parish.
Names of neighbouring owners. Hall, manor house,
church and farms shown in plan form. Open fields showing
owner's strips; common; acreages of land belonging to
estate; roads; River Granta; site of mill; park; woods.
Scale bottom left; compass above scale showing 8 plain
points. Boundary of estate coloured red.
Numbers on plots suggest map originally accompanied
by a terrier. Pencil notes filling in details of land, land use
and acreages. Rough draft drawn between 1815, when
Elizabeth Chalk married to become Elizabeth Reeve and a
neighbouring landowner, and 1829, when William
Stutfield, a neighbouring landowner, became owner of
Hildersham Hall estate through marriage. Owner was John
or Mary Burgoyne, the latter from 1827–9 [VCH, 6, 63].

Hinxton – [c. 1804] – HIN80401 – CRO R57/24/1/57a
The Plan to which the annexed Abstract refers.
Scale: 1:1,140; **Size**: (i) 12 7/16 x 16 1/8in.; **Top** is
N; Manuscript(i), parchment, coloured.
Hinxton Hall, TL498448, and c. 30a. S of village,
bounded by roads from Ickleton in S and from London to
Cambridge in E, and 'South Meadow' and pond in W.
Names of fields, roads and former owners. Closed fields
showing owner's land; tenure; roads including turnpike;
watercourses; garden and kitchen garden; ponds; cold bath;
sites of features including buildings, dovecote, greenhouse,
yards and plantation.
Border of 1 narrow band; title at top; cardinal points
stated in border. Details of land tenure, plot number and
land conveyed to Thomas Fawcett given in red.
Numbers on plots refer to sale documents. Some plots
are ticked, pencil notes, note top right: 'The Cottage and
pieces of Land surrounded by the double Red Ink Lines are
not included in the Sale to Mr Miles, but have been conveyed to Thomas Fawcett Esqr'. On dorse: 'Plan of
Hinxton. Mem. The Spots of Ground though small in
themselves form very material Part of the Place, which
would be spoilt, by the Loss of either Piece (as No 11 for
instance). G.W.' Later note: 'about year 1800 and

previous to that period'. In 1804, Edward Green, owner of the Hall, died and estate was sold to Jonathan Miles; map probably drawn about this time [*VCH*, 6, 224].

Hinxton – [1831] – HIN83101 – CRO R57/24/1/57b
Plan of an Estate in the Parish of Hinxton in the County of Cambridge.
Surveyor: [A.H.]; **Scale:** 1:1,490; **Size:** (ii) 16 3/8 x 19 3/16in.; **Top** is NNW; Manuscript(i), paper, coloured.
Hinxton Hall, TL498448, and c. 86a. S of village bounded by road from Cambridge to London in E and River Granta in W, and extending N and S of road from Ickleton.
Names of fields and former owners. Hinxton Hall, dovecote, bath house, cottages and farm shown in plan form. Closed fields showing owner's land; wood showing deciduous and coniferous trees; meadow; tenure; roads including turnpike; watercourses; gardens; ponds and bridges.
Title top left; compass top left showing 4 points. Roads coloured yellow, water coloured blue, hall coloured light pink.
Numbers on plots suggest map originally accompanied by a terrier. Numbers are same as those on HIN80401. Date and surveyor's initials on dorse. Some details about former owners, as on HIN80401.

Hinxton – [c. 1835] – HIN83501 – CRO 296/P18
[Hinxton Grange.]
Scale: 1:1,860; **Size:** (ii) 29 1/8 x 35 3/4in.; **Top** is N; Manuscript(i), paper mounted on cloth, coloured.
Hinxton Grange, TL503465, and c. 320a. bounded by Great Abington Parish in E, Pampisford Parish in N, and roads from Great Chesterford to Cambridge in W and running E from village towards Great Abington in S.
Names of areas around house. Hinxton Grange and greenhouse shown in plan form. Closed fields; wood and trees; acreages; road; gates; gardens, orchard and lawn; paddock, stack yard and drying ground; sunken fence.
Road coloured brown, paddock outlined in green.
Pencil notes. Owner was probably Wedd William Nash, who built Hinxton Grange c. 1835 [*VCH*, 6, 223].

Hinxton – [c. 1835] – HIN83502 – CRO 124/P58
The Lordship and Rectorial Estate Hinxton Camb's.
Scale: Six Chains to an Inch, 1:4,752; **Size:** (ii) 28 x 31 1/8in.; **Top** is NNE; Manuscript(ii), tracing paper mounted on cloth, coloured.
Lordship Farm, TL494453, and c. 1,400a. in N of parish bounded by Pampisford Parish in N, Duxford Parish in W, Great Abington Parish in E and road running E from village to Great Abington in S.
Names of farms and fields. Hinxton Grange, Lordship Farm, cottages, farm buildings and building which may be a mill shown in plan form, church shown in perspective. Closed fields showing owner's land; common and meadow; wood and trees; acreages; roads, toll bar on road from Royston to Newmarket; footpaths; watercourses including River Granta; gardens and orchard; yard; gravel and turf pits; bridges; moat.
Title bottom right; scale bottom left; compass middle right showing 8 plain points with a decorated N. Water coloured blue, trees coloured green, buildings coloured red, roads coloured brown.
A few pencil notes. Owner was probably Wedd William Nash, who built Hinxton Grange c. 1835 [*VCH*, 6, 223].

Histon – [c. 1806] – HIS80601 – CRO 132/T515
Abstract of the Title of Mr John Watson to a Piece of Freehold Ground at Histon whereon a Windmill lately [stood], and also to an Allotment of Freehold Land lately made thereto.
Surveyor: [William Collisson]; **Draughtsman:** [R. Vitty]; **Scale:** 1:2,160; **Size:** (iii) 4 1/2 x 3 1/4in.; **Top** is NE; Manuscript(i), paper, uncoloured.
7a.2r.21p. in W of parish at TL429639, junction of Meadow Road and Park Lane.
Names of roads, neighbouring owners and claimant of land. Closed fields showing owner's land; roads; site of mill.
Title at top of sheet; compass in centre of map showing 2 points, incorrectly giving top as N.
Beneath map, signed 'R.V.', is note of acreages of allotments, and: 'The dotted line A shewed the reduced state of Copyhold Lot of St Etheldred as bought by Mr Radford'. On dorse: 'For Mr Randall's Perusal. Not approved; but from the small Quantity of land consented to with a Bond of Indemnity. Ed. R.V.' At bottom of this note: 'Vitty Cambridge'. Map probably drawn in connection with 1806 inclosure award; numbers on plots refer to award, inclosure surveyor was William Collisson. Paper has a watermark of 1806.

Histon – [1809] – HIS80901 – BLO Johnson.b.62(5), CRO 65/04, L42/1, L75/10, CUL Maps.PSQ.18.457
Plan of Histon Estate.
Auctioneer: John Swan; **Engraver:** F. Hodson; **Scale:** 1:9,748; **Size:** (ii) 9 1/2 x 12 1/4in.; **Top** is NW; Engraved, paper, coloured.
Abbey Farm, TL433641, and 604a.2r.32p. in NW of parish W of village, bounded by Westwick Parish in N, Oakington Parish in NW and Girton Parish in SW.
Names of neighbouring owners and parishes. Buildings shown in plan form, particulars of sale identify 'Drage's Farm', Abbey Farm, tithe barn and outbuildings. Closed fields; roads and footpaths; watercourses; responsibility for boundaries; gardens and orchard identified on particulars of sale.
Title top left; compass middle bottom showing 4 points. Lot outlined in red.
Accompanies: 'Particulars and conditions of sale of a ... freehold And small part Copyhold Estate situate in the several parishes of Barnwell, Fen Ditton, Horningsea, Teversham, Histon and Waterbeach, in the County of Cambridge ... will be sold by auction ... November, 1809'. On dorse: 'Particulars of the late Mr Panton's Estate at Barnwell'. Particulars of sale give lot number, present occupant, state of cultivation, land tax, tithes and common rights. Scale given on map of land in Barnwell Parish, Cambridge. This is Plate 2. Mr Panton's 1st name was Thomas [Venn, I, 3, 303]. See also FDI80901–4 and HRN80901–6.

Horningsea – 1791 – HRN79101 – SJC MPS 36
A Plan of the Lands &c appertaining to the Parsonage of Horningsea in the County of Cambridge; belonging to St John's College Cambridge. made in the Year 1791.
Surveyor: [Joseph Freeman?]; **Scale:** 8 chains per Inch, Scale bar 0–12 chains (= 1 1/2in.), 1:6,336; **Size:** (i) 18 7/8 x 25 3/4in.; **Top** is ENE; parchment, coloured.

Horningsea Church, TL493627, farm in village to N, and 65a.2r.20p. in strips scattered throughout parish mainly S of village, and in N of Fen Ditton Parish S of road from Cambridge to Newmarket.

Names of fields, roads, river and neighbouring owners. Farm buildings, barn and church shown in plan form. Open fields showing owner's strips; closes; glebe; state of cultivation shown by colour; acreages; roads and milestone; watercourses, ponds and bridge; hedges; churchyard, rick yard and 'green yard'.

Border of 1 broad and 1 narrow band; title bottom right in a cartouche of leaves and flowers; scale beneath title; compass middle top showing 8 points which extend over left-hand part of map. Table middle bottom giving acreages in each field and a summary of arable and pasture. Roads coloured brown, strips coloured yellow, hedges and grass coloured green, buildings coloured red.

Pencil notes. Accompanying terrier at SJC MPS 35 has a drawing of the farm at 1:243. Top is W, shows 27a.25p. bounded by Church Lane in S. Buildings shown in plan form and include house, granary, 'hog stye', 'cow house', 'cart lodge', 'hen house', wheat barn, stables and barley barn. Also shows garden, farmyard and nature of walls and roofs. Map is in style of Joseph Freeman, who surveyed for the College in the 1790s. Photograph of SJC MPS 36 at CRO TR869/P20 at 1:8,448.

Horningsea – [1809] – HRN80901 – B L O Johnson.b.62(5), CRO 65/04, L42/1, L75/10, CUL Maps.PSQ.18.457
Horningsea. Lot 1.
Auctioneer: John Swan; **Engraver:** F. Hodson; **Scale:** 1:9,748; **Size:** (ii) 9 3/8 x 11 1/2in.; **Top** is N; Engraved, paper, uncoloured.
Clayhithe Farm, TL501642, and 145a.1r.25p. extending from Clayhithe in W to Bottisham Parish [Lode Parish since 1894] in E.
Names of parishes and neighbouring owners. Farm buildings and cottages shown in plan form. Closes and old inclosures; roads and footpaths; watercourses; garden identified on particulars of sale.
Title middle top; compass middle right showing 4 points.
Accompanies: 'Particulars and conditions of sale of a ... freehold And small part Copyhold Estate situate in the several parishes of Barnwell, Fen Ditton, Horningsea, Teversham, Histon and Waterbeach, in the County of Cambridge ... will be sold by auction ... November, 1809'. On dorse: 'Particulars of the late Mr Panton's Estate at Barnwell'. Particulars of sale give lot number, present occupant, state of cultivation, land tax, tithes and common rights. Scale given on map of land in Barnwell Parish, Cambridge. This is Plate 3. Mr Panton's 1st name was Thomas [Venn, I, 3, 303]. See also FDI80901–4, HIS80901 and HRN80902–6.

Horningsea – [1809] – HRN80902 – B L O Johnson.b.62(5), CRO 65/04, L42/1, L75/10, CUL Maps.PSQ.18.457
Horningsea. Lot 2.
Auctioneer: John Swan; **Engraver:** F. Hodson; **Scale:** 1:9,748; **Size:** (ii) 9 3/8 x 11 7/16in.; **Top** is N; Engraved, paper, uncoloured.

Eye Hall Farm, TL499637, and 219a.3r.12p. in NW of parish bounded by River Cam in W and crossing road running N from Horningsea.
Names of neighbouring owners. Farm buildings shown in plan form. Closed fields; roads and footpaths; watercourses; pightle and orchard identified on particulars of sale.
Title centre top; compass top left showing 4 points.
Accompanies particulars of sale of Thomas Panton's estate in 1809; see HRN80901 for details. This is Plate 4. See also FDI80901–4, HIS80901 and HRN80903–6.

Horningsea – [1809] – HRN80903 – B L O Johnson.b.62(5), CRO 65/04, L42/1, L75/10, CUL Maps.PSQ.18.457
Horningsea. Lots 3, 6, 7, 10 and 11.
Auctioneer: John Swan; **Engraver:** F. Hodson; **Scale:** 1:9,748; **Size:** (ii) 14 1/4 x 9 1/4in.; **Top** is N; Engraved, paper, uncoloured.
Junction of Horningsea Road and Biggin Lane, TL491615, and 221a.2r.29p. divided into plots SE of junction bounded by Fen Ditton Parish in S, NW of junction bounded by River Cam in NW, and land N and E through village.
Names of parishes and neighbouring owners. Farm buildings and cottages shown in plan form. Closed fields; roads; watercourses; rick yard and pightle identified on particulars of sale.
Title middle top; compass middle left showing 4 points.
Accompanies particulars of sale of Thomas Panton's estate in 1809; see HRN80901 for details. This is Plate 5. See also FDI80901–4, HIS80901 and HRN80902,4–6.

Horningsea – [1809] – HRN80904 – B L O Johnson.b.62(5), CRO 65/04, L42/1, L75/10, CUL Maps.PSQ.18.457
Horningsea & Fen Ditton. Lot 4.
Auctioneer: John Swan; **Engraver:** F. Hodson; **Scale:** 1:9,748; **Size:** (ii) 8 3/4 x 11 1/8in.; **Top** is N; Engraved, paper, coloured.
230a.3r.0p. in TL4962 and TL5062 in Fen Ditton and Horningsea parishes, extending from Horningsea Main Street in W to Stow cum Quy Parish in E.
Names of neighbouring owners. Farm buildings and cottages shown in plan form. Closed fields; roads and footpaths; garden, pightle, milking and rick yards identified on particulars of sale.
Title middle top; compass bottom right showing 4 points. Boundary between Horningsea and Fen Ditton parishes coloured yellow.
Accompanies particulars of sale of Thomas Panton's estate in 1809; see HRN80901 for details. This is Plate 6. See also FDI80901–4, HIS80901 and HRN80902–3,5–6.

Horningsea – [1809] – HRN80905 – B L O Johnson.b.62(5), CRO 65/04, L42/1, L75/10, CUL Maps.PSQ.18.457
Horningsea & Fen Ditton. Lots 5, 8 and 9.
Auctioneer: John Swan; **Engraver:** F. Hodson; **Scale:** 1:9,748; **Size:** (ii) 8 3/4 x 14 1/16in.; **Top** is N; Engraved, paper, coloured.
104a.2r.7p. in TL4962 and TL5062 in NE of Fen Ditton Parish bounded by Stow cum Quy Parish in E and Horningsea Parish in N, and land to W in Horningsea Parish SW of village and bounded by River Cam in W.

Names of neighbouring owners and parishes. Particulars of sale identify farm buildings, cottage and public house, which are shown in plan form. Closed fields; roads; watercourses and pond; garden identified on particulars of sale.

Title middle top; compass top left showing 4 points. Boundary between Horningsea and Fen Ditton parishes coloured yellow.

Accompanies particulars of sale of Thomas Panton's estate in 1809; see HRN80901 for details. This is Plate 7. See also FDI80901-4, HIS80901 and HRN80902-4,6.

Horningsea – [1809] – HRN80906 – B L O Johnson.b.62(5), CRO 65/04, L42/1, L75/10, CUL Maps.PSQ.18.457

Horningsea & Fen Ditton. Lot 12.

Auctioneer: John Swan; **Engraver:** F. Hodson; **Scale:** 1:9,748; **Size:** (ii) 8 13/16 x 10 7/8in.; **Top** is N; Engraved, paper, coloured.

Biggin Farm, TL488618, and 146a.0r.26p. bounded by River Cam in NW, Horningsea Road in E and Fen Ditton Parish in S.

Names of neighbouring owners. Farm buildings shown in plan form. Closed fields; roads and footpaths; watercourses; clay pit.

Title middle top; compass middle right showing 4 points. Boundary between Fen Ditton and Horningsea parishes coloured yellow.

Accompanies particulars of sale of Thomas Panton's estate in 1809; see HRN80901 for details. This is Plate 8. See also FDI80901-4, HIS80901 and HRN80902-5.

Horningsea – [c. 1810] – HRN81001 – SJC MPS 218

Plan of Estates situate at Horningsea in the County of Cambridge Belonging to the Master, Fellow & Scholars of St John's College in the University of Cambridge.

Scale bar 0–20 chains (= 3 5/16in.), 1:4,782; **Size:** (i) 26 5/8 x 20 3/8in.; **Top** is N; Manuscript(i), parchment, coloured.

Horningsea Church, TL493627, farmhouse in village to N, and 365a.1r.7p. in plots in NE corner of parish bounded by Bottisham Parish in E and River Cam in W, to S of village bounded by Horningsea Road in W, and SE of village bounded by Low Fen Drove Way in N.

Names of river, parishes and neighbouring owners. Farm buildings and cottage shown in plan form, church shown in perspective. Closed fields showing owner's land; old inclosures; roads; watercourses; ponds; hedges; hop ground; state of cultivation shown by colour.

Border of 1 broad band with 1 narrow band on either side; title top left; scale beneath title; compass middle top showing 8 points with a decorated N. Table on right giving tenants, land use, description of land and acreages. Water coloured blue, roads coloured brown, buildings coloured red, closes coloured green or outlined in yellow.

Probably drawn at time of 1810 inclosure award. Photograph at CRO TR869/P21, at 1:9,051.

Horningsea – [c. 1810] – HRN81002 – SJC MPS 224

[Farm at Horningsea, owned by St John's College, Cambridge and occupied by John Moore.]

Scale: 1:3,680; **Size:** (i) 20 5/8 x 23 3/8in.; **Top** is N; Manuscript(ii), parchment, coloured.

Horningsea Church, TL493627, farmhouse to N and 148a.3r.9p. bounded by River Cam in W, and plots S of

village bounded by Horningsea Road in W, and SE of village bounded by Low Fen Drove Way in N.

Farm buildings shown in plan form, church shown in perspective. Closed fields showing owner's land; hedges; state of cultivation shown by colour; roads; watercourses; pond.

Border of 1 narrow band; compass top left showing 4 points. Table on right giving acreages. Grass coloured green.

Probably based on HRN81001, which was probably drawn at time of 1810 inclosure award and shows farms occupied by Moore and Horner [HRN81003 shows land let to Horner].

Horningsea – [c. 1810] – HRN81003 – SJC MPS 223

[Farm at Horningsea, owned by St John's College, Cambridge and occupied by Charles Horner.]

Scale: 1:5,670; **Size:** (ii) 14 7/8 x 17 3/4in.; **Top** is N; Manuscript(ii), parchment, uncoloured.

Horningsea Church, TL493627, farmhouse in village to N, and 246a.1r.38p. in NE of parish bounded by Bottisham Parish in NE and River Cam in SW.

Closed fields showing owner's strips; hedges; roads; watercourses.

Compass middle top showing 4 points. Table top left giving acreages.

Pencil notes. Probably based on HRN81001, which was probably drawn at time of 1810 inclosure award and shows farms occupied by Moore [see HRN81002] and Horner.

Horningsea – [c. 1810] – HRN81004 – SJC MPS 279

Plan of Estate at Horningsea Cambs.

Scale bar 0–20 chains (= 3 5/16in.), 1:4,782; **Size:** (i) 46 11/16 x 24 3/8in.; **Top** is N; Manuscript(i), paper mounted on cloth, coloured.

Horningsea Church, TL493627, farmhouse in village to N, and 368a.3r.33p. in plots in NE of parish bounded by Bottisham Parish in E and River Cam in W, to S of village bounded by 'Horningsey Road' in W, and SE of village bounded by Low Fen Drove Way in N, and 2a.3r.9p. in Bottisham Parish.

Names of neighbouring owners. Buildings shown in plan form and include 'North Hill Farm', farm buildings, cottages, Horningsea Church, vicarage and blacksmith's shop. Closed fields showing owner's land; state of cultivation shown by colour; plantation; roads and footpaths; watercourses; bridge; gardens; hop ground; 'Reed bed'.

Border of 1 narrow band with decorated corners; title top left; scale at bottom; compass in centre showing 8 points. Table on right giving field names, acreages and land use. Water coloured blue, fields coloured brown and blue/green, roads coloured brown.

Probably drawn at time of 1810 inclosure award; estate owned by St John's College, Cambridge.

Horningsea – [1810] – HRN81005 – SJC MPS 282

Plan of the Parish of Horningsea in the County of Cambridge Made on the Inclosure.

Surveyor: [George Cole]; **Scale bar** 0–40 chains (= 6 5/8in.), 1:4,782; **Size:** (i) 48 7/16 x 25 1/16in.; **Top** is NNE; Manuscript(ii), tracing paper mounted on cloth, coloured.

Horningsea Church, TL493627, farmhouse in village to N, and 368a.3r.33p. in plots in NE of parish bounded by Bottisham Parish in E and River Cam in W, to S of village bounded by 'Horningsey Road' in W, and SE of village bounded by Low Fen Drove Way in N.

Names of owners and allotments. Houses, farm buildings and church shown in plan form. Closed fields; acreages; roads and footpaths; watercourses.

Border of 1 narrow band; title at top; scale bottom left; compass on left showing 16 points. Land owned by St John's College, Cambridge outlined in red, roads coloured brown, water coloured blue.

Pencil notes and later addition of railway. Copy of map by George Cole which accompanied 1810 inclosure award, shows land allotted to St John's College. Accompanied by an abstract of inclosure award, SJC D110.303.

Horningsea – [Post 1810] – HRN81006 – CUL MS Plans 387

[Map of part of Horningsea Parish.]

Scale: 1:4,800; **Size:** (ii) 20 1/4 x 23 5/8in.; **Top** is S; Manuscript(ii), tracing paper mounted on paper, uncoloured.

Eye Hall Farm, TL499637, and c. 720a. bounded by Milton and Waterbeach parishes in W and Clayhithe in N, and extending S of farm.

Names of neighbouring owners. Farm buildings shown in plan form. Closed fields; acreages; roads and watercourses; hedges; responsibility for boundaries; ferry; location of trees.

Numbers on plots suggest map originally accompanied by a terrier. On dorse: 'Bishop of Hereford – Horningsea'. Drawn after sale of Thomas Panton's estate in 1809 [see HRN80902] and 1810 inclosure award.

Horseheath – [1769–70] – HRS77001 – CUL MS Plans a.5(i)

A Plan of the Demense [sic.] Horseheath Cambridgeshire.

Surveyor: [John Mackown]; **Scale bar** 1–0–100 perches (= 2 5/8in.), 1:7,476; **Size:** (i) 11 3/4 x 9 5/8in.; **Top** is E; Manuscript(i/ii), paper, coloured.

Horseheath Hall, TL624473, and 741a.0r.7p. in Horseheath and West Wickham parishes and in Withersfield Parish [Suffolk], crossed by road to West Wickham in W and bounded by road from Linton to Haverhill in S.

Names of fields. Buildings shown in plan form and include Horseheath Hall, summer-house, cold bath, icehouse, menagerie ['Managery'] and cottages. Open fields; wood; waste; paddock; roads; footpaths and gates; park; garden and its layout; lawns; fences; rookery; bank.

Border of 2 narrow bands; title bottom left; scale above title. Fields outlined in green, roads coloured brown, buildings coloured red, water coloured blue.

Accompanying table gives names of house, acreages and state of cultivation. In volume entitled on flyleaf: 'Particulars of a survey of the Parishes of Horseheath & West Wickham together with Lands adjoining in the Several Parishes of Bartlow & Shudy Camps, in the County of Cambridge & Wethersfield parish in the County of Suffolk, the Estate of the Rt Honble Thomas Lord Montfort. Surveyed, Regulated & particularized by John Mackown, 1769 & 1770'. Volume used for land tax of tenants, contains 8 maps which cover 3,017a.2r.29p. in Horseheath and neighbouring parishes. The other maps in volume are copies and drawn on tracing paper, this map may also be a copy though not drawn on tracing paper. See also HRS77002–7 and SHU77001. Photograph in CRO.

Horseheath – [1769–70] – HRS77002 – CUL MS Plans a.5(ii)

['Valley Field' in Horseheath and West Wickham, owned by Thomas Bromley, Lord Montfort.]

Surveyor: [John Mackown]; **Scale:** 1:8,000; **Size:** (i) 12 1/8 x 7in.; **Top** is W; Manuscript(ii), tracing paper mounted on paper, coloured.

Churchyard, TL613474, and 270a.0r.1p. W of Horseheath village, bounded by main road in village in E and roads to Linton in S and to Cambridge in N.

Names of fields and some tenants. Houses and barns shown in plan form. Open fields; glebe; closes; common; wood and trees; roads and footpaths; watercourses; gates; park; fences; pond; bank; garden identified on table.

Border of 1 narrow band. Fields outlined in green, roads coloured brown, buildings coloured red, water coloured blue.

Accompanying table gives names of houses and tenants, acreages and state of cultivation. In volume which gives surveyor and date; see HRS77001 for details. See also HRS7703–7 and SHU77001. Photograph in CRO.

Horseheath – [1769–70] – HRS77003 – CUL MS Plans a.5(iii)

A plan of Heath Farm, situate in the Parishes of Horseheath & Bartlow.

Surveyor: [John Mackown]; **A scale** of Perches, 1:6,900; **Size:** (i) 13 5/8 x 6 3/8in.; **Top** is N; Manuscript(ii), tracing paper mounted on paper, coloured.

Heath Farm, TL586477, and 245a.1r.35p. to SE extending into Bartlow Parish in S, and bounded by road from Linton to West Wratting in E.

Names of fields and tenants. Barn shown in plan form. Open fields showing owner's strips; closes; glebe; common; waste; roads and footpaths; gates; 'old gravell pitt' and 'chalk pitt'.

Border of 1 narrow band; title top left; scale middle right. Roads coloured brown, buildings coloured red.

Accompanying table gives names of fields, acreages and state of cultivation. In volume which gives owner, surveyor and date; see HRS77001 for details. See also HRS77002,4–7 and SHU77001. Photograph in CRO.

Horseheath – [1769–70] – HRS77004 – CUL MS Plans a.5(iv)

[Land in Horseheath, owned by Thomas Bromley, Lord Montfort and let to John Twinn.]

Surveyor: [John Mackown]; **Scale:** 1:8,800; **Size:** (i) 11 1/4 x 8 3/8in.; **Top** is W; Manuscript(ii), tracing paper mounted on paper, coloured.

Dovecote, TL611471, and 431a.0r.22p. bounded by village in W and road to Linton in N.

Names of fields and neighbouring owners. Houses and barns shown in plan form. Open fields showing owner's strips; glebe; closes; common and meadow; roads and footpaths; gates; watercourses; moat; garden identified on table.

Border of 1 narrow band. Roads coloured brown, buildings coloured red, water coloured blue.

Accompanying table gives names of farm and fields, acreages and state of cultivation. Inset bottom left at 1:9,000 and measuring 5 5/8 x 3 1/4in. of land bounded by roads from Horseheath to Haverhill in N and to Cardinal's Green in S. In volume which gives surveyor and date; see

HRS77001 for details. See also HRS77002–3,5–7 and SHU77001. Photograph in CRO.

Horseheath – [1769–70] – HRS77005 – CUL MS Plans a.5(v)
[Lower Cardinal's Farm and land in Horseheath and Shudy Camps, owned by Thomas Bromley, Lord Montfort and let to Sam. Pollentine.]
Surveyor: [John Mackown]; **Scale:** 1:8,400; **Size:** (i) 12 7/8 x 5 5/8in.; **Top** is W; Manuscript(ii), tracing paper mounted on paper, coloured.
Lower Cardinal's ['Home'] Farm, TL614467, and 268a.1r.6p. bounded by road from Horseheath to Haverhill in N, Cardinal's Green in E and footpath from Cardinal's Green in S, and extending into Shudy Camps Parish.
Names of fields and neighbouring owners. Farm buildings and cottage shown in plan form. Open fields showing owner's strips; glebe; closes; common; roads and gates; fences; gravel pit; moat; garden and orchard identified on table.
Border of 1 narrow band. Roads coloured brown, buildings coloured red, water coloured blue.
Accompanying table gives names of farm and fields, acreages and state of cultivation. In volume which gives surveyor and date; see HRS77001 for details. See also HRS77002–4,6–7 and SHU77001. Photograph in CRO.

Horseheath – [1769–70] – HRS77006 – CUL MS Plans a.5(vi)
A Plan of Carnell Green Farm in the Parishes of Horseheath & Shudy Camps.
Surveyor: [John Mackown]; **Scale:** 1:4,200; **Size:** (i) 11 1/2 x 8 1/4in.; **Top** is W; Manuscript(ii), tracing paper mounted on paper, coloured.
Cardinal's ['Carnell Green'] Farm, TL619459, and 207a.0r.25p. bounded by road from Cardinal's Green to Mill Green in W and by footpath running W from Cardinal's Green in N.
Names of fields and neighbouring owners. House and barn shown in plan form. Open fields; closes; glebe; 'sawpitt meadow'; roads and gates; watercourses; pond; moat; garden identified on table.
Border of 1 narrow band; title top left. Roads coloured brown, buildings coloured red, water coloured blue.
Accompanying table gives names of farm and fields, acreages and state of cultivation. In volume which gives owner, surveyor and date; see HRS77001 for details. See also HRS77002–5,7 and SHU77001. Photograph in CRO.

Horseheath – [1769–70] – HRS77007 – CUL MS Plans a.5(vii)
A Plan of Limberhurst Farm in the Parishes of Horseheath, Shudy Camps and Wethersfield.
Surveyor: [John Mackown]; **Scale:** 1:2,770; **Size:** (i) 10 3/4 x 8 3/8in.; **Top** is W; Manuscript(ii), tracing paper mounted on paper, coloured.
Limberhurst Farm, TL634469, and 291a.0r.28p. bounded by road from Horseheath to Haverhill in N, and extending S of farm.
Names of fields and neighbouring owners. House and barns shown in plan form. Open fields showing owner's strips; closes; meadow; roads and gates; watercourses; fences; moat; banks; garden and orchard identified on table.
Border of 1 narrow band; title top left. Roads coloured brown, buildings coloured red, water coloured blue.

Accompanying table gives names of fields, acreages and state of cultivation. In volume of maps which gives owner, surveyor and date; see HRS77001 for details. See also HRS77002–6 and SHU77001. Photograph in CRO.

Horseheath – 1827 – HRS82701 – PCC Horseheath C15
Plan of an Estate in the Parishes of Horseheath Shudy Camps, Bartlow and West Wickham in the County of Cambridge belonging to the Master and Fellows of Pembroke Hall in the University of Cambridge and Stanlake Batson Esqr their Lessee as settled and adjusted in the Year 1827.
Surveyor: [Alexander Watford jr]; **Scale** of 5 Chains to the Inch, 1:3,960; **Size:** (ii) 31 7/8 x 41 1/8in.; **Top** is N; Manuscript(i), paper mounted on cloth, coloured.
Horseheath Church, TL613473, and 88a.1r.21p. [statute measure] or 84a.3r.0p. [computed measure] scattered throughout parishes, bounded by Streetly End in N and boundary between Horseheath and Linton parishes in W, and land in N of Shudy Camps and Bartlow parishes S of Cardinal's Green.
Names of fields, wood, roads, tenants and neighbouring owners. Cottages shown in plan form, Horseheath Church and post mill shown in perspective. Open fields showing owner's strips; closes; common and meadow; wood including Hare Wood; acreages; responsibility for boundaries; dimensions of some boundaries; roads; watercourses; ponds; moat; 'Middle of the World'.
Title top right; scale beneath title; compass above title showing 4 plain points. Roads coloured yellow, land belonging to College coloured blue.
Refers to: 'A Terr\e/ar of certain Lands and Premises belonging to the College or Hall of Mary Valence, commonly called Pembroke Hall, in the University of Cambridge now in Lease to the Right Honorable Thomas Lord Montfort: lying and being in Horseheath, Shudy Camps and Bartlow, in the County of Cambridge. Taken this Twenty first Day of June 1788 By us whose Names are hereunto subscribed'. Note to terrier: 'NB This Terrier copied from the Terrier of 1788 was drawn up by me and the Statute Quantities and the Numbers corresponding to the College Plan (as settled & approved) were introduced into the Old Description in order more fully to identify the situation of the Property Alexr Watford'. Above note: 'To the original Terrier made in 1788 there is a Plan of the 4A2R0P and 5A2R0P prefixed, but it was deemed unnecessary by me to be copied in this. 24th Novr 1827 Alex Watford'. For this plan, see WEV78801.

Horseheath – 1828 – HRS82801 – CRO 124/P62
Estate in the Parishes of Horseheath Shudy Camps Bartlow and West Wickham in the County of Cambridge belonging to the Master and Fellows of Pembroke Hall in the University of Cambridge in lease to Stanlake Batson Esqr as adjusted & settled in the Year 1828.
Surveyor: James Richardson; **Scale bar** 0–30 chains (= 6in.), 1:3,960; **Size:** (i) 30 1/2 x 39 5/8in.; **Top** is N; Manuscript(i), parchment, coloured.
College Farm, TL615476, and 88a.1r.21p. scattered throughout parishes, bounded by Streetly End in N and boundary between Horseheath and Linton parishes in W, and land in N of Shudy Camps and Bartlow parishes S of Cardinal's Green.
Names of fields, roads and neighbouring land. Farm buildings, cottages and 'Chequers Public House' shown in

plan form, church and post mill shown in perspective. Open fields showing owner's strips; closes; common; pasture and meadow; glebe; wood including Hare Wood; trees; state of cultivation shown by colour; acreages; roads including turnpike; watercourses and ponds; 'Middle of the World'.

Border of 1 blue band 3/16in. wide with 2 narrow bands on either side; title middle bottom with decorative lettering and line-work; scale right of title; compass middle top showing 8 points. Table on right with a border which imitates a scroll of paper showing acreages of open and inclosed land. Roads and arable coloured brown, meadow coloured green, water coloured blue.

Note bottom right: 'We do hereby testify our approval of this Plan and agree to be bound thereby S Batson Henry Tasker Treasurer of Pembroke Hall 18th March 1828'.

I

Ickleton – 1795 – ICK79501 – CLC ACC.1985/5
Plan of Estates at Ickleton in the County of Cambridge belonging to the Revd the Master & Fellows of Clare Hall and to Mr John Pytches Surveyed in the Year. 1795.
Surveyor: [Joseph Freeman?]; **Scale bar** 5–0–20 chains (= 3 1/8in.), 1:6,336; **Size:** (i) 22 1/16 x 43 5/8in.; **Top** is N; Manuscript(i), paper, coloured.
Ickleton Church, TL495438, and 265a.2r.30p. scattered throughout parish. Of this, 148a.0r.36p. by computation or 122a.3r.28p. by admeasurement owned by Clare College.
Names of fields, roads and neighbouring owners. Church, farm buildings and cottages shown in plan form. Open fields showing owner's strips; closes; meadow; state of cultivation shown by colour; roads; watercourses including direction of flow of River Granta; ditch; 'Black Well'; spring; balks; 'Chesterford Bridge'; hedges and fences; 'Clay Pitts'; gardens; orchards identified on table.
Border of 1 broad band with 1 narrow band on inside; title bottom right; scale centre bottom; compass top left showing 4 points. Table bottom left giving field names and acreages. Roads and some arable strips coloured brown, other arable strips outlined in brown, water coloured blue, hedges coloured green, buildings coloured red, garden coloured yellow.
Ink note under table, possibly added in 1798: 'Note All the Lands coloured Green are belonging to the College. The rest are Mr Pytches' private Estate. There is a Sheep~Walk for 9 Score Sheep which belongs to the College'. Table on right, possibly added in 1798: 'Supplementary reference of all the College Lands seperated and distinguished from those of Mr Pytches', which shows areas by computation and admeasurement. Pencil notes of land 'Wanting in New Survey'. Map is in style of Joseph Freeman, and endorsed: 'We Joseph Freeman of the Town of Cambridge in the County of Cambridge Surveyor being duly authorized by and on the behalf of the Master Fellows and Scholars of Clare Hall in the University of Cambridge and Samuel Hanchett of Ickleton in the County of Cambridge Farmer being duly authorized by and on the behalf of John Pytches the Younger late of Gazely but now of Alderton in the County of Suffolk Gentleman to divide the Lands belonging to each which cannot be ascertained by the Terriers which mention Lands the names of which are totally forgotten and lost do hereby certify that we have carefully examined and compared the within Chart or Map

with the Lands therein mentioned and do declare that the same is a true correct and accurate Map and description of all the Lands belonging to each And We do further declare that we have agreed and determined that the several Lands therein coloured green shall hereafter be the property of the said Master Fellows and Scholars and that the residue of the said Lands therein mentioned coloured Yellow shall be here after the property of the said John Pytches Witness our hands this Nineteenth Day of May 1798 Joseph Freeman Saml Hanchett'. Rough copy on paper mounted on cloth, whole sheet measures 21 7/8 x 36 3/4in., title and ink note on right. At CLC Safe B:64/6 is a valuation by Joseph Freeman, made in 1798.

Ickleton – 1803 – ICK80301 – CRO, CUL Maps.bb.53(1).93.52
A Plan of the Grange Farm in the Manors of the Priory Cauldrees Hovels and Durham within the Parish of Ickleton in the County of Cambridge being in the Possession of The Honourable Percy Charles Wyndham Lord of the aforesaid Manors.
Surveyor: Edward Laurence; **Draughtsman:** W. Haydell; **Scale bar** 0–30 chains (= 3 13/16in.), 1:6,232; **Size:** (i) 21 1/8 x 16 11/16in.; **Top** is N; Positive and negative photostat, paper, uncoloured.
Ickleton Old Grange ['Grange Farm'], TL462419, and c. 970a. in W of parish bounded by Duxford Parish in N and Chrishall Parish ['Creswell Lordship', Essex] in S.
Names of fields and neighbouring owners. Farm buildings shown in plan form; farmhouse probably shown in perspective [indistinct]. Open fields showing owner's strips; common; waste; trees; roads; garden and orchard.
Border of 1 broad and 1 narrow band; title top left; scale bottom left; compass middle top showing 4 points.
Inset top right of 2 plots. Numbers on fields suggest map originally accompanied by a terrier. Note bottom right: 'Reduced from the Survey taken by Edwd Laurence in 1719 W. Haydell Oct. 1803'. Manuscript original [category iv] owned by G.W.H. Bowen Esq of Ickleton Grange in 1937; not found in 1988. Photostats are poor quality.

Ickleton – [c. 1810] – ICK81001 – CLC ACC.1985/5
An Estate belonging to Mrs Susan Brooke in the Parish of Ickleton in the County of Cambridge.
Surveyor: [Edward Gibbons]; **Scale bar** 6–0–24 chains (= 5in.), 1:4,752; **Size:** (i) 25 3/4 x 14in.; **Top** is N; Manuscript(ii), tracing paper, coloured.
Ickleton Church, TL495438, and 200a.0r.27p., in plots to N and E, and 1 plot mostly W of road from Duxford to Strethall bounded by Strethall and Littlebury parishes [Essex] in S.
Names of roads and neighbouring owners. Cottages shown in plan form; church shown in perspective. Closed fields showing owner's land; state of cultivation probably shown by colour; acreages; roads and watercourses; responsibility for boundaries.
Border of 1 narrow band; title middle right in an oval cartouche of 2 narrow bands with dots in-between; scale under title; compass in centre showing 4 points. Roads coloured brown, some plots coloured green.
Under scale: 'Note * In Dispute'. Tracing of part of map by Edward Gibbons which accompanied 1810 inclosure award; made before Susan Brooke died in 1812 [*VCH*, 6,

236] and Clare College, Cambridge bought estate in 1819 [CLC Handlist].

Ickleton – 1811 – ICK81101 – TCC Box 21 Ickleton 141

An Estate belonging to Trinity College in the University of Cambridge in the Parish of Ickleton 1811.

Scale bar 1–0–30 chains (= 5 1/8in.), 1:4,791; **Size:** (i) 13 7/8 x 31in.; **Top** is NE; Manuscript(i), paper, coloured.

Vallance Farm, TL485419, and 250a.3r.12p. in plots E and N of church, and in S of parish bounded by roads from Elmdon to Ickleton in NW and to Strethall in S.

Names of roads, parishes and neighbouring owners. Farm buildings and houses shown in plan form, church shown in perspective. Closed fields showing owner's land; acreages; roads and watercourses; responsibility for boundaries.

Border of 1 narrow band; title bottom right; scale centre bottom; compass in centre showing 4 points. Roads coloured brown, old inclosures coloured green.

Note under title: 'This ... Mark denotes the Fence belongs to the Piece in which it is made The Old Inclosures are distinguished by Green Color'. Pencil notes. Numbers on plots refer to map which accompanied inclosure award.

Ickleton – 1812 – ICK81201 – CRO R60/21/1

Estate belonging to The Honble Percy C. Wyndham in the Parish of Ickleton in the County of Cambridge (1812).

Scale bar 2–0–28 chains (= 5in.), 1:4,752; **Size:** (i) 14 7/8 x 9 1/8in.; **Top** is NE; Manuscript(i), paper mounted on board, coloured.

Caldrees Manor House, TL493438, and 29a.2r.39p. in village extending along Abbey Street in W and Frog Street in S, bounded by church in E and brook in N.

Names of tenants and neighbouring owners. Farm buildings, cottages and vicarage shown in plan form, church shown in perspective. Closes showing owner's land; acreages; tenure; roads and watercourses; park, gardens and 'pleasure grounds'; pond; yard; gates; land exchanged on or after inclosure.

Border of 1 narrow band; title middle bottom in an oval cartouche of 1 narrow band with 1 broad band on inside and dots in-between; scale beneath title. Table on dorse giving field names, acreages of land both in village and open fields, and rents of land in village. Roads coloured brown, park coloured green, some buildings striped, others stippled.

Numbers on fields refer to inclosure award. May be a tracing and hence in category (ii).

Ickleton – 1815 – ICK81501 – CLC ACC.1985/5

Estate in Ickleton 1815.

Surveyor: Edward Gibbons; **Scale bar** 6–0–12 chains (= 2 15/16in.), 1:4,853; **Size:** (i) 14 5/8 x 21 1/4in.; **Top** is NW; Manuscript(i), parchment, coloured.

Tenement at TL492436, and 79a.3r.36p. mostly E of road from Duxford to Strethall, bounded by Duxford Parish in N and Hinxton Parish in E.

Names of roads, parishes and neighbouring owners. Houses in village shown in plan form. Closed fields showing owner's land; acreages; roads and watercourses; hedges.

Border of 1 narrow band; title bottom left in a cartouche of drapery; scale top left; compass in centre showing 4 points. Table bottom right giving acreages. Roads

coloured brown, hedges coloured green, water coloured blue, buildings coloured red.

Pencil notes. Shows estates allotted to Clare College, Cambridge on inclosure.

Ickleton – 1818 – ICK81801 – WIN CC.11213

A Plan of an Estate the Property of the Dean and Canons of Windsor in the Parish of Icklington and County of Cambridge 1818.

Scale bar 0–36 chains (= 6in.), 1:4,752; **Size:** (i) 28 9/16 x 33 1/8in.; **Top** is N; Manuscript(i), paper mounted on cloth, coloured.

Ickleton Church, TL495438, and 640a.3r.3p. scattered throughout parish.

Names of tenants, neighbouring owners and roads. Buildings in village shown in plan form, church shown in perspective. Closed fields showing owner's land; acreages; roads and watercourses; hedges showing hedgerow trees; pit; reasons for allotments.

Border 1/2in. wide of 1 narrow grey band, 1 narrow uncoloured band inside and 1 broad blue band in-between; title top right; scale bottom left; compass in centre showing 4 points. Roads coloured brown, hedges and trees coloured green, water coloured blue, buildings coloured grey, 1 plot coloured green.

Ickleton – 1819 – ICK81901 – CRO R60/20/8/5

Plan of a Pightle called Housens, in the Parish of Ickleton, and County of Cambridge; belonging to Mr Saml Hanchett.

Surveyor: John King; **Scale bar** 0–3 chains (= 6in.), 1:396; **Size:** (i) 7 11/16 x 12 5/8in.; **Top** is NW; Manuscript(i), paper, coloured.

2r.33p. S of village, probably in TL4742, bounded by line of 'Old Marsh Brook' in W and N, and crossed in N by 'New Brook'.

Names of fields and neighbouring owners. Closed fields; trees including 2 ash trees; state of cultivation shown by colour and given in words; acreages; watercourses; hedges; pightle.

Border of 1 broad and 1 narrow band; title top right; scale bottom right marking 50 links as well as chains; compass bottom left showing 4 points with a feathered tail. Water coloured blue, line of former brook coloured brown, grass and trees coloured green.

Close was part of Mowbrays Manor [*VCH*, 6, 236].

Ickleton – [1824] – ICK82401 – TCC Box 21 Ickleton 161a

['Plan of House at Ickleton'.]

Surveyor: [William Savill]; **Scale:** 1:97; **Size:** (ii) 20 5/8 x 19 1/4in.; Manuscript(i), paper, coloured.

c. 1r. in Ickleton Parish.

Names of areas. Buildings shown in plan form and include barns, cart shed, 'Calfs Pens', 'Cow House', pigsty, stable, 'Chaff House', kitchen, dairy, cellar and 'Privy'. Gates; yards; stairs; dimensions of areas.

Walls coloured pink and yellow.

Title and pencil note of date on dorse. Accompanies: 'Specification and estimate for a cottage and farm buildings proposed to be erected upon an allotment of land in the parish of Ickleton Cambridgeshire agreeably to a plan proposed for that purpose belonging to the Master and Fellows of Trinity College Cambridge' [TCC Box 21 Ickleton

161b]. At end of specification: 'Measured & Valued by Wm Savill 13th May 1824'.

Ickleton – [1824] – ICK82402 – TCC Box 21 Ickleton 162
['Plan of Ickleton Farm with the state of Cropping and adjustment of Shifts'.]
Scale: 1:4,760; **Size:** (ii) 13 x 16 1/4in.; **Top** is NE; Manuscript(i), paper, coloured.
Vallance Farm, TL485419, and 234a.1r.14p. bounded by Elmdon and Strethall parishes [Essex] in S and road from Elmdon to Ickleton in NW.
Closed fields showing owner's land; heath; crops for previous and following years, including tares, seeds, trefoil, wheat, spring wheat, oats, clover ley, 'turnips fed off with sheep', barley, potatoes, fallow, 'Arable Heath', and wheat, rye and pease stubble; roads and watercourses; tumulus ['Hill'].
Table bottom right giving acreages. Fields outlined in yellow or green, roads coloured brown, water coloured blue.
Top right: 'Abstract of Cropping & Seed' gives crops, acreages, bushels of grain, and space to enter corn delivered. Title and date on dorse. Estate owned by Trinity College, Cambridge.

Impington – [c. 1806] – IMP80601 – CCC Drawer 100
Tracing of Estate in the Parish of Impington Cambs:
Surveyor: [William Collisson]; **Scale:** 1:6,340; **Size:** (ii) 20 3/16 x 24 5/16in.; **Top** is E; Manuscript(ii), tracing paper, uncoloured.
Impington Church, TL448632, farm to W and c. 1,200a. to S, bounded by roads to Cambridge in E and from Histon to Milton in W.
Farm buildings shown in plan form, church shown in perspective. Closed fields showing owner's land; roads and watercourses; pond.
Title bottom left; compass in centre showing 4 points.
Traced from map by William Collisson which accompanied 1806 inclosure award, to which numbers on plots refer. Shows land owned by Christ's College, Cambridge.

Impington – [c. 1806] – IMP80602 – CUM Doc.706
[Allotment in Impington, probably Uriah Taylor's farm.]
Surveyor: [William Collisson]; **Scale:** 1:5,010; **Size:** (ii) 15 1/4 x 18 7/8in.; **Top** is NE; Manuscript(ii), paper, uncoloured.
Impington Church, TL448632, and 24a.3r.27p. to SW.
Names of neighbouring owners. Houses shown in plan form, church and windmill shown in perspective. Closed fields; acreages; roads and footpath; gravel pit; responsibility for boundaries.
Compass top right showing 4 points. Table on right giving acreages.
Numbers on plots refer to inclosure award. Pencil note bottom left: '8 chain to an Inch', 1:6,336. Copied after 1810 from map by William Collisson which accompanied 1806 inclosure award; drawn on paper with watermark of 1810.

Impington – [c. 1806] – IMP80603 – EDR CC.12331
Impington.
Surveyor: [William Collisson]; **Scale:** 1:5,190; **Size:** (ii) 18 1/2 x 15 3/8in.; **Top** is NE; Manuscript(ii), paper, uncoloured.

Impington Church, TL448632, and 160a.1r.30p. to NE bounded by Landbeach Parish in NE.
Names of roads. Farm buildings shown in plan form, church shown in perspective. Closed fields; acreages; roads; watercourses and pond; responsibility for boundaries.
Title top right; compass middle right showing 8 points.
Later ink and pencil notes, including ink note on dorse: 'Impington Rectory Farm'. Numbers on fields refer to inclosure award. Based on map by William Collisson which accompanied 1806 inclosure award, shows land allotted to Dean and Chapter of Ely.

Impington – [c. 1806] – IMP80604 – CRO 132/T467
Plan and dimentions of Mr. Collins' allotment in Impington field.
Surveyor: Richard Matthews; **Scale:** 1:2,340; **Size:** (ii) 7 1/4 x 4 1/2in.; **Top** is NW; Manuscript(i), paper, uncoloured.
4a.0r.3p. at TL451635 in NE of parish, bounded by road to Milton in W and watercourse in N.
Names of road and neighbouring owners. Closed field; acreage and dimension of field; roads and watercourses; gates; hedges.
Title at top. Cuffed hands point along road to Milton.
At bottom: 'Sir, The above is the plan and dimentions of your Allotment in Impington field; but to make it of the required size, (4A:0R:3P,) you must remove your marks 22 links, or about 14ft. 6in. nearer towards Impington and make it so much wider on the longest side. Rd Matthews'. Shows land allotted to William Collin under 1806 inclosure award [CRO 132/T464 gives his 1st name].

Impington – [Post 1806] – IMP80605 – CRO 132/T466
Elizabeth Drage Impington.
Scale: 1:2,540; **Size:** (ii) 9 3/8 x 15 1/4in.; **Top** is NW; Manuscript(ii), tracing paper, uncoloured.
12a.3r.5p. at TL450635 NE of church, bounded by Clay Close Lane in S and E and Public Drain in N, and 2 fields further NE along Clay Close Lane just S of turning at TL455638.
Cottage shown in plan form. Closed fields showing owner's land; acreages; roads and watercourses; bridge; hedges; responsibility for boundaries.
Title top right; compass middle top showing 4 plain points. Table bottom right giving field names, acreages, reasons for allotment of land and tenure.
Pencil calculations. On dorse: 'Plan of Impington Estate' and note of quit rent. Drawn after 1806 inclosure award and before estate was sold to William Collin in 1820 [CRO 132/T464].

Impington – [c. 1828] – IMP82801 – CUL MS Plans y.1(19)
Chantry Close, at Impington taken from the Award at Mr Pemberton's.
Draughtsman: [Elliot Smith]; **Scale:** 1:2,720; **Size:** (iii) 7/8 x 1 5/8in.; **Top** is N?; Manuscript(iv), paper, coloured.
Chantry Close, TL437616, and 7a.12r.7 1/2p. in SW of parish bounded by Woodhouse Farm in S.
Names of neighbouring owners. Close; trees; acreage.
Title top left. Field outlined in green, trees coloured green.

Numbers on plot refer to inclosure award. Land owned by Storey's Charity. Drawn for fire insurance purposes, in volume from Elliot Smith and Sons, Auctioneers and Estate Agents; most maps in volume drawn c. 1828. Mr Pemberton was the Cambridge solicitor, Christopher Pemberton [Jackson, 1990, 313].

Isleham – 1779 – ISL77901 – WRO CR114/2/ii
Isleham Map.
Surveyors: [John] Lund [sr and jr]; A **Scale** of Four Chains in One Inch, Scale bar 0–21 chains (= 5 1/4in.), 1:3,168; **Size:** (i) 3 11/16 x 3 5/16in.; **Top** is N; Manuscript(i), paper, coloured.
c. 3a. bounded by a road in E.
Name of neighbouring owner. Buildings shown in plan form. Closed field; roads; gate.
Border of 1 broad band; title at top; scale bottom right of whole sheet; compass at top of whole sheet showing 4 points. Buildings coloured red, land outlined in yellow, green and red.
Number on plot suggests map originally accompanied by a terrier. Top right of sheet which also contains maps of Soham [SOH77901-2]. Entitled centre right: 'A Map of the Estates of the Right Honourable Lady Viscountess Irwin at Barroway. Soham and Isleham in the County of Cambridge. Surveyed by Messrs Lunds in 1779'. Surveyors' 1st names were John [Eden L294 and L294.1].

Isleham – [Ante 1780] – ISL78001 – KCC L8
A Survey and Plan of an Estate at Isleham in the County of Cambridge belonging to the Provost and Scholars of Kings College Cambridge.
Scale bar 1–0–40 chains (= 6 13/16in.), 1:4,767; **Size:** (i) 28 3/4 x 23 5/16in.; **Top** is N; Manuscript(i), parchment, coloured.
129a.1r.1p. SW of village and church, which is at TL643744.
Names of fields and neighbouring owners. Buildings in village shown in plan form. Open fields showing owner's strips; closes; fen; roads and watercourses; chalk pit.
Border of 1 broad and 1 narrow band; title at top; scale middle bottom; compass centre top showing 8 points. Table bottom left giving field names, acreages and land use in inclosures. Roads coloured yellow; field boundaries coloured yellow and red.
3 insets of land in 'West Fenn', 'Cross Causy' and 'Hockle Corner' in E of parish. Probably drawn before 1780, when a neighbouring owner died.

Isleham – [c. 1787–1806] – ISL78701 – CRO 311/P1
A Plan of Isleham Lordship in Cambridgeshire belonging to The Honourable John Buller Esqr.
Scale bar 1–0–20 Gunter's chains (= 5 1/8in.), 1:3,245; **Size:** (i) 117 x 54 7/16in.; **Top** is NW; Manuscript(i), parchment mounted on cloth, coloured.
Isleham Church, TL644744, and c. 5,200a. in whole parish and some strips in Fordham Parish and in Freckenham Parish [Suffolk].
Names of fields, parishes and droves. Isleham and Freckenham churches, farms and houses in village, priory, ferry house, windmill and post mills in Fordham, Freckenham and Isleham shown in perspective, Buller's house N of church shown in exaggerated perspective. Open fields showing all strips; closes; mere; meadow; roads and footpaths; watercourses; gates; 'Gerard's Well'; 'Beggar's

Bush'; layout of gardens of Buller's house; fences; 'sand pin'; chalk pits; osier beds.
Border of 1 broad and 1 narrow band; title bottom right; scale beneath title; compass rose bottom left showing 8 points with a decorated N. Person standing in field S of Buller's house. Roads coloured brown, water coloured blue, balks coloured green, some closes outlined in grey.
Accompanied by a undated terrier at CRO R85/113: 'Particulars of \Open Field Lands and Inclosures & Fen Lands and reference to/ the Map of Isleham'. Drawn after 1787 and probably before 1790 [taken from dates of death of former and current owners]. However, owner was then James Buller. By 1806, John had become the owner; loose sheet inside terrier dated 26 March 1806 says that William Leonard, land surveyor, has 'borrowed the Map and Field Book of the Parish of Isleham, the property of John Buller Esqr ...' John Buller sold the estate in 1807 [Lysons, 221].

K

Kingston – 1720 – KIN72001 – CRO R52/12/5/1
Kingston Wood In the County of Cambridge For the Right Honourable Lord Edward Harley. Surveyed and Delineated in the year of our Lord God 1720 by John Cory.
Surveyor: John Cory; **Scale bar** 0–60 perches = 1–0–14 chains (= 3 1/16in.), 1:3,879; **Size:** (ii) 31 3/4 x 27 3/4in.; **Top** is E; Manuscript(i), parchment, coloured.
Kingston Wood Farm, TL328540, and 598a.0r.9p. in S of parish bounded by Wimpole Parish in S, Great Eversden Parish in E, Bourn Parish in W and a line running WNW from N of Great Eversden Wood in N, and crossed by Crane's Lane.
Names of farms, fields and neighbouring owners. Kingston Wood Farm and farm buildings, dovecote, 'Mr Pains' house and kiln shown in perspective. Closed fields; pightle; Kingston and 'Harron' woods; 'Pin~coat' and Lady Pastures spinneys; trees; meadow; state of cultivation shown by colour and symbols; acreages; roads and footpaths; watercourses; 'Bourn prossessioning way'; gates; orchards; moat; hedges with hedgerow trees.
Title top right in a leafy baroque cartouche; scale bottom left surmounted by yellow and grey dividers; compass rose bottom right showing 32 red, green, yellow and blue points with a decorated N. Table top left giving field names and descriptions, and acreages. Wood and pasture coloured green, houses coloured red, barns and other farm buildings coloured yellow, land outlined in green, red, blue or brown, 'Pains Farm' outlined in yellow.
Pencil notes and alterations.

Kingston – 1792 – KIN79201 – QCC 328
A Plan of an Estate situated in the Parish of Kingston and County of Cambridge Belonging to the Master Fellows and Scholars of Queens College Cambridge.
Surveyor: A[lexander] Watford [sr]; **Scale bar** 1–0–15 chains (= 5 5/16in.), 1:2,385; **Size:** (i) 22 1/8 x 24 1/8in.; **Top** is NW; Manuscript(i), parchment, coloured.
Farm at TL345554 and 58a.0r.34p. to E and NE, bounded in N by Bourn Brook and Toft and Caldecote parishes.
Names of some fields, roads, owner and neighbouring owners. Farm buildings shown in plan form. Closed fields showing owner's land; common; meadow; 'Lammas Ground'; trees; state of cultivation shown by colour; acreages of 2 plots; hedges and fences; roads and verges; watercourses; moat.

Border of 1 broad and 1 narrow band; title at bottom in a cartouche of green leaves; scale bottom left; compass top right showing 16 points, incorrectly giving top as NE. Table top left giving field names and acreages. Closes coloured green and yellow, water coloured blue, roads coloured yellow, buildings coloured red, 1 plot outlined in red.

Pencil addition of 1 allotment. At QCC 336 is a terrier of Kingston in 1793 by Alexander Watford sr.

Kingston – [1825] – KIN82501 – QCC 355 A16, B16
Estate at Kingston In The County of Cambridge.
Surveyor: [Alexander Watford jr]; **Scale bar** 0–30 chains (= 5in.), 1:4,752; **Size:** (i) 25 5/16 x 38 9/16in.; **Top** is NNE; Manuscript(ii), paper, coloured.
Kingston Church, TL346554, and 149a.3r.6p. in N of parish W of village, bounded by Bourn Brook in NW and Toft Parish in NE.
Names of roads, fields and neighbouring owners. Kingston Church, farm and cottages shown in plan form. Closed fields showing owner's land; meadow; small areas of wood; state of cultivation shown by colour; acreages; hedges; roads; watercourses and public drain; moat; allotments; 'Kingston Stones'.
Border of 1 broad band with 1 narrow band on either side; title top left; scale bottom left; compass middle bottom showing 8 points. Table on right giving field names, acreages, land use and land exchanged. Roads coloured brown, fields coloured yellow and green, water coloured blue.
In volume drawn in 1825: 'Plans of the Several Estates in England and Wales belonging to the President and Fellows of the College of St Margaret and St Bernard commonly called Queen's College in the University of Cambridge Delineated from Authentic Documents in the possession of the said President and Fellows and from actual Surveys taken By their most obedient and obliged Servant Alexr Watford'. Title page drawn by James Richardson [Watford's nephew]. This is the Bursar's copy; 2nd, finer, copy [the Master's copy] at QCC 355 B16 measures 24 3/4 x 36 9/16in. and is drawn on parchment. Border 7/16in. wide of a central blue band with 1 broad band on either side, scale has gothic lettering, compass top right. Table has a border imitating a scroll of paper and red lines. Fields coloured in yellow and brown stripes, roads have red/brown edges.

Knapwell – 1776 – KNA77601 – CRO R60/24/2/46b
A Map of the Lordship of Knapwell with Lands adjoining in Boxworth in the County of Cambridge belonging chiefly to Wright Squire Esqr 1776.
Surveyor: Edward Hare; **Scale bar** 10–0–30 statute chains (= 6 5/8in.), 1:4,782; **Size:** (i) 29 1/2 x 23in.; **Top** is NE; Manuscript(i), parchment, coloured.
Manor house N of church, TL336631, and c. 760a. in whole parish and extending into Boxworth Parish in NE.
Names of fields and neighbouring owners. Farm buildings and dovecote shown in plan form, church shown in perspective. Closed fields; wood including Knapwell Wood; trees; acreages; tenure; roads, including turnpike from St Neot's to Cambridge; moated mound; hedges; pound; gravel pit.
Border of 1 broad and 1 narrow band; title top right in a rococo cartouche with branches; scale beneath title; compass top left showing 4 points with a decorated N. 5th [PB,

226] Duke of Bedford's land outlined in red, rectory land outlined in blue, James Rust's land outlined in yellow.
Numbers on Squire's land suggest map originally accompanied by a terrier.

L

Landbeach – [1808] – LAB80801 – CUA D.XXI.13(1)
Plan of the Farm let to Mr John Headley.
Scale: 1:9,900; **Size:** (i) 20 5/8 x 13 5/8in.; **Top** is NE; Manuscript(i), parchment, coloured.
Site of Landbeach Church, TL477653, and 351a.3r.34p. in plots in S of parish bounded by Milton Parish in E and Impington Parish in S, to N of village bounded by roads from Ely to Cambridge in NE and from Milton through Landbeach in NW, and in N of parish bounded by Cottenham Parish in NW.
Names of roads and neighbouring owners. Buildings shown in plan form. Closed fields showing owner's land; state of cultivation shown by colour; acreages; roads and watercourses; hedges; responsibility for boundaries; yard, garden, pightle, spinney, fen and meadow identified on lease.
Border of 2 narrow bands; title top left as an ink note; compass top right showing 4 points. Roads coloured brown, pasture coloured green.
Accompanied by note of acreages and land use, and landlord's and tenants' covenants. On lease endorsed: 'Dated 26th September 1808 Reverend Joseph Turner and others surviving Trustees of Worts Charity to Mr John Headley Counterpart Lease of a Farm at Landbeach for 15 years from Michaelmas 1808'.

Landbeach – [1808] – LAB80802 – CUA D.XXI.13(2)
Plan of the Farm let to Mr William Wilson.
Scale: 1:7,770; **Size:** (i) 18 1/4 x 15 1/8in.; **Top** is NE; Manuscript(i), parchment, coloured.
Site of Landbeach Church, TL477653, and 311a.1r.3p. in SW of parish bounded by Histon Parish in S and road from Landbeach to Waterbeach in N, and N of village E and W of road from Landbeach to Ely.
Names of roads and neighbouring owners. Buildings shown in plan form and include dovecote and blacksmith's shop [identified on lease]. Closed fields showing owner's land; state of cultivation shown by colour; acreages; roads; watercourses; hedges; moat; responsibility for boundaries; garden, yard, meadow and sheepwalk identified on lease.
Border of 2 narrow bands; title top left as an ink note; compass top right showing 4 points. Roads coloured brown, pasture coloured green.
On lease endorsed: 'Dated 26th September 1808 Revd Joseph Turner and others surviving Trustees of Wort's Charity to Mr William Willson Counterpart Lease of a Farm at Landbeach for Fifteen years from Michaelmas 1808'.

Leverington – 1782 – LEV78201 – PRI
A Map of part of the Estate of Daniel Swaine Esqr, in Leverington in the Isle of Ely Being the Homestead and the Lands thereto belonging taken AD 1782.
Surveyor: John Watte; **Scale bar** 0–20 chains (= 5in.), 1:3,168; **Size:** (i) 18 1/2 x 23 5/8in.; **Top** is E; Manuscript(i), parchment, coloured.
Leverington Hall, TF447112, and 225a.2r.33p. bounded by road from Leverington Common to Wisbech in S and road to Holbeach in E.

Names of roads and neighbouring owners. Buildings shown in perspective and include church, hall, houses, cottages and barns, post mill and 4 dovecotes. Closed fields showing owner's land; deciduous and coniferous trees; avenue of trees in park; roads and turnpike; watercourses, drains and ponds; 'Old Gull'; bridges including Dowgate Bridge; gates including ornamental gates to hall and its park; stiles; garden; walls and fences; 'The Old Sea or Roman Bank'; village sign.

Border of 1 broad brown ink band with 1 narrow band on inside; title top left in a rococo cartouche with red roses and green leaves; scale bar centre bottom; compass in centre showing 4 points. Table bottom left giving field names and acreages. Land outlined in blue, now faded to green, roads outlined in brown.

Inset right of title of land labelled: 'This lies detached', with N at top. Beneath table: 'Note, In the Number one 9a 3r 16p is intermixed a Lott belonging to Bends Feoffees Parson drove of 1a 3r 21p'. Beneath note is an explanation which includes symbols for each type of fence: 'The Lands of Mr Swaine are shaded round on the Inside with light Blue. The Ditch Fences are done with a black Line — The dry Fences with Post & Rails, [symbol]. The Baulk Fences are dotted only ...' Note bottom right: 'Jno Watte Surveyed & Delineated 1782'.

Leverington – [Early 19th century] – LEV80001 – WM DIV.31
['J Webster's Estate Newton Corner'.]
Scale 9 chains per Inch, 1:7,128; **Size:** (i) 8 x 10 1/4in.; **Top** is NNW; Manuscript(i), paper, coloured.
c. 180a. in E of parish bounded by West Walton Parish [Norfolk] in E and 'Old Roman Bank' leading to Newton Parish in W, and 8a.1r.8p. in W of West Walton Parish.
Names of roads and neighbouring owners. Farm buildings shown in plan form. Closed fields; acreages; roads and turnpike; bank; pond.
Border of 1 narrow band; scale centre bottom; compass top left showing 8 points. Roads coloured brown, land coloured red.
Title on dorse. Ink draft at same scale and, on tracing paper, copy which measures 19 3/4 x 29 3/4in. and at 3 chains per inch, 1:2,376. Original drawn in early 19th century.

Leverington – [c. 1811] – LEV81101 – WM DIV.40
['A Plan of the Estates, late of Lawrence Banyer Esq. deceased; in the Parishes of Emneth, Walsoken, Terrington, & in Marshland Smeeth and Fen, in the County of Norfolk; and in the Parishes of Wisbech, Leverington, Tid St Giles & Upwell, in the Isle of Ely, in the County of Cambridge'.] In Leverington.
Scale bar 0–40 chains (= 5in.), 1:6,336; **Size:** (i) 4 7/8 x 7 1/4in.; **Top** is N; Manuscript(i), paper, coloured.
13a.0r.16p. bounded by 'The Sea Dike Bank' in S and 'Bony Lane' in E.
Names of fields, bank, roads and neighbouring owners. House shown in perspective. Closed fields showing owner's land; roads; bank.
Border of 2 narrow bands; title at top; scale bottom right of whole sheet; compass rose centre bottom of whole sheet showing 4 points. Table right of scale giving acreages, land use and occupiers. Land outlined in green, field names written in red, now faded.

On left of sheet beneath WSM81101. Sheet measures 23 3/8 x 25in. and title, as given above, is top right in a cartouche with brown and yellow vases and blue and yellow edges. Bottom left of sheet is a note: 'NB The Letters a and p in the second Column in the Table of References, distinguish the arable from the Pasture Lands'. Probably drawn in connection with sale of Lawrence Banyer's estate in 1811 [*Cambridge Chronicle*, 8 February 1811]. See also TYD81101, UPW81101 and WSM81101.

Leverington – [1825] – LEV82501 – BL Maps.c.8.a.15
Leverington Marsh, Containing 14a.2r.6p.
Surveyor: [John Grimsby Lenny]; **Scale bar** 1–0–10 chains (= 3 5/8in.), 1:2,403; **Size:** (ii) 10 3/16 x 8in.; **Top** is N; Manuscript(i), paper, coloured.
14a.2r.6p., probably in TF4412, bounded by 'Old Roman Sea Bank' and road from Leverington to Newton in E and 'Parson Drove Lane' in S.
Names of roads and neighbouring owners. Buildings shown in plan form. Closed fields; copse; hedges and hedgerow trees; acreages of land for 'Neat' [cattle] and 'Neat with Yards &c.'; roads; gates and fences; ponds; 'Old Roman Sea Bank'.
Title at top; scale at bottom; compass bottom right showing 8 points. Buildings coloured red and grey, paths coloured brown, water coloured blue, land coloured pale brown.
Note top right: 'II'. On preceding page is a view of Leverington Church. In volume: 'The Estates of Mr Josiah Rumball, at Wisbech, Leverington, and Parson Drove, in the Isle of Ely, and County of Cambridge. J.G. Lenny, Surveyor, Bury St Edmund's, 1825'. Summary of acreage of whole estate: 56a.3r.31p. Surveyor's 1st names were John Grimsby [Eden L148]. See also LEV82502–3 and WSP82501.

Leverington – [1825] – LEV82502 – BL Maps.c.8.a.15
Parson Drove Pieces, Containing North Inham Field 13a.0r.37p. South Inham Field 9a.0r.8p. Total 22a.1r.5p.
Surveyor: [John Grimsby Lenny]; **Scale bar** 1–0–20 chains (= 3 5/16in.), 1:7,173; **Size:** (ii) 10 3/16 x 16in.; **Top** is WSW; Manuscript(i), paper, coloured.
22a.1r.5p., probably in TF3808 and TF3809, bounded by Harold's Bank in N and crossing 'Parson Drove Green'.
Names of fields and neighbouring owners. Building shown in plan form. Trees; acreages of land for grass and 'neat' [cattle]; watercourses; gates; hedges; rough ground or bushes; 'Parson Drove Green'; 'Harrold Bank'; yards.
Title top right; scale bottom right; compass bottom left showing 8 points. Building coloured grey, water coloured blue, yards coloured brown, land coloured green or pale brown.
Note top right: 'III'. Pencil notes. In volume which gives owner, surveyor and date; see LEV82501 for details. See also LEV82503 and WSP82501.

Leverington – [1825] – LEV82503 – BL Maps.c.8.a.15
Lands in Parson Drove Fen, Containing 18a.1r.24p.
Surveyor: [John Grimsby Lenny]; **Scale bar** 1–0–7 chains (= 2 5/8in.), 1:2,414; **Size:** (ii) 10 3/16 x 8in.; **Top** is N; Manuscript(i), paper, coloured.
18a.1r.24p., probably in TF3607, bounded by Long Drove in NW and 'Short Drove' in E.
Names of droves and neighbouring owners. Buildings shown in plan form. Waste; trees; acreages of land for

grass and 'neat' [cattle]; watercourses; bridge; gates; hedges and fences; droves.

Title top left; scale bottom right; compass middle left showing 8 points. Water coloured blue, fields coloured pale brown, buildings coloured grey.

Note top right: 'IV'. Pencil note. In volume which gives owner, surveyor and date; see LEV82501 for details. View of Parson Drove Church and vicarage on preceding page. See also LEV82502 and WSP82501.

Linton – [1581] – LIN58101 – CRO L95/19b
[Land owned by Ferdinand Parys in 'Dernpath' and 'Vichyns bush' shots.]
Scale: 1:4,090; **Size:** (ii) 11 13/16 x 8in.; **Top** is NE; Manuscript(i), paper, uncoloured.

c. 210a. NE of Barham Manor, bounded by roads to Bartlow in S and to Horseheath in N.

Names of owners, tenants and shotts. Open fields showing all strips; acreages; tenure; roads and watercourses.

Table on recto and verso of next sheet giving date, tenants and acreages of strips in 'Barham Field', owners in 'Tyll Field' and land belonging to 'myself – Linton: Land'.

'Myself' was probably Ferdinand Parys, Lord of Linton Manor. In 1581, he was concerned with distinguishing rights of sheep-walk between Barham and Linton manors [*VCH*, 6, 93].

Linton – 1600 – LIN60001 – PCC Linton T1c
Lynton towne Mapp: with the mapp of the whole Manour of Bergham alias Berkham in the sayd towne of Lynton, conteyned in six sheats or leaues of paper on bothe sides, as hereafter you may perceive, in manner following: per: R.M. armigerium Dominum dicti Manerij. 20 Maij 1600 & 42o Eliz: Regine [?].
Surveyor: R[obert] M[illicent]; **Scale:** 1:1,150; **Size:** (ii) 12 1/16 x 15 7/8in.; **Top** is NW; Manuscript(i), paper, uncoloured.

Linton Church, TL562467, and c. 37a. to W bounded by road to Great Abington in SW and River Granta in NE.

Names of fields, owners, tenants and roads. Buildings shown in perspective and include houses, 'Lynton Manour', almshouses, school house, vicarage and farm buildings, church shown in exaggerated perspective and has a weather vane pointing W. Closes; pasture and meadow; tenure; roads and watercourses; gates and fences; walls and doors; gardens and orchards; market cross and 'market staules'; pound; 5 bridges including 'Bartons brige' and 'Church brige'.

Title top left.

Note top right: 'Thes sides are both in Lynton fee, all sauing Wm Redgwells house, which is custom to Bergham Manor As maye appere'. Owner was Robert Millicent [*VCH*, 6, 87]. Bridges described and named at CRO L95/14 ff.1v–3v,10. Positive and negative photostats at CUL Maps.bb.53(1).95.64 and in CRO, negative photostat at CUM Palmer B.64. See also LIN60002-6.

Linton – [1600] – LIN60002 – PCC Linton T1c
The Mapp of whole Bergham Manour in Lynton parishe conteyned in fyue Leafes on bothe sides therof, as followeth. wherin ys set downe every persons land or tenement in the sayd Manour particularly as yt lyeth in the fields therof & by what nature the same ys holden, either of the sayd Manor or otherwise.

Surveyor: [Robert Millicent]; **Scale:** 1:8,030; **Size:** (ii) 12 1/16 x 15 7/8in.; **Top** is N; Manuscript(i), paper, uncoloured.

c. 2,000a. N of town extending as far N as Balsham Parish, bounded in W by Chilford Hall and in E by Borley Wood; road from Balsham to Linton ['Balsham way beyond Ballydon hyll'] and Roman road ['Woolstreate waye on Bergham Fee'] cross at TL575491.

Names of fields, woods, roads, owners and tenants. Open fields showing all strips; small inclosures of pasture; Borley and 'Short' woods; pasture and leys; tenure; acreages; roads and footpaths; gates and fences.

Title top left.

Owner was Robert Millicent [*VCH*, 6, 87]. Date and surveyor given on LIN60001. Positive and negative photostats at CUL Maps.bb.53(1).95.68 and in CRO, negative photostat at CUM Palmer B.64. See also LIN60003-6.

Linton – [1600] – LIN60003 – PCC Linton T1c
[Land N and E of Linton Church, owned by Robert Millicent.]
Surveyor: [Robert Millicent]; **Scale:** 1:1,080; **Size:** (ii) 12 1/16 x 15 7/8in.; **Top** is N; Manuscript(i), paper, uncoloured.

c. 37a. N and E of church, TL562467, bounded by Hadstock Parish [Essex] in S, and extending N of High Street ['Cambridge Waye'].

Names of fields, roads, owners and tenants. Houses, cottages, farm buildings, church, vicarage, parsonage and Hadstock Mill shown in perspective with some tiled roofs, church has a weathervane pointing E. Open fields showing all strips; closes; waste; meadow and pasture; tenure; acreages; roads and footpaths; watercourses; gates; orchard; 'Londons crosse' and 'Bergham cross'; fences; old market; 'Mill dam'; hill shown as a mound.

Sketch based on map at PCC Ainslie, 2, p.138, bounded by roads from Linton to Bartlow in N and to Hadstock Mill in W, and by Hadstock Mill in S. Sketch measures 1 1/2 x 5 3/8in. and compass on left showing 4 points. Robert Millicent owned Barham Manor [*VCH*, 6, 87]. Date and surveyor given on LIN60001. Positive and negative photostats at CUL Maps.bb.53(1).95.65 and in CRO, negative photostat at CUM Palmer B.64. See also LIN60002,4-6.

Linton – [1600] – LIN60004 – PCC Linton T1c
[Barham Hall, Linton, owned by Robert Millicent.]
Surveyor: [Robert Millicent]; **Scale:** 1:1,920; **Size:** (ii) 12 1/16 x 15 7/8in.; **Top** is NE; Manuscript(i), paper, uncoloured.

Barham Hall, TL574461, and c. 120a. bounded by River Granta in W, and extending E of road to Bartlow.

Names of fields, roads, owners and tenants. Barham Hall and outbuildings, 'Myll' and barns shown in perspective. Open fields showing all strips; closes; pasture and meadow; tenure; acreages; roads and footpaths; watercourses; gates; gardens; fences; bowling alley; 'pounde'; 'ozier ground' and 'hop grounde'; yards named [e.g. 'hogyarde']; 'great orchard'.

Owner was Robert Millicent [*VCH*, 6, 87]. Date and surveyor given on LIN60001. Positive and negative photostats at CUL Maps.bb.53(1).95.66 and in CRO, negative photostat at CUM Palmer B.64. See also LIN60002-3,5-6.

Linton – [1600] – LIN60005 – PCC Linton T1c
[Land in NE of Linton, owned by Robert Millicent.]
Surveyor: [Robert Millicent]; **Scale:** 1:5,670; **Size:**
(ii) 12 1/16 x 16 3/8in.; **Top** is N; Manuscript(i), paper,
uncoloured.

c. 1,000a. bounded by Balsham Parish in N, Horseheath
Parish in E, Borley Wood in W and road to Horseheath in S;
roads from Linton to Horseheath ['Haverell or Horseheath
way from Lynton'] and from Bartlow to West Wickham
['Waye to the oakes gate and so to Wickham'] cross at
TL589466.
Names of fields, woods, roads, owners and tenants.
Open fields showing all strips; closes; 'Short' and Borley
woods; pasture; 'late heath'; tenure; acreages; roads and
gates; fences.
Robert Millicent owned Barham Manor [*VCH*, 6, 87].
Date and surveyor given on LIN60001. Positive and nega-
tive photostats at CUL Maps.bb.53(1).95.69 and in CRO,
negative photostat at CUM Palmer B.64. See also
LIN60002–4,6.

Linton – [1600] – LIN60006 – PCC Linton T1c
[Land in SE of Linton, owned by Robert Millicent.]
Surveyor: [Robert Millicent]; **Scale:** 1:8,230; **Size:**
(ii) 12 1/16 x 15 7/8in.; **Top** is N; Manuscript(i), paper,
uncoloured.

c. 2,100a. in SE of parish bounded by River Granta in W
and road from Linton to Horseheath in N; tributary to River
Granta is crossed by Bartlow ['Berklowe'] Bridge at
TL584452.
Names of fields, roads, owners and tenants. Houses,
barns and 'The little myll' shown in perspective. Open
fields showing all strips; meadow and pasture; tenure;
acreages; roads and watercourses; gates; gardens and orchards; fences; osier ground; 'Berklowe Bridge'; 'Bergham
swan nest'.
Robert Millicent owned Barham Manor [*VCH*, 6, 87].
Date and surveyor given on LIN60001. Positive and negative photostats at CUL Maps.bb.53(1).95.67 and in CRO,
negative photostat at CUM Palmer B.64. See also
LIN60002–5.

Linton – 1600 – LIN60007 – CRO, CUL
Maps.bb.53(1).95.25–33
F.P. Supervisus et exacta Descriptio manerio*rum* de
lynton magna et parva cu*m* Chilforde et michaellottes Nec
no o*mn*ium ali*arum* ter*rarum* et tene*m*ento*rum* iac*entium* et
existent*ium* in Lynton p*re*dicta viz infra feod*um* de Lynton
p*re*dicta ibid*em* cap*ta* et fac*ta* mense Aprilis Anno Regni
Domine no*st*re Elizabethe Re*gi*ne &c xlijo tam per exam-
inationem o*mn*ium singul*arum* eviden*ci*a*rum* p*re*dicto*rum*
manerio*rum* quam per informa*ti*onem Tene*n*ti*um* eorum viz
Roberti Richardson Barnabe Richman Ric*ardi* Lawrance
Will*elmi* Townsend P*hilippi* Thayke Will*elmi* Casbolte
Alexa*ndri* Holte Millesent Hockley Jo: Brand Jo: Fulwell
Will*elmi* Redgwell Roberti Toftes Roberti Warryn P*hilippi*
Payne Jo: Newman Roberti Brand Will*elmi* Cooke Jo:
Burman Jo: Pettytt Will*elmi* Malyn Nich*olai* Ward Roberti
Glascocke Tho*m*e Salman Franc*isci* Hockley Tho*m*e Thorpe
Roberti Brand et alio*rum* 1600 per T.W.
Surveyor: T[homas] W[aterman?]; **Scale bar** 0–60
perches (= 3 3/4in.), 1:3,168; **Size:** (ii) 29 7/8 x 64
3/4in.; **Top** is SE; Positive and negative photostat, paper,
uncoloured, 6+3 sheets.

Little Linton Farm, TL555474, and c. 1,900a. in W of
parish E of town.
Names of fields, woods, roads, owners and tenants.
Little Linton Farm, church, houses, farm buildings and 2
mills shown in perspective. Open fields showing all strips
of manor land; closes; common; 'The Warryne'; 'Lynton'
and 'Hildersham' woods and trees; acreages; roads; watercourses; gardens and orchards; crosses; moat around Little
Linton Farm; hills shown as mounds; 'Henxston gappe';
'The Hop Ground'; tenure; yards; 'Newe Parke'.
Title bottom right in a decorated cartouche; scale middle
bottom surmounted by dividers with floral decoration; cardinal points stated at edge. Table middle bottom of tenants:
'Index earu*m* reru*m* quae ob angustiam loci non convenien-
ter scribi queant'; top left: 'A Table shewyinge the Tenure
of every several p*ar*cell of grounde *w*ithin this description
by the coloure only', showing land of each manor, and
vicarage, rectory and freehold land.
Owner was Ferdinand Parys [*VCH*, 6, 85–6,88]. 19th-
century paper copy, attributed to Robert Arber, in PCC,
measures 32 3/4 x 70in. and has scale bar 0–100 perches (=
6 1/8in.), 1:3,233. Hills not shown. Land owned by
Michaelotts Manor coloured pink, vicarage land coloured
blue, rectory land coloured red, demesne land coloured
green, indenture coloured light blue, copyhold land
coloured yellow, freehold land coloured white or left uncoloured, water coloured blue, roads and boundaries
coloured pink. Table of tenants bottom left. Surveyor of
original may be Thomas Waterman [P. G. Eden, personal
communication]. William Cole describes original at BLM
Add.5842 p.388. Negative photostat is only in CUL and is
reduced to 3 sheets. Original manuscript map not found in
1988.

Linton – [1731/2] – LIN73201 – CUM Palmer MS C.9
['A Particular Survey of the Capital Mesuage of
Barrington Flacke Esqr ...']
Surveyor: [[unidentified] Maling]; **Scale bar** 1–0–7
poles (= 2 1/8in.), 1:1,755; **Size:** (i) 12 3/8 x 15 1/8in.;
Top is ESE; Manuscript(i), paper mounted on cloth,
coloured.

10a.3r.36p. in S of parish bounded by Hadstock Parish
[Essex] in E and S.
Names of fields. Farm buildings shown in plan form.
Closed fields; trees; acreages; gardens and orchards; yards.
Border of 2 narrow bands; yellow and brown scale bar
top right surmounted by yellow dividers; compass below
scale bar showing 8 blue and yellow points. Fields out-
lined in yellow, green and red, trees coloured green,
buildings coloured grey.
Accompanying terrier gives field names and acreages of
273a.1r.7p., of which 11a.1r.35p. are in Hadstock Parish.
Pencil and ink notes of field names and owner or occupier.
In volume: 'A Particular Survey of the Capital Mesuage of
Barrington Flacke Esqr with the Yards Gardens Orchards
Closes & Inclosed Grounds thereto adjoyning in Lynton
Com: Cantebr: And of all other the Inclosures of him the
Said Barrington Flacke Esqr within the several Fees of the
respective Manors of Great Lynton Barham and Hadstock
with the Contents of each upon a just Admeasurement And
also a Terrar of all and every the several Pecies and Parcells
of Common Field Arable Land & of Common Meads of him
the said Barrington Flack Esqr within the said several Fees
in Lynton & Hadstock aforesaid with their Descriptions
Abuttals & Contents upon an Actual Mensuration as

aforesaid. The same made taken and Digested in the Years (1731 & 1732) By me Maling'. On verso of title: 'Note. That the several Meadow Grounds and Land herein mentioned to lye within the Fee of the Mannor of Hadstock are annexed to and used with the Farms of the Said Barrington Flacke in Lynton'.

Linton – [1777] – LIN77701 – CRO R59/14/11/11e

['Boundary between Catley Park Grounds belonging to Benjamin Keene Esqr & Burton Wood Land belonging to Thomas Wolfe Esqr'.]
Arbitrator: Thomas Pennystone; **Scale:** 1:1,580; **Size:** (ii) 11 3/4 x 14 3/4in.; **Top** is S; Manuscript(i), paper, coloured.

Catley Park, TL541419, and c. 400a. in SW of parish bounded by Hadstock Parish [Essex] in S, and extending into N of Great Chesterford Parish [Essex] as far W as Burton Wood.

Names of fields and owners. Burton and Linton woods and trees; length of boundary; roads and watercourses; site of gate into park; park and gardens; fence, walls and hedges.

Trees coloured green.

Bottom right are details of course of ditch showing hedge in dispute. Date and title on accompanying judgment.

Linton – [1777] – LIN77702 – CRO R59/5/9/177

[Messuage of James Doo in Linton village.]
Scale: 1:266; **Size:** (i) 7 1/16 x 4 9/16in.; **Top** is N; Manuscript(i), parchment, uncoloured.

c. 30p. in village in TL5546 or TL5646.

House and outbuildings shown in plan form. Dimensions of areas; yard.

Border of 1 narrow red band; cardinal points stated in border.

Date on deed: 'Mr Essex, Mr Moore and Mr Geldard by Mr Moore's direction to Mr Doo: Assignment of Term and Conveyance of a house and premises at Linton in Cambridgeshire'.

Linton – 1779 – LIN77901 – CRO 124/P64

Survey of Catley Estate (in part) being in the Parish of Linton & County of Cambridge belonging to Benjn Keene Esqr taken by J. Freeman 1779.
Surveyor: J[oseph] Freeman; **Scale bar** 1–0–28 Gunter's chains (= 9 5/8in.), 1:2,386; **Size:** (i) 70 3/4 x 30 7/8in.; **Top** is SW; Manuscript(i), parchment, coloured.

Catley Park, TL541449, and 976a.2r.1p. in W of parish bounded by Great Chesterford Parish [Essex] in SW and Hildersham Parish in W and NW, and extending E of Little Linton Farm.

Names of fields. Catley Park House, Little Linton Farm and buildings, Hildersham and Little Linton mills and dovecote shown in perspective. Closed fields and old inclosures; Linton Wood, 'The Warren Grove' and trees; meadow and fishery; state of cultivation shown by 'p' for pasture; acreages; roads and watercourses; gates; park; hedges and fences; pond and bridge; moats.

Border of 1 broad and 1 narrow band; title top left in a rococo cartouche; scale bottom right; compass top left showing 8 points. Table top right giving tenants, field names and acreages. Fields outlined in green, woods and trees coloured green.

Pencil sketches of roads and acreages. Surveyor's 1st name was Joseph [Eden F209].

Linton – 1785 – LIN78501 – PCC

A Map of the Manor of Barham in the Parish of Linton in the County of Cambridge belonging to Sarah Lonsdale.
Surveyor: Charles Wedge [sr]; **Scale bar** 1–0–19 chains (= 3 3/4in.), 1:4,224; **Size:** (i) 30 1/2 x 38 3/8in.; **Top** is W; Manuscript(i), parchment, coloured.

Barham Hall, TL574460, and 194a.2r.34p. bounded by road from Hadstock to Balsham in W, Balsham Parish in N, Horseheath and Bartlow parishes in E and Hadstock Parish [Essex] in S.

Names of fields, roads and neighbouring owners. Barham Hall, mill, houses and 'Post house' shown in plan form, Bartlow Church and post mill [SE of mill, no longer extant] shown in perspective. Open fields showing all strips; closes; 'Michaelots' and Borley woods and trees; meadow; acreages; roads and footpaths; watercourses and bridge; gardens; crosses; 'Nan Saxbys Grave'; 'Fullwels Hedge'; 'Shortwood Corner'; 'Rivyden'; 'Smallage Gap'; limekiln; ducking stool; 'Lamb Fair' and 'Old Lamb Fair'; 'Cart~wheel or Swans nest'.

Border of 1 broad band with 1 narrow band on either side; title top left in a rococo cartouche with a pagoda, leaves and fences; scale bottom right surmounted by dividers; compass rose in centre showing 16 points, incorrectly giving top as N. Top right are coats of arms of families of Sarah Lonsdale's father, William Disbrow [PCC Barham V10], and 1st husband, Robert Millicent [*VCH*, 6, 87]. Roads coloured brown, red lines.

Accompanied by 2 copies of a terrier at PCC S16 and S17. Pencil notes.

Linton – [1794] – LIN79401 – PCC Ly p.32

[Land in Linton, owned by Pembroke College, Cambridge.]
Surveyor: [Joseph Freeman]; **Scale:** 1:2,440; **Size:** (ii) 16 3/8 x 11in.; **Top** is E; Manuscript(i), paper, uncoloured.

Linton Church, TL562467, and 34a.1r.0p. in village bounded by church and river in S, 'Linton Street' in N and 'Mill Field' in W.

Names of roads and neighbouring owners. Church, farm and stable to N of church shown in perspective. Closed fields showing owner's land and some other closes; trees; meadow; state of cultivation given in words; acreages; hedges; roads; watercourses.

Compass middle left showing 4 points.

Note top right: 'The House that Mr Thackerays Tenant lives in is called the Old Vicarage and the Rectory House – Guild Hall. The Almshouses are supposed to belong to the Parish'. Pencil notes referring to Wedge's plan, LIN78501. Accompanies: 'Valuation of the Rectory of Linton in the County of Cambridge', dated 1794. In a book of College estates surveyed by Joseph Freeman.

Linton – [c. 1797–1810] – LIN79701 – CRO L95/40c

A Survey of Little Linton farm.
Scale: 1:6,860; **Size:** (ii) 16 x 19 7/8in.; **Top** is W; Manuscript(i), paper, uncoloured.

Little Linton Farm, TL555474, and 657a.3r.30p. bounded by River Granta in N, Catley Park in S, Hildersham Parish in W, and road running S from road to Cambridge to allotments in E.

Farm buildings shown in plan form. Closed fields showing owner's land; meadow; pasture; warren; roads and footpaths; watercourses; yard and moats.

Title at top. Table top left giving field names and acreages.

Calculations, notes at bottom of land subject to tithes. Notes on dorse of acreages of land let to tenants, and value of land. Drawn between 1797, when a previous tenant died, and 1810, when a current tenant died. Owner was Benjamin Keene [*VCH*, 6, 85].

Linton – 1816 – LIN81601 – PCC Barham V10
Plan of the Premises at Barham.
Surveyor: Charles Humfrey; **Scale bar** 0–70 feet (= 2 1/2in.), 1:336; **Size:** (i) 9 3/4 x 12 7/8in.; **Top** is S; Manuscript(i), paper, coloured.
Barham Hall, TL574462, and c. 2a. surrounding it.
Farm buildings shown in plan form. Gate; yards; state of cultivation shown by colour.
Border of 1 broad black band; title at top; scale beneath title; compass in centre showing 4 points. Buildings coloured red and grey, grass coloured green.
Letters on plots suggest map originally accompanied by a terrier. Manor owned by Pembroke College, Cambridge.

Linton – [c. 1836] – LIN83601 – CRO G/L/AP2
Linton Central Workhouse. General plan.
Surveyors: William Bell and Sons; **Scale bar** 10–0–60 feet (= 8 3/4in.), 1:96; **Size:** (ii) 19 15/16 x 26 15/16in.; **Top** is N; Manuscript(i), paper, coloured.
Hospital ['workhouse'] at TL559472, and c. 2r. NW of village bounded by Union Lane in S.
Descriptions of areas. School, rooms, laundry, brew house, W.C., governor's room, clerk's room, committee room and stores shown in plan form. Dimensions of areas; yards; sinks and pumps; copper.
Title top left; scale middle bottom. Walls coloured pink or yellow.
Shows sites of cross-sections on other plans. Workhouse built in 1836 [*VCH*, 6, 99].

Litlington – 1782 – LIT78201 – CRO R60/12/1
A Plan of an Estate called Bedwells & Courses lying in the parishes of Littlington & Steeple Morden Cambridgeshire Belonging to Sir Tho. Spenr Wilson Bart. Surveyed by J. Storer of Halsted Essex Anno 1782. No. 1.
Surveyor: J[ohn] Storer; **Scale bar** 10–0–30 perches (= 3 5/16in.), 1:2,391; **Size:** (i) 21 1/16 x 29 3/4in.; **Top** is NNW; Manuscript(i), paper mounted on paper, uncoloured.
Bedwells Farm, TL310467, and 52a.2r.1p. NE of village and around church.
Names of fields, owners and neighbouring owners. Buildings shown in plan form and include Bedwells house, farm buildings, 'cart lodge', stables, granary, pigsty, malting office and dovecote. Open fields showing owner's strips; closes; common; trees; roads and gates; orchards; hedges; moat; responsibility for boundaries.
Border of 1 narrow band; title bottom right; scale bottom left; compass in centre showing 16 points which extend over whole sheet. Tables on left giving total acreages of estate [363a.1r.38p.], acreages of land on this map, acreages of inclosed land and function of buildings.
Note under title: 'N.B. This plan is contained in Six Sheets'. Note left of title: 'N.B. The Boundary Fences

marked with Dots thus .... do not belong to this Estate the others do. Nos 129. 135 & 391 are in the Parish of Steeple Morden, all the rest in the Parish of Littlington.' Pencil notes of some acreages. Surveyor's 1st name was John [Eden S542]. Positive and negative photostats at 1:3,520 at CUL Maps.bb.53(1).95.9. See also LIT78202–6.

Litlington – [1782] – LIT78202 – CRO R60/12/1
[Bedwells estate, Litlington, owned by Sir Thomas Spencer Wilson.] No. 2.
Surveyor: [John Storer]; **Scale:** 1:2,391; **Size:** (i) 21 1/8 x 29 5/8in.; **Top** is NNW; Manuscript(i), paper mounted on paper, uncoloured.
47a.3r.12p. in E of parish, extending S of road from Litlington to Bassingbourn into Bassingbourn Parish and N of road from Ashwell to Melbourn ['Ashwell Street'].
Names of fields and neighbouring owners. Open fields showing owner's strips; roads; hedges.
Border of 1 narrow band; compass middle top showing 4 points. Table on left giving acreages.
Pencil notes of acreages. Title, surveyor, scale and date given on LIT78201. Positive and negative photostats at 1:3,520 at CUL Maps.bb.53(1).95.10,12. See also LIT78203–6.

Litlington – [1782] – LIT78203 – CRO R60/12/1
[Bedwells estate, Litlington, owned by Sir Thomas Spencer Wilson.] No. 3.
Surveyor: [John Storer]; **Scale:** 1:2,391; **Size:** (i) 20 3/4 x 29 5/8in.; **Top** is NW; Manuscript(i), paper mounted on paper, uncoloured.
62a.2r.39p. in TL3043 and TL3143 in N and W of parish, and a few strips in Steeple Morden Parish.
Names of fields and neighbouring owners. Open fields showing owner's strips; roads.
Border of 1 narrow band; compass top right showing 4 points. Table bottom left giving acreages.
Pencil notes of orientation and acreages. Title, surveyor, scale and date given on LIT78201. Positive and negative photostats at 1:3,520 at CUL Maps.bb.53(1).95.13. See also LIT78202,4–6.

Litlington – [1782] – LIT78204 – CRO R60/12/1
[Bedwells estate, Litlington, owned by Sir Thomas Spencer Wilson.] No. 4.
Surveyor: [John Storer]; **Scale:** 1:2,391; **Size:** (i) 21 1/8 x 29 5/8in.; **Top** is N; Manuscript(i), paper mounted on paper, uncoloured.
Limlow Hill, TL323417, and 96a.2r.19p. in SE of parish, bounded by road from Ashwell to Melbourn in N and Bassingbourn Parish in E.
Names of fields, roads, hills and neighbouring owners. Open fields showing owner's strips; roads.
Border of 1 narrow band; compass middle top showing 4 points. Table on left giving acreages.
Pencil notes. Title, surveyor, scale and date given on LIT78201. Positive and negative photostats at 1:3,520 at CUL Maps.bb.53(1).5.11,14. See also LIT78202–3,5–6.

Litlington – [1782] – LIT78205 – CRO R60/12/1
[Bedwells estate, Litlington, owned by Sir Thomas Spencer Wilson.] No. 5.
Surveyor: [John Storer]; **Scale:** 1:2,391; **Size:** (i) 21 x 29 5/8in.; **Top** is NNW; Manuscript(i), paper, uncoloured.

38a.2r.2p. in SE of parish N and E of TL329401, junction between roads from Royston to Baldock and to Litlington ['Ashwell'].

Names of fields and neighbouring owners. Open fields showing owner's strips.

Border of 1 narrow band; compass middle top showing 4 points. Table on left giving acreages.

Pencil notes. Bottom half of sheet is missing. Title, surveyor, scale and date given on LIT78201. Positive and negative photostats at 1:3,520 at CUL Maps.bb.53(1).95.11–12. See also LIT78202–4,6.

Litlington – [1782] – LIT78206 – CRO R60/12/1

[Bedwells estate, Litlington, owned by Sir Thomas Spencer Wilson.] No. 6.

Surveyor: [John Storer]; **Scale:** 1:2,391; **Size:** (i) 21 1/4 x 29 11/16in.; **Top** is W; Manuscript(i), paper mounted on paper, uncoloured.

51a.0r.3p. in TL3140 and TL3141 in SW of parish, bounded by Steeple Morden Parish in W, and including 1 strip in Steeple Morden Parish E of road from Baldock to Litlington.

Names of fields, roads and neighbouring owners. Open fields showing owner's strips; roads.

Border of 1 narrow band; compass top right showing 4 points. Table bottom left giving acreages.

Pencil notes. One further blank sheet with a few pencil notes. Title, surveyor, scale and date given on LIT78201. Positive and negative photostats at 1:3,520 at CUL Maps.bb.53(1).95.14. See also LIT78201–5.

Litlington – [1782] – LIT78207 – ERO D/DFr A3/6

Plan of the Thrift at Odsey Heath in the Parishes of Litlington & Steeple Morden Cambridgeshire.

Surveyor: [John Storer]; **Scale:** 1 Chain to an Inch, 1:792; **Size:** (ii) 11 x 7 3/4in.; **Top** is NNE; Manuscript(i), paper, uncoloured.

The Thrift, TL318395, and c. 2a. bounded by roads from Royston to Baldock in S and to Ashwell in N, and Steeple Morden Parish in W.

Names of fields and roads. House, stables, barns, 'Cartlodge' and dovecote shown in plan form [all identified on table]. Closed fields; meadow; boundary between Steeple Morden and Litlington parishes; fences; roads.

Title at bottom of sheet; scale above title; compass showing 4 points top right. Table on right giving buildings.

On letter dated 5 November 1782 from J. Storer of Halstead [Essex] to Sir Thomas Spencer Wilson Bart, describing land owned by Mr Hodge and that owned by Sir Thomas and let to Hodge. Surveyor's 1st name was John [Eden S542].

Litlington – 1794 – LIT79401 – CRO

Plan of the Parsonage Farm at Litlington. in the County of Cambridge. belonging to Clare Hall; Cambridge. Surveyed in 1794.

Surveyor: [Joseph Freeman?]; **Scale bar** 5–0–15 chains (= 2 3/8in.), 1:6,669; **Size:** (i) 26 x 18 3/4in.; **Top** is NNW; Manuscript(i), parchment, coloured.

Litlington Church, TL309427, and 51a.3r.21p. scattered throughout parish.

Names of fields, roads and neighbouring owners. Farm buildings, church, mill and 'Alehouse' shown in plan form. Open fields showing owner's strips; closes; common; state

of cultivation shown by colour; roads; watercourses; clunch pit and 'old Clay Pitts'; churchyard; moat; gates and fences.

Border of 1 broad band with 1 narrow band on inside; title centre top; scale top left; compass top right showing 8 points. Table left of scale giving field names and acreages. Buildings coloured red, water coloured blue, hedges and pasture coloured green, arable strips coloured brown.

In style of Joseph Freeman, who valued estate in 1797 [CLC Safe B:66/2].

Litlington – 1828 – LIT82801 – CRO R58/16/2

Plan of Estate belonging to J.M. Wilson Esqr in the Parish of Litlington in the County of Cambridge As allotted by the Commissioners 1828.

Surveyor: Alexander Watford [jr]; **Scale:** 6 Chains to the Inch, 1:4,752; **Size:** (i) 49 3/4 x 28 5/8in.; **Top** is NW; Manuscript(i), paper, coloured.

Church Farm, TL311428, and 465a.3r.24p. in plots NE of village bounded by Bury Farm in W and extending 1 field W of road to Bassingbourn, and in S of parish E and W of road to Royston bounded by county boundary with Hertfordshire in S.

Names of roads, owner and neighbouring owners. Church, Church Farm, cottages and Thrift Public House shown in plan form. Closed fields showing owner's land; common; acreages; tenure; roads including turnpike; footpaths; watercourses; orchards; responsibility for boundaries; pond.

Border of 1 narrow band; title top left; scale middle bottom; compass top right showing 4 plain points. Table bottom right giving field names and acreages. Land coloured yellow, green, brown, blue, red or grey to indicate different occupiers.

Pencil notes giving more details of surrounding land, pencil additions to table indicating from whom land was received and giving further descriptions of the plots. Note that small variations of quantity caused by: 'give & take lines with Coll. Pigott'. Positive and negative photostats in 3+3 sheets at CUL Maps.bb.53(1).95.42–4. Owner's 1st names were John Maryon [Venn, II, 6, 524].

Little Abington – 1603 – LLA60301 – BL 1690.(1), CUL Maps.bb.53(1).93.58–61

Manerii De Abbington Parva, Desc[r]iptio in qua precipue destinguntur Capitale Mesuagium vocatum Cardinnalls in tenura Edmundi Marshe, et Leonerdi Swann Tenentis Thomae Bucke Cum uno Tenemento in manibus Domini cognito per nomen de Leuerers Quae sunt parcella terrarum et possessionium Iohannis Spencer Militis sparsim in isto Manerio Iacentia. Facta Mense Augusti Anno Domini millesimo sexcentesimo tertio per Iohannem Norden. Dictarum terrarum tenentibus associatis.

Surveyor: John Norden; **Scala** perticarum 16 1/2 pedum, Scale bar 0–80 perches (= 3 7/8in.), 1:4,088; **Size:** (ii) 33 5/8 x 35 7/8in.; **Top** is E; Positive and negative photostat, paper, uncoloured, 4+4 sheets.

Little Abington Church, TL529492, and 640a.3r.21p. in whole parish.

Names of parishes, roads, owners and tenants. Little and Great Abington churches, 'Great Abbington hall', cottages and farm buildings shown in perspective. Open fields showing owners' strips in each of 3 farms; trees; meadow; roads and watercourses; hedges; 'chalk pitt'; 'Bourn Bridg'.

Title middle top in an ornamental cartouche; scale bottom left; compass bottom left showing 4 points, incorrectly giving top as NNE. Tables top left and right giving acreages of land in 'Cardinalls' and 'Leuerers' respectively.

Note bottom right: 'Theis Landes are solde after the determynation of Marshes Lease unto mr Pallyvesyne [Sir Horatio Palavicino; *VCH*, 6, 11]'. Middle bottom: 'The destinction of the three fermes following by Coulers Leuerers not Leased, with yollow thus Leased to Edmond Marsh being part of Cardinalls Leased to Buck in the tenure of Leonerd Swan Other mens' land in generall thus'. At CRO 619/M56 is a survey and rental of the manor by John Norden, dated 1 James I, and at CRO 619/M66 is a terrier of Little Abington, unsigned and undated. 2nd part of terrier is of Great Abington, by John Norden, so 1st part was probably also drawn up by him in 1603–4. Original map owned by Mrs Alice Mortlock of Great Abington in 1930s; not found in 1988. Copy in BL is positive photostat only, at 1:3,168.

Little Abington – [c. 1791] – LLA79101 – C L C ACC.1985/5

Map of the College Farm at Little Abington, in the County of Cambridge. belonging to Clare Hall.

Surveyor: [Joseph Freeman?]; **Scale bar** 10–0–20 chains (= 3 3/4in.), 1:6,336; **Size:** (i) 19 1/8 x 25 7/8in.; **Top** is NNE; Manuscript(i), parchment, coloured.

100a.3r.13p. scattered throughout parish, all, except for 3 plots, N of road from Cambridge to Hildersham and bounded by Balsham Parish in N, Babraham Parish in W and Hildersham Parish in E.

Names of fields, roads and neighbouring owners. Open fields showing owner's strips; closes; state of cultivation shown by colour; roads; hedges; balks; clay and sand pits; 'Church Meadow' adjoining map to S.

Border of 2 narrow bands; title centre bottom; scale bottom left; compass centre left showing 4 points. Table on right giving field names and acreages. Balks, closes and hedges coloured green, arable strips coloured yellow or brown.

Pencil notes. Date written in pencil under title. In style of Joseph Freeman, who valued estate in 1791 [CLC Safe B:34/1].

Little Abington – 1803 – LLA80301 – C L C ACC.1985/5

Estate in the Parish of Little Abington belonging to The Master, Fellows & Scholars of Clare Hall College in the County of Cambridge 1803.

Scale bar 0–10 chains (= 3 5/16in.), 1:2,391; **Size:** (i) 25 3/8 x 19 9/16in.; **Top** is NNE; Manuscript(i), parchment, coloured.

Farm at TL532492, and 56a.1r.26p. N of road from Cambridge to Hildersham.

Names of owners, tenants, neighbouring owners and roads. Farm buildings shown in plan form. Closed fields showing owner's land; acreages; roads; responsibility for boundaries.

Border of 1 narrow band; title middle left; scale under title; compass top right showing 4 points with a decorated N. Table on right giving tenants and acreages. Buildings coloured red, roads coloured brown, some boundaries coloured red.

Later red lines altering boundaries. Shows allotments to be made to College under 1807 inclosure award. At CLC Safe B:34/1: 'An Estimate of the Dilapidations of a

Farm=House and outbuildings situate at Abington, Cambs belonging to the Society of Clare Hall in the University of Cambridge; and under Lease to Mr Fairchild; 20 Aug 1803'.

Little Eversden – 1827 – LLE82701 – CUL MS Plans y.1(9)

Plan of the Old Farm Little Eversden Taken from the Commissioners of Inclosures Plan, July 1827.

Surveyor: [Samuel Kempson Simmons]; **Draughtsman:** [Elliot Smith]; **Scale:** 1:8,350; **Size:** (iii) 7 5/8 x 11in.; **Top** is NE; Manuscript(iii), paper, coloured.

'Old Farm', TL376533, and 87a.3r.35p. extending NE of village and bounded by Haslingfield Parish in S and Harlton Parish in SE.

Names of roads and neighbouring owners. Closed fields showing owner's land; roads and footpaths; spinney identified on table.

Title top right. Table on left giving field names and acreages. Table outlined in red.

Samuel Kempson Simmons was surveyor for inclosure of Great and Little Eversden. Drawn for fire insurance purposes, in volume from Elliot Smith and Sons, Auctioneers and Estate Agents.

Little Gransden – [1821] – LLG82101 – CUL MS Plans 326a

Sketch of part of the Allotment belonging to the Rector of Little Gransden in the Parish of Little Gransden in the County of Cambridge. Intended to be sold by Auction, in Lots, on Thursday the 9th of August next, under the provisions of the Act of Parliament for the Inclosure of the said Parish.

Surveyor: [Anthony Jackson]; **Scale:** Six Chains to an Inch, 1:4,752; **Size:** (i) 14 1/4 x 17 11/16in.; **Top** is NNW; Manuscript(i), paper mounted on paper, coloured.

49a.1r.10p. in SE of TL2755 in SE of village, bounded in N and W by road running SE from village centre to Mill Hill.

Names of roads and neighbouring owners. Little Gransden Church shown in perspective. Closed fields showing owner's land; trees; acreages; roads and watercourses; hedges; responsibility for boundaries.

Border of 1 broad and 1 narrow band coloured brown inbetween; title middle bottom; scale beneath title; compass top right showing 4 points. Roads coloured brown, land to be sold outlined in blue.

Particulars of sale of allotment, to be sold on 9 August 1821, at CUM Doc.636(157–65). Anthony Jackson was asked to draw this plan on 15 May 1821 [CUM Add.6041 f.73v]. Rector was Thomas Briggs [Venn, II, 1, 379]. See also LLG82102, which shows same area at a larger scale.

Little Gransden – [1821] – LLG82102 – CUL MS Plans 326b

Sketch of part of the Allotment belonging to the Rector of Little Gransden in the Parish of Little Gransden in the County of Cambridge, intended to be sold by Auction, in Lots, on Thursday the 9th of August next, under the provisions of the Act of Parliament for the Inclosure of the said Parish.

Surveyor: [Anthony Jackson]; **Scale:** Three Chains to an Inch, 1:2,376; **Size:** (i) 15 9/16 x 19 15/16in.; **Top** is NNW; Manuscript(i), paper mounted on paper, coloured.

49a.1r.10p. in SE of TL2755 in SE of village, bounded in N and W by road running SE from village centre to Mill Hill.

Names of roads and neighbouring owners. Closed fields showing owner's land; trees; acreages; roads and watercourses; hedges; responsibility for boundaries.

Border of 1 broad and 1 narrow band coloured brown inbetween; title bottom left; scale beneath title; compass middle top showing 4 points. Roads coloured brown.

See LLG82101, which shows same area at a smaller scale, for further details.

Little Gransden – [1821] – LLG82103 – CUL MS Plans 579

Part of 4th Allotment awarded to the Rector of Little Gransden Sold to the Revd Thomas Briggs for the Expences of Buildings & Subdivision Fences.
Surveyor: [Anthony Jackson]; **Scale:** 3 Chains to an Inch, 1:2,376; **Size:** (ii) 14 15/16 x 18 3/16in.; **Top** is NNW; Manuscript(ii), tracing paper, coloured.
42a.3r.6p. in SE of TL2755 in SE of village, bounded in N and W by road running SE from village centre to Mill Hill; and part of 3rd Allotment, SW of church.

Names of neighbouring owners. Closed fields; acreages; roads; responsibility for boundaries; small inclosure, possibly a yard.

Title at centre; compass middle top showing 4 points, 2 of which coloured blue. Road coloured brown.

Pencil notes, note after title: 'The Boundaries will be the same as described in the Award.' Note bottom right: 'NB. If the above Allotment of 0.2.6 is given up to Mr Briggs it should be awarded in respect of his private Estate and the Quantity added to the Rectory Allotment in Mill Field'. Agreement of sale of this allotment in August 1821 to Rev. Thomas Briggs at CUM Doc.636(169). Anthony Jackson was asked on 15 May 1821 to draw 2 maps of land to be sold [CUM Add.6041 f.73v]; map based on Jackson's maps at LLG82101–2.

Little Gransden – [1822] – LLG82201 – CUM Doc.636(179)

[Land at Little Gransden exchanged between Rev. Thomas Briggs and John Spring.]
Surveyor: [Anthony Jackson]; **Scale:** 1:2,770; **Size:** (ii) 6 x 7in.; **Top** is N; Manuscript(i), paper, coloured.
1a.3r.18p. at TL271552 N of church and W of road to Great Gransden, and at TL272542 SE of church and E of road to Gamlingay.

Names of owners and neighbouring owners. Closed fields; acreages; roads; responsibility for boundaries.

'Part of Sandpit Close exchanged to John Spring' coloured red.

Note at bottom: 'The Fence next Sandpit Close to be made by the Revd Thos Briggs'. Numbers on plots refer to inclosure award; inclosure surveyor was Anthony Jackson. Accompanies request for exchange, dated 4 January 1822; description of exchange is at CUM Doc.636(228).

Little Gransden – [c. 1826] – LLG82601 – CRO 87/P1
[Estates in Little Gransden.]
Scale: 1:4,320; **Size:** (ii) 8 1/2 x 15 1/4in.; **Top** is N; Manuscript(ii), tracing paper, coloured.
Site of farm at TL271553, N of church and E of road to Great Gransden, and 103a.1r.25p. bounded by Waresley

Parish [Huntingdonshire] in W, road to Gamlingay in E and Fuller's Hill Farm in S.

Names of fields, roads, parishes and neighbouring owners. Farm buildings shown in plan form, church and post mill shown in perspective. Closed fields showing owner's land; acreages of some plots; roads and footpaths; watercourses; responsibility for boundaries, some of which are shown with pecked lines.

Table bottom right giving field names and acreages. Roads coloured brown, farmhouse and homestead coloured red.

Pencil notes, note beneath table: 'The Allotment in Mill Field containing 2a.1r.38p. is in lieu of an acre of Land by Gamlingay Parish set out upon the Waresley Inclosure and the Tithes of two Fields sold to John Spring'. Probably drawn at time of 1826 inclosure award.

Littleport – [c. 1796] – LLP79601 – CRO P109/22/1
A Plan Shewing the situation of Mr Airs's House and the roads leading thereto.
Scale: 1:16,800; **Size:** (ii) 8 15/16 x 14 13/16in.; **Top** is N; Manuscript(i), paper, coloured.
Primrose Hill Farm ['Mr Airs' house], TL561894, and c. 1,300a. to E bounded by River Ouse in E, Croft Drove in N and Littleport town in S.

Names of roads. Littleport Church and Primrose Hill Farm shown in perspective. Closed fields showing owner's and surrounding land; roads and footpaths; watercourses; gates; 'Black Lake' and 'Mowfen' bridges; river bank shown by hachures.

Title top left. Roads coloured brown, footpath coloured yellow/brown, river coloured grey.

Note top left beneath title in a border of 2 parallel lines, giving neighbouring owners, explanation of colours used and distance from 'Feoffee Gate' to Croft River. Beneath note is another giving distance from Mr Airs' house to Littleport by 2 routes. Accompanied by documents dated 1796.

Littleport – 1797 – LLP79701 – CRO 283/P
A Survey of the two Farms lying in Whelpmoor in the Parish of Littleport in the Great Level of the Fens, marked C and D in the General Plan, belonging to Mr Edmd Tattersall, Taken July 1797 by Thos Warren Bury.
Surveyor: Thomas Warren [jr]; **Scale bar** 0–40 chains (= 4 7/16in.), 1:7,139; **Size:** (i) 33 5/16 x 24in.; **Top** is ESE; Manuscript(i), parchment, coloured.
White Hall Farm, TL581881, and 978a.3r.2p. in Burnt Fen bounded by River Ouse ['Cam'] in W and White House Drove in E.

Names of drains, droves and neighbouring owners. White Hall Farm, barn, farm buildings and windmill shown in perspective. Closes; wood; deciduous and coniferous trees; acreages; roads including turnpike; watercourses; gates; yard.

Border of 1 broad and 1 narrow band; title top right in a rococo cartouche; scale bottom right; compass middle left showing 16 points. Fields outlined in green and yellow, trees and roads coloured green.

Numbers on fields suggest map originally accompanied by a terrier. Note bottom left of acreages and symbol for each farm. Pencil notes of occupiers and crops in 1802, which include barley, grass, fallow, turnips and wheat. Surveyor was Thomas Warren jr [Eden W123].

Littleport – 1822 – LLP82201 – CRO R59/31/40/77

The Estate of Mr J. Seaber Junr lying in Burnt Fen 1822.

Scale bar 1–4 chains (= 3/4in.), 1:4,224; **Size**: (ii) 19 3/8 x 18 1/4in.; **Top** is NW; Manuscript(ii), tracing paper fragments mounted on paper, uncoloured.

c. 380a. in TL6087 and TL6188 in centre of parish, bounded by River Ouse in N and crossed by White House ['White Top Mill'] Drain and Drove.

Names of neighbouring owners and droves. Closes showing owner's land; acreages; roads and watercourses.

Title top left; scale middle top; compass bottom left showing 4 plain points.

Some parts of map are missing, including part of scale bar.

Little Shelford – 1748 – LLS74801 – CRO 305/P2

A Survey Of an Estate lying in Little Shelford in the County of Cambridge Surveyed in Ap: 1748 By F. Warren.

Surveyor: F[rancis] Warren; **Scale bar** 40–0 perches (= 3 5/16in.), 1:2,391; **Size**: (i) 18 3/8 x 23 5/8in.; **Top** is WSW; Manuscript(i), parchment, coloured.

Manor house, TL455518, and 138a.2r.16p. bounded by river in E, road to Hauxton in S, Hauxton Parish in W and Great Shelford Parish in N.

Names of areas. Manor house, barns, church, parsonage, dovecote, outbuildings and offices shown in plan form, mill shown in perspective. Closes; trees and groves; meadow; roads and watercourses; gates and stiles; gardens and their layout; kitchen garden; orchards; barn yard; churchyard; courtyard; 'rails' [fence?].

Border of 1 broad and 1 narrow band; title top left in a 3-dimensional oval cartouche; scale middle bottom surmounted by dividers; compass rose top right showing 8 points. Tables bottom left giving field names and acreages for upland, bottom right giving field names and acreages for meadow and middle bottom giving acreages for houses and outbuildings. Water coloured blue, trees coloured green, estate outlined in red, meadow outlined in green, upland outlined in yellow.

Surveyor's 1st name was Francis [Eden W119]. Owner was William Finch, a Cambridge ironmonger, who bought manor from Roger Gillingham in 1745 [*VCH*, 8, 222].

Little Shelford – 1813 – LLS81301 – CRO P138/26/3

A Map of Little Shelford in the County of Cambridge 1813.

Surveyor: Edward Gibbons; **Scale bar** 5–0–25 [chains] (= 3 1/4in.), 1:7,311; **Size**: (i) 22 3/8 x 20 7/8in.; **Top** is NE; Manuscript(i), parchment, coloured.

'Shelford House', TL454516, and c. 1,200a. in whole parish; land belonging to Charles Wale in 1 plot NE of road from Whittlesford to Cambridge and 1 plot SW of road from Little Shelford to Hauxton.

Names of fields, roads, parishes, owner, tenants and neighbouring owners. 'Shelford House' and houses in village shown in plan form, Little Shelford Church shown in perspective. Closed fields; common; wood and trees; meadow and moor; acreages; roads and footpaths; watercourses; hedges; bridge; pit.

Border of 1 broad and 1 narrow band; title middle top in a cartouche of flowers and a ribbon; scale at bottom with scale bar repeated upside-down; compass left of title showing 4 points with decorated N. Table on right giving landowners and acreages. Roads coloured brown, old

inclosures outlined in green, Wale's land outlined in red, footpaths coloured yellow.

Pencil notes of acreages and crops in 1815–17, including oats, clover, barley, fallow and wheat. Ink notes of names of Wale's fields, acreages, summary of acreages of plantations and stipples on some plots. 'Shelford House' also known as 'Shelford Hall' or 'Old House' [*VCH*, 8, 222].

Lolworth – [c. 1730s] – LOL73001 – CLC ACC.1985/5

The Plan of the College Farm at Lolworth likewise the Measurement of all the Field Lands and Sward belonging to the same the home Closes Included.

Surveyor: [William] Harrington; **Scale**: 1:1,650; **Size**: (i) 8 9/16 x 14 7/8in.; **Top** is NW; Manuscript(ii), parchment, coloured.

Farm at TL369645, and 17a.1r.30p. bounded by road to Cambridge in S and common in E.

Names of fields, roads and neighbouring owners. Farm buildings shown in plan form. Closes; grove and trees; acreages; roads and gates; garden; spring and ponds; yard and churchyard; common adjoining map.

Border of 2 narrow bands; title at top of sheet; compass rose on right showing 4 points. Buildings and boundaries coloured red.

Middle left of sheet which also contains a terrier of the land. Notes bottom left: 'Acres of Soard and Land Belonging to the abovesaid Colledge Farm at Lolworth', and, 'Copy of Thomas Churchman's Terrar & Harrington's Plan'. Copy probably made in late 18th century. Original probably drawn in 1730s, when William Harrington surveyed in Suffolk [Eden H140]. Farm owned by Clare College, Cambridge.

Lolworth – 1792 – LOL79201 – CLC ACC.1985/5

A Plan of a Farm at Lolworth in the County of Cambridge. belonging to the Master, Fellows and Scholars of Clare Hall Surveyed in 1792.

Surveyor: [Joseph Freeman]; **Scale bar** 10–0–30 chains (= 4 15/16in.), 1:6,416; **Size**: (i) 19 9/16 x 26in.; **Top** is N; Manuscript(i), parchment, coloured.

Lolworth Church, TL369642, farm to N and 94a.3r.33p. scattered throughout parish.

Names of fields, roads, parishes and neighbouring owners. Farm buildings shown in plan form, church shown in perspective. Open fields showing owner's strips; closes; grove and trees; common and meadow; state of cultivation shown by colour; roads and gates; watercourses; spring; 'Meadow Ditch'; ponds; bridges; hedges, 'Starve Goose Hedge' and fences; number of lands between each strip; balks.

Border of 1 broad band with 1 narrow band on inside; title centre top in a cartouche of a stone with a tree beside; scale centre bottom; compass top left showing 4 points. Table on left giving field names, acreages and number of lands; summary table top right. Hedges, balks and grass coloured green, water coloured blue, arable coloured in brown stripes, buildings owned by Clare College coloured red, other buildings coloured black.

Top right: 'Note. In the Common Cowpasture, there is 3A 2R 2P, belonging to this Farm; but its situation cannot be ascertained.'; 'The Lott Grass belonging to the Farm, is the length of Six Cart Ropes on the Headens in each Field.'; 'The Right of Common to this Farm, is Five Cow commons in the Cowpasture; and Sixty Sheep commons in the Fields, with right of Folding to the same'. Note middle right: 'The Buildings on this Farm, are, A Dwelling House, now lett in Three Tenements; clay walls and Thatched. Great Barn, Weather boarded and Thatched; contains four mows and midstye. Small Barn with a Leantoo on the West side. Boarded on the west side and both ends, the last side clayed. A Cart Lodge – boarded on the south side'. Bottom right: 'Note The present Lords of the Manor of Lolworth, are Coll: Orchard and – Hawley Esqrs' [Paul Orchard and Henry Hawley; *VCH*, 9, 159]. Rough copy on paper mounted on cloth measures 18 5/8 x 22in. and without a border. Another copy cut from a 1797 lease measures 17 7/8 x 27 1/16in. Does not show hedges and has no title, but shows a green and churchyard and labels road from Huntingdon to Cambridge as a turnpike. Note bottom right is slightly different: 'Note The Lands of this Farm lay between lands belonging to Orchards and Hawley Esqrs Lords of the Manor, except where the abuttals are expressed to the contrary in the plan'. In style of Joseph Freeman, who valued estate in 1792 [CLC Safe B:68/6].

Long Stanton All Saints' – [c. 1816–38] – LSA81601 – CRO 124/P70

[Draft plan of Long Stanton All Saints' and Long Stanton St Michael, showing land owned by Hatton family.]

Scale: 1:4,800; **Size:** (i) 44 1/16 x 29 1/4in.; **Top** is NW; Manuscript(i), paper, coloured.

Long Stanton All Saints' Church, TL399664, and c. 1,500a. in whole parish and in W of Long Stanton St Michael Parish.

Buildings in village, including Manor Farm in Long Stanton St Michael, manor house in Long Stanton All Saints' and Fishpond Cottages, shown in plan form. Closed fields; roads and watercourses; hedges.

Border of 1 broad band with 1 narrow band on either side. Roads coloured brown, buildings coloured blue.

Pencil notes giving names of neighbouring owners, tenants, acreages, responsibility for boundaries, reasons for some allotments of land and strip of common. Misses Anne, Frances and Elizabeth Ann Hatton were the main landowners. Probably drawn soon after they inherited estate after 9 April 1816 [date from Inclosure Commissioners' minute book], and before Frances Hatton died in 1838 [*VCH*, 9, 224; C. P. Lewis, personal communication].

Long Stanton All Saints' – [c. 1816–38] – LSA81602 – CRO 124/P68

[Land owned and let by Misses Frances, Elizabeth Ann and Anne Hatton in Long Stanton All Saints' and Long Stanton St Michael parishes.]

Scale of Chains 12 in an Inch, 1:9,504, Scale bar 0–40 [chains] (= 3 1/4in.), 1:9,748; **Size:** (i) 22 x 32 1/2in.; **Top** is NNE; Manuscript(i), parchment, coloured.

Long Stanton All Saints' manor house, TL397667, and 1,755a.1r.37p. in whole of both parishes.

Names of parishes and neighbouring owners. Long Stanton All Saints' Church, cottages, Home Farm, Long Stanton St Michael manor house, farms, farm buildings and 'Tollbar house' shown in plan form. Closed fields; tenure; roads and watercourses; fishponds; 2 gravel pits; park and gardens identified on table.

Border of 1 broad band with 1 narrow band on either side; scale middle bottom; compass above scale showing 16

points. Table on right giving owners, field names, acreages, allotments and land leasehold from Bishop of Ely and from Pembroke Hall, Cambridge. Summary table bottom left. Roads coloured yellow, buildings and allotment numbers shown in pink, Frances Hatton's land shown in blue, Elizabeth Ann Hatton's land shown in pink, Anne Hatton's land shown in yellow.

Pencil notes. See LSA81601 for probable date. Above is BAS81601, which shows estate owned by Hale Wortham, who married Mary Hatton [*VCH*, 8, 15].

Long Stanton All Saints' – [c. 1816–38] – LSA81603 – CUL MS Plans 274

Plan of the Parishes of Long Stanton All Saints & St Michael.

Scale: 1:4,530; **Size:** (ii) 45 5/8 x 33 5/16in.; **Top** is NNE; Manuscript(i), paper mounted on cloth, coloured.

Long Stanton All Saints' Church, TL399664, and c. 1,500a. in whole parish and in W of Long Stanton St Michael Parish.

Names of parishes and neighbouring owner. Buildings in village including churches shown in plan form. Closed fields; tenure; acreages of some plots; roads and watercourses; moat.

Title top left; compass top left showing 4 points. Roads coloured brown, boundary between Long Stanton All Saints' and Long Stanton St Michael parishes coloured deep brown, Frances Hatton's land coloured blue, Elizabeth Ann Hatton's land coloured pink, Anne Hatton's land coloured yellow.

Note below title giving key to colours. Red ink numbers on plots suggest map originally accompanied by a terrier, black ink numbers refer to inclosure award. Pencil notes of crops in 1821 and 1822. Edges of map are missing. See LSA81601 for probable date.

Longstowe – [1800] – LSW80001 – SJC MPS 286

A Map of an Estate situate in the Parish of Long Stow. in the County of Cambridge the the [sic.] property of the Society of St. Johns College Cam*bridge*.

Scale bar 0–9 chains (= 3in.), 1:2,376; **Size:** (i) 19 5/8 x 15 11/16in.; **Top** is W; Manuscript(i), parchment, coloured.

91a.2r.32p. in W of TL3054, S of village and bounded by road to Little Gransden in E.

Names of neighbouring owners. Farm buildings, public house and dovecote shown in plan form. Closed fields showing owner's land; roads; gates; orchard; hedges; ponds.

Border of 1 narrow band; title bottom left surrounded by decorative line-work; scale bottom right; compass top right showing 4 plain points with a decorated N, incorrectly giving top as NNE. Table top left giving field names and descriptions, and acreages. Fields outlined in yellow and blue, water coloured blue.

Pencil notes of crops: '73, 74, 75', including beans, wheat, barley, roots, peas, seeds and fallow. Date on dorse. Photograph at CRO TR869/P22.

Longstowe – [1809] – LSW80901 – CRO R53/22/151

[Cottage and land in Longstowe.]

Scale: 1:162; **Size:** (i) 8 1/8 x 8 1/8in.; **Top** is W; Manuscript(i), parchment, uncoloured.

House, probably in TL3154, and c. 15p. bounded by Ermine Street in E and a pond in W.

Names of areas. House, shop, 'Trade shop', kitchen and back kitchen, parlour, barn and pantry shown in plan form. Poplar tree; dimensions of areas; roads and watercourses; garden; yard.

Border of 2 narrow red bands.

Above map is a drawing of house in elevation. Drawn on deed of 1809: 'Dr Thomson to Mr Newman: Lease of plot of Ground at Longston for 50 years'. Dr Thomson's 1st name was Robert [VCH, 5, 122].

Longstowe – 1828 – LSW82801 – CRO P113/3/2
Long Stow Rectory.
Surveyor: R[ichard] G[rey] Baker; **Scale bar** 0–18 chains (= 6in.), 1:2,376; **Size:** (i) 49 1/4 x 34 7/16in.; **Top** is N; Manuscript(i), paper mounted on cloth, coloured.

Rectory, TL311553, and c. 630a. bounded by church in N, Ermine Street ['Old North Road'] in E, main street through village ['Stow Street'] in W and Arrington Parish in S.

Names of fields, some buildings and neighbouring owners. Copy Yard, 'Coomb Grove', and 'Dr Thompson's' farms, 'Fox' and 'Red Lion' public houses, rectory, church and cottages shown in plan form. Closed fields showing owner's land; wood and trees; acreages; roads and footpaths; watercourses; garden and orchard; ponds; pound and yards; bridges; fences; responsibility for boundaries.

Border of 1 broad and 1 narrow band; title top left; scale bottom left; compass middle left showing 4 plain points with a decorated N. Roads coloured brown, water coloured blue, some buildings coloured pink.

Numbers on plots suggest map originally accompanied by a terrier. Pencil notes of roads and neighbouring owners. Surveyor's 1st names were Richard Grey [Eden B49]; Rector in 1828 was Ralph Tatham, President of St John's College, Cambridge [VCH, 5, 126].

Longstowe – [c. 1833] – LSW83301 – CRO R53/22/238
['Great Papworth' and 'Wright's' farms, Longstowe.]
Scale: 1:4,730; **Size:** (ii) 12 15/16 x 15 1/2in.; **Top** is N; Manuscript(i), paper mounted on cloth, coloured.

Middle ['Great Papworth'] Farm, TL308548, and c. 640a. mostly W of street running N–S through Longstowe village, and bounded in N by road from Ermine Street to rectory and in W by Little Gransden Parish.

Names of farms, fields, roads and neighbouring owners. Middle ['Great Papworth'] and 'Wright's' farms, farm buildings and cottages shown in plan form. Closed fields showing owner's land; wood and trees; state of cultivation shown by colour; acreages; roads and watercourses; garden; yards.

Compass top right showing 4 plain points. Roads and arable coloured brown, pasture coloured green, wood coloured bottle green, cottages coloured red.

Crossed-out numbers on plots suggest map originally accompanied by a terrier. Later additions of names, including modern names of farms. Probably drawn at same time as sale plan of 1833, LSW83307. Estate held by trustees of Dr Robert Thomson, who died in 1827 [VCH, 5, 122].

Longstowe – [c. 1833] – LSW83302 – CRO R53/22/239
[Tracing of map of 'Great Papworth' and 'Wright's' farms, Longstowe.]
Scale: 1:4,730; **Size:** (ii) 13 5/8 x 17in.; **Top** is N; Manuscript(ii), tracing paper, uncoloured.

Middle ['Great Papworth'] Farm, TL308548, and c. 640a. mostly W of street running N–S through Longstowe village, bounded in N by road from Ermine Street to rectory and in W by Little Gransden Parish.

Names of farms and fields. Middle ['Great Papworth'] and 'Wright's' farms shown in plan form. Closed fields showing owner's land; acreages; roads and watercourses; garden; yards.

Numbers on plots suggest map originally accompanied by a terrier. Later additions of 1 neighbouring owner. Tracing of LSW83301; see this entry for details of date and owner.

Longstowe – [c. 1833] – LSW83303 – CRO R53/22/240
['Great Papworth Farm', Longstowe.]
Scale: 1:4,730; **Size:** (ii) 15 3/8 x 22 9/16in.; **Top** is N; Manuscript(iii), paper, coloured.

Middle ['Great Papworth'] Farm, TL308548, and c. 640a. mostly W of road running N–S through Longstowe village, bounded by Little Gransden Parish in W and extending to N as far as 1 field S of road running from Ermine Street to rectory.

Names of fields. Closed fields showing owner's land; state of cultivation shown by colour; acreages; roads and watercourses; yard; site of house, barn, cottages and plantation.

Pasture indicated by patches of green.

Numbers on plots suggest map originally accompanied by a terrier. Based on LSW83301; see this entry for details of date and owner.

Longstowe – [c. 1833] – LSW83304 – CRO R53/22/241
[Longstowe Hall estate.]
Scale: 1:4,530; **Size:** (ii) 11 7/8 x 16 1/8in.; **Top** is NE; Manuscript(i), paper mounted on cloth, coloured.

Longstowe Hall, TL308557, and c. 430a. W of Ermine Street bounded by Caxton Parish in N, extending into Great Gransden Parish [Huntingdonshire] and Little Gransden Parish in W, and S of road running from Ermine Street to rectory.

Names of fields, buildings, roads and neighbouring owners. Longstowe Hall and 'Gas house' shown in plan form. Closed fields showing owner's land; pightle; wood including Hare Plantation [Great Gransden] and 'Great Wood'; trees; pasture; warren; glebe; state of cultivation shown by colour; acreages; roads and watercourses; garden, kitchen garden and 'flouer garden'; fishponds; stackyard; sites of lodge, cottages, brick kiln and Home Farm.

Compass middle top showing 4 points. Roads and arable coloured brown, pasture and wood coloured green.

Later additions of neighbouring owners and some names of features. Probably accompanies LSW83301; see this entry for details of date and owner.

Longstowe – [c. 1833] – LSW83305 – CRO R53/22/242
[Tracing of map of Longstowe Hall estate.]
Scale: 1:4,530; **Size:** (ii) 13 5/8 x 21 1/2in.; **Top** is NE; Manuscript(ii), tracing paper, uncoloured.

Longstowe Hall, TL308557, and c. 430a. W of Ermine Street, bounded by Caxton Parish in N, extending into Great Gransden Parish [Huntingdonshire] and Little Gransden Parish in W, and S of road from Ermine Street to rectory.

Names of fields. Longstowe Hall and 'Gas house' shown in plan form. Closed fields showing owner's land; pasture;

warren; acreages; roads and watercourses; fishponds; site of brick kiln, woods and Home Farm.

Tracing of LSW83304, drawn c. 1833. Very rough tracing of same map on dorse. Estate held by trustees of Dr Robert Thomson, who died in 1827 [VCH, 5, 122].

Longstowe – [c. 1833] – LSW83306 – C U L Maps.PSQ.18.89, Maps.PSQ.x.18.135
A Plan of the Manor and Estate of Long Stow.
Lithographer: [unidentified] Yorston; **Scale:** 1:15,000; **Size:** (i) 11 x 7 1/16in.; **Top** is N; Lithograph, paper, coloured.

Longstowe Hall, TL308557, and 442a.2r.22p. S of church and N of road to Little Gransden.

Names of fields, roads and neighbouring owners. Church shown in perspective, other buildings shown in plan form and include Longstowe Hall, Middle ['Great Papworth'], 'Wright's', Bellam ['Hawkes's'] and Lower ['Purser's'] farms, outbuildings and 'Golden Lion' and 'Fox' public houses. Closed fields showing owner's land; roads and footpaths; milestones; orchard, gardens, trees, meadow and pond all identified on particulars of sale.

Border of 1 broad and 1 narrow band; title top left with decorative lettering; compass bottom left showing 4 points. Lot 1 coloured green, lot 2 coloured pink, lot 3 coloured yellow, lot 4 coloured blue.

Note beneath title about lot colouring. Accompanies: 'Cambridgeshire. To be sold by Private Contract, entire or in lots. A valuable Freehold and Tithe Free Estate situate in the Parish of Long Stow on the North Road, about 10 miles from Cambridge, 10 from Royston, 11 from Huntingdon, and 48 from London, consisting of lot. 1 ...' Particulars of sale give details of land use, state of cultivation, tenants, acreages and rent. Sale probably took place in 1833 [see LSW83307]. Estate held by trustees of Dr Robert Thomson, who died in 1827 [VCH, 5, 122].

Longstowe – 1833 – LSW83307 – CRO R53/22/237
Plan 2 of Part of Long Stow Estate, in the County of Cambridge, not comprised in Lease to Francis Pym Esqr for Sale by Auction by Mr. George Robins, ... July 9th 1833.
Auctioneer: George Robins; **Lithographer:** C. Ingrey; **Scale bar** 1–0–40 chains (= 6 11/16in.), 1:4,856; **Size:** (i) 18 3/4 x 21 3/8in.; **Top** is N; Lithograph, paper, uncoloured.

Middle ['Great Papworth'] Farm, TL308548, and c. 1,100a. bounded by Ermine Street in E, Little Gransden Parish in W and road running E from Ermine Street to Longstowe Church in N, and extending just S of road from Ermine Street to Little Gransden ['Cambridge Way'].

Names of farms, fields, roads and neighbouring owners. Middle ['Great Papworth'], Bellam ['Hawkes''], Lower ['Purser's'] and 'Wright's' farms, 'Fox' public house and stables shown in plan form. Closed fields showing owner's land; common; wood and trees; acreages; roads and footpaths; watercourses; garden; hedges; ponds and bridge; 'Hen Pen'; site of cottages.

Border of 1 broad and 1 narrow band; title centre top; scale middle bottom; compass top left showing 4 points with a feathered tail.

Note bottom left saying Mr Wallis's farm coloured red, Messrs Wright's, Hawkes' and Purser's farms coloured green and Mr Wither's farm coloured yellow. This map is uncoloured. Pencil notes. Lot numbers suggest map originally accompanied particulars of sale. Estate held by

trustees of Dr Robert Thomson, who died in 1827 [VCH, 5, 122].

M

Madingley – 1811 – MAD81101 – CUL MS Plans 558
Plan of Estates in the Parishes of Madingley, Girton, &c. in the County of Cambridge belonging to Admiral Sir Charles Cotton Bart.
Surveyor: William Custance; **Scale bar** 0–20 chains (= 2 3/8in.), 1:6,670; **Size:** (i) 23 3/8 x 39 1/2in.; **Top** is N; Manuscript(i), parchment, coloured.

Madingley Hall, TL392604, and 3,309a.0r.29p. in all of Madingley and Girton parishes, bounded by road from St Neot's to Cambridge in S and Oakington and Histon parishes in N.

Names of some neighbouring owners. Buildings shown in plan form and include Madingley Church, Madingley Hall, vicarage, public house and post mill in Madingley Parish, Girton Church and public house in Girton Parish, and farms, cottages and farm buildings in both parishes. Closed fields; glebe; wood and trees; meadow; state of cultivation shown by shading and given in words; roads and footpaths; watercourses; park, gardens and orchards; moat; ponds; pightle; hedges and fences; bath.

Border of 1 broad and 1 narrow band; title top right with decorative line-work; scale bottom left; compass combined with scale and showing 8 points. Tables top left and right giving tenants, field names, descriptions of land use and acreages. Buildings owned by estate coloured red, roads coloured pale yellow, water coloured blue.

Photograph in CRO.

March – 1732 – MAR73201 – CRO 283/P
A Survey of Lynwood Farm and the Lands thereto belonging in Tenure of Mr John Simons And also a Survey of Coneywood Farm and the Lands thereto belonging In Tenure of Robert Bawser And also a Survey of Several Lands in Ranson Meer belonging to John Waddington Esq & others All which Lands are in the Parishes of March and Wimblington in the Isle of Ely and County of Cambridge.
Surveyor: Joseph Smith; A **Scale** of Chains 6 in 1 Inch, Scale bar 0–30 chains (= 5in.), 1:4,752; **Size:** (i) 25 5/8 x 28 3/8in.; **Top** is N; Manuscript(i), parchment, coloured.

Linwood House ['Lynwood Hall'], TL408938, and c. 1,300a. in E of Ranson Moor in March Parish bounded by Millhill Drove in E, and extending into N of Sedge Fen in Wimblington Parish.

Names of farms, closes and neighbouring land. Linwood House, Toll Farm and 'Water Engine' [a windmill] shown in perspective. Closes; trees; roads and watercourses; gardens and orchards; bridge.

Border of 5/16in.-wide yellow band; title along top; scale bottom right surmounted by red and yellow dividers; compass rose bottom left showing 4 red points. Roads and buildings coloured brown, water coloured blue, fields outlined in yellow, red and green.

Numbers on plots suggest map originally accompanied by a terrier. Pencil note of land adjoining map and owned by Mr [John] Waddington.

March – [c. 1766–89] – MAR76601 – HRO SM22/146

A Plan of the Estate lying in March Fen in the Isle of Ely & County of Cambridge belonging to Sir Robert Bernard Bart.

Scale bar [0–28 chains] (= 3 1/2in.), 1:6,336; **Size:** (i) 15 15/16 x 24in.; **Top** is S; Manuscript(i), parchment, coloured.

Infields Farm, TL359994, and c. 400a. in W of parish bounded by Shaw's Dike ['Short Dyke'] in W and Plantwater Drain in E, and extending N and S of Twenty Foot River ['River Bavil'].

Names of fields, roads, watercourses and neighbouring owners. Farm buildings shown in plan form, windmills shown in perspective. Closed fields; roads, 'Old Cawsway'; gates; watercourses.

Border of 1 broad band with 1 narrow band on inside; title bottom left in an uncoloured baroque cartouche; scale middle top; compass rose bottom right showing 8 red, yellow, green and grey points. Roads coloured brown, buildings coloured red, fields outlined in green, blue, red and yellow.

Numbers on fields suggest map originally accompanied by a terrier. HRO catalogue suggests map drawn c. 1780; Sir Robert Bernard was baronet from 1766 to 1789 [*EDB*, 59]. Positive and negative photostats at 1:11,960 at CUL Maps.bb.53(1).93.113 and positive photostat at CRO TR373/P4.

March – [c. 1766–89] – MAR76602 – HRO LR24/369

A Plan of High and Low Rainsey Moors in the Parishes of March and Doddington in Isle [sic.] of Ely and County of Cambridge belonging to Sir Robt Bernard Bart.

Scale bar 1–0–25 chains (= 3 1/4in.), 1:6,336; **Size:** (i) 13 x 32 1/4in.; **Top** is E; Manuscript(i), parchment, coloured.

c. 690a. in High Ranson Moor in Doddington Parish and Low Ranson ['Rainsey'] Moor in March Parish, bounded by road from Doddington to Benwick in TL3790 in S and River Nene in N and W.

Names of fields, river, drains, roads and neighbouring owners. Farm buildings shown in plan form, windmill shown in perspective. Closed fields; roads and gates; watercourses and drains.

Border of 1 broad band with 1 narrow band on inside; title middle right in a purple and green cartouche with rococo decoration of a vase and leaves; scale bottom right; compass rose middle bottom showing 8 red, yellow, green and blue points. Roads coloured brown, river outlined in blue, buildings coloured red, fields outlined in red, green, blue and yellow.

Numbers on fields suggest map originally accompanied by a terrier. Pencil notes. HRO catalogue suggests map drawn c. 1780; Sir Robert Bernard was baronet from 1766 to 1789 [*EDB*, 59]. Positive and negative photostats at 1:8,337 at CUL Maps.bb.53(1).93.112 and negative photostat at CRO TR373/P6.

March – 1794 – MAR79401 – SJC MPS 56

The Map of a Farm called Estover in the parish of March in the Isle of Ely: belonging to St. John's College in the University of Cambridge. Surveyed in 1794.

Surveyor: Joseph Freeman; **Scale bar** 5–0–10 chains (= 4 7/8in.), 1:2,437; **Size:** (i) 25 x 20 11/16in.; **Top** is N; Manuscript(i), parchment, coloured.

Estover Farm, TL421982, and 171a.1r.9p. bounded by road running N from March to Elm in W and including 115a. to NW bounded by Twenty Foot River in N.

Names of fields, droves and neighbouring owners. Farm buildings shown in plan form. Closed fields showing owner's land; common; wood; waste and 'The Slamp' [slump, bog]; arable shown by stripes, pasture shown by symbols representing tufts of grass; roads and watercourses; gates; gardens and orchards; hedges; bridges.

Border of 1 broad and 1 narrow band; title bottom left in a rococo cartouche with a face at the top; scale beneath title; compass middle right showing 8 points. Table top right giving field names and acreages of land for fen and upland. Grass coloured green, arable coloured in yellow stripes, buildings coloured red, water coloured blue.

Accompanies terrier and surveyed by Joseph Freeman and Nicholas King, 1791 [SJC D31.45]. On dorse of terrier is enlarged drawing of farm at 1:243 and showing 1a.0r.17p. Top is W, bounded by common in W and a close in E. Shows house, barn, 'turf house', 'bullock house', 'cart lodge', garden, orchard, farmyard and nature of walls and roofs. Photograph of 1794 map at 1:3,586 at CRO TR869/P23.

March – 1805 – MAR80501 – CUL MS Plans 645

Map of an Estate the Property of the Honorable General Sparrow lying in march Cambridgeshire which contains 434a.1r.9p.

Surveyor: W[illiam] Peak; **A Scale** of 32 Chains (= 4in.), 1:6,336; **Size:** (i) 18 9/16 x 26 5/8in.; **Top** is NW; Manuscript(i), parchment, coloured.

Infields Farm, TL359994, and 434a.1r.9p. bounded by Shaw's Dike in W and Plantwater Drain in E, and extending N and S of Twenty Foot River ['Bevils Leam'].

Names of watercourses and neighbouring owners. Farm buildings shown in plan form, 2 windmills shown in perspective. Closed fields showing owner's land; acreages; roads and footpaths; watercourses; gates; bridge over river.

Border of 1 narrow band; title top left in an ornamental cartouche which includes vases and has reeds underneath; scale middle bottom coloured green; compass top right showing 8 points coloured green and black with a very colourful N point. 2 tables bottom left giving tenants and acreages. William Clarke's land shaded green, William Waudeby's land shaded yellow, boundary between March and Whittlesey parishes coloured red.

Pencil notes. Surveyor's 1st name was William [Eden P142]; owner was probably the Honourable General Robert Bernard Sparrow [Army List, 1805], who died on 29 August 1805 while returning by ship from Barbados [memorial in Brampton Church, Huntingdonshire]. Photograph in CRO.

March – 1824 – MAR82401 – CRO 515/P

Plan of Estates in March, the Property of Mr Nathan Gray. [In Burrow Moor.]

Surveyor: Joseph Jackson; **Scale:** 3 Chains to an Inch, 1:2,376; **Size:** (iii) 15 x 11in.; **Top** is N; Manuscript(i), paper, coloured.

39a.2r.7p. in Burrow Moor E of TL394959, junction of Burrowmoor Road ['Drove'] with Cross Road, bounded by Burrowmoor Road in S.

Names of roads, fen and neighbouring owners. Closed fields showing owner's land; acreages; roads and watercourses; gates; responsibility for boundaries.

For whole sheet: border of 1 broad and 1 narrow band; title centre top; scale middle right. Land outlined in yellow, green and red.

On middle of sheet containing 4 maps; see also MAR82402–4. Whole sheet measures 27 13/16 x 50 3/4in. Note under scale about symbol denoting responsibility for fences. Lot numbers on plots. Pencil notes. Accompanied by a pencil map.

March – 1824 – MAR82402 – CRO 515/P
Plan of Estates in March, the Property of Mr Nathan Gray. [E of March town.]
Surveyor: Joseph Jackson; **Scale:** 3 Chains to an Inch, 1:2,376; **Size:** (iii) 6 x 11in.; **Top** is W; Manuscript(i), paper, coloured.
c. 36a. E of town and S of TL443986, where Binnimoor Road ['Drove'] reaches River Nene.
Names of fields, roads, river and neighbouring owners. 3 windmills shown in perspective. Closed fields showing owner's land; acreage of 1 lot; roads and watercourses; bridges.
For whole sheet: border of 1 broad and 1 narrow band; title centre top; scale middle right. Lots coloured red, green and yellow.
Top left of sheet containing 4 maps; see MAR82401 for details. Lot numbers on plots. See also MAR82403–4.

March – 1824 – MAR82403 – CRO 515/P
Plan of Estates in March, the Property of Mr Nathan Gray. [NE of March town.]
Surveyor: Joseph Jackson; **Scale:** 3 Chains to an Inch, 1:2,376; **Size:** (iii) 13 x 13in.; **Top** is W; Manuscript(i), paper, coloured.
c. 97a. NE of town and W of TL445986, confluence of River Nene and Twenty Foot River, bounded by Twenty Foot River in N, River Nene in S and road from March to Chain Bridge in W.
Names of fields, rivers, roads and neighbouring owners. 5 windmills shown in perspective. Closed fields showing owner's land; roads and watercourses; bridges including Chain Bridge.
For whole sheet: border of 1 broad and 1 narrow band; title centre top; scale middle right. Plots coloured yellow, green and pink.
Bottom left of sheet containing 4 maps; see MAR82401 for details. Lot numbers on plots. Pencil notes of acreages. See also MAR82402,4.

March – 1824 – MAR82404 – CRO 515/P
Plan of Estates in March, the Property of Mr Nathan Gray. [SW of March town.]
Surveyor: Joseph Jackson; **Scale:** 3 Chains to an Inch, 1:2,376; **Size:** (iii) 6 x 10in.; **Top** is N; Manuscript(i), paper, coloured.
c. 43a. in 'Sumps', N of TL415965, junction of Gall Road ['Drove'] with Burrowmoor Road ['Drove'], bounded by River Nene in N and 'red bridge' over river and main road running S from town in E.
Names of roads, river and neighbouring owners. Houses shown in plan form. Closed fields showing owner's land; acreages; roads including turnpike; watercourses; garden; bank and bridge; gates; hedge and fences; responsibility for boundaries.

For whole sheet: border of 1 broad and 1 narrow band; title centre top; scale middle right. Land outlined in red, green, yellow and orange.
Centre right of sheet containing 4 maps; see MAR82401 for details. Lot numbers on plots. Pencil and ink notes. See also MAR82401–3.

March – 1824 – MAR82405 – CRO 515/P
Plan of an Estate in March, the Property of Mr Nathan Gray, called the Chequer row.
Surveyor: Joseph Jackson; **Scale bar** 0–40 feet (= 4in.), 1:120; **Size:** (i) 26 1/8 x 50 7/8in.; **Top** is W; Manuscript(i), paper mounted on cloth, uncoloured.
c. 2a. in TL4196, bounded by River Nene in S and road to Elm in E.
Names of tenants, buildings and roads. Buildings shown in plan form and include houses, privies, pigsties, stables, 'Wood~house', 'Calf~house', 'Soot~house', 'Turf hovel', 'Open~hovel', 'Liquor House' and 'Old Brewhouse'. Roads and 'causeway'; watercourses and 'Old Dike'; gates; gardens; passages; frontages; ash pit; yards; oven; sign to 'Chequers' [public house].
Border of 1 broad band with 1 narrow band on inside; title bottom left; scale centre bottom.
Pencil notes extending area and giving responsibility for boundaries. Lot numbers.

March – 1832 – MAR83201 – CRO 515/P
Plan of Botany Bay Farm in the Parish of March the Property of Stokely Hutchinson.
Surveyor: Richard Mackley; **Scale:** 1:2,230; **Size:** (i) 28 x 32 1/4in.; **Top** is N; Manuscript(i), paper mounted on cloth, coloured.
Botany Bay Farm, TL378959, and 512a.0r.13p. bounded by River Nene in N and W, Knight's End Road in S and drove running S from TL389964 in E.
Names of river and neighbouring owners. Farm and farm buildings shown in plan form, 2 windmills shown in perspective. Closed fields showing owner's land; wood and trees; wash; acreages and dimensions of plots; roads and watercourses; hedges.
Border of 1 broad band with 1 narrow band on outside and 3 narrow bands on inside; title top left with decorative linework above; compass below title showing 8 points. Buildings coloured red, water probably coloured blue.
Numbers on plots suggest map originally accompanied by a terrier. Note bottom left of acreages. Map very discoloured, so colouring difficult to establish.

March – [1834] – MAR83401 – CRO R61/17/4/B4
[Land S of March Chain Bridge, owned by the late Thomas Richardson.]
Scale: Four Chains to an Inch, 1:3,168; **Size:** (i) 11 1/4 x 7 5/16in.; **Top** is N; Manuscript(i), parchment, coloured.
Chain Bridge, TF421002, and 47a.0r.13p. bounded by Twenty Foot River in N, road from March to bridge in E and The Chase ['Norwood private road'] in S.
Names of tenants, roads and neighbouring owners. 'Chain House' shown in plan form. Closed fields showing owner's land; trees; slump and bank; state of cultivation shown by colour; acreages and dimensions of plots; tenure; roads and watercourses; gates; responsibility for boundaries.

Border of 1 narrow red band; scale at bottom; cardinal points stated in border. Roads and arable coloured brown, pasture and trees coloured green, water coloured blue.

Note at bottom explaining symbol for denoting responsibility for boundaries. Date on lease: 'Mr William Ground surviving Trustee under Mr Thomas Richardsons Will to Mr John Doncaster: Release of Freehold Land in March with Covenant to Surrender Copyholds'.

Melbourn – 1792 – MEB79201 – SJC MPS 59

A Map of Lands situate in the Parishes of Melbourn and Meldreth in the County of Cambridge; belonging to the College of St John the Evangelist in that University. Surveyed in 1792.

Surveyors: [Nicholas King] [and Joseph Freeman?]; **Scale bar** 10–0–40 chains (= 3 1/8in.), 1:12,670; **Size:** (i) 24 15/16 x 21 1/8in.; **Top** is N; Manuscript(i), parchment, coloured.

Melbourn Church, TL382448, and 93a.2r.4p. in strips scattered throughout Melbourn and Meldreth parishes.

Names of fields, roads and neighbouring owners. Melbourn and Meldreth churches shown in perspective. Open fields showing owner's strips; closes; common; trees; 'moor'; roads including turnpike from Cambridge to Royston; footpaths; watercourses; hedges; gravel pit; bridge; 'Hogs hole'.

Border of 1 broad and 1 narrow band; title bottom right in a cartouche of leaves with a ribbon at top and fruit and flowers underneath; scale bottom left; compass top left showing 4 points. Tables top left and top right giving field numbers, number of strips and acreages of land leased by William Ellis and William Scruby. Roads coloured green or brown, strips coloured yellow or red, buildings coloured red, hedges coloured green, water coloured blue, Ellis' land coloured yellow, Scruby's land coloured red.

At SJC D31.46 is a terrier, surveyed by Nicholas King, of land in Melbourn leased to Ellis. On dorse is enlarged drawing of the farm, showing 2r.21p. at 1:151 with top pointing N and bounded by church in W and road in S. Shows house, 'cow house', stables, hovel, barn, 'hogstye', yard, orchard, garden and nature of walls and roofs. Map of whole estate is in style of Joseph Freeman; possibly produced in Freeman's office and King was his assistant [see MAR79401]. Photograph at 1:13,770 at CRO TR869/P24.

Melbourn – 1834 – MEB83401 – CRO R78/39

A Map of Melbourn Open Field before the inclosure and the land belonging to the Lordship Farm of 500 acres Occupied by My Father John Newling.

Surveyor: Jo. Newling; **Scale:** 1:1,600; **Size:** (ii) 10 9/16 x 13 1/16in.; **Top** is E; Positive photostat, paper, uncoloured.

Farm at TL385451, and c. 4,700a. in whole parish except for far NE.

Names of farms, fields and roads. Mill, church, Melbourn Bury, cottages, farms, windmill and 'North Hall' shown in perspective, Lordship Farm shown in exaggerated perspective. Open fields showing owner's strips; closes; common; trees; heath; pasture; roads and footpaths; watercourses; gardens; 'Botly Hill Bush'; moat; clunch pits and 'old pits'; tumulus at Grinnel ['Grindle'] Hill shown as a mound.

Title top right.

Very crude drawing. Land owned by Wortham Hitch [d. 1834] and then by John Hitch [*VCH*, 8, 71]. Manuscript original not found in 1988.

Melbourn – 1834 – MEB83402 – CRO P117/3/2

Plan of the Vicarage House and Homestead with Pasture Close adjoining thereto situate at Melbourn, Camb's November, 1834.

Surveyors: [unidentified] Cockett, [unidentified] Nash; **Scale:** One Inch to a Chain, 1:792; **Size:** (ii) 20 x 14 5/16in.; **Top** is NW; Manuscript(i), paper, coloured.

Melbourn Vicarage, TL383448, and 8a.3r.39p. E of church and NW of road from Royston to Cambridge.

Names of fields, roads and neighbouring owners. Vicarage, barn, stables and wash house shown in plan form, outlines of neighbouring buildings. Closes; pasture; large tree at corner of churchyard; state of cultivation shown by colour; acreages; roads and footpaths; watercourses; gates; garden and its layout; pond; footbridge; responsibility for boundaries; orchard adjoining map.

Title middle left; scale bottom left; compass top right showing 4 plain points with a decorated N. Garden coloured yellow, pasture coloured green, water coloured blue, buildings coloured purple, buildings adjoining map coloured grey.

Pencil additions. Note of garden belonging to Hale Wortham, to be exchanged with another plot.

Melbourn – 1835 – MEB83501 – CRO 296/SP11

Plan of Building Ground to be sold by Auction by Cockett & Nash at Melbourn Novr 19th 1835.

Auctioneers: [unidentified] Cockett, [unidentified] Nash; **Scale:** One inch to a Chain, 1:792; **Size:** (ii) 17 x 13 5/8in.; **Top** is S; Manuscript(i), paper, uncoloured.

2a.0r.36p. in TL3844, bounded by road from Cambridge to Royston in N and Back Street ['Melbourn Backside'] in S.

Names of areas, roads and neighbouring owners. Cottages shown in plan form, edge of White House Farm homestead. Closed fields showing owner's land; roads; gardens and orchard; responsibility for boundaries.

Title top left; scale bottom left.

Pencil notes of acreages. Lot numbers suggest map originally accompanied particulars of sale. On dorse: 'Mr Thos Scruby – Plan of Orchard at Melbourn'.

Meldreth – 1774 – MED77401 – GLC H1/ST/E115/23

A Survey of the Scite of the Manor of Topcliffs, and the Water Mill and Lands adjoining; at Mildrid in Cambridgeshire belonging to St Thomas's Hospital taken in 1774 by O. Swan.

Surveyor: O[wen] Swan; **Scale bar** 0–80 statute perches (= 4 7/8in.), 1:3,249; **Size:** (i) 7 7/8 x 18in.; **Top** is N; Manuscript(i), parchment, coloured.

Meldreth Church, TL378468, and 8a.1r.1p. to S and W, bounded by river in E.

Names of fields. Buildings shown in perspective and include water mill, manor house and outbuildings, church shown in exaggerated perspective. Closes; pightle; wood, Elm grove and trees; 'church pasture'; roads and watercourses; gates; garden and orchard; hedges; millpond.

Border 3/16in. wide with a leaf motif with 2 narrow brown bands on either side and rosettes in the corners; title on left in a rococo cartouche; scale bottom left in a border with the leaf motif; compass at bottom showing 8 points with 4 main points having decorated arms. Table on right giving field names and acreages. Houses coloured brown, fields outlined in green, trees coloured green or brown, buildings have red roofs, water coloured blue/grey.

Surveyor's 1st name was Owen [Eden S617].

Meldreth – [c. 1820] – MED82001 – EDR CC.12333
Meldreth.
Surveyor: [Edward Gibbons]; **Scale:** 1:4,740; **Size:** (ii) 23 5/8 x 20 3/8in.; **Top** is NW; Manuscript(ii), paper, uncoloured.

Meldreth Church, TL378468, and 339a.3r.21p. to N bounded by Orwell Parish in N and Shepreth Parish in E, and land to S and E bounded by road to Whaddon in W.

Names of fields, owner, tenants and roads. Farm buildings shown in plan form, church shown in perspective. Closed fields; roads and watercourses; responsibility for boundaries; reasons for allotments.

Title top right; compass bottom right showing 4 points.
Ink note on dorse: 'Meldreth Rectory'. Copied from map by Edward Gibbons which accompanied 1820 inclosure award, shows land allotted to Dean and Chapter of Ely.

Meldreth – [Post 1820] – MED82002 – CCC Box 46
Sketch of Meldreth Estate in tenure of Mr Bun.
Surveyor: M[artin] Nockolds; **Scale:** 1:5,790; **Size:** (ii) 15 1/4 x 9 1/2in.; **Top** is N; Manuscript(ii), tracing paper, uncoloured.

Christ's College ['Chard'] Farm, TL381469, and c. 160a. bounded by road from Shepreth to Whaddon in S and land owned by Harvey's Charity in E.

Names of neighbouring owners. Farm buildings shown in plan form. Closed fields showing owner's land; acreages of some plots; roads.

Title bottom left.
Note after title: 'the Red line shows the boundary of the College Property next Harveys Charity; where dotted it is not fenced, from A to B. the fence belongs to Christ College from B to C. the fence belongs to the Charity Estate. M. Nockolds. The Black Lines show the present fences'. Drawn after 1820 inclosure award. Surveyor's 1st name was Martin [Eden N110].

Milton – 1793 – MIL79301 – CRO L3/26(a)
['Rough plan of Church Yard at Milton and alterations made therein'.]
Scale bar 60–0 yards (= 12 11/16in.), 1:170; **Size:** (ii) 13 3/8 x 15 3/8in.; **Top** is NE; Manuscript(i), paper, uncoloured.

Milton Church, TL480629, and c. 2r. in churchyard.
Names of areas and neighbouring owners. Church shown in plan form. Roads; lengths of boundaries; plantation adjoining map.

Scale on right; cardinal points stated along church walls.
Notes of boundaries to be altered and their lengths. Note added in 1857 of boundaries which were altered. Title on dorse. Land owned by Bishop of Ely.

Milton – 1816 – MIL81601 – PCC Milton G1
A Sketch of an Estate situate in the Parish of Milton in the County of Cambridge belonging to the Master and Fellows of Pembroke Hall.
Scale: 1:5,090; **Size:** (ii) 16 3/8 x 20 3/8in.; **Top** is NE; Manuscript(iv), tracing paper, uncoloured.

Milton Church, TL480629, and 69a.0r.27p. S of crossroads to S.

Names of roads and neighbouring owners. Cottages shown in plan form, church shown in perspective. Closed fields showing owner's land; 'Lug Fen'; responsibility for boundaries; roads; watercourses; acreages given on table.

Title middle top; compass top left showing 4 plain points. Table bottom right giving acreages and allotments in fields and fen.

Numbers refer to inclosure award. Notes at end of table of allotments in Landbeach, and: 'Note. This is on the left going to Ely, at the end of a green lane about 1/2 a mile from Milton'. This allotment not shown on plan. Later pencil notes of land taken by railway.

N

Newmarket All Saints' – 1756 – NEA75601 – PRO MPE 410
[Land in Newmarket leased by John Manners, Marquis of Granby, from the Crown.]
Surveyor: Charles Evans; **Scale:** 1:358; **Size:** (i) 20 3/8 x 17 1/4in.; **Top** is S; Manuscript(i), paper, uncoloured.

c. 2a. in TL6463, bounded by Newmarket Street and 'Common Church Way' in N.

Names of occupiers, areas, buildings and neighbouring owners. Buildings shown in plan form and include houses, stables, barns, 'wood house', 'hen house', 'coach house', forge, 'offices that are carcased but were never finished'. Dimensions of areas; footpaths and 'Common Church Way'; gardens; yards and courts.

Border of 1 broad band with 1 narrow band on either side; cardinal points stated in border. Table on left giving tenants and value of areas, table bottom left of houses 'to be excepted'.

Note: 'Vine Coachhouses Six of wich are for his Majestys use'. At bottom: 'I have this day Surveyed a Piece or Parcell of Ground Situate at New Markett in Cambridgeshire belonging to [Marquis of Granby] Abutting North on New Markett Street South on the Road leading to Wooditton East on the Road from New Markett to Chevely and on William Brand and Samuel Buckle and West on Mrs Boswell and William Brand, where four Yards four Brick Messuages and several Stable Brick buildings and allso two Timber Messuages. All wich are coloured Red and the Yards to the same enclosed with red Lines, most of the aforesaid Buildings are in Middling repair and cannot be Valued at more than One Hundred Pounds per Annum to make up the present Term Fifty Years. Chas Evans'. Tenant was probably Marquis of Granby as he leased the other properties on this sheet; land owned by the Crown [see NEA75602 and SWB75601]. Map is at top of sheet.

Newmarket All Saints' – 1756 – NEA75602 – PRO MPE 410
The two closes called the King's Closes Containing Nine Acres – Situate at Newmarket In the County of Cambridge.
Surveyor: Charles Evans; **Scale:** 1:1,400; **Size:** (i) 15 1/4 x 10 1/4in.; **Top** is S; Manuscript(i), paper, uncoloured.

All Saints' churchyard, TL644633, and c. 15a. to S bounded by road to Cheveley in E, Newmarket Heath in S and 'Saxon Lane' in W.

Closes; dimensions of areas; hedges and fences.

Border of 1 broad band with 1 narrow band on either side; title in centre; cardinal points stated in border.

Note at bottom: 'I have this day Surveyed two Closes of Land belonging to the Rt Honble the Marquis of Granby & the Earle of Guernsey. Worth about Seven pounds per Annum Chas Evans'. John Manners, Marquis of Granby [PB, 2,328] and Heneage Finch, 2nd Earl of Aylesford and Lord Guernsey [PB, 143] leased land from the Crown. Bottom right of sheet; see also NEA75601 and SWB75601.

Newmarket All Saints' – 1786 – NEA78601 – PRO K T1/639 [To become MFQ 756]

Surveyed a piece or parcel of Ground, situate at Newmarket, in the County of Cambridge, belonging to the Duke of Rutland, and the Countess Dowager of Aylesford, on which stands One large Brick Messuage with Coach=houses, Stables, Out Houses, Yards and Gardens thereto belonging – Also one small Brick Messuage near the same. – One Brick and Two Timber Messuages next the Street, and several Stables in the Yard, behind the same, as described by the dark Colour on the above Plan. – The large Messuage is Substantial, the others are slight buildings but in Tenantable repair, and the whole may be Valued at Ninety Pounds Per Annum for a term of 50 Years Jno Marquand Ap: 22nd. 1786.

Surveyor: John Marquand; **Scale:** 1:492; **Size:** (i) 15 x 11 1/2in.; **Top** is S; Manuscript(i), paper, coloured.

c. 2a. in TL6463, bounded by roads to Wood Ditton in S and to Cheveley in E, and 'Newmarket Street' in N.

Names of tenants, neighbouring owners, roads and buildings. Buildings shown in plan form and include 'Dwelling House', 'Messuages', 'Wash=house', coach houses, shop, houses, barns, stables, 'Room' and site of almshouses. Roads; dimensions of areas; gardens; yards; 'Dung~hole'.

Border of 2 narrow bands; title at bottom; cardinal points stated at edge of map. Buildings coloured black and red, gardens coloured green, yards coloured yellow.

Note under title: 'NB. The Buildings coloured Red are excepted out of the Lease'. Accompanies report by the Surveyor General, C. Augustus Selwyn, on 'Ground at Newmarket whereon the Old Palace \formerly/ stood', following a petition from [4th] Duke of Rutland [PB, 2,329] and Lady Louisa Aylesford [PB, 144] for a renewal of their leases from the Crown. See also NEA78602 and SWB78601.

Newmarket All Saints' – 1786 – NEA78602 – PRO K T1/639 [To become MFQ 756]

Surveyed a piece or parcel of Land, situate at Newmarket, in the County of Cambridge, belonging to the Duke of Rutland and Countess Dowager of Aylesford, consisting of two Closes, containing about 9 Acres worth a Rent of Fifty Shillings per Acre amounting to twenty two Pounds ten shillings per Annum Jno Marquand Ap: the 22nd 1786.

Surveyor: John Marquand; **Scale:** 1:1,790; **Size:** (i) 14 x 11 1/4in.; **Top** is S; Manuscript(i), paper, coloured.

c. 9a. S of All Saints' churchyard, TL644633, bounded by road to Cheveley in E, 'Saxon Lane' in W and Newmarket Heath in S.

Names of roads. Closes; roads; dimensions of areas; site of almshouses.

Border of 2 narrow bands; title at bottom; cardinal points stated at edge of map. Close coloured green, site of almshouses coloured yellow.

Drawn following a petition from [4th] Duke of Rutland [PB, 2,329] and Lady Louisa Aylesford [PB, 144] for a renewal of their leases from the Crown. See also NEA78601 and SWB78601.

Newmarket All Saints' – 1803 – NEA80301 – PRO CRES 2/115

Plan of 6 Inclosures at Newmarket belonging to the Crown on Lease to His Grace of Rutland and others made in 1803.

Scale: 1:1,540; **Size:** (i) 13 1/2 x 9 3/4in.; **Top** is N; Manuscript(ii), tracing paper, uncoloured.

9a.1r.37p. S of All Saints' churchyard, TL644633, bounded by roads to Cheveley in E and to Saxon Street in W, and a road in S.

Names of roads. Buildings shown in plan form and include site of almshouse and 'King's Store House'. Closes; acreages; roads; hedges; garden.

Border of 1 broad band with 1 narrow band on inside; title top left; compass centre right showing 4 points, and cardinal points stated at edge of map. Table top right giving tenants and acreages.

'No 2' right of title. Many estimates of repair to buildings added 1815–17.

Newmarket All Saints' – [c. 1815–17] – NEA81501 – PRO MPE 630

[Land in Newmarket, owned by the Crown.]

Scale: 1:188; **Size:** (i) 17 7/16 x 22 9/16in.; **Top** is W; Manuscript(i), paper, coloured.

All Saints' churchyard, TL644633, and c. 3r. to S bounded by road to Saxon ['Saxham'] Street in E.

Names of areas and roads. Buildings shown in plan form and include workshops, wash house, 'Coalhouse', 'Privy', 'Hovel', 'Store Sheds', 'New ladder Shed and House for Tarpaulins', 'The Labourer in Trusts' Apartments'. Roads; dimensions of areas; gardens; paddocks; 'Dung hole'; 'Cinder hole'; 'His Majesty's Store Yard Office Yard &c'; 'The old Slaughter house Yard but now a Paddock'.

Border of 2 narrow bands. Buildings coloured pink.

Note on right referring to 1 plot: 'N.B. Crown Land late the Prince of Wales' Paddocks, but now in the Occupation of John Douglas Esqr by Permission of His Grace the Duke of Rutland'. Note at top referring to another plot: 'N.B. Crown Land late the Prince of Wales' Paddocks &c but now occupied by Mr Smallman'. In collection of maps drawn between 1815 and 1817, draughtsman probably drew NEA81502 as well.

Newmarket All Saints' – [c. 1815–17] – NEA81502 – PRO MPE 630

[Newmarket Palace, owned by the Crown.]

Scale bar 100–0 feet (= 6 5/16in.), 1:190; **Size:** (i) 17 1/2 x 26 1/4in.; **Top** is S; Manuscript(i), paper, coloured.

c. 2a. in TL6463, bounded by roads to London in E and to Cheveley in NE.

Names of areas, roads, neighbouring owners and neighbouring features. Buildings shown in plan form and include 'Engine House', 'Great Stables', larder, 'The Grooms House &c', 'Late Prince of Wales' Stables', 'Privy', 'Coal House', 'Entrance House', 'Back Stables occupied by His Royal Highness the Duke of York'. Roads; gardens; dimensions of areas; 'Kitchen' and 'Engine' courts; 'Fire Engines';

'late the Old Chamberlains Office &c'; 'His Majestys' Stable Yard'.

Border of 2 narrow bands; scale at bottom. Buildings coloured pink.

Note on Great Stables: 'Out of repair'. In collection of maps drawn between 1815 and 1817, draughtsman probably drew NEA81501 as well.

Newmarket All Saints' – 1815 – NEA81503 – PRO MPE 630

Plan of Newmarket Palace. Ground Floor.

Draughtsman: G[eorge] R[ussell]; **Scale bar** 0–100 feet (= 12 1/2in.), 1:96; **Size:** (i) 34 x 25 11/16in.; **Top** is S; Manuscript(ii), paper, coloured.

c. 1a. in TL6463, bounded by road to London in N.

Names of areas and roads. Buildings shown in plan form and include 'Engine House'. Gardens; 'Engine' and 'Kitchen' courts; fire engines; engines.

Border of 1 narrow band; title centre top; scale bottom left. 'Apartments occupied by the Housekeeper' coloured pink, 'Apartments occupied by Mr Newell' coloured yellow.

Note on right explaining colour scheme and that 'A' marks 'Rooms in a very dilapidated state'. Note bottom right: 'Copied December 1815 G.R. Office of H.M. Works'. See also NEA81601, another copy which labels rooms and shows slight changes in occupancy. Draughtsman's name was George Russell [PRO map catalogue]; palace owned by the Crown.

Newmarket All Saints' – 1816 – NEA81601 – PRO MPE 630

Plan of Newmarket Palace. Ground Floor.

Draughtsman: Thomas Chawner; **Scale bar** 10–0–70 feet (= 5in.), 1:192; **Size:** (i) 21 5/8 x 17 3/16in.; **Top** is S; Manuscript(ii), paper, coloured.

c. 1a. in TL6463, bounded by road to London in N.

Names of areas and roads. Buildings shown in plan form and include stables, coach house, 'Lumber~place', stoves, 'Old Confectionary', cellars, store rooms, shed, sitting room, 'Bed Closet', 'Temporary Stable', 'Great Kitchen', 'Second Kitchen', larders, 'Knife & Shoe Room', 'Landry', pantry, 'Portico', 'The Old Hazard Room now a Bed Room', 'Lofty Cellar', wash houses, scullery, kitchens, house-keeper's and footman's rooms, lobbys, parlours, bedroom, 'Second Hall', 'Closet' and 'Water Closet', entrances and entrance hall, 'Queen Anne's Dining Room', 'Queen Anne's Drawing Room', 'Engine House'. Roads; gardens; courtyard; greenhouse; 'Fire Engines'; 'Engine'; 'Engine Court'; 'Great Stairs'; posts and railings; 'Site of an Old Building lately pulled down, called, The Lord Chamberlains Office &c'.

Border of 2 narrow bands; title at top; scale bottom left. 'Coach~house and Stable, in possession of The Duke of York' coloured blue, 'Apartments occupied by John Douglas Esqr' coloured pink, 'Apartments occupied by Mrs Nowell, Deputy Housekeeper' coloured yellow.

Note on right explaining colour scheme and that 'A' marks 'Rooms in a very dilapidated state'. Pencil additions. Palace owned by the Crown. See also NEA81503, another copy which does not label rooms.

Newmarket All Saints' – 1817 – NEA81701 – PRO MPE 630

Plan of part of Newmarket Palace, Ground Floor

Surveyor: W[illiam] A[lexander] Arnold; **Scale bar** 0–80 feet (= 9 7/8in.), 1:97; **Size:** (i) 22 5/8 x 26 3/8in.; **Top** is S; Manuscript(i), paper, coloured.

c. 3r. in TL6463, bounded by 'Ram Lane' in S.

Names of features, roads and occupiers. Buildings shown in plan form and include 'Coach~house and stable', 'Back Kitchen', 'Brewhouse &c', 'The Old Confectionary', 'The late Housekeepers', 'Formerly the Master of the Horse Apartments = but now the Deputy Housekeepers', 'Hothouse'. 'Large Garden'; 'Fire Engine'.

Border of 2 narrow bands; title centre top; scale bottom left. Some areas coloured red.

Red notes of new walls, 'New fire place for Hot house', 'Ground allotted for new Water Closet' and 'New doorway'. These notes incorporate pencil notes on N part of NEA81601. Pencil notes. Surveyor's 1st names were William Alexander [see NEA81702]. Palace owned by the Crown.

Newmarket All Saints' – [1817] – NEA81702 – PRO CRES 2/115

[Newmarket Palace, owned by the Crown.]

Surveyor: William Alexander Arnold; **Scale:** 1:115; **Size:** (ii) 12 1/2 x 8in.; **Top** is S; Manuscript(i), paper, uncoloured.

30p. in TL6463, bounded by 'Ram Lane' in S and High Street in N.

Names of areas, roads and neighbouring owners. Buildings shown in plan form and include 'Green~house', 'late Master of the Horse Apartments, but now occupied by the deputy Housekeeper', and 'late His Royal Highness the Duke of Yorks, Apartments, but now occupied by John Douglas Esqr'. Roads; gardens; courtyard.

Notes: 'late the Old Chamberlains Offices, Yard &c', 'Temporary intended Post and Railing', 'Proposed Entrance from Ram Lane', 'Allotted for Sale' and 'Proposed Entrance from High Street'. On dorse of letter from W. A. Arnold to James Pillar Esqr at Land Revenue Office, dated 27 April 1817. Letter concerned with preparations for sale of property. Letters on map refer to this letter.

Newmarket All Saints' – [Post 1818] – NEA81801 – PRO CRES 2/115

[Newmarket Palace, owned by the Crown.]

Scale: 1:344; **Size:** (i) 7 3/8 x 9in.; **Top** is SE; Manuscript(i), paper, coloured.

c. 1r. in TL6463, bounded by 'Ram Lane' in S and High Street in N.

Names of tenants and roads. Buildings shown in plan form and include offices and 'Late The Greyhound Inn'. Roads.

Border of 1 narrow band; compass on left showing 4 points. 2 buildings coloured red, 1 plot coloured green.

Pencil notes. On paper with watermark of 1818.

Newmarket All Saints' – [Post 1818] – NEA81802 – PRO CRES 2/115

[Newmarket Palace, owned by the Crown.]

Scale: 1:551; **Size:** (iii) 3 x 4in.; **Top** is SE; Manuscript(i), paper, coloured.

c. 1r. in TL6463, bounded by 'Sun Lane' in W and High Street in N.

Names of roads and neighbouring owners. Buildings shown in plan form. Roads; gates; gardens; well; 'Fore Court'; 'Duke of York's new boundary Wall'.

Land outlined in green, buildings coloured blue.

Note under map: 'A. The part of the Palace formerly occupied by Queen Anne B. Front doorway C. Greenhouse'. Pencil notes. On paper with watermark of 1818.

Newmarket All Saints' – [Post 1818] – NEA81803 – PRO CRES 2/115

[Newmarket Palace, owned by the Crown.]

Scale: 1:689; **Size:** (i) 8 7/8 x 9 1/8in.; **Top** is SE; Manuscript(i), paper, coloured.

c. 1r. in TL6463, bounded by 'Ram Lane' in N, and roads to Saxon Street ['Saxon Lane'] in W and to Cheveley in E.

Names of roads and areas. Buildings shown in plan form and include house, sheds, stable and church. Roads; garden; yard.

Border of 1 narrow band; compass on left showing 4 points. Garden coloured green, buildings coloured blue, yards coloured yellow, church coloured grey.

On paper with watermark of 1818.

Newmarket All Saints' – [Post 1818?] – NEA81804 – PRO CRES 2/115

[Paddock in Newmarket, owned by the Crown.]

Scale: 1:1,320; **Size:** (ii) 7 1/2 x 7 7/8in.; **Top** is S; Manuscript(i), paper, uncoloured.

2r.30p. in TL6463, bounded by All Saints' churchyard in N, road to Cheveley in E and 'His Majestys Store Yard' in W.

Names of areas. 'Hovel' shown in plan form. Roads; dimensions of area; 'The New Burial Ground'.

Cardinal points stated at edge of map.

Note top right of acreage. Note: 'This strip for the National School'. Probably drawn at similar time to NEA81801–3.

Newmarket All Saints' – 1831 – NEA83101 – PRO MPEE 81

Plan of Newmarket Palace and Lands adjacent in the County of Cambridge & Sold to Stephen Piper Esqr 1831.

Scale: 1:721; **Size:** (ii) 30 5/16 x 27in.; **Top** is NNE; Manuscript(i), parchment, coloured.

c. 15a. S of All Saints' Church, TL644633, bounded by road to Cheveley in E and Park ['Dog Kennel'] Lane in W.

Names of roads, areas and neighbouring owners. Buildings shown in plan form and include houses, stables, sheds, 'Coach House', church, shop, 'Wash[?] House', 'Old Palace House', 'Work~Shops', 'Room'. Acreages of some areas; gardens; yard; passage; pound; 'Dung Hole'.

Title top right; compass centre top showing 4 points. Areas outlined in brown and pink.

Pencil and ink notes, including identification of almshouses and 'The new Churchyard'.

Newmarket All Saints' – 1834 – NEA83401 – CRO 101/P4

Plan of an estate, situate in Newmarket, All Saints', In the County of Cambridge, the property of Mr Stephen Piper, Miss Sarah Piper, & Miss Elizth Piper, 1834.

Surveyor: R[ichard] Harwood; **Scale:** One Chain to an Inch, Scale bar 0–6 chains = 0–396 feet (= 5 13/16in.), 1:792; **Size:** (i) 20 1/8 x 29 3/8in.; **Top** is SE; Manuscript(i), parchment, coloured.

All Saints' Church, TL644633, and c. 17a. bounded by road from Cambridge to Bury St Edmunds in N, All Saints'

['Cheveley'] Road in E, Park ['Dog Kennel'] Lane in W and Granby Street ['road to the training ground'] in S.

Names of roads and neighbouring owners. All Saints' Church, houses, 'Old Palace', 'Chaise House', wash house, stable, coach house, blacksmith's shop and 'outoffices' shown in plan form. Closed fields showing owner's land; pasture; state of cultivation shown by colour; roads; gardens and layout of Old Palace lawn; yards and churchyard; fences and hedges.

Border of 1 broad band with 2 narrow bands on inside; title top left with decorative lettering; scale middle bottom; compass middle top showing 8 points with a N decorated with a crown. Table bottom right giving descriptions of areas and tenants. Roads coloured brown, buildings coloured red, pasture coloured green, gardens outlined in green.

Note top right: 'N.B. The Houses are distinguished by Black figures; The Outoffices and other buildings, by Red figures; The Yards and Gardens, by Blue figures.' Surveyor's 1st name was Richard [Eden H188].

Newton – [1834] – NEC83401 – CRO R51/17/20(b)

[Camps Park, Newton.]

Auctioneer: [Benjamin Bridges]; **Lithographer:** W[illiam] Metcalfe; **Scale:** 1:3,090; **Size:** (i) 7 1/4 x 11 1/4in.; **Top** is SW; Lithograph, paper, uncoloured.

Camps Park, TL446485, and 4a.1r.0p. in E of parish along boundary with Whittlesford Parish.

Names of fields, parishes and neighbouring owners. Open fields showing owner's strips; common; roads and watercourses.

Border of 1 broad and 1 narrow band; compass middle top showing 4 plain points, incorrectly giving top as NE.

Accompanies: 'Particulars and Conditions of Sale of several valuable freehold and copyhold estates, in the parishes of Harston, Hauxton, Newton, Foxton, Little Shelford, and Thriplow, in the County of Cambridge. To be Sold by Auction, by Benjamin Bridges, ... May, 1834'. Particulars of sale give date and details of land, acreages and tenure. Land sold by Seagrave Faircloth, mostly to William Hurrell [VCH, 8, 197]. Lithographer's 1st name was William [CRO EPR CW 1825 WR C52:178]. See also NEC83402–4.

Newton – [1834] – NEC83402 – CRO R51/17/20(b)

[Cockle Hill, Newton.]

Auctioneer: [Benjamin Bridges]; **Lithographer:** W[illiam] Metcalfe; **Scale:** Three chains to an inch, 1:2,376; **Size:** (i) 18 x 10 3/4in.; **Top** is NNE; Lithograph, paper, uncoloured.

Cockle Hill, TL4449, and 50a.0r.0p. in E of parish extending from Hoffer ['Newton'] Brook in S to just S of boundary with Harston Parish in N, and bounded by Little Shelford Parish in E.

Names of fields, roads and neighbouring owners. Closed fields showing owner's land; roads and watercourses.

Border of 1 broad and 1 narrow band; scale bottom right; compass top left showing 4 plain points.

Accompanies particulars of sale of Seagrave Faircloth's estate in 1834; NEC83401 gives details and auctioneer. See also NEC83403–4.

Newton – [1834] – NEC83403 – CRO R51/17/20(b)

[Land in far SW of Newton Parish.]

Auctioneer: [Benjamin Bridges]; **Lithographer:** W[illiam] Metcalfe; **Scale:** 1:2,400; **Size:** (i) 11 3/8 x 7 5/16in.; **Top** is NW; Lithograph, paper, uncoloured.

10a.0r.0p. in SW of parish, bounded by Foxton Parish in W, S and E; Hoffer Brook reaches boundary of Newton Parish at TL421485.

Names of neighbouring owners and parishes. Open fields showing owner's strips; wood; watercourses; responsibility for boundaries.

Border of 1 broad and 1 narrow band; compass top left showing 4 plain points, incorrectly giving top as N.

Accompanies particulars of sale of Seagrave Faircloth's estate in 1834; NEC83401 gives details and auctioneer. See also NEC83402,4.

Newton – [1834] – NEC83404 – CRO R51/17/20(b)
[Top Farm, Newton.]

Auctioneer: [Benjamin Bridges]; **Lithographer:** W[illiam] Metcalfe; **Scale:** 1:2,570; **Size:** (i) 7 3/8 x 12 1/8in.; **Top** is NNE; Lithograph, paper, uncoloured.

Top Farm, TL438494, and 23a.0r.17p. crossing main road in Newton village, bounded by roads to Thriplow in E and to Harston in N.

Names of roads and neighbouring owners, descriptions of areas. Farm buildings shown in plan form and include granaries, pigsties, 'cow houses', 'cart house', stable, 'harness room' and 'chaise house'. Closed fields showing owner's land; wood and trees; state of cultivation and crops given in words; acreages; roads and watercourses; gates; garden; fishpond; hedge; pound; yards and drying ground; bridge; bath; responsibility for boundaries.

Border of 1 broad and 1 narrow band; plain compass top left showing 4 points, incorrectly giving top as N.

Accompanies particulars of sale of Seagrave Faircloth's estate in 1834; NEC83401 gives details and auctioneer. See also NEC83402–3.

O

Oakington – [1825] – OAK82501 – QCC 355 A22, B22
Plan of Estate at Oakington In The County of Cambridge.

Surveyor: [Alexander Watford jr]; **Scale bar** 0–30 chains (= 5in.), 1:4,752; **Size:** (i) 25 3/4 x 38 3/16in.; **Top** is NNW; Manuscript(ii), paper, coloured.

Oakington Church, TL414648, and strips scattered throughout parish.

Names of fields, roads and neighbouring owners. Cottages and church shown in plan form. Open fields showing owner's strips; closes; common and meadow; state of cultivation shown by colour; acreages; hedges; roads; watercourses and bridges; balks.

Border of 1 broad band with 1 narrow band on either side; title bottom right; scale beneath title; compass left of title showing 8 points. Fields outlined in red, brown and blue, fields coloured yellow and green, balks coloured green, water coloured blue, roads coloured brown.

Numbers on plots suggest map originally accompanied by a terrier. In volume drawn in 1825: 'Plans of the Several Estates in England and Wales belonging to the President and Fellows of the College of St Margaret and St Bernard commonly called Queen's College in the University of Cambridge Delineated from Authentic Documents in the possession of the said President and Fellows and from actual Surveys taken By their most obedient and obliged

Servant Alexr Watford'. Title page drawn by James Richardson [Watford's nephew]. This is the Bursar's copy; 2nd, finer, copy [the Master's copy] at QCC 355 B22, entitled: 'Estate In the Parish of Oakington in the County of Cambridge'. It measures 24 13/16 x 36 3/16in. and is drawn on parchment. Border 7/16in. wide of a central blue band with 1 broad band on either side, title has gothic lettering, scale bottom left. Fields coloured in brown and yellow stripes and have green edges. Positive photostat of this copy at 1:10,560 at BL 1640.(24).

Oakington – [c. 1834] – OAK83401 – QCC Box 116
[Sketch map to show fences on land at Oakington allotted to Queens' College, Cambridge.]

Scale: Not drawn to scale; **Size:** (ii) 13 5/8 x 17in.; Manuscript(i), paper, coloured.

3 plots of land in Oakington Parish showing a total of 440 chains 42 links of fencing.

Windmill shown in perspective. Roads; lengths of fences; hedges.

Fence coloured red.

On dorse: 'Fencing at Oakington'. Accompanied by 2 pen sketches on separate sheets of paper. 2 plots have notes above: 'W. Harradine's <assessment> length of quicking and fencing at Oakington', and 'Sandy Hill Farm'. Drawn in connection with inclosure of Oakington; award made in 1834.

Oakington – 1834 – OAK83402 – QCC 355 B22
Plan of the Parish of Oakington. in the County of Cambridge As Awarded by the Commissioners.

Surveyor: James Richardson; **Scale bar** 0–30 chains (= 5in.), 1:4,752; **Size:** (i) 24 1/2 x 36 1/8in.; **Top** is NW; Manuscript(ii), parchment, coloured.

Oakington Church, TL414648, and c. 1,700a. in whole parish.

Names of fields, owners, neighbouring owners and roads; buildings in village, including church, shown in plan form. Closed fields; meadow; acreages; responsibility for boundaries; hedges; roads; bridleway, footpaths and stile; watercourses; drain; pond; bridges; tunnel; reasons for allotments.

Border 7/16in. wide of a central blue band with 1 broad band on either side; title bottom right with gothic lettering and decorative line-work; scale bottom left; compass on right showing 8 points. Roads coloured brown with a red border, some fields coloured yellow and green, water coloured blue, land owned by Queens' College, Cambridge coloured pink.

Note centre bottom: 'NB The College Property is coloured Pink'. Map added to the Master's copy of volume drawn in 1825; see OAK82501. Positive photostat at 1:10,560 at BL 1640.(23).

Oakington – 1834 – OAK83403 – CRO P126/6/9
Oakington Town Land.

Surveyor: Thomas Jukes; **Scale:** 1:3,310; **Size:** (ii) 7 7/8 x 6 5/16in.; **Top** is SE; Manuscript(i), paper, uncoloured.

21a.1r.10p. in TL4063, bounded in NW by road from Long Stanton to Oakington.

Names of roads and neighbouring owners. Closed field; roads; gates.

Title at top. Table on right giving acreages.

Note after title: 'Contains inside Land without fences & Road'. On dorse is surveyor's bill and: 'Revd Ths Webster, Oakington'. Sheet torn in half.

Orwell – [Ante 1686] – ORW68601 – C U L Maps.Deposited.R.a.1
[Estate at Orwell, owned by Thomas Chicheley.]
Scale bar 1–0–10 [chains] (= 6 13/16in.), 1:1,279; **Size:** (i) 54 x 42 3/4in.; **Top** is NNE; Manuscript(i), parchment, coloured.
Orwell Church, TL362504, and c. 2,100a. in whole parish.
Names of fields and occupiers of closes. Church and cottages shown in perspective. Open fields; closes; trees; common; 'The Greene'; meadow; marsh; state of cultivation shown by colour; acreages; roads and watercourses; fences; 2 springs.
Border of 1/16in.-wide band coloured yellow and enclosed in brown lines; title cartouche middle left coloured red and yellow, with no title inside; yellow scale bar bottom left surmounted by brown dividers with blue points; compass rose bottom right showing 8 blue and yellow points with brown flowers. Thomas Chicheley's coat of arms middle right. Meadow coloured yellow, arable outlined in brown, grass outlined in green.
Pencil notes, including 'The scale is 4 chains to an Inch', 1:3,168. Drawn before Sir John Cutler bought estate from Thomas Chicheley in 1686 [*VCH*, 5, 243]. CUL map catalogue suggests date of c. 1686. Positive photostat in CRO.

Orwell – 1820 – ORW82001 – CCC Drawer 47
Rough Sketch of Malton Farm in order to Show the separate Pieces contained in the Valuation of Mr Dugmore and the Variation of Quality 1820.
Scale: 1:2,540; **Size:** (i) 19 1/4 x 15 1/4in.; **Top** is W; Manuscript(i), paper, coloured.
Malton Farm, TL372483, and 272a.3r.0p. bounded by Meldreth Parish to S.
Names of fields. Malton Farm shown in perspective. Closed fields showing owner's land; pightle; wood, trees, 'Turpins' and 'Chapel' groves; meadow; acreages; roads and watercourses; bridges; holt; state of cultivation possibly shown by colour.
Border of 2 narrow bands separated by a 1/16in. grey strip; title bottom left. Water coloured blue; fields outlined in yellow and green.
Numbers on plots either suggest map originally accompanied by a terrier or may refer to valuation by [John; Eden D344] Dugmore. Farm owned by Christ's College, Cambridge.

Over – 1797 – OVE79701 – CUL MS Plans 548
A Plan of the homestead and adjoining Grounds belonging to Mr Thos Robinson of Over, in the County of Cambridge. Surveyed by T.L. Clerk to Mr Jenkinson 1797.
Surveyor: T[homas] L[ovell]; **Scale:** One Chain to an Inch, 1:792; **Size:** (i) 26 x 20 3/4in.; **Top** is NE; Manuscript(i), parchment, coloured.
Homestead at TL378708, corner of Wante Lane ['Wance Lane' and 'Little Street'] in N of village, and 23a.3r.26p. bounded by Hawcroft Lane in N and High Street in S.
Names of fields, roads and neighbouring owners. Farm buildings shown in plan form. Closes; trees; meadow and

pasture; roads and gates; garden and its layout; ponds; functions of yards; orchard identified on table.
Border of 1 broad and 2 narrow bands; title middle top with decorative lettering and in an oval cartouche with a bow; scale bottom left; compass top left showing 8 points. Table middle left with decorative lettering giving field names, acreages and leased land. Buildings outlined in red, water coloured blue, gardens and trees coloured green, roads and yards coloured brown, other land coloured yellow.
Surveyor was Thomas Lovell [Eden L267], who drew a map of Gamlingay with John Jenkinson in 1801 [see GAM80101].

Over – [Early 19th century] – OVE80001 – NRO D.S.391
Over.
Scale: 1:5,070; **Size:** (i) 19 5/16 x 14 11/16in.; **Top** is N; Manuscript(i), paper mounted on cloth, coloured.
Plots scattered throughout parish.
Names of roads and neighbouring owners. Chapel and cottage shown in plan form. Closed fields; roads; responsibility for boundaries.
Border of 1 narrow band; title bottom left; compass in centre showing 4 points. Fields coloured yellow, orange, green and pink, roads coloured brown.
Notes that these are 'Lot 1', 'Lot 2', 'Lot 3', and 'Lot 4'. On left and bottom of sheet; see also BOT80001 and RAM80001. Drawn in early 19th century: a neighbouring owner had an estate mapped in 1797 [OVE79701] and died in 1828.

Over – [c. 1803–29] – OVE80301 – CUA D.P.III.1.a–c
B Over Estate.
Scale: 1:4,810; **Size:** (i) 8 x 10 7/8in.; **Top** is N; Printed, paper mounted on cloth, uncoloured.
25a.0r.37p. around TL381704, junction of road to Willingham with main road through village, and NE of village, bounded by roads to Bare Hill in W and to Willingham in S; and 1 plot of land in TL3970 E of Public Drain.
Names of roads, fen and neighbouring owners. Fields; acreages; roads and watercourses; responsibility for boundaries.
Border of 1 narrow band; title at top; compass bottom left showing 8 points.
Middle top of sheet entitled at bottom: 'Plan of the estates in Cambridge, Over, Cottenham and Rampton Belonging to Hobsons Charity'. Sheet has a border of 1 broad and 1 narrow band. Probably drawn after 1803, the date of death of William Linton's father Salmon [a copyholder on RAM80301; *VCH*, 9, 109], and before 1829, when the Gaol shown on the map of the Cambridge estate ceased to be used. 2 unmounted paper copies. See also COU80301 and RAM80301.

Over – 1805 – OVE80501 – SCC XVIII/2
Close of Pasture at Over 1R.15P by Admeasurement Fences included leased to John Robertson for 21 years from Michaelmas 1805.
Scale: 1:401; **Size:** (ii) 6 x 7 7/8in.; **Top** is W; Manuscript(i), paper, coloured.
1r.15p. bounded by a road in W.
Names of features. Close; roads; ditch; pond; hedge and fence.
Title at bottom; 'West.' written at top of map. Hedge, fence, ditch and pond coloured grey, road coloured yellow.
Land owned by St Catharine's College, Cambridge.

Over – 1816 – OVE81601 – CRO R59/31/40/103

Plan of a Bank belonging to the Bedford Level Corporation in the Occupation of Mr Saml Wells Junior Situate in the Parishes of Over & Swavesey, in the County of Cambridge Surveyed & Planned by William Smith 1816.

Surveyor: William Smith; **Scale bar** 4–0–36 chains (= 10in.), 1:3,168; **Size:** (i) 11 13/16 x 62 1/8in.; **Top** is W; Manuscript(i), paper, coloured.

53a.0r.32p. along Bedford Level Corporation Barrier Bank NE and SW of TL363711, junction of the bank and Over and Swavesey parishes, bounded by River Ouse in NW, in NW of Over Parish bounded by Willingham Parish in NE and extending into Swavesey Parish in SW.

Names of features and parishes. Roads and watercourses; site of 'Over Engine'; tunnels; 'Great Gull' and 'Little Gull'; Swavesey sluice; ferry; bridge.

Border of 1 broad and 1 narrow band; title middle bottom; scale beneath title; plain compass on left showing 4 points with a feathered tail. Bank coloured green, water coloured blue, roads coloured yellow.

Note of acreages of bank in Over and Swavesey, and of width of bank. Pencil note of land adjoining map in Swavesey Parish.

P

Pampisford – 1799 – PAM79901 – QCC 328

Estate belonging to The Master, Fellows, & Scholars of Queens College, Cambridge, and Alexr Ross Esq in the Parish of Pampisford and County of Cambridge as Allotted and Exchanged 1799.

Surveyor: [Alexander Watford sr]; **Draughtsman:** [Richard Summerfield]; **Scale bar** 0–20 chains = 0–2 Furlongs (= 3 5/16in.), 1:4,782; **Size:** (i) 23 1/16 x 18 3/4in.; **Top** is N; Manuscript(i), paper mounted on cloth, coloured.

Pampisford Church, TL498482, and 198a.3r.1p. owned by Queens' College, Cambridge and 105a.0r.22p. owned by Alexander Ross to SW, bounded by river and Whittlesford Parish in W and by road from Whittlesford to Bourn Bridge in SE, and to NE bounded by Babraham Parish in N.

Names of owners, tenants, neighbouring owners and roads. Farm buildings, mill and toll house shown in plan form, church shown in perspective. Closed fields showing owners' land; trees; waste; acreages; responsibility for boundaries; hedges; roads and former course of road; turnpike and toll gate; watercourses; bridges; moats.

Border of 1 narrow band with 1 broad band on inside; title on right; scale at bottom; compass on left showing 8 points. Table bottom right giving acreages of land owned by Ross and by Queens' College. Roads coloured brown, buildings coloured red and black, fields coloured pink, green, yellow and blue.

Note left of table: 'NB The Enclosures coloured Red are given in exchange [The Enclosures coloured] Blue, are received in exchange'. Pencil notes. Alexander Watford sr valued estate and paid Richard Summerfield for map on 30 December 1799 [QCC Box 87].

Pampisford – 1799 – PAM79902 – QCC Box 135

Estate belonging to The Master Fellows and Scholars of Queens College, Cambridge, in the Parish of Pampisford and County of Cambridge as allotted in 1799.

Surveyor: [Alexander Watford sr]; **Draughtsman:** [Alexander Watford jr]; **Scale** is 6 Chains to the inch, 1:4,752; **Size:** (i) 17 1/4 x 23 1/8in.; **Top** is N; Manuscript(ii), parchment, coloured.

College Farm, TL502485, and 198a.3r.1p. NW of road to Bourn Bridge.

Names of roads and neighbouring owners. Farm buildings shown in plan form. Closed fields; trees; state of cultivation shown by colour; acreages; roads and watercourses; length of boundaries and responsibility for their maintenance.

Border of 1 narrow band; title on right; scale at bottom; compass top left showing 4 points. Table bottom left giving acreages. Roads coloured brown, grass coloured green, water coloured blue.

Note under title: 'N.B. The Pieces numbered, 3, 4, 9, 11, 16, 20, 22, 23, have been received in Exchange, and the Plan is numbered irregularly that it may agree with the Original in the hands of the College' [PAM79901]. On lease and counterpart: 'The Master and Fellows of Queens College To Alexander Ross Esqre Lease of a Farm at Pampisford in Cambridgeshire for 21 years from Michaelmas 1801 Dated 14 January 1803'. Alexander Watford jr was paid £14 15s 8d for making maps on 22 May 1802 [QCC Box 104].

Pampisford – [1825] – PAM82501 – QCC 355 A19, B19

Estate at Pampisford In The County of Cambridge.

Surveyor: [Alexander Watford jr]; **Scale bar** 0–30 chains (= 5in.), 1:4,752; **Size:** (i) 25 7/16 x 21 5/8in.; Top is NNE; Manuscript(ii), paper, coloured.

Pampisford Church, TL492482, and 199a.0r.31p. N of village.

Names of neighbouring owners and roads. Farm buildings and cottages shown in plan form, church shown in perspective. Closed fields showing owner's land; spinneys; former common land; 'Allotment on the Cow Common'; state of cultivation shown by colour; acreages; hedges; roads and turnpike; watercourses; bridges; moat.

Border of 1 broad band with 1 narrow band on either side; title top left; scale bottom left; compass middle left showing 4 points. Table bottom right giving field names, acreages and land use. Fields coloured green and yellow, roads coloured brown, water coloured blue.

On left of sheet which also contains map of Coveney [COV82501], in volume drawn in 1825: 'Plans of the Several Estates in England and Wales belonging to the President and Fellows of the College of St Margaret and St Bernard commonly called Queen's College in the University of Cambridge Delineated from Authentic Documents in the possession of the said President and Fellows and from actual Surveys taken By their most obedient and obliged Servant Alexr Watford'. Title page drawn by James Richardson [Watford's nephew]. This is the Bursar's copy; 2nd, finer, copy [the Master's copy] at QCC 355 B19, has 'Sold' added at end of title, measures 24 3/4 x 18 1/8in., is drawn on parchment and top points NE. Border 3/8in. wide of a central blue band with 1 broad band on either side, scale at bottom, compass on right shows 8 points. Table has gothic lettering and red lines. Fields coloured in brown and yellow stripes and have green edges, roads have red/brown edges.

Papworth Everard – 1815 – PAP81501 – B L M
Add.36278E

Plan of The Parish of Papworth St. Everard In the County of Cambridge.

Scale bar 0–30 chains (= 2 7/16in.), 1:9,748; **Size:** (i) 24 3/16 x 24 1/8in.; **Top** is N; Manuscript(i), paper mounted on cloth, coloured.

Papworth Hall, TL288626, and c. 1,100a. in whole parish.

Names of fields, roads and neighbouring owners. Cottages, church and hall shown in plan form. Fields; wood; roads; watercourses and ponds; park and lawn; moat; bridges.

Border of 1 narrow band; title top right; scale bottom right; compass top left showing 4 points. Roads coloured brown, water coloured blue, grass coloured green, buildings coloured red or grey, trees coloured green, land belonging to hall outlined in red.

Papworth Hall estate owned by Charles Madryll Cheere [*VCH*, 9, 360].

R

Rampton – 1754 – RAM75401 – CUL MS Plans R.a.6

Survey of the Lordship and Manor of Rampton in the County of Cambridge Belonging to Iohn Leman Esqr Taken by Henry Fensham 1754.

Surveyor: Henry Fensham; **Scale bar** 10–0–80 perches = 0–2 furlongs (= 7 1/2in.), Scale bar 100–0–500 yards (= 9 1/8in.), 1:2,376; **Size:** (i) 70 1/2 x 54in.; **Top** is ENE; Manuscript(i), parchment mounted on cloth, coloured.

Manor Farm, TL427680, and c. 1,400a. in whole parish and strips in 'Cottenham Holm' in W of Cottenham Parish.

Names of fields and parishes. Church, Manor Farm and cottages shown in plan form. Open fields showing all strips; closes; common; wood and trees; meadow and fen; state of cultivation shown by colour; roads; bridleway; park; garden and its layout; orchards; watercourses; ditch; moat; ponds; bridges; site of former mill; hedges; fences; 'Patten Pitts'; churchyard.

Uncoloured border of 1 broad band with 1 narrow band on each side enclosing a floral design; title top right in a highly-coloured baroque cartouche with leaves and flowers; scale bottom left coloured yellow and grey; compass middle left showing 16 decorated points. Table bottom left giving tenants, the colour of their strips and referring to a field book. Leman's coat of arms middle top. Common coloured green, each tenant's land shown by a different colour.

Abstract of terrier at CUL S696.b.91.4. Notes indicating change of name of fen, key to boundary types, explanation of colour of common, and, 'This boundary of the Fenn was antiently a Water course, and is now caled the Lake'. John Granger was left estate in 1753, on condition that he took the name and arms of Leman [*V C H Hertfordshire*, 2, 359]; he did this in 1754 [27 George II Cap 1].

Rampton – [Early 19th century] – RAM80001 – N R O D.S.391

Rampton.

Scale: 1:5,070; **Size:** (i) 9 3/8 x 10 5/8in.; **Top** is N; Manuscript(i), paper mounted on cloth, coloured.

c. 41a. in TL4168, W of village and N and S of road to Willingham.

Names of roads and neighbouring owners. Buildings shown in plan form. Closed fields; roads and watercourses; responsibility for boundaries.

Border of 1 narrow band; title on right; compass top right showing 4 points. Roads coloured brown, water coloured blue, fields coloured green and pink.

Notes that these are 'Lot 5' and 'Lot 6'. On centre right of sheet; see also BOT80001 and OVE80001. Drawn in early 19th century: a neighbouring owner on OVE80001 had an estate mapped in 1797 and died in 1828.

Rampton – [c. 1803–29] – RAM80301 – CUA D.P.III.1.a–c

Rampton estate.

Scale: 1:768; **Size:** (i) 18 5/16 x 10 3/4in.; **Top** is NE; Printed, paper mounted on cloth, coloured.

Cuckoo Bridge, TL432679, and 26a.3r.31p. in E of parish, bounded by Long Stanton St Michael Parish in SW, Westwick Parish in SE and Cottenham Parish in E.

Names of roads, drains and neighbouring owners. Fields; hedges; acreages and dimensions of bridleway; roads and watercourses; bridge; responsibility for boundaries.

Border of 1 narrow band; title at top; compass on left showing 8 points. Land belonging to Hobson's Charity coloured green, 2 plots of land coloured red.

Notes of William Linton's copyhold and 'Part colored green'. On right of sheet, entitled at the bottom: 'Plan of the estates in Cambridge, Over, Cottenham and Rampton Belonging to Hobsons Charity'. Sheet has a border of 1 broad and 1 narrow band. Probably drawn after 1803, the date of death of William Linton's father Salmon [*VCH*, 9, 109], and before 1829, when the Gaol shown on the map of the Cambridge estate ceased to be used. 2 unmounted paper copies. See also COU80301 and OVE80301.

Rampton – 1825 – RAM82501 – CUL MS Plans 17

Plan of the Manor Farm at Rampton in the County of Cambridge.

Surveyor: [Indecipherable signature]; **Scale bar** 1–0–30 chains (= 7 3/4in.), 1:3,168; **Size:** (i) 32 1/4 x 20 11/16in.; **Top** is NE; Manuscript(i), paper mounted on paper, coloured.

Manor Farm, TL427680, and c. 310a. N and W of village bounded by Cottenham Parish in E.

Names of commons, meadows and neighbouring owners. Church, farm buildings, houses and 'Chequers' public house shown in plan form. Open fields showing owner's strips; glebe; inclosed meadow; common; wood and trees; state of cultivation shown by colour; roads and watercourses; garden and its layout; moat; ponds; hedges and wall.

Border of 1 narrow band; title top left; scale bottom right; compass middle left showing 4 points. Buildings coloured red, roads coloured yellow, water coloured blue, arable coloured brown, pasture coloured green, boundaries internal to estate coloured red, some hedges coloured red, others coloured black.

Numbers on fields suggest map originally accompanied by a terrier. Land owned by John Mann [*VCH*, 9, 214].

S

Sawston – [c. 1828] – SAW82801 – CUL MS Plans y.1(22)

Oil and Trefoil Mills at Darnford.

Draughtsman: [Elliot Smith]; **Scale:** 20ft in an Inch, 1:240; **Size:** (iii) 10 x 8 1/2in.; **Top** is N; Manuscript(i), paper, uncoloured.

Demford Mill, TL472493, and c. 21p. W of village.

Names of parts of mill and tenants. Furnaces, stables, 2 cottages and building which houses mill stones shown in plan form. Watercourses.

Title middle left; scale beneath title.

Note on left: 'Oil Mill works one pair of stones No kiln adjoining or communicating 5 Furnaces used marked thus [red cross] The Mill is used only for making Oil Oats are not shelled therein'. Similar note for Trefoil Mill [N of Oil Mill]. Notes about fabric [brick and tile] and presence of rooms above ground floor. Drawn for fire insurance purposes, in volume from Elliot Smith and Sons, Auctioneers and Estate Agents; most maps in volume drawn c. 1828.

Sawston – [c. 1832] – SAW83201 – CUL MS Plans 388
Plan of Property at Sawston, Cambs.
Scale: 1 Chain to 1 Inch, 1:792; **Size:** (ii) 19 5/8 x 12 11/16in.; **Top** is ESE; Manuscript(i), cloth mounted on paper, coloured.

Tannery, TL486488, and 64a.1r.1p. S of village, crossed by watercourse and bounded by road from Cambridge to Linton in W.

Names of neighbouring owners. House, almshouses and factory buildings shown in plan form. Closed fields; acreages; tenure shown by colour; roads and milestones; watercourses.

Title middle top; scale middle bottom; compass middle left showing 4 points with a decorated N. Water coloured blue, roads coloured brown, most buildings coloured grey.

Note below title about colour indicating land tenure. Dotted lines may indicate planned, unbuilt buildings. Thomas Evans leased land from Huntington's Charity and had built the buildings shown by 1832 [Teversham, 1947, 264].

Shepreth – 1764 – SHE76401 – CRO R53/4/160
A Plan of all the Inclosures belonging to Mr William Woodham at Shepreth in the County of Cambridge: Taken by Jeremiah Slade 1764.
Surveyor: Jeremiah Slade; **Scale bar** 1–0–10 chains (= 5 7/16in.), 1:1,602; **Size:** (ii) 29 13/16 x 21 1/2in.; **Top** is N; Manuscript(i), paper mounted on cloth, coloured.

Docuraies Manor, TL392479, and 43a.1r.1p. to SE bounded by road from Barrington to Harston in NE and moat in S.

Names of fields. Docuraies Manor, farm, mill, barns, stables, 'malting', 'cow~lodges', 'wheat~cases', cart shed, 'hen house' and dovecote shown in plan form. Closes; pightle; wood and trees; meadow; osier holt; acreages; roads and footpaths; watercourses; gates and stiles; gardens and orchards; moats; bridges; yards and courtyard.

Title along top with decorated initial letters; scale middle bottom; compass rose in centre showing 8 points. Table top right giving descriptions of buildings. Roads coloured black, water coloured blue, trees coloured green, buildings coloured brown.

Shudy Camps – 1721 – SHU72101 – CRO L86/83
A Mapp of An Estate Belonging to James Reynolds Esqr Serjeant at Law Lying and Being in Shedicampes in Cambridgeshire, and now in the Occupation and use of

William Purkise. Surveyed in The year of Our Lord God One Thousand Seven Hundred and Twenty one by Wm Tallemach.
Surveyor: William Tallemach; **Scale bar** 1–0–11 [chains] (= 3 13/16in.), 1:2,492; **Size:** (i) 30 3/8 x 28 3/4in.; **Top** is N; Manuscript(i), parchment, coloured.

Barsey Farm, TL640455, and 169a.3r.19p. in E of parish around farm and scattered throughout Haverhill Parish [Suffolk].

Names of fields and neighbouring owners. Farm and buildings shown in perspective. Open fields showing owner's strips in Haverhill Parish; closes; wood and trees; meadow; acreages; moat; yard.

Border of 1 broad brown band outlined by narrow dark brown lines; title middle top in a brown oval cartouche; scale bottom left coloured yellow and surmounted by dividers; compass middle bottom showing 16 yellow, green and red points which extend all over map. Table top left giving field names and acreages. Land outlined in green, brown or yellow, trees coloured green, buildings coloured yellow with brown roofs, strips coloured grey.

Notes of calculations of acreages in closes and in open fields.

Shudy Camps – [1769–70] – SHU77001 – CUL MS Plans a.5(viii)
A Plan of the Manor Farm, called Noster Field End, otherwise Prior, in the Parish of Shudycamps in the County of Cambridge.
Surveyor: [John Mackown]; **Scale:** 1:8,400; **Size:** (i) 10 3/4 x 9 3/8in.; **Top** is NE; Manuscript(ii), tracing paper mounted on paper, coloured.

Nosterfield End Farm, TL639443, in W of parish, and c. 260a. bounded in S by road from Shudy Camps to Haverhill and by Castle Camps Parish.

Names of fields and neighbouring owners. Farm buildings, barns and pigsty shown in plan form. Open fields showing tenant's land; closes; wood and trees; meadow; roads and footpaths; watercourses; gates; ponds; fences; garden and orchard identified on table.

Border of 1 narrow band; title middle top. Roads coloured brown, buildings coloured red, water coloured blue.

Accompanying table gives field names, acreages and state of cultivation. In volume entitled on flyleaf: 'Particulars of a survey of the Parishes of Horseheath & West Wickham together with Lands adjoining in the Several Parishes of Bartlow & Shudy Camps in the County of Cambridge & Wethersfield parish in the County of Suffolk, the Estate of the Rt Honble Thomas Lord Montfort. Surveyed, Regulated & particularized by John Mackown, 1769 & 1770'. Volume used for land tax of tenants, contains 8 maps which cover 3,017a.2r.29p. in Horseheath and neighbouring parishes. See also HRS77001–7. Photograph in CRO.

Shudy Camps – 1794 – SHU79401 – TCC Box 2 Shudy Camps 27
A Map of the Parish and Rectory of Shudy~Camps distinguishing the Lands tithable thereto, in the Parishes of Horsheath and Bartlow in the County of Cambridge belonging to the Master Fellows and Scholars of Trinity College Cambridge Taken by A. Watford 1794.
Surveyor: A[lexander] Watford [sr]; **A Scale of** Chains, Scale bar 0–2,640 [feet] (= 4in.), 1:7,920; **Size:**

(i) 33 1/8 x 42in.; **Top** is NNE; Manuscript(i), parchment, coloured.

Shudy Camps Park, TL624447, and 2,423a.0r.22p. in whole parish, in S of Horseheath Parish and in NE of Bartlow Parish.

Names of fields, parishes, roads and neighbouring owners. Shudy Camps Park shown in perspective, farm buildings and cottages shown in plan form. Open fields showing owner's strips in Horseheath and Bartlow parishes; closes; common; wood and trees; meadow and pasture; roads and footpaths; gates; watercourses; park; crosses; fences; moat; gravel pit; balks.

Border of 1 narrow band; title bottom left; scale bottom right; compass centre bottom showing 32 points. Roads coloured yellow, buildings coloured red, trees coloured blue, land outlined and coloured blue, yellow and pink.

Pencil notes. Accompanying terrier at TCC Box 28 Shudy Camps 34 gives acreages of arable, pasture, meadow and wood: 'References To a Map of the Rectory of Shudy Camps in the County of Cambridge distinguishing the Land tithable thereto in the Parishes of Bartlow &c. The Rectory of which belonging to the Master Fellows and Scholars of Trinity College Cambridge Taken in the Year 1794 By A. Watford'. Map and terrier accompany: 'Valuation of Shudy Camps Rectory in the County of Cambridge. Belonging to the Master Fellows and Scholars of Trinity College Cambridge made Septr 19th 1794', by Alexander Watford [TCC Box 28 Shudy Camps 35]; 'Valuation of the Vicarage of Shudy Camps in the County of Cambridge belonging to the Master Fellows & Scholars of Trinity College Cambridge made Septr 19th 1794', by Alexander Watford [TCC Box 28 Shudy Camps 36]; and 'Valuation of Shudy Camps. Sept 1794 by A.W.' [TCC Box 28 Shudy Camps 37]. Surveyor's 1st name was Alexander [Eden W141].

Shudy Camps – 1812 – SHU81201 – CRO 346/T18
Plan of Camp's Farm, Cambridgeshire.
Surveyor: P[aul] Padley; **Auctioneer:** [Richard] Peyton; **Scale bar** 1–0–10 statute chains (= 2 3/8in.), 1:3,668; **Size:** (ii) 13 7/8 x 8 1/4in.; **Top** is NNE; Photocopy, paper, uncoloured.

279a.0r.6p. in N of parish E of TL619463, junction of roads running N from Shudy Camps from Cardinal's Green to Haverhill, bounded by roads from Horseheath to Haverhill in N and running N from Shudy Camps in W, and extending into S of Horseheath Parish and E of Bartlow Parish.

Names of neighbouring owners and roads. Shardelow's Farm, cottages and farm buildings shown in plan form. Open fields and closes showing owner's land; 'North Way' and 'Great' woods; meadow; roads and footpaths; watercourses; gates; pond; moat; responsibility for boundaries; site of 'Manor of Shardelows Allington, or Northway'.

Title top left with decorative line-work; scale bottom left.

Accompanies: 'Specification of the very desirable Manor of Shardelows Allington, otherwise Northway, in Shudy Camps, together with a respectable messuage ... (for the most part enclosed) known by the names of Camps Farm, High Waters, and North Way, situate in the Parishes of ShudyCamps, Horseheath and Bartlow, in the County of Cambridge ... will be sold by auction, by Mr. Peyton ... May, 1812'. Particulars of sale give details of state of cultivation, tenants and acreages; contract shows owner to be Heneage Finch, 4th Earl of Aylesford, and lots 6 and 8 were

sold to Marmaduke Dayrell. Land in Horseheath sold to Stanlake Batson [*VCH*, 6, 74]. Surveyor's 1st name was Paul [Eden P11]; auctioneer's 1st name given on contract.

Shudy Camps – [1818] – SHU81801 – TCC Box 2 Shudy Camps 28
Map of the Parish of Shudy Camps In the County of Cambridge Also of sundry Lands in the Parishes of Bartlow and Horseheath.
Scale bar 0–40 chains (= 5 3/8in.), 1:5,894; **Size:** (i) 48 1/2 x 25 5/8in.; **Top** is WNW; Manuscript(i), paper, coloured.

Shudy Camps Church, TL620444, and 2,422a.2r.29p. in whole parish, in S of Horseheath Parish and in NE of Bartlow Parish.

Names of fields, neighbouring owners, parishes and roads. Farm buildings and cottages shown in plan form, church shown in perspective. Open fields showing owner's strips in Horseheath and Bartlow parishes; closes; wood; meadow and green; state of cultivation shown by colour; park; roads; watercourses, ponds and moat.

Border of 1 broad band with 1 narrow band on either side; title top left; scale bottom right; compass centre left showing 8 points. Roads coloured brown, fields coloured yellow or green, wood coloured green, water coloured blue, some fields outlined in red, brown, green or grey.

Pencil notes. Accompanying terrier at TCC Box 28 Shudy Camps 44 gives acreages of arable, pasture and wood with: 'Reference To The Map of Shudy Camps in the County of Cambridge With the Division of Tithes as agreed upon in the Year 1818' on the cover. Date of map given on dorse and on terrier. Land owned by Trinity College, Cambridge.

Shudy Camps – [1825] – SHU82501 – QCC 355 A9, B9
Lancelets and Drapers Farm In The Parishes of Bumpstead Helions and Haverhill together with Lacey Fields In The Parish of Shudy Camps.
Surveyor: [Alexander Watford jr]; **Scale bar** 0–20 chains (= 5 1/8in.), 1:3,091; **Size:** (i) 25 1/2 x 38 3/8in.; **Top** is NW; Manuscript(ii), paper, coloured.

Drapers Farm, TL627425, and 366a.2r.35p. in S and W of Helions Bumpstead Parish [Essex] and S of Haverhill Parish [Suffolk], and 40a.3r.33p. in SE of Shudy Camps Parish.

Names of farms, fields and neighbouring owners. Farm buildings shown in plan form. Closed fields showing owner's land; 'Holy Wood' and trees; state of cultivation shown by colour; acreages; hedges; roads; rights of way; gates; watercourses; ponds; gardens and orchards; farmyard.

Border of 1 broad band with 1 narrow band on either side; title top left; scale middle bottom; compass top right showing 4 points. Table on left giving field names, acreages and land use. Roads coloured brown, fields coloured yellow and green, wood coloured green, water coloured blue.

Pencil notes. Centre top are maps of: 'Drapers Farm Homestead, Buildings &c on Scale of two Chains to the Inch', and 'Lancelets Farm Homestead, Buildings &c on scale of two Chains to the Inch', 1:1,584. In volume drawn in 1825: 'Plans of the Several Estates in England and Wales belonging to the President and Fellows of the College of St Margaret and St Bernard commonly called Queen's College in the University of Cambridge Delineated from Authentic Documents in the possession of the said President and

Fellows and from actual Surveys taken By their most obedient and obliged Servant Alexr Watford'. Title page drawn by James Richardson [Watford's nephew]. This is the Bursar's copy; 2nd, finer, copy [the Master's copy] at QCC 355 B9 measures 24 3/4 x 36 3/8in. and is on parchment. Scale bar shows 0–30 chains (= 7 3/8in.), 1:3,222. Name of each field is given. Border 3/8in. wide of a blue central band and 1 broad band on either side, title top right has gothic lettering, compass in centre shows 8 points. Table has border imitating a scroll of paper, red lines and does not include Lacey Fields. Fields coloured in yellow and brown stripes with green edges, roads coloured brown with a red/brown outline. Plan of homestead shows both farms together, and is entitled: 'Homesteads Buildings &c on a Scale of two Chains to an Inch'. Photograph of this copy at ERO T/M 137 at 1:5,137, and positive photostat at BL 1640.(17) at 1:10,560.

Snailwell – [Ante 1806] – SNA80601 – C R O R55/7/48/3
[Glebe in 'North Field', Snailwell.]
Scale: 1:2,200; **Size:** (ii) 28 7/8 x 20 1/16in.; **Top** is S; Manuscript(i), paper mounted on paper, coloured.
c. 400a. in 'North Field' in TL6467 and TL6468, bounded by road to Chippenham ['Port Road'] in S, Chippenham Parish in E, Snailwell Fen in W and Poor's Fen in N.
Names of owners and roads. Open field showing all strips; closes; acreages; roads.
Balks, glebe and closes coloured yellow, roads coloured black.
Name of field on dorse. Pencil note of cottage and garden. Drawn before 1806 inclosure award. See also SNA80602–4.

Snailwell – [Ante 1806] – SNA80602 – C R O R55/7/48/1
['Plan of Snailwell Grounds near the House let from year to year'.]
Scale: 1:1,760; **Size:** (ii) 15 x 9 3/16in.; **Top** is S; Manuscript(i), paper, coloured.
Manor house, TL642675, and 45a. W of village, bounded by River Snail and mill in NE, Exning Parish [Suffolk] in W and road from Snailwell to Exning in S.
Names of fields and buildings. 'Mansion house', offices and stables shown in plan form. Closes; common; acreages, 1 plot measured by pole, others estimated; River Snail and springs; gardens including 'kitchen or lower garden', 'little garden', 'house garden' and 'upper garden'; 'The canal' [a moat]; mill yard; common fen adjoining map.
Table top left giving fields and acreages. Water coloured black, land outlined in yellow, buildings outlined in red.
Title on dorse. Drawn before 1806 inclosure award. See also SNA80601,3–4.

Snailwell – [Ante 1806] – SNA80603 – C R O R55/7/48/2
['A Description of the little field called Westons'.]
Scale: 1:1,570; **Size:** (ii) 12 1/2 x 15 3/8in.; **Top** is S; Manuscript(i), paper mounted on paper, coloured.
c. 39a. in TL6367 and TL6467 W of village, bounded by road to Exning in S.
Names of owners and footpaths. Open field showing all strips; common; acreages; roads and footpaths.

Parsonage land coloured yellow, hall land coloured blue.
Title on dorse. Drawn before 1806 inclosure award. See also SNA80601–2,4.

Snailwell – [Ante 1806] – SNA80604 – C R O R55/7/48/3
['Markett Field', Snailwell, showing parsonage and hall lands.]
Scale: 1:2,430; **Size:** (ii) 39 1/4 x 15 5/8in.; **Top** is NW; Manuscript(i), paper mounted on paper, coloured.
c. 490a. in TL6466 SW of village, crossed by road to Newmarket and bounded by road to Exning in N, heath in S, Exning Parish [Suffolk] in W and Chippenham Parish in E.
Names of owners, closes and roads. Open fields showing all strips; closes; heath; acreages; roads; gates to hall; hall garden adjoining map.
Roads coloured black, parsonage land and closes coloured yellow, hall land coloured blue.
Field name on dorse, with notes of exchanges of land. Drawn before 1806 inclosure award. See also SNA80601–3.

Snailwell – [c. 1820] – SNA82001 – CRO R55/7/114/10
Ground floor of Mr Laughtons Old House.
Surveyor: [William Young?]; **Scale:** 1:77; **Size:** (ii) 12 3/4 x 7 7/8in.; **Top** is S?; Manuscript(i), paper, uncoloured.
House at TL642675, and c. 11p. next to churchyard.
Names of buildings. House, dovecote, tool house, wash house and coal house shown in plan form. Lengths of some plots; garden; yard and churchyard; wall; pump.
Title at bottom.
Numbers on plots suggest map originally accompanied by a terrier. Pencil notes of features. Accompanied by drawing of front and side elevations, plan of bedroom floor and document signed by William Young about repairs to a house in 1820. Owner's 1st names were William Hyde [Venn, II, 4, 104].

Soham – [c. Elizabeth I] – SOH55801 – PRO MPC 62
[Soham Park and Mere showing land owned by Duchy of Lancaster.]
Scale: 1:50,250; **Size:** (ii) 25 3/4 x 30 7/8in.; Manuscript(i), parchment, coloured.
Soham Church, TL594732, and c. 13,000a. in whole parish.
Names of fields, fens, features and roads. Wicken, Soham and Fordham churches shown in perspective. Open fields; closes; fen; roads; watercourses, ditches, drains and lodes; bridges; 'Soham Meare'; 'Whight Lane' and its hedges.
Cardinal points stated at edge of map. Water coloured blue, churches have blue roofs, roads coloured brown, trees and fen coloured green, fields coloured in brown stripes, background of map coloured green.
Verbal description of bounds written around edge of map; any side could be top. Some areas marked that they pay rent to the Crown. Some fen areas marked by symbols representing tufts of grass. Date taken from PRO map catalogue.

Soham – 1626 – SOH62601 – R A Y
A description and Platt of the south parte of the lordship of Sohame in the Countie of Cambridge ...

Surveyor: William Hayward; **Scale bar** 0–80 perches (= 4in.), 1:3,960; **Size:** (i) 38 1/2 x 52 3/8in.; **Top** is SSE; Manuscript(i), parchment in 4 sheets, coloured.

Land in S of Soham Parish and in W of Fordham Parish.

Names of fields, tenants, neighbouring owners and roads. Cottages and mill shown in perspective. Open fields showing owner's strips; closes; common; trees; fen, waste and meadow; acreages; roads and footpaths; watercourses; bridges; hedges; 'a bank called Rogers Wall'.

Border of 2 narrow bands; title top right in a rectangular cartouche; green and yellow scale bar bottom right surmounted by yellow dividers; 'The Meridian lines' at bottom and top right. Land outlined in red, blue, yellow, green and orange, buildings coloured red, roads coloured brown, water coloured blue.

Occupiers of cottages noted at edge of map if no room by cottage. Map very rubbed and much of title now illegible. William Hayward spells his name 'Gvlielm Haiward'. Estate held in trust by Robert and Edward Ramsay for Sir John Ramsay, Viscount Haddington and Earl of Holderness, from 1624 [Lysons, 254] until sold by Robert Ramsay to Sir Robert Heath in 1633 [CRO R77/25/190]. See also SOH62602, which shows land further N.

Soham – [1626] – SOH62602 – RAY
[Northern part of the Lordship of Soham.]
Surveyor: [William Hayward]; **Scale bar** 0–120 perches = 0–3 furlongs (= 5 3/4in.), 1:4,132; **Size:** (i) 34 3/4 x 41 1/2in.; **Top** is ESE; Manuscript(i), parchment in 2 sheets, coloured.

Soham Church, TL594732, and land N of village.

Names of fields, tenants and neighbouring owners. Church and cottages shown in perspective. Open fields showing owner's strips; closes; common and waste; acreages; roads and footpaths; watercourses; bridges; banks; hedges; 'Great Meare' shown by stipples; 'Shoulder Hill'.

Border of 1 narrow band; pink scale bar bottom right surmounted by dividers; 'The meridian line' on right. Land outlined in red, green and yellow, water coloured blue, buildings coloured red.

Occupiers of cottages noted at edge of map if no room by cottage. Pencil grid. See SOH62601, companion map which shows land further S, for details of owner, surveyor and date.

Soham – [1628–30] – SOH63001 – PRO MPB 27
[Disputed lands in Attorney-General and Ramsay v. Thornton.]
The Scale is of 40 poles in an inch: 16 foote dimi: to the Pole, 1:7,920; **Size:** (ii) 12 1/4 x 20 3/4in.; **Top** is S; Manuscript(i), parchment, uncoloured.

Hainey Farm, TL557753, and c. 1,600a. bounded by Stuntney in N, River Ouse in W and Wicken Parish in S.

Names of farm, fen, river and neighbouring land. Hainey Farm ['A Seuerall called Hennee'] shown in perspective. Common and fen; roads and watercourses.

Scale bottom left; cardinal points stated in border.

Damaged on left. Drawn to accompany a legal dispute, 4–5 Charles I; disputants were Edward and Robert Ramsay on behalf of Sir John Ramsay [see SOH62601] and Roger Thornton, who died in 1630 [PRO map catalogue; CRO R55/7/20/2]. See also SOH63002.

Soham – [1628–30] – SOH63002 – PRO MPB 27
Greate Metlam.
Scale bar 0–120 poles = 0–3 furlongs (= 2 13/16in.), 1:8,448; **Size:** (ii) 16 3/4 x 26 1/4in.; **Top** is E; Manuscript(i), parchment, uncoloured.

c. 4,400a. in NE of parish, bounded by Isleham Parish in E, Ely Trinity Parish in W and River Lark ['Millenhall River'] in NE.

Names of neighbouring land. Watercourses.

Title in centre; scale bottom right; cardinal points stated at edge, incorrectly giving top as N.

Note under title: 'The 1500 acres taken out of this great fenne, and devided from the Residue by the pricked line'. Note above this line: 'That Parte of Great Meltham [Mettleham] which is left for the Tenants conteininge 840 acres'. See SOH63001 for reasons for drawing map.

Soham – [c. 1656] – SOH65601 – RAY
[Land in Soham and Fordham parishes, showing manor owned by Duchy of Lancaster, part of possessions of Thomas Chicheley and Adventurers' land.]
Surveyor: [William Palmer]; **Scale:** 1:4,040; **Size:** (i) 122 3/4 x 60 5/8in.; **Top** is S; Manuscript(i), parchment in 7 sheets, coloured.

Soham Church, TL594732, and land in Soham and Fordham parishes bounded by Ely Trinity Parish in N, and Isleham Parish and Mildenhall Parish [Suffolk] in E.

Names of fields, owners, tenants, neighbouring owners and roads. Soham Church, mill and cottages shown in perspective. Open fields showing owner's strips; closes; common; waste; 'Soham Meare a severall Fishing of the Lords'; acreages; roads and footpaths; watercourses and lodes; 'Shell Lake'; 'Mildenhall River'; bridges; 'Greene'; 'Mill's Bushe'.

Border 1/2in. wide of 1 broad yellow band with 1 narrow brown band on outside. Land outlined in green, yellow, red, brown and blue, buildings coloured red, water coloured blue.

Numbers on lots. W, SW and NW sheets of map are missing. Drawn at very similar scale to FOR65601–7 and SOH65603–12 which were by William Palmer, and is probably original upon which tracings are based. At Raynham Hall Box 100 is a sketch of land in 'Great Fen' in E of Soham Parish, at same scale and measuring 38 x 21in. Probably a draft for final map, with ink notes, calculations, measurements and score lines.

Soham – [1656] – SOH65602 – CRO
['Comonable houses Cottages Yards Gardens Orchards Tofts Crofts meadows pastures meares mearegroundes Fengrounds Lakes Hoults Groves hempegrounds and Arable Lands in Fordham Soham and Barway And all Wasts Moores Fennes Comons Intercomons therto belonging being within the precincts of the Lordship or Manor of Soham in the County of Cambridge being parcel of the Duchie of Lancaster and part of the possessions of Thos Chichelie Esqre together with the Adventurers grounds being within the same precincts'.] [Soham Manor.]
Surveyor: [William Palmer]; **Scale:** 1:15,900; **Size:** (ii) 30 x 19 7/8in.; **Top** is SSE; Manuscript(ii), tracing paper, coloured.

Soham Church, TL593732, and c. 13,000a. in Soham and Fordham parishes.

Names of fields, commons, fens and closes. Soham Church shown in perspective. Open fields; closes; common and fen; acreages; roads and watercourses.

Compass rose top right showing 16 green, blue, brown, yellow and pink points. Fields outlined in green, yellow, pink and blue, water coloured blue, coloured lettering.

At end of volume of tracings of maps of manor of Soham; title, surveyor and date are given on front flyleaf, and note: 'Copied by W.A.G. 1860'. See also FOR65601 [which gives scale], 2–7 and SOH65603–12.

Soham – [1656] – SOH65603 – CRO
D. [Clipsall Field.]
Surveyor: [William Palmer]; **Scale:** 1:3,960; **Size:** (ii) 20 x 14 7/8in.; **Top** is SE; Manuscript(ii), tracing paper, coloured.
c. 310a. in TL6172, bounded by River Snail in E.
Names of fields, roads, owners and tenants. Open fields showing all strips; closes; acreages; roads and watercourses.

Compass rose bottom right showing 8 yellow, blue and brown points. Fields outlined in green, yellow, pink and blue, water coloured blue, coloured lettering.

In volume of tracings made in 1860; title, surveyor, date and copyist given on front flyleaf [see SOH65602]. See also FOR65601 [which gives scale], 2–7 and SOH65604–12.

Soham – [1656] – SOH65604 – CRO
I. [Mill Croft.]
Surveyor: [William Palmer]; **Scale:** 1:3,960; **Size:** (ii) 20 x 14 7/8in.; **Top** is NE; Manuscript(ii), tracing paper, coloured.
c. 340a. in TL5972 and TL6072 in Mill Croft SW of town, bounded by Horse Croft Fen in W and river in N.
Names of fields, roads, owners and tenants. Houses shown in perspective. Open fields showing all strips; closes; acreages; roads and footpaths; watercourses.

Compass bottom left showing 2 plain points. Fields outlined in green, yellow, pink and blue, water coloured blue, coloured lettering.

In volume of tracings made in 1860; title, surveyor, date and copyist given on front flyleaf [see SOH65602]. See also FOR65601 [which gives scale], 2–7 and SOH65603,5–12.

Soham – [1656] – SOH65605 – CRO
K. [Soham town.]
Surveyor: [William Palmer]; **Scale:** 1:3,960; **Size:** (ii) 20 x 14 7/8in.; **Top** is SW; Manuscript(ii), tracing paper, coloured.
Soham Church, TL593732, and c. 420a. in town bounded by river in S and W and Hall Street in N.
Names of fields, owners and tenants, common and fen. Church, cottages and mill shown in perspective. Closes; common; wash; acreages; roads and footpaths; watercourses and bridges; orchards; fen.

Compass top left showing 2 plain points. Fields outlined in green, yellow, pink and blue, water coloured blue, coloured lettering.

In volume of tracings made in 1860; title, surveyor, date and copyist given on front flyleaf [see SOH65602]. See also FOR65601 [which gives scale], 2–7 and SOH65603–4,6–12.

Soham – [1656] – SOH65606 – CRO
L. [N of town.]
Surveyor: [William Palmer]; **Scale:** 1:3,960; **Size:** (ii) 20 x 14 7/8in.; **Top** is NE; Manuscript(ii), tracing paper, coloured.
c. 160a. in TL5974, bounded by road to Ely in W and Hall Street in S.
Names of fields, roads, owners and tenants. Cottages shown in perspective. Closes; acreages; roads.

Compass top left showing 2 points with a yellow decorated N with a crown and 'Robert H. Peck' in ribbon at bottom of N. Fields outlined in green, yellow, pink and blue, coloured lettering.

In volume of tracings made in 1860; title, surveyor, date and copyist given on front flyleaf [see SOH65602]. See also FOR65601 [which gives scale], 2–7 and SOH65603–5,7–12.

Soham – [1656] – SOH65607 – CRO
M. [North Field.]
Surveyor: [William Palmer]; **Scale:** 1:3,960; **Size:** (ii) 20 x 14 7/8in.; **Top** is SE; Manuscript(ii), tracing paper, coloured.
c. 350a. in TL5975 in North Field, bounded by road to Ely in W and Bancroft Drove ['Lane'] in E.
Names of fields, roads, owners and tenants. Open fields showing all strips; closes; acreages; roads.

Compass rose bottom right showing 8 yellow, blue and brown points. Fields outlined in green, yellow, pink and blue, coloured lettering.

In volume of tracings made in 1860; title, surveyor, date and copyist given on front flyleaf [see SOH65602]. See also FOR65601 [which gives scale], 2–7 and SOH65603–6,8–12.

Soham – [1656] – SOH65608 – CRO
N. [S of Redland Field.]
Surveyor: [William Palmer]; **Scale:** 1:3,960; **Size:** (ii) 20 x 14 7/8in.; **Top** is S; Manuscript(ii), tracing paper, coloured.
c. 270a. in TL5774, SW of Soham Cotes.
Names of fields, owners and tenants. Cottages shown in perspective. Open fields showing all strips; closes; acreages; roads.

Compass at bottom showing 2 plain points. Fields outlined in green, yellow, pink and blue, coloured lettering.

In volume of tracings made in 1860; title, surveyor, date and copyist given on front flyleaf [see SOH65602]. See also FOR65601 [which gives scale], 2–7 and SOH65603–7,9–12.

Soham – [1656] – SOH65609 – CRO
O. [NE of town.]
Surveyor: [William Palmer]; **Scale:** 1:3,960; **Size:** (ii) 20 x 14 7/8in.; **Top** is SE; Manuscript(ii), tracing paper, coloured.
c. 250a. in TL5874, bounded by Hall Street in S and E, Soham Lode in W and common in N.
Names of fields, roads, owners and tenants. Cottages shown in perspective. Closes; common; waste; acreages; roads and watercourses.

Compass bottom left showing 2 plain points. Fields outlined in green, yellow, pink and blue, water coloured blue, coloured lettering.

In volume of tracings made in 1860; title, surveyor, date and copyist given on front flyleaf [see SOH65602]. See also FOR65601 [which gives scale], 2–7 and SOH65603–8,10–12.

Soham – [1656] – SOH65610 – CRO
P. [Redland Field.]
Surveyor: [William Palmer]; **Scale:** 1:3,960; **Size:** (ii) 20 x 14 7/8in.; **Top** is S; Manuscript(ii), tracing paper, coloured.
c. 230a. in TL5775, in Redland Field W of Soham Cotes, bounded by river in W and common in E.
Names of fields, roads, owners and tenants. Cottages shown in perspective. Open fields showing all strips; common; acreages; roads and watercourses.
Compass on left showing 2 points with a yellow decorated N with a crown and 'Robert H. Peck' in ribbon at bottom of N. Fields outlined in green, yellow, pink and blue, water coloured blue, coloured lettering.
In volume of tracings made in 1860; title, surveyor, date and copyist given on front flyleaf [see SOH65602]. See also FOR65601 [which gives scale], 2–7 and SOH65603–9,11–12.

Soham – [1656] – SOH65611 – CRO
Q. [Crow Fen.]
Surveyor: [William Palmer]; **Scale:** 1:3,960; **Size:** (ii) 20 x 14 7/8in.; **Top** is NE; Manuscript(ii), tracing paper, coloured.
c. 140a. in TL5476, Crow Fen, bounded by river in W, Barway Fen in E and Soham Cotes in S.
Names of fields, rivers, owners and tenants. Closes; common; waste; fen; acreages; roads and watercourses.
Compass rose bottom right showing 8 yellow, blue and brown points. Fields outlined in green, yellow, pink and blue, water coloured blue, coloured lettering.
In volume of tracings made in 1860; title, surveyor, date and copyist given on front flyleaf [see SOH65602]. See also FOR65601 [which gives scale], 2–7 and SOH65603–10,12.

Soham – [1656] – SOH65612 – CRO
R. [Barway.]
Surveyor: [William Palmer]; **Scale:** 1:3,960; **Size:** (ii) 20 x 14 7/8in.; **Top** is N; Manuscript(ii), tracing paper, coloured.
c. 160a. in Barway in TL5475, bounded by Crow Fen in N, river in S and W and Barway Road ['The Drove Way'] in E.
Names of fields, roads, owners and tenants. Cottages and chapel shown in perspective. Closes; common; fen; acreages; roads and watercourses.
Compass middle left showing 2 points with a yellow decorated N with a crown and 'Robert H. Peck' in ribbon at bottom of N. Fields outlined in green, yellow, pink and blue, water coloured blue, coloured lettering.
In volume of tracings made in 1860; title, surveyor, date and copyist given on front flyleaf [see SOH65602]. See also FOR65601 [which gives scale], 2–7 and SOH65603–11.

Soham – 1779 – SOH77901 – WRO CR114/2/ii
Barroway Map.
Surveyors: [John] Lund [sr and jr]; **A Scale** of Four Chains in One Inch, Scale bar 0–21 chains (= 5 1/4in.),

1:3,168; **Size:** (i) 13 15/16 x 23 7/8in.; **Top** is N; Manuscript(i), paper, coloured.
Barway Church, TL545758, and c. 72a. in Barway.
Names of roads and neighbouring owners. Farm buildings shown in plan form, church shown in perspective. Closes; trees; roads and gates.
Border of 1 broad band; title at top; scale bottom right of whole sheet; compass at top of whole sheet showing 4 points. Buildings coloured red, trees coloured green, fields outlined in green, red, yellow and brown.
Numbers on plots suggest map originally accompanied by a terrier. Fields not shown in correct positions. At bottom of sheet which also contains maps of Isleham [ISL77901] and Soham [SOH77902] and entitled centre right: 'A Map of the Estates of the Right Honourable Lady Viscountess Irwin at Barroway. Soham and Isleham in the County of Cambridge. Surveyed by Messrs Lunds in 1779'. Surveyors' 1st names were John [Eden L294 and L294.1].

Soham – 1779 – SOH77902 – WRO CR114/2/ii
Soham Map.
Surveyors: [John] Lund [sr and jr]; **A Scale** of Four Chains in One Inch, Scale bar 0–21 chains (= 5 1/4in.), 1:3,168; **Size:** (i) 17 15/16 x 23 13/16in.; **Top** is N; Manuscript(i), paper, coloured.
c. 240a. in Soham Parish.
Names of roads and neighbouring owners. Buildings shown in plan form. Closes; trees; roads and footpaths; gates and stiles.
Border of 1 broad band; title in centre; scale bottom right of whole sheet; compass at top of whole sheet showing 4 points. Buildings coloured red, trees coloured green, roads coloured brown, fields outlined in green, brown, yellow and brown.
Numbers on plots suggest map originally accompanied by a terrier. Fields not shown in correct positions. At bottom of sheet which also contains maps of Isleham [ISL77901] and Barway [SOH77901]; see SOH77901 for details.

Soham – [c. 1790] – SOH79001 – SJC MPS 296, 296(2)
Plan of certain Estates at Barway, belonging to St Johns the Evangelists College in the University of Cambridge.
Surveyor: [Joseph Freeman?]; **Scale:** 1:4,180; **Size:** (i) 17 9/16 x 12 9/16in.; **Top** is N; Manuscript(i), parchment, coloured.
Barway Church, TL545758, and 27a.2r.33p. N and S of Soham Lode and extending E along Harrimere Drain, bounded by River Ouse in W and Harrimere ['Soham Mere'] Drain in S.
Names of farms, fields, neighbouring owners and drains. Houses and other buildings in Barway shown in plan form, 'Highfield' windmill shown in perspective. Closed fields showing owner's land; wash; state of cultivation given in words; land quality, e.g. 'sometime drowned'; acreages; roads; River Ouse and drains showing direction of flow; bank; tunnel; bridge.
Border of 1 narrow band; title bottom right; compass top right showing 4 points. Table on right giving acreages and land use. Water coloured blue, land outlined in yellow.
Note below title: 'NB The Lands coloured Yellow belong to the College And also a Moiety of the Fishing in the River Ouse from Marr Ware to Twissels Ware about 3 1/2 Furlongs together with the Part of the Wash on each side included within the Yellow Lines, And also about 3 3/4

Furlongs of Fishing in the West River'. Inset bottom left of fishing rights in Stretham [see STR79001]. Cut from lease and drawn c. 1790; very similar to SOH79002 except that does not extend so far E. In style of Joseph Freeman, who was employed by the College in the 1790s. 2nd copy at SJC MPS 296(2), with pencil notes.

Soham – 1790 – SOH79002 – SJC MPS 287
A Plan of certain Lands and Fisheries at Barway belonging to St Johns the Evangelist College in the University of Cambridge. 1790.
Surveyor: [Joseph Freeman?]; **Scale bar** 0–15 chains (= 3in.), 1:3,960; **Size:** (i) 19 7/8 x 33in.; **Top** is N; Manuscript(i), parchment, coloured.
Barway Church, TL545758, and 27a.2r.33p. N and S of Soham Lode, bounded by River Ouse in W, Harrimere ['Soham Mere'] Drain in S and Goose Fen ['Cobs'] Drove in E.
Names of fields, droves and neighbouring owners. Barway Church and buildings in Barway village shown in plan form, windmills shown in perspective. Closed fields showing owner's land; fen and wash; state of cultivation given in words on some plots; acreages; roads; watercourses showing direction of flow; bridges; tunnel; banks shown by hachures.
Border of 1 broad and 1 narrow band; title middle top in a cartouche of leaves and flowers with a ribbon; scale left of title; compass right of title showing 8 points. Table top right giving field names, acreages and state of cultivation. Houses coloured red, arable outlined in yellow, pasture and wash outlined in green.
Note at bottom: 'The Lands Coloured with Green or Yellow belong to the College. And also a Moiety of the Fishing in the River Ouse, from Marr Ware to Twissel's Ware, about 3 1/2 furlongs, together with part of the wash on each side, included within the Green Lines. And also about 3 3/4 furlongs of Fishing in the West River, vide Plan'. Inset bottom left of fishing rights in Stretham [see STR79002]. In style of Joseph Freeman, who was employed by the College in the 1790s. Photograph at 1:6,789 at CRO TR869/P27.

Soham – [c. 1795] – SOH79501 – BLM Add.35686 f.159
[Soham Mere and Middle Fen District, showing land owned by George, 1st Marquis Townshend.]
Scale: 1:34,900; **Size:** (ii) 12 7/16 x 7 13/16in.; **Top** is N; Manuscript(i), paper, uncoloured.
c. 1,300a. in Soham Mere and 'Middle Fen District' in E of parish, S of Soham Lode.
Name of owner. 2 windmills shown in perspective. Watercourses and drain; bank of mere.
Note on mere: 'Soham Meer and Mill belonging to Marquiss Townsend'. In volume of Hardwicke papers; accompanying documents dated 1795.

Soham – [1825] – SOH82501 – CUL Maps.PSQ.18.80
Plan of Saint John's Farm. Lot 3.
Auctioneer: Elliot Smith; **Printer:** C[harles] Hullmandel; **Scale:** 1:1,080; **Size:** (ii) 14 13/16 x 8 11/16in.; **Top** is W; Printed, paper, uncoloured.
St John's Farm, TL594778, and c. 200a. N of village, bounded by Great Fen Drove ['Main Drain'] in S and W.
Names of roads, drains and neighbouring owners. Farmhouse shown in perspective, farm buildings and mill shown in plan form. Closes; roads and watercourses; ponds.
Title at top.
Accompanies: 'Plans, Particulars and Conditions of Sale, of important freehold and copyhold (fine certain) estates, consisting of Spinney Abbey Farm, in the parish of Wicken, St. John's Farm, in the parish of Soham and County of Cambridge, and a valuable Farm at King's Ripton, in the County of Huntingdon; which will be sold by auction, by Elliot Smith ... July, 1825'. Particulars of sale mention: 'powerful Water Engine, erected within the last four years', date, tenants, tenure, rents and taxes. Printer's 1st name was Charles [*DNB*, 15, 199]. Owner was probably Sarah Rayner, who owned estates at Swaffham Prior and Wicken sold at same time [SWP82501 and WIC82501; Knowles, 1902, 38].

Soham – [1831] – SOH83101 – CUL Maps.PSQ.18.87
Plan of an Estate in the Parish of Soham in the County of Cambridge for Sale by Mr Hoggart in Lots.
Auctioneer: [unidentified] Hoggart; **Lithographer:** C.M. Firth; **Scale bar** 0–18 chains (= 3 3/8in.), 1:4,224; **Size:** (i) 13 13/16 x 17 1/4in.; **Top** is NNW; Lithograph, paper, uncoloured.
Little Hasse Farm, TL605753, and 117a.2r.23p. in NE of parish along Great Hasse ['Hurst'] Drove and Little Hasse ['Hurst'] Drove bounded by Isleham Parish in E, and 1 strip of land in North Field bounded by Horse Fen Drove in W and Northfield Road ['Jointway leading to Crow Hall'] in E.
Names of roads and neighbouring owners. Little Hasse Farm, outbuildings and 'Edward Howlet's' house shown in plan form. Closed fields; acreages; roads and gates; watercourses; fence; garden identified on particulars of sale.
Border of 2 narrow bands; title top left; scale bottom right; compass middle top showing 4 points with a decorated N. Table bottom right giving field names and acreages.
Accompanies: 'Particulars of valuable Freehold and Copyhold Estates, Soham, near Ely, and Newmarket, Which will be Sold by Auction, by Mr Hoggart ... 27th August, 1831 ...' Particulars of sale give date, tenure, state of cultivation and rents.

Soham – 1832 – SOH83201 – CRO P142/3/9
Plan of the Vicarage, Gardens, &c, belonging to The Revd H. Tasker, Vicar of Soham, Cambs.
Surveyor: W[illiam] Warren; **Scale bar** 1–0–5 chains (= 7 1/2in.), 1:634; **Size:** (i) 19 11/16 x 15 15/16in.; **Top** is NNE; Manuscript(i), paper, coloured.
Soham Vicarage, TL593731, and 3a.0r.39p. bounded by Churchgate Street in E, Clay Street ['Bull Lane'] in S, path to church in W and church in N.
Names of neighbouring owners, roads and buildings. Vicarage, rectory, coach house, Baptist Chapel, Red Lion Public House, cottages and stable shown in plan form, church shown in perspective. Closes; acreages of vicarage land; roads; gates; gardens, lawn and kitchen garden; pond and pump; fences; yards.
Border of 1 broad and 1 narrow band; title top right with decorative lettering; scale at bottom; compass rose middle top showing 4 points. Vicarage land coloured yellow and blue, lawn coloured green.
Pencil notes of land exchanged. Surveyor's 1st name was William [Eden W126], owner's 1st name was Henry [Venn, II, 6, 112].

Soham – [c. 1833–61] – SOH83301 – CUL MS Plans R.a.9

The Estate of James Drage Merest Esqre at Soham Cambridgeshire.

Surveyor: John Croft; **Scale bar** 1–0–20 chains (= 3 1/2in.), 1:4,752; **Size:** (i) 61 5/8 x 46 5/8in.; **Top** is N; Manuscript(i), paper mounted on cloth, coloured.

The Moat, TL592728, and 694a.3r.33p. scattered throughout parish.

Names of fields and neighbouring owners. Church, farm and farm buildings shown in plan form. Open fields showing owner's strips; common; wood; waste and fen; state of cultivation shown by colour; tenure; acreages; roads; toll bar on turnpike; footpaths; watercourses; gardens and their layout; moat; ponds; bridge and dam; fences.

Border of 1 narrow band; title middle left; scale middle bottom; plain compass bottom left showing 8 points. Water coloured blue, house coloured red, other buildings coloured grey, arable coloured brown, pasture coloured green.

Numbers on fields suggest map originally accompanied by a terrier. Pencil notes of acreages. Inset at bottom of 10a.2r.30p. arable in Fordham Parish and inset on left of 10a.3r.29p. pasture in Wicken Parish. Address of John Croft given as Bury St Edmunds; map probably drawn while he practised there 1833–61 [Eden C550].

Stapleford – 1740–1 – STL74101 – EDR CC.12334

A Survey of Stapleford Heath, Taken in Decbr 1740/1. by Thos Warren, of Bury.

Surveyor: Thomas Warren [sr]; **Scale bar** 0–40 perches (= 2 7/16in.), 1:13,000; **Size:** (i) 22 1/4 x 26 5/8in.; **Top** is NE; Manuscript(i), parchment, uncoloured.

Wandlebury Ring, TL494534, and 561a.1r.22p. bounded by Great Shelford Parish in NW, Roman Road in NE and Babraham Parish in SE.

Names of fields and roads. Heath; acreages; roads and 'Old Roman Way'; gates; milestones; clunch and sand pits; well; hills shown as mound with tree on top; site of gardens, yards and buildings.

Border of 1 broad band with 1 narrow band on inside; title in centre in a square cartouche of 1 broad band with 1 narrow band on inside; scale bottom left; compass rose bottom right showing 4 points.

Dotted line dividing area, note along it: 'This Streight Line drawn from Stapleford Field on the S:W: Side the Heath through the Middle of the Bush on Clunchpitt Hill through Severall Hills as Markes to a Mark or Stone to be Erected at Haverill Road on the N:E: Side the Heath Divides the Said Heath into two Equall parts'. Drawn in connection with division of heath between Dean and Chapter of Ely and Francis, 2nd Earl Godolphin [*VCH*, 8, 233]. Crosses on map mark survey and division of land. Surveyor was Thomas Warren sr [Eden W122].

Stapleford – [c. 1814] – STL81401 – EDR CC.12334

Stapleford.

Surveyor: [Edward Gibbons]; **Scale bar** 0–24 chains (= 4in.), 1:4,752; **Size:** (ii) 37 x 26 5/8in.; **Top** is ENE; Manuscript(ii), paper, uncoloured.

665a.1r.27p. scattered throughout parish; junction of road from Stapleford to Heath Farm ['Hills Road'] and footpath is at TL476516.

Names of fields, owner, tenants and roads. Buildings shown in plan form. Closed fields; heath; acreages;

meadow; roads, Roman Road and turnpike; footpaths; watercourses; responsibility for boundaries; reasons for allotments; 'Telegraph' [signalling station?; Reaney, 1943, 89].

Title bottom right; scale top right.

Copied from map by Edward Gibbons which accompanied 1814 inclosure award, shows land allotted to Dean and Chapter of Ely.

Steeple Morden – [1767] – STM76701 – JCC Steeple Morden

The Plan of No 45.

Surveyor: John Smith; **Scale:** 1:1,060; **Size:** (iii) 8 3/4 x 11 1/2in.; **Top** is S; Manuscript(i), paper, coloured.

c. 5a. at Flecks Lane Farm, TL295456, bounded by road to Shingay in NW and Abington Pigotts Parish in SE.

Names of buildings and roads. Buildings shown in plan form and include farmhouse, 'hen house', 'cartlodge', granary, oat barn, 'hogsty', stables and 'Great Barn'. Roads; gateway; orchards; pond; road; hedge; passage; farmyard; kitchen.

Title at top; cardinal points stated at edge. Red lines on map.

On explanation to a terrier, which says map shows 3r.24p. at 1:731, gives date and: 'It appears to me the Farm House, The Kitchen, the little yard, Henhouse, Waggon Lodge, Granary, Oat Barn and part of Cow Yard being all on the left hand side of Red Stroke, going in from Shingay Road strait to end of Oat Barn, or between Oat Barn and Hogsty are on College Ground and are part of the Close or Orchard by Estimation one Acre and a half – in Terrier Number 45. – and the Buildings on the Right hand side probably may be on Mrs Akehursts Free Land Therefore upon the whole the Terrier is so Imperfect on College part, I think there ought to be a new one. John Smith'. Notes of Great Barn on Mrs Akehurst's free land. Farm owned by Jesus College, Cambridge. See also STM76702.

Steeple Morden – [1767] – STM76702 – JCC Steeple Morden

['Barns on Flex Farm'.]

Surveyor: [John Smith]; **Scale:** 1:1,060; **Size:** (iii) 6 x 12 5/8in.; **Top** is S; Manuscript(i), paper, uncoloured.

c. 7a. at Flecks Lane ['Flex'] Farm, TL295456.

Name of land. Barns shown in plan form. Closes showing owner's land; acreages 'by estimation'; roads; grove.

Cardinal points stated at edge.

Notes describing necessity for Jesus College, Cambridge [the owner] to have a barn, and stating whether land is freehold or copyhold. Accompanies explanation to a terrier of 1767; see also STM76701 which names surveyor.

Steeple Morden – 1793 – STM79301 – SJC MPS 219

Plan of Two Farms at Steeple~Morden in the County of Cambridge belonging to St. Johns the Evangelists College in the University of Cambridge Surveyed in 1793.

Surveyor: [Joseph Freeman]; **Scale bar** 0–20 chains (= 2 1/8in.), 1:7,454; **Size:** (i) 28 1/2 x 23 7/8in.; **Top** is N; Manuscript(i), parchment, coloured.

Farm at TL289442 in North Brook End, and 206a.0r.37p. in strips scattered throughout parish.

Names of fields, roads and neighbouring owners. Farm buildings shown in plan form. Open fields showing owner's strips; closes; pightles; wood and trees; 'Mere';

pasture closes shown by symbol representing tufts of grass; roads; watercourses; orchard; hedges; pond.

Border of 1 broad band with 1 narrow band on inside; title bottom right with decorative lettering; scale beneath title; compass middle left showing 4 points. Table on right giving acreages, field names and descriptions of inclosures for farm leased by Wilson and farm leased by John Strickland, and summarizing acreages for open and inclosed land, and for arable and pasture. Strips and roads coloured brown, grass and trees coloured green, buildings coloured red, water coloured blue.

In style of Joseph Freeman and accompanies terrier by him, SJC D31.49, which has on dorse a plan of farm leased to Wilson with its barns and stables at 1:240. Photograph of map at 1:9,856 at CRO TR869/P25.

Steeple Morden – [1822] – STM82201 – JCC Steeple Morden

Plan of an Estate, situate in the Parish of Steeple Morden in the County of Cambridge; belonging to the Master, Fellows, and Scholars of Jesus College, in the University of Cambridge; in Lease to Wescomb.

Surveyor: [Samuel Kempson Simmons]; **Scale:** 1:5,110; **Size:** (i) 30 3/4 x 21 1/2in.; **Top** is N; Manuscript(i), parchment, coloured.

Farm in TL2941 and 198a.3r.4p. to N, mostly S of road from Guilden Morden to Shingay, 1 plot to N towards Tadlow Parish and 10a.1r.32p. in Abington Pigotts Parish ['Abington in the Clay'].

Names of neighbouring owners. Farm buildings and cottages shown in plan form. Closed fields showing owner's land; woods, 'Nut' and 'Offal' groves and spinney; roads and watercourses; moat; land allotted in exchange.

Border of 2 narrow bands; title top left. Roads coloured brown, buildings coloured red, water coloured blue.

Probably map for which Samuel Kempson Simmons was paid £8 in 1822, and a further 12s 6d in 1824 [JCC A/C.1.10].

Steeple Morden – 1827 – STM82701 – CRO L60/39

Sketch of Lands exchanged between the Earl of Hardwicke and New College Oxford, under the Steeple Morden Inclosure Act.

Surveyor: S[amuel] K[empson] Simmons; **Scale:** 1:6,340; **Size:** (i) 13 9/16 x 17 1/8in.; **Top** is NNE; Manuscript(ii), tracing paper, coloured.

c. 210a. in N of parish in North Brook End E of TL289449, junction of roads from Guilden Morden to Shingay and to Steeple Morden.

Names of owners and neighbouring owners. Homestead belonging to New College shown in perspective. Closed fields showing all land; 'Nut Grove'; acreages; roads; 2 pightles; responsibility for boundaries.

Border of 1 broad band with 1 narrow band on inside; title on right; compass in centre showing 8 plain points. Roads and numbers referring to inclosure award coloured brown.

Note under title: 'From the Inclosure Map February 1827 S.K. Simmons'. Notes of land exchanged and old inclosures. Surveyor's 1st names were Samuel Kempson [Eden S226].

Steeple Morden – [1828] – STM82801 – B L M Add.Eg.2987 f.241b

Plan of the Right Honble Lord Willoughby de Broke's Estate. in the Parish of Steeple Norton [sic.] and County of Cambridge.

Auctioneer: [Thomas Harmston]; **Lithographers:** [unidentified] Ingrey, [G.E.] Madeley; **Scale** of 16 Chains to an Inch, 1:12,672; **Size:** (i) 20 x 12 1/4in.; **Top** is N; Lithograph, paper, uncoloured.

'Chenies Manor', TL293425, and 439a.2r.35p. scattered throughout parish.

Names of roads and neighbouring owners. Cottages, farm buildings and church shown in plan form. Closed fields showing owner's land; acreages; roads and turnpike; watercourses; spinney, garden and orchard identified on particulars of sale.

Border of 1 narrow band with 1 broad band on inside; title bottom right; scale under title; compass in centre showing 4 points.

Note under scale: 'NB. The Portions dotted off part of the Allotments are Tythe free'. Ink note correcting parish name. Accompanies particulars of sale [BLM Add.Eg.2987 f.243]: 'Particulars of An Estate at Steeple Morden, Cambridgeshire, and an Estate at Cottered, Herts. which will be Sold by Auction, by Mr. Thos. Harmston, ... On Saturday, 11th of October, 1828 ...' Particulars printed by [unidentified] Creasey and give field names, acreages, land use and land tax. Lithographers were [unidentified] Ingrey [Eden I16.5] and G.E. Madeley [Eden M117].

Stetchworth – 1770 – STN77001 – CUL MS Plans 345

A Plan and Survey of the Lordship of Stetchworth in the County of Cambridge chiefly belonging to John Flemming Esqr who is Lord of the said Manor. Surveyed in the Year 1770 by Geoe Salmon.

Surveyor: George Salmon; **Scale bar** 1–0–50 chains (= 7 7/8in.), 1:5,129; **Size:** (i) 27 1/4 x 69 3/8in.; **Top** is NE; Manuscript(i), paper mounted on paper, coloured.

Stetchworth Church, TL643590, and 3,010a.3r.28p. in whole parish and some meadow in Dullingham Parish.

Names of parishes. Church, hall, park, farms and farm buildings, 'stand' [for racing], stable and houses in village all shown in plan form. Open fields showing owner's strips; old inclosures; common; wood and trees; waste and heath; state of cultivation shown by colour; acreages of some plots; roads and footpaths; gates; watercourses; park; ponds; hedges and fences.

Border of 2 narrow bands; title top right in a rococo cartouche with grasses; scale bottom right; compass middle top showing 4 points. Table at bottom giving farms, tenants, field names, woods, inclosures and acreages. 'Hall Farm' outlined in pink, 'Park Farm' outlined in yellow, 'Place Farm' outlined in blue, fields outlined in colour, pasture strips coloured green.

Pencil notes, mainly of acreages, some extensions to map and notes about scale. Owner's surname was spelled Fleming [*VCH*, 6, 172]. Photograph in CRO.

Stow cum Quy – 1737 – STO73701 – CRO 107/P

A Map of the Manor of Stow cum Quij in the County of Cambridge Surveyed for James Martin Esqr by Joseph Colbeck 1737.

Surveyor: Joseph Colbeck; **A Scale** of Gunter's Chains four in an Inch, 1:3,168, Scale bar 1–0–20 chains

(= 5 1/8in.), 1:3,245; **Size:** (i) 35 x 58 7/16in.; **Top** is ENE; Manuscript(i), parchment, coloured.

Quy Hall, TL515611, and c. 2,500a. in whole parish except for Quy Fen.

Names of fields. Cottages, Quy Hall, Quy Mill and church shown in perspective. Open fields showing all strips; closes; common; wood and trees including avenue of trees to hall; meadow and fen; roads and watercourses; park; gardens including layout of garden to hall; kitchen garden; bridges; hedge.

Border of 5/16in.-wide red band; title middle right in a yellow and red ornamental cartouche with a green background; scale bottom left surmounted by yellow dividers in a green and pink cartouche with a vase of flowers above scale bar; compass rose bottom right showing 16 red and blue points with a yellow border and green background. Roads coloured brown, fields outlined in green, yellow, blue and red, wood and park coloured green, water coloured blue, buildings coloured grey.

Numbers on plots suggest map originally accompanied by a terrier. Note middle bottom in a rectangular red and green cartouche giving boundaries of estate. Pencil additions and crayon notes of acreages.

Stow cum Quy – 1779 – STO77901 – WRO CR114/2/i

A Map of the Estate of the Right Honourable Lady Viscountess Irwin at Anglesea Abbey, in the County of Cambridge. Surveyed by Messrs Lunds in 1779.

Surveyors: [John] Lund [sr and jr]; **A Scale** of Four Chains in One Inch, Scale bar 0–21 chains (= 5 1/4in.), 1:3,168; **Size:** (i) 23 x 23 7/8in.; **Top** is N; Manuscript(i), paper, coloured.

Anglesea Abbey, TL530622, and c. 270a. around it and scattered throughout parish.

Names of neighbouring owners. Anglesea Abbey, outbuildings and mill shown in plan form. Open fields showing owner's strips; closes; trees; roads and gates; watercourses and bridge; 'Sheep~Walk'.

Border of 1 broad band; title bottom right; scale bottom left; compass top left showing 4 points. Trees coloured green, roads coloured brown, water coloured green, fields outlined in yellow, green, blue, red and brown, Thomas Caine's freehold coloured red, William Newman's and Mr Tattersall's freeholds coloured green.

Numbers on plots suggest map originally accompanied by a terrier. Strips in open fields shown as insets. Surveyors' 1st names were John [Eden L294 and L294.1].

Stow cum Quy – 1804 – STO80401 – EDR CC.10110

Ground Plan of Stow cum Quy Parsonage by Joseph Truslove Camb*ridge* 1804.

Surveyor: Joseph Truslove; **Scale:** 0–70 [feet] (= 7 3/4in.), 1:108; **Size:** (i) 20 7/8 x 29 1/4in.; Manuscript(i), paper, coloured.

c. 3r. bounded by glebe on right and a road on left.

Buildings shown in plan form and reference table identifies 'Best' and 'Middle' parlours, privy, passage, kitchen and 'Back Kitchen', 'Smallbeer Cellar', dairy, 'Lumber Room', 'hen house', 'Old Maltkiln', 'Wheat Case', wheat and barley barns, 'Waggon' and 'Cart' hovels, 'Hay house', 'Duck house', 'Chaff~house', 'Best Cart' and 'Old Cart' stables, 'cow house', 'Cart house & Granary over it'. Deciduous and coniferous trees; roads and footpaths; gardens; 'Cellar Stairs'; 'Stair Case'.

Border of 1 narrow band; title bottom left; scale centre left. 'Reference to Buildings' bottom right. Walls coloured red and yellow, grass coloured green, paths coloured yellow.

Land owned by Bishop of Ely.

Stow cum Quy – 1827 – STO82701 – PRI

A Map of the Manor and Parish of Stow cum Quy, in the County of Cambridge. surveyed for James Thomas Martin, Esquire. By William Womack, Land Surveyor, Worcester. 1827.

Surveyor: William Womack; **Scale** Three Chains in one Inch, 1:2,376, Scale bar 1–0–30 chains (= 10 1/4in.), 1:2,395; **Size:** (i) 66 7/8 x 89in.; **Top** is ENE; Manuscript(i), paper mounted on cloth, coloured.

Quy Hall, TL515612, and 2,011a.1r.32p. in whole parish and including 4a.0r.10p. in Fen Ditton Parish, 3a.0r.32p. in Teversham Parish and 41a.1r.1p. in Bottisham Parish.

Names of fields and neighbouring owners. Hall, church, mill, 'The Kennell', farm buildings and cottages shown in plan form. Open fields showing all strips; closes; common, meadow and fen; wood, plantation, trees and avenue of trees; state of cultivation shown by colour; roads, footpaths and gates; milestones; watercourses; ponds; bridges; park; gardens and orchards; cross; 'Boundary' marked by 'Quy Water Bar'; hedges and fences; 2 pumps; 'The Fishery'; 2 posts.

Border of 1 13/16in.-wide geometrical pattern coloured black, white and grey; title bottom left; scale centre bottom; compass middle right showing 8 points. Table bottom right giving field names, land use and acreages in Stow cum Quy, Fen Ditton, Teversham and Bottisham parishes. Roads coloured brown, trees, hedges and pasture coloured green, water coloured blue, buildings coloured red, arable coloured in brown stripes.

Pencil notes. 'Cledge [clay] Weight [canal basin?]' written along footpath in N of parish [path leading to dock?]. Accompanied by: 'Terrier of the Parish of Stow cum Quy in the County of Cambridge from an actual Admeasurement taken by William Womack, Surveyor, of Claines near Worcester for James Thomas Martin Esqre 1827'. Terrier gives owner, occupier, land use, field names and acreages. 2nd terrier gives land of each owner.

Stretham – [c. 1790] – STR79001 – SJC MPS 296, 296(2)

[Fishing rights belonging to St John's College, Cambridge, along River Great Ouse in Stretham Parish.]

Surveyor: [Joseph Freeman?]; **Scale:** 1:19,800; **Size:** (i) 4 9/16 x 5 1/8in.; **Top** is W; Manuscript(i), parchment, coloured.

3 3/4 furlongs along River Great Ouse ['West River'] in TL5274 and land W of river, bounded by Thetford Parish in N and E.

Names of owner, neighbouring owners and river. Common water; watercourses; length of river.

Border of 1 narrow band. Water coloured blue, College land coloured yellow.

Note at top: 'NB This West River branches from the Cam at Thetford, & extends from the Cam, to the Hundred foot River which it Joins at the Hermitage'. Inset at bottom left to SOH79001. Cut from lease and drawn c. 1790; very similar to SOH79002 and STR79002. In style of Joseph

Freeman, who was employed by the College in the 1790s. 2nd copy at SJC MPS 296(2).

Stretham – [1790] – STR79002 – SJC MPS 287
[Fishing rights belonging to St John's College, Cambridge, along River Great Ouse in Stretham Parish.]
Surveyor: [Joseph Freeman?]; **Scale:** 1:19,600; **Size:** (i) 5 3/16 x 6 11/16in.; **Top** is E; Manuscript(i), parchment, coloured.
3 3/4 furlongs along River Great Ouse ['West River'] in TL5274 and land W of river, bounded by Thetford Parish in N and E.
Names of owners, neighbouring owners and river. Common water; watercourses; length of river.
Border of 1 broad and 1 narrow band. College land outlined in green.
Note on right: 'This is planed out of Scale'. Note at bottom: 'This West River branches from the Cam at Thetford and extends from the Cam to the Hundred Foot River, which it joins at the Hermitage'. Inset at bottom left to SOH79002, dated 1790. In style of Joseph Freeman, who was employed by the College in the 1790s. Photograph at 1:23,900 at CRO TR869/P27.

Sutton – 1639 – SUT63901 – EDR CC.12315
An exact Survey of the Lordshipp of Sutton in the Isle of Ely caled or knowne by the name of the Berristedd.
Surveyor: Thomas Crawley; **Draughtsmen:** Jo[hn?] Cole, Jo. Pegg; **Scale bar** 0–5 [furlongs] (= 4 15/16in.), 1:8,020; **Size:** (ii) 16 1/2 x 12 15/16in.; **Top** is S; Manuscript(ii), paper mounted on cloth, uncoloured.
Burystead Farm, TL433788, and c. 1,400a. to N.
Names of fields. Site of cottage. Closes; West Fen; acreages; 'dove coate way'; garden and orchard; yard.
Title bottom right; scale above title; 'N' written at bottom, faces of sun at other edges.
Note top right of 33a. in 'Lammas Meadowe beyond the River in iiij parcells ...' Note left of this note: 'A peece of fenn called the Gull Lott adioyneinge to these four peeces on the south=west: and contains by estimation xiiij Acres but is not surueyed, beinge taken at the time of the survey, for the dreyners, & since returned as was also the peece in Greate fenn Close 6l 0s 0d'. Pencil outlines of fields, notes of rents of some fields. Map was 'Measured or Surveyed according to this forme by Thomas Crawley of [?] in winter Anno 163<8>\9/. Jo. Cole Script: 1645 And renewed by Jo Pegg 1649'. Note on dorse of 'Tymber upon the farme'. Lordship owned by Dean and Chapter of Ely. Jo. Cole may have been the John Cole of Downham who died in 1649 [CRO EPR CW 1649 WR C28:233].

Swaffham Bulbeck – 1756 – SWB75601 – PRO MPE 410
Hare Park Lodge.
Surveyor: Charles Evans; **Scale:** 1:185; **Size:** (i) 15 3/8 x 6 5/8in.; Manuscript(i), paper, uncoloured.
c. 10p. in SW of TL5859.
Close; dimensions of areas.
Border of 1 broad band with 1 narrow band on either side; title in centre.
Note at bottom: 'I have this Day Surveyed a piece or parcell of Ground Situate on new Markett Heath in the Parish of [Swaffham Bulbeck] belonging to the Marquis of Granby & Lord Guernsey Abutting East, West, North and South on the Heath wheron now Stands one Brick Building which is

called Hare Park Lodge and is in a very bad State of Repair cannot be value'd at more than five pounds *per* Ann*um* Chas Evans'. John Manners, Marquis of Granby [*PB*, 2,328] and Heneage Finch, 2nd Earl of Aylesford and Lord Guernsey [*PB*, 143], leased land from the Crown. Bottom left of sheet; see also NEA75601–2.

Swaffham Bulbeck – 1786 – SWB78601 – PRO K T1/639 [To become MFQ 756]
Surveyed a p<ea>\ie/ce or parcel of Ground, situate on Newmarket Heath\/ in the County of Cambridge\/ belonging to the Duke of Rutland and Countess Dowager of Aylesford, on which stands one small Brick Messuage called Hare Park Lodge\/ with Stables adjoining thereto\/ as described on the plan\/ the Buildings are out of repair\/ & may be Valued at Ten pounds *per* Annum for a term of fifty Years. Jno Marquand Ap: the 22nd 1786.
Surveyor: John Marquand; **Scale bar** 400–0 links (= 5 3/8in.), 1:589; **Size:** (i) 13 7/8 x 10 5/8in.; **Top** is N; Manuscript(i), paper, coloured.
c. 2a. in SW of TL5859.
Names of buildings. Buildings shown in plan form and include house, stables, 'Hare Park Lodge' and 'Room'. Dimensions of areas; garden; 'well paled round'.
Border of 2 narrow bands; title at bottom; cardinal points stated at edge of map. Garden coloured green, buildings coloured grey, well coloured blue.
Drawn following a petition from [4th] Duke of Rutland [*PB*, 2,329] and Lady Louisa Aylesford [*PB*, 144] for a renewal of their leases from the Crown. See also NEA78601–2.

Swaffham Bulbeck – 1800 – SWB80001 – CUL MS Plans 547
Plan of an Estate the Property of William, Parker, Hamond Esqr: within the Parish of Swaffham Bulbeck, in the County of Cambridge.
Surveyor: Thomas Norfolk; **Scale bar** 0–40 chains = 4 furlongs (= 4 3/8in.), 1:7,241; **Size:** (i) 42 1/4 x 20 3/8in.; **Top** is NW; Manuscript(i), parchment, coloured.
Mitchell Hall Farm, TL556624, and 315a.3r.36p. bounded by Swaffham Prior Parish in E, Dullingham and Burrough Green parishes in S, Swaffham Heath Road in W and junction of Long Meadow Road with White Droveway in N.
Names of farms, roads and neighbouring owners. Farm and farm buildings, Upper and Lower Hare Park, and '4 mile stable' shown in plan form, post mill and smock mill shown in perspective. Fields showing owner's land; old inclosures; wood and trees; heath; state of cultivation given in words; roads and watercourses; feature which may be an orchard; gravel; responsibility for fences; Beacon Course [racecourse].
Border of 1 broad and 1 narrow band; title middle left in an oval cartouche of 2 concentric rings; scale beneath title; compass middle left showing 8 points. Roads coloured brown, fences to be maintained by owner coloured red.
Lot numbers and some acreages marked in pencil.

Swaffham Bulbeck – [c. 1801–8] – SWB80101 – DCC Map Cabinet Drawer 4 E11
Reduced Plan of a Farm the Property of Jacob John Whittington Esqr situate in the Parish of Swaffham Bulbeck in the County of Cambridge Henry King (Tenant) Surveyed by Thos Norfolk.

Surveyor: Thomas Norfolk; **Scale** of Half a Mile, Scale bar 0–40 chains = 0–4 furlongs (= 4 3/8in.), 1:7,241; **Size:** (ii) 20 1/2 x 14 1/8in.; **Top** is NW; Manuscript(ii), paper mounted on cloth, coloured.

Four Mile Stable Farm, TL585600, and 538a.0r.8p. in S of parish bounded by Dullingham and Burrough Green parishes in S and Bottisham Parish in SW, and c. 56a. in N of parish bounded by River Cam in NW and Bottisham Parish in SW.

Names of roads, rivers and neighbouring owners. Four Mile Stable and Upper and Lower Hare Park shown in plan form. Closed fields showing owner's land; state of cultivation given in words; heath and fen; acreages; roads; watercourses, bank and wash; 'Old gravel pit'; Beacon Course [racecourse]; responsibility for boundaries; common in Bottisham Parish adjoining map.

Title top right; scale middle bottom; compass centre top showing 4 points. Roads coloured yellow, plots outlined in brown, water coloured blue.

Pencil notes. Probably drawn between 1801 inclosure award and 1808 award of Bottisham Parish.

Swaffham Bulbeck – 1813 – SWB81301 – CRO 305/P

Map of an Estate in the Parishes of Little Swaffham and Bottisham in the County of Cambridge belonging to John Hemington Esqr.

Surveyor: T[homas] Lilburne; **A Scale** of 8 Chains in an Inch, Scale bar 1–30 chains (= 3 11/16in.), 1:6,336; **Size:** (i) 22 x 18 5/8in.; **Top** is NW; Manuscript(i), parchment, coloured.

Chalk Farm, TL568605, bounded by road from Cambridge to Newmarket in S and Swaffham Heath Road in N, and Lythel's ['Fen'] Farm, TL531663, bounded by Swaffham Bulbeck Lode in SW and River Cam in NW. Both farms together extend over 656a.3r.22p.

Names of farms, fields, rivers, roads and neighbouring owners. Buildings shown in plan form and include Lythel's Farm, Chalk Farm and cottages. Closed fields showing owner's land; wash; state of cultivation shown by colour; roads including turnpike; watercourses; gates; pond; osier bank; hedges; responsibility for boundaries; garden identified on table.

Border of 1 broad blue band with 1 narrow uncoloured band on either side; title top right in a cartouche with decorative line-work; scale top left; compass middle top showing 4 points with a feathered tail, N has a crown and Prince of Wales' feathers. Table above scale giving field names, acreages of land and ditches and state of cultivation. Water and grass coloured blue, arable coloured white, roads coloured brown, buildings coloured red.

Pencil extension to Lythel's Farm, and notes of tenure in Chalk Farm. Surveyor's 1st name was Thomas [Eden L199].

Swaffham Prior – 1808 – SWP80801 – EDR CC.10105

Plan of an Estate. situate in the Parish of Swaffham Prior in the County of Cambridge. belonging to The Lord Bishop of Ely in Lease to Mr Edward Elliston and the Revd William Gooch.

Scale bar 0–40 chains (= 3 5/16in.), 1:9,564; **Size:** (i) 47 1/2 x 10 9/16in.; **Top** is NNW; Manuscript(i), parchment, coloured.

Swaffham Prior Church, TL569639, and 434a.1r.24p. scattered throughout parish.

Names of roads and neighbouring owners. Houses and cottages in village and farm buildings shown in plan form, church shown in perspective. Closed fields showing owner's land; acreages; roads and watercourses; bridges; responsibility for boundaries; Beacon Course [racecourse].

Border of 1 narrow band; title top left; scale centre bottom; compass bottom right showing 8 points. Table bottom left giving field names and acreages. Buildings coloured red.

'See of Ely' written at top. Only 1 of the 2 churches in the churchyard is shown.

Swaffham Prior – [c. 1814] – SWP81401 – CUL MS Plans 280

In the parishes of Swaffham Prior & Swaffham Bulbeck Cambs.

Surveyor: [Edward Gibbons]; **Scale:** 6 chains to an inch, 1:4,752; **Size:** (ii) 92 1/4 x 28 1/4in.; **Top** is NW; Manuscript(ii), tracing paper mounted on paper, coloured.

Manor Farm, TL565639, and c. 5,200a. in N and E of Swaffham Prior Parish bounded by Waterbeach Parish in N, Swaffham Bulbeck Parish in W, Stetchworth Parish in S and Swaffham Field ['Middle'] Road and Rand Drove in E, and some land in E of Swaffham Bulbeck Parish.

Names of neighbouring owners, tenants and roads. Church shown in perspective, Swaffham Prior House, manor house, houses, farms and farm buildings shown in plan form. Closed fields showing owner's land; trees; state of cultivation given in words; tenure; acreages; roads and footpaths; watercourses; orchards; moat; 'Barston Bridge'; responsibility for boundaries.

Title top right; scale middle bottom; compass middle left showing 4 points. Houses coloured red, other buildings coloured black, plots outlined in blue, red or yellow.

Pencil notes. Top left corner is missing. Numbers on plots suggest map originally accompanied by a terrier. Probably drawn to show land allotted to John Peter Allix and based on map by Edward Gibbons which accompanied 1814 inclosure award.

Swaffham Prior – [c. 1814] – SWP81402 – EDR CC.12335

Swaffham Prior.

Surveyor: [Edward Gibbons]; **Scale:** 1:5,130; **Size:** (ii) 37 3/8 x 26 5/8in.; **Top** is ENE; Manuscript(ii), paper, uncoloured.

Swaffham Prior Church, TL569639, and 759a.3r.22p. scattered throughout parish.

Names of owner, tenants and roads. Houses shown in plan form, church shown in perspective. Closed fields; acreages; roads and droves; watercourses; bank; gravel pit; responsibility for boundaries; reasons for allotments.

Title top left.

Later ink note bottom left: 'Scale Six Chains to one Inch', 1:4,752. Numbers on plots refer to inclosure award. Shows land allotted to Dean and Chapter of Ely on inclosure, probably based on map by Edward Gibbons which accompanied 1814 award. Only 1 of the 2 churches in the churchyard is shown.

Swaffham Prior – [c. 1814] – SWP81403 – EDR CC.12336

['Plan of Swaffham Allotments to the Dean & Chapter of Ely under the Act 45 Geo 3. 1805'.]

Surveyor: [Edward Gibbons]; Scale: 1:5,160; Size: (ii) 23 9/16 x 19 1/4in.; Top is NW; Manuscript(ii), paper, coloured.

127a.1r.13p. in Swaffham Prior Fen bounded by River Cam in NW and Reach in E.

Names of droves, lodes and neighbouring owners. Windmill shown in perspective. Closed fields; droves; lodes and watercourses; bank; responsibility for boundaries.

Table bottom left giving acreages. Droves coloured green, water coloured blue, bank coloured yellow.

Title on dorse. Pencil notes, pencil compass in centre giving top as N. Probably based on map by Edward Gibbons which accompanied 1814 inclosure award.

Swaffham Prior – [1825] – SWP82501 – C U L Maps.PSQ.18.80

Fishery belonging to Spinney Abbey. Lot 1.

Auctioneer: Elliot Smith; **Printer:** C[harles] Hullmandel; **Scale:** 1:8,640; **Size:** (i) 10 1/2 x 16 15/16in.; **Top** is W; Printed, paper, uncoloured.

1 mile, 5 furlongs, 34 perches along River Cam, SW of TL531689, where Rand Drove reaches the River Cam, and extending W to Mill Drain in Bottisham Parish.

Names of fields, lodes, droves and neighbouring owners. Sluice house, farm buildings and cottages shown in plan form, 2 smock mills shown in perspective. Closed fields; wash; roads; watercourses; stiles; bridge.

Border of 1 narrow band; title top left.

Accompanies: 'Plans, Particulars and Conditions of Sale, of important freehold and copyhold (fine certain) estates, consisting of Spinney Abbey Farm, in the parish of Wicken, St. John's Farm, in the parish of Soham, and a valuable Farm, at King's Ripton, in the County of Huntingdon; which will be sold by auction, by Elliot Smith ... July, 1825'. Particulars of sale give date and fish stocks. Printer's 1st name was Charles [*DNB*, 15, 199]; owner was Sarah Rayner [Knowles, 1902, 38]. See also SOH82501 and WIC82501.

Swaffham Prior – [1825] – SWP82502 – QCC 355 A21, B21

Estate at Swaffham Prior In The County of Cambridge.

Surveyor: [Alexander Watford jr]; **Scale bar** 0–40 chains (= 3 3/8in.), 1:9,387; **Size:** (i) 9 5/8 x 38 5/8in.; Top is N; Manuscript(ii), paper, coloured.

Farm and 162a.1r.15p. in TL5664 and TL5764, and plots extending from Beacon Course in SE to Swaffham Bulbeck Parish in NW.

Names of roads and neighbouring owners. Buildings shown in plan form. Closed fields showing owner's land; state of cultivation shown by colour; acreages; hedges; roads; watercourses; grove and fence 'stubbed up' identified on table.

Border at bottom and 2 sides of 1 broad band with 1 narrow band on either side; title top left; scale at bottom; compass above scale showing 4 points. Table at bottom giving field names, acreages, land use and allotments. Roads coloured brown, fields coloured yellow and green, water coloured blue.

Numbers on some plots refer to the inclosure award. Vertical dimensions measured to top of drawing. At bottom of sheet which also contains maps of Burwell [BUW82501], Chesterton [CHF82501] and Dullingham [DUL82501], and in volume drawn in 1825: 'Plans of the

Several Estates in England and Wales belonging to the President and Fellows of the College of St Margaret and St Bernard commonly called Queen's College in the University of Cambridge Delineated from Authentic Documents in the possession of the said President and Fellows and from actual Surveys taken By their most obedient and obliged Servant Alexr Watford'. Title page drawn by James Richardson [Watford's nephew]. This is the Bursar's copy; 2nd, finer, copy [the Master's copy] at QCC 355 B21 measures 11 3/8 x 36 5/8in. and is drawn on parchment. Border 7/16in. wide of a central blue band with 1 broad band on either side, title on right has gothic lettering, scale at bottom, compass bottom left has 8 points. Table above scale and has a border imitating a scroll of paper and red lines. Fields coloured in yellow and brown stripes, roads have red/brown edges. Positive photostat of this copy at 1:21,900 at BL 1640.(28).

Swavesey – 1799 – SWV79901 – TCC Box 23 Swavesey 152

Plan of the Old Inclosures belonging to the Society of Trinity College in the Parish of Swavesey in the County of Cambridge 1799.

Surveyor: [Joseph Truslove]; **Scale:** 1:5,020; **Size:** (i) 12 13/16 x 21 3/4in.; **Top** is E; Manuscript(i), parchment, coloured.

Pond at TL365690, and 27a.3r.17p. to S along road from Swavesey to Huntingdon.

Names of roads and neighbouring owners. Buildings shown in plan form. Closed fields showing owner's land; roads; pond; spinney and gardens identified on table.

Border of 1 narrow band; title top right. Table bottom left giving tenants, field names and acreages. Buildings coloured pink, roads coloured yellow, fields coloured and outlined in green, water coloured blue.

Surveyor was probably Joseph Truslove, who drew up terrier at TCC Box 23 Swavesey 153 with note at end: 'The foregoing account is a true Terrier and description of all the Common Field arable Land, Lays and Meadow Ground situate in the bounds of Swavesey in the County of Cambridge belonging to the Society of Trinity College in the University of Cambridge in the occupation of Mrs Susannah Anderson called Late Taylors Farm Dated this 22nd day of December 1799 Joseph Truslove'.

T

Tadlow – 1750 – TAD75001 – DCC

A Survey of China Dairy, in the Parishes of Tadlow & Croydon, and County of Cambridge The Estate of Sir Iacob Garrard Downing Bart Surveyed by Jos Cole 1750.

Surveyor: Joseph Cole; **Scale bar** 10–0–80 perches (= 5 5/8in.), 1:3,168; **Size:** (i) 20 3/4 x 13 15/16in.; **Top** is NNW; Manuscript(i), parchment, coloured.

116a.0r.27p. in TL2847 and TL2947 bounded by Shingay Parish in S; 27a.1r.34p. are in SW of Croydon Parish.

Names of fields and parishes. Farm buildings shown in plan form. Closed fields showing owner's land; trees; meadow; hedges; roads and gates; watercourses and ponds; 'Drift Way'; boundary between Croydon and Tadlow parishes not shown; acreages given on table.

Border of 1 broad band with 1 narrow band on inside; title top left in a rococo cartouche with leaves and flowers and coloured red, green, purple and gold; yellow scale bar centre bottom; compass rose centre right showing 8 red, blue, yellow and green points. Table top right giving field names and acreages in each parish. Above scale bar is a perspective drawing of the farmhouse. Water coloured blue, roads coloured yellow, buildings coloured red, trees and hedges coloured green, fields outlined in green.

'Leasehold' added later on 1 plot in ink and pencil. Numbers on edges of map refer to adjacent sheets. This is number 12 in a volume of maps of the Downing estate. See also CRY75001–11, EAS75001–8 and TAD75002–9.

Tadlow – 1750 – TAD75002 – DCC

A Survey. of Simon's Farm, in the Parishes of Tadlow & Croydon, in the County of Cambridge. The Estate of S*ir* Iacob Garrard Downing Bart By Jos. Cole 1750.

Surveyor: Joseph Cole; **Scale bar** 10–0–80 perches (= 5 5/8in.), 1:3,168; **Size:** (i) 20 5/8 x 13 13/16in.; **Top** is N; Manuscript(i), parchment, coloured.

137a.1r.19p. in TL2847 bounded by TAD75001 in S; 20a.1r.35p. are in Croydon Parish.

Names of fields. Farm buildings shown in plan form. Closed fields showing owner's land; trees, in 1 area bounded by an ink line; state of cultivation shown by colour; hedges; roads and gates; ponds and moats; balks; boundary between Croydon and Tadlow parishes not shown; acreages given on table.

Border of 1 broad band with 1 narrow band on inside; title top left in a cartouche of red drapery with gold edges; yellow scale bar bottom left; compass rose top right showing 8 red, blue, yellow and green points. Table bottom right giving field names, acreages and land use for each parish. Left of table is a perspective drawing of the farmhouse. Fields outlined in green, arable coloured in yellow stripes, hedges coloured green, water coloured blue, buildings coloured red, roads coloured yellow.

'Leasehold' added later to 1 close in ink and pencil. Numbers on edges of map refer to adjacent sheets. This is number 13 in a volume of maps of the Downing estate. See also CRY75001–11, EAS75001–8 and TAD75001,3–9.

Tadlow – 1750 – TAD75003 – DCC

A Survey. of Tilton's Farm, In the Parish of Tadlow In the County of Cambridge The Estate of The Honble S*ir* Iacob Garrard Downing Brt By Jos. Cole 1750.

Surveyor: Joseph Cole; **Scale bar** 10–0–80 perches (= 5 1/2in.), 1:3,240; **Size:** (i) 17 13/16 x 22 11/16in.; **Top** is N; Manuscript(i), parchment, coloured.

Bridge ['Tilton's'] Farm, TL285466, and 243a.2r.10p. bounded by Guilden Morden and Steeple Morden [incorrectly called 'Shingay Lordship'] parishes in S and Wrestlingworth Parish [Bedfordshire] in NW.

Names of fields and parishes. Farm buildings shown in plan form. Closed fields showing owner's land; 'pyghtle'; trees; meadow; state of cultivation shown by colour; hedges; roads and gates; watercourses, ponds; balks; acreages given on table; orchard and bridge indicated by words.

Border of 1 broad band with 1 narrow band on inside; title centre top in a rococo cartouche with leaves and flowers and coloured red, blue, green, yellow and gold; yellow scale bar bottom right; compass rose bottom left showing 8 red, blue, yellow and green points. Table top right giving field names, land use and acreages of fields and lanes. Beneath compass rose is a perspective drawing of the farmhouse. Roads coloured yellow, water coloured blue, fields outlined

in green, arable coloured in yellow stripes, buildings coloured red, hedges coloured green.

'Leasehold' added later in ink and pencil on 2 fields. Numbers on edges of map refer to adjacent sheets. This is number 14 in a volume of maps of the Downing estate. See also CRY75001–11, EAS75001–8 and TAD75001–2,4–9.

Tadlow – 1750 – TAD75004 – DCC

A Survey. of Lunnis's Home Farm, In the Parish of Tadlow, and County of Cambridge. The Estate of S*ir* Iacob Garrard Downing Bart Surveyed by Jos. Cole 1750.

Surveyor: Joseph Cole; **Scale bar** 10–0–80 perches (= 5 11/16in.), 1:3,133; **Size:** (i) 20 5/8 x 13 15/16in.; **Top** is N; Manuscript(i), parchment, coloured.

100a.1r.3p. in TL2646, bounded by Guilden Morden Parish in S and Wrestlingworth Parish [Bedfordshire] in W.

Names of fields, parishes, roads and neighbouring owner. Farm buildings shown in plan form. Closed fields showing owner's land; trees; meadow; state of cultivation shown by colour; hedges; roads and gates; watercourses and ponds; balks; acreages given on table.

Border of 1 broad band with 1 narrow band on inside; title top left in a rococo cartouche with leaves and flowers and coloured red, green, purple and gold; yellow scale bar centre bottom; compass rose centre right showing 8 red, blue, yellow and green points. Table top right giving field names, acreages and land use. Bottom right is a perspective drawing of the farmhouse. Water coloured blue, hedges coloured green, fields outlined in green, arable coloured in yellow stripes, buildings coloured red, roads coloured yellow.

Numbers on edges of map refer to adjacent sheets. This is number 15 in a volume of maps of the Downing estate. See also CRY75001–11, EAS75001–8 and TAD75001–3,5–9.

Tadlow – 1750 – TAD75005 – DCC

A Survey. of Rich*d* Lunnis's, Stocks Farm In the Parish of Tadlow, and County of Cambridge. The Estate of S*ir* Jacob Garrard Downing Bart By Jos. Cole. 1750.

Surveyor: Joseph Cole; **Scale bar** 10–0–80 perches (= 5 5/8in.), 1:3,168; **Size:** (i) 20 3/4 x 13 15/16in.; **Top** is WNW; Manuscript(i), parchment, coloured.

137a.0r.7p. in TL2847, bounded by TAD75003 in S and TAD75001 in E.

Names of fields. Farm buildings shown in plan form. Closed fields showing owner's land; trees; state of cultivation shown by colour; hedges; roads and gates; orchards; ponds; balks; acreages given on table.

Border of 1 broad band with 1 narrow band on inside; title top left in a cartouche with purple drapery, green leaves, red flowers and gold decoration; yellow scale bar bottom left; compass rose centre left showing 8 red, blue, yellow and green points. Table top right giving field names, land use and acreages of fields and lanes. Above scale bar is a perspective drawing of the farmhouse. Roads coloured yellow, fields outlined in green, arable coloured in yellow stripes, trees and hedges coloured green, water coloured blue, buildings coloured red.

'Leasehold' written in ink and pencil on 1 close. Numbers on edges of map refer to adjacent sheets. This is number 16 in a volume of maps of the Downing estate. See also CRY75001–11, EAS75001–8 and TAD75001–4,6–9.

Tadlow – 1750 – TAD75006 – DCC

A Survey. of Swans Farm In the Parish of Tadlow, and County of Cambridge. The Estate of The Honble Sir Jacob Garrard Downing Brt By Ios. Cole 1750.

Surveyor: Joseph Cole; **Scale bar** 10–0–80 perches (= 5 11/16in.), 1:3,133; **Size:** (i) 22 3/4 x 16 5/16in.; **Top** is N; Manuscript(i), parchment, coloured.

Church ['Swans'] Farm, TL280475, and 298a.1r.31p. S of church, bounded by Wrestlingworth Parish [Bedfordshire] in W and TAD75005 in S.

Names of fields and parishes. Farm and vicarage shown in plan form, church shown in perspective. Closed fields showing owner's land; trees; state of cultivation shown by colour; hedges; roads and gates; ponds; balks; 'The Pightles'; acreages given on table.

Border of 1 broad band with 1 narrow band on inside; title top left in a rococo cartouche with purple drapery, green, red and blue leaves and flowers and gold ornament; yellow scale bar bottom right; compass rose bottom left showing 8 red, blue, yellow and green points. Table top right giving field names, land use and acreages of fields and lanes. Centre top is a perspective drawing of the farmhouse. Roads coloured yellow, fields outlined in green, arable coloured in yellow stripes, hedges and trees coloured green, water coloured blue, buildings coloured red.

Pencil notes. Numbers at edges of map refer to adjacent sheets. This is number 17 in a volume of maps of the Downing estate. See also CRY75001–11, EAS75001–8 and TAD75001–5,7–9.

Tadlow – 1750 – TAD75007 – DCC

A Survey. of the Tower Farm In the Parish of Tadlow In the County of Cambridge The Estate of The Honble Sir Jacob Garrard Downing Bt By Jos. Cole. 1750.

Surveyor: Joseph Cole; **Scale bar** 10–0–80 perches (= 5 5/8in.), 1:3,168; **Size:** (i) 20 15/16 x 14in.; **Top** is N; Manuscript(i), parchment, coloured.

Tadlow Tower Farm, TL284484, and 196a.2r.16p. bounded by TAD75006 in W, CRY75009 in E and TAD75002 in S.

Names of fields. Farm buildings shown in plan form. Closed fields showing owner's land; state of cultivation shown by colour; hedges showing hedgerow trees; gates; ponds; balks; acreages given on table.

Border of 1 broad band with 1 narrow band on inside; title top left in a rococo cartouche with leaves and flowers and coloured red, purple, blue, green, yellow and gold; yellow scale bar bottom left; compass rose above scale showing 8 red, blue, yellow and green points. Table bottom right giving field names, acreages and land use. Beneath title is a perspective drawing of the farmhouse. Buildings coloured red, water coloured blue, hedges coloured green, fields outlined in green, arable coloured in yellow stripes.

Numbers on edges of map refer to adjacent sheets. This is number 18 in a volume of maps of the Downing estate. See also CRY75001–11, EAS75001–8 and TAD75001–6,8–9.

Tadlow – 1750 – TAD75008 – DCC

A Survey. of New England Farm In the Parish of Tadlow In the County of Cambridge The Estate of The Honble Sir Iacob Garrard Downing Bart Surveyed By Jos. Cole. 1750.

Surveyor: Joseph Cole; **Scale bar** 10–0–80 perches (= 5 5/8in.), 1:3,168; **Size:** (i) 20 3/4 x 14 1/16in.; **Top** is E; Manuscript(i), parchment, coloured.

New England Farm, TL275485, and 191a.2r.26p. bounded by Cockayne Hatley Parish [Bedfordshire] in W and TAD75006 and TAD75007 in S.

Names of fields and parishes. Farm buildings shown in plan form. Closed fields showing owner's land; wood, 'Poplar Grove' and trees; state of cultivation shown by colour; hedges; gates; ponds; balks; acreages given on table.

Border of 1 broad band with 1 narrow band on inside; title top right in a rococo cartouche with leaves and flowers and coloured gold, purple, red, green and blue; yellow scale bar centre bottom; compass rose bottom left showing 8 red, blue, yellow and green points. Table middle left giving field names, acreages and land use. Above table is a perspective drawing of the farmhouse. Fields outlined in green, arable coloured in yellow stripes, water coloured blue, wood, trees and hedges coloured green, buildings coloured red.

Pencil notes. Numbers on edges of map refer to adjacent sheets. This is number 19 in a volume of maps of the Downing estate. See also CRY75001–11, EAS75001–8 and TAD75001–7,9.

Tadlow – 1750 – TAD75009 – DCC

A Survey of Pincote Dairy, in the Parish of Tadlow. and County of Cambridge. The Estate of Sir Iacob Garrard Downing Bart By Jos. Cole 1750.

Surveyor: Joseph Cole; **Scale bar** 10–0–80 perches (= 5 5/8in.), 1:3,168; **Size:** (i) 20 5/8 x 14 1/16in.; **Top** is N; Manuscript(i), parchment, coloured.

250a.2r.11p. in TL2749 and TL2750 bounded by Cockayne Hatley Parish [Bedfordshire] in W, Hatley St George Parish in N and TAD75008 in E and S.

Names of fields and parishes. 'Cow~house' shown in plan form. Closed fields showing owner's land; pightle; 'Pincote Wood' and trees; hedges; gates; watercourses, ponds and moats; acreages given on table.

Border of 1 broad band with 1 narrow band on inside; title top right in a rococo cartouche coloured red, green and purple; yellow scale bar bottom right; compass rose top left showing 8 red, blue, green and yellow points. Table above scale giving field names and acreages. Fields outlined in green, water coloured blue, wood, trees and hedges coloured green, building coloured red.

Pencil and ink notes. Numbers on edges of map refer to adjacent sheets. This is number 20 in a volume of maps of the Downing estate. See also CRY75001–11, EAS75001–8 and TAD75001–8.

Tadlow – 1832 – TAD83201 – KCC K81

Estate Tadlow In the County of Cambridge Belonging to the Provost & Scholars of Kings College as set out by the High Court of Chancery from the Estate of the late Sir Jacob Garrard Downing.

Surveyor: James Richardson; **Scale bar** 5–0–40 chains (= 7 1/2in.), 1:4,752; **Size:** (i) 38 3/16 x 25 3/8in.; **Top** is N; Manuscript(i), paper mounted on cloth, coloured.

Moat at TL284476, and 76a.2r.32p. in whole parish, bounded by Croydon Parish in E, Guilden and Steeple Morden parishes in S [incorrectly called Morden and

Shingay parishes] and Wrestlingworth and Cockayne Hatley parishes [Bedfordshire] in W.

Names of farms and neighbouring owners. Buildings shown in plan form and include 'Tadlow Tower Farm', 'Mr James Kings'', 'Mr Rich White' and 'Mr Jas Holders' [farms]; and cottages. Closed fields; wood and trees; hedges; state of cultivation shown by colour; acreages; roads, turnpike and footpaths; watercourses; gates; ponds and moat.

Border 3/16in. wide of 1 broad and 2 narrow bands; title at top with blue lettering of 'Estate Tadlow' and decorative line-work; scale at bottom; compass top right showing 8 points. Table top left with a border imitating a scroll of paper giving field names and acreages. Water coloured blue, roads coloured yellow, fields coloured green with brown strips at edges, parish boundary coloured red, lettering of parishes coloured blue and shadowed.

Teversham – [1688] – TEV68801 – GLC H1/ST/E107/5
['A Survey of Certaine Lands lyeing in the Parish of Teversham In the County of Cambridgeshire Being Lands belonging to St Thomas' Hospital Surveyed Anno Domini 1688 By Richard Browne'.] Number 1 [In 'Scales' and 'Priest Dicth' [sic.] furlongs.]
Surveyor: [Richard Browne]; **Scale bar** 40–0–10 perches (= 4 1/16in.), 1:2,467; **Size:** (ii) 14 x 16 1/4in.; **Top** is NW; Manuscript(i), parchment, coloured.
5a.2r.29p. in TL4956, bounded by 'Hinton~Fulbourn Way' in S.
Names of roads and neighbouring owners. Open fields showing owner's strips; acreages; roads; 'Preist Dicth' [sic.].
Title at top; scale bottom right; compass rose at top showing 4 plain points. Table bottom left giving acreages and furlongs. Strips coloured yellow.
In volume with title on 1st paper leaf. At end of volume is a note of total acreage, 129a.0r.24p., and: 'Note the 1th Figure or Map begins at the West Side of the Town and the 2th Map and so the Rest goes East in Order one from the other &c Note that about 30:Acres of the *said* 128A.3R.22P. are Inclosed'. See also TEV68802–7.

Teversham – [1688] – TEV68802 – GLC H1/ST/E107/5
Number II In Mill Field.
Surveyor: [Richard Browne]; **Scale:** 1:2,467; **Size:** (ii) 13 7/8 x 16in.; **Top** is SW; Manuscript(i), parchment, coloured.
6a.2r.16p. in TL4957, S of village.
Names of fields and neighbouring owners. Open fields showing owner's strips; acreages; roads.
Title at top; compass rose top left showing 4 plain points. Table bottom right giving acreages and furlongs. Strips coloured yellow.
Acreage has been corrected from 6a.0r.36p. In volume with title, date and surveyor on 1st paper leaf; see TEV68801 for details. See also TEV68803–7.

Teversham – [1688] – TEV68803 – GLC H1/ST/E107/5
Number III In Mill Field.
Surveyor: [Richard Browne]; **Scale:** 1:2,467; **Size:** (ii) 13 15/16 x 15 1/2in.; **Top** is W; Manuscript(i), parchment, coloured.
15a.2r.23p. in NW of TL4957, bounded by road from Cherry Hinton to Teversham in E, and S of village.

Names of fields, roads and neighbouring owners. House shown in perspective. Open fields showing owner's strips; 'Town land' adjoining map; acreages; roads; 'A Balke'; 'the Town Gate'.
Title at top; compass rose on right showing 4 plain points. Table top left giving acreages and furlongs. Strips coloured brown.
In volume with title, date and surveyor on 1st paper leaf; see TEV68801 for details. See also TEV68802,4–7.

Teversham – [1688] – TEV68804 – GLC H1/ST/E107/5
Number IIII this lyeth all in Causie Feild.
Surveyor: [Richard Browne]; **Scale bar** 80–0–10 perches (= 3 11/16in.), 1:4,833; **Size:** (ii) 13 1/2 x 15 9/16in.; **Top** is WNW; Manuscript(i), parchment, coloured.
25a.1r.30p. in TL4858, W of village.
Names of neighbouring owners. Open fields showing owner's strips; 'Town leys' adjoining this sheet; acreages; roads; 'Swans Bridge Close'.
Title top right; scale bottom right; compass rose bottom left showing 4 plain points. Tables top left and bottom right giving acreages and furlongs. Strips coloured brown.
In volume with title, date and surveyor on 1st paper leaf; see TEV68801 for details. See also TEV68802–3,5–7.

Teversham – [1688] – TEV68805 – GLC H1/ST/E107/5
Number V [In Teversham village N of TEV68803.]
Surveyor: [Richard Browne]; **Scale:** 1:2,467; **Size:** (ii) 13 15/16 x 17 1/8in.; **Top** is NNE; Manuscript(i), parchment, coloured.
Teversham Church, TL496585, and 17a.1r.7p. in village and to N.
Names of field, lands, buildings and neighbouring owners. Buildings shown in perspective and include houses, Teversham Church, manor house and barns. Open fields showing owner's strips; closes; crofts; 'Lamas Land'; common; state of cultivation given in words; 'Richards Meadow'; acreages; roads and watercourses; gates; moat; pond; tree in village; 'Town Gate'; churchyard wall.
Title top right; compass rose top left showing 4 plain points. Table bottom left giving acreages and furlongs. Closes outlined in yellow, strips coloured brown.
In volume with title, date and surveyor on 1st paper leaf; see TEV68801 for details. See also TEV68802–4,6–7.

Teversham – [1688] – TEV68806 – GLC H1/ST/E107/5
Number VI ['Fresh Lake Furlong' and 'Mannor Closes' E of TEV68805.]
Surveyor: [Richard Browne]; **Scale:** 1:2,467; **Size:** (ii) 13 13/16 x 15 3/8in.; **Top** is NNE; Manuscript(i), parchment, coloured.
24a.1r.23p. in TL5058, E of village.
Names of fields and neighbouring owners. House shown in perspective. Open fields showing owner's strips; closes; wood; acreages; roads and watercourses; Teversham Fen ['Fresh Lake Common or Fenn'] adjoins map to N.
Title top right; compass rose in centre showing 4 points. Table at bottom giving acreages and furlongs. Strips coloured yellow.
In volume with title, date and surveyor on 1st paper leaf; see TEV68801 for details. See also TEV68802–5,7.

Teversham – [1688] – TEV68807 – GLC H1/ST/E107/5
Number VII [S of 'Fresh Lake Fenn'.]

Surveyor: [Richard Browne]; **Scale:** 1:2,467; **Size:** (ii) 13 3/4 x 15 3/8in.; **Top** is N; Manuscript(i), parchment, coloured.

22a.1r.1p. in TL5158 in E of parish, S of Teversham ['Fresh Lake'] Fen.

Names of neighbouring owners. Open fields showing owner's strips; common; acreages; roads and watercourses.

Title top right; compass rose bottom right showing 4 plain points. Tables bottom right, bottom left and top right giving field names, acreages and furlongs. Strips coloured brown.

In volume with title, date and surveyor on 1st paper leaf; see TEV68801 for details. See also TEV68802–6.

Teversham – [c. 1772] – TEV77201 – GCC XV.25

['A Survey of a Farm called Dengains (belonging to Gonvel and Cajus College in Cambridge,) in the Parish of Teversham and County of Cambridge'.] [No. 1. 'Dengains Farm' in 'Mill Field'.]

Surveyor: [Joseph Freeman?]; **Scale:** 1:3,220; **Size:** (ii) 12 1/2 x 8in.; **Top** is E; Manuscript(ii), paper, coloured.

'Dengains Farm' and 47a.1r.22p., probably in TL4957 in 'Mill Field', bounded by road to Cherry Hinton in W.

Names of fields and neighbouring owners. Farm buildings shown in perspective. Open fields showing owner's strips; closes; wood and trees; fen; state of cultivation shown by colour; distances between strips; roads and gates; watercourses and ponds; gardens and orchards; hedges; moats.

'East' written at top of map. Table on facing page giving field names and acreages. Roads coloured brown, water coloured blue, farmhouse has a red roof, barns have yellow roofs, arable coloured in yellow stripes, trees coloured green.

Under table: 'Note, the Figures under the red dotted Lines are the Measured distance from each Piece for Instance the 12 Rood is 86 Links from the 8 Acre Balk on the East side of the Road and 609 Links from the Acre in the Same Furlong'. This is number 1 in a volume of maps showing 142a.3r.30p. in Teversham Parish. Probably surveyed by Joseph Freeman, who was paid for surveying and mapping Teversham in the half year ending at Lady Day 1773, and Mr Gee was paid for transcribing the survey in the half year ending at Michaelmas 1777 [GCC Bursar's Book 1758–75 and 1775–91]. Title taken from beginning of volume. CAX77201 is also copied into volume. See also TEV77202–14.

Teversham – [c. 1772] – TEV77202 – GCC XV.25

[Land in 'Mill Field', Teversham, owned by Gonville and Caius College, Cambridge.]

Surveyor: [Joseph Freeman?]; **Scale:** 1:3,170; **Size:** (ii) 12 1/2 x 8in.; **Top** is E; Manuscript(ii), paper, coloured.

2a.0r.30p. in 'Mill Field', probably in TL4957, bounded by 'Priest Ditch' in E, 'Mallards Hedge' in S and 'Garland Green' in N.

Names of fields, features and neighbouring owners. Open fields showing owner's strips; state of cultivation shown by colour; distances between strips; 'Priest Ditch'; 'Mallards Hedge'.

'East' written at top of map. Table on facing page giving acreages and bounds of land. Water coloured blue, arable coloured in yellow stripes.

This is number 2 in a volume of maps; see TEV77201 for details. See also TEV77203–14.

Teversham – [c. 1772] – TEV77203 – GCC XV.25

[Land in 'Mill Field', Teversham, owned by Gonville and Caius College, Cambridge.]

Surveyor: [Joseph Freeman?]; **Scale:** 1:2,600; **Size:** (ii) 12 1/2 x 8in.; **Top** is S; Manuscript(ii), paper, coloured.

1a.0r.26p. in 'Fulburn Crosses' in 'Mill Field', probably in TL4956, bounded by road from Fulburn to Cherry Hinton in S and 'Garland Green' in E.

Names of fields, headlands, road and neighbouring owners. Open fields showing owner's strips; state of cultivation shown by colour; distances between strips; road.

'South' written at top of map. Table on facing page giving acreages. Road coloured brown, arable coloured in yellow stripes.

This is number 3 in a volume of maps; see TEV77201 for details. See also TEV77202,4–14.

Teversham – [c. 1772] – TEV77204 – GCC XV.25

[Land in 'Mill Field', Teversham, owned by Gonville and Caius College, Cambridge.]

Surveyor: [Joseph Freeman?]; **Scale:** 1:3,330; **Size:** (ii) 12 1/2 x 8in.; **Top** is S; Manuscript(ii), paper, coloured.

3a.0r.13p. in 'Fulburn Crosses' in 'Mill Field', probably in TL4956, bounded by Fulbourn Parish in S and extending N and S of road from Fulburn to Cherry Hinton.

Names of fields, headlands, road and neighbouring owners. Open fields showing owner's strips; state of cultivation shown by colour; balks; distances between strips; road.

'South.' written at top of map. Table on facing page giving acreages and bounds of 1 strip. Road coloured brown, arable coloured in yellow stripes, balks coloured green.

This is number 4 in a volume of maps; see TEV77201 for details. See also TEV77202–3,5–14.

Teversham – [c. 1772] – TEV77205 – GCC XV.25

[Land in 'Mill Field', Teversham, owned by Gonville and Caius College, Cambridge.]

Surveyor: [Joseph Freeman?]; **Scale:** 1:3,100; **Size:** (ii) 12 1/2 x 8in.; **Top** is E; Manuscript(ii), paper, coloured.

13a.3r.5p. in 'Frith Furlong' in 'Mill Field', probably in TL4957, bounded by Cherry Hinton Parish in S, and including 6a.0r.25p. in 'Causey Field'.

Names of fields and neighbouring owners. Open fields showing owner's strips; close; state of cultivation shown by colour; distances between strips; balks; hedges; 'Marsh Ditch'.

'East.' written at top of map. Table on facing page giving acreages. Water coloured blue, arable coloured in yellow stripes, close outlined in green, balks coloured green.

This is number 5 in a volume of maps; see TEV77201 for details. See also TEV77202–4,6–14.

Teversham – [c. 1772] – TEV77206 – GCC XV.25

[Land in 'Causey Field', Teversham, owned by Gonville and Caius College, Cambridge.]

Surveyor: [Joseph Freeman?]; Scale: 1:3,300; Size: (ii) 12 1/2 x 8in.; Top is S; Manuscript(ii), paper, coloured.

9a.2r.6p. in 'Causey Field', probably in TL4858, bounded by Cherry Hinton Parish in S.

Names of fields, roads, headlands and neighbouring owners. Open fields showing owner's strips; state of cultivation shown by colour; roads; distances between strips; 'Kings Bush'; drain.

'South.' written at top of map. Table on facing page giving acreages in each furlong. Roads coloured brown, arable coloured in yellow stripes, hedges and bush coloured green.

This is number 6 in a volume of maps; see TEV77201 for details. See also TEV77202–5,7–14.

Teversham – [c. 1772] – TEV77207 – GCC XV.25

[Land in 'Causey Field', Teversham, owned by Gonville and Caius College, Cambridge.]

Surveyor: [Joseph Freeman?]; Scale: 1:3,190; Size: (ii) 12 1/2 x 8in.; Top is S; Manuscript(ii), paper, coloured.

1a.3r.32p. in 'Clare Ditch Furlong' in 'Causey Field', probably in TL4859, bounded by Fen Ditton Parish in N.

Names of fields, headlands and neighbouring owners. Open fields showing owner's strips; state of cultivation shown by colour; road; balks; distances between strips.

'South' written at top of map. Table on facing page giving acreages and bounds of strips. Road coloured brown, arable coloured in yellow stripes, balks coloured green.

This is number 7 in a volume of maps; see TEV77201 for details. See also TEV77202–6,8–14.

Teversham – [c. 1772] – TEV77208 – GCC XV.25

[Land in 'Causey Field', Teversham, owned by Gonville and Caius College, Cambridge.]

Surveyor: [Joseph Freeman?]; Scale: 1:3,820; Size: (ii) 12 1/2 x 8in.; Top is N; Manuscript(ii), paper, coloured.

3r.7p. in 'Pond Furlong' and 'Widdows Dole' in 'Causey Field', probably in TL4858, bounded by Cherry Hinton Parish in S.

Names of fields, headlands and neighbouring owners. Open fields showing owner's strips; state of cultivation shown by colour; distances between strips.

'North' written at top of map. Table on facing page giving acreages and bounds of 1 strip. Arable coloured in yellow stripes.

This is number 8 in a volume of maps; see TEV77201 for details. See also TEV77202–7,9–14.

Teversham – [c. 1772] – TEV77209 – GCC XV.25

[Land in 'Causey Field', Teversham, owned by Gonville and Caius College, Cambridge.]

Surveyor: [Joseph Freeman?]; Scale: 1:3,300; Size: (ii) 12 1/2 x 8in.; Top is N; Manuscript(ii), paper, coloured.

41a.3r.24p. in 'Hole in the Field Furlong' in 'Causey Field', probably in TL4859, bounded by road from Cambridge to Newmarket in N.

Names of fields and neighbouring owners. Open fields showing owner's strips; state of cultivation shown by colour; road; balks; distances between strips.

'North' written at top of map. Table on facing page giving acreages. Road coloured brown, balks coloured green, arable coloured in yellow stripes.

This is number 9 in a volume of maps; see TEV77201 for details. See also TEV77202–8,10–14.

Teversham – [c. 1772] – TEV77210 – GCC XV.25

[Land in 'Causey Field', Teversham, owned by Gonville and Caius College, Cambridge.]

Surveyor: [Joseph Freeman?]; Scale: 1:3,030; Size: (ii) 12 1/2 x 8in.; Top is N; Manuscript(ii), paper, coloured.

6a.2r.7p. in 'Long', 'Short' and 'Rushbush' furlongs in 'Causey Field', probably in TL4859, crossed E–W by 'Cambridge Road to Newmarket Alias Dr Harvey's Charity', and bounded by 'Green Way' in E and Fen Ditton Parish in N.

Names of fields, headlands, roads and neighbouring owners. Open fields showing owner's strips; state of cultivation shown by colour; roads; distances between strips; balks and 'Procession Balk'.

'North.' written at top of map. Table on facing page giving acreages in each furlong and bounds of 1 strip. Roads coloured brown, arable coloured in yellow stripes, balks coloured green.

This is number 10 in a volume of maps; see TEV77201 for details. See also TEV77202–9,11–14.

Teversham – [c. 1772] – TEV77211 – GCC XV.25

[Land in 'Brook Field', Teversham, owned by Gonville and Caius College, Cambridge.]

Surveyor: [Joseph Freeman?]; Scale: 1:3,780; Size: (ii) 12 1/2 x 8in.; Top is E; Manuscript(ii), paper, coloured.

12a.1r.16p. in 'Brook Field', probably in TL5058, bounded by Fen Ditton Parish in N and 'Freslake Fen' in S.

Names of fields, headlands and neighbouring owners. Open fields showing owner's strips; closes; trees; state of cultivation shown by colour; distances between strips; balks; hedges; 'New Ditch'.

'East.' written at top of map. Table on facing page giving acreages and land use in each furlong. Arable coloured in yellow stripes, pasture outlined in green, trees and balks coloured green.

This is number 11 in a volume of maps; see TEV77201 for details. See also TEV77202–10,12–14.

Teversham – [c. 1772] – TEV77212 – GCC XV.25

[Land in 'Mill Ditch Field', Teversham, owned by Gonville and Caius College, Cambridge.]

Surveyor: [Joseph Freeman?]; Scale: 1:3,550; Size: (ii) 12 1/2 x 8in.; Top is S; Manuscript(ii), paper, coloured.

12a.1r.26p. in 'Cote', 'Middle' and 'Freslake' furlongs in 'Mill Ditch Field', probably in TL5058, bounded by 'Road through the Town' in W and 'Freslake Fen' in N.

Names of fields, roads and neighbouring owners. Open fields showing owner's strips; closes; state of cultivation shown by colour; distances between strips; balks; hedges.

'South.' written at top of map. Table on facing page giving acreages in each furlong. Arable coloured in yellow stripes, roads coloured brown, balks coloured green, fen outlined in green.

This is number 12 in a volume of maps; see TEV77201 for details. See also TEV77202–11,13–14.

Teversham – [c. 1772] – TEV77213 – GCC XV.25

[Land in 'Mill Ditch Field', Teversham, owned by Gonville and Caius College, Cambridge.]

Surveyor: [Joseph Freeman?]; **Scale:** 1:6,100; **Size:** (ii) 12 1/2 x 8in.; **Top** is W; Manuscript(ii), paper, coloured.

23a.0r.14p. in 'Mill Ditch Field', probably in TL5158, bounded by 'Fishouse Fen' in N, Wilbraham Fen in NE, 'Fulburn Fen' in S and 'Mill Ditch' in W, and crossed E–W by 'Mill Ditch Way'.

Names of fields, fens, roads and neighbouring owners. Open fields showing owner's strips; state of cultivation shown by colour; roads; 'Mill Ditch'; balks; distances between strips.

'West,' written at top of map. Table on facing page giving acreages in each furlong. Roads coloured brown, water coloured blue, fen outlined in green, balks coloured green, arable coloured in yellow stripes.

This is number 13 in a volume of maps; see TEV77201 for details. See also TEV77202–12,14.

Teversham – [c. 1772] – TEV77214 – GCC XV.25

[Land in 'Riches Meadow', Teversham, owned by Gonville and Caius College, Cambridge.]

Surveyor: [Joseph Freeman?]; **Scale:** 1:2,990; **Size:** (ii) 12 1/2 x 8in.; **Top** is S; Manuscript(ii), paper, coloured.

3r.2p. in 'Riches Meadow', probably in TL4958, bounded by 'Church Field' and a watercourse in N.

Names of fields and neighbouring owners. Open fields showing owner's strips; watercourse; hedges.

'South,' written at top of map. Table on facing page giving acreages. Water coloured blue, plots outlined in green.

Note beneath table giving neighbouring owners in the meadow and: 'Note, these are Equally divided'. This is number 14 in a volume of maps; see TEV77201 for details. See also TEV77202–13.

Teversham – 1812 – TEV81201 – GCC Drawer 1 Map 1 (Teversham)

Plan of the Estates at Teversham in the County of Cambridge, belonging to the Master Fellows and Scholars of Gonville and Caius College in the University of Cambridge. Made AD 1812, By Alexdr Watford.

Surveyor: Alexander Watford [jr]; **Scale:** 1:4,730; **Size:** (i) 22 1/8 x 14 1/4in.; **Top** is NE; Manuscript(i), parchment, coloured.

Manor Farm, TL501578, and 218a.2r.22p. E of church bounded by Fulburn Parish in E, Cherry Hinton Parish in S and road from Teversham to Fulburn in N.

Names of tenants, neighbouring owners and roads. Manor Farm and cottages shown in plan form, church shown in perspective. Closed fields showing owner's land; acreages; roads and watercourses; hedges; 'Caudle Head'; moat; reasons for allotments.

Border of 1 broad band with 1 narrow band on inside; title centre top; compass bottom left showing 8 points. Tables bottom left below compass and bottom right giving tenants, field names and acreages. Roads coloured yellow, hedges coloured green, buildings coloured red, water coloured blue.

Pencil notes and grid.

Teversham – 1813 – TEV81301 – CRO P153/25/21

Plan of The Charity Allotment at Teversham.

Surveyor: Thomas Pursell; **Scale bar** 1–0–9 chains (= 3 5/16in.), 1:2,391; **Size:** (i) 6 9/16 x 9 7/8in.; **Top** is NW; Manuscript(i), paper, coloured.

11a.0r.5p. in TL4859 in N of parish, bounded by road from Cambridge to Newmarket in S and Fen Ditton Parish in N.

Names of fields, owner, neighbouring owners and parish. Closed fields; acreages; width of land between 2 boundary lines; roads; hedges.

Border of 2 narrow bands; title top left with decorative line-work; scale bottom right; compass top right showing 4 points with a decorated N. Cuffed hand points to Cambridge. Roads coloured brown, boundaries coloured red and blue.

Note under title: 'N.B. The Red Line is the proper Boundary – and not the Blue Line where Walker has placed the Fence'. 2 pencil notes of dimensions.

Teversham – 1824 – TEV82401 – PCC Teversham A17

Sketch of Estate at Teversham drawn by Mr Watford our Surveyor, in 1824.

Surveyor: [Alexander] Watford [jr]; **Scale:** 1:4,980; **Size:** (i) 12 3/8 x 7 9/16in.; **Top** is NE; Manuscript(iv), tracing paper, uncoloured.

c. 110a. in SE of TL4958, bounded by roads to Cherry Hinton in SW and to Fulbourn in NE.

Names of roads and neighbouring owners. Buildings shown in plan form. Closed fields showing owner's land; acreage of 1 field; roads; watercourses and public drain; responsibility for boundaries; hedges; orchard; reasons for allotments; tenure.

Border of 1 narrow band; title at top; compass top left showing 4 plain points.

Numbers on fields refer to inclosure award. Estate owned by Pembroke College, Cambridge. Surveyor's 1st name was Alexander [Eden W141.1]. See also TEV82402, a similar map accompanied by a valuation.

Teversham – [1824] – TEV82402 – PCC LE p.79

[Estate at Teversham, owned by Pembroke College, Cambridge.]

Surveyor: [Alexander Watford jr]; **Scale:** 1:2,790; **Size:** (iii) 9 1/2 x 3 1/4in.; **Top** is NE; Manuscript(ii), paper, uncoloured.

60a.2r.17p. in SE of TL4958, in S of village.

Names of areas and neighbouring owners. Homestead shown in plan form. Closed fields; acreages; roads; orchard; responsibility for boundaries; subdivision of allotments.

Compass top left showing 4 points.

Note bottom left: 'This is an exact copy of Mr Watfords Plan. He was a Commissioner of the Inclosure' [either TEV82401, which shows a field of 55a.1r.22p. and other areas, or map by Alexander Watford which accompanied 1815 inclosure award]. This map accompanies: 'A Valuation of an Estate belonging to the Master & Fellows of Pembroke Hall & Situate at Teversham in Cambridgeshire in the occupation of W.J. Foote. by Mr Alexr Watford. March 10. 1824. Cambridge'.

Thorney – [c. 1609] – THO60901 – HRO LR24/370

A description of the groundes of Thornea Abbey with their seuueral contents by statute measure set downe within them ...

Scale bar 0–320 perches = 0–8 furlongs (= 3 7/8in.), 1:16,350; **Size:** (i) 22 1/4 x 28in.; **Top** is S; Manuscript(i), paper mounted on cloth, uncoloured.

Thorney Abbey, TF282042, and c. 18,000a. in whole parish.

Names of fens, closes and roads. Thorney Abbey, houses and a windmill shown in perspective. Fen; acreages; roads and watercourses; bridges.

Border of 2 narrow bands; title bottom right in a cartouche of 2 plain rectangles; 3-dimensional scale bar middle bottom surmounted by dividers.

Writing very feint and map is damaged. Catalogue in HRO suggests date of 1609. Land owned by Edward Russell, 3rd Earl of Bedford [*VCH*, 4, 221]. Positive and negative photostats at CUL Maps.bb.66.95.11–14 and CRO R86/112.

Thorney – 1652 – THO65201 – BRO R1/144A

The true Platt and Linear Description of the Mannor of Thorney Abbey in the Isle of Ely and Countie of Cambridge being the Inheritance and Possession of the Right Honourble the Earle of Bedford with the Content and quantity of everie particular parcell of Highground and Fenn land thereto belonginge according to a Survey and admensurement thereof made Anno Domini 1652 per me Benj: Hare.

Surveyor: Benjamin Hare; **Scale bar** 0–320 perches (= 7 7/8in.), 1:8,046; **Size:** (i) 47 1/2 x 59 1/4in.; **Top** is N; Manuscript(i), parchment, coloured.

Thorney Church, TF282042, and c. 18,000a. in whole parish.

Names of fields, fen, dykes and droves. Houses, church and Toneham Farm ['Tonam hous'] shown in perspective. Fields; fen; wood and trees; 'Deere parke'; acreages; roads and gates; watercourses; dyke and drains; 'Ashly poole'; 'Thorney Mill Bridge'; pump; 'Thorney' and 'Knarr' crosses; decoy.

Border 15/16in. wide with red and yellow shells on a green background; title top left in a strapwork cartouche with *putti* and flowers and coloured red, yellow and green; yellow scale bar surmounted by dividers bottom left, with yellow shells and decoration; compass rose middle left showing 32 red, yellow, green and blue points. 5th [*PB*, 226] Earl of Bedford's coat of arms above title. Water coloured blue, roads coloured brown, fields outlined in green, blue and yellow, trees coloured green, buildings have red roofs except for church which is coloured yellow with a blue roof, gold lettering.

Bottom right in a strapwork cartouche with fruit and flowers and coloured red, yellow, green and blue: 'Note that such Grounds as are shadowed about with the Seagreene colour and devided with the Yellow are all Fenn~lands. those with the Sapp greene Highlands and fenn skirts; the Rivers and cheife Draynes with the Azure, and the Highwaies & droves with the Russett'. Numbers on plots refer to terrier in CRO: 'The Survey of the Mannor of Thorney in the Isle of Ely and County of Cambridge being the possession of the Right Honble William Earle of Bedford with the Content & Quantity of every particular parcell thereto belonging haueing relacon to a Mapp or Plott thereof drawne whereby this more plainly Appeareth

Taken Anno Domini 1652 per me Benj: Hare'. At end of terrier is note: 'surveyed, at 16 1/2 feet to the Pole'. Copy measuring 46 7/8 x 58 3/8in. at BRO R1/144B, with: 'Transcribed per Tho: Gressam Anno Domini 1710' added at end of title. Buildings coloured yellow. Copyist was probably Thomas Gresham [Eden G291].

Thorney – [Early 18th century] – THO70001 – BRO R1/298

[Thorney Lordship, owned by Wriothesley Russell, 2nd Duke of Bedford.]

Scale: 1:19,000; **Size:** (ii) 18 1/8 x 22in.; **Top** is N; Manuscript(i), paper mounted on cloth, uncoloured.

c. 18,000a. in whole parish and in 'BasingHall Moor' in N of Whittlesey Parish; Thorney Church, which is not shown, is at TF282042.

Names of fen, closes, drove, dykes and some occupiers. Houses and farm buildings shown in plan form. Roads; watercourses; decoy.

Note bottom left about land in 'BasingHall Moor': 'N.B. This is opposite Cross Thorney Dike to Pieces N4 & 012.12.15 no XLIV but omitted there for want of Room'. Numbers on plots suggest map originally accompanied by a terrier. Top left corner missing. Some droves are hatched rather than shown in ink wash. Drawn in early 18th century.

Thorney – 1728 – THO72801 – BLO Gough Maps 2 11B

A Plan of the Town of Thorney in the Isle of Ely, Com: Cantab. Belonging to the most Noble Wriothsley Duke of Bedford. Surveyed by John Sanderson, 1728.

Surveyor: John Sanderson; **Scale bar** 300–0 feet (= 2 1/2in.), 1:1,440; **Size:** (ii) 13 1/4 x 11 9/16in.; **Top** is NNW; Manuscript(i), paper, uncoloured.

Thorney Abbey, TF282042, and c. 27a. in town.

Buildings shown in plan form, Thorney Abbey, houses, barns, ale house, shed, shop and offices all identified on table. Roads; watercourses and bridge; walls; market cross.

Title bottom left in a cartouche of a tombstone with human figures; scale bottom right in a rustic scene; compass rose centre left showing 8 points. 3rd [*PB*, 226] Duke of Bedford's coat of arms bottom right with the scale. Table bottom right with a border imitating a scroll of paper, identifying buildings. Top left is a view of W front of Abbey, top right: 'A Plan for building the Town in a regular manner'.

Note above table explaining symbols and 'The Middle Isle of the Abby yet left standing'. Note beneath table: 'NB That all the Houses are double Hatched, the Barns, Turf Sheds, Hovels, &c single Hatched'. Engraved version of map, signed 'Gerrd Vander Gucht sculp*sit*', at BLO Gough Maps 2 12B. Border of 1 narrow band, vignette of W front of Abbey has no people.

Thorney – 1731/2 – THO73201 – BRO R1/145

A Map of the Mannor or Lordship of Thorney in the Isle of Ely and County of Cambridge Estate of the most Noble Wriothesley Duke of Bedford As the same was Actually Surveyed and Drawn in the Year 1731, and 1732. By John Halsey.

Surveyor: John Halsey; **Scale bar** 2–0–39 chains (= 6 3/4in.), 1:4,811, Scale bar 10–0–130 poles (= 6 3/4in.), 1:4,107; **Size:** (i) 79 1/8 x 85 1/2in.; **Top** is N; Manuscript(i), parchment, coloured.

Blue Bell Bridge, TF276082, and c. 18,000a. in whole parish and in 'Bassinghall Moore' in N of Whittlesey Parish.

Names of fields, fen, droves and neighbouring owners. 'French School' and homesteads shown in plan form, windmills shown in perspective. Fields; fen; acreages of fields and droves and number of pieces; roads; watercourses; dykes; bank; holts; pightles; 'Deer Park', 'The Hay Park'; 'Knarr' and 'Thorney' crosses; 'Stack Yard'; 'Vesey's Corner'; decoy; 'Anchors Bridge' and 'Blue Bell' [bridge].

Border 5/8in. wide, coloured red, yellow and green and marked in furlongs and miles [1 furlong = 1 5/8in., 1:4,874]; title top left; scale bottom left. Droves coloured green, fields outlined in green, buildings coloured red, water coloured blue.

Numbers on plots suggest map originally accompanied by a terrier. Pencil notes. Ink notes on scale indicating that poles are 16 1/2 feet, and adding arks for 18-foot poles. Land owned by 3rd Duke of Bedford [*PB*, 226].

Thorney – [1738] – THO73801 – BRO R5/4007
A Map of the Lordship of Thorney the Estate of his Grace the Duke of Bedford.

A **Scale** of Furlongs and Miles NB 10 Chains is a Furlong, Scale bar 0–2 miles (= 6 1/4in.), 1:20,280; **Size:** (ii) 20 7/8 x 24in.; **Top** is N; Manuscript(i), paper mounted on paper, coloured.

c. 18,000a. in whole parish and in 'Bassinghall Moore' in N of Whittlesey Parish; Thorney Church, which is not shown, is at TF282042.

Names of fields, fen and droves. Farms and 'new Inn' shown in plan form. Fields; pightles; fen; wood; number of pieces of land; roads and droves; watercourses and dyke; bank; decoy; 'Deer Park'; 'Knarr Cross'.

Title top left in a cartouche with reeds, fish and flowers and coloured red, blue and green; scale bottom left; compass rose centre top showing 8 red, yellow, green and pink points. Duke of Bedford's coat of arms above title. Fields coloured brown, green, pink, red, blue, orange and yellow.

Pencil notes. Accompanies: 'An Explanation of the following Particulars of the Pieces of Ground in the Lordship of Thorney as described in a Map at the End of this Book The 1st Column on the left hand contains a Series of Numbers in Roman Characters with the general Name of each Fen &c referring to the The 2d Column shews the Letters of the Alphabet into which most of the foregoing Numbers are divided the 3d Column Shews the Number of Pieces into which each Letter is Subdivided The 4th Column shews the Number of Acres each Piece contains, The 5th Column is a Continued series in Arithmetical Progression from 1 to 1499 which are also expressid in the Margin of the Tenants particular Accompt in order to refer here and to the Map the 6th Column shews the Names of the Tenants who rent each Piece of Ground from Lady Day 1738 & to whom from time to time the same was transferred NB LD stands for Lady Day & Mi stands for Michalmass'; on cover: 'Thorney Ledger from Lady Day 1738 To Lady Day 1755'. Land owned by John Russell, 4th Duke of Bedford [*PB*, 226].

Thorney – [1749] – THO74901 – PRO MPE 741
An exact Map ... The Honourable the Earl, of Lincolns ... Low Borough Fen ... Four Hundred Acres in the Manor ... Crowland, And ... New South Eau ... Ely [and land belonging to 4th Duke of Bedford in Thorney Fen.]

Surveyor: [John Grundy]; **Scale bar** 0–2 furlongs (= 5 1/4in.), 1:3,017; **Size:** (i) 16 7/8 x 23 5/8in.; **Top** is N; Manuscript(i), parchment, coloured.

Singlesole Farm, TF256070, and c. 270a. to E, extending into Crowland Parish [Lincolnshire].

Names of farms, fields, fen and neighbouring owners. Buildings shown in perspective and include farm buildings, cottages, 'Low~Borough Fen Engine' and 'Engines'. Closed fields; common; fen; roads and droves; watercourses; drains; dyke; bank; hedges; bridges.

Border of 1 broad band with 1 narrow band on inside; title centre bottom; scale bottom left; compass bottom right showing 4 points. Earl of Lincoln's land outlined in green, 'Corporation Bank' coloured red.

Note centre top: 'Explanation. The Levells are incerted in the Red Circles which are placed on the part to which the said Levells are taken and are all of them compared with the primary Observations (which is on the Medium point of Land in Low Borough Fen behind the Engine) Those on the Drains are in two Columns the Upper of which denotes the Rise or Fall of that Particular point from the Primary one and is taken to the Surface of the Water, the Lower Column is the Depth of the Water in that point. NB R signifies Rise and F. Fall. – The Corporation Bank is described by Red and the Right Honble the Earl of Lincolns Land by Green'. Title very rubbed. Surveyor and date taken from PRO map catalogue. Land owned by Henry Fiennes Clinton, 9th Earl of Lincoln [*PB*, 1,961] and John Russell, 4th Duke of Bedford [*PB*, 226].

Thorney – [Mid-18th century] – THO75001 – CRO R77/38
['Plan of Thorney Lordshipp'.]

Scale: 1:33,700; **Size:** (ii) 13 1/8 x 16 5/8in.; **Top** is N; Manuscript(i), paper, coloured.

c. 18,000a. in whole parish; Thorney Church, which is not shown, is at TF282042.

Names of fields, fen, drains, droves and drainage engines. Fen; acreages; droves; drains; 'Knarr cross'; engines 'which have been used this season'; engines 'rendered useless'; 'places from whence Engines were removed by Mr Butchers order's'; 'places to which they [engines] were removed'.

Table centre top giving key to symbols for engines and the 'Successive order in which these remarks should be read'. Land outlined in yellow and red, symbols for engines which have worked this season coloured red.

Extensive notes around map of need to alter distribution of engines to improve drainage, and plan and costs of implementing changes. Title on dorse. Land owned by 4th Duke of Bedford. Drawn in mid-18th century; Robert Butcher was the Duke's Agent-in-chief c. 1738–71 [BRO Catalogue of Russell Estate Records].

Thorney – 1752–3 – THO75301 – BRO R1/146
An Actual Survey of the Mannor and Lordship of Thorney in the Isle of Ely and County of Cambridge Belonging to The Most Noble Iohn Duke of Bedford Taken in 1752 & 1753 By Vincent Wing.

Surveyor: Vincent Wing; **A Scale** of Gunters Chains 80 in a Statute Mile, A Scale of Perches 18[?] feet to a Perch, Scale bar 10–0–80 chains (= 11 1/4in.), 1:6,336; **Size:** (i) 57 3/4 x [65]in.; **Top** is N; Manuscript(i), paper mounted on cloth, coloured.

Thorney Church, TF282042, and c. 18,000a. in whole parish.

Names of fields, fen and watercourses. Farm buildings and church shown in plan form, windmills shown in perspective. Fields; fen; waste; 'Stray Pasture'; trees; acreages and number of pieces; roads; watercourses; hedges; 'Stack Yard'; pightle; 'Thorney', 'Tarketuls' and 'St Vincents' crosses; 'Charters Corner'.

Border of 1 broad band with 1 narrow band on either side; title top left in a rococo cartouche with leaves, flowers and shell ornament and coloured blue, green, red, yellow and pink; scale bottom left; compass rose under title showing 16 points and 'Variation 17° Westerly'. Duke of Bedford's coat of arms above title. Buildings coloured red.

Map very fragile, only western half, which measures 57 3/4 x 32 3/4in., could be consulted. Numbers on plots refer to terrier [BRO R2/140]: 'Index to the Map of Thorney Lordship with the Tenants Names &c at Lady Day 1753', which describes land and gives acreages and tenants. THO76701 based on this map.

Thorney – 1756 – THO75601 – BRO R1/147
A Map of the Lordship of Thorney.
Surveyor: A[lexander] Hughes; **Scale:** 1:19,300; **Size:** (i) 18 1/8 x 22 3/16in.; **Top** is N; Manuscript(iii), paper mounted on cloth, coloured.
17,631a.1r.38p. in whole parish; Thorney Church, which is not shown, is at TF282042.
Names of fields, fen, dykes, droves and roads. Houses and farm buildings shown in plan form, windmills shown in perspective. Fields; pasture; number of pieces of land; roads and droves; watercourses, dykes and bank; holt; hedges; 'Knar', 'Thorney', 'St Vincents' and 'Turketuls' crosses; decoy; 'Deer Park'; 'Lordship Corner'; ponds.
Border of 1 broad band with 1 narrow band on inside; title bottom left; compass top left showing 16 points. 4th [*PB*, 226] Duke of Bedford's coat of arms above compass. Water coloured blue, fields outlined in green and yellow, buildings coloured red, hedges coloured green.
Numbers on plots suggest map originally accompanied by a terrier, perhaps that at BRO R2/141 which has: 'An Index to the Survey of Thorney Lordship from Lady Day 1756' on cover but: 'The Particulars of a Survey of the Lordship of Thorney, taken in the Years 1752 and 1753' as title on inside. Surveyor's 1st name was Alexander; in 1756 he was clerk to John Wing, Agent for Thorney [BRO R5/4008]. See also THO75602–3.

Thorney – [1756] – THO75602 – BRO R1/148
[Thorney Lordship, owned by 4th Duke of Bedford.]
Surveyor: [Alexander Hughes]; **Scale:** 1:19,700; **Size:** (i) 17 3/4 x 21 5/16in.; **Top** is N; Manuscript(iii), paper mounted on cloth, coloured.
17,631a.1r.38p. in whole parish; Thorney Church, which is not shown, is at TF282042.
Names of fields, fen, roads, droves and dykes. Houses and farm buildings shown in plan form, windmills shown in perspective. Fields; waste; pasture; trees; number of pieces of land; roads and droves; watercourses and dykes; bank; ponds; holt; hedges; 'Thorney', 'Knar', 'St. Vincents' and 'Turktuls' crosses; 'Lordship Corner'; decoy; 'Deer Park'.
Border of 1 broad band with 1 narrow band on inside; scale middle left; compass rose top right showing 16

points. Water coloured blue, buildings coloured red, fields outlined in green and yellow.
Inset top left: 'An exact Plan of the Town of Thorney', at a 'Scale of Gunter's Chains, 10 to a Furlong', scale bar 1–0–6 chains (= 2 5/16in.), 1:2,397. Shows roads, river and following buildings in plan form and coloured grey: 'Dukes Head Inn', 'Hall', office, church and churchyard, and 'Shambles'. Numbers on plots suggest map originally accompanied by a terrier, perhaps that at BRO R2/141 [see THO75601 for details]; it does not refer to numbers on plots in inset. Map is very similar to THO75601 and THO75603, drawn by Alexander Hughes in 1756 [see THO75601].

Thorney – 1756 – THO75603 – BRO R1/299
A Map of the Lordship of Thorney.
Surveyor: A[lexander] H[ughes]; **Scale:** 1:19,700; **Size:** (i) 17 15/16 x 24 1/8in.; **Top** is N; Manuscript(iii), paper mounted on cloth, coloured.
17,631a.1r.38p. in whole parish; Thorney Church, which is not shown, is at TF282042.
Names of fields, fen, droves, roads and dyke. Farm buildings and houses shown in plan form, windmills shown in perspective. Fields; waste; pasture; number of pieces of land; roads and droves; watercourses; dyke; bank; holt; hedges; 'Thorney', 'Knar', 'Turketuls' and 'St. Vincents' crosses; 'Lordship Corner'; decoy; 'Deer Park'; 'Martins Hill'; ponds.
Border of 1 broad band with 1 narrow band on either side; title top left; compass rose beneath title showing 16 points. Water coloured blue, buildings coloured red, fields outlined in green and yellow, hedges coloured yellow.
Numbers on plots suggest map originally accompanied by a terrier, perhaps that at BRO R2/141 [see THO75601 for details]. Land owned by John Russell, 4th Duke of Bedford. Surveyor was probably Alexander Hughes [see THO75601]. See also THO75602.

Thorney – 1767 – THO76701 – BRO R1/149
A Plan Of the Manor and Lordship of Thorney In the Isle of Ely and County of Cambridge Belonging to his Grace the most Noble John Duke of Bedford From a Late Survey of Mr Vinct Wings By Wm Walton Junr 1767.
Surveyors: Vincent Wing, William Walton jr; A **Scale** of one Statute Mile or Eighty of Gunters Chains, Scale bar 0–1 mile (= 11 1/8in.), 1:5,695; **Size:** (i) 59 1/8 x 64 3/4in.; **Top** is N; Manuscript(iii), parchment, coloured.
Thorney Church, TF282042, and c. 18,000a. in whole parish.
Names of fields and fen. Farm buildings shown in plan form, church, corn mill [post mill] and windmills [possibly smock mills] shown in perspective. Fields; fen; waste; trees; holt; 'Stray Pasture'; acreages and number of pieces; roads; watercourses and 'Stone Bridge'; hedges; bank; pightle; decoy; 'Stack Yard'; 'Thorney', 'Knar', 'Tarketulluss', 'St Vincent' and unnamed crosses; 'Charters Corner'.
Border of 1 broad band with 1 narrow band on inside; title top left in a rococo cartouche; scale bottom left; compass rose under title showing 8 points and 'Variation 17° Westerly'. Land outlined in red, green, yellow, blue, pink and orange, buildings coloured red, waste coloured green, water coloured blue.

Based on THO75301 and numbers on plots probably refer to its terrier [BRO R2/140; see THO75301 for details].

Thorney – [c. 1771] – THO77101 – CRO 283/P
A Map of Thorney Farm, the property of Iohn Waddington of Ely Esqr.
Surveyor: [J. Porter]; **Scale:** Grid of chains, furlongs and miles in border, 1 furlong = 2 1/2in., 1:3,168; **Size:** (i) 25 1/8 x 29 15/16in.; **Top** is N; Manuscript(i), parchment, coloured.
Farm, probably in TF2702 S of village, and 353a.3r.5p. bounded by 'Crooked Drain' in E and drain in N.
Names of drains. Farm buildings and 2 windmills shown in perspective. Closes; wood and trees; roads and watercourses; gates; banks.
Border of 1 broad band with 2 broad yellow bands inside forming grid; title middle bottom in a rococo cartouche with a knight's helmet at top; scale in border; compass top left showing 16 points. Table top right giving field numbers and acreages. Trees coloured green, land outlined in yellow and green.
Right of title is summary of acreages. Note of surveyor bottom right in a plain rectangular border. Pencil notes. Probably drawn soon after John Waddington inherited estate in 1771 [Waddington, 1934, 119].

Thorney – [1822] – THO82201 – BRO R5/4200
A Sketch of Thorney Lordship.
Surveyor: [Tycho Wing jr]; **Scale:** 1:26,600; **Size:** (ii) 15 3/8 x 18 3/4in.; **Top** is N; Manuscript(i), paper, coloured.
c. 18,000a. in whole parish; Thorney Church, which is not shown, is at TF282042.
Names of fields, roads and dykes. Buildings shown in plan form. Roads and dykes.
Border of 1 broad band with 1 narrow band on inside; title top left. Roads coloured brown, buildings coloured red.
Numbers on fields use numbering system of the 18th-century surveys of lordship. At front of: 'A Valuation of his Grace the Duke of Bedford's Estate at Thorney in the Isle of Ely and County of Cambridge, also of his Grace's Estates in the Parishes of Whittlesea, Eye, Newborough. Ramsey, Parson Drove & Wisbech Saint Mary in the Counties of Northampton, Huntingdon and Isle of Ely aforesaid in 1822', signed at end by Tycho Wing. Land owned by John Russell, 6th Duke of Bedford [PB, 226].

Toft – [Ante 1799] – TOF79901 – SJC MPS 79
[Land at Toft, owned by St John's College, Cambridge.]
Surveyor: [Joseph Freeman?]; **Scale:** 1:5,850; **Size:** (i) 22 x 29 1/8in.; **Top** is N; Manuscript(i), parchment, coloured.
Pond at TL359562, junction of roads from Toft to Hardwick and to Comberton, and 33a.2r.10p. scattered throughout parish, including 1a.1r.28p. in N of Kingston Parish S of Bourn ['Kingston'] Brook and 1 strip in Caldecote Parish W of Hardwick Wood.
Names of fields, roads, rivers and neighbouring owners. Buildings in village shown in plan form. Open fields showing owner's strips; old inclosures; Hardwick Wood; waste; meadow; pasture shown by symbols depicting tufts of grass; roads and watercourses; bridge; pond; hedges.
Border of 2 narrow bands. Table on left giving field names, acreages and number of lands. Grass coloured

green, water coloured blue, strips coloured yellow, roads coloured yellow/green, wood coloured green and brown.
In style of Joseph Freeman, who was employed by the College in the 1790s and died in 1799 [*Gentleman's Magazine*, 69.I, 1799, 260], though handlist in SJC suggests map drawn in 1801. Photograph at 1:9,900 at CRO TR869/P28.

Toft – [c. 1815] – TOF81501 – CRO R86/6
[Land in Toft allotted to John Haggerston.]
Surveyor: [William Smith]; **Scale:** 1:4,860; **Size:** (ii) 20 3/4 x 16 1/2in.; **Top** is N; Manuscript(ii), paper, coloured.
Farm at TL362561 and 244a.0r.34p. to SE and NE in TL3655 and TL3656, bounded by Bourn Brook in S and Comberton Parish in NE.
Names of owners and neighbouring owners. Farm buildings shown in plan form, windmill shown in perspective. Closed fields showing owner's land; acreages; roads and watercourses.
Compass bottom right showing 4 points. Land coloured green or pink and outlined in pink, roads coloured brown, water coloured blue.
Numbers on plots refer to inclosure award. Note under compass: 'The Windmill does not belong'. Copied, after 1832 [date of watermark of paper], from map by William Smith which accompanied 1815 inclosure award.

Toft – [1815] – TOF81502 – CRO R86/6
An extract from the Plan of the Parish of Toft in the County of Cambridge As divided and Allotted by the Commissioners appointed to Inclose the said Parish A.D. 1812. William Smith, Surveyor; John Dugmore, Joseph Truslove and Charles Wedge Commissioners.
Surveyor: William Smith; **Draughtsman:** Henry Sayer; **Scale bar** 0–40 chains (= 6 5/8in.), 1:4,746; **Size:** (i) 15 15/16 x 16 1/16in.; **Top** is N; Manuscript(ii), paper mounted on cloth, coloured.
Toft Church, TL362558, farm to N, and land bounded by road to Comberton in N, church in W, Great Eversden Parish in S and Comberton Parish in E.
Names of owner and former owner. Buildings shown in plan form, church shown in perspective. Closed fields showing owner's land; acreages; roads and watercourses; hedges; responsibility for boundaries.
Border of 1 narrow band with 1 broad band and 2 narrow bands on inside; title top right; scale bottom right; compass centre left showing 4 points. Table bottom left giving acreages. Land coloured pink, water coloured blue, buildings coloured red, roads coloured brown.
Note above scale: 'Extracted by order of Messrs Boodle & Company Hy Sayer, Surveyor 5th March 1842'. Shows land allotted to Revd Samuel Smith, purchased of Thomas Day and H. B. King. Numbers on plots refer to 1815 inclosure award.

Trumpington – [1780] – TRU78001 – CRO P158/28/1
['Fire at Trumpington 1780'.]
Draughtsman: [Rev. Thomas Heckford?]; **Scale:** 1:300; **Size:** (ii) 8 x 10 1/2in.; **Top** is W; Manuscript(i), paper, uncoloured.
c. 3r. at TL446549 in centre of village, W of road from Cambridge to Harston and probably N of road to Grantchester.

Names of neighbouring owners with land affected by fire, roads and buildings. Granary, barns, greenhouse, stables, outhouses, cart lodge and 'Mr Stonebridge's House' shown in plan form. Roads; gates; 'hog styes'; hay stack and rick.

Compass centre top showing 4 plain points.

Notes about where fire started and how each building was affected. Top right-hand corner torn off. Title, date and some calculations on dorse. Thomas Heckford may have drawn map as handwriting is similar to that on accompanying documents by him.

Trumpington – [c. 1801] – TRU80101 – CUL MS Plans 590

Plan of Vicarage & Rectory – Homestalls.

Surveyor: [Alexander Watford jr?]; **Scale:** 1:667; **Size:** (iii) 7 7/8 x 12 11/16in.; **Top** is N; Manuscript(i), paper mounted on paper, coloured.

Trumpington Church, TL443549, and c. 2a. to E in centre of village.

Functions of buildings and yards. Church, house, offices, barn and stable shown in plan form. Roads and watercourses; gates; garden; yard; pond and common pond.

Title bottom right. Church, barn and stable coloured grey, house and offices coloured red, garden and road coloured yellow, pond coloured blue.

Letters suggest map originally accompanied by an explanation. Note top right: 'DEF Vicarage Fence the other Fences round the Pond, yard, & between Farm yard & Garden to be maintained by Lessee'. Accompanied by documents at CUM Doc.659 dated 1801; at Doc.659(29) is Alexander Watford's rough proposal of allotments to the Vicar, dated 24 March 1801. Vicar was Rev. Thomas Heckford [*VCH*, 8, 264]. See also TRU80102, probably drawn slightly later.

Trumpington – [c. 1801] – TRU80102 – CUL MS Plans 591

Plan of Rectory and Vicarage – Homestalls at Trumpington.

Surveyor: [Alexander Watford jr?]; **Scale:** 1:960; **Size:** (ii) 9 1/8 x 6 1/2in.; **Top** is SE; Manuscript(i), paper mounted on paper, uncoloured.

Trumpington Vicarage, TL444549, and c. 1a. to E in centre of village.

Names of neighbouring owners, road and functions of land. Buildings shown in plan form, barn, stables, house and offices identified on TRU80101. Roads and gates; pond; open field adjoining map to S; old inclosure adjoining map to E.

Title bottom left. Barn, stables and other buildings stippled, house and offices shaded.

Pencil notes. Probably drawn after TRU80101 as shows new buildings, garden has become vicarage and farmyard has become rectory. Accompanying documents at CUM Doc.659 suggest date and surveyor [see TRU80101 for details]. Vicar was Rev. Thomas Heckford [*VCH*, 8, 264].

Trumpington – [c. 1801] – TRU80103 – C U M Doc.659(254)

['Description of the Impropriators & Vicars Allotments sold under the Trumpington Inclosure Act'.]

Surveyor: [Edward Gibbons?]; **Scale:** 1:2,430; **Size:** (ii) 16 1/8 x 12 7/8in.; **Top** is N; Manuscript(i) paper, uncoloured.

40a.0r.0p. bounded by Great Shelford Parish in S and road from Cambridge to Linton in E.

Names of roads and neighbouring owners. Closed fields; acreages; roads; responsibility for boundaries.

Table top left giving acreages and value.

Lot numbers and names of tenants or purchasers. Pencil extensions to allotment for tithes. Title on dorse. Paper has watermark of 1801. Part of collection of documents of 1801 associated with inclosure of Trumpington, probably by inclosure surveyor, Edward Gibbons. Vicar was Rev. Thomas Heckford [*VCH*, 8, 264].

Trumpington – [1801] – TRU80104 – C U M Doc.659(46)

['Mr Anstey's land at Trumpington'.]

Surveyor: [Edward Gibbons]; **Scale:** 1:2,710; **Size:** (ii) 9 3/4 x 8in.; **Top** is E; Manuscript(i), paper, uncoloured.

c. 19a. at TL442549, W of road to Hauxton.

Names of owner and roads. Farmhouse, rectory, vicarage and outbuildings shown in plan form. Closes; acreages of 2 plots; roads and turnpike.

Compass middle left showing 4 points.

Note on 1 plot: 'Vicar requests 10 Acres may be laid here'. Title on dorse. Accompanies letter dated 1801 from Edward Gibbons to Christopher Pemberton relating to request by Vicar for 10a. of land. Anstey's 1st name was Christopher [Venn, I, 1, 34].

Trumpington – 1802 – TRU80201 – TCC Box 20 Trumpington 44

Plan of an Estate, situate in the Parish of Trumpington in the County of Cambridge belonging to the Society of Trinity College in the University of Cambridge.

Scale bar 0–30 chains (= 4 15/16in.), 1:4,812; **Size:** (i) 28 x 22in.; **Top** is NNW; Manuscript(i), parchment, coloured.

Trumpington Church, TL432549, and 394a.1r.4p. to S bounded by roads to Great Shelford in SE and to Royston in SW, and to N bounded by road to Royston in W and Cherry Hinton Parish in E.

Names of roads, parishes and neighbouring owners. Vicarage and farm buildings shown in plan form, church shown in perspective. Closed fields showing owner's land; state of cultivation may be shown by colour; acreages; roads; watercourses and bridge; hedges; churchyard.

Border of 1 narrow band; title top left in a cartouche of a green and grey decorative line; blue scale bar centre bottom; compass rose top right showing 16 red and yellow points. Table above scale giving acreages. Roads coloured brown, fields coloured yellow and green, water coloured blue, buildings coloured red.

Pencil notes.

Trumpington – 1804 – TRU80401 – CUL MS Plans R.b.11

A Map of the Parish of Trumpington in the County of Cambridge.

Surveyor: Edward Gibbons; **Scale bar** 6–0–30 statute chains (= 5 15/16in.), 1:4,802; **Size:** (i) 29 3/8 x 43 7/8in.; **Top** is NW; Manuscript(i), parchment, coloured.

Trumpington Hall, TL441451, and c. 2,300a. in whole parish.

Names of roads, parishes and neighbouring owners. Trumpington Hall, Trumpington Manor, Anstey Hall, cottages and farm buildings shown in plan form, church shown in perspective. Closed fields; wood and trees; waste; acreages; roads, turnpike and toll bar; watercourses; ponds and fishponds; bridge; 'Mortar' and gravel pits.

Border of 1 narrow and 1 broad band; title top left in an ornate cartouche with flowers and leaves; scale middle bottom with decorative lettering; compass top left showing 4 points with an ornate N. Roads coloured brown, land not owned by F.C.J. Pemberton outlined in green, some buildings stippled, others shaded.

Numbers on fields suggest map originally accompanied by a terrier of Pemberton's land. Note centre left: 'Such of the peices that have not the Owners Name inserted therein are the property of F.C.J. Pemberton Esqr'. Railway lines sketched later in pencil. Owner's 1st names were Francis Charles James [VCH, 8, 252]. Positive photostat mounted on cloth at BL 1640.(7).

Trumpington – [Post 1809] – TRU80901 – JCC St Giles
Plan of an Estate situate in the Parish of Trumpington in the County of Cambridge; belonging to the Master, Fellows, and Scholars of Jesus College; in the University of Cambridge.
Scale: 1:4,840; **Size:** (i) 9 1/2 x 19 7/8in.; **Top** is NE; Manuscript(i), parchment, coloured.
20a.0r.12p. in TL4656, bounded by Cherry Hinton Parish in E.
Names of neighbouring owners and roads. Closed fields showing owner's land; acreages; hedges; roads and watercourses.
Border of 2 narrow bands; title top right; compass on right showing 4 points with a feathered tail. Water coloured blue.
At bottom of sheet beneath a map of 'Rifle Range Farm' in St Giles' Parish, Cambridge. Drawn after 1809 inclosure award.

Trumpington – 1820 – TRU82001 – TCC Box 20
Trumpington 71
Plan of the Trumpington Estate 1820.
Surveyor: [Alexander Watford jr]; **Scale:** 1:4,920; **Size:** (i) 20 x 15 3/4in.; **Top** is NNW; Manuscript(i), paper, coloured.
313a.1r.35p. in TL4556, bounded by roads to London in W and to Haverhill ['The Hills Road'] in E.
Names of roads and neighbouring owners. Buildings including mill shown in plan form. Closed fields showing owner's land; acreages; roads and watercourses; 'The Moor'; hedges; responsibility for boundaries; 'Line of Reservation'.
Border of 1 narrow band; title bottom left; compass top right showing 4 plain points. Roads coloured brown, buildings coloured red, water coloured blue, 'The Moor' outlined in green.
Accompanies: 'Valuation of an Estate at Trumpington in the County of Cambridge belonging to the Master, Fellows, and Scholars of Trinity College, and Francis Charles James Pemberton Esqr, their Lessee. Dated Jany 4th 1820', signed 'Alexr Watford' at end.

Trumpington – [c. 1829] – TRU82901 – C U L
Maps.PSQ.aa.18.1(2)
Plan of the Trumpington Estate in the County of Cambridge. belonging to Christopher John Anstey Esqre.
Surveyor: George Morris; **Publisher:** C. Richards; **Scale bar** 0–20 chains (= 2 5/16in.), 1:6,850; **Size:** (i) 13 1/2 x 12 3/16in.; **Top** is NNE; Lithograph, paper, coloured.
Anstey Hall, TL444548, and 422a.0r.30p. bounded by river in W and roads to Grantchester in N and to Cambridge in E.
Names of roads, river and neighbouring owners. Church shown in perspective, farm buildings and Anstey Hall shown in plan form. Closed fields; trees; state of cultivation shown by colour; acreages; roads and turnpike road; footpaths; watercourses; pond, 'Turf pond' and fishponds; 'Old mills'; spring; 'New bridge'; hedges.
Border of 2 narrow bands; title middle right with decorative lettering; scale beneath title; compass top left showing 4 points with feathered tail. Roads coloured yellow, water coloured blue, meadow and pasture coloured green.
Manuscript notes of acreages, field names and 'plan of 1816 or thereabouts'. Vignette of Anstey Hall above lithograph. Accompanies: 'Particular of the valuable and very desirable Freehold and Tithe Free Estate, ... called Trumpington, Huntingtons, & Crouchmans'. Land sold after Anstey inherited estate in 1827 [VCH, 8, 255]; CUL map catalogue suggests date of 1829.

Trumpington – [1829] – TRU82902 – TCC Box 20
Trumpington 72b
[Land at Trumpington, owned by Mrs Martha Humphreys.]
Scale: 1:419; **Size:** (i) 6 x 5 1/8in.; **Top** is N; Manuscript(i), parchment, coloured.
c. 1r. W of a road.
Names of neighbouring owners. Buildings shown in plan form. Closed field; roads; dimensions of area.
Border of 2 red lines; compass bottom right showing 4 points. Land coloured blue.
On lease: 'Dated 9th June 1829 Mrs M. Humphreys to Mr Benjamin Bridges Release of a freehold estate at Trumpington in the County of Cambridge', which gives Mrs Humphreys' 1st name.

Tydd St Giles – [1772] – TYD77201 – PRO MR 604
Land lying in Tidd St Giles Cambridgeshire.
Surveyor: [Robert Lowde]; **Scale bar** 0–18 chains (= 5 15/16in.), 1:2,401; **Size:** (i) 7 3/4 x 11in.; **Top** is N; Manuscript(i), parchment, coloured.
12a.2r.38p., probably in TF4216 or TF4316, bounded by 'Church Lane' in W.
Names of road and neighbouring owners. Closed fields; roads.
Border 3/8in. wide of 1 broad yellow band and 1 narrower uncoloured band on either side; title at top; scale centre bottom of whole sheet and surmounted by dividers; compass centre top of whole sheet showing 8 points. Table top left of whole sheet giving tenants and acreages. Land outlined in grey.
Map is inset to right of scale on map entitled: 'A Plan of Lands in the Parish of Sutton St James Lincolnshire'. Accompanied by letter of commission from Duchy of

Lancaster for map, and certificate for it signed by Robert Lowde on 13 November 1772. See also TYD77202.

Tydd St Giles – [1772] – TYD77202 – PRO MR 604
Land lying in Tidd St Giles Cambridgeshire.
Surveyor: [Robert Lowde]; **Scale bar** 0–18 chains (= 5 15/16in.), 1:2,401; **Size:** (i) 15 7/8 x 11 3/4in.; **Top** is N; Manuscript(i), parchment, coloured.
11a.3r.6p. in N of parish, bounded by 'Shire Drain' in N and Tydd St Mary Parish [Lincolnshire] in N and W.
Names of droves and neighbouring owners. Closed field; roads; watercourses and 'Shire Drain'; feature which may be a bank.
Border 3/8in. wide of 1 broad yellow band and 1 narrower uncoloured band on either side; title centre top; scale centre bottom of whole sheet; compass centre top of whole sheet showing 8 points. Table top left of whole sheet giving tenants and acreages. Land outlined in yellow.
Map is inset to left of scale on map of land in Sutton St James, Lincolnshire; see TYD77201 for details of title and accompanying documents which give date and surveyor.

Tydd St Giles – [c. 1779] – TYD77901 – WM DIV.32
['Map of Tydd St Giles, showing the Trafford estates (unsettled) belonging to Sir Clement Trafford & sold by him'.]
Scale: 1:6,000; **Size:** (iii) 15 x 56in.; **Top** is NW; Manuscript(ii), tracing paper mounted on paper, coloured.
c. 4,700a. in whole parish.
Names of roads, drains, bank and neighbouring owners. Closed fields; roads and droves; watercourses and drains.
Land either outlined and coloured red or outlined in green.
Title on wrapper of map. Unsettled properties of Trafford estate were conveyed to trustees for sale in 1779 [*VCH*, 4, 228].

Tydd St Giles – 1779 – TYD77902 – WRO CR114/2/v
Tid St, Giles Map. 1
Surveyors: [John] Lund [sr and jr]; A **Scale** of Four Chains in One Inch, **Scale bar** 0–21 chains (= 5 1/4in.), 1:3,168; **Size:** (i) 17 7/8 x 24in.; **Top** is N; Manuscript(i), paper, coloured.
c. 260a. scattered throughout parish.
Names of roads and neighbouring owners. Farm buildings shown in plan form. Open fields showing owner's strips; closes; roads and gates; watercourses including Kindersley's ['Kimberley'] Cut and direction of flow; drains; sluice marked by 2 arrows; county boundary between Lincolnshire and Cambridgeshire; common adjoining map.
Border of 1 broad band; title centre top; scale at bottom of whole sheet; compass top left of whole sheet showing 4 points. Roads coloured brown, buildings coloured red, Sir Clement Trafford's land coloured green, Messrs Lumpkin and Leasey's land coloured red, fields outlined in yellow, green, red and blue.
Note on 1 plot: 'N:B: Lady Irwin has Half of this Close supposed on the last side the remainder of it belongs to Sir Clemont Trafford & the Clergy Widows'. Numbers on plots suggest map originally accompanied by a terrier. Fields not shown in correct positions. Map at bottom of sheet entitled top right: 'A Map of the Estate of the Right Honourable Lady Viscountess Irwin at Sutton St, Edmonds in the County of Lincoln. & Tid St. Giles in the Isle of Ely.

Surveyed by Messrs, Lund's in 1779'. Surveyors' 1st names were John [Eden L294 and L294.1].

Tydd St Giles – [c. 1808] – TYD80801 – E D R CC.10121
Mrs Hannath's Land lying in Tidd St Gile's High Marsh.
Scale: 1:4,870; **Size:** (i) 6 3/4 x 8 1/16in.; **Top** is NNE; Manuscript(i), paper mounted on paper, coloured.
40a.1r.13p., bounded by Shire Drain in NE and 'Buckworths Drain' in S.
Names of drains. Closed fields; tree; roads and watercourses.
Border of 2 narrow bands; title top left; compass middle right showing 8 points. Table below title giving acreages. Land outlined in red, blue and yellow, water coloured grey.
Probably drawn in connection with renewal of one of Mrs Hannath's leases of land from Bishop of Ely in 1808, 1816, 1823, 1830 or 1837 [formerly at EDR CC.94672–6].

Tydd St Giles – [c. 1811] – TYD81101 – WM DIV.40
['A Plan of the Estates, late of Lawrence Banyer Esq. deceased; in the Parishes of Emneth, Walsoken, Terrington, & in Marshland Smeeth and Fen, in the County of Norfolk; and in the Parishes of Wisbech, Leverington, Tid St Giles & Upwell, in the Isle of Ely, in the County of Cambridge'.] In Tid Saint Giles.
Scale bar 0–40 chains (= 5in.), 1:6,336; **Size:** (i) 6 7/8 x 7 1/4in.; **Top** is N; Manuscript(i), paper, coloured.
16a.1r.11p. scattered throughout parish.
Names of fields, roads and neighbouring owners. Closed fields showing owner's land; roads and droves; banks; drains.
Border of 2 narrow bands; title at top; scale bottom right of whole sheet; compass rose centre bottom of whole sheet showing 4 points. Table of scale giving acreages, land use and occupiers. Fields outlined in brown with names written in red, now faded.
Pencil notes. On left of sheet, above map of Upwell [UPW81101]. Sheet measures 23 3/8 x 25in. and title, as given above, is top right in a cartouche with brown and yellow vases and blue and yellow edges. Bottom left of sheet is note: 'NB The Letters a and p in the second Column in the Table of References, distinguish the arable from the Pasture Lands'. Probably drawn in connection with sale of Lawrence Banyer's estate in 1811 [*Cambridge Chronicle*, 8 February 1811]. See also LEV81101, UPW81101 and WSM1101.

Tydd St Giles – [1811] – TYD81102 – G L C A/CSC/1101/9
A Map of Two Fields in Tid St Giles, Isle of Ely, Cambridgeshire.
Surveyor: [W.P. Attfield]; **Scale bar** 0–10 chains (= 2 1/2in.), 1:3,168; **Size:** (i) 11 7/8 x 7 1/8in.; **Top** is N; Manuscript(i), parchment, coloured.
6a.1r.33p., bounded by Shire Drain in N and crossed by road running E–W.
Names of watercourses and neighbouring owners. Closed fields; state of cultivation shown by colour; acreages; roads and gates; watercourses.
Border of 1 broad band with 1 narrow band on inside; title top right in an oval cartouche of 1 broad band with 1 narrow band on inside; scale centre bottom; compass in

centre showing 4 points. Roads coloured brown, water coloured blue, grass coloured green.

Centre top is note of parish. Pencil notes. Later ink note under title: 'In occupation of Robert Hill – 1841'. In volume: 'Maps of the Wisbeach Estate in the Counties of Cambridge, Lincoln and Norfolk. belonging to the Corporation of The Sons of the Clergy. Surveyed by W.P. Attfield Whetstone & Hadley MDCCCXI'. At end is table of acreages and land use with ink notes added in 1841, and valuation by Attfield. See also TYD81103, UPW81102–4, WEL81101, WSM81102–5 and WSP81101.

Tydd St Giles – [1811] – TYD81103 – G L C A/CSC/1101/10
A Map of Three Fields in Tid St Giles, Isle of Ely, Cambridgeshire.
Surveyor: [W.P. Attfield]; **Scale bar** 0–10 chains (= 2 1/2in.), 1:3,168; **Size:** (i) 13 1/16 x 8 1/16in.; **Top** is NW; Manuscript(i), parchment, coloured.
19a.1r.28p., along 'Sandy Lane' and W of road from Wisbech to Long Sutton.
Names of roads and neighbouring owners. Closed fields; common; state of cultivation shown by colour; acreages; roads and turnpike; gates.
Border of 1 broad band with 1 narrow band on inside; title top right in a cartouche of a stone edged in brown and with green bushes and grass; scale at bottom; compass centre right showing 4 points. Roads coloured brown, pasture coloured green, arable coloured in dark brown stripes.
Above map is note of parish. Note bottom left: 'In No 3 Mr Long claims 2 Roods, but there are no Boundaries remaining'. Pencil notes, ink notes of land sold in 1835 and, under title, 'In occupation of Robert Hill 1841'. In volume which gives date, owner and surveyor; see TYD81102 for details. See also UPW81102–4, WEL81101, WSM81102–5 and WSP81101.

Tydd St Giles – 1832 – TYD83201 – CRO R76/92
Particulars of Land at Tid Gote belonging to the North Level Commissioners – 1832 Oct 2d.
Surveyor: H[enry] Wilson; **Scale:** 1:2,570; **Size:** (ii) 12 5/8 x 8in.; **Top** is NE; Manuscript(i), paper, coloured.
3a.1r.16p. in TF4417, bounded by North Level Main Drain in E and 'Old Shire Drain' in W.
Names of roads, drains and neighbouring owners. Buildings shown in plan form. Roads; watercourses including North Level Main Drain and 'Old Shire Drain'; bank; sluice.
Title at top; compass top left showing 4 points. Table on right giving acreages. Buildings and subdivisions of land coloured red.
In commonplace book of John and Tycho Wing, agents to 6th Duke of Bedford; surveyor's 1st name was Henry [Eden W435.5].

U

Upwell – 1774 – UPW77401 – CRO 283/P
A Plan of the Estate of John Hagar Esqr lying in Eusimoor in Upwell in the Isle of Ely taken MDCCLXXIV.
Surveyor: John Watte; **Scale bar** 0–40 chains = half a mile (= 4 15/16in.), 1:6,416; **Size:** (i) 24 x 17 3/4in.; **Top** is NW; Manuscript(i), parchment, uncoloured.

Farm at TL472995, and 195a.0r.31p. in Euximoor Fen bounded by Euximoor Drove in E, Sixteen Foot Drain in S, River Nene ['Nine'] in N and 'Outring Drove' in W.
Names of river, droves and neighbouring owners. Farm buildings, cottages, 'Boarded House' and 5 windmills shown in perspective. Closes; trees; roads; watercourses; banks.
Border of 1 broad and 1 narrow band; title top left in a rococo cartouche with a person, bird and flowers as decoration; scale bottom right; compass in centre showing 4 plain points. Table on left giving field numbers and acreages.

Upwell – [Late 18th century] – UPW77501 – E D R CC.10122
[Land in Upwell Fen, owned by Bishop of Ely.]
Scale: 1:13,700; **Size:** (i) 9 3/8 x 12 1/4in.; **Top** is W; Manuscript(i), parchment, uncoloured.
466a.1r.28p. in Upwell Fen, bounded by Darcey Lode and 'Old Chair' in W, 'District Drain' in SW, and 'Run Drove' and Padgett's ['Patchets'] Drove in E.
Names of fields, watercourses, droves and neighbouring owners. Cottages and outbuildings shown in perspective. Closed fields; acreages; roads and droves; watercourses.
Border of 2 narrow red bands; 'North' written on right.
Note bottom right of total acreage. Pencil compass top right. 'Eusimore & Welney Reeve' in pencil on dorse.

Upwell – [c. 1811] – UPW81101 – WM DIV.40
['A Plan of the Estates, late of Lawrence Banyer Esq. deceased; in the Parishes of Emneth, Walsoken, Terrington, & in Marshland Smeeth and Fen, in the County of Norfolk; and in the Parishes of Wisbech, Leverington, Tid St Giles & Upwell, in the Isle of Ely, in the County of Cambridge'.] In Upwell.
Scale bar 0–40 chains (= 5in.), 1:6,336; **Size:** (i) 4 11/16 x 7 1/4in.; **Top** is N; Manuscript(i), paper, coloured.
5a.3r.34p., W of village in Laddus Fen.
Names of fen, drove and neighbouring owners. 2 windmills drawn in pencil and shown in perspective. Closed field; road.
Border of 2 narrow bands; title at top; scale bottom right of whole sheet; compass rose centre bottom of whole sheet showing 4 points. Table right of scale giving acreages, land use and occupiers. Field outlined in green, fen shown in red, now very faded.
Bottom left of whole sheet, which measures 23 3/8 x 25in. and title, as given above, top right in a cartouche with brown and yellow vases and blue and yellow edges. Bottom left of sheet is note: 'NB The Letters a and p in the second Column in the Table of References, distinguish the arable from the Pasture Lands'. Probably drawn in connection with sale of Lawrence Banyer's estate in 1811 [*Cambridge Chronicle*, 8 February 1811]. See also LEV81101, TYD81101 and WSM81101.

Upwell – [1811] – UPW81102 – GLC A/CSC/1101/11
A Map of Two Fields in Upwell.
Surveyor: [W.P. Attfield]; **Scale bar** 0–10 chains (= 2 1/2in.), 1:3,168; **Size:** (i) 13 x 8 3/16in.; **Top** is NW; Manuscript(i), parchment, coloured.
8a.2r.33p. in Upwell Parish in Cambridgeshire along Well Stream [former course of River Nene] NW of county

boundary, and 1a.3r.9p. SE of county boundary in Upwell Parish [Norfolk].

Names of watercourses. Building shown in plan form. Common; state of cultivation shown by colour; acreages; roads and droves; watercourses; garden; county boundary with Norfolk; gates.

Border of 1 broad band with 1 narrow band on inside; title top right in a cartouche of a stone edged in brown with green grass and bushes; scale centre bottom; compass centre right showing 4 points. Water coloured blue, roads coloured brown, arable coloured in dark brown stripes, building coloured red, garden coloured green, county boundary shown by a red dotted line.

Above map is note of parish. Pencil notes. Later ink note below title: '1841. In occupation of Thomas Bundy'. In volume: 'Maps of the Wisbeach Estate in the Counties of Cambridge, Lincoln and Norfolk. belonging to the Corporation of The Sons of the Clergy. Surveyed by W.P. Attfield Whetstone & Hadley MDCCCXI'. At end is table of acreages and land use with ink notes added in 1841, and valuation by Attfield. See also TYD81102–3, UPW81103–4, WEL81101, WSM81102–5 and WSP81101.

Upwell – [1811] – UPW81103 – GLC A/CSC/1101/12
A Map of a piece of Land in Laddis Fen Upwell, Cambridgeshire.
Surveyor: [W.P. Attfield]; **Scale bar** 0–10 chains (= 2 1/2in.), 1:3,168; **Size:** (i) 12 1/4 x 7 3/8in.; **Top** is NE; Manuscript(i), parchment, coloured.
6a.1r.5p. in Laddus Fen.
Closed field; state of cultivation shown by colour; acreage; gate.
Border of 1 broad band with 1 narrow band on inside; title at top; scale at bottom; compass on left showing 4 points. Land coloured green.
Centre top is note of parish. Pencil notes. Later ink note under title: 'In the occupation of Thomas Bundy 1841'. In volume which gives date, owner and surveyor; see UPW81102 for details. See also TYD81102–3, UPW81104, WEL81101, WSM81102–5 and WSP81101.

Upwell – [1811] – UPW81104 – GLC A/CSC/1101/14
A Map of Two Fields in Upwell High Fen Isle of Ely, Cambridgeshire.
Surveyor: [W.P. Attfield]; **Scale bar** 0–10 chains (= 2 1/2in.), 1:3,168; **Size:** (i) 12 5/16 x 7 5/16in.; **Top** is NE; Manuscript(i), parchment, coloured.
17a.3r.14p. in Upwell Fen in S of parish, bounded by Padgett's Drove in NE and 'to Brimstone Hill' in SE.
Names of roads and neighbouring owners. Closed fields; state of cultivation shown by colour; acreages; droves; gates.
Border of 1 broad band with 1 narrow band on inside; title centre top in a shield; scale at bottom; compass centre left showing 4 points. Roads coloured brown, pasture coloured green, arable coloured in dark brown stripes.
Centre top is note of parish. Site of barn on land adjoining map is marked. Later ink note below title: 'In occupation of Joseph Bennington (late Ward) 1841'. In volume which gives date, owner and surveyor; see UPW81102 for details. See also TYD81102–3, UPW81103, WEL81101, WSM81102–5 and WSP81101.

Upwell – 1821 – UPW82101 – CRO R59/31/40/66
A Plan and Survey of 36 acres of Adventurers Land lying in Upwell Fen the Property of Messrs Richd & Thos Orton Esqrs. Shewing the Quantity belonging to Each. Surveyed March 14th 1821 by John Pope.
Surveyor: John Pope; **Scale:** 4 Chains to an inch, 1:3,168; **Size:** (i) 11 x 8 7/16in.; **Top** is NE; Manuscript(i), paper mounted on paper, uncoloured.
36a. in TL4599, bounded by River Nene in NW and Reed Fen in S.
Names of owners, river and neighbouring fen. House belonging to Thomas Orton and windmill shown in perspective. Closed fields showing owners' land; acreages; watercourses.
Border of 1 broad and 1 narrow band; title top right; scale bottom right.
Note on dorse: 'Sketch of part of Mr Thos Orton's Farm'.

W

Waterbeach – [1680/1] – WAT68101 – BLM Add.62711 f.31
['Waterbeach Rectory Demised to Mr John Robson March the 18th Anno 1680 during the lives of the said John Robson and William Robson and Jeremy Robson Brothers to the said John Robson'.]
Scale: 1:396; **Size:** (ii) 11 1/4 x 14 3/8in.; Manuscript(i), paper, uncoloured.
c. 2a. in TL4965, bounded by a garden on left.
Rectory shown in plan form and shows layout of ground floor. Trees; garden; walls; steps.
Pencil notes. Title and date on dorse.

Waterbeach – [c. 1828] – WAT82801 – ECC FEL.5.10
Rough sketch of lands in Waterbeach subject to the rent charge of £9 a year to the College.
Scale: 1:6,340; **Size:** (ii) 7 7/16 x 6in.; Manuscript(i), paper, uncoloured.
43a.1r.34p. in Waterbeach Parish.
Names of fields and tenants. Closed fields; acreages; roads.
In volume of accounts of Holbeach estate of Emmanuel College, Cambridge; probably drawn when book started in 1828, accounts continue to 1861.

Waterbeach – 1828 – WAT82802 – CUL MS Plans y.1(14)
Mrs Francis. Waterbeach.
Draughtsman: [Elliot Smith]; **Scale:** 1:182; **Size:** (ii) 14 1/2 x 20 15/16in.; **Top** is W; Manuscript(i), paper, coloured.
Public house, TL496653, and c. 1a. in centre of village bounded by road to Cambridge in N.
Functions of land, names of roads. Dairy and cellar, barn, public house, 'Cowhouse' and 2 stables shown in plan form. Lengths of plots; roads and gates; garden; yard; feature in garden wall.
Title bottom right. Land outlined in yellow and brown.
Drawn for fire insurance purposes, in volume from Elliot Smith and Sons, Auctioneers and Estate Agents.

Waterbeach – 1829 – WAT82901 – CUL Maps.53.82.4
Plan of a freehold estate belonging to Samuel Peach Esq: situate at Waterbeach, Cambridgeshire. To be Let by Auction by E. & G.N. Driver, 1829.

Auctioneers: E[dward E.] Driver, G[eorge] N[eale] Driver; **Scale:** 1:26,280; **Size:** (i) 11 15/16 x 8 3/16in.; **Top** is NNE; Lithograph, paper, uncoloured.

Denny Abbey, TL492685, and 1,563a.1r.28p. NE of village, bounded by road from Landbeach to Stretham in W and Bannold Drove in E, and 1 plot in Clayhithe in Horningsea Parish.

Names of farms, fields and neighbouring owners. 'Winfold', Denny Abbey and 'Denny Lodge' farms, farm buildings, Denny Abbey and cottage shown in plan form, windmill shown in perspective. Closed fields; common; trees; fen; acreages; roads and footpaths; watercourses; gravel pits; site of new farm at 'Winfold Farm'; proposed site of homestead.

Border of 1 narrow band with decorated corners; title beneath border; compass bottom left showing 4 points. Table giving total acreages of 3 farms.

Lot numbers refer to particulars of auction [not found in 1988]. Auctioneers' 1st names were Edward E. and George Neale [Eden D319 and D320].

Welney – [1811] – WEL81101 – GLC A/CSC/1101/15

A Map of a Field called Buckshot, in Welney Fen, Isle of Ely, Cambridgeshire.

Surveyor: [W.P. Attfield]; **Scale bar** 0–10 chains (= 2 7/16in.), 1:3,249; **Size:** (i) 12 5/16 x 7 3/8in.; **Top** is NE; Manuscript(i), parchment, coloured.

6a.0r.5p. in Welney Fen, bounded by droves in NE and NW.

Names of neighbouring owners. Closed field; state of cultivation shown by colour; acreages; droves; drain; gates.

Border of 1 broad band with 1 narrow band on inside; title at top in a shield; scale centre bottom; compass centre left showing 4 points. Roads coloured brown, pasture coloured green, water coloured blue.

Centre top is note of parish. Pencil notes. Later ink note under title: '1841 In occupation of Joseph Bennington (late Ward)'. In volume: 'Maps of the Wisbeach Estate in the Counties of Cambridge, Lincoln and Norfolk. belonging to the Corporation of The Sons of the Clergy. Surveyed by W.P. Attfield Whetstone & Hadley MDCCCXI'. At end is table of acreages and land use with ink notes added in 1841, and valuation by Attfield. See also TYD81102–3, UPW81102–4, WSM81102–5 and WSP81101.

Wendy – 1813 – WEN81301 – CUM Palmer MS C.2

A Plan of the Parish of Wendy in the County of Cambridge the Property of the Honble Tho. Windsor 1813.

Surveyors: [William?] Hollingworth, [unidentified] Day; **Scale:** 1:9,170; **Size:** (i) 11 3/8 x 15 1/4in.; **Top** is NNW; Manuscript(i), parchment, coloured.

Wendy Church, TL323476, and c. 1,400a. bounded by road from Royston to Caxton in E and a watercourse in N and W.

Names of roads and neighbouring owners. Farm buildings shown in plan form. Closed fields; acreages; roads and gates; watercourses; moat; hedges and fences.

Border of 1 broad band with 1 narrow band on inside; title top left in a cartouche of a scroll hanging from a column; compass centre top showing 8 points. Top right is vignette of church in exaggerated perspective. Roads coloured brown, hedges coloured green, buildings coloured

red, water coloured blue, farms outlined in green, pink, orange, brown, yellow, black and red.

Note bottom left of colours of each farm. Pencil notes. Hollingworth's 1st name was William [Eden H456.5].

Wentworth – [c. 1830] – WEO83001 – EDR CC.12319

Wentworth.

Surveyor: [William Newton]; **Scale:** 1:6,340; **Size:** (ii) 27 1/16 x 17in.; **Top** is N; Manuscript(ii), paper, uncoloured.

Wentworth Church, TL481785, and c. 510a. to S and E, and land bounded by roads from Mepal to Ely in S and from Wentworth to Coveney in W.

Names of roads. Farm buildings shown in plan form, church shown in perspective. Closed fields; roads and turnpike; watercourses; 'New Cut Bridge'.

Title top left; compass below title showing 8 points.

Copy of part of map by William Newton which accompanied 1830 inclosure award, shows land allotted to Dean and Chapter of Ely. Numbers on plots refer to inclosure award. Pencil notes of neighbouring owners.

Wentworth – [c. 1830] – WEO83002 – EDR CC.12320

Plan of the Wold Farm in the Parish of Wentworth held under lease of the Dean and Chapter of Ely.

Surveyor: [William Newton]; **Scale bar** 0–20 chains (= 3 5/16in.), 1:4,782; **Size:** (ii) 13 9/16 x 9 3/16in.; **Top** is NNE; Manuscript(ii), paper, coloured.

c. 110a. N and E of TL481789, junction of roads from Wentworth to Coveney and from Mepal to Ely; 1 plot is W of road from Wentworth to Coveney.

Names of roads and neighbouring owners. Closed fields; state of cultivation shown by colour; roads; watercourses and bridges.

Title top left; scale centre bottom. Arable coloured brown, pasture coloured green.

Copy of part of map by William Newton which accompanied 1830 inclosure award.

Wentworth – 1831 – WEO83101 – NRO D.S.392

Map of an Estate situate at Wentworth and adjoining Parishes in the Isle of Ely the Property of Henry Francis Esq. 1831.

Surveyor: William Newton; **Scale bar** 1–0–30 chains (= 5 1/8in.), 1:4,791; **Size:** (i) 28 5/8 x 19 15/16in.; **Top** is NNE; Manuscript(i), paper mounted on cloth, coloured.

Wentworth Church, TL481786, and 676a.0r.29p., including 4a.0r.16p. in W of Witchford Parish and 1a.1r.27p. in E of Witcham Parish.

Names of fields, former owners, neighbouring owners and roads. Cottages and 'Red Lion' shown in plan form, church shown in perspective. Closed fields; wood; acreages of some plots; roads and drove; watercourses; bridge; pond; banks; tenure.

Border of 1 broad band with 1 narrow band on inside; title top left; scale bottom right; compass centre top showing 4 points. Table bottom left giving acreages and identifying land leasehold of Dean and Chapter of Ely and of Dean and Canons of Windsor. Fields coloured green and red, water coloured blue, roads coloured brown.

Bottom right: 'Explanation Mr Francis' Estate coloured Pink Leasehold of the Dean & Chapter coloured Green The Nos Names & Quantities &c in Red, refer to the Commissioners Award under the Inclosure Act. The Black

Nos refer to the Schedule annexed'. Schedule not found in 1988.

Weston Colville – 1794 – WET79401 – SJC MPS 260
Plan of a Farm at Weston Colvill in the County of Cambridge. belonging to the College of St. John the Evangelist in the University of Cambridge. Surveyed in the Year 1794. John Hall Esqr. Lessee.
Surveyor: [Joseph Freeman]; **Scale bar** 100 links–0–15 chains (= 4in.), 1:3,168; **Size:** (i) 18 1/8 x 21 1/16in.; **Top** is NW; Manuscript(i), parchment, coloured.
College Grove ['The Grove'], TL638517, and 70a.3r.3p. bounded by Weston Green in NW and roads from Carlton Green to West Wickham in E and from Weston Green to Carlton Green in S, and extending nearly as far as Carlton cum Willingham Parish in N.
Names of roads and neighbouring owners. Farm buildings shown in plan form. Closed fields showing owner's land; pightle; wood; meadow; arable shown by stripes and pasture shown by symbols representing tufts of grass; roads and watercourses; garden; hedges; pond.
Border of 1 broad and 1 narrow band; title middle bottom; scale bottom right; compass top left showing 4 points, incorrectly giving top as N. Table bottom left giving field names and acreages. Arable coloured brown, grass, trees and hedges coloured green, water coloured blue, buildings coloured red.
In style of Joseph Freeman, who drew up accompanying terrier, with plan of the house, stables and barn at 1:442 [SJC D31.50]. Photograph of map, at 1:4,055, at CRO TR869/P29.

Weston Colville – [c. 1828] – WET82801 – CRO 124/P82
Plan of an Estate in the Parishes of Weston Colville & Carlton in the County of Cambridge <The Property of John Hall Esqre>.
Scale: 6 Chains to the Inch, 1:4,752; **Size:** (ii) 50 9/16 x 24 5/16in.; **Top** is NNW; Manuscript(i), paper mounted on paper, coloured.
Weston Colville Hall, TL612530, and c. 3,200a. in whole parish except for far NW and SE, and a small area in Carlton cum Willingham Parish SW of church.
Names of farms, groves and neighbouring owners. Finchley Gate ['Finchley'], Pound, Mines and Church farms, hall, Linnet Hall, Weston Colville Church and houses in Weston Colville and Weston Green shown in plan form. Closed fields showing owner's land; woods including Lower and Great Coven's ['Great' and 'Little Colville'] and groves; trees including belts of coniferous trees in NW of parish; state of cultivation indicated by 'gr' for grass and 'ar' for arable; roads and watercourses; gardens and orchards; churchyard; ponds and moats.
Title bottom right; scale beneath title; compass bottom right showing 4 plain points. Water coloured blue, roads coloured yellow.
Numbers on fields suggest map was originally accompanied by a terrier. Pencil notes, notes bottom right about final map [this is a rough draft], numbering on plots and colouring of arable, grass and fences. Sketch of farm buildings on dorse. John Hall succeeded to estate in 1809 [*VCH*, 6, 184]; probably drawn at same time as WET82802–3.

Weston Colville – 1828 – WET82802 – CRO 124/P83b
John Hall Esqr Estate at Weston Colville 1828.
Scale: 1:2,150; **Size:** (ii) 73 3/8 x 46in.; **Top** is SE; Manuscript(i), paper, coloured.
Pound Farm, TL625522, and c. 1,200a. in all of parish SE of Weston Green except for far SE, and in Carlton Green hamlet in SW of Carlton cum Willingham Parish.
Names of fields, parishes, some tenants and neighbouring owners. Pound, Street and Finchley Gate farms, houses in Weston Green and outbuildings shown in plan form. Closed fields showing owner's land; pightle; common and pasture; state of cultivation indicated by 'ar' for arable and 'gr' for pasture; acreages; roads and watercourses; gardens and orchards; ponds; brick kiln; yards; sites of woods.
Title top left; compass middle bottom showing 2 points, incorrectly giving top as E. Some buildings and lines coloured blue.
Numbers on fields suggest map originally accompanied by a terrier. Pencil notes filling in details and calculations. Some parts of map backed with paper. On dorse is plan of Downham Parish, Essex. See also WET82803, which shows rest of Hall's estate.

Weston Colville – [1828] – WET82803 – CRO 124/P83a
[Land in Weston Colville, owned by John Hall.]
Scale: 1:2,270; **Size:** (ii) 75 5/8 x 34 1/8in.; **Top** is SE; Manuscript(i), paper, coloured.
Weston Colville Hall, TL613530, and c. 1,200a. in all of parish NW of Weston Green, except for far NW.
Names of fields and tenants. Weston Colville Hall, parsonage, windmill, Linnet ['Lennards'] Hall, house and outbuildings shown in plan form. Closed fields showing owner's land; pightles; meadow and pasture; acreages; roads and watercourses; gardens, lawn and orchards; ponds and moat; yards and churchyard; sites of plantations and grove including Great Covens ['Covins'] and 'Little Covins' woods.
Some buildings coloured blue, some blue lines, some red writing.
Numbers on fields suggest map originally accompanied by a terrier. Pencil and ink alterations and calculations. Pencil notes on dorse including titheable land. Accompanies WET82802, drawn in 1828.

West Wickham – [1788] – WEV78801 – PCC Horseheath C9
[Land in West Wickham, owned by Pembroke College, Cambridge.]
Surveyors: [Thomas Talbot, Jeremiah Lagden]; **Scale:** 1:1,550; **Size:** (ii) 12 1/4 x 7 15/16in.; **Top** is S; Manuscript(i), paper, uncoloured.
11a. in SE of TL6148, bounded by road from Streetly End to West Wickham in NW.
Names of fields, roads and neighbouring owners. Closed fields showing owner's land; trees; roads, gates; hedges and fences.
Compass rose top right showing 4 points. Vignette at top of trees and a fence.
Bottom right is note of tenants and acreages. Pencil notes. Bound with terrier: 'A Terr\e/ar of certain Lands and Premises belonging to the College or Hall of Mary Valence commonly called Pembroke Hall in the University of Cambridge now in Lease to the Right Honorable Thomas

Lord Montfort: lying and being in Horseheath Shudy Camps and Bartlow in the County of Cambridge. Taken this Twenty first Day of June 1788 By us whose Names are hereunto subscribed'. Notes at end of terrier that surveyors were: 'Tho. Talbot on the part of Pembroke Hall Jeremiah Lagden on the Part of Stanlake Batson Esqr', and, dated 1799: 'Note, the three last Lots lay in West Wickham Parish – Wm Custance'. Tracing of map and copy of terrier at CUL MS Plans a.5(ix), photograph in CRO.

West Wickham – [c. 1813] – WEV81301 – CUL MS Plans 337a, 592
West Wickham, Cambs.
Scale: 1:5,040; **Size:** (i) 14 3/8 x 17 15/16in.; **Top** is W; Manuscript(ii), tracing paper mounted on paper, coloured.
c. 210a. W of TL692494, most easterly part of Cadge's Wood in E of parish, bounded by Roman Road to Horseheath in S, and extending into Withersfield Parish [Suffolk].
Names of fields, roads, wood and parishes. Closed fields; Cadge's and Over woods and trees; pasture; acreages; roads; park; hedges and fences; responsibility for boundaries.
Border of 1 narrow band; title bottom right; compass middle top showing 4 points, incorrectly giving top as N. County boundary with Suffolk coloured yellow, pasture coloured green.
2 copies of map accompany documents dated 1813 at CUM Doc.660.

West Wickham – [c. 1822] – WEV82201 – P C C Horseheath C14
The Plan of a field in the Parish of West Wickham in the County of Cambridge in the occupation of William H Rust of West Wickham aforesaid Belonging to the Master Fellows and Scholars of the College or hall of Mary Valence commonly called Pembroke hall in the University of Cambridge.
Surveyor: [Alexander Watford jr]; **Scale:** 1:2,330; **Size:** (iii) 6 7/8 x 6 3/4in.; **Top** is SE; Manuscript(ii), paper, uncoloured.
17a.3r.8p. in TL6148, bounded by Hare Wood in SE and road from Streetly End to West Wickham in W.
Name of field. Closed field; acreage; hedges; roads.
Title at bottom. Red dotted lines.
Note beneath title: '(Description) The dotted lines within the field shews how the fields laid before the inclosure and also the names of the said fields The dotted line against hare wood is part of the 12th Public footway The Red dotted line shews the hedge now standing and which was Planted in the wrong place and making the said field contain 13 Acres 3 Roods 2 perches And the other fence Intended to be planted 286 links of a chain towards the north west which contain the Remaining part to be added to the said 13a 3R. 2p to make it Right according as it is set out in the award for Inclosing the said Parish as follows' [extract from inclosure award follows on verso of sheet and on recto of next leaf]. On dorse: 'Copy of award of land at West Wickham'. Map copied from that by Alexander Watford which accompanied 1822 inclosure award.

West Wickham – 1824 – WEV82401 – PCC LE p.67
Plan of West Wickham Taken from the Award Plan by me G.A. 1824.
Surveyor: [Alexander Watford jr]; **Draughtsman:** G[ilbert] A[inslie]; **Scale:** 1:4,500; **Size:** (iii) 7 x 5in.; **Top** is NW; Manuscript(iv), paper, uncoloured.
17a.3r.8p. in TL6247, bounded by Hare Wood in W, Horseheath Parish in S and Withersfield Parish [Suffolk] in E.
Closed fields; acreages; responsibility for boundaries; roads and footpaths.
Title right; plain compass at top showing 2 points.
Beneath map is sketch of same area, with top pointing SW, which extends roads and refers to: 'Valuation of an Estate in Horseheath Wickham belonging to the Master & Fellows of Pembroke Hall and in Lease in the Earl of Hardwick', dated 1845. Map based on that by Alexander Watford which accompanied 1822 inclosure award; Gilbert Ainslie was a Fellow of Pembroke College, Cambridge [Venn, II, 1, 20].

West Wickham – [1825] – WEV82501 – QCC 355 A18, B18
Estate at West Wickham In The County of Cambridge.
Surveyor: [Alexander Watford jr]; **Scale bar** 0–30 chains (= 5in.), 1:4,752; **Size:** (i) 25 5/8 x 17 1/16in.; **Top** is NW; Manuscript(ii), paper, coloured.
West Wickham Church, TL612492, and 124a.2r.17p. NW of village bounded by Balsham Parish in NW.
Names of fields, neighbouring owners and roads. Houses shown in plan form, church shown in perspective. Closed fields showing owner's land; state of cultivation shown by colour; acreages; hedges; roads and footpaths; watercourses and bridge; 'Allotment with Plan of Subdivisions' in 2 fields.
Border at top, bottom and left of 1 broad band with 1 narrow band on either side, border at right of 2 narrow bands; title top left; scale bottom left; compass in centre showing 4 points. Table bottom right giving acreages, land use and allotments. Fields coloured yellow and green, roads coloured brown, water coloured blue.
On left of sheet which also contains a map of Coton [COT82501]. In volume drawn in 1825: 'Plans of the Several Estates in England and Wales belonging to the President and Fellows of the College of St Margaret and St Bernard commonly called Queen's College in the University of Cambridge Delineated from Authentic Documents in the possession of the said President and Fellows and from actual Surveys taken By their most obedient and obliged Servant Alexr Watford'. Title page drawn by James Richardson [Watford's nephew]. This is the Bursar's copy; 2nd, finer, copy [the Master's copy] at QCC 355 B18, measures 24 3/8 x 18 3/8in. and drawn on parchment. Top points N. Border 7/16in. wide of a central blue band with 1 broad band on either side, title top right has gothic lettering, compass on right shows 8 points. Table has a border imitating a scroll of paper and has red lines. Fields coloured in yellow and brown stripes and have green borders, roads have red/brown edges.

West Wickham – [c. 1827] – WEV82701 – P C C Horseheath C14
I A Plan of the Demesne shewing the situation of the House and the Road in order to reconcile the Description of the 4a2r0p & 5a2r0p.

Surveyor: [Alexander Watford jr]; **Scale:** 1:1,020; **Size:** (iii) 4 x 5 1/2in.; **Top** is NW; Manuscript(ii), paper, uncoloured.

10a. in TL6148, bounded by Hare Wood in SE and road from Streetly End to West Wickham in NW.

Names of fields and wood. 'Mansion House' shown in plan form. Closed fields showing owner's land; trees and Hare Wood; state of cultivation given in words; roads; gates; lawn.

Title at top.

Copy probably drawn in 1827 of map drawn to help settle land dispute between Pembroke College, Cambridge and Stanlake Batson, and to assess value of land. Accompanies correspondence with Mr Batson and: 'Memoranda to be attended to at the Bursar's Rooms relative to the Papers of Horseheath Hall Property in Lease to Mr Batson', 16 May 1827, which mention 'Plans relating to the Lands in dispute'. Referred to in: 'Mr Watford's Report, relative to the final investigation of the Quantity of the Horseheath Estate. Dated 24th Novr 1827'. See HRS82701 for plan accompanying this report. See also WEV82702–3.

West Wickham – [c. 1827] – WEV82702 – P C C Horseheath C14

II. Plan of Saghouse, New Fields & Overyards.

Surveyor: [Alexander Watford jr]; **Scale:** 1:6,400; **Size:** (iii) 2 x 3 3/8in.; **Top** is W; Manuscript(ii), paper, uncoloured.

19a.0r.22p. in E of TL6147, bounded by road from Streetly End to West Wickham in W and Horseheath Parish in S.

Closed fields showing owner's land; acreages; roads.

Title at top. Table at top giving field names, acreages and land use.

Note at bottom: 'NB I have substituted my own admeasurement of the West Wickham Lands for this as it will accord with the Plan made for Mr Batson'. Copy probably drawn in 1827 of map drawn to help settle land dispute between Pembroke College, Cambridge and Stanlake Batson, and to assess value of land. See WEV82701 for details of accompanying documents which suggest date. See also WEV82703.

West Wickham – [c. 1827] – WEV82703 – P C C Horseheath C14

['Sketch of the 5a 1/2 as measured by Mr Watford'.]

Surveyor: [Alexander] Watford [jr]; **Scale:** 1:2,320; **Size:** (ii) 8 1/2 x 14in.; **Top** is NW; Manuscript(i), paper, uncoloured.

9a.0r.18p. statute measure [10a.0r.0p. computed measure] in TL6148, bounded by road from Streetly End to West Wickham in NW and Hare Wood in SE.

Names of fields, roads, tenants and neighbouring owners. Building shown in plan form. Closed fields; acreages and dimensions of areas; roads; hedges.

Pencil sketch of compass top right showing 4 points.

Note on left of computed and statute acreages. Title on dorse. Drawn to help settle land dispute between Pembroke College, Cambridge and Stanlake Batson, and to assess value of land. Accompanies: 'Description of the College 5a2r0p supposing that Mr Watford is correct in his Conclusions', and: 'Mr Watford's Report, relative to the final investigation of the Quantity of the Horseheath Estate. Dated 24th Novr 1827'. See HRS82701 for plan accompanying this report. See also WEV82701–2.

West Wickham – [1829] – WEV82901 – C U L Maps.PSQ.18.81

Plan of the estate.

Auctioneer: W.W. Simpson; **Lithographer:** J.M. Johnson; **Scale bar** 0–30 chains (= 4 15/16in.), 1:4,812; **Size:** (i) 8 7/16 x 12 1/4in.; **Top** is NE; Lithograph, paper, coloured.

Streetly End Farm, TL613481, and c. 170a. crossed by road to Streetly Hall, and bounded by road from Horseheath to West Wickham in E and field boundary running from TL609486 to TL616486 in N.

Names of closes, roads and neighbouring owners. Buildings shown in plan form, particulars of sale identify farm buildings, houses, cottages, brick kiln, tan yard, tower mill and malting office. Closed fields; trees; state of cultivation shown by colour; acreages; roads and watercourses; hedges; responsibility for boundaries; bridges.

Border of 1 narrow band; title bottom right; scale beneath title; plain compass middle right with a feathered tail showing 4 points and indicating 16 subdivisions. Yards coloured red, pasture coloured 2 shades of green, arable coloured brown.

Inset of 23a.0r.4p. around brick kiln. Accompanies 'Particular and conditions of sale of a Valuable Estate, principally freehold, and altogether tithe free, Pleasantly situated at Streetly End, in the parish of West Wickham, Cambridgeshire, which will be sold by auction by Mr W.W. Simpson ... July, 1829'. Particulars of sale give date and details about buildings, occupiers, rents and taxes. Sold by Daniel Taylor [*VCH*, 6, 12; this is the map referred to in footnote 11].

West Wratting – 1719 – WEW71901 – CUL MS Plans 713

An Actual Survey of the manner of Rands in the Parish of West Wrattin in the Comp [sic] of Cambridge purchased by the Corporation of the Sons of the Clergy of Esqr Dalten for the reliefe of poor Widows and Children of Clergy~men Surveyed and measured December 1719 by A. Frogly.

Surveyor: A[rthur] Frogley; **Scale bar** 4–0–84 rods (= 5 7/16in.), 1:3,204; **Size:** (ii) 34 7/8 x 23 13/16in.; **Top** is W; Manuscript(i), parchment, coloured.

West Wratting Church, TL606524, and 187a.0r.33p. scattered in plots to W along road to Cambridge and to E as far as West Wratting common.

Names of roads. Church, post mill and farm buildings shown in perspective. Open fields showing owner's strips; closes; common; wood and trees; pasture and meadow; acreages of some plots; roads and gates; orchard; pond.

Title top left in a cartouche with classical columns; scale middle left; compass rose middle bottom showing 16 points in a plain circular border. Table in same cartouche as title giving tenants, field names and acreages for 2 farms. Land belonging to Mr Whitaker's farm outlined in green, land belonging to Mr Flake's farm outlined in green and red, houses have red roofs.

Pencil notes, note of 1844 attached top right: 'Though Inaccurate in many Points – has been of much service in identifying Lands on Bowles' Map of 1737 Richard Harwood'. Pencil alterations to a plot number are corrected on WLL71901. Previous owner was Tyrell Dalton [*VCH*, 6, 193]. Surveyor's 1st name was Arthur [Eden F228].

West Wratting – [1719] – WEW71902 – C U L Maps.FR.y.12

A Survey of Lands at West~Wratting Cambridgeshire belonging to the Corporation of the Sons of the Clergy.

Surveyor: [Arthur Frogley]; **Draughtsman:** J[ohn] Newton; **Scale bar** 0–40 chains (= 3 7/8in.), 1:8,175; **Size:** (i) 9 3/8 x 15 1/2in.; **Top** is N; Manuscript(ii), parchment, coloured.

187a.0r.33p. scattered throughout parish bounded by Balsham common in W.

Names of roads. Farm buildings and windmill shown in perspective. Closes; wood and trees; 'West Wratting Common, alias Little Shrubs'; acreages of some fields; roads; pond; hop ground, orchards and meadow identified on terrier.

Border of 1 broad band with 1 narrow band on inside; title top left in a cartouche of leaves; yellow and grey scale bar bottom left; compass top right showing 8 points. Roads coloured yellow, trees coloured green, fields coloured green or red, water coloured blue, wood coloured green and brown.

Note by 1 building: 'A House lett to D. Woodland'. Top right: '10' in later ink note. Map is framed; attached to back of frame is a terrier which gives field names, acreages and land use. Note at bottom of terrier: 'NB Whitaker's Farm is green And Flax Farm green, & red'. Map signed by J[ohn] Newton, 97 Chancery Lane, where he practised c. 1807–18 [Eden N69]; as in WSM71601, Newton copied map from original by Arthur Frogley in 1719 [WEW71901], but numbering of plots has changed.

West Wratting – 1737 – WEW73701 – BL Maps R.a.2

A Map of An Estate Lying in the Parish of West Wratting in the County of Cambridge Belonging to the Governours of the Charity for Relief of the Poor Widows and Children of Clergymen. Taken in September and October Anno Domini 1737 by Jn Bowles surveyer.

Surveyor: John Bowles; **Scale bar** 5–0–100 poles or perches (= 4 1/4in.), 1:4,892; **Size:** (i) 27 1/2 x 59 7/8in.; **Top** is NE; Manuscript(i), parchment, coloured.

West Wratting Church, TL606524, and 187a.0r.33p. in scattered plots extending S and E to West Wratting common, and bounded by Balsham Parish in W, Weston Colville Parish in E and heath in N.

Names of fields. Farms and farm buildings, cottage, houses, churches, West Wratting Hall, West Wratting Park House, Brook Farm ['The Shrub House'; identified on table] and post mill shown in perspective. Open fields showing owner's strips; common; wood and trees; heath; pasture; land ploughed from heath; roads and footpaths; watercourses; gates; pond; chalk pits; 'The grave'; 'The White post'; fences; responsibility for boundaries.

Border of 1 narrow and 1 broad band; title bottom right in a gold baroque cartouche; scale bottom left; compass top left showing 4 blue and gold points. Table middle bottom showing tenants and their land, homesteads of Mr Whitaker and Mr Gellson, and key to symbols. Strips outlined in green, yellow and red, trees coloured green, ditch coloured grey, roads coloured brown.

'West Wratting' written in a scroll in centre of village. Pencil notes. Positive photostat at CUL Atlas.0.97.9.

West Wratting – [c. 1757] – WEW75701 – JCC West Wratting

['Valley Farm House & Stables.']

Scale to the Ground Plan 10–0–40 [feet] (= 4 7/8in.), 1:123, Scale for the Stable 10–0–20 [feet] (= 7 5/8in.), 1:47; **Size:** (ii) 19 x 26 7/8in.; **Top** is S; Manuscript(ii), tracing paper mounted on paper, coloured.

Valley Farm, TL561541, and c. 3r. around it.

Names of areas. Buildings shown in plan form and include hall, pantry, parlours, kitchen, 'Back house', coal house, 'Harnes house' and stable. Dimensions of some areas; roads and gates; ditches; kitchen yard; 'Durt Bin', 'Cole Bing', 'Dung Pitt'; door; 'Brick wall'; 'petty', 'several petty privies'; school yard; gravel.

Scale bottom left. Walls of buildings coloured yellow and grey.

Top right is plan of stable, with front and side elevations underneath. Shows buildings are timber-framed. Title and date on label to map. May accompany William Elstobb's survey and valuation of 1757 [JCC West Wratting 2]. Owned by Jesus College, Cambridge.

West Wratting – 1771 – WEW77101 – CRO 305/P1

A Map of an Estate situate at West Wratting in the County of Cambridge belonging to Robt Shaftoe Esqr. Surveyed in the Year 1771.

A Scale of four Chains to an Inch, Scale bar 0–18 chains (= 4 1/2in.), 1:3,168; **Size:** (i) 22 1/8 x 29 1/4in.; **Top** is N; Manuscript(i), parchment, coloured.

Oxcroft Farm, TL592514, and 167a.3r.27p. bounded by Balsham Parish in S and road to village in N and W, and some land to W on heath.

Names of fields and owners of leasehold land. Oxcroft Farm, farm buildings and house in paddock shown in plan form. Closes; heath; Conger's ['Congary'] Well and 'High Ocklers' plantations; meadow; roads; gates.

Border of 3/16in.-wide green band with 2 narrow bands on either side; title middle bottom in a rococo cartouche; scale in middle surmounted by yellow and blue dividers and a green ribbon; compass middle top showing 8 green, yellow and grey points. Table bottom right giving field names and acreages. Fields outlined in green, red, blue and yellow.

Note under table: 'N.B. This Estate is all Freehold, except No. 9, 12, 13, 14 and 15 which are specified on the Plan. Note also, the Numbers 1, 2, 3, 4, 5, 6, 7 and 8 are not Freehold but Jesus College'. Pencil notes of acreages on table. Drawn when Robert Shaftoe inherited estate as a result of his brother Jenison's suicide in 1771 [VCH, 6, 194].

West Wratting – 1793 – WEW79301 – JCC ES.4.10.29

Plan of Lands and Houses called the Valley, in the Parish of West~Wratton; belonging to Jesus College Cambridge. Surveyed in the Year 1793.

Surveyor: [Joseph Freeman]; **Scale bar** 0–10 chains (= 5in.), 1:1,584; **Size:** (i) 20 1/8 x 28 5/8in.; **Top** is NE; Manuscript(i), paper, coloured.

Valley Farm, TL561541, and 14a.3r.16p. around it.

Farm buildings and barns shown in plan form. Closed fields showing owner's land; trees; acreages; features which may be gardens or orchards; heath adjoining map.

Border of 2 narrow bands; title top right; scale at bottom. Buildings coloured red, trees and land coloured green, gardens coloured brown.

Bottom left: 'Map of the Buildings' at 1:469 showing offices, hovels, 'Dwelling House', stables and granary, all coloured red. Pencil notes of allotments on inclosure. In style of Joseph Freeman; in volume whose contents list suggests drawn by [unidentified] Freeman.

West Wratting – 1794 – WEW79401 – JCC ES.4.10.15
Plan of an Estate in the Parishes of West Wratting and West Wickham, in the County of Cambridge. belonging to Jesus College, Cambridge. Surveyed in 1794.
Surveyor: [Joseph Freeman]; **Scale bar** 5–0–15 chains (= 2 1/2in.), 1:6,336; **Size:** (i) 25 3/4 x 19 7/8in.; **Top** is N; Manuscript(i), parchment, coloured.
West Wratting Church, TL606524, and 93a.0r.35p. N and W of village, bounded by Oxcroft Farm in S.
Names of farms, fields, neighbouring owners and roads. Houses and farm buildings shown in plan form. Open fields showing owner's strips; closes; state of cultivation shown by colour; roads; Conger's ['Congary'] Well Plantation, 'Mill Wood' in West Wickham Parish and trees; paddocks; ditches.
Border of 1 narrow and 1 broad band; title bottom left; scale in centre; compass centre top showing 4 points. Table bottom left giving field names, acreages and land use. Trees coloured green, land coloured brown, buildings coloured red.
Inset bottom right of land N of village bounded by Weston Colville Parish, with top as NNE. Inset on left of land in NW of West Wickham Parish bounded by Balsham Parish in W, with top as ENE. Pencil notes. In style of Joseph Freeman; in volume whose contents list suggests drawn by [unidentified] Freeman.

West Wratting – 1794 – WEW79402 – BRO R1/153
No. 1 Plan and Survey of an Estate; at West Wratting, Balsham and West Wickham; in the County of Cambridge. the Property of the most noble Francis, Duke of Bedford. Surveyed in the Year 1794.
Surveyor: [Joseph Freeman]; **Scale bar** 10–0–25 chains (= 4 3/8in.), 1:6,336; **Size:** (i) 23 3/8 x 26 7/8in.; **Top** is N; Manuscript(i), parchment, coloured.
Scarlett's Farm, TL605515, and land to E, N and S of road to Withersfield, in NE of West Wickham Parish and in E of Balsham Parish.
Names of fields, roads and neighbouring owners. Farm buildings, 'The Mill' and 'Mill House' shown in plan form. Open fields showing owner's strips; closes; wood and trees; state of cultivation shown by colour; roads; watercourses and ponds; moat; hedges and fences.
Border of 1 broad band with 1 narrow band on inside; title bottom left; scale under title; compass in centre showing 4 points. 5th [PB, 226] Duke of Bedford's coat of arms centre bottom. Roads coloured yellow, hedges coloured green, arable coloured in brown stripes, pasture and trees coloured green, buildings coloured red.
Numbers on plots suggest map originally accompanied by a terrier. Note right of coat of arms: 'Mr Archer says this Plan is incorrect'. Centre right: 'Note. For Corporation read Corporation of Clergimen'. Inset bottom right of land in West Wickham and Balsham parishes, with top as NW. Joseph Freeman was paid £44 6s 9d in 1796 for surveying and planning estate [BRO Russell Box 279]. See also WEW79403.

West Wratting – 1794 – WEW79403 – BRO R1/154
No. 11 Plan and Survey of an Estate at West Wratting, Balsham and West Wickham; in the County of Cambridge.

the Property of the most noble Francis Duke of Bedford. Surveyed in the Year 1794.
Surveyor: [Joseph Freeman]; **Scale bar** 10–0–20 chains (= 3 3/4in.), 1:6,336; **Size:** (i) 36 1/4 x 30 5/16in.; **Top** is NW; Manuscript(i), parchment, coloured.
West Wratting Church, TL606524, and land to NW bounded by Weston Colville Parish in N and Balsham Parish in S, and some strips in Balsham and West Wickham parishes.
Names of farms, fields, roads and neighbouring owners. Cottages, Oxcroft, Valley and Dungate farms and church shown in plan form. Open fields showing owner's strips; closes; wood and trees; heath; intercommon; state of cultivation shown by colour; roads and watercourses; 'Balsham Great Ditch and Bank'; bridge; hedges; earthworks; bank shown by hachures.
Border of 1 broad band with 1 narrow band on inside; title bottom left; scale under title; compass top right showing 4 points, incorrectly giving top as N. 5th [PB, 226] Duke of Bedford's coat of arms above title. Hedges coloured green, roads coloured brown, buildings coloured red, heath and pasture coloured green, arable coloured in brown stripes, land coloured blue, yellow, red and brown.
Note beneath coat of arms: 'Mr Archer says this Plan is incorrect'. Right of scale: 'Note. For Corporation read Corporation of Clergymen'. Beneath title: 'Note The Lordship Farm is held by Lease from Peter House College, and Coloured with Blue The Manor called Le Great Nuns, held by Lease from Jesus College ... Yellow The Manor or Reputed Manor of Oxcroft, Freehold ... Red The Remaining Lands are Freehold and Copyhold intermixed ... Brown To this Plan belongs a Book of Reference, which gives the best information that could be obtained of the different Tenures'. Joseph Freeman was paid £44 6s 9d in 1796 for surveying and planning estate [BRO Russell Box 279]. See also WEW79402.

West Wratting – 1796 – WEW79601 – JCC ES.4.10.20
A Plan of Wratting Park in the County of Cambridge. 1796.
Surveyor: [Joseph Freeman]; **Scale bar** 100 links– 0–5 chains (= 3in.), 1:1,584; **Size:** (i) 23 9/16 x 20 1/2in.; **Top** is N; Manuscript(i), parchment, coloured.
West Wratting House, TL609518, and 86a.0r.33p. in park to S.
Names of neighbouring owners. House, blacksmith's cottage and other cottages shown in plan form. Closed fields; wood and trees; acreages of land belonging to Jesus College; roads; gates; gardens; blacksmith's yard; tenure.
Border of 1 broad and 1 narrow band; title at top; scale bottom right; compass in middle showing 4 points. Table top right giving acreages, landowners and tenure. Roads coloured brown, trees coloured green, buildings coloured red, land owned by Jesus College outlined in yellow.
Note beneath scale: 'The Buildings are Coloured with Red. Jesus College Lands with Yellow'. In style of Joseph Freeman; in volume whose contents list suggests drawn by [unidentified] Freeman.

West Wratting – 1809 – WEW80901 – CUL MS Plans 715
Plan of Estate the Property of John Chester Pern Esqr lying within the Parish of Westwratting in the County of Cambridge, Divided and Allotted under an Act of Parliament

for Inclosing the said Parish Passed Anno Domini 1809. T. Norfolk, surveyor.

Surveyor: T[homas] Norfolk; **Scale bar** 0–20 chains (= 3 1/4in.), 1:4,874; **Size:** (i) 29 1/2 x 15 1/4in.; **Top** is NNW; Manuscript(i), paper mounted on cloth, coloured.

Scarlett's Farm, TL605516, and 176a.2r.32p. in SW of village, bounded by Scarlett's Lane in S, road to Balsham in N and High ['Town'] Street in E, and 1 plot further S along road to Withersfield.

Names of roads and neighbouring owners. Church and post mill shown in perspective, farm buildings including 'hay lock' [loft] shown in plan form. Closed fields showing owner's land; wood and trees; state of cultivation shown by colour; roads and footpaths; watercourses; garden; moat; hedges.

Border of 1 broad band with 1 narrow band on either side; title middle right in an oval cartouche of 1 broad band with 1 narrow band on either side; scale beneath title; compass above title showing 8 points. Table bottom left giving acreages and description of land, and indicating which land was exchanged, sold or bought on inclosure. Roads and arable coloured brown, pasture and wood coloured green.

Pencil notes and note under table: 'The Whole is Freehold except the 6th Allotment which is Copyhold of the Manor of Escaliers otherwise Charles in Westwratting, Dean Piper Tenant'. Surveyor's 1st name was Thomas [Eden N115].

West Wratting – [c. 1813] – WEW81301 – JCC West Wratting 3

Plan of an Estate situate in the Parish of West Wratting in the County of Cambridge belonging to the Master, Fellows, and Scholars of Jesus College in the University of Cambridge.

Scale: 1:4,320; **Size:** (i) 26 x 18 1/8in.; **Top** is NW; Manuscript(i), parchment, coloured.

Valley Farm, TL561541, and 198a.1r.3p. in NW of parish, bounded by Great Wilbraham Parish in N and Balsham Parish in S.

Names of neighbouring owners, roads and areas. Farm buildings and barns shown in plan form. Closed fields showing owner's land; hedges; acreages; roads; watercourses including Fleam Dyke ['Balsham Ditch']; allotments 'in Exchange with C. Pern for Land in Abington'.

Border of 1 narrow band; title top right; compass middle right showing 4 points. Table at bottom giving acreages and reasons for allotments. Roads coloured brown.

Probably drawn at time of 1813 inclosure award for West Wratting when land in Little Abington exchanged with John Chester Perne [*VCH*, 6, 8; WEW80901]; catalogue in JCC suggests drawn between 1809 and 1821.

West Wratting – 1815 – WEW81501 – CUL MS Plans 714

Plan of an Estate belonging to the Corporation for the Relief of Poor Widows and Children of Clergymen, lying within the Parish of Westwratting in the County of Cambridge as Divided, Allotted, and Inclosed under and by an Act of Parliament Passed Anno Domini 1809, 1815. Taken from the Award Plan of the Commissioners in January 1815.

Surveyor: Thomas Norfolk; **Scale bar** 0–40 chains = 0–4 furlongs (= 6 1/2in.), 1:4,874; **Size:** (ii) 54 3/4 x 24

1/4in.; **Top** is NW; Manuscript(iv), paper mounted on cloth, coloured.

West Wratting Church, TL606524, and 644a.0r.1p. bounded by Balsham Parish in NW and Weston Colville Parish in SE.

Names of tenants and neighbouring owners. Church and post mill shown in perspective, farm buildings shown in plan form. Closed fields showing owner's land; Rand's Wood and trees; state of cultivation shown by colour; tenure; acreages of copyhold land; roads and footpaths; watercourses; park and garden; pond; bridges; hedges.

Title middle right; scale beneath title; compass middle left showing 8 points. Table beneath scale giving tenants and acreages of land of each tenant and of land in hand. Roads coloured yellow, water coloured blue, arable coloured brown, pasture coloured green.

Pencil notes.

Whaddon – [c. 1820–41] – WHA82001 – CCC

Plan of a Portion of the Parish of Whaddon, showing the Old Inclosures belonging to the Master and Fellows of Christ College Cambridge; and the whole of the Open Field Lands in the Parish.

Scale bar 1–0–50 chains (= 5 3/16in.), 1:7,786; **Size:** (i) 33 5/16 x 22 3/4in.; **Top** is NNW; Manuscript(i), paper mounted on cloth, coloured.

Whaddon Church, TL350466, and 144a.0r.20 1/2p. scattered throughout parish.

Names of fields. Farm buildings shown in plan form. Open fields; closes; common and meadow; acreages of land belonging to Christ's College; roads and footpaths; watercourses; bridges; 'Basin'.

Border of 1 broad and 1 narrow band; title top right; scale at bottom; compass bottom left showing 8 points. Roads coloured brown, buildings coloured purple and red, water coloured blue, fields outlined in green, blue, red, purple, brown and yellow.

Accompanying terrier gives acreages and number of pieces in open fields and 'new closes', and refers to a plan and terrier of 1796. 'New closes' implies some land recently inclosed, possibly under 1820 award, but final inclosure award of 1841 had not yet occurred.

Whittlesey – 1683/4 – WHR68401 – BRO R1/300

A Perfect Survey of these Grounds herein Specified lying in the Mannor of Whittlesey in the Isle of Ely and County of Cambridge aforesaid (in a place there Called the Wash) the lands aforesaid was late in the Possession of Stretchley and now are belonging to Christ Hospital London the said Survey taken in March 1683 by Robt Smith.

Surveyor: Robert Smith; **Scale:** 1:4,150; **Size:** (i) 8 5/8 x 12 5/8in.; **Top** is S; Manuscript(i), paper, coloured.

107a.3r.34p., probably in TL9928 and TL9929, bounded by Morton's Leam in S and North Bank in N.

Names of neighbouring owners. Closed fields showing owner's land; acreages; roads and 'The Drove through the Middle of the Wash'; Morton's Leam; banks; 'the new Cutt Land' and 'the old Cutt Land'.

Border of 1 narrow red band; title top left in a red square cartouche; compass rose top right showing 16 red and uncoloured points. Left of title is a printed coat of arms of Christ's Hospital with 'ChrisHospital' written in ink underneath. Roads and Morton's Leam coloured brown.

Whittlesey – 1706 – WHR70601 – BLO MS Rolls Cambridgeshire 10

Ground Surveyed for Arthur Rit Hon, Earl of Torington Lying in Whitlsy & Wisbidg fenns Contaning 1844a:2r:04p, of which theire is 14a:3r:03p, of Cutt Land, with the Tennants Names, now occupyng & theire number of Ackers which they haue upon Rent, By Val: Deepup in Peterborow Nouth:2:1706 [November 2].

Surveyor: Val. Deepup; **Scale bar** 10–0–90 [perches] (= 3 1/8in.), 1:6,336; **Size:** (i) 32 1/8 x 22 1/2in.; **Top** is E; Manuscript(i), parchment, coloured.

Junction of Shaw's Dike with S bank of Morton's Leam, TF351008, and 1,844a.2r.4p. bounded by Twenty Foot River ['Bevill's Leam'] in S and Wisbech High Fen in N.

Names of drains. Houses, barns and windmill shown in perspective. Closed fields showing owner's land; trees; acreages; watercourses, dykes and drains; banks; gate.

Border 3/8in. wide of 1 green band with 1 yellow band with ink decoration on inside; title in centre in a cartouche of fruit and flowers coloured green, yellow and red; red and yellow scale bar above title surmounted by yellow dividers with a red, green and yellow top. Table on left giving tenants and acreages. Banks coloured green, trees coloured green, buildings and gate coloured yellow.

Whittlesey – [c. 1710] – WHR71001 – BLO MS Rolls Cambridgeshire 8

An Esate [sic] in Whitlsey Late of Geo Vnderwood Esq Deceased Consisting Of A Free hold Containing § with out Hoults 216a:1r:18 with Hoults 227:2:30 And A Leas=hold belonging to The Right Honovrable Arthvr Earl Of Torrington Containing § With out Hoults 1095a:2r:30p: Hoults 29:0:27 With Hoults 1124:3:17 Surveyed by Tho Boyce.

Surveyor: Thomas Boyce; **Scale bar** 0–10 [chains] (= 3in.), 1:2,640; **Size:** (i) 22 13/16 x 34in.; **Top** is E; Manuscript(i), parchment, coloured.

Underwood's Farm, TL269926, and 1,352a.2r.7p. bounded by Whittlesey Dike in N and Bevill's Leam in S.

Names of rivers. Houses, barns and 2 windmills [possibly smock mills] shown in perspective. Closed fields; wood; acreages; roads; watercourses and bridges; earthworks.

Border of 3/16in.-wide red band; title centre bottom in a cartouche of a yellow stone slab; scale bottom left surmounted by yellow dividers. Roads coloured yellow, trees coloured green, water coloured grey.

Numbers on plots suggest map originally accompanied by a terrier. Date suggested in BLO map catalogue.

Whittlesey – [c. 1716] – WHR71601 – BLO MS Rolls Cambridgeshire 11

Land In Whitlessey Belonging To The Right Honovrable The Earle of Lincoln Containing In The Whole 1134a:3r Surveyed by Tho Boyce.

Surveyor: Thomas Boyce; **Scale:** 1:4,490; **Size:** (i) 25 x 33 7/8in.; **Top** is NE; Manuscript(i), parchment, coloured.

1,134a.3r.0p. W of TL308956, bounded by Whittlesey Dike in N and Bevill's Leam in S.

Names of dykes and neighbouring owners. Cottages, barns and windmills shown in perspective. Trees; acreages; roads and dykes; bridges; pasture shown by colour.

Border of 3/16in.-wide yellow band with 1 narrow brown band on each side; title centre bottom in a cartouche of yellow columns; compass rose bottom left showing 4 points. Table on left with a green border 3/16in. wide with 1 brown line on each side giving tenants and acreages. Roads coloured yellow, trees and grass coloured green, water coloured grey.

Drawn after Henry Clinton, 7th Earl of Lincoln, inherited Earl of Torrington's estate in 1716 [*DNB*, 26, 169–72]; BLO map catalogue suggests date of 1715.

Whittlesey – 1775 – WHR77501 – BRO R5/4006

A Plan of the Reed~Bush along the Sides of Smiths~Leam in Whittlesea~Wash, from The Dog~in~a~Doublet, to Knar~Lake, taken A.D. 1775.

Surveyor: John Watte; **Scale bar** 0–40 chains (= 5in.), 1:6,336; **Size:** (i) 4 x 47 3/4in.; **Top** is NNW; Manuscript(i), paper, uncoloured.

Junction of River Nene and Delph Dike, TL275994, and 121a.1r.25p. to E extending as far as boundary with Thorney and Wisbech St Mary parishes.

Names of buildings, gulls and neighbouring owners. Buildings shown in perspective and include 'The Dog~in~a~Doublet' and 'The Three Fishes' public houses, 'Poplar Tree House' and 'Jacklin's House'. Closed fields; poplar tree; roads and drove; watercourses; bank; 'Bradley's Gull' and Popley's Gull; 'gravel' [ford]; 2 inn signs.

Border of 2 narrow bands; title bottom left in a cartouche of 1 narrow band with 1 broad band on inside; scale bottom right; compass in centre showing 4 points. Table bottom left giving tenants and acreages.

Notes at bottom: '(In this Survey half the Ditch next the Wash Lands is Included)'; 'Note, The true Distance from the Dog~in~a~Doublet Sluice to Knar Lake, in a direct Line, is 4 Miles, 5 Furlongs, 2 Chains, & 60 Links, equal 372,60 Chains, or 4,6575 Miles'. In: 'The Particulars of a Survey of the Lordship of Thorney, taken in the Years 1752 and 1753'. Land owned by Francis Russell, 5th Duke of Bedford.

Whittlesey – [c. 1786–8] – WHR78601 – CUL MS Plans 554

[Whittlesey Manors, owned by Laura, Elizabeth and Charlotte Maria Waldegrave.]

Surveyor: [Thomas Moore?]; **Scale:** 1:32,200; **Size:** (ii) 9 7/8 x 15 1/4in.; **Top** is N; Manuscript(i), paper, coloured.

c. 21,000a. in Whittlesey and N of Benwick parishes, S of TL308955, junction of Bevill's Leam and Whittlesey Dike and bounded by River Nene in E, Cnut's ['Delf'] Dyke in SW and Whittlesey Dike in N.

Names of fields, fen, droves, dykes, owners and tenants. Open fields showing all strips; common; waste; 'Glassmoore', 'Pulver and Turff Fen', Whittlesey and Ramsey meres; acreages of some fields; roads and footpaths; watercourses.

Roads coloured brown, river and meres coloured green.

Accompanies: 'A Particular of the three mannors or Lordships of Whittlesey within the Isle of Ely to wit Whittlesey St Mary Whittlesey St Andrew and the Rectory of Whittlesey St Mary called Coquenary with the Impropriate Tythes belonging to the said severall Mannors lying in the fields of Whittlesey and Eastrea and Coats being Hamletts belonging to Whittlesey aforesaid and the Tythes of Ferm Lands lying in the said three severall

Mannors and also the Profitts arising to the Lord of the said Mannors on admittances of the Copyhold Tenants by Fines and amerciaments imposed & sett by the Jurys at the Courts Leet and Courts Baron held twice in the Year for the said Mannors with the Estrays & Royalty of Fishing in Mortons Leams & with the supposed Vallue to apurchasor', signed by Thomas Moore [surname unclear] and gives details of tenants, acreages, state of cultivation, tenure, tithes, buildings to be repaired, rents and fines. Owned by 3 Waldegrave sisters: Laura, Elizabeth and Charlotte Maria [*VCH*, 4, 128]. Probably drawn in connection with chancery dispute when husbands of Charlotte Maria [m. 1784] and Horatia [m. 1786] tried to retrieve part of their wives' inheritance [Biddulph, 1938, 153]. Shows a rent charge to Lady Catherine Petre, who died in 1788 [*PB*, 2,109].

Whittlesey – [c. 1822] – WHR82201 – C R O R59/31/40/77

[Land in Flag Fen, owned by William David Grounds, Robert Searle and Whittlesey Charity.]

Scale: 1:7,730; **Size:** (ii) 10 3/8 x 15 5/16in.; **Top** is N; Manuscript(ii), tracing paper mounted on paper, uncoloured.

464a.0r.35p. in Flag Fen, bounded by junction of Whittlesey Dike and Bevill's Leam, TL308954, in E, Turningtree Road ['Turn Tree Drove'] in W, Whittlesey Dike in N and Bevill's Leam in S.

Names of owners, watercourses and droves. Farm buildings shown in plan form, 2 windmills shown in perspective. Closed fields showing owner's land; acreages; roads and watercourses; bridges.

Table bottom right giving acreages and owners.

Numbers on fields suggest map originally accompanied by a terrier. In similar style to and classified with LLP82201, so probably drawn at about same time.

Whittlesey – 1823 – WHR82301 – CRO 515/P

Survey of Nos 49 and 50 in Whittlesea Fourth District, belonging to Messrs Waddelow, Roslyn and Blunt, made in pursuance of an Order of the Eau Brink Commissioners of Appeal by Joseph Jackson Land Surveyor, March, 1823.

Surveyor: Joseph Jackson; **Scale:** 4 Chains to an Inch, 1:3,168; **Size:** (ii) 29 11/16 x 21 7/8in.; **Top** is N; Manuscript(i), paper, uncoloured.

Beggar's Bridge, TL323968, and 219a.3r.13p. in The Turves bounded by Turf Drove in W and Burnthouse Drove in E.

Names of owners, droves and bridge. Farm buildings shown in plan form. Closes; acreages; roads and watercourses; gates; Beggar's Bridge; fences.

Title bottom left; scale bottom right; compass middle top showing 4 plain points. Table top right giving acreages and landowners.

Pencil notes and calculations. On dorse: 'No. 41. Mr Waddlows Farm in Whittlesea fen'. Owners were John Waddelow [CRO EPR CW 1843 WR C57:71], Thomas Roslyn [CRO EPR CW 1833 WR C54:245] and Henry Layton Blunt [CRO EPR CW 1845 WR C57:323].

Whittlesford – [Post 1815] – WHV81501 – PCC

Plan of an Estate situate in the Parishes of Whittlesford and Duxford in the County of Cambridge belonging to The Master and Fellows of Pembroke Hall in the University of Cambridge.

Scale bar 0–20 chains (= 3 1/4in.), 1:4,874; **Size:** (i) 18 1/2 x 24 3/8in.; **Top** is W; Manuscript(i), parchment, coloured.

61a.3r.27p. in TL4648 in centre of parish, bounded by roads to Newton in NW and to Cambridge in NE, and 1a.1r.18p. in N of Duxford Parish.

Names of roads, neighbouring owners and former tenants. Cottages shown in plan form. Closed fields showing owner's land; meadow; acreages; hedges; roads, footpaths and bridleway.

Border of 1 narrow band; title centre top; scale at bottom; compass in centre showing 4 plain points. Table top left giving field names and acreages. Roads coloured brown, College land coloured green.

Numbers on fields suggest map originally accompanied by a terrier. Drawn after 1815 inclosure award.

Whittlesford – [c. 1819] – WHV81901 – CRO R58/5/9 p.165

The River and North Boundary of Whittlesford Cambridgeshire.

Surveyor: [Anthony Jackson?]; **Scale:** 1:9,000; **Size:** (i) 15 5/8 x 33 3/4in.; **Top** is NE; Printed, paper, coloured.

Whittlesford Manor, TL476486, and c. 2,000a. in NE of parish, bounded by Sawston Parish in NE, Pampisford Parish in SE, Little Shelford Parish in W and road from Great Shelford to Duxford in S, including land in SW of Sawston Parish.

Names of fields, roads, owners and tenants. Cottages, church, Pampisford, Whittlesford ['Hollick's'] and Dernford ['Danser'] mills and buildings, probably toll houses, on turnpike road from Royston to Newmarket shown in plan form, 'Martindale's Mill' shown in perspective, Whittlesford Manor and stables shown in exaggerated perspective. Open fields showing owner's land; closes; common; trees; meadow; roads including turnpike; footpaths; watercourses including River Cam and mill-streams; gates; parks and gardens; fences and hedges; bridges; 'Abrahams shoals'; 'floodgates or sluice'; 'Stank' [pool; Reaney, 1943, 262]; churchyard.

Border of 1 broad and 1 narrow band; title top right. Cuffed hands indicate directions of some roads. Land in Whittlesford coloured green, river coloured blue, buildings except for manor coloured red, boundary of manor coloured red, ditch coloured yellow.

Pencil notes of owners of cottages and some features. Ink notes about field once belonging to Roger Ascham, additions of descriptions, owners and tenants, red ink addition of a path. Bottom right is key to colours and letters indicating 'Ancient Ditch' filled by Mr Martindale, area of soil erosion and earth thrown out of river upon Mr Hollick's land. Map cut out of a larger sheet. Accompanies letter with note: 'A letter from Anthony Jackson Esqr of Barkway Hertfordshire one of the commissioners appointed in 1813 to enclose the parish of Whittlesford, – dated 1819 – to Ebenezer Hollick Esquire of the 'Lodge House' Whittlesford – giving some particulars of land in that parish belonging to Mr Martindale about which there appears to be some dispute. This and others respecting the water course &c between Hollicks Oil Mill at Whittlesford and Martindales Paper Mill – ultimately led to a law suit between the parties, and for which purposes I presume the accompanying map was produced'. Manuscript notes on map and letter probably in same hand, and in Volume IX of the '"Maynard Collection." M.S. Papers, &c. principally relating, to Whittlesford Manor. From the time of the Saxon King Edward the Confessor, to the time of the Hollick & Tickell Family's, I.E. from A.D. 1024 to A.D. 1895. A period of 871 years'. Martindale's 1st name was Charles [VCH, 6, 255].

Whittlesford – 1833 – WHV83301 – CUL MS Plans y.1(27)
Whittlesford Oil Mills taken 15 April 1833.
Draughtsman: [Elliot Smith]; **Scale:** 1:450; **Size:** (iii) 5 x 8 1/4in.; **Top** is N; Manuscript(i), paper, uncoloured.
Oil Mill, TL473494, and c. 1a. surrounding it.
Functions of buildings. Rape Cake, Oil and 'Old' mills, dairy, coach house, stables and 2 'Lean toos' shown in plan form. Watercourses; gates; site of waterwheel.
Title top left.
Pencil notes, notes on buildings about overhead rooms, furnaces and number of mill stones. Owned by Charles Thurnall [VCH, 6, 270]. Drawn for fire insurance purposes, in volume from Elliot Smith and Sons, Auctioneers and Estate Agents.

Wicken – 1770 – WIC77001 – CRO P172/28
A Map of the Estate of the Right Honble: the Earl of Besborough, at Wicken in Cambridge Shire Surveyed by Jas Parker of Thetford Norfolk – 1770.
Surveyor: James Parker; **Scale bar** 0–80 perches (= 5in.), 1:3,168; **Size:** (i) 36 7/8 x 33 1/8in.; **Top** is N; Manuscript(i), parchment, coloured.
Hall Farm, TL578705, and c. 1,800a. in W of parish, bounded by River Cam in W, Padney Drove in E and village in N.
Names of fields, roads and neighbouring owners. Church and smock mill shown in perspective, Hall Farm and farm buildings shown in plan form. Open fields showing owner's strips; closes; common; wood and trees; waste; fen; osier beds; acreages; roads and footpaths; gates and stiles; watercourses; ponds; moat; responsibility for boundaries.
Border of 1 broad and 1 narrow band; title top left in a cartouche of 3 *putti* holding a scroll; red scale bar beneath title in a gold rococo cartouche; red and gold compass rose in centre of map showing 16 points which extend all over map. Explanation top right in a gold cartouche with green leaves giving key to symbols, location of fishing rights and referring to a terrier. Fields outlined in red, yellow or green, trees coloured green, roads coloured brown, buildings coloured red.
Note under explanation: 'N:B: The Lands that are not adjoining are not laid down at their proper distance some of them being a Considerable distance from each other'. Pencil additions and lot numbers. Positive and negative photostats at 1:4,782 at CUL Maps.bb.53(1).95.70–1.

Wicken – 1825 – WIC82501 – CUL Maps.PSQ.18.80
Plan of Spinney Abbey Estate 1825 exclusive of Open Field Lands. Lot 1.
Auctioneer: Elliot Smith; **Printer:** C[harles] Hullmandel; **Scale:** Six Chains to the Inch, 1:4,752; **Size:** (ii) 14 7/8 x 16 1/4in.; **Top** is NE; Printed, paper, uncoloured.

Spinney Abbey, TL553718, and 377a. E of village bounded by road from Stretham to Wicken in E and Wicken Sedge Fen in S.
Names of roads and neighbouring owners. Spinney Abbey, tithe barn, mill ['Water Engine'] and dovecote shown in plan form. Closed fields; acreages; roads and watercourses; ponds; hedges; wood, gardens and orchards identified on particulars of sale.
Title bottom left; scale bottom right; compass above title showing 4 points with a feathered tail.
Inset bottom right of 'Lot 2', 4a.0r.16p. in Soham Parish, which shows responsibility for fences. Accompanies: 'Plans, Particulars and Conditions of Sale, of important freehold and copyhold (fine certain) estates, consisting of Spinney Abbey Farm, in the parish of Wicken, St. John's Farm, in the parish of Soham and County of Cambridge, and a valuable Farm at King's Ripton, in the County of Huntingdon, which will be sold by auction, by Elliot Smith ... July, 1825'. Particulars of sale give details of occupant, tenure, acreages, open-field land, rents and taxes. Printer's 1st name was Charles [DNB, 15, 199]. Owner was Sarah Rayner [Knowles, 1902, 38]. See also SOH82501 and SWP82501.

Wilburton – 1805 – WLB80501 – CRO 515/P
The Plan of an Estate at Wilburton, Isle of Ely, Cambridgeshire. The Property of Mrs Catharine Buckle 1805.
Surveyor: John Bransby; **Scale bar** 10–0–100 rods (= 4 5/8in.), 1:4,709; **Size:** (ii) 33 1/8 x 25 7/8in.; **Top** is N; Manuscript(i), paper mounted on cloth, coloured.
Farm at TL487749, junction of road from Haddenham to Stretham with Berristead ['Berry Stead'] Lane, and 288a.0r.26p. in strips scattered throughout parish.
Names of fields, roads, rivers and neighbouring owners. Farm buildings and cottages shown in plan form. Open fields showing owner's strips; closes; common; groves and trees; wash; state of cultivation shown by colour; roads; watercourses including River Ouse and New Cut; gardens and orchard; ponds and bridge; stack yard; bank shown by hachures.
Title top left in an oval cartouche with a green and yellow border and a red band on outside; scale middle bottom; compass underneath title showing 4 points with a decorated N and S. Tables at bottom giving acreages of open field, fen and inclosed land. River coloured blue, arable outlined in yellow, pasture outlined in green, farm coloured red and orange.
Note by bridge about distance between land S of New Cut and bridge. Note on 1 plot: 'When the Lord of the Manor intends to plough up this Piece, he may command all the Copyhold Tenants to assist with their Ploughs and Horses'. Pencil addition of 12a.3r.28p. in Haddenham Fen, and acreages added to table in ink. Note on dorse: 'Map of Wilburton Estate belonging to Mr [Sir] {Albert} Pell' [VCH, 4, 169]. 2nd, unmounted, copy at CRO 515/P.

Willingham – 1719 – WLL71901 – CUL MS Plans 716
An Actual Survey of the Farm called Queenins in Willingham in the Compt of Cambridge, & the mannor of Parris in Westratting in the Compt of Cambridge, with the farms & lands thereunto belonging that are inclosed. belonging to the Corporation of the Sons of the Clergy in Quinnings Containing [sic.] 192A 1R 33P in the

inclosures of Westratting Containing 187A 0R 33P. Surveyed & measured December by A. Frogley 1719.

Surveyor: A[rthur] Frogley; **Scale bar** 20–0–100 rods (= 7 7/16in.), 1:3,195; **Size:** (ii) 35 1/4 x 30 1/4in.; **Top** is N; Manuscript(i), parchment mounted on cloth, coloured.

Queenholme Farm, TL429723, and 385a.2r.26p. in N of parish S of River Ouse, and Brook Farm, West Wratting Parish.

Names of farms and roads. Farm buildings and post mill in West Wratting Parish and smock mill in Willingham Parish shown in perspective. Closes showing owner's land; common; wood and trees, number of trees in fields in Willingham Parish; roads and gates; watercourses.

Title top right in a cartouche with classical columns and a pediment; scale beneath title; compass rose middle top showing 8 points. Table in same cartouche as title giving tenants, field names and acreages. 'Whitaker's Farm', West Wratting coloured green, 'Flax Farm', West Wratting coloured green and red, roads coloured orange.

Pencil notes. Includes pencil alterations to plot number on WEW71901. Drawn on acquisition of Willingham farm by Corporation of the Sons of the Clergy according to Samuel Saywell's will, proved in 1709 and effective by 1719 [*VCH*, 9, 404]. Surveyor's 1st name was Arthur [Eden F228].

Willingham – 1719 – WLL71902 – CUL MS Plans 718

A Survey of Queenhams Farm at Willingham in the County of Cambridge belonging to the Corporation of the Sons of the Clergy. Made by A. Frogley 1719.

Surveyor: A[rthur] Frogley; **Draughtsman:** J[ohn] Newton; **Scale bar** 0–40 chains (= 3 7/8in.), 1:8,176; **Size:** (i) 9 3/8 x 15 3/8in.; **Top** is N; Manuscript(ii), parchment, coloured.

Queenholme Farm, TL429723, and 198a.0r.37p. in NE of parish S of River Ouse.

Names of roads and watercourses. Windmill shown in perspective. Closes; trees; roads and watercourses.

Border of 1 narrow and 1 broad band; title top right in a cartouche with leaves and a ribbon tied into a bow; scale middle right coloured yellow and grey with decorative lettering; compass middle left showing 8 points. River coloured blue, fields outlined in green, roads coloured brown.

Site of farmhouse marked in pencil. Top right: '11' in later ink note. Accompanied by list of field names and acreages. Copy of part of WLL71901 made by J[ohn] Newton [Eden N69], Chancery Lane, c. 1811 [date suggested in CUL map catalogue]. Surveyor's 1st name was Arthur [Eden F228].

Willingham – 1754 – WLL75401 – CUL MS Plans 18

A Map of some Lands belonging to The Revrd Mr Saml: Knight lying in The Parish of Wilingham in The County of Cambridge Surveyed 1754 by Wm Elstobb.

Surveyor: William Elstobb [jr]; **Scale bar** 1–0–15 Gunter's chains (= 6 7/16in.), 1:1,704; **Size:** (i) 14 1/2 x 18 3/8in.; **Top** is NE; Manuscript(i), paper mounted on paper, coloured.

51a.2r.22p. in N of TL3948, bounded by Stanton Mere Way ['Long Stanton Mear Way'] in S and Over Parish in W.

Names of fields, roads, fens and neighbouring owners. Closes; trees; state of cultivation shown by colour;

acreages; roads and watercourses; gates; banks shown by hachures.

Border of 1 narrow and 1 broad band; title top right in a cartouche of red drapery and ropes; scale middle bottom coloured yellow and black; compass left of centre showing 16 yellow, red and green points. Pasture and trees coloured green, arable coloured brown.

Numbers on plots suggest map originally accompanied by a terrier. Surveyor was probably William Elstobb jr as in CAR75401 [Eden E83]. Photograph in CRO.

Willingham – 1790 – WLL79001 – SJC MPS 158

Plan of a Close of Pasture called Ashman's & Two Cottages in the Occupation of William Hon and also of an inclosed Holt of Pasture with a Piece of Common Meadow in Belsis Meadow in the occupation of Elizabeth Lack widow The above mentioned premises are in the Parish of Willingham in the County of Cambridge & belong to St John the Evangelist's College in Cambridge.

Surveyor: Joseph Freeman; **Scale:** 1:1,460; **Size:** (i) 11 3/4 x 13 3/4in.; **Top** is E; Manuscript(i), parchment, coloured.

6a.2r.14p., probably in TL6941 E of village.

Names of fields, neighbouring owners and roads. Cottages shown in plan form. Closes showing owner's land; strip of meadow; state of cultivation shown by colour; acreages; roads; hedges and trees.

Border of 2 narrow bands; title top left; compass in centre showing 4 points. Table top right giving field names and rent due. Grass coloured green.

Pencil notes.

Willingham – 1795 – WLL79501 – CUL MS Plans R.b.14

Plan of Lands at Willingham in the County of Cambridge belonging to Jesus College, in the University of Cambridge According to Surveys of the Parish taken in 1575 & 1603 Revised in 1795.

Surveyor: [Joseph Freeman]; **Scale:** 1:4,220; **Size:** (i) 28 7/8 x 49 5/8in.; **Top** is S; Manuscript(iii), parchment, coloured.

Willingham Church, TL405705, and c. 2,700a. in S of parish bounded by Cottenham Parish in E, Long Stanton All Saints' Parish in W and Rampton Parish in S.

Names of fields and owners. Church, houses and farm buildings shown in plan form. Open fields showing owner's strips and number of strips in-between; closes; common; state of cultivation shown by colour; acreages; roads and watercourses; hedges; earthworks; Belsar's ['Belsies''] Hill; 'Black pitt', 'Common Pitts'.

Border of 1 narrow and 1 broad band; title middle bottom with decorative line-work. Table bottom right giving colour code for each tenant's land [sand, yellow, blue, pink or brown]. Houses coloured red, water coloured blue, roads coloured brown and pasture outlined in green.

Pencil notes. E part unfinished. Mr Freeman was paid £6 13s 0d in 1796 for making a plan of Willingham [JCC A/C.1.9]; his 1st name was Joseph [Eden F209]. Photograph in CRO.

Willingham – 1811 – WLL81101 – CUL MS Plans 717

Plan of a Farm called Queenholmes at Willingham in the County of Cambridge belonging to the Governors of the Sons of the Clergy surveyed in the Year 1811.

Scale bar 1–0–19 chains (= 4 13/16in.), 1:3,291; **Size:** (i) 18 11/16 x 15 1/8in.; **Top** is N; Manuscript(i), parchment mounted on cloth, coloured.

Queenholme Farm, TL429723, and 198a.0r.37p. in NE of parish S of River Ouse.

Names of river, roads and neighbouring owners. Windmill shown in perspective. Closes; wash; state of cultivation shown by colour; roads and watercourses; bank shown by hachures.

Border of 1 narrow and 1 broad band; title bottom left over a stone bridge with fishing tackle and reeds, and vignette of King's College Chapel, Cambridge above; scale middle bottom; compass top right showing 4 points with a decorated N. Table bottom right giving field names and acreages. Water coloured blue, wash coloured yellow/green, arable coloured very pale brown, grass coloured very pale green.

Pencil notes. Note along 1 plot: 'The Herbage of Queenholmes Way belongs to the Poor of The Parishes of Willingham & Bluntisham'. Probably drawn in connection with visitation of Corporation's estates in 1811 by John Bacon [Pearce, 1928, 121].

Willingham – [Post 1811] – WLL81102 – CUL MS Plans 719

Plan of the Willingham Farm.

Scale: 8 Chains to an Inch, Scale bar 0–16 chains (= 2in.), 1:6,336; **Size:** (i) 10 3/16 x 13 1/2in.; **Top** is NE; Manuscript(iii), tracing paper, uncoloured.

Queenholme Farm, TL429723, and 197a.1r.34p. in NE of parish S of River Ouse.

Names of roads, rivers and neighbouring owners. Closes; roads and watercourses.

Border of 1 broad and 1 narrow band; title top right in a rectangular cartouche of 2 lines; scale bottom left; plain compass middle right showing 4 points. Table top left giving field names and acreages.

Note by 1 plot: 'The Herbage of Queenholm Way belongs to the Poor of the Parishes of Willingham and Bluntisham'. Altered copy of WLL81101, showing subdivision of fields in greater detail and site of homestead, but no windmill. Land owned by Corporation of the Sons of the Clergy [VCH, 9, 404].

Willingham – [1825] – WLL82501 – QCC 355 A20, B20

Estate at Willingham In The County of Cambridge.

Surveyor: [Alexander Watford jr]; **Scale bar** 3–0–30 chains (= 5 1/2in.), 1:4,752; **Size:** (i) 25 1/2 x 38 5/8in.; **Top** is SE; Manuscript(ii), paper, coloured.

Belsar's Hill, TL423703, and c. 1,700a. in S of parish, bounded by Over Parish in W, Long Stanton All Saints' Parish in S, Rampton Parish in E and The Irams and Hempsals Fen in N.

Names of fields, hills, fens, roads and neighbouring owners. Farm shown in plan form. Open fields showing owner's strips; closes; meadows and fen; land quality; state of cultivation shown by colour; acreages of homestead close; hedges, roads and watercourses; balks.

Border of 1 broad band with 1 narrow band on either side; title top left; scale at bottom. Fields outlined in blue, red and green, strips coloured brown and green, balks coloured green, water coloured blue, roads coloured brown.

Numbers on plots suggest map originally accompanied by a terrier. Pencil notes. In volume drawn in 1825: 'Plans

of the Several Estates in England and Wales belonging to the President and Fellows of the College of St Margaret and St Bernard commonly called Queen's College in the University of Cambridge Delineated from Authentic Documents in the possession of the said President and Fellows and from actual Surveys taken By their most obedient and obliged Servant Alexr Watford'. Title page drawn by James Richardson [Watford's nephew]. This is the Bursar's copy; 2nd, finer, copy [the Master's copy] at QCC 355 B20 measures 24 13/16 x 36 1/8in., is drawn on parchment, and has scale bar 0–30 chains (= 5in.), 1:4,752. Top points WNW. Acreages are given. Border 3/8in. wide of a central blue band with 1 broad band on either side, title bottom right, scale bottom left has gothic lettering, compass top left shows 8 points. Roads have red/brown edges. Positive photostat of this copy at BL 1640.(25).

Wimblington – 1637 – WMB63701 – CRO L39/3

The description of all such grounds belonging to Stoney in the Isle of Ely & County of Cambridge as were latelie purchased of Robert Paiton Esqr: taken: 1637 Per me: Ben: Hare.

Surveyor: Benjamin Hare; **Scala** 40 [perches]: Ben: Hare: 1637:, 1:7,920; **Size:** (i) 21 1/4 x 30 5/8in.; **Top** is NNE; Manuscript(i), paper mounted on paper, coloured.

Gravel pit W of Stonea Grange, TL448938, and 1,302a.3r.30p. in Latches Fen bounded by Horse Moor in N, Boot's Road in S, road running E of Wimblington in W and Manea Parish in E.

Names of roads, neighbouring owners and neighbouring fen. Houses in Stonea shown in perspective. Open fields; acreages and dimensions of some plots; roads and watercourses; old lake; gravel pits; 'The sluce'; common and fen adjoining map.

Border of 3/8in.-wide yellow band with 1 brown line on inside; title top left in a strapwork cartouche with flowers coloured red, yellow and blue; scale note middle bottom; N half of compass bottom right showing 8 points coloured yellow, red and blue. Land outlined in red, green and brown, houses have red roofs.

Note bottom left in a red and blue frame about acreages bought. Letters on map crossed out. Note on dorse: 'We whose names are subscribed to these presente; are all agreed upon this Mapp; and are Content to Cast and take our lottes; accordinge to the devisions set out by A: B: C: D: E: upon the same, and the lock spitting and dikeinge is to goe on, and to be regulated acordingly as they are sett out in black lynes by equall apporcions and Stoney Grange and Hamlett Stampe are to be set out indifferently into five parts and devided by lottes acordinglie amongst us. Oli. StJohn, F. Vernatt, John Latch, Abraham Vernatt, Rt Henley. Lottes were cast by the parties underwritten this 6t day of June 1638 and the Land marked withe the lettre A did fall to Mr Williamson and Mr Talbot and the land Marked with the lettre B did fall to Mr StJohn and the land marked with the lettre C did fall to Mr Vernatt Mr Tho. Knyvett and Nath. Knyvett and the land marked with the lettre D did fall to Mr Latch and the land marked with the lettre E did fall to Sir T.S: Vernatt and Sir Abraham Dawes who are content therewith and doe accept of their parte and shares accordinglye. Abraham Vernatt pro se est Thomam est Nathenieln Knyvett, F. Vernatt, Fra. Williamson, John Latch, Oli. StJohn, Tho: Talbott'. Former owner was Robert Peyton [VCH, 4, 112].

Wimblington – [1770] – WMB77001 – PRI

A Farm In the Tithing of Wimblington In the Parish of Doddington And County of Cambridge Also, A Close near Merch Chain Bridge.

A Scale of 20 Chains Or 1/4 of a Mile, Scale bar 0–20 chains (= 1 13/16in.), 1:8,739; **Size:** (i) 12 7/8 x 8 13/16in.; **Top** is W; Manuscript(i), parchment, coloured.

226a.1r.1p. in Wimblington Green, TL417921, and land to W bounded by Chatteris Parish in SW and March Parish in NE; and a plot in N of March Parish at Chain Bridge.

Names of fields, tenants, neighbouring owners and roads. Farm buildings shown in plan form. Open fields showing owner's strips; closes; glebe; wood and trees; roads; watercourses and drains; 'The Wheel Bank'; gates and stiles; hedges; pond; garden; Chain Bridge; yard; common adjoining map; holt identified on table.

Border 1/4in. wide of 1 broad blue band with 1 broad and 1 narrow uncoloured band on inside; title bottom right in a rococo cartouche with flowers; scale middle right; compass in centre showing 16 points which extend all over map. Farm coloured red, water coloured blue.

On p.197 of a volume bound in red leather with gold tooling: 'Map's Of Estates in The Counties of Dorset, Devon, & Wilts. Belonging to Humpry, Sturt, Esqr; Surveyed In the Year's 1765, 1766, 1767. And the Drawings Compleated, In January, 1770. by Isaac Taylor. Of Ross, Herefordshire.' Tables on DOD77001 include this map, probably drawn at same time. See also DOD77002. Humphry Sturt inherited estate in 1765 [Pevsner, 1972, 298]. Positive photostats at BL 1640.(20), CRO 382/P3.

Wimblington – 1775 – WMB77501 – CUL MS Plans 164

Lands belonging to J. Waddington Esqr except which is inclosed with red lines surveyed by J. Porter, 1775.

Surveyor: J. Porter; **Scale:** Grid of 1 mile intervals, 1 mile = 4 7/8in., 1:13,000; **Size:** (i) 19 1/8 x 24 5/16in.; **Top** is N; Manuscript(i), parchment, coloured.

Stonea Grange, TL449938, and 841a.0r.3p. in E of village in Latches Fen crossed by drain to Latches Fen pumping station in N, bounded by Sixteen Foot Drain in SE, road to Manea ['Maney'] in S and village in W.

Names of roads, drains, neighbouring fields and neighbouring owners. Houses in town, 'new corn mill' [smock mill], 2 windmills and Stonea Grange shown in perspective. Closes; common; trees; acreages; roads and watercourses; gates.

Border of 1 broad band; title bottom left in a cartouche decorated with leaves and flowers; scale of 1 mile grid with border divided into 8 blocks to each mile, alternately coloured yellow and uncoloured; compass top left showing 8 points with a decorated N. Table bottom right giving fields and acreages for each mile to E. Drains coloured blue or brown, fields coloured green.

Photograph in CRO. Owner's 1st name was John [Waddington, 1934, 119]. See also WMB77502.

Wimblington – 1775 – WMB77502 – CRO 283/P

Lands belonging to John Waddington Esqr except what is inclosed with red Lines Surveyed by J. Porter 1775.

Surveyor: J. Porter; **Scale:** Grid of 1 mile intervals, 1 mile = 5in., 1:12,670; **Size:** (i) 21 1/4 x 23 7/8in.; **Top** is N; Manuscript(i), parchment, coloured.

Stonea Grange, TL449938, and 836a.0r.18p. bounded by Sixteen Foot Drain in E, drain to Latches Fen pumping

station in N, and roads to Manea ['Maney'] in S and to E of Wimblington running N–S in W.

Names of former owners and neighbouring land. Stonea Grange, house and 2 windmills shown in perspective. Closes; trees; acreages; roads and watercourses; gates; fences; bridge and banks.

Border of 1 broad band with 2 broad yellow bands inside; title bottom left in a rococo cartouche with fruit and flowers; scale in border; compass top left showing 16 points. Table left of title in a cartouche of 1 narrow band giving acreages for each mile to E. Fields outlined in green and red, drains coloured black.

Numbers on fields suggest map originally accompanied by a terrier. Later ink notes of a landowner, 'error in gravel' on table, and: 'part of Stonea farm'. See also WMB77501.

Wimpole – 1638 – WMP63801 – CRO R77/1

A description of the Mannour of Wimple in the Countie of Cambridge, being part of the possessions of the right worshipfull Tho: Chicheley Esquire: Anno. Domini 1638. Performed by Ben: Hare Sen: Surveyour.

Surveyor: Benjamin Hare sr; **Scale:** 1:2,730; **Size:** (i) 36 1/4 x 67 3/8in.; **Top** is ENE; Manuscript(i), parchment, coloured, 5+1 sheets.

Wimpole Old Hall ['Manor House'], TL 338509, and c. 2,500a. in whole parish except for land S of boundary with Kingston Parish [on missing sheet].

Names of roads and tenants. Manor house, stables, dovecote, post mill, church, and cottages in village, in 'Thresham End' and in Arrington Parish E of Ermine Street, shown in perspective. Open fields showing all strips; closes; pightle; common; woods including Cobb's and 'Ratford' woods; trees; meadow; acreages and number of lands; tenure; roads; gates; parks and gardens; watercourses; moat; ponds and bridge; pound.

Border of 5/16in.-wide grey band; title top left in a decorative red and blue cartouche; compass rose top right showing 16 points with red and blue decoration. Water coloured blue, roads coloured brown, trees coloured yellow, houses have red roofs.

Letters on furlongs suggest map originally accompanied by a terrier. Drawn on 6 sheets, most NW is missing. Infra-red photograph in 7 sheets mounted on cloth at BL Maps 6.c.55.

Wimpole – [c. 1721] – WMP72101 – BLO MS.Gough Drawings.a.4 f.69

[Park at Wimpole Hall.]

Surveyor: [Charles Bridgeman?]; **Scale bar** 0–20 chains (= 3 1/4in.), 1:4,874, Scale bar 100–0–1,500 feet (= 4 1/16in.), 1:4,726; **Size:** (ii) 26 7/8 x 15 1/4in.; **Top** is N; Manuscript(i), paper, coloured.

Wimpole Hall, TL336510, and c. 1,400a. in park in W of parish and N of TL337502.

Hall and farm buildings shown in plan form, church and 2 houses shown in perspective. Closed fields; trees, plantation and wood; roads; watercourses, ponds and fishponds; bridges; gardens and water garden; hill shown by pencil hachures.

Scale bottom left. 2 areas outlined in green, 1 area outlined in orange.

Pencil notes and marks of trees. Drawn in connection with landscaping of park by Charles Bridgeman c. 1721 [VCH, 5, 265]. Owner was Edward Harley, Earl of Oxford.

WMP72102 is possibly a draft of this map. See also WMP72103–4, drawn at same time.

Wimpole – [c. 1721] – WMP72102 – BLO MS.Gough Drawings.a.4 f.35

[Park at Wimpole Hall.]

Surveyor: [Charles Bridgeman?]; **Scale bar** 100–0–1,500 feet (= 8in.), 1:2,400; **Size:** (i) 39 3/8 x 28in.; **Top** is N; Manuscript(i), paper, pencil.

Wimpole Hall, TL336510, and c. 1,400a. in park in W of parish and N of TL337502.

Wimpole Hall, church and farm buildings shown in plan form. Closed fields; trees; roads; watercourses, ponds and fishponds; bridges; gardens and water garden.

Border of 1 narrow band; scale centre bottom.

Survey marks. Possibly draft of WMP72101; see this entry for probable date and owner. See also WMP72103–4, drawn at same time.

Wimpole – [c. 1721] – WMP72103 – BLO MS.Gough Drawings.a.4 f.30

Wimpole No. 1.

Surveyor: [Charles Bridgeman?]; **Scale bar** 100–0–500 feet (= 10in.), 1:720; **Size:** (ii) 21 3/8 x 28 3/4in.; **Top** is S; Manuscript(i), paper, uncoloured.

Wimpole Hall, TL336510, and c. 26a. in avenue to S.

Wimpole Hall shown in plan form. Trees; dimension of area in front of hall; fishponds; water garden.

Title top left; scale at bottom.

Pencil lines and lines of sight. Survey marks. Drawn at same time as WMP72101–2,4; see WMP72101 for details of date and owner.

Wimpole – [c. 1721] – WMP72104 – BLO MS.Gough Drawings.a.4 f.31

Wimpole No. 3.

Surveyor: [Charles Bridgeman?]; **Scale bar** 100–0–1,000 feet (= 6 3/4in.), 1:1,956; **Size:** (ii) 86 1/2 x 18 1/2in.; **Top** is S; Manuscript(i), paper, uncoloured.

Wimpole Hall, TL336510, and c. 320a. in avenue to S and in NW of Whaddon Parish.

Wimpole Hall shown in plan form. Trees; watercourses and 'Bason'.

Title top left and bottom left; scale bottom right.

Note middle left of dimensions of 'Bason'. Note bottom left of number of trees in avenue, 1,216 in total. Lines of sight. Drawn at same time as WMP72101–3; see WMP72101 for details of date and owner.

Wimpole – 1790 – WMP79001 – BLM Add.36278G

A Plan of the Park and Demesne Lands &c. at Wimpole the Seat of The Right Honble the Earl of Hardwicke with some Alterations.

Surveyor: William Emes; **Scale bar** 1–0–15 chains (= 3 11/16in.), 1:3,436; **Size:** (i) 32 1/4 x 20 3/4in.; **Top** is N; Manuscript(i), parchment, coloured.

Wimpole Hall, TL335510, and c. 1,100a. E of road from Royston to Huntingdon.

Buildings shown in plan form and table identifies hall, church, inn, vicarage, stables, cottages, 'Gardeners House', 'Belvidere farm' and ruins. Closed fields; wood and trees; roads; footpaths; gates; watercourses; ponds; bridges; gardens; hedges; hill shown by hachures; yards, farmyard, churchyard, cow pastures, meadow, kitchen garden,

'Pleasure Garden', 'Melon~Ground', 'sunk~fences', deer park, 'Rideings' and site of maypole all identified on table.

Border of 1 broad brown band; title top left in a rococo cartouche; scale bottom right; compass rose above scale showing 8 yellow and grey points. Reference to map between scale and compass in a rococo cartouche. Water coloured blue, buildings coloured red, grass and trees coloured green, roads coloured brown.

Owned by Philip Yorke, 2nd Earl of Hardwicke [*PB*, 1,246].

Wimpole – 1800 – WMP80001 – CUL MS Plans 609

A Map of the Park, Pleasure~grounds and Home Farm at Wimpole in the County of Cambridge belonging to the Earl of Hardwicke 1800.

Scale: 1:12,400; **Size:** (i) 12 9/16 x 10 7/16in.; **Top** is N; Manuscript(i), parchment, coloured.

Wimpole Hall ['Mansion'], TL336510, and c. 2,500a. bounded by roads to Orwell in S and from Royston to Huntingdon in W, and Kingston Parish in N.

Names of roads, features and buildings. Wimpole Hall, lodge, parsonage, stables, farm and buildings shown in plan form. Closed fields; wood; deciduous and coniferous trees; roads and gates; watercourses; deer park; garden; fishponds and ponds; fences and hedges; bridges.

Border of 1 broad and 1 narrow band; title top right with decorative lettering and surmounted by a crown; compass bottom right showing 8 points with a lion on the N. Roads coloured brown, fishponds coloured blue.

Accompanying terrier at CUL MS Plans 610 gives field names with course of cropping and observations to be filled in. Owned by Philip Yorke, 3rd Earl of Hardwicke [*PB*, 1,246].

Wimpole – [c. 1815] – WMP81501 – WMP

Map of Wimpole Park and Farm, situate in The Parishes of Wimpole and Arrington, and County of Cambridge; the Property of The Right Honourable Philip Earl of Hardwicke. K.G.

Surveyor: Robert Withers; **Draughtsman:** B[radbury] Last; **Scale** of 8 Chains to an Inch, Scale bar 0–40 chains (= 5in.), 1:6,336; **Size:** (i) 20 5/8 x 23 1/4in.; **Top** is N; Manuscript(i), paper, coloured.

Wimpole Hall, TL355510, and c. 2,500a. bounded by roads to Orwell in S and from Royston to Caxton in W, and Kingston Parish in N.

Names of features and neighbouring occupiers. Wimpole Hall, lodge, 'The Tower', 'Hill House', ice house and farm buildings shown in plan form, church shown in perspective. Closed fields; wood, trees and avenue of trees; roads and footpaths; watercourses, ponds, 'Spring Ponds' and fishponds; bridges; park; fences; garden; boundary between Wimpole and Arrington parishes.

Border of 1 broad band with 1 narrow band on inside; title bottom right in a rococo cartouche; scale bottom left; compass top right showing 8 blue and red points with a yellow fleur-de-lys. Buildings coloured red and black, water coloured blue, trees coloured green, edge of neighbouring land shaded green, roads coloured brown.

Top left of map is missing. Numbers on plots suggest map originally accompanied by a terrier. Note bottom left: 'Map*pe*d by B. Last, Whepstead', and bottom right: 'Surveyed by Robert Withers'. Draughtsman's 1st name was Bradbury, he practised in Norfolk and Suffolk 1801–19 [Eden L64]. Probably 1815 map referred to in ARR82801–

4 and WMP82801–11; 3rd Earl of Hardwicke owned estate 1796–1834 [PB, 1,246].

Wimpole – [1828] – WMP82801 – COL C43.C32.3
[Wimpole Park and Plantations and Wimpole Farm, owned by 3rd Earl of Hardwicke.]
Surveyor: [Robert Withers]; **Scale:** 1:9,504; **Size:** (i) 8 9/16 x 14 5/16in.; **Top** is E; Manuscript(iii), paper, coloured.
Wimpole Hall, TL335510, and 852a.1r.19p. bounded by road from Royston to Huntingdon in W and Kingston Parish in N, including 1 plot in E of Arrington Parish.
Names of farms, roads and neighbouring owners. Buildings shown in plan form and include hall, church, 'Hardwicke Arms Inn', 'Hill House', 'Collins's' and Home ['Wimpole'] farms, folly ['Tower'] and cottages. Closed fields; wood and trees; state of cultivation shown by colour; roads and turnpike; footpaths; watercourses and ponds; gardens and orchards; bridge; fences; plantations; 'Inclosed Garden', deer park, 'Ozier Ground' and meadow identified on terrier.
Border of 1 broad band with 1 narrow band on inside; compass on right showing 8 points. Water coloured blue, roads coloured brown, buildings coloured red or grey, grass coloured green, arable coloured brown.
Bottom left: 'I Letter. A. Wimpole Park and Plantations', top right: 'I Letter. B. Wimpole Farm'. In volume: 'Survey of Estates belonging to the Right Honourable Philip Earl of Hardwick. K.G. Situate in the Parishes of Wimpole and Arrington in the County of Cambridge. By Robert Withers. 1815. Reviewed and adjusted. 1828.' On following page: 'Note. All the Maps in the following Survey are upon a Scale of Twelve Chains to an Inch', 1:9,504. At end is abstract of survey [3,816a.1r.18p. in total]. Accompanying terrier gives field names, acreages and tenant. See also ARR82801–4 and WMP82802–11.

Wimpole – [1828] – WMP82802 – COL C43.C32.3
II Pateman's Farm.
Surveyor: [Robert Withers]; **Scale:** 1:9,504; **Size:** (i) 8 3/8 x 10 3/4in.; **Top** is E; Manuscript(iii), paper, coloured.
'Pateman's Farm' and 240a.0r.10p. in E of parish, bounded by Orwell Parish in S and Great Eversden Parish in E.
Names of roads and neighbouring owners. Farm buildings shown in plan form. Closed fields; Cobb's Wood; state of cultivation shown by colour; roads and watercourses; bridge; hedges and fences; orchard and meadow identified on terrier.
Border of 1 broad band with 1 narrow band on inside; title bottom left. Roads coloured brown, water coloured blue, buildings coloured red or grey, wood and pasture coloured green, arable coloured brown.
In volume which gives owner, surveyor, date and scale; see WMP82801 for details. Accompanying terrier gives field names, acreages and tenant. See also ARR82801–4 and WMP82803–11.

Wimpole – [1828] – WMP82803 – COL C43.C32.3
III Part of Kingston Pastures.
Surveyor: [Robert Withers]; **Scale:** 1:9,504; **Size:** (i) 8 7/16 x 10 3/4in.; **Top** is N; Manuscript(iii), paper, coloured.

97a.1r.30p. in N of Wimpole Parish, bounded by Kingston Pastures Farm, TL329529, in Kingston Parish in N and road to Wimpole in E.
Names of roads and neighbouring owners. Buildings shown in plan form. Closed fields; wood and trees; state of cultivation shown by colour; roads.
Border of 1 broad band with 1 narrow band on inside; title at top. Roads coloured brown, wood and grass coloured green, arable coloured brown, buildings coloured grey.
In volume which gives owner, surveyor, date and scale; see WMP82801 for details. Accompanying terrier gives field names, acreages and tenant. See also ARR82801–4 and WMP82802,4–11.

Wimpole – [1828] – WMP82804 – COL C43.C32.3
IV Coomb Grove Farm.
Surveyor: [Robert Withers]; **Scale:** 1:9,504; **Size:** (i) 8 7/16 x 10 3/4in.; **Top** is N; Manuscript(iii), paper, coloured.
Coombe Grove Farm, TL321528, and 299a.2r.29p. in Wimpole and Arrington parishes bounded by Longstowe Parish in N, Croydon Parish in W and Kingston Parish in NE.
Names of farm, roads and neighbouring owners. Farm buildings shown in plan form. Closed fields; wood and trees; state of cultivation shown by colour; roads and turnpike; milestone; watercourses and bridge; Decoy Pond ['Reservoir']; fences; garden identified on terrier.
Border of 1 broad band with 1 narrow band on inside; title top left. Roads coloured brown, water coloured blue, buildings coloured red, arable coloured brown, wood and pasture coloured green.
Pencil notes. In volume which gives owner, surveyor, date and scale; see WMP82801 for details. Accompanying terrier gives field names, acreages and tenant. See also ARR82801–4 and WMP82802–3,5–11.

Wimpole – [1828] – WMP82805 – COL C43.C32.3
V Wimpole Hole Farm.
Surveyor: [Robert Withers]; **Scale:** 1:9,504; **Size:** (i) 8 5/16 x 10 3/4in.; **Top** is N; Manuscript(iii), paper, coloured.
Valley ['Wimpole Hole'] Farm, TL325519, and 407a.1r.2p. in Wimpole and Arrington parishes E and W of road from Royston to Huntingdon, and bounded by Wimpole Park in E.
Names of roads and neighbouring owners. Farm buildings, mill and cottages shown in plan form. Closed fields; wood and trees; state of cultivation shown by colour; roads; watercourses, ponds and bridges; hedges and fences; meadow identified on terrier.
Border of 1 broad band with 1 narrow band on inside; title bottom left; compass top left showing 8 points. Roads and arable coloured brown, grass and trees coloured green, water coloured blue, buildings coloured red or grey.
In volume which gives owner, surveyor, date and scale; see WMP82801 for details. Accompanying terrier gives field names, acreages and tenant. See also ARR82801–4 and WMP82802–4,6–11.

Wimpole – [1828] – WMP82806 – COL C43.C32.3
IX Eight Elms Farm.
Surveyor: [Robert Withers]; **Scale:** 1:9,504; **Size:** (i) 8 5/16 x 10 3/4in.; **Top** is N; Manuscript(iii), paper, coloured.

Eight Elms Farm, TL332495, and 244a.2r.22p. in Wimpole and Arrington parishes, bounded by Croydon Parish in W and road to Cambridge in S.

Names of roads and neighbouring owners. Farm buildings shown in plan form. Closed fields; spinney and trees; state of cultivation shown by colour; roads, turnpike and 'Intended Road'; watercourses and pond; Arrington Bridge; hedges and fences; meadow identified on terrier.

Border of 1 broad band with 1 narrow band on inside; title top left. Roads and arable coloured brown, grass coloured green, water coloured blue, buildings coloured red or grey.

In volume which gives owner, surveyor, date and scale; see WMP82801 for details. Accompanying terrier gives field names, acreages and tenant. See also ARR82801–4 and WMP82802–5,7–11.

Wimpole – [1828] – WMP82807 – COL C43.C32.3
X Letter. P. Thornberry Hill Farm.
Surveyor: [Robert Withers]; **Scale:** 1:9,504; **Size:** (i) 8 3/8 x 5 1/4in.; **Top** is N; Manuscript(iii), paper, coloured.

Thornberry Hill Farm, TL351511, and 156a.3r.21p. bounded by Orwell Parish in SE.

Names of roads and neighbouring owners. Farm buildings shown in plan form. Closed fields; spinney and trees; state of cultivation shown by colour; roads; watercourses and bridge; hedges and fences; meadow identified on terrier.

Border to top, bottom and right of 1 broad band with 1 narrow band on inside; title at bottom; compass bottom left showing 4 points. Roads and arable coloured brown, water coloured blue, buildings coloured red or grey.

On right of sheet which also contains ARR82804. In volume which gives owner, surveyor, date and scale; see WMP82801 for details. Accompanying terrier gives field names, acreages and tenant. See also ARR82802–6,8–11.

Wimpole – [1828] – WMP82808 – COL C43.C32.3
XI Porter's Farm.
Surveyor: [Robert Withers]; **Scale:** 1:9,504; **Size:** (i) 8 7/16 x 10 3/4in.; **Top** is N; Manuscript(iii), paper, coloured.

River Cam ['Porter's'] Farm, TL341488, and 154a.2r.8p. mostly S of road to Cambridge and bounded by Whaddon Parish in S.

Names of roads and neighbouring owners. Farm buildings shown in plan form. Closed fields; trees; state of cultivation shown by colour; roads, turnpike and 'Intended Road'; watercourses and bridge; hedges and fences; meadow identified on terrier.

Border of 1 broad band with 1 narrow band on inside; title top right. Arable and roads coloured brown, grass coloured green, water coloured blue, buildings coloured red or grey.

In volume which gives owner, surveyor, date and scale; see WMP82801 for details. Accompanying terrier gives field names, acreages and tenant. See also ARR82801–4 and WMP82802–7,9–11.

Wimpole – [1828] – WMP82809 – COL C43.C32.3
XII Arber's Farm.
Surveyor: [Robert Withers]; **Scale:** 1:9,504; **Size:** (i) 8 7/16 x 10 11/16in.; **Top** is N; Manuscript(iii), paper, coloured.

Hoback ['Arber's'] Farm, TL347491, and 138a.1r.12p. bounded by Whaddon Parish in S, Orwell Parish in E and road to Cambridge in N.

Names of roads and neighbouring owners. Farm buildings shown in plan form. Closed fields; spinney and trees; state of cultivation shown by colour; roads; watercourses and pond; bridges; hedges and fences; meadow identified on terrier.

Border of 1 broad band with 1 narrow band on inside; title top left; compass bottom left showing 8 points. Roads and arable coloured brown, water coloured blue, grass coloured green, buildings coloured red or grey.

In volume which gives owner, surveyor, date and scale; see WMP82801 for details. Accompanying terrier gives field names, acreages and tenant. See also ARR82801–4 and WMP82802–8,10–11.

Wimpole – [1828] – WMP82810 – COL C43.C32.3
XIII Titchmarsh's Farm.
Surveyor: [Robert Withers]; **Scale:** 1:9,504; **Size:** (i) 8 7/16 x 10 11/16in.; **Top** is N; Manuscript(iii), paper, coloured.

Cambridge Road ['Titchmarsh's'] Farm, TL339497, and 178a.3r.14p. bounded by road to Cambridge in S and Wimpole Avenue in W.

Names of roads and neighbouring owners. Farm buildings shown in plan form. Closed fields; spinney and trees; state of cultivation shown by colour; roads, turnpike and 'Intended Road'; watercourses and ponds; bridges; hedges and fences; 'Brick kiln Ground'; meadow identified on terrier.

Border of 1 broad band with 1 narrow band on inside; title bottom right; compass top left showing 8 points. Roads and arable coloured brown, water coloured blue, grass coloured green, buildings coloured red or grey.

In volume which gives owner, surveyor, date and scale; see WMP82801 for details. Accompanying terrier gives field names, acreages and tenant. See also ARR82801–4 and WMP82802–9,11.

Wimpole – [1828] – WMP82811 – COL C43.C32.3
XIV Cottages and Tenements in Wimpole and Arrington.
Surveyor: [Robert Withers]; **Scale:** 1:9,504; **Size:** (i) 12 9/16 x 18 1/8in.; **Top** is NW; Manuscript(iii), paper, coloured.

Wimpole Hall, TL335510, and 103a.3r.9p. scattered throughout parish and in E of Arrington Parish.

Names of farms, roads and neighbouring owners. Buildings shown in plan form and include Wimpole and Arrington churches, hall, cottages, 'Hardwicke Arms Inn', mill, 'Hill House', 'Wimpole Hole', 'Wimpole', 'Pateman's' and Thornberry Hill farms; brick kiln, toll house, 'Octagon Lodge', public house, 'Smith's Shop', dog kennel, lodges, shop and parsonage identified on terrier. Closed fields; wood and trees; state of cultivation shown by colour; roads, turnpike and 'Intended Road'; watercourses and ponds; bridges and Arrington Bridge; hedges and fences; garden, meadow, plantation and churchyard identified on terrier.

Border of 1 broad band with 1 narrow band on inside; title top right; compass bottom left showing 8 points. Roads and arable coloured brown, water coloured blue, grass coloured green, buildings coloured red or grey.

Accompanying terrier gives field names, acreages and tenants; at end: 'Note. Beside the Glebe Land, of part of which the quantity by statute measure appears in the preceding page, there are included in the foregoing Survey the following Leasehold Estates, of which the situation and boundaries are unknown. Glebe belonging to the Rectory of Arrington; held, (together with the Parsonage as before stated,) by Lease of Trinity College, Cambridge, as under: viz. ... Total by computation or customary measure – 22:2:20. There is also an Estate held by Lease of Peter House College, Cambridge; which is described as consisting of 27A:1R:0P of Arable Land in the Common Fields of Wimpole and Orwell'. Map is in volume which gives owner, surveyor, date and scale; see WMP82801 for details. See also ARR82801–4 and WMP82802–10.

Wisbech St Mary – 1662 – WSM66201 – C R O R56/9/2
[Guyhirn Hamlet, Wisbech St Mary, and Waldersey Fen, Elm.]
Surveyor: Theophilus Byrd; **Scale bar** 1–0–110 perches (= 5 3/4in.), 1:3,822; **Size:** (i) 23 11/16 x 40 5/8in.; **Top** is S; Manuscript(i), parchment mounted on paper, coloured.
c. 1,700a. bounded in NW by Guyhirn Bridge, TF399035, and extending along River Nene in W and along Waldersey Main Drain and Long Drove in S.
Names of fields and droves. Houses in Guyhirn shown in perspective. Open fields; common; wash; trees; acreages; roads and watercourses.
Border of 7/16in.-wide brown band; scale middle bottom with a yellow scale bar; cardinal points stated in border, incorrectly giving top as E. Lettering coloured red, blue or brown, droves coloured green, field boundaries coloured yellow.
Letters may indicate ownership of plots. Notes of acreages, symbols which may indicate windmills, and 'Monks feild'. Much faded.

Wisbech St Mary – 1716 – WSM71601 – G L C A/CSC/1101
A Survey of the Manor of Ripes in Wisbeach, Tid St Mary Tid St Giles and Upwell belonging to the Corporation of the Sons of the Clergy Surveyed by A: Frogley 1716.
Surveyor: A[rthur] Frogley; **Draughtsman:** J[ohn] Newton; **Scale bar** 0–60 chains (= 2 11/16in.), 1:17,680; **Size:** (i) 9 1/4 x 15 1/16in.; **Top** is NE; Manuscript(ii), parchment, coloured.
Wisbech St Mary Church, TF419082, and 188a.1r.25p. in Cambridgeshire, 24a.1r.23p. in Norfolk part of Upwell Parish and 22a.1r.5p. in Tydd St Mary [Lincolnshire], extending from Tydd Gote in N to Ely in S.
Names of fields, roads and rivers. Ely Cathedral, 'Gyhern Chapel', Upwell, Wisbech St Mary and Wisbech St Peter churches, windmills, houses, 'St Edmund Mill' in Tydd St Mary and 'The Wool Pocket at Tid Goat' shown in perspective. Fields; acreages; roads and droves; watercourses including direction of flow of 'Gyherne Flue'; banks; bridges shown in perspective; 'Gyhern cross'.
Border of 1 broad band with 1 narrow band on inside; title at top in a cartouche of reeds; yellow and grey scale bar bottom left; compass centre bottom showing 8 points. Water coloured blue, roads coloured yellow, land outlined in red, blue and green.
Numbers on fields suggest map originally accompanied by a terrier. Note at bottom: 'NB. The Fields bordered with Green, are in Cambridge in the Isle of Ely. Red, are in

Lincolnshire. Blue, are in the County of Norfolk'. Land in Lincolnshire shown as inset on left. Red lines separate off land in Lincolnshire and Norfolk. Surveyor's 1st name was Arthur [Eden F228]. Copied by John Newton of 97 Chancery Lane, where he practised c. 1807–18 [Eden N69].

Wisbech St Mary – 1769 – WSM76901 – CRO 283/P
A Plan of the estate of John Waddington Esqr lying in Wisbech St Marys in the Isle of Ely.
Surveyor: John Watte; **Scale bar** 1–0–10 [chains] (= 2 11/16in.), 1:3,242; **Size:** (i) 24 7/8 x 19 5/8in.; **Top** is NNW; Manuscript(i), parchment, coloured.
Site of house at TF411076, junction of main road running E–W through Wisbech St Mary with Sand Bank running S, and 129a.2r.55p. S of church bounded by main road in N and Sand Bank in W.
Names of neighbouring owners. Church, house and cottages in village shown in perspective. Closes; trees; roads and gates; fences.
Border of 1 broad green band with 1 broad yellow band inside; title middle right in a rococo cartouche with open book, theodolite, dividers, globe, protractor and staff at bottom; scale middle bottom; compass bottom left showing 4 points. Table left of scale giving field numbers and acreages. Land outlined in green and yellow, trees coloured green.
Above is map of 'The Fenland': 64a.2r.20p. in Wisbech High Fen bounded by Cant's Drove in N, at same orientation and scale.

Wisbech St Mary – [1787] – WSM78701 – E D R CC.10116
A Survey of a Farm, commonly called Bishop Lands, in the Parish of Wisbeach St Maries in the Isle of Ely and County of Cambridge. belonging to Mr Wm Hemment of Thorney Abby.
Scale: 1:6,540; **Size:** (ii) 15 13/16 x 12 3/4in.; **Top** is N; Manuscript(i), paper, coloured.
Farm in TF3404, and 591a.0r.38p. bounded by Gold Dike in W, Inkerson Fen in N and Peakirk Drain in S.
Name of neighbouring land. Cottage and farm buildings shown in perspective. Closed fields; acreages; droves and dykes.
Title top left; compass bottom left showing 4 points. Table on right giving acreages. Buildings coloured yellow, fields outlined in yellow and green.
Notes on some fields, for example: 'Burnt up by bad management formerly', 'Part cut up for fuel', 'Cut up for fuel'. Date on dorse. Land owned by Bishop of Ely. Accompanies: 'The Lord Bishop of Ely to Mr William Hemment Lease of Wisbech High Fen', 14th February 1787 [EDR CC.94958].

Wisbech St Mary – [c. 1794] – WSM79401 – E D R CC.10118
A Plan of Mr Iohn Reams Estate Situate in Wisbech St Peters [sic.] in Inham Field.
Scale: 1:5,940; **Size:** (i) 10 11/16 x 14 11/16in.; **Top** is NNW; Manuscript(i), parchment, coloured.
122a.2r.28p. in Wisbech St Mary Parish S of church, bounded by 'A Common Road' in N and Bevis Lane in E, which meet at TF423082.
Names of fields, roads and neighbouring owners. Closed fields; roads.

Border of 1 broad band with 1 narrow band on inside; title top right in a rococo cartouche with a figure at the top; compass top left showing 8 points. Table bottom right giving acreages. Field outlined in red, subdivisions outlined in yellow, land adjoining map outlined in green.

Probably drawn at same time as WSM79403; both show same area and neighbouring owners. Bishop of Ely let land to John Ream in 1794 [EDR CC.10319] and 1800 [EDR CC.10321].

Wisbech St Mary – [1794] – WSM79402 – E D R CC.10126/1
Map of Lands In Lease, No: 1. to Oglethorpe Wainman M:D Mr Robert Hardwicke and Mr Joseph Howell lying in the Parish of Wisbech St Mary.
Scale bar 0–20 chains (= 1 5/8in.), 1:9,748; **Size:** (i) 8 13/16 x 6 1/2in.; **Top** is NW; Manuscript(i), parchment, coloured.
147a.2r.14p. in Inlay's Field, bounded by River Nene ['Wisbech River'] in SE and High Road ['Guyhirn Lane'] in W; High Road turns to run along river at TF405042.
Names of roads, river and neighbouring owners. Farm buildings shown in plan form. Closed fields; roads; watercourses and direction of flow of river.
Border of 1 broad band with 1 narrow band on inside; title top left in an oval cartouche of 1 broad band with 1 narrow band on inside; scale bottom left; compass under title showing 4 points. Table bottom right giving field names, acreages 'by the Particular of Sale' and 'By Mr Watte's Survey' [149a.1r.15p.; John Watte, Eden W164]. Land coloured green, road from Peterborough to Wisbech coloured yellow, river coloured grey.
Probably accompanied by lease formerly at EDR CC.94859. In volume: 'Maps of the Demesne Lands of the Manor of Wisbech Barton, lying in the Parishes of Wisbech St Peter and Wisbech St Mary in the Isle of Ely in the County of Cambridge, belonging to the See of Ely, as now divided and leased in ten Lots, or separate Leases by the Honble, & Right Reverend James Lord Bishop of Ely, pursuant to an Act of Parliament for that Purpose passed in the year 1794'. See also WSM79403 and WSP79403–10.

Wisbech St Mary – [1794] – WSM79403 – E D R CC.10126/6
Map of Lands In Lease No: 6. to Mr John Ream lying in the Parish of Wisbech St Mary.
Scale: 1:9,820; **Size:** (i) 8 13/16 x 6 7/16in.; **Top** is NNW; Manuscript(i), parchment, coloured.
Wisbech St Mary Church, TF419082, and 122a.2r.28p. in Inham Field to S and W of Bevis Lane.
Names of roads and neighbouring owners. Buildings in village shown in plan form, church shown in perspective. Closed fields; roads.
Border of 1 broad band with 1 narrow band on inside; title top right in an oval cartouche of 1 broad band with 1 narrow band on inside; compass centre right showing 4 points. Table at bottom giving field names and acreages 'by the Particular of Sale' and 'By Mr Watte's Survey' [122a.2r.22p.; John Watte, Eden W164]. Land coloured green.
Probably accompanied by lease at EDR CC.10319 [missing 1988]. In volume which gives owner and date; see WSM79402 for details. See also WSP79403–10. Probably drawn at same time as WSM79401; both show same area and neighbouring owners.

Wisbech St Mary – 1808 – WSM80801 – E D R CC.10106
Plan of an Estate situate in Wisbeach High Fen in the Isle of Ely and County of Cambridge. belonging to The Lord Bishop of Ely in Lease to Mr John Hemment 1808.
Scale: 1:6,540; **Size:** (i) 23 3/16 x 20 1/8in.; **Top** is N; Manuscript(i), parchment, coloured.
Junction of Gold Dike with southern boundary of Inkerson Fen, TF338054, and 600a.0r.0p. in Bishop Lands bounded by Thorney Parish in W, Inkerson Fen in N, Peakirk Drain in S and Bishoplands Drain in E.
Names of droves, dykes and neighbouring fen. Farm buildings shown in plan form. Closes; acreages; roads and watercourses.
Border of 1 narrow band; title top left; compass bottom left showing 8 points. Table on right giving field names and acreages. Water coloured blue, buildings coloured red.
'See of Ely' at top. Copy at 1:13,600 on: 'The Honourable and Right Reverend James Lord Bishop of Ely to Mr John Hemment Lease', 14 February 1808 [EDR CC.94961]. Measures 7 7/8 x 5 5/8in. Border of 2 narrow red bands, no title, compass on left showing 4 points. Land coloured green, buildings uncoloured. Numbers on plots refer to table on original, summary of acreage at bottom.

Wisbech St Mary – [c. 1811] – WSM81101 – W M DIV.40
['A Plan of the Estates, late of Lawrence Banyer Esq. deceased; in the Parishes of Emneth, Walsoken, Terrington, & in Marshland Smeeth and Fen, in the County of Norfolk; and in the Parishes of Wisbech, Leverington, Tid St Giles & Upwell, in the Isle of Ely, in the County of Cambridge'.] In Wisbech.
Scale bar 0–40 chains (= 5in.), 1:6,336; **Size:** (i) 5 x 7 1/4in.; **Top** is N; Manuscript(i), paper, coloured.
17a.0r.32p. in Wisbech St Mary and Wisbech St Peter parishes, bounded by Nettle Bank in Elm Parish in W, 'Drove to White Engine' and 'Barton Lane' in N and 'Abbots Lane' in S.
Names of fields, roads and neighbouring owners. Closed fields showing owner's land; roads and drove; bank.
Border of 2 narrow bands; title at top; scale bottom right of whole sheet; compass rose centre bottom of whole sheet showing 4 points. Table right of scale giving acreages, land use and occupiers. Land outlined in yellow, field names written in red, now faded.
Notes of land tenure. Top left of whole sheet, which measures 23 3/8 x 25in. and title, as given above, is top right in a cartouche with brown and yellow vases and blue and yellow edges. Bottom left of sheet is note: 'NB The Letters a and p in the second Column in the Table of References, distinguish the arable from the Pasture Lands'. Probably drawn in connection with sale of Lawrence Banyer's estate in 1811 [*Cambridge Chronicle*, 8 February 1811]. See also LEV81101, TYD81101 and UPW81101.

Wisbech St Mary – [1811] – WSM81102 – G L C A/CSC/1101/1
A Map of Two Fields abutting on Black Drove, in Wisbeach High Fen, Wisbeach St Mary, Isle of Ely, Cambridgeshire.
Surveyor: [W.P. Attfield]; **Scale bar** 0–10 chains (= 2 7/16in.), 1:3,249; **Size:** (i) 11 11/16 x 6 3/4in.; **Top** is NNW; Manuscript(i), parchment, coloured.

9a.0r.4p. in W of parish, bounded by Black Drove in W and road from Peterborough to Wisbech in S, which meet at TF355037.

Names of roads and neighbouring owners. Closed fields; state of cultivation shown by colour; acreages; roads and turnpike; gates.

Border of 1 broad band with 1 narrow band on inside; title middle top in a cartouche of a stone arch with decorative lettering; scale at bottom; compass middle right showing 4 points. Fields coloured green, roads coloured brown.

Centre top is note of crops. Pencil notes of crops. Later note below title: 'In the occupation of Mr Robt Abbott 1841'. In volume: 'Maps of the Wisbeach Estate in the Counties of Cambridge, Lincoln and Norfolk. belonging to the Corporation of The Sons of the Clergy. Surveyed by W.P. Attfield Whetstone & Hadley MDCCCXI'. At end is table of acreages and land use with ink notes added in 1841, and valuation by Attfield. See also TYD81102–3, UPW81102–4, WEL81101, WSM81103–5 and WSP81101.

Wisbech St Mary – [1811] – WSM81103 – G L C A/CSC/1101/2

A Map of a Field abutting on Goold or Gould Drove in Wisbeach High Fen, Wisbeach St Mary, Isle of Ely, Cambridgeshire.

Surveyor: [W.P. Attfield]; **Scale bar** 0–10 chains (= 2 7/16in.), 1:3,249; **Size:** (i) 11 11/16 x 6 13/16in.; **Top** is NNW; Manuscript(i), parchment, coloured.

8a.1r.26p. in Wisbech High Fen, bounded by Gull ['Gould'] Drove in S and 'Mill Drain' in N.

Names of roads and neighbouring owners. Closed field; state of cultivation shown by colour; acreage; roads and gates.

Border of 1 broad band with 1 narrow band on inside; title centre top in a cartouche of a stone arch with decorative lettering; scale at bottom; compass middle right showing 4 points. Roads coloured brown, field coloured in dark brown stripes.

Centre top is note of parish. Pencil notes. Later note below title: 'In occupation of Mr Robert Abbott – 1841'. In volume which gives date, owner and surveyor; see WSM81102 for details. See also TYD81102–3, UPW81102–4, WEL81101, WSM81104–5 and WSP81101.

Wisbech St Mary – [1811] – WSM81104 – G L C A/CSC/1101/3

Wisbeach St Mary. Isle of Ely, Cambridgeshire.

Surveyor: [W.P. Attfield]; **Scale bar** 0–20 chains (= 2 1/2in.), 1:6,336; **Size:** (i) 12 x 7 13/16in.; **Top** is NW; Manuscript(i), parchment, coloured.

87a.0r.30p. in Guyhim Field in W of parish, bounded by River Nene in S, 'Guyhern Chapel' in SE and 'Follys or Followes Drove' in NW.

Names of buildings, roads and neighbouring owners. Guyhim Chapel, 'Chequers Public House' and 'Ferry House' shown in plan form. Closed fields; state of cultivation shown by colour; acreages; roads and gates; watercourses.

Border of 1 broad band with 1 narrow band on inside; title at top; scale at bottom; compass in centre showing 4 points. Water coloured blue, roads coloured brown, pasture coloured green, arable shown by dark brown stripes.

Centre top is note of parish. Pencil notes of crops in 1816–18. Later ink note below title: 'In occupation of Mr

Robert Abbott – 1841'. In volume which gives date, owner and surveyor; see WSM81102 for details. See also TYD81102–3, UPW81102–4, WEL81101, WSM81103,5 and WSP81101.

Wisbech St Mary – [1811] – WSM81105 – GLC A/CSC/1101/4

A Map of seven Fields abutting on Morrow Lane & Tolemies Drove in Wisbeach St Mary, Isle of Ely, Cambridgeshire.

Surveyor: [W.P. Attfield]; **Scale bar** 0–20 chains (= 2 1/2in.), 1:6,336; **Size:** (i) 12 13/16 x 6 3/4in.; **Top** is NW; Manuscript(i), parchment, coloured.

72a.2r.32p. in Murrow Field, bounded by 'Morrow Lane' in NW and Tholomas ['Tolemies'] Drove in SE.

Names of roads and neighbouring owners. Site of house. Closed fields; state of cultivation shown by colour; acreages; roads and gates; gardens.

Border of 1 broad band with 1 narrow band on inside; title top left in an oval cartouche of 1 broad band with 1 narrow band on inside; scale bottom right; compass top right showing 4 points. Roads coloured brown, pasture coloured green, arable coloured dark brown.

Centre top is note of parish. Later pencil notes of crops, acreages and railway; ink notes of land use and railway and, under parish and title, 'In occupation of Mr Robert Abbott 1841'. In volume which gives date, owner and surveyor; see WSM81102 for details. See also TYD81102–3, UPW81102–4, WEL81101, WSM81103–4 and WSP81101.

Wisbech St Mary – 1834 – WSM83401 – CRO 515/P

Plan and Survey of the Estate belonging to The Co~heirs of Mr Thomas Marriott deceased Situate in Wisbech High Fen in the Parish of Wisbech St Mary's Isle of Ely.

Surveyor: Joseph Jackson; **Scale:** 3 Chains to an Inch, 1:2,376; **Size:** (ii) 30 5/16 x 26in.; **Top** is N; Manuscript(i), paper, uncoloured.

234a.2r.32p. in Wisbech High Fen, bounded by toll road to Thorney in N and Counter Drain along N bank of River Nene in S.

Names of roads, drains and neighbouring owners. Cottage shown in plan form. Closed fields showing owner's land; wash; trees; acreages; roads including turnpike; watercourses; gates; gardens; responsibility for boundaries.

Title top left; scale beneath title; 'North' at top of map. Table middle left giving owners, field names and acreages.

Pencil table bottom left giving state of cultivation, field numbers and acreages. Land owned by Mr Wilkins and Mr Skell. Outline of map on dorse. Accompanied by scale drawing of area with survey lines marked in pencil.

Wisbech St Peter – 1792 – WSP79201 – CRO 408/E6

A Survey of the Castle Gardens and Premises in Wisbech St Peters belonging to his Lordship the Bishop of Ely, in Right of his See, of Ely.

Surveyor: John Watte; **Scale bar** 0–10 chains (= 9 7/8in.), 1:802; **Size:** (i) 18 x 9 7/8in.; **Top** is NW; Manuscript(i), parchment, coloured.

Wisbech Castle, TF462097, and 4a.0r.2p. bounded by River Nene in NW, churchyard in SE, The Crescent ['Deadman's Lane'] in SW and Castle Ditch in NE.

Names of areas, roads and neighbouring owners. Buildings shown in plan form and include castle, parsonage, theatre, stables, offices and 'Custom House'. Acreage of whole area; roads; gates to castle shown in detail; 'West', 'East' and 'Pleasure' gardens; churchyard; 'Green Yard'; watercourses; pond; ditch shown by hachures; bridge over River Nene shown in perspective; walls.

Border of 1 broad and 1 narrow band; title at top; scale at bottom; compass middle right showing 4 points with a decorated N. Walls coloured green.

Drawn in connection with sale of castle by Bishop of Ely [EDR D9.6]; see also WSP79411.

Wisbech St Peter – [c. 1794] – WSP79401 – EDR CC.10120

Wisbich S<a>nt Peters and Wisbich *Saint* Maries Isle of Ely County of Cambridge.

Scale: 1:12,900; **Size:** (ii) 15 x 18 3/4in.; **Top** is N; Manuscript(i), paper, coloured.

Wisbech St Mary Church, TF419082, and at least 933a.0r.19p. scattered throughout parish and in E of Wisbech St Mary Parish.

Names of rivers and roads. Wisbech St Mary Church shown in perspective, cottages shown in plan form. Closed fields showing owner's land; roads; River Nene, with arrow showing direction of flow.

Title top left. Areas outlined in blue, red and green and coloured yellow.

Note under title: 'N.B. The Closes marked M are in Wisbich St Maries'. Later ink note above title: 'Wisbech Barton'. Pencil notes of lot numbers and of compass. Land owned by Bishop of Ely; map is related to WSM79402–3 and WSP79403–10, drawn to accompany leases of 1794.

Wisbech St Peter – [c. 1794] – WSP79402 – EDR CC.10119

A Plan of Mr John Reams Est*ate* Situate in Wisbech St Peters in Hirn Field.

Scale: 1:5,510; **Size:** (i) 10 5/8 x 14 3/16in.; **Top** is NNW; Manuscript(i), parchment, coloured.

100a.2r.33p. in far SW of parish NW of TF437078, junction of Cross Lane and Lords Lane, bounded by Bevis Lane in W; most NW plot is in Wisbech St Mary Parish.

Names of field, roads and neighbouring owner. Closed field; droves and lanes.

Border of 1 narrow band with 1 broad band on inside; title bottom right in a rococo cartouche; compass top right showing 8 points. Table bottom left giving acreages. Field outlined in red, plots outlined in yellow or green.

Arrows point along NW part of Lords Lane. Probably drawn at same time as WSP79407; both show same area and neighbouring owner. Land owned by Bishop of Ely.

Wisbech St Peter – [1794] – WSP79403 – EDR CC.10126/2

Map of Lands In Lease No: 2. to Oglethorpe Wainman M:D: lying in the Parish of Wisbech St Peter.

Scale: 1:9,670; **Size:** (i) 8 7/8 x 6 1/2in.; **Top** is NW; Manuscript(i), parchment, coloured.

Junction of Barton Road and Mile Tree Lane, TF438088, and 95a.2r.3p. to E in Fenland Field.

Names of roads and neighbouring owners. Closed fields; roads.

Border of 1 broad band with 1 narrow band on inside; title top left in an oval cartouche of 1 broad band with 1 narrow band on inside; compass centre right showing 4 points. Table at bottom giving field names and acreages

'by the Particular of Sale' and 'By Mr Watte's Survey' [98a.3r.36p.; John Watte, Eden W164]. Land coloured green.

Accompanies lease: 'The Bishop of Ely to Dr Wainman', 14 June 1794 [EDR CC.94868]. In volume: 'Maps of the Demesne Lands of the Manor of Wisbech Barton, lying in the Parishes of Wisbech St Peter and Wisbech St Mary in the Isle of Ely in the County of Cambridge, belonging to the See of Ely, as now divided and leased in ten Lots, or separate Leases by the Honble, & Right Reverend James Lord Bishop of Ely, pursuant to an Act of Parliament for that Purpose passed in the year 1794'. See also WSM79402–3 and WSP79404–10.

Wisbech St Peter – [1794] – WSP79404 – EDR CC.10126/3

A Map of Lands In Lease No: 3, to Oglethorpe Wainman M:D, lying in the Parish of Wisbech St Peter.

Scale: 1:10,200; **Size:** (i) 8 7/8 x 6 1/2in.; **Top** is NNE; Manuscript(i), parchment, coloured.

92a.1r.19p. in a plot in TF4510, bounded by River Nene in E and road from Wisbech to Holbeach in W, and land to SW extending as far as TF445092, junction of Barton Road with 'Mill Lane'.

Names of river, roads and neighbouring owners. 2 post mills and 'Red Engine' [a smock mill] shown in perspective. Closed fields; roads, turnpike and toll bar; watercourses and direction of flow of river; bridge.

Border of 1 broad band with 1 narrow band on inside; title top left in an oval cartouche of 1 broad band with 1 narrow band on inside; compass on right showing 4 points. Table bottom right giving field names and acreage 'by the Particular of Sale' and 'By Mr Watte's Survey' [95a.2r.17p.; John Watte, Eden W164]. Roads coloured yellow, fields coloured green, river coloured grey.

Accompanies lease: 'The Bishop of Ely to Dr Wainman', 14 June 1794 [EDR CC.94875]. In volume which gives owner and date; see WSP79403 for details. See also WSM79402–3 and WSP79405–10.

Wisbech St Peter – [1794] – WSP79405 – EDR CC.10126/4

Map of Lands In Lease No: 4. to Mr Samuel Stanton lying in the Parish of Wisbech St Peter.

Scale: 1:8,910; **Size:** (i) 8 13/16 x 6 7/16in.; **Top** is NNE; Manuscript(i), parchment, coloured.

Junction of Gadd's Lane and Barton Road, TF440092, and 140a.1r.1p. to W and S in Nymandole and Wheatmath fields.

Names of roads and neighbouring owners. Closed fields; roads.

Border of 1 broad band with 1 narrow band on inside; title top left in an oval cartouche of 1 broad band with 1 narrow band on inside; compass on left showing 4 points. Table bottom right giving field names and acreages 'by the Particular of Sale' and 'By Mr Watte's Survey' [144a.1r.17p.; John Watte, Eden W164]. Fields coloured green.

Accompanies lease: 'The Bishop of Ely to Samuel Stanton', 14 June 1794 [EDR CC.94882]. In volume which gives owner and date; see WSP79403 for details. See also WSM79402–3 and WSP79404,6–10.

Wisbech St Peter – [1794] – WSP79406 – E D R CC.10126/5

Map of Lands In Lease No: 5. to Mr James Bellamy lying in the Parish of Wisbech St Peter.

Scale: 1:10,300; **Size:** (i) 8 7/8 x 6 7/16in.; **Top** is NW; Manuscript(i), parchment, coloured.

Junction of Mile Tree Lane and 'High Lane', TF438087, and 137a.0r.35p. in Nymandole and North Bridge fields bounded by Lords Lane in SW.

Names of roads and neighbouring owners. Closed fields; roads.

Border of 1 broad band with 1 narrow band on inside; title top left in an oval cartouche of 1 broad band with 1 narrow band on inside; compass centre left showing 4 points. Table bottom right giving field names and acreages 'by the Particular of Sale' and 'By Mr Watte's Survey' [140a.0r.18p.; John Watte, Eden W164]. Fields coloured green.

Accompanies lease: 'The Bishop of Ely to Mr Jas Bellamy', 14 June 1794 [EDR CC.95180]. In volume which gives owner and date; see WSP79403 for details. See also WSM79402-3 and WSP79404-5,7-10.

Wisbech St Peter – [1794] – WSP79407 – E D R CC.10126/7

Map of Lands In Lease No: 7, to Mr John Ream lying in the Parishes of Wisbech St Peter and Wisbech St Mary.

Scale: 1:10,410; **Size:** (i) 8 13/16 x 6 7/16in.; **Top** is NW; Manuscript(i), parchment, coloured.

Junction of Cross Lane and Lords Lane, TF436078, and 100a.2r.33p. in Hirn Field bounded by Bevis Lane in W; 1 plot is in far E of Wisbech St Mary Parish.

Names of roads and neighbouring owners. Buildings in Wisbech St Mary village shown in plan form, Wisbech St Mary Church shown in perspective. Closed fields; roads.

Border of 1 broad band with 1 narrow band on inside; title top right in an oval cartouche of 1 broad band with 1 narrow band on inside; compass centre left showing 4 points. Table at bottom giving field names and acreages 'by the Particular of Sale' and 'By Mr Watte's Survey' [100a.2r.33p.; John Watte, Eden W164]. Fields coloured green.

Note left of table: 'Note, No: 29 lies in the Parish of Wisbech Saint Mary'. Buildings in Wisbech St Mary not identical to those in WSM79403. In volume which gives owner and date; see WSP79403 for details. See also WSM79402-3 and WSP79404-6,8-10. Probably drawn at same time as WSP79402; both show same area and neighbouring owner.

Wisbech St Peter – [1794] – WSP79408 – E D R CC.10126/8

Map of Lands In Lease No: 8, to Messrs Isaac Jecks, and Richard Bunbury Dawbarn lying in the Parish of Wisbech St Peter.

Scale: 1:6,390; **Size:** (i) 8 7/8 x 6 7/16in.; **Top** is N; Manuscript(i), parchment, coloured.

17a.1r.11p. in 'East Field' E of town, bounded by River Nene in W and 'Old Sea or Roman Bank' in E.

Names of river and neighbouring owners. 2 windmills shown in perspective. Closed fields; watercourses and direction of flow of River Nene; gate; 'Old Sea or Roman Bank'.

Border of 1 broad band with 1 narrow band on inside; title top right in an oval cartouche of 1 broad band with 1

narrow band on inside; compass top left showing 4 points. Table at bottom giving field names and acreages. Fields coloured green, water coloured grey.

Pencil additions of 2 plots which are included on WSP79401. Accompanies lease: 'The Bishop of Ely to Messrs Jecks and Dawbarn', 14 June 1794 [EDR CC.94895]. In volume which gives owner and date; see WSP79403 for details. See also WSM79402-3 and WSP79404-7,9-10.

Wisbech St Peter – [1794] – WSP79409 – E D R CC.10126/9

Map of Lands In Lease No: 9. to Mr William Clark lying in the Parish of Wisbech St Peter.

Scale: 1:6,910; **Size:** (i) 8 13/16 x 6 7/16in.; **Top** is NNW; Manuscript(i), parchment, coloured.

29a.3r.5p. in 'Marsh Field' W of TF462099, where road from King's Lynn turns to run along River Nene, bounded by 'The Old River' in E.

Names of river, roads and neighbouring owners. Buildings in Wisbech shown in plan form, post mill and smock mill shown in perspective. Closed fields; roads, turnpike and toll bar; gate; watercourses, 'Wisbech Canal' and 'The Old River' and its direction of flow; bridge.

Border of 1 broad band with 1 narrow band on inside; title top left in an oval cartouche of 1 broad band with 1 narrow band on inside; compass in centre showing 4 points. Table at bottom giving field names and acreages. Fields coloured green, river and buildings coloured grey, turnpike coloured yellow.

Pencil line. Accompanies lease: 'The Bishop of Ely to Wm Clark Esqr', 14 June 1794 [EDR CC.94901]. In volume which gives owner and date; see WSP79403 for details. See also WSM79402-3 and WSP79404-8,10.

Wisbech St Peter – [1794] – WSP79410 – E D R CC.10126/10

Map of Lands In Lease No: 10. to Mr William Clark lying in the Parish of Wisbech St Peter.

Scale: 1:6,700; **Size:** (i) 8 13/16 x 6 7/16in.; **Top** is NNW; Manuscript(i), parchment, coloured.

49a.2r.29p. in 'Marsh Field' E of town, bounded by Walsoken Parish [Norfolk] and 'The Old River' in S and E and 'Wisbech Canal' in W.

Names of watercourses and neighbouring owners. Buildings in Wisbech shown in plan form. Closed fields; 'Wisbech Canal'; 'The Old River'.

Border of 1 broad band with 1 narrow band on inside; title top right in an oval cartouche of 1 broad band with 1 narrow band on inside; compass top left showing 4 points. Table at bottom giving field names and acreages. Fields coloured green.

Accompanies lease: 'The Bishop of Ely to Mr Willm Clark', 14 June 1794 [EDR CC.94910]. In volume which gives owner and date; see WSP79403 for details. See also WSM79402-3 and WSP79404-9.

Wisbech St Peter – [1794] – WSP79411 – EDR D9.6 [Wisbech Castle.]

Surveyor: [John Watte]; **Scale:** 1:800; **Size:** (i) 16 1/8 x 12 1/4in.; **Top** is NW; Manuscript(i), paper, coloured.

Wisbech Castle, TF462096, and c. 2a. bounded by churchyard in SE, Market Place in NE and The Crescent ['Deadmans Lane'] in NW and SW.

Names of roads and functions of areas. Brew house, stable, 'Wash house', 'coal house', privy, castle, coach house, dog kennel and theatre shown in plan form. Roads; garden, 'Blue gardens' and kitchen garden; 'wilderness'; pond; ditch; yards; 'Ancient Wall'; stable yard; office yard; fore court; landing.

Border of 1 broad and 1 narrow band; compass top left showing 4 points. Roads outlined in yellow, buildings outlined in red, walls outlined in green, water outlined in blue.

John Watte surveyed castle prior to its sale by Bishop of Ely, see WSP79201; in letter at EDR D9.6, Watte refers to plan of castle drawn in connection with its sale. Photocopy of map at CRO R73/73, with later note top left: 'Copy from Bargain & Sale of 6th December 1794 Lord Bishop of Ely to Mr Joseph Medworth', tracing at CUL MS Plans 581 also dated 1794.

Wisbech St Peter – [1811] – WSP81101 – G L C A/CSC/1101/5
A Map of two Fields abutting on the North Bank, Wisbeach St Peter Isle of Ely Cambridgeshire.
Surveyor: [W.P. Attfield]; **Scale bar** 0–10 chains (= 2 7/16in.), 1:3,249; **Size:** (i) 12 3/4 x 7 1/16in.; **Top** is NW; Manuscript(i), parchment, coloured.
5a.1r.3p. NE of River Nene.
Names of river and neighbouring owners. Closed fields; state of cultivation shown by colour; acreages; roads and gates; watercourses.
Border of 1 broad band with 1 narrow band on inside; title at top in a oval cartouche of 1 broad band with 1 narrow band on inside; scale at bottom; compass centre right showing 4 points. Water coloured blue, roads coloured brown, fields coloured green.
Centre top is note of parish. Pencil notes. Later ink note below title: 'In occupation of Robt Abbott – 1841'. In volume: 'Maps of the Wisbeach Estate in the Counties of Cambridge, Lincoln and Norfolk. belonging to the Corporation of The Sons of the Clergy. Surveyed by W.P. Attfield Whetstone & Hadley MDCCCXI'. At end is table of acreages and land use with ink notes added in 1841, and valuation by Attfield. See also TYD81102-3, UPW81102-4, WEL81101 and WSM81102-5.

Wisbech St Peter – [c. 1820–39] – WSP82001 – W M DIV.33
Plan of an Estate in the Parishes of Wisbech and Elm in the Isle of Ely belonging to the Misses Percival.
Scale bar 10–0–40 chains (= 5 1/2in.), 1:7,200; **Size:** (i) 22 1/8 x 33 5/8in.; **Top** is NW; Manuscript(i), paper mounted on cloth, coloured.
Wood House Farm, TF457048, and 1,379a.2r.4p. to N and W bounded by River Nene ['Wisbech River'] in NW.
Names of farms, fields, roads and river. Wood House and Jew House farms and outbuildings and steam engine shown in plan form. Closed fields showing owner's land; acreages; roads and watercourses; hedges.
Border of 1 narrow band; title top left; scale bottom right; compass top right showing 4 points. Table above scale giving acreages, tenure and key to colours. Roads coloured brown, freehold land coloured green, leasehold land coloured red, water coloured blue.
Numbers on plots suggest map originally accompanied by a terrier. Drawn after steam engines introduced into Cambridgeshire Fens in 1820 [Darby, 1983, 174] and

before later additions in pencil and ink of land sold in 1839 and 1840.

Wisbech St Peter – [1825] – WSP82501 – B L Maps.c.8.a.15
Estate in Wisbech Saint Peter's, Containing 1a.2r.36p.
Surveyor: [John Grimsby Lenny]; **Scale bar** 1–0–5 chains (= 2in.), 1:2,376; **Size:** (ii) 10 3/16 x 8in.; **Top** is N; Manuscript(i), paper, coloured.
1a.2r.36p., possibly in TF4510, bounded by River Nene in E.
Names of roads and neighbouring owners. Buildings shown in plan form. Trees; acreages of land under 'grass' and 'neat' [cattle]; roads; gates; watercourses including direction of flow of River Nene; fences; banks including 'Little East Field Bank'.
Title at top; scale centre bottom; compass bisecting scale showing 2 points. Buildings coloured red and grey, paths coloured brown, water coloured blue, grass coloured green.
Note top right: 'I'. On preceding page is a view of Wisbech, the river and bridge. In volume: 'The Estates of Mr Josiah Rumball, at Wisbech, Leverington, and Parson Drove, in the Isle of Ely, and County of Cambridge. J. G. Lenny, Surveyor, Bury St Edmund's, 1825'. Summary of acreage of whole estate: 56a.3r.31p. Surveyor's 1st names were John Grimsby [Eden L148]. See also LEV82501-3.

Witcham – 1795 – WTC79501 – CLC ACC.1985/5
A Plan of an Estate at Witcham in the Isle of Ely belonging to Clare Hall in the University of Cambridge Surveyed in the Year 1795.
Surveyor: [Joseph Freeman]; **Scale bar** 5–0–10 chains (= 2 3/4in.), 1:4,320; **Size:** (i) 24 5/16 x 27 1/4in.; **Top** is N; Manuscript(i), parchment, coloured.
63a.2r.34p. scattered throughout parish, and 2a.1r.3p. in Sutton Parish.
Names of fields, roads, watercourses and neighbouring owners. Cottages, Witcham Hive ['Hive'], 'Mr Upshaw's House' and 'Meeting House' in Sutton Parish [identified on WTC79701] shown in plan form. Open fields showing owner's strips; closes; roads and droves; watercourses, Hundred Foot River and direction of flow; hedges; number of lands between each strip; balks; meadow.
Border of 1 broad band with 1 narrow band on inside; title top left; scale below title; compass above title with a red fleur-de-lys as N. Table on left giving tenants, field names, acreages, land use and number of ridges. Grass and hedges coloured green, water coloured blue, land leased to Mr Sanxter coloured red, land leased to R. Poole coloured yellow.
Note in table: 'N.B. The Dam Heads and Cow Croft in Mr Sanxters Occupation, could not be Measured on Account of the Fens being covered with Water when the Survey was made. the Measurement is taken from a Field Book of the Fens'. Insets at top of land in Sutton Parish and fen in Witcham Parish. Pencil notes. Rough copy drawn on paper mounted on cloth with no border measures 18 7/8 x 22in. and does not show all the insets. Copy drawn on paper with a watermark of 1801 of lands leased to Mr Poole in Sutton, Witcham Meadlands and The Wash, and of all the tables, with no border, measures 9 1/4 x 14 3/4in.. Original is in style of Joseph Freeman and is accompanied by a valuation by him dated 1795 [CLC W.J. Harrison's notes on Clare College's estates].

Witcham – [1797] – WTC79701 – CLC ACC.1985/5 ['Witcham Jellings lease 1797'.]

Surveyor: [Joseph Freeman?]; **Scale:** 1:4,320; **Size:** (i) 24 1/8 x 30 5/8in.; **Top** is N; Manuscript(ii), parchment, uncoloured.

32a.0r.13p. scattered throughout parish, and including 2a.1r.3p. in Sutton Parish.

Names of fields, roads, watercourses and neighbouring owners. Cottages and 'Meeting House' in Sutton Parish shown in plan form. Open fields showing owner's strips; closes; roads and drove; watercourses and ditch; meadow; wash; number of lands between each strip.

Border of 1 narrow band. Table bottom left giving field names, acreages, land use and number of ridges.

Probably copy of part of WTC79501 which shows land leased by Clare College, Cambridge to Mr Sanxter, surveyed by Joseph Freeman. Title on dorse in pencil. 2nd copy in CLC.

Witchford – 1779 – WTF77901 – WRO CR114/2/vi Whichford Map.

Surveyors: [John] Lund [sr and jr]; **A Scale** of four Chains in One Inch, Scale bar 0–21 chains (= 5 1/4in.), 1:3,168; **Size:** (i) 23 1/8 x 12 1/16in.; **Top** is N; Manuscript(i), paper, coloured.

c. 100a. bounded by Ely St Mary Parish in E.

Names of roads and neighbouring owners. Closed fields; trees; roads and gates; tenure of 2 plots.

Border of 1 broad band; title on left; scale centre bottom of whole sheet; compass in centre of sheet showing 4 points. Trees coloured green, roads coloured brown, fields outlined in yellow, red, brown, green and blue.

Numbers on plots suggest map originally accompanied by a terrier. On right of sheet which also contains map of Ely [EYT77901], entitled at centre top: 'A Map of the Estates of the Right Honourable Lady Viscountess Irwin at Stuntney and Whichford in the Isle of Ely and County of Cambridge. Surveyed by Messrs Lund's in 1779'. Surveyors' 1st names were John [Eden L294 and L294.1].

Witchford – 1793 – WTF79301 – CLC ACC.1985/5

Plan of a Farm at Witchford In the Isle of Ely belonging to Clare Hall in the University of Cambridge Surveyed in 1793.

Surveyor: [Joseph Freeman]; **Scale bar** 2–0–20 chains (= 2 7/8in.), 1:6,061; **Size:** (i) 21 1/8 x 25 13/16in.; **Top** is N; Manuscript(i), parchment, coloured.

Farm N of road to Ely, and 117a.3r.16p. bounded by Grunty Fen in S and Sedge Fen in NE.

Names of fields, roads and neighbouring owners. Farm buildings shown in plan form. Open fields showing owner's strips; closes; meadow and fen; roads and droves; gates; hedges and fences; state of cultivation shown by colour.

Border of 1 broad band with 1 narrow band on inside; title middle right; scale bottom right; compass top right showing 4 points. Table top left giving field names, acreages and number of ridges. Hedges and grass coloured green, arable coloured in brown stripes, buildings coloured red.

By 1 plot: 'Note. in this pightle (No. 1) the College have a small parcel of Land containing about 1/6 of an Acre'. Rough copy drawn on paper mounted on cloth with no border measures 18 3/16 x 21 3/4in. Table is divided between top left and bottom right. Another, uncoloured,

copy with no title, cut from a lease possibly dated 1797 [date of other leases with maps of Cambridgeshire estates], measuring 22 3/8 x 27 1/4in. Surveyor of original was Joseph Freeman, who also valued estate in 1793 [CLC Safe A:18/1].

Woodditton – [1810] – WYD81001 – CRO 101/T326

[Land at Woodditton leased by 5th Duke of Rutland to Mary Panton.]

Scale bar 0–18 chains (= 3in.), 1:4,752; **Size:** (i) 6 1/8 x 9 5/16in.; **Top** is NW; Manuscript(i), parchment, coloured.

Building, TL639625, and 30a.2r.7p. bounded by road from Dullingham to Newmarket in NW and Woodditton open fields in SE.

Names of roads and neighbouring owners. Building shown in plan form. Closed fields; acreages; roads; footpath; watercourse; pond; pleasure grounds identified on lease.

Border at left and bottom of 1 broad ink band with 1 narrow ink band on inside, border at top and right of 2 red lines; scale centre bottom; compass centre top showing 4 points. Roads coloured yellow, water coloured blue, building coloured red, fields outlined in green or red, pasture coloured in green stripes, pleasure grounds coloured green and with symbol depicting tufts of grass.

Pencil notes. On lease: 'His Grace the Duke of Rutland to Mrs Panton Lease of Lands in Wood Ditton in the County of Cambridge', 21 July 1810. Lease gives Mrs Panton's 1st name. Owner was 5th Duke of Rutland [*PB*, 2,329].

Addendum (April 1992)

Grantchester – 1806 – CRC

Plan of an Estate situate in the Parishes of St Giles, Grantchester, and Coton in the County of Cambridge belonging to The Master, Fellows, and Scholars of the College of Corpus Christi; and of Blessed Mary the Virgin; commonly called Benet College; in the University of Cambridge. 1806. [463a.1r.19p.]

Kirtling – 1816 – CRO 101/T1295

[Plan on release of 3a.3r.17p.]

Landbeach – [c. 1813] – CRC XXXV.60

Plan of an Estate situate in the Parish of Landbeach in the County of Cambridge belonging to the Master, Fellows & Scholars of Benet College in the University of Cambridge. [289a.1r.25p.]

Little Wilbraham – 1806 – CRC XXIII.32

Plan of an Estate, situate in the Parish of Little Wilbraham, in the County of Cambridge belonging to The Master, Fellows, and Scholars of the College of Corpus Christi and Blessed Mary the Virgin, commonly called Benet College, in the University of Cambridge 1806. [562a.3r.5p.]

Little Wilbraham – 1806 – CRC

Plan of Buildings at Little Wilbraham, in the County of Cambridge belonging to The Master Fellows & Scholars, of Benet College, in the University of Cambridge. in Lease to Doctor Temple, and in the Occupation of Richard Kent 1806. [c. 1a.]

CHRONOLOGICAL LIST OF MAPS

c. Elizabeth I	SOH55801	c. 1730s	LOL73001
1581	LIN58101	Ante 1731/2	FDI73201–4
1600	LIN60001–7	1731/2	LIN73201, THO73201
1601/2	GAM60201–16	1732	MAR73201
1603	LLA60301	1733	CHE73301–4
c. 1609	THO60901	c. 1735	CHG73501
1612	CAR61201	1737	STO73701, WEW73701
1617	BAL61701–6, CAS61701–5	1738	THO73801
1626	SOH62601–2	c. 1740–50	BAP74001
1628–30	SOH63001–2	1740	DRY74001
1631	COU63101	1740–1	STL74101
c. 1634–9	BUR63401–4	1741	CAS74101–2
1637	WMB63701	1747	CRY74701–3
1638	WMP63801	c. 1748	CAS74801
1639	SUT63901	1748	LLS74801
c. 1650	EYM65001	1749	THO74901
1650	BOX65001	Mid-18th century	
1652	THO65201		THO75001
1654	GRT65401	1749/50	CAX75001
c. 1656	SOH65601	1750	CRY75001–11, EAS75001–8,
1656	FOR65601–7, SOH65602–12		TAD75001–9
1659	CHP65901	1751	GUI75101
1662	WSM66201	1752	GAM75201
1666	GRT66601	1752–3	THO75301
1674	BUR67401	1754	CAR75401, RAM75401, WLL75401
1680/1	WAT68101	1756	NEA75601–2, SWB75601,
1683/4	WHR68401		THO75601–3
Ante 1686	ORW68601	c. 1757	WEW75701
1688	TEV68801–7	1759	BOT75901
Early 18th century		1764	SHE76401
	CHA70001, GRT70001, THO70001	c. 1766–89	MAR76601–2
1700	DOD77001–2	1766	GRV76601
1706	WHR70601	1767	CAR76701, STM76701–2,
c. 1710	WHR71001		THO76701
1712	CHP71201–8	1769	WSM76901
c. 1716	WHR71601	1769–70	HRS77001–7, SHU77001
1716/17	GTA71701	1770	HIL77001, STN77001, WIC77001,
1716	WSM71601		WMB77001
1719	WEW71901–2, WLL71901–2	c. 1771	BEN77101, THO77101
1720	KIN72001	1771	CAS77101, WEW77101
c. 1721	WMP72101–4	c. 1772	CAX77201, TEV77201–14
1721	SHU72101	1772	TYD77201–2
1723	COM72301–4	c. 1773	GTS77301–2
1728	THO72801	1773	CAS77301, HAD77301

1774	MED77401, UPW77401
Late 18th century	
	CHA77501, ELM77501, EYM77501, UPW77501
1775	CHG77501, WHR77501, WMB77501–2
1776	KNA77601
1777	HAS77701, LIN77701–2
c. 1779	TYD77901
1779	EYT77901, ISL77901, LIN77901, SOH77901–2, STO77901, TYD77901, WTF77901
Ante 1780	ISL78001
1780	CHA78001, TRU78001
1782	LEV78201, LIT78201–7
1783	COV78301
c. 1784	EYT78401
1785	BAB78501, LIN78501
c. 1786–8	WHR78601
1786	CAX78601, DUL78601, NEA78601–2, SWB78601
c. 1787–1806	ISL78701
1787	WSM78701
1788	CAL78801, WEV78801
c. 1790	SOH79001, STR79001
1790	CHF79001–3, SOH79002, STR79002, WLL79001, WMP79001
c. 1791	GTS79101, LLA79101
1791	BAL79101, BOU79101, COU79101–3, HRN79101
c. 1792–5	CAS79201
1792	EYM79201, FDY79201, KIN79201, LOL79201, MEB79201, WSP79201
1793	BOT79301, CHF79301, DOW79301–2, GAM79301, MIL79301, STM79301, WEW79301, WTF79301
c. 1794	DOW79401, WSM79401, WSP79401–2
1794	CAS79401, CHF79401–2, COM79401, GAM79401, LIN79401, LIT79401, MAR79401, SHU79401, WET79401, WEW79401–3, WSM79402–3, WSP79403–11
c. 1795	FOX79501, SOH79501
1795	BOU79501, FOR79501, GRT79501–2, HIL79501, ICK79501, WLL79501, WTC79501
c. 1796	LLP79601
1796	BAR79601, BUR79601–2, FDI79601, HAS79601, WEW79601
c. 1797–1810	LIN79701
1797	COU79701, DUL79701, GUI79701, LLP79701, OVE79701, WTC79701
c. 1798	EYM79801–6, EYT79801–3
1798	BAP79801, CHA79801
Ante 1799	TOF79901
1799	PAM79901–2, SWV79901
Early 19th century	
	BOT80001, BOU80001, CAS80001, DOW80001, LEV80001, OVE80001, RAM80001
c. 1800	CAS80002–6, CHA80001
1800	BAP80001, LSW80001, SWB80001, WMP80001
c. 1801–8	SWB80101
c. 1801	GTW80101, HAU80101–2, TRU80101–3
1801	CHP80101, COT80101, GAM80101, GTE80101–5, HAR80101, TRU80104
Post 1801	HIL80101
c. 1802	CHI80201
1802	BOT80201, COU80201, TRU80201
c. 1803–29	COU80301, OVE80301, RAM80301
c. 1803	BAR80301
1803	BAR80302, DOD80301–3, GAM80301, ICK80301, LLA80301, NEA80301
c. 1804	HIN80401
1804	ABI80401, CHF80401, GRT80401, STO80401, TRU80401
1805	BAR80501, MAR80501, OVE80501, WLB80501
Ante 1806	SNA80601–4
c. 1806–28	GAM80601
c. 1806	BAS80601–3, HIS80601, IMP80601–4
1806	BUW80601, GRT80601
Post 1806	IMP80605
1807	CHA80701, EYT80701, GAM80701, GRV80701
c. 1808	TYD80801
1808	CAS80801, LAB80801–2, SWP80801, WSM80801
c. 1809	FOR80901
1809	FDI80901–4, FOR80902, HIS80901, HRN80901–6, LSW80901
Post 1809	TRU80901
c. 1810	HRN81001–4, ICK81001
1810	BAS81001, CAS81001, HRN81005, WYD81001
Post 1810	HRN81006
c. 1811	LEV81101, TYD81101, UPW81101, WSM81101
1811	ICK81101, MAD81101, TYD81102–3, UPW81102–4, WEL81101, WLL81101, WSM81102–5, WSP81101
Post 1811	WLL81102
1812	CHE81201, ICK81201, SHU81201, TEV81201

c. 1813	COM81301, WEV81301, WEW81301
1813	BOU81301, CHE81301, FUL81301, HAR81301, LLS81301, SWB81301, TEV81301, WEN81301
c. 1814	GIR81401–2, STL81401, SWP81401–3
1814	BOT81401–3, BUR81401, CHP81401, ELT81401
Post 1814	FUL81401, GIR81403–4
c. 1815–17	NEA81501–2
c. 1815–29	HIL81501
c. 1815	TOF81501, WMP81501
1815	HAU81501, ICK81501, NEA81503, PAP81501, TOF81502, WEW81501
Post 1815	WHV81501
c. 1816–38	BAS81601, LSA81601–3
1816	BUW81601, CHF81601, CHP81601, DRY81601, ELT81601, HAQ81601, LIN81601, MIL81601, NEA81601, OVE81601
1817	BAP81701, BRI81701, BUW81701, CHI81701, COV81701–2, NEA81701–2
1818	ELM81801, GTA81801–2, HAD81801, ICK81801, SHU81801
Post 1818?	NEA81804
Post 1818	BUW81801, NEA81801–3
c. 1819	WHV81901
1819	GTA81901, ICK81901
c. 1820–39	WSP82001
c. 1820–41	WHA82001
c. 1820	BOU82001, BUR82001–2, MED82001, SNA82001
1820	DOD82001, ORW82001, TRU82001
Post 1820	HAS82001, MED82002
c. 1821–63	BUW82101
1821	FOR82101–2, HAD82101, LLG82101–3, UPW82101
c. 1822	WEV82201, WHR82201
1822	LLG82201, LLP82201, STM82201, THO82201
1823	BEN82301, CRX82301, WHR82301
1824	HAQ82401, ICK82401–2, MAR82401–5, TEV82401–2, WEV82401
c. 1825	ELM82501
1825	BAL82501, BUW82501, CAS82501, CHF82501, COT82501, COV82501, DUL82501, FUL82501, GTE82501, HAD82501, HAQ82501, HAS82501,

	KIN82501, LEV82501–3, OAK82501, PAM82501, RAM82501, SHU82501, SOH82501, SWP82501–2, WEV82501, WIC82501, WLL82501, WSP82501
c. 1826	LLG82601
1826	BOU82601, DUX82601, EYM82601, FOR82601–2
c. 1827	CAS82701, WEV82701–3
1827	CHI82701, EYM82701, HAD82701, HRS82701, LLE82701, STM82701, STO82701
c. 1828	GTS82801, IMP82801, SAW82801, WAT82801, WET82801
1828	ARR82801–4, HRS82801, LIT82801, LSW82801, STM82801, WAT82802, WET82802–3, WMP82801–11
c. 1829	TRU82901
1829	BAB82901, BAL82901, BAR82901, CAR82901, CHP82901–2, COV82901–2, GTE82901, HAQ82901, TRU82902, WAT82901, WEV82901
c. 1830	WEO83001–2
1830	CHE83001, COM83001, DUX83001, FOX83001–2
1831	BAL83101, CAS83101, CHE83101, FUL83101, HAP83101, HIN83101, NEA83101, SOH83101, WEO83101
c. 1832	SAW83201
1832	MAR83201, SOH83201, TAD83201, TYD83201
c. 1833–61	SOH83301
c. 1833	LSW83301–6
1833	BAL83301, BOT83301–5, BUR83301, CAS83301, LSW83307, WHV83301
c. 1834	ARR83401, GTA83401, OAK83401
1834	BAL83401, BAR83401, GTA83402–3, HAP83401, MAR83401, MEB83401–2, NEA83401, NEC83401–4, OAK83402–3, WSM83401
c. 1835–48	ASH83501
c. 1835	CAX83501, GTS83501, HIN83501–2
1835	GAM83501, GTS83502–3, MEB83501
c. 1836	CHA83601, LIN83601
1836	BAL83601, CHF83601, GTE83601, HAP83601

NOTES

CHAPTER 1. INTRODUCTION

1   ECC SUR.13.

CHAPTER 2. ART, MAPS AND COMMUNICATION

1   See pp.xxi–xxiv for an explanation of the map codes, which refer to entries in the carto-bibliography.

CHAPTER 3. CAMBRIDGESHIRE AND ITS ESTATE MAPS

1   VAM T.65–1954.
2   QCC Box 20 Letter of 31 March 1785.
3   QCC 328.
4   QCC Box 99 Letter of 15 October 1810.
5   SJC D99.1.
6   QCC Box 15/22.
7   SJC D70.4.
8   ESRO V5/22/1.
9   QCC 328.
10   *Gazetteer and New Daily Advertiser*, 1 November 1766; D. Hodson, personal communication.
11   Personal observation of map in private hands.
12   QCC Box 25 Letter of 12 February 1808.
13   ECC GBX 44 Letter of 8 February 1815.
14   JCC Over 6.
15   CUA CUR.34.36.
16   *Norwich Gazette*, 29 March 1729; P. G. Eden, personal communication.

CHAPTER 4. ESTATE SURVEYORS AND THEIR EMPLOYMENT

1   *Norwich Mercury*, 18 November 1843; D. Cubitt, personal communication.
2   BRO Catalogue of the Russell estate papers.
3   *Cambridge Chronicle*, 19 October 1771, 1; 27 September 1777, 1; 21 November 1778, 1; 26 June 1779, 3; 9 September 1780, 1; 21 June 1777, 3.
4   *Cambridge Chronicle*, 6 February 1790, 3.
5   TCC Box 6 Shillington 83, TCC Box 5 Eaton Bray 18, TCC Box 5 Felmersham 78.
6   CUA VCV.43(1), VCV.42(2).
7   QCC Box 126.
8   TCC Box 44 Ware 130.
9   CUA CUR.39.27.2.
10   QCC Box 28/52; CUA CUR.65,177.
11   TCC Box 35 Barrington 464.
12   QCC Box 22/31.
13   TCC Box 85,1 p.1.
14   QCC 328.
15   JCC TRU.2.3
16   CRO P107/13/1/52.
17   CRO P22/5/6, CRO P31/4/1.
18   *Cambridge Chronicle*, 23 August 1783, 2.
19   *Cambridge Chronicle*, 11 January 1806, 1; EPR CW1829 WR C53:157.
20   CRO P26/11/8; CUA CUR.33.5,17.
21   CRO P26/11/9, CRO City/St Andrew the Less/Rate Book 1838; *Cambridge Chronicle*, 30 September 1831, 3.
22   GCC LXV.31.
23   *Universal British Directory*, 1793; CRO P26/11/8.
24   *Cambridge Chronicle*, 12 September 1834, 3.
25   BRO Catalogue of the Russell estate papers.
26   Personal observation of estate atlas in private hands.

27   BLM Add.35641 f.181.
28   BLM Add.35641 ff.178 and 181, Add.35685 f.80.
29   TCC Shelf 29.33.
30   QCC Box 27.
31   SJC C5.3 p.48, SJC D110.5.
32   *Cambridge Chronicle*, 24 January 1812, 1.
33   *Cambridge Chronicle*, 23 February 1805, 3.
34   *Cambridge Chronicle*, 22 May 1829, 3.
35   *Cambridge Chronicle*, 31 March 1787, 3.
36   *Cambridge Chronicle*, 23 March 1793, 2; TCC Shelf 30.12.
37   GCC Drawer 5 Map 3.
38   SJC D31.45.
39   *Cambridge Chronicle*, 15 March 1833, 3.
40   SJC D99.133.
41   *Gazetteer and New Daily Advertiser*, 1 November 1766; D. Hodson, personal communication.
42   CUA VCV.42(2).
43   *Cambridge Chronicle*, 27 January 1826, 3.
44   *Cambridge Chronicle*, 13 September 1833, 3.
45   TCC Great Iron Chest Lawyers Bills 1b.
46   QCC Box 113 Letter of 6 August 1823.
47   BRO R5/4007B.
48   ECC BUR.0.4a.
49   SJC D99.133.
50   SJC D100.6.
51   *Cambridge Chronicle*, 30 May 1778, 3.
52   *Cambridge Chronicle*, 23 August 1783, 2.
53   *Cambridge Chronicle*, 18 November 1831, 3; 12 September 1834, 3.
54   *Cambridge Chronicle*, 24 December 1830, 3.
55   *Cambridge Chronicle*, 20 November 1802, 1.
56   *Cambridge Chronicle*, 31 October 1801, 3; 28 August 1812, 2; 2 December 1825, 3.
57   QCC Box 27 Letters of 15 and 20 July 1775.
58   QCC 328.
59   ECC GBX 44 Letter of 6 November 1806.
60   ECC GBX 44 Letter of 12 November 1825.
61   ECC GBX 44 Letter of 17 April 1816.
62   ECC GBX 67 Letter of 4 November 1811.
63   PRO CRES 2/115.
64   *Cambridge Chronicle*, 30 November 1771, 3.
65   *Cambridge Chronicle*, 20 May 1780, 3.

CHAPTER 5. ESTATE SURVEYORS: THEIR STATUS, TRAINING AND TECHNIQUES

1   *Norwich Mercury*, 5 April 1828.
2   *Norfolk Chronicle*, 14 October 1837; D. Cubitt, personal communication.
3   QCC Conclusions Book 1787–1832.
4   ECC GBX 44 Letter of 2 October 1816.
5   ECC GBX 44 Letter of 6 November 1806.
6   PRO PROB 6/175/398r.
7   CUA Misc.Collect.15, 30.
8   PRO PROB 6/177/436r.
9   *Cambridge Chronicle*, 22 February 1828, 3.
10   CUA U.Ac.2(4) and (5).
11   *Cambridge Chronicle*, 26 November 1819, 3.
12   *Cambridge Chronicle*, 10 January 1834, 3.
13   QCC Box 115 Letter of 17 April 1836.
14   LPL MS.1262.
15   PRO PROB 6/220/f.332v.
16   *Cambridge Chronicle*, 22 June 1844, 2; *Gentleman's Magazine*, 22, 1844, 329.
17   *Cambridge Chronicle*, 14 September 1844, 3.
18   *Cambridge Chronicle*, 11 January 1806, 1.
19   *Cambridge Chronicle*, 28 April 1770, 3.
20   *Cambridge Chronicle*, 30 May 1778, 3.
21   BRO R1/268.
22   BLM Add.5823 ff.147–52.
23   CUM Add.5970.2 Letter of 30 May 1844.
24   EPR CW 1853 WR C59:116.
25   TCC Box 21 Ickleton 160.
26   CUA CUR.79,20.
27   *Cambridge Chronicle*, 23 September 1831, 3.
28   *Cambridge Chronicle*, 25 November 1831, 3.
29   CUA CUR.79,19.
30   *Cambridge Chronicle*, 25 January 1828, 3.
31   QCC Book 6, QCC 328.
32   QCC 328.
33   *Cambridge Chronicle*, 21 July 1764, 3.
34   CUL MS Plans 712(5); CRO P22/5/6.
35   BLM Add. 35623 ff.25 and 46, Add.35641 ff.178 and 181.
36   BLM Add.35641 f.181.
37   CUA Geol.2/8(11).
38   EPR 1782 AR C3:49n.
39   *Cambridge Chronicle*, 20 April 1771, 3.
40   *Cambridge Chronicle*, 22 September 1815, 3.

41 *Cambridge Chronicle*, 22 July 1814, 1; 29 December 1815, 3.
42 *Cambridge Chronicle*, 23 September 1831, 1.
43 *Cambridge Chronicle*, 13 December 1777, 3.
44 *Cambridge Chronicle*, 14 May 1774, 3; 9 January 1802, 3; 11 June 1808, 3.
45 *Cambridge Chronicle*, 15 July 1825, 3.
46 *Cambridge Chronicle*, 3 January 1767, 3; 11 July 1807, 3.
47 *Cambridge Chronicle*, 4 July 1807, 2.
48 *Cambridge Chronicle*, 10 January 1789, 3.
49 BRO R5/4498.
50 ECC BUR.0.3d.
51 TCC Box 35 Barrington 468.
52 *Cambridge Chronicle*, 16 November 1810, 3.
53 *Cambridge Chronicle*, 7 December 1832, 2.
54 BRO R3/23.
55 GCC Bursar's Book 1758–75.
56 QCC Box 104 Bill paid 3 April 1802.
57 TCC Box 28 Over 23.
58 TCC Shelf 84.19.
59 QCC Box 104 Bill paid 3 April 1802.
60 ERO D/DFr A3/6.
61 QCC Box 104 Bill paid 3 March 1802.
62 QCC Box 113 Letters of 12 September 1823 and 16 April 1824.
63 QCC Box 113 Note on valuation of Chesterton.
64 CUA VCV.42(2).

CHAPTER 6. LANDOWNERS AND THEIR INTERESTS

1 I am grateful to Dr M. Gleeson-White for looking at the catalogue for me.
2 CUA V.C.Ct.III.7(42).
3 QCC Book 3 pp.154 and 160.
4 CLC Safe A:1/6 p.158, Safe A:1/7 p.127.
5 CLC Safe A:1/6 p.116.
6 CLC Safe A:1/5 p.106.
7 CLC Safe A:25/41.
8 CLC Safe A:1/5 p.178.
9 CUA U.Ac.2(2)297v.
10 QCC Book 6.
11 PRO PROB 5/1056.
12 HRO.
13 ECC BUR.8.4, BUR.8.5; JCC A/C.1.7; QCC Book 7, Book 8.

14 ECC BUR.8.5.
15 *Daily Post*, 7 June 1733; D. Hodson, personal communication.
16 Quarry Bank Mill, Styal, personal observation.
17 EPR CW 1786 WR C45:17.
18 CRO Handlist to the Tharp family papers; R55/7/75/33–4.
19 CRO 132/M/28.
20 CRO P107/13/1/66.
21 EPR CW 1821 WR C51:244.
22 EPR CW 1828 WR C53:36.
23 EPR CW 1845 WR C57:323.
24 CRO 132/T464–5.
25 *Cambridge Chronicle*, 28 March 1807, 3; 6 May 1831, 3.
26 EPR CW 1840 WR C56:125.
27 EPR W 1836 WR 20:239.
28 *Cambridge Chronicle*, 21 September 1799, 3.
29 EPR CW 1824 WR C52:8.
30 EPR CW 1833 WR C54:538.
31 BRO Catalogue of the Russell estate papers.

CHAPTER 7. LANDOWNERS, THEIR ESTATES AND USES OF MAPS

1 WRO Ra 1/3/vi.
2 BRO Catalogue of the Russell estate papers.
3 BRO R5/4023.
4 BRO R4/4030/14.
5 BRO Catalogue of the Russell estate papers.
6 CRO R76/61(b) Letter of 4 September 1833.
7 BRO R5/4105.
8 ECC BUR.8.4.
9 SJC SB1.1.
10 QCC Box 27 Letter of 11 August 1775.
11 QCC Box 27 Letter of 21 February 1776.
12 CLC Safe C:3/2 pp.173 and 178.
13 SJC M1.8; SJC SB4.50.
14 QCC Conclusions Book 1733–87 p.127.
15 QCC Account Book 'Coll. No. 2' pp.3–9.
16 QCC Box 113.
17 CLC Cupboard:6/8.
18 ECC SCH.1.17.
19 QCC Conclusions Book 1733–87 p.64.

20 TCC Catalogue of the archives.
21 SJC C5.2 f.236r.
22 JCC Tempsford 2.
23 See, for example, ECC BUR.0.4b.
24 SJC C5.3.
25 QCC Conclusions Book 1733–87, 1787–1832 and 1832–88.
26 JCC A/C.1.7.
27 QCC 355 A and B; QCC Book 8.
28 PCC Barham W6.
29 SJC C5.3.
30 TCC Shelf 85.3.
31 SJC MPS 124.
32 ECC SCH.1.17.
33 ECC BUR.8.4.
34 CRO R79/44 Box marked 'Duke of Rutland 15'.
35 *Cambridge Chronicle*, 8 February 1811, 2.
36 SJC D55.13.
37 ECC BUR.0.4c.
38 QCC Box 28.
39 ECC BUR.6.1.
40 GCC Gesta Book 1751–84.
41 LBH Ha 1/15 p.240.
42 CLC Safe A:3/43.
43 QCC Box 113 Letter of 15 October 1825.
44 *Cambridge Chronicle*, 21 January 1825, 1.
45 GLC MP3/79.
46 HRO.
47 PRO CP25/2/539/1657/MICH.
48 QCC Conclusions Book 1787–1832.
49 QCC 355 A (Bursar's copy) and B (Master's copy).
50 TCC Shelf 85.3 15 December 1826.
51 CRO Q/RLv5.
52 BRO Catalogue of the Russell estate papers.
53 BRO R5/4008.
54 BRO R5/4009.
55 BRO R5/4007B.
56 BRO R5/4007B.
57 BRO R5/4009.

BIBLIOGRAPHY

PRIMARY SOURCES

Unpublished

Principal unpublished sources are listed here; full reference is made in footnotes to documents which have been consulted but are not part of the following collections. Locations of estate maps are given in each entry in the carto-bibliography in Appendix 2.

Bedfordshire County Record Office

Archives of the Russell estate:

Accounts for Dry Drayton estate 1703–95 (R5/4482–92, 4496–9).
Accounts for farms in hand in Cambridgeshire 1742–67 (R5/4313–9, 4500).
Accounts for West Wratting estate 1791–9 (Russell Box 279).
Correspondence about Dry Drayton estate 1740 (R3/23).
Objections to Mr Scribo's management of Thorney 1743 (R4/4030/14).
Rentals for Thorney estate 1719–1840 (R5/4001, 4006–19, 4060–115).
Rental cash books for Thorney estate 1729–88 (R5/4204–11, 4228–52).
Valuation of Thorney 1809, 1810 (R4/4129–30).
Valuation of Thorney 1822 (R5/4200).

Cambridgeshire County Record Office, Cambridge Branch

Archives of the Russell estate:

Account book of Thorney steward 1751–64, 1769–1809 (R76/92).
Commonplace book of Thorney steward 1804–28 (R76/92).
Correspondence of Thorney steward 1833 (R76/61(b)).
Steward's letter book for Thorney 1755–60, 1764–77, 1799–1853 (R77/38).

Archives of the Rutland estate:

Packet of deeds dated c.1716–1860, in uncatalogued box marked 'Duke of Rutland' (R79/44).

Cambridgeshire County Record Office, Huntingdon Branch

Catalogue of books in the Library at Thorp Park; as they stood at the decease of Sir Robert Bernard. 1789. Catalogue of the Books at Brampton Hall.
A Plan of the Estate of John Leman Esqr; Mrs Elizth Newnham and John Newnham Esqr; in; the Parish of Warboys, and County of Huntingdon with the divisions of the same as made by Mr Thos Browne & Agreed to by all parties Decr, 23 1755.

Bibliography

Cambridge University Archives

Botanic Garden accounts and minutes 1766–1844 (Char.II.13, Misc.Collect.21–2, Prem.I.2–4).

Financial board deed 1825 (FB.10.A.5).

Grace book N 1823–36.

Minutes of syndicates 1736–1834 (Min.VI.I).

Register of leases 1719–1844 (D.I.2–3).

Registry files of correspondence and papers about estates (CUR.30.1, 32.1, 33.5, 34, 39.17.1–3, 39.25.1–2, 39.27.2, 65, 79).

Title deeds (D.XI.7–10, XIII.24, 116–7, XV.83).

University memoranda 1795–9 (Misc.Collect.15).

Vice-Chancellor's accounts 1770–1845 (U.Ac.2(3)–(5), U.Ac.3).

Vouchers to Vice-Chancellor's accounts 1776–1843 (VCV.23–61).

Woodwardian estate correspondence and valuations 1794–1809 (Geol.2.8, 14–6).

Worts charity accounts, correspondence, minutes and reports 1709–1844 (Char.II.6a, 7a, 10, 19, 24, 32).

Clare College, Cambridge

Accounts 1735–1844 (Safe A:1/20–25).

Accounts of Blithe estate 1713–1844 (Safe A:3/2–3, Safe C:5/7).

Accounts of Samuel Blithe as Fellow and with his pupils and tradesmen 1658–1701 (Safe A:1/4–8, 25/41).

College order book 1759–1840 (Safe C:3/2).

Estate papers for Cambridgeshire estates (Above Cupboard:8, Cupboard:5–6, Safe A:3, 18–19, Safe B:34, 38–9, 43–5, 49–50, 55–6, 58, 60, 62, 64–8, Safe C:5–6).

Master's or Bursar's accounts 1762–1802 (Cupboard:6/16).

Miscellaneous notes about estates 1715–1840 (Safe C:5/4).

Summary estate accounts 1731–82 (Cupboard:6/8).

Survey of college estates c. 1830–50 (Cupboard:6/21).

Emmanuel College, Cambridge

Ash estate accounts 1720–1844 (SCH.1.2–3).

Bursar's accounts

Bursar's accounts 1699–1844 (BUR.8.2–9).

Bursar's accounts (vouchers) 1775–1844 (BUR.0.3, 4, 9).

College order book 1742–1844 (COL.14.2–3).

Consideration on the nature and value of leases 1721 (BUR.6.1).

Dixie estate accounts 1735–1844 (SCH.1.15).

Estate documents and correspondence 1799–1844 (GBX 5, 19, 29, 35, 38, 43–4, 46–8, 54, 67).

Gillingham estate accounts 1729–1844 (FEL.5.7).

Lusby estate accounts 1832–44 (FEL.5.11).

Richards' exhibition accounts 1718–1844 (SCH.1.10).

Say and Seal exhibition accounts 1736–1844 (SCH.1.4–5).

Thorpe estate accounts 1720–1844 (SCH.1.17).

Wood money 1720–1844 (FEL.5.1, 12).

Fitzwilliam Museum, Cambridge

Catalogue of the Founder's Library.

Gonville and Caius College, Cambridge

Bursar's book 1758–75.

Deeds of property in Free School Lane, Cambridge 1800–21 (LXV.3k–l).

Gesta book 1751–84.

Jesus College, Cambridge

Accounts 1700–1844 (A/C.1.5–10).

Accounts of Proby fund and Hundon estate 1819–44 (TRU.5.1).

Accounts of Rustat trust estate 1727–1844 (TRU.1.4–5).

Accounts of Rustat trust, Eltisley estate 1757–1807 (TRU.1.10).

Accounts of Rustat widows trust, Harston estate 1773–1837 (TRU.2.3).

Accounts of Sutton trust estate 1738–81 (TRU.4.1–3).

College order book 1753–1844 (COL.4.1–3).

Estate surveys 1788–1836 (ES.4.10).

Primary sources

Lambeth Palace Library, London

The Collects of the Church of England rendered into Verse by Alexander Watford of Cambridge 1842 (MS.1262).

Queens' College, Cambridge
(in Manuscripts Room, Cambridge University Library)

Account book c. 1818 (Coll. No. 2).
Account of Mr Hughes' benefaction 1779–1844 (Book 82).
Auditor's book 1700–72 (Book 12).
Bursar's accounts 1823–9, 1839–45 (Book 19, 33, 306–7).
College orders concerning lands 1622–1864 (Book 49).
Conclusions books 1733–1836 (In President's Lodge).
Dr James' book 1652–1700 (Book 80).
Estate documents (Box 13, 15–18, 20–3, 25–8, 87–8, 92, 98–100, 104–5, 113–16, 123, 126).
Estate surveys (300, 361–2, 364–6).
Leases (Box 48, 55).
Magnum journale 1660–1835 (Book 6–8).
Maps (328, 333, 348, 350–3, 355).
Register of leases 1762–1831 (Book 48).
Treasurer's accounts 1733–1840 (322–3).
Wood book 1691–1830 (Book 40).

St John's College, Cambridge

Conclusions book 1736–1844 (C5.2–3).
Estate correspondence and reports (D35, 99, 109–10).
Estate survey by Rev. James Wood, Fellow, 1787–8 (SB1.1).
Lawyers' bills 1842–50 (SB20.1).
Quarterly accounts 1803–5 (SB10.1).
Rentals 1734–1845 (SB4.15–53).
Reports of visits of James Wood, Master, to estates 1816–20 (M1.8).

Trinity College, Cambridge

Accounts 1760–1844 (Shelf 29.24–39, 30.1–56).

Estate documents (Box 21, 23, 28, 35).
Lawyers' bills (Great Iron Chest 1b).
Senior Bursar's day book 1812, 1837–44 (Shelf 32.11, 18–19).
Senior Bursar's letter book 1834–44 (Shelf 42.2–5).
Senior Bursar's minutes 1791–1844 (Shelf 84.18–28, 85.1–8).

Published

Act, 1754. *An Act to Enable John Grainger Esquire and his Heirs to Take and Use the Surname of Leman and to Bear the Arms of Sir William Leman Deceased.* 27 George II Cap. 1.
Agas, R., 1596. *A Preparative to Platting of Landes and Tenements for Surveigh Shewing the Diversitie of Sundrie Instruments Applyed Thereunto* ... London: Printed by Thomas Scarlet.
Ainslie, J., 1812. *Comprehensive Treatise on Land Surveying: Comprising the Theory and Practice in all its Branches* ... Edinburgh: Printed ... by John Brown.
Army List, 1805. *A List of all the Officers of the Army and Royal Marines on Full and Half-Pay.* 53rd ed. London: War Office.
Atwell, G., 1658. *The Faithfull Surveyour: Discovering Divers Errours in Land-measuring* ... [Cambridge]: Printed for the author by Nathanael Rowls.
Baily, F., 1802. *Tables for the Purchasing and Renewing of Leases for Terms of Years Certain and for Lives.* London: the author.
Beckett, J., 1804. *Elements and Practice of Mensuration and Land Surveying* ... London: Printed for Lackington, Allen, and Co.
Benese, R., [c. 1550]. *This Boke Newely Imprynted Sheweth the Maner of Measuyinge of all Maner of Lande* ... 2nd ed. [1st ed. 1537.] London: Imprynted by me Robert Myer.
Bibliotheca Angleseiana, 1686. *Bibliotheca Angleseiana, sive, Catalogus Variorum Librorum ... Procuravit Honoratiss. Arthur Comes D'Anglesey* ... London: Per Thomam Philippum.
Bibliotheca Hoblyniana, 1769. *Bibliotheca Hoblyniana, sive, Catalogus Librorum ... Robertus Hoblyn, Armiger.* London: J. Murray.

357

Bibliotheca Illustris, 1687. *Bibliotheca Illustris, sive, Catalogus Variorum Librorum* ... [of William Cecil, Lord Burleigh]. London: Per T. Bentley and B. Walford.

Bibliotheca Nobilissimi, 1719. *Bibliotheca Nobilissimi Principio Johannis Ducis de Novo-Castro &c.: Being a Large Collection of Books Contain'd in the Libraries of the most Noble William and Henry Cavendish and John Hollis, late Dukes of Newcastle ... Which will be sold by Nath. Noel* ... [London: Nath. Noel, 1719].

Bodger, J., [c. 1787]. *This View of the Noblemen's and Gentlemen's Trains of Running Horses, with the Grooms and Horses in their Full Liveries, Taking their Exercise up the Warren Hill, East of the Town of Newmarket, Is by Permission Dedicated by His Royal Highnesses devoted and most obedient humble servant, John Bodger.* Stilton: Bodger.

Brunton, J., 1939. *John Brunton's Book: Being the Memories of John Brunton, Engineer, From a Manuscript in his Own Hand Written for his Grandchildren and Now First Printed.* Introduction by J. H. Clapham. Cambridge: Cambridge University Press.

Burns, A., 1771. *Geodaesia Improved, or, A New and Correct Method of Surveying Made Exceeding Easy.* Chester: Printed for the author.

Burton, R., 1621. *Anatomy of Melancholy: What It Is, With all the Kindes, Causes, Symptomes, Prognostickes, and Severall Cures of It ... Philosophically, Medicinally, Historically, Opened and Cut Up by Democritus Junior, etc.* Oxford: John Lichfield and James Short for Henry Cripps.

Cambridge Chronicle, 1762–1844. *The Cambridge Chronicle and Journal and General Advertiser for the Counties of Cambridge, Huntingdon, Lincoln, Rutland, Bedford, Herts, Isle of Ely, &c.* Cambridge.

Catalogue, [c. 1726]. *Catalogus Bibliothecae Kingstonianae.* [s.l.: s.n.].

Catalogue, 1771. *Catalogus Librorum in Bibliotheca Osterleiensi.* [s.l.: s.n.].

Catalogue, [1772]. *A Catalogue of the Entire Library of the Late Eminent Antiquary Mr. Thomas Martin, of Palgrave, in the County of Suffolk ... Which will Begin to be Sold ... By Martin Booth and John Berry.* [Norwich: Martin Booth and John Berry].

Catalogue, 1790. *A Catalogue of the Books in the Library of Ralph Willett, Esq. at Merly, in the County of Dorset.* London: [s.n.].

Catalogue, 1798. *A Catalogue of Optical, Mathematical, and Philosophical Instruments, Made and Sold by W. and S. Jones, [No. 135,] next Furnival's-Inn, Holborn, London,* At end of: *Essays on the Microscope,* by G. Adams, 2nd ed. by F. Kanmacher. London: Jones.

Catalogue, 1812. *A Catalogue of the Magnificent Library, Books of Prints, and Manuscripts, of the Late Most Noble George, Marquis of Townshend, &c. P.S.A. and F.R.S. Brought from his House at Richmond, Which will be Sold by Auction By Leigh and Sotheby* ... [London: Leigh and Sotheby].

Catalogue, 1813a. *A Catalogue of the Entire Library of the Late Charles Long, Esq. of Hurt's Hall, Suffolk ... Which will be Sold by Auction By Leigh and Sotheby* ... [London: Leigh and Sotheby].

Catalogue, 1813b. *A Catalogue of the Well Known and Celebrated Library of the Late Ralph Willett, Esq. Brought from his Seat at Merly, in the County of Dorset ... Which will be Sold by Auction By Leigh and Sotheby* ... [London: Leigh and Sotheby].

Catalogue, 1826. *A Catalogue of the Valuable Library of the Right Honourable Lord Bayning ... Which will be Sold by Auction By Stewart, Wheatley, & Adlard* ... [London: Stewart, Wheatley and Adlard].

Catalogue, 1831. *A Catalogue of the Valuable and Highly Interesting Library of Printed Books and MSS Removed from Leeds Castle in Kent, a Great Part of Which was Collected at Different Times by the Lords Fairfax, and Added to by the Rev. Dr. Wilkins, of Suffolk ... Which will be Sold by Auction By Mr Christie* ... [London: Christie].

Catalogue, 1850. *Catalogue of Optical, Mathematical, and Philosophical Instruments, Made and Sold by W. and S. Jones, Lower Holborn, London.* London: Jones.

Catalogue, 1867. *Catalogue of the Books in the Library of Woburn Abbey.* London: Printed by Yates and Alexander.

Catalogue, 1879. *Catalogue of the Library at Chatsworth.* London: Chiswick Press. 4 vols.

Charity Commission, 1837. *Report of the Commissioners Appointed in Pursuance of an Act of Parliament Made and Passed in the 5th and 6th Years of King William the 4th, c. 71, Intituled, 'An Act for Appointing Commissioners to Continue the Inquiries Concerning Charities in England and Wales, Until the First Day of March One Thousand Eight Hundred and Thirty-Seven (Dated 4th February 1837.) 31.* London: HMSO.

Chart Park Library, 1814. *Chart Park Library: a Catalogue of the Entire and Splendid Library of the Late Sir Charles Talbot, Bt. Removed from Chart Park, Surrey ... Which will be Sold by Auction By Leigh and Sotheby ...* [London: Leigh and Sotheby].

Clare, J., 1931. *Sketches in the Life of John Clare Written by Himself*, edited by E. Blunden. London: Cobden-Sanderson.

Clare, J., 1951. The Autobiography 1793–1824, In: *The Prose of John Clare*, by J.W. and A. Tibble. London: Routledge and Kegan Paul, 11–100.

Clare, J., 1984. [Autobiographical Passages], In: *John Clare*, edited by E. Robinson and D. Powell. Oxford: Oxford University Press, 429–31.

Correct, Brief and Interesting Account, 1840. *A Correct, Brief, and Interesting Account of the Leman Case ... from the Nottingham Review of April 17, 1840 with Extensive Additions.* Nottingham: Printed by Richard Sutton.

Crocker, A., 1806. *The Elements of Land-Surveying: Designed Principally for the Use of Schools and Students.* London: Printed for Richard Phillips.

Davis, W., 1798. *A Complete Treatise of Land Surveying: by the Chain, Cross, and Offset Staffs Only ...* London: Printed for the author.

Dee, J., [1570]. Preface, In: *The Elements of Geometrie of the Most Auncient Philosopher Euclide of Megara: Faithfully (now first) Translated into the Englishe Toung by H. Billingsley ...* London: John Daye.

Defoe, D., 1724. *A Tour Through the Whole Island of Great Britain.* 1971 ed., abridged and edited with an introduction and notes by Pat Rogers. Harmondsworth: Penguin.

Digges, L., 1562. *A Boke Named Tectonicon ...* 2nd ed. [1st ed. 1556.] London: Thomas Gemini.

Digges, L., 1571. *A Geometrical Practise Named Pantometria, ... Framed by Leonard Digges Gentleman, Lately Finished by Thomas Digges his Sonne ...* London: Henrie Bynneman.

Eliot, G., 1859. *Adam Bede.* 1980 ed., edited with an introduction by Stephen Gill. Harmondsworth: Penguin.

Emerson, W., 1770. *The Art of Surveying or Measuring Land ...* London: Printed for J. Nourse.

Fisher, G., 1809. *The Instructor, or, Young Man's Best Companion ...* New ed. Gainsborough: for H. Mozley.

Fitzherbert, J., 1523. *Here Begynneth a Ryght Frutefull Mater: and Hath to Name the Boke of Surveyeng and Improvmentes.* London: Richard Pynson.

Folkingham, W., 1610. *Feudigraphia: the Synopsis or Epitome of Surveying Methodized ...* London: Printed for Richard Moore.

Gardner, R., 1851. *History, Gazetteer, and Directory of Cambridgeshire ...* Peterborough: Gardner.

Gentleman's Diary, 1741–1800. *The Gentleman's Diary, or, The Mathematical Repository ... Containing Many Useful and Entertaining Particulars Peculiarly Adapted to the Ingenious Gentleman Engaged in the Study and Practice of the Mathematics.* London: Davis and Dickson. 3 vols.

Gentleman's Magazine, 1731–1844. *The Gentleman's Magazine, and, Historical Chronicle.* London.

Goldsmith, O., 1770. *The Deserted Village: A Poem.* London: Printed for W. Griffin.

Gooch, W., 1811. *General View of the Agriculture of the County of Cambridge: Drawn Up for the Consideration of the Board of Agriculture and Internal Improvement.* London: Board of Agriculture.

Gough, R., 1701. *Observations Concerning the Seates in Myddle and the Familyes to Which They Belong.* 1981 ed.: *The History of Myddle*, edited with an introduction and notes by David Hey. Harmondsworth: Penguin.

Green, J., 1717. *The Construction of Maps and Globes ...* London: Printed for T. Horne ... [et al.].

Hammond, J., 1725. *The Practical Surveyor ...* London: Printed for T. Heath.

Hawney, W., [1735]. *The Compleat Measurer, or, The Whole Art of Measuring ...* 4th ed. London: for J. J. and P. Knapton.

Holwell, J., 1678. *A Sure Guide to the Practical Surveyor ...* London: Printed by W. Godbid for Christopher Hussey.

Hopton, A., 1611. *Speculum Topographicum, or, The Topographicall Glasse ...* London: by N. O[kes] for Simon Waterson.

Hornby, T., 1827. *A Treatise on the New Method of Land Surveying ...* London: Printed for Baldwin, Cradock and Joy ... [et al.].

Huntar, A., [1624]. *A Treatise of Weights, Mets and Measures of Scotland ...* Edinburgh: Printed by John Wreittoun.

Hutton, C., 1770. *A Treatise on Mensuration both in Theory and Practice.* Newcastle upon Tyne: Printed by T. Saint for the author.

Knight, R.P., 1795. *The Landscape: a Didactic Poem in Three Books Addressed to Uvedale Price, Esq.* 2nd ed. [1st ed. 1794.] London: G. Nicol.

Laurence, E., 1716. *The Young Surveyor's Guide, or, A New Introduction to the Whole Art of Surveying Land Both by the Chain and All Instruments Now in Use ...* London: Printed for James Knapton.

Laurence, E., 1727. *The Duty of a Steward to his Lord: Represented Under Several Plain and Distinct Articles ...* London: John Shuckburgh.

Leedham-Green, E.S., 1986. *Books in Cambridge Inventories: Book-lists from Vice-Chancellor's Court Probate Inventories in the Tudor and Stuart Periods.* Cambridge: Cambridge University Press. 2 vols.

Leigh, V., 1577. *The Moste Profitable and Commendable Science of Surveying of Landes, Tenements and Hereditamentes ...* London: for Andrew Maunsell.

Ley, C., 1786. *The Nobleman, Gentleman, Land Steward, and Surveyor's Compleat Guide ...* [s.l.]: Printed for and sold by the author.

Leybourn, W., 1650. *Planometria, or, The Whole Art of Surveying of Land ...* London: Nathaniel Brooks.

Leybourn, W., 1653. *The Compleat Surveyor ...* London: R. and W. Leybourn for E. Brewster and G. Sawbridge.

Lucar, C., 1590. *A Treatise Named Lucarsolace ...* London: Richard Field for John Harrison.

Lysons, D. and Lysons, S., 1808. *Magna Britannia. Vol. 2.i: Cambridgeshire.* London: Printed for T. Cadell and W. Davies.

Marshall, W., 1806. *On the Management of Landed Estates: a General Work for the Use of Professional Men, Being an Abstract of the More Enlarged Treatise on Landed Property Recently Published.* London: Printed for Longman, Hurst, Rees and Orme.

Martindale, A., 1702. *The Country-Survey-Book, or, Land-Meters Vade-Mecum ...* 3rd ed. [1st ed. 1682.] London: Printed for R. Clavel and G. Sawbridge.

Mordant, J., 1761. *The Complete Steward, or, The Duty of a Steward to his Lord.* London: Printed for W. Sandby.

Norden, J., 1610. *The Surveiors Dialogue ...* 2nd ed. [1st ed. 1607.] London: Printed by W. S[tansby] for J. Busby.

Peacham, H. sr, 1577. *Garden of Eloquence ...* London: H. Jackson.

Peacham, H. jr, 1612. *The Gentlemans Exercise ...* London: Printed for I.M.

Peacham, H. jr, 1622. *The Compleat Gentleman ...* London: for Francis Constable.

Rathborne, A., 1616. *The Svrveyor in Foure Bookes.* London: Printed by W. Stansby for W. Burre.

Richards, J., 1730. *The Gentleman's Steward and Tenants of Manors Instructed ...* London: Printed for John Senex and William Innys.

Sleeman, T., 1806. *A Practical Treatise on the Description and Uses of Portable Mathematical Instruments ... to Which is Added, A Complete System of Land-Surveying ...* London: Printed for W.J. and J. Richardson.

Smith, J., 1705. *The Art of Painting in Oyl ... to Which is Added, The Whole Art and Mystery of Colouring Maps and Other Prints with Water Colours.* 4th ed. London: Printed for Samuel Crouch.

Society of Antiquaries of London, 1849. *Proceedings of the Society of Antiquaries of London,* 1, 46.

Stephenson, W., 1805. *The System of Land Surveying at Present Adopted by Surveyors and Commissioners in Old and New Inclosures ...* London: Symonds.

Stone, T., 1785. *An Essay on Agriculture: With a View to Inform Gentlemen of Landed Property Whether their Estates are Managed to the Greatest Advantage.* Lynn: Printed by W. Whittingham and sold by J. Robson, New-Bond-Street, and R. Baldwin, Pater-Noster-Row, London.

Talbot, B., 1784. *The Compleat Art of Land-Measuring, or, A Guide to Practical Surveying ...* London: Printed for T. and W. Lowndes.

Universal British Directory of Trade, Commerce and Manufacture. Vol. 1, 1793. Promoted by P. Barfoot and J. Wilkes. London: Champante and Whitrow.

Vancouver, C., 1794. *General View of the Agriculture in the County of Cambridge with Observations on the Means of its Improvement: Drawn Up for the Consideration of the Board of Agriculture and Internal Improvement.* London: Printed by W. Smith.

Venn, J., ed., 1891. *The Register of Baptisms, Marriages and Burials in St Michael's Parish, Cambridge (1538–1837).* Cambridge: Cambridge Antiquarian Society.

Vyse, C., 1770. *The Tutor's Guide: Being a Complete System of Arithmetic, with Various Branches in the Mathematic* ... London: for Robinson and Roberts.

Walford, E., 1860. *The County Families of the United Kingdom.* London: Robert Hardwicke.

Wilson, H., 1731. *Surveying Improv'd, or, The Whole Art, Both in Theory and Practice, Fully Demonstrated* ... 2nd ed. [1st ed. 1725.] London: Printed for J. Batley.

Wing, J., 1700. *Geodaetes Practicus Redivivus: the Art of Surveying Formerly Publish'd by Vincent Wing, Math. Now Much Augmented and Improv'd* ... London: Printed by J. Matthews for Awnsham and John Churchill.

Wingate, E., 1630. *Arithmetique Made Easie, in Two Bookes.* London: For Phil. Stephen and Chr. Meredith.

Worsop, E., 1582. *A Discoverie of Sundrie Errours and Faults Daily Committed by Landemeaters Ignorant of Arithmetike and Geometrie* ... London: Printed by Henrie Middleton for Gregorie Seton.

Wyld, S., 1764. *The Practical Surveyor, or, The Art of Land-Measuring Made Easy* ... 5th ed. [1st ed. 1725.] London: Printed for W. Johnston.

SECONDARY SOURCES

Unpublished

Bennett, J.A., 1990. Mathematical instruments in Harriot's time. Paper presented at a joint meeting of the Thomas Harriot Seminar and the British Society for the History of Mathematics, Cambridge, 18 – 20 September.

Buisseret, D., 1988. The estate plan in North America. Nebenzahl Lecture, Newberry Library, Chicago.

Catalogue of the archives of Emmanuel College Cambridge. [Lists maps, surveys, terriers and valuations.]

Catalogue of the archives of Jesus College Cambridge. [Lists maps, surveys, terriers and valuations.]

Catalogue of the archives of St John's College Cambridge. [Lists maps, surveys, terriers and valuations.]

Catalogue of the archives of Trinity College Cambridge. [Lists maps, surveys, terriers and valuations.]

Catalogue of the Founder's Library in the Fitzwilliam Museum, Cambridge.

Catalogue of the Russell estate papers in the Bedfordshire and Devon County Record Offices. [Lists maps, surveys, terriers and valuations.]

Eden, P.G., 1983a. Estate surveyors in Britain 1550–1850: a study in the structure of occupations. Paper presented at the 10th International Conference on the History of Cartography, Dublin, 29 August – 2 September.

Evans, R.J., 1982. The diffusion of science: the geographical transmission of natural philosophy into the English provinces 1660–1760. Ph.D. Thesis, University of Cambridge.

Haas, J.M., 1960. The rise of the Bedfords 1741–1757: a study in the politics of the reign of George II. Ph.D. Thesis, University of Illinois.

Handlist to the Tharp family papers in the Cambridgeshire County Record Office, Cambridge Branch.

Harley, J.B., 1989a. 'The myth of the great divide': art, science and text in the history of cartography. Paper presented at the 13th International Conference on the History of Cartography, Amsterdam, 26 June – 1 July.

Harvey, P.D.A., 1988. The origins and early development of the estate plan in England. Nebenzahl Lecture, Newberry Library, Chicago.

Higman, B.W., 1988a. Jamaican estate plans and their use to the historian. Nebenzahl Lecture, Newberry Library, Chicago.

Howell, D.W., 1965. The landed gentry of Pembrokeshire in the eighteenth century. M.A. Thesis, University of Wales.

Bibliography

Konvitz, J.W., 1988. The nation-state, Paris, and cartography in 18th and 19th century France. Paper presented at a conference of the Historical Geography Research Group of the Institute of British Geographers: Politics and place: French revolutionary ideals and historical geography, Emmanuel College, Cambridge, 30 June – 2 July.

Parish, C., 1983. Boxworth (Cambridgeshire): some notes on its history. Typescript in County Record Office, Shire Hall, Cambridge.

Postgate, M.R., 1964. Field systems of Cambridgeshire. Ph.D. Thesis, University of Cambridge.

Startin, E., [c. 1988]. The evolution of Isleworth: mapping of the area, 1607 – 1746. Typescript in Guildhall Library, London.

Willmoth, F.H., 1985. The employment of surveyors in the fen drainage scheme of 1649–1656: their status, roles and achievements. M.Phil. Thesis, University of Cambridge.

Willmoth, F.H., 1990. Sir Jonas Moore (1617–79): practical mathematician and patron of science. Ph.D. Thesis, University of Cambridge.

Wolter, J.A., 1987. The development of map collections. Paper presented at the 12th International Conference on the History of Cartography, Paris, 7 – 11 September.

Published

Aalen, F.H.A. and Hunter, R.J., 1964. The estate maps of Trinity College, *Hermathena*, 98, 85–96.

Adams, I.H., 1968. The land surveyor and his influence on the Scottish rural landscape, *Scottish Geographical Magazine*, 84, 248–55.

Adams, I.H., 1971. *The Mapping of a Scottish Estate*. Edinburgh: Department of Educational Studies, University of Edinburgh.

Adams, I.H., 1975. Economic processes and the Scottish land surveyor, *Imago Mundi*, 27, 13–18.

Adams, I.H., 1976. Estate plans, *The Local Historian*, 12, 26–30.

Airs, M., 1975. *The Making of the English Country House 1500–1640*. London: Architectural Press.

Airy, W., 1909. The history of land measurement in England, Reprinted in: *The Chartered Surveyor*, 107, 1975, 267–8.

Alfrey, N. and Daniels, S., eds., 1990. *Mapping the Landscape: Essays on Art and Cartography*. Nottingham: Department of Art History, University of Nottingham.

Alpers, S., 1983. *The Art of Describing: Dutch Art in the Seventeenth Century*. London: Murray.

Alpers, S., 1987. The mapping impulse in Dutch art, In: *Art and Cartography: Six Historical Essays*, edited by D. Woodward. Chicago: University of Chicago Press, 51–96.

Anderson, A.H., 1966. The books and interests of Henry Lord Stafford (1501–1563), *The Library*, 21, 87–114.

Anderson, A.H., 1975. The books of Thomas, Lord Paget (c. 1544–1590), *Transactions of the Cambridge Bibliographical Society*, 6, 226–42.

Anderson, B.L., 1969. Provincial aspects of the financial revolution of the eighteenth century, *Business History*, 11, 11–22.

Andrews, C.B., 1934. A book-collector of the eighteenth century, *Book Collector's Quarterly*, 4, 23–30.

Andrews, J.H., 1967. The French school of Dublin land surveyors, *Irish Geography*, 5, 275–92.

Andrews, J.H., 1974. The maps of the escheated counties of Ulster, 1609–10, *Proceedings of the Royal Irish Academy*, 74C, 133–69.

Andrews, J.H., 1978. Local maps and the Irish archivist, *Irish Archives Bulletin*, 8, 5–14.

Andrews, J.H., 1980a. Henry Pratt, Surveyor of Kerry Estates, *Journal of the Kerry Archaeological and Historical Society*, 13, 5–38.

Andrews, J.H., 1980b. Science and cartography in the Ireland of William and Samuel Molyneux, *Proceedings of the Royal Irish Academy*, 80C, 231–50.

Andrews, J.H., 1985. *Plantation Acres: An Historical Study of the Irish Land Surveyor and his Maps*. Belfast: Ulster Historical Foundation.

Andrews, J.H., 1986. Mapping the past in the past: the cartographer as antiquarian in pre-Ordnance Survey Ireland, In: *Rural Landscapes and Communities: Essays Presented to Desmond McCourt*, edited by C. Thomas. Blackrock: Irish Academic Press, 31–63.

Armytage, W.H.G., 1960. Coffee houses and science, *British Medical Journal*, 2, 213.

Ashton, T.S., 1955. *An Economic History of England: The Eighteenth Century*. London: Methuen.

Aylmer, G.E., 1986. The economics and finances of the colleges and university c. 1530–1640, In: *The History of the University of Oxford. Vol. 3: The Collegiate University*, edited by J. McConica. Oxford: Oxford University Press, 521–58.

Babington, C.C., 1853. *Ancient Cambridgeshire, or, An Attempt to Trace Roman and Other Ancient Roads that Passed Through the County of Cambridge: With a Record of the Places Where Roman Coins and Other Remains Have Been Found*. Cambridge: Deighton.

Baigent, E., 1990. Swedish cadastral mapping 1628–1700: a neglected legacy, *Geographical Journal*, 156, 62–9.

Baker, A.R.H. and Butlin, R.A., 1973. *Studies of Field Systems in the British Isles*. Cambridge: Cambridge University Press.

Barber, P., 1985. Pageantry, defence and government: maps at court to 1550, In: Publication of 1985 series of Nebenzahl Lectures, Monarchs, ministers and maps. Chicago: University of Chicago Press [forthcoming].

Barrell, J., 1972. *The Idea of Landscape and the Sense of Place 1730–1840: An Approach to the Poetry of John Clare*. Cambridge: Cambridge University Press.

Bartlett, J., 1894. *A New and Complete Concordance ... in the Dramatic Works of Shakespeare With a Supplementary Concordance to the Poems*. London: Macmillan.

Barty-King, H., 1975. *Scratch a Surveyor: the Nearest Anyone Will Ever Get to Telling the Story of Drivers Jonas, Traced Through the Diaries, Letters, Memos, Reports Which Might Have Been Written – and Some That Were – Between 1725 and 1975*. London: Heinemann.

Batho, G.R., 1957. The finances of an Elizabethan nobleman: Henry Percy, ninth Earl of Northumberland (1564–1632), *Economic History Review*, 9, 433–50.

Batho, G.R., 1960. The library of the 'wizard' Earl: Henry Percy ninth Earl of Northumberland (1564–1632), *The Library*, 15, 246–61.

Baxandall, M., 1972. *Painting and Experience in Fifteenth Century Italy: A Primer in the Social History of Pictorial Style*. Oxford: Clarendon Press.

Baxandall, M., 1985. *Patterns of Intention: On the Historical Explanation of Pictures*. New Haven: Yale University Press.

Beckett, J.V., [1978]. Landownership: its relation to social, economic and political development in Cumbria, c. 1680–1750, In: *Landownership and Power in the Regions: Papers Submitted to the Conference of Regional History Tutors Held at Himley Hall in May 1978*, edited by M.D.G. Wanklyn. Wolverhampton: Centre for West Midlands Historical Studies for CORAL, 15–25.

Beckett, J.V., 1984. The pattern of landownership in England and Wales 1660–1880, *Economic History Review*, 37, 1–22.

Beckett, J.V., 1986. *The Aristocracy in England 1660–1914*. Oxford: Blackwell.

Beckett, J.V., 1989. Landownership and estate management, In: *The Agrarian History of England and Wales. Vol. 6: 1750–1850*, edited by G.E. Mingay. Cambridge: Cambridge University Press, 545–640.

Bedford, H.A. 11th Duke of, 1897. *A Great Agricultural Estate: Being the Story of the Origin and Administration of Woburn and Thorney*. London: Murray.

Bennett, H.S., 1965. *English Books and Readers 1558 to 1603: Being a Study in the History of the Book Trade in the Reign of Elizabeth I*. Cambridge: Cambridge University Press.

Bennett, H.S., 1969. *English Books and Readers 1475–1557: Being a Study in the History of the Book Trade from Caxton to the Incorporation of the Stationers' Company*. 2nd ed. Cambridge: Cambridge University Press.

Bennett, H.S., 1970. *English Books and Readers 1603 to 1640: Being a Study in the History of the Book Trade in the Reign of James I and Charles I*. Cambridge: Cambridge University Press.

Bennett, J.A., 1987. *The Divided Circle: A History of Instruments for Astronomy, Navigation and Surveying*. Oxford: Phaidon Christie's.

Bennett, J.A. and Brown, O., 1982. *The Compleat Surveyor*. Cambridge: Whipple Museum of the History of Science.

Beresford, J., 1925. *The Godfather of Downing Street: Sir George Downing 1623–1684: An Essay in Biography*. London: Richard Cobden-Sanderson.

Bibliography

Beresford, M.W., 1946. Commissioners of enclosure, *Economic History Review*, 16, 130–40.

Beresford, M.W., 1948. Ridge and furrow and the open fields, *Economic History Review*, 1, 34–46, Reprinted in: *Time and Place: Collected Essays.* London: Hambledon Press, 1984, 111–22.

Beresford, M.W., 1971. *History on the Ground: Six Studies in Maps and Landscapes.* London: Methuen.

Berman, M., 1975. 'Hegemony' and the amateur tradition in British science, *Journal of Social History*, 8, Winter, 30–50.

Berman, M., 1978. *Social Change and Scientific Organization: The Royal Institution, 1799–1844.* London: Heinemann.

Biddulph, V., 1938. *The Three Ladies Waldegrave (and their Mother).* London: Peter Davies.

Bill, E.G.W., 1988. *Education at Christ Church, Oxford, 1660–1800.* Oxford: Clarendon Press.

Black, A., compiler, 1972. *Guide to Education Records in the County Record Office Cambridge.* Cambridge: Cambridgeshire and Isle of Ely County Council.

Blakemore, M.J. and Harley, J.B., 1980. Concepts in the history of cartography: a review and perspective, *Cartographica*, 17, Monograph 26.

Bloch, M., 1929. Les plans parcellaires, *Annales d'histoire économique et sociale*, 1, 60–70, 390–8.

Boelhower, W., 1988. Inventing America: a model of cartographic semiosis, *Word and Image*, 4, 475–97.

Bohannon, M.E., 1938. A London bookseller's bill 1635–1639, *The Library*, 18, 417–46.

Bönisch, F., 1967. The geometrical accuracy of the 16th and 17th century topographical surveys, *Imago Mundi*, 21, 62–9.

Boud, R.C., 1975. The early development of British geological maps, *Imago Mundi*, 27, 73–96.

Bowden, P.J., 1985. Agricultural prices, wages, farm profits, and rents, In: *The Agrarian History of England and Wales. Vol. 5.II. 1640–1750: Agrarian Change*, edited by J. Thirsk. Cambridge: Cambridge University Press, 1–118.

Brassley, P., Lambert, A. and Saunders, P., eds., 1988. *Accounts of the Reverend John Crakanthorp of Fowlmere 1682–1710.* Cambridge: Cambridgeshire Records Society.

Brauer, G.C., 1959. *The Education of a Gentleman: Theories of Gentlemanly Education in England 1660–1775.* New York: Bookman Associates.

Broc, N., 1986. *La Géographie de la Renaissance.* Paris: Les Editions du CTHS.

Brodrick, G.C., 1885. *Memorials of Merton College with Biographical Notices of the Warden and Fellows.* Oxford: Oxford Historical Society.

Brooke, C., 1985. *A History of Gonville and Caius College.* Woodbridge: Boydell Press.

Buchanan, R.A., 1989. *The Engineers: A History of the Engineering Profession in Britain, 1750–1914.* London: Jessica Kingsley.

Burke's Genealogical and Heraldic History of the Landed Gentry, 1952. 17th ed. by L. G. Pine. London: Burke's Peerage.

Burke's Genealogical and Heraldic History of the Peerage, Baronetage and Knightage, 1970. 105th ed. by P. Townsend. London: Burke's Peerage.

Burke, B., 1883. *A Genealogical History of the Dormant, Abeyant, Forfeited, and Extinct Peerages of the British Empire.* New ed. London: Harrison.

Burke, J. and Burke, J.B., 1844. *A Genealogical and Heraldic History of the Extinct and Dormant Baronetcies of England, Ireland, and Scotland.* 2nd ed. London: John Russell Smith.

Bushell, W.D., 1938. *Hobson's Conduit: The New River at Cambridge Commonly Called Hobson's River.* Cambridge: Cambridge University Press.

Butlin, R., 1990a. Drainage and land use in the fenlands and fen-edge of northeast Cambridgeshire in the seventeenth and eighteenth centuries, In: *Water, Engineering and Landscape: Water Control and Landscape Transformation in the Modern Period*, edited by D. Cosgrove and G. Petts. London: Belhaven Press, 54–76.

Butlin, R., 1990b. Small-scale urban and industrial development in north-east Cambridgeshire in the nineteenth and early twentieth centuries, In: *The Transformation of Rural Society, Economy and Landscape: Papers from the 1987 Meeting of the Permanent European Conference for the Study of the Rural Landscape*, edited by U. Sporrong. Stockholm: Department of Human Geography, Stockholm University, 217–26.

Buxton, J. and Williams, P., 1979. *New College Oxford 1379–1979*. Oxford: Warden and Fellows of New College.

Byrne, M. St C. and Thomson, G.S., 1931. 'My Lord's books': the library of Francis, second Earl of Bedford, in 1584, *Review of English Studies*, 7, 385–405.

Caird, J.B., 1989. Early 19th century estate plans, In: *Togail Tir Marking Time: The Map of the Western Isles*, edited by F. Macleod. Stornoway: Acair Ltd and An Lanntair, 49–77.

Cam, H.M., 1939. John Mortlock III: 'Master of the town of Cambridge' 1755–1816, *Proceedings of the Cambridge Antiquarian Society*, 40, 1–12.

Campbell, E.M.J., 1952. The development of the characteristic sheet 1533–1822, *Proceedings of the Eighth General Assembly and Seventeenth International Congress of the International Geographical Union*. Washington: US National Committee of the International Geographical Union, 426–30.

Campbell, E.M.J., 1962. The beginnings of the characteristic sheet to English maps, *Geographical Journal*, 128, 411–15.

Cantor, L., 1983. *The Medieval Parks of England: A Gazetteer*. Loughborough: Department of Education, Loughborough University of Technology.

Capp, B., 1979. *Astrology and the Popular Press: English Almanacs 1500–1800*. London: Faber.

Carr, A.P., 1962. Cartographic record and historical accuracy, *Geography*, 47, 135–45.

Carter, E., 1819. *History of the County of Cambridge, from the Earliest Account to the Present Time …* London: Bentley.

Chardon, R., 1982. A best-fit evaluation of DeBrahm's 1770 chart of Biscayne Bay, *American Cartographer*, 9, 47–67.

Charlton, K., 1965. *Education in Renaissance England*. London: Routledge and Kegan Paul.

Chartres, J.A., 1989. Country trades, crafts and possessions, In: *The Agrarian History of England and Wales. Vol. 6: 1750–1850*, edited by G.E. Mingay. Cambridge: Cambridge University Press, 416–66.

The Cholmleys of Whitby, *Annual Report of the North Riding Record Office*, 1970, 5–14.

Chrisman, M.U., 1982. *Lay Culture, Learned Culture: Books and Social Change in Strasbourg, 1480–1599*. New Haven: Yale University Press.

Clark, K., 1976. *Landscape into Art*. London: Murray.

Clarke, G.N.G., 1988. Taking possession: the cartouche as cultural text in eighteenth-century American maps, *Word and Image*, 4, 455–74.

Clarke, M., 1981. *The Tempting Prospect: A Social History of English Watercolours*. London: British Museum Publications.

Clark-Kennedy, A.E., 1983. *Cambridge to Botany Bay: A Victorian Family Tragedy*. Cambridge: A.E. Clark-Kennedy.

Clay, C., 1968. Marriage, inheritance and the rise of large estates in England 1660–1815, *Economic History Review*, 21, 503–18.

Clay, C., 1985. Landlords and estate management in England, In: *The Agrarian History of England and Wales. Vol. 5.II. 1640–1750: Agrarian Change*, edited by J. Thirsk. Cambridge: Cambridge University Press, 119–251.

Clemenson, H.A., 1982. *English Country Houses and Landed Estates*. London: Croom Helm.

Clutton, E., 1982. Some seventeenth century images of Crete: a comparative analysis of the manuscript maps by Francesco Basilicata and the printed maps by Marco Boschini, *Imago Mundi*, 34, 48–65.

Combs, H.C. and Sullens, Z.R., 1940. *A Concordance to the English Poems of John Donne*. Chicago: Packard and Company.

Connor, R.D., 1987. *The Weights and Measures of England*. London: HMSO.

Coombs, D., 1978. *Sport and the Countryside in English Paintings, Watercolours and Prints*. Oxford: Phaidon.

Corbett, M. and Lightbown, R., 1979. *The Comely Frontispiece: The Emblematic Title-Page in England 1550–1660*. London: Routledge and Kegan Paul.

Corbett, W.J., 1897. Elizabethan village surveys, *Transactions of the Royal Historical Society*, 11, 67–87.

Cosgrove, D.E., 1984. *Social Formation and Symbolic Landscape*. London: Croom Helm.

Costello, W.T., 1958. *The Scholastic Curriculum at Early Seventeenth-Century Cambridge*. Cambridge, Mass.: Harvard University Press.

County of Cambridge Local Education Committee, 1908. *Educational Endowments (excluding Cambridge Borough)*. Cambridge: Cambridgeshire County Council.

Cox, N., 1978. *Bridging the Gap: A History of the Corporation of the Sons of the Clergy Over 300 Years 1655–1978*. Oxford: Becket Publications.

Cranfield, G.A., 1951. The first Cambridge newspaper, *Proceedings of the Cambridge Antiquarian Society*, 45, 5–16.

Crawforth, M.A., 1985. Evidence from trade cards for the scientific instrument industry, *Annals of Science*, 42, 453–554.

Cressy, D., ed., 1975. *Education in Tudor and Stuart England*. London: Arnold.

Croft-Murray, E., 1962. *Decorative Painting in England 1537–1837. Vol. 1: Early Tudor to Sir James Thornhill*. London: Country Life.

Curl, J.S., 1979. *Moneymore and Draperstown: The Architecture and Planning of the Estates of the Drapers' Company in Ulster*. Belfast: Ulster Architectural Heritage Society.

Curl, J.S., 1981. *The History, Architecture and Planning of the Estates of the Fishmongers' Company in Ulster*. Belfast: Ulster Architectural Heritage Society.

Daniels, S., 1988. The political iconography of woodland in later Georgian England, In: *The Iconography of Landscape: Essays on the Symbolic Representation, Design and Use of Past Environments*, edited by D. Cosgrove and S. Daniels. Cambridge: Cambridge University Press, 43–82.

Daniels, S., 1990. Goodly prospects: English estate portraiture, 1670–1730, In: *Mapping the Landscape: Essays on Art and Cartography*, edited by N. Alfrey and S. Daniels. Nottingham: Department of Art History, University of Nottingham, 9–12.

Darby, H.C., 1933. The agrarian contribution to surveying in England, *Geographical Journal*, 82, 529–35.

Darby, H.C., 1948a. Cambridgeshire in the nineteenth century, In: *Victoria History of the Counties of England. Cambridgeshire, Vol. 2*, edited by L.F. Salzman. Oxford: Oxford University Press, 111–23.

Darby, H.C., 1948b. Political history, In: *Victoria History of the Counties of England. Cambridgeshire, Vol. 2*, edited by L.F. Salzman. Oxford: Oxford University Press, 377–419.

Darby, H.C., 1983. *The Changing Fenland*. Cambridge: Cambridge University Press.

Darley, G., 1980. The ideal village, In: *The Shell Book of English Villages*, edited by J. Hadfield. London: Joseph, 60–7.

Daumas, M., 1972. *Scientific Instruments of the Seventeenth and Eighteenth Centuries and their Makers*, translated and edited by M. Holbrook. London: Batsford.

Davies, O.R.F., 1965. The wealth and influence of John Holles, Duke of Newcastle 1694–1711, *Renaissance and Modern Studies*, 9, 22–46.

Davies, R., 1982. *Estate Maps of Wales 1600–1836*. Aberystwyth: National Library of Wales.

Deane, P. and Cole, W.A., 1967. *British Economic Growth 1688–1959: Trends and Structure*. 2nd ed. Cambridge: Cambridge University Press.

De Boer, G. and Carr, A.P., 1969. Early maps as historical evidence for coastal change, *Geographical Journal*, 135, 17–39.

Delano Smith, C., 1985. Cartographic signs on European maps and their explanation before 1700, *Imago Mundi*, 37, 9–29.

Delano Smith, C., 1989. Art or cartography? The wrong question, *History of the Human Sciences*, 2, 89–93.

Delderfield, E.R., 1970. *West Country Historic Houses and their Families. Vol. 2: Dorset, Wiltshire and North Somerset*. Newton Abbot: David and Charles.

Dictionary of National Biography, 1885–1900. Edited by L. Stephen. London: Smith, Elder and Co. 63 vols.

Donno, E.S., ed., 1985. *Twelfth Night, or, What You Will*, by W. Shakespeare. Cambridge: Cambridge University Press.

Douglas, D.C., 1951. *English Scholars 1660–1730*. 2nd ed. London: Eyre and Spottiswoode.

Dunbabin, J.P.D., 1986. College estates and wealth 1660–1815, In: *The History of the University of Oxford. Vol. 5: The Eighteenth Century*, edited by L.S. Sutherland and L.G. Mitchell. Oxford: Oxford University Press, 269–307.

Duncan, G.D., 1986. An introduction to the accounts of Corpus Christi College, In: *The History of the University of Oxford. Vol. 3: The Collegiate University*, edited by J. McConica. Oxford: Oxford University Press, 574–96.

Dunthorne, H., 1988. Seeing the past through paintings, *History and Archaeology Review*, 3, Spring, 13–23.

Dymond, D., [1987]. *Israel Amyce's Map of Melford Manor, 1580*. Long Melford: Long Melford Historical and Archaeological Society.

Eden, P.G., 1973. Land surveyors in Norfolk 1550–1850. Part I: The estate surveyors, *Norfolk Archaeology*, 35, 474–82.

Eden, P.G., 1975. Land surveyors in Norfolk 1550–1850. Part II: The surveyors of inclosure, *Norfolk Archaeology*, 36, 119–48.

Eden, P.G., 1983b. Three Elizabethan estate surveyors: Peter Kempe, Thomas Clerke and Thomas Langdon, In: *English Map-Making 1500–1650*, edited by S. Tyacke. London: British Library, 68–84.

Eden, P.G., ed., forthcoming. *Dictionary of Land Surveyors and Local Cartographers of Great Britain and Ireland c.1540–1850*, 2nd ed. by A.S. Bendall. (1st edition published by Dawson, Folkestone, 1975–9.)

Edwards, A.C. and Newton, K.C., 1984. *The Walkers of Hanningfield: Surveyors and Mapmakers Extraordinary*. London: Buckland Publications.

Ehrensvärd, U., 1987. Color in cartography: a historical survey, In: *Art and Cartography: Six Historical Essays*, edited by D. Woodward. Chicago: University of Chicago Press, 123–46.

Eland, G., ed., 1935. The annual progress of New College by Michael Woodward – Warden 1659–1675, *Records of Buckinghamshire*, 13, 77–137.

Elvey, E.M., 1963. *A Handlist of Buckinghamshire Estate Maps*. [s.l.]: Buckinghamshire Record Society.

Emmison, F.G., 1938. Jacobean household inventories, *Publications of the Bedfordshire Historical Record Society*, 20, 1–143.

Emmison, F.G., 1963. Estate maps and surveys, *History*, 48, 34–7.

Emmison, F.G., 1974. *Archives and Local History*. 2nd ed. Chichester: Phillimore.

Emmison, F.G., ed., 1947. *Catalogue of Maps in the Essex Record Office 1566–1855*. Chelmsford: Essex County Council.

Emmison, F.G., ed., 1952. *Catalogue of Maps in the Essex Record Office 1566–1855*. *1st Supplement*. Chelmsford: Essex County Council.

Emmison, F.G., ed., 1964. *Catalogue of Maps in the Essex Record Office 1566–1855*. *2nd Supplement*. Chelmsford: Essex County Council.

Emmison, F.G., ed., 1968. *Catalogue of Maps in the Essex Record Office 1566–1855*. *3rd Supplement*. Chelmsford: Essex County Council.

Evans, I.M. and Lawrence, H., 1979. *Christopher Saxton: Elizabethan Map-Maker*. Wakefield: Wakefield Historical Publications, and London: The Holland Press.

Evans, J., 1855. Extracts from the private account book of Sir W. More, *Archaeologia*, 36, 284–92.

Evans, M.C.S., 1977. The pioneers of estate mapping in Carmarthenshire, *Carmarthenshire Antiquary*, 13, 52–64.

Fairhurst, H., 1968. An old estate plan of Auchindrain, mid-Argyll, *Scottish Studies*, 12, 183–7.

Feather, J., 1985. *The Provincial Book Trade in Eighteenth-Century England*. Cambridge: Cambridge University Press.

Feingold, M., 1984. *The Mathematicians' Apprenticeship: Science, Universities and Society in England, 1560–1640*. Cambridge: Cambridge University Press.

Finch, M.E., 1956. *The Wealth of Five Northamptonshire Families 1540–1640*. Lamport Hall, Northamptonshire: Northamptonshire Record Society.

Forbes, M.D., ed., 1928. *Clare College 1326–1926: University Hall 1326–1326, Clare Hall 1346–1856. Vol. 1*. Cambridge: Clare College.

Foster, J., 1888–92. *Alumni Oxonienses: The Members of the University of Oxford. Early Series 1500–1714*. 1891–2, 4 vols. *1715–1886*. 1888. 4 vols. Oxford: Parker.

Foster, J.W., 1974. The topographical tradition in Anglo-Irish poetry, *Irish University Review*, 4, 169–87.

Foster, J.W., 1975–6. The measure of paradise: topography in eighteenth-century poetry, *Eighteenth-Century Studies*, 9, 232–56.

Fowkes, D.V. and Potter, G.R., eds., 1988. *William Senior's Survey of the Estates of the First and Second Earls of Devonshire c. 1600–28*, with a biographical note on William Senior by P. Eden. Chesterfield: Derbyshire Record Society.

Fowler, G.H., 1928. The strip-map of Aspley Guise, c. 1745 with an analysis of the enclosure award, 1761, *Quarto Memoirs, Bedfordshire Historical Record Society*, 2, 21–35.

Fowler, G.H., 1936. The strip-map of Eversholt, 1764, with notes on the strip-map of Houghton Regis, 1762, *Quarto Memoirs, Bedfordshire Historical Record Society*, 2, 38–53.

French, S., 1978. *The History of Downing College*. [Cambridge]: Downing College Association.

Fussell, G.E., 1947. *The Old English Farming Books from Fitzherbert to Tull 1523–1730*. London: Crosby Lockwood.

Fussell, G.E., 1950. *More Old English Farming Books from Tull to the Board of Agriculture 1731 to 1793*. London: Crosby Lockwood.

Fussell, G.E., 1983. *The Old English Farming Books. Vol. 3: 1793–1839*. London: Pindar Press.

Geertz, C., 1983. *Local Knowledge: Further Essays in Interpretative Archaeology*. New York: Basic Books.

Gerber, R., 1984. The development of competence and performance in cartographic language by children at the concrete level of map-reasoning, In: New insights in cartographic communication, edited by C. Board, *Cartographica*, 21, Monograph 31, 98–119.

Gerrit, P.J., 1955. *Members of Parliament 1734–1832*. New Haven: Yale University Press.

Girouard, M., 1980. *Life in the English Country House*. Harmondsworth: Penguin.

Glass, J.B., 1975. A survey of native Middle American pictorial manuscripts, In: *Handbook of Middle American Indians. Vol. 14: Guide to Ethnohistorical Sources Part 3*, edited by H.F. Cline. Austin: University of Texas Press, 3–80.

Gombrich, E.H., 1972. *Art and Illusion: A Study in the Psychology of Pictorial Representation*. 4th ed. London: Phaidon.

Gombrich, E.H., 1982. *The Image and the Eye: Further Studies in the Psychology of Pictorial Representation*. Oxford: Phaidon.

Gonner, E.C.K., 1912. *Common Land and Inclosure*. London: Macmillan.

Goodison, J.W., 1955. *Catalogue of Cambridge Portraits. Vol. 1: The University Collection*. Cambridge: Cambridge University Press.

Goodison, J.W., 1985. *Catalogue of the Portraits in Christ's, Clare and Sidney Sussex Colleges*.

Cambridge: Cambridge Antiquarian Records Society.

Goshawk, E., 1948. Old Lincolnshire maps, *The Lincolnshire Historian*, 78–91.

Grewe, K., 1984. *Bibliographie zur Geschichte des Vermessungswesens = Bibliography of the History of Surveying*. Stuttgart: Konrad Wittwer.

Grierson, P., 1972. *English Linear Measures: An Essay in Origins*. Reading: University of Reading.

Gross, E.J., 1912. Chronicle of the college estates, In: *Biographical History of Gonville and Caius College. Vol. 4.II*, compiled by J. Venn. Cambridge: Cambridge University Press.

Gruzinski, S., 1988. *La Colonisation de l'imaginarie: sociétés indigènes et occidentalisation dans la Mexique espagnol XVIe–XVIIIe siècle*. Paris: Gallimard.

Guelke, L., 1977. Cartographic communication and geographic understanding, In: The nature of cartographic communication, edited by L. Guelke, *Cartographica*, Monograph 19, 129–45.

Guelke, L., 1979. Perception, meaning and cartographic design, *Canadian Cartographer*, 16, 61–9.

Gunasena, D., 1982. Nicholas Lane: seventeenth-century land surveyor and cartographer, *Wandsworth Historian*, 34, 1–8.

Habakkuk, H.J., 1940. English landownership 1680–1740, *Economic History Review*, 10, 2–17.

Habakkuk, H.J., 1979. The rise and fall of English landed families 1600–1800: Part I, *Transactions of the Royal Historical Society*, 29, 187–207.

Habakkuk, H.J., 1980. The rise and fall of English landed families 1600–1800: Part II, *Transactions of the Royal Historical Society*, 30, 199–221.

Hainsworth, D.R., 1987. The estate steward, In: *The Professions in Early Modern England*, edited by W. Prest. London: Croom Helm, 154–80.

Hale, J.R., 1971. *Renaissance Europe 1480–1520*. London: Collins.

Hall, A.R., 1962. *The Scientific Revolution 1500–1800: The Formation of the Modern Scientific Attitude*. 2nd ed. London: Longman.

Hall, A.R., 1969. *The Cambridge Philosophical Society: A History 1819–1969*. Cambridge: Cambridge Philosophical Society.

Hall, T.W., 1932. *The Fairbanks of Sheffield 1688 to 1848*. Sheffield: J.W. Northend.

Hall, T.W., 1937. The Fairbanks of Sheffield, In: *Incunabula of Sheffield History*, by T.W. Hall. Sheffield: J.W. Northend, 203–21.

Hampson, E.M., 1934. *The Treatment of Poverty in Cambridgeshire 1597–1834*. Cambridge: Cambridge University Press.

Hampson, E.M., 1948. Social history 1500–1900, In: *Victoria History of the Counties of England. Cambridgeshire, Vol. 2*, edited by L.F. Salzman. Oxford: Oxford University Press, 90–110.

Hans, N., 1951. *New Trends in Education in the Eighteenth Century*. London: Routledge and Kegan Paul.

Harding, D., 1972. Mathematics and science education in eighteenth-century Northamptonshire, *History of Education*, 1, 139–59.

Harley, J.B., 1963. William Yates and Peter Burdett: their role in the mapping of Lancashire and Cheshire in the 18th century, *Transactions of the Historical Society of Lancashire and Cheshire*, 115, 107–31.

Harley, J.B., 1964. The Society of Arts and the surveys of English counties 1759–1809. Part III: The response to the awards 1759–1766, *Journal of the Royal Society of Arts*, 112, 119–24.

Harley, J.B., 1966. English county map-making in the early years of the Ordnance Survey: the map of Surrey by Joseph Lindley and William Crosley, *Geographical Journal*, 132, 372–8.

Harley, J.B., 1970. Introduction, In: *Britannia. Volume the First*, by J. Ogilby, 1675. Amsterdam: Theatrum Orbis Terrarum, v–xxxi.

Harley, J.B., 1972. *Maps for the Local Historian: A Guide to the British Sources*. London: Bedford Square Press for the Standing Conference for Local History.

Harley, J.B., 1975. *Ordnance Survey Maps: A Descriptive Manual*. Southampton: Ordnance Survey.

Harley, J.B., 1983. Meaning and ambiguity in Tudor cartography, In: *English Map-Making 1500–1650*, edited by S. Tyacke. London: British Library, 22–45.

Harley, J.B., 1985. The iconology of early maps, In: *Imago et Mensura Mundi: Atti del IX Congresso Internazionale di Storia della Cartographica*, edited by C. Marzoli. 2 vols. Rome: Encyclopedia Italiana, 1, 29–38.

Harley, J.B., 1987. The map and the development of the history of cartography, In: *The History of Cartography. Vol. 1: Cartography in Prehistoric, Ancient, and Medieval Europe and the Mediterranean*, edited by J.B. Harley and D. Woodward. Chicago: University of Chicago Press, 1–42.

Harley, J.B., 1988a. L'histoire de la cartographie comme discours, *Préfaces*, 5, 70–5.

Harley, J.B., 1988b. Silences and secrecy: the hidden agenda of cartography in early modern Europe, *Imago Mundi*, 40, 57–76.

Harley, J.B., 1988c. Power and legitimation in the English geographical atlases of the eighteenth century, In: *History of the Atlas* [forthcoming].

Harley, J.B., 1988d. Maps, knowledge and power: an historical essay, In: *The Iconography of Landscape: Essays in the Symbolic Representation, Design and Use of Past Environments*, edited by D. Cosgrove and S. Daniels. Cambridge: Cambridge University Press, 277–312.

Harley, J.B., 1989b. Deconstructing the map, *Cartographica*, 26, 1–20.

Harley, J.B. and Stuart, E.A., 1982. George Withiell: a West Country surveyor of the late seventeenth century, *Devon and Cornwall Notes and Queries*, 35, 45–58.

Harley, J.B. and Walters, G., 1978. English map collecting 1790–1840: a pilot study of the evidence in Sotheby sale catalogues, *Imago Mundi*, 30, 31–55.

Harris, A., 1973. An East Yorkshire land surveyor: William Watson of Seaton Ross, *Yorkshire Archaeological Journal*, 45, 149–57.

Harris, J., 1979. *The Artist and the Country House: A History of Country House and Garden View Painting in Britain 1540–1870*. London: Sotheby Parke Burnet.

Harrison, J.F.C., 1984. *The Common People: A History from the Norman Conquest to the Present*. London: Fontana.

Harrison, W.J., 1958. *Life in Clare Hall Cambridge 1658–1713*. Cambridge: Heffer.

Harvey, J.H., 1966. Thomas Clay's plan of the manor of Great Bookham, Surrey, 1614, *Proceedings of the Leatherhead and District Local History Society*, 2, 281–3.

Harvey, P.D.A., 1965. An Elizabethan map of manors in North Dorset, *British Museum Quarterly*, 29, 82–4.

Harvey, P.D.A., 1980. *The History of Topographical Maps: Symbols, Pictures and Surveys*. London: Thames and Hudson.

Harvey, P.D.A., 1987. Local and regional cartography in medieval Europe, In: *The History of Cartography. Vol. 1: Cartography in Prehistoric, Ancient and Medieval Europe and the Mediterranean*, edited by J.B. Harley and D. Woodward. Chicago: University of Chicago Press, 464–501.

Haslam, G., 1985. John Norden's survey of the manor of Kennington, 1616, *London Topographical Record*, 25, 59–62.

Hassall, W.O., 1950a. The books of Sir Christopher Hatton at Holkham, *The Library*, 5, 1–13.

Hassall, W.O., ed., 1950b. *A Catalogue of the Library of Sir Edward Coke*. London: Yale University Press.

Hay, D., 1977. *Annalists and Historians: Western Historiography from the Eighth to the Eighteenth Centuries*. London: Methuen.

Hazlitt, W.C., ed., 1875. *Poetical and Dramatic Works of Thomas Randolph: Now First Collected and Edited from the Early Copies and from MSS., with some Account of the Author and Occasional Notes*. London: Reeves and Turner. 2 vols.

Head, C.G., 1984. The map as natural language: a paradigm for understanding, In: New insights in cartographic communication, edited by C. Board, *Cartographica*, 21, Monograph 31, 1–32.

Heidenreich, C.E., 1975. Measures of distance employed in 17th and early 18th century maps of Canada, *Canadian Cartographer*, 12, 121–37.

Helgerson, R., 1986. The land speaks: cartography, chorography and subversion in Renaissance England, *Representations*, 16, 51–85.

Henderson, W.O., 1982. The college estates, In: *Aspects of Downing History*, [edited by S. French]. Cambridge: Downing College Association, 19–54.

Hervey, M.F.S., 1921. *The Life, Correspondence and Collections of Thomas Howard Earl of Arundel 'Father of Vertu in England'*. Cambridge: Cambridge University Press.

Higman, B.W., 1986. Jamaican coffee plantations, 1780–1860: a cartometric analysis, *Caribbean Geography*, 2, 73–91.

Higman, B.W., 1987. The spatial economy of Jamaican sugar plantations: cartographic evidence from the eighteenth and nineteenth centuries, *Journal of Historical Geography*, 13, 17–39.

Higman, B.W., 1988b. *Jamaica Surveyed: Plantation Maps and Plans of the Eighteenth and Nineteenth Centuries*. Kingston: Institute of Jamaica Publications.

Hindle, B.P., 1988. *Maps for Local History*. London: Batsford.

Hodson, D., 1978. *Maps of Portsmouth before 1801*. Portsmouth: City of Portsmouth.

Holderness, B.A., 1972. Landlords' capital formation in East Anglia 1750–1870, *Economic History Review*, 25, 434–47.

Holderness, B.A., [1978]. The land market in the East Midlands, 1670–1820, In: *Landownership and Power in the Regions: Papers Submitted to the Conference of Regional History Tutors Held at Himley Hall in May 1978*, edited by M.D.G. Wanklyn. Wolverhampton: Centre for West Midlands Historical Studies for CORAL, 27–41.

Holderness, B.A., 1984. East Anglia and the Fens: Norfolk, Suffolk, Cambridgeshire, Ely, Huntingdonshire, Essex and the Lincolnshire Fens, In: *The Agrarian History of England and Wales. Vol. 5.I. 1640–1750: Regional Farming Systems*, edited by J. Thirsk. Cambridge: Cambridge University Press, 197–238.

Holmes, G., 1982. *Augustan England: Professions, State and Society 1680–1730*. London: Allen and Unwin.

Holmes, M., 1986. *The Country House Described: An Index to the Country Houses of Great Britain and Ireland*. Winchester: St Paul's Bibliographies in association with the Victoria and Albert Museum.

Hooke, J. and Perry, R.A., 1976. The planimetric accuracy of tithe maps, *Cartographic Journal*, 13, 177–83.

Hopper, J.H., 1980. The two John Grundys, *Lincolnshire Life*, 20, June, 24–7.

Hore, J.P., 1899. *Sporting and Rural Records of the Cheveley Estate*. London: Printed for private circulation by Horace Cox.

Horner, A.A., 1971. Cartouches and vignettes on the Kildare estate maps of John Rocque, *Quarterly Bulletin of the Irish Georgian Society*, 14, 57–76.

Horner, A.A., 1974. Some examples of the representation of height data on Irish maps before 1750, including an early use of the spot-height method, *Irish Geography*, 7, 68–80.

Horner, A.A., 1978. Two eighteenth-century maps of Carlow Town, *Proceedings of the Royal Irish Academy*, 78C, 115–26.

Houghton, W.E., 1942. The English virtuoso in the seventeenth century, *Journal of the History of Ideas*, 3, 51–73, 190–219.

Howard, H.F., 1935. *An Account of the Finances of the College of St John the Evangelist in the University of Cambridge 1511–1926*. Cambridge: Cambridge University Press.

Howell, D.W., 1986. *Patriarchs and Parasites: The Gentry of South-West Wales in the Eighteenth Century*. Cardiff: University of Wales Press.

Howson, G., 1982. *A History of Mathematics Education in England*. Cambridge: Cambridge University Press.

Hughes, E., 1949. The eighteenth-century estate agent, In: *Essays in British and Irish History in Honour of James Eadie Todd*, edited by H.A. Cronne, T.W. Moody and D.B. Quinn. London: F. Muller, 185–99.

Hughes, S.S., 1979. *Surveyors and Statesmen: Land Measuring in Colonial Virginia*. Richmond, Virginia: The Virginia Surveyors' Foundation and the Virginia Association of Surveyors.

Hull, F., 1973. *Catalogue of Estate Maps 1590–1840 in the Kent County Archives Office*. Maidstone: Kent County Council.

Hull, F., 1987. Aspects of local cartography in Kent and Essex, 1585–1700, In: *An Essex Tribute: Essays Presented to Frederick G. Emmison as a Tribute to his Life and Work for Essex History and Archives*, edited by K. Neale. London: Leopard's Head Press, 241–52.

Hull, P.L., 1955. Some Bedfordshire surveyors of the eighteenth century, *Journal of the Society of Archivists*, 1, 31–7.

Hussey, C., 1967. *The Picturesque: Studies in a Point of View*. London: Frank Cass.

Hutchins, J., 1861–74. *The History and Antiquities of the County of Dorset*, 3rd ed. by W. Shipp and J.W. Hodson. Westminster: J.B. Nichols and Sons.

Hyde, R., 1977. Thomas Hornor: pictural land surveyor, *Imago Mundi*, 29, 23–34.

Irwin, R., 1958. General introduction, In: *The English Library Before 1700: Studies in its History*, edited by F. Wormald and C.E. Wright. London: Athlone Press, 1–14.

Irwin, R., 1966. *The English Library: Sources and History*. London: Allen and Unwin.

Isham, G., ed., 1955. *The Correspondence of Bishop Brian Duppa and Justinian Isham 1650–60*. Lamport Hall, Northamptonshire: Northamptonshire Record Society.

Jackson, C., 1990. *A Cambridge Bicentenary: The History of a Legal Practice 1789–1989*. Bungay: Morrow and Co.

James, C.W., 1931. Some notes on the library of printed books at Holkham, *The Library*, 11, 435–60.

Jayne, S., 1983. *Library Catalogues of the English Renaissance*. Godalming: St Paul's Bibliographies.

Jayne, S. and Johnson, F.R., 1956. *The Lumley Library: The Catalogue of 1609*. London: British Museum.

Jenkins, P., 1984. Cambridgeshire and the gentry: the origins of a myth, *Journal of Local and Regional Studies*, 4, 1–17.

Johnson, F.R., 1950. Notes on English retail book-prices 1550–1640, *The Library*, 5, 83–112.

Johnston, S.A., Willmoth, F.H. and Bennett, J.A., 1985. *The Grounde of Artes: Mathematical Books of 16th-Century England*. Cambridge: Whipple Museum of the History of Science.

Jones, A., 1979. Land measurement in England 1150–1350, *Agricultural History Review*, 27, 10–18.

Jones, F., 1943. Some farmers of bygone Pembrokeshire, *Transactions of the Honourable Society of Cymmrodorion*, 133–51.

Jones, W.H.S., 1936. *A History of St Catharine's College Once Catharine Hall Cambridge*. Cambridge: Cambridge University Press.

Kain, R.J.P. and Prince, H.C., 1985. *The Tithe Surveys of England and Wales*. Cambridge: Cambridge University Press.

Kaufman, P., 1960. *Borrowings from the Bristol Library 1773–1784: A Unique Record of Reading Vogues*. Charlottesville: Bibliographical Society of the University of Virginia.

371

Kearney, H., 1970. *Scholars and Gentlemen: Universities and Society in Pre-Industrial Britain 1500–1700*. London: Faber.

Kenney, C.E., 1947. *The Quadrant and the Quill: A Book Written in Honour of Captain Samuel Sturmy, 'A Tryed and Trusty Sea-man', and Author of The Mariner's Magazine, 1669*. London: Printed and produced by Metchim and Son Ltd.

Kenney, C.E., 1950. William Leybourn 1626–1716, *The Library*, 5, 159–71.

Kerling, N.J.M., 1974a. Administration, In: *The Royal Hospital of Saint Bartholomew 1123–1973*, edited by V.C. Medvei and J.L. Thornton. London: St Bartholomew's Hospital, 1974, 19–35.

Kerling, N.J.M., 1974b. Archives, In: *The Royal Hospital of Saint Bartholomew 1123–1973*, edited by V.C. Medvei and J.L. Thornton. London: St Bartholomew's Hospital, 1974, 299–307.

Kerridge, E., ed., 1953. *Surveys of the Manors of Philip, First Earl of Pembroke and Montgomery, 1631–2*. Devizes: Wiltshire Archaeological and Natural History Society Records Branch.

Kettle, A.J., 1979. Agriculture 1500 to 1793, In: *Victoria History of the Counties of England. Staffordshire Vol. 6*, edited by M.W. Greenslade and D.A. Johnson. Oxford: Oxford University Press for the Institute of Historical Research, University of London, 49–90.

Kiely, E.R., 1947. *Surveying Instruments: Their History and Classroom Use*. New York: Bureau of Publications, Teachers College, Columbia University.

Kingston, A., 1906. *A History of Royston Hertfordshire: With Biographical Notes of Royston Worthies, Portraits, Plans and Illustrations*. London: Elliot Stock.

Knowles, M., 1902. *History of Wicken*. London: Elliot Stock.

Konvitz, J.W., 1987. *Cartography in France 1660–1848: Science, Engineering and Statecraft*. Chicago: University of Chicago Press.

Latham, R., ed., 1978. *Catalogue of the Pepys Library at Magdalene College Cambridge. Vol. 1: Printed Books*, compiled by N.A. Smith, assisted by H.M. Adams and D. Pepys Whiteley, with an appendix on Incunabula by J.C.T. Oates. Cambridge: D.S. Brewer.

Latham, R. and Matthews, W., eds., 1970–83. *The Diary of Samuel Pepys: A New and Complete Transcription*. London: Bell and Hyman. 11 vols.

Lawrence, H., 1985. John Norden and his colleagues: surveyors of Crown lands, *Cartographic Journal*, 22, 54–6.

Laxton, P., 1976. The geodetic and topographical evaluation of English county maps 1740–1840, *Cartographic Journal*, 13, 37–54.

Lears, T.J., 1985. The concept of cultural hegemony: problems and possibilities, *American Historical Review*, 90, 567–93.

Lievsay, J.L. and Davis, R.B., 1954. A cavalier library – 1643, *Studies in Bibliography*, 6, 141–60.

Lindert, P.H. and Williamson, J.G., 1983. English workers' living standards during the Industrial Revolution: a new look, *Economic History Review*, 36, 1–25.

Lindsay, J.M., 1980. The assessment of transient patterns on historic maps: a case study, *Cartographic Journal*, 17, 16–20.

List of Catalogues of English Book Sales 1676–1900 Now in the British Museum, 1915. London: British Museum.

Lloyd, R. and Gilmartin, P., 1987. The South Carolina coastline on historical maps: a cartometric analysis, *Cartographic Journal*, 24, 19–26.

Lockhart, D.G., 1978. The land surveyor in Northern Ireland before the coming of the Ordnance Survey circa 1840, *Irish Geography*, 11, 102–9.

Longfield, A.K., 1977. A County Sligo estate map of 1768, *Quarterly Bulletin of the Irish Georgian Society*, 20, 57–70.

Lynam, E., 1945. Period ornament, writing and symbols on maps, 1250–1800, *Geographical Magazine*, 18, 323–6, 365–8.

Lynam, E., 1950. English maps and map-makers of the sixteenth century, *Geographical Journal*, 116, 7–28.

MacCulloch, D., 1975. Radulph Agas: virtue unrewarded, *Proceedings of the Suffolk Institute of Archaeology*, 33, 275–84.

McIntosh, M., 1987. New College, Oxford and its Hornchurch estate, 1391–1675, In: *An Essex Tribute: Essays Presented to Frederick G. Emmison as a Tribute to his Life and Work for Essex History and Archives*, edited by K. Neale. London: Leopard's Head Press, 171–83.

McKenzie, D.F., 1986. *Bibliography and the Sociology of Texts.* London: British Library.

McKerrow, R.B., 1927. *An Introduction to Bibliography for Literary Students.* Oxford: Clarendon Press.

McKitterick, D., 1986. *Cambridge University Library: A History. Vol. 2: The Eighteenth and Nineteenth Centuries.* Cambridge: Cambridge University Press.

Maclagan, M., 1956. Genealogy and heraldry in the sixteenth and seventeenth centuries, In: *English Historical Scholarship in the Sixteenth and Seventeenth Centuries: A Record of the Papers Delivered at a Conference Arranged by the Dugdale Society to Commemorate the Tercentenary of the Publication of Dugdale's Antiquities of Warwickshire,* edited by L. Fox. London: Oxford University Press for the Dugdale Society, 31–48.

McLean, A., 1972. *Humanism and the Rise of Science in Tudor England.* London: Heinemann.

Madge, S.J., 1938. *The Domesday of Crown Lands: A Study of the Legislation, Surveys, and Sales of Royal Estates Under the Commonwealth.* London: George Routledge and Sons.

Manners, W.E., 1899. *Some Account of the Military, Political and Social Life of The Right Hon. John Manners Marquis of Granby.* London: Macmillan.

Manning, C.S., 1988. The farm or grange of New Barns in the manor of Ely: and Richard Tattersall (1724–1795), *Cambridgeshire Local History Society Bulletin,* 43, 20–8.

Manning, C.S., 1989. The farm or grange of New Barns in the manor of Ely. Part 2: Christopher Potter (c. 1751–1817), *Cambridgeshire Local History Society Bulletin,* 44, 9–19.

Marchant, H., 1986. A memento mori or vanitas emblem on an estate map of 1612, *Mapline,* 44, 1–4.

Margary, H., 1977. A proposed photographic method of assessing the accuracy of old maps, *Imago Mundi,* 29, 78–9.

Maslen, K., 1987. Parson Lister's library, *Transactions of the Cambridge Bibliographical Society,* 9, 155–73.

Mason, A.S., 1989. The 1745 parish map of Shoreditch, *The Terrier: The Friends of Hackney Archives Newsletter,* 16, 3–6.

Mason, A.S., 1990. *Essex on the Map: The 18th Century Land Surveyors of Essex.* Chelmsford: Essex Record Office.

Mason, R.A., 1985. 'Scotching the Brut': the early history of Britain, *History Today,* 35, 26–31.

Masters, R., [1790]. *A Catalogue of the Several Pictures in the Public Library and Respective Colleges, in the University of Cambridge: Intended as a Companion to the Concise and Accurate Description of the University and Town, &c.* Cambridge: Printed by J. Archdeacon ... for J. and J. Merrill.

Mendyk, S.A.E., 1986. Early British chorography, *The Sixteenth Century Journal,* 17, 459–81.

Mendyk, S.A.E., 1989. *'Speculum Britanniae': Regional Study, Antiquarianism, and Science in Britain to 1700.* Toronto: University of Toronto Press.

Miller, S.T., 1987. Rain's eye plan: unique historical source? *The Local Historian,* 17, 417–22.

Mingay, G.E., 1963. *English Landed Society in the Eighteenth Century.* London: Routledge and Kegan Paul.

Mingay, G.E., 1967. The eighteenth-century land steward, In: *Land, Labour and Population in the Industrial Revolution: Essays Presented to J.D. Chambers,* edited by E.L. Jones and G.E. Mingay. London: Arnold, 3–27.

Mingay, G.E., 1976. *The Gentry: The Rise and Fall of a Ruling Class.* London: Longman.

'A Minority Interest': Science in Cambridge Before 1800: Catalogue of an Exhibition of University Archives Held in Association with the Cambridge Festival 21–27 July 1982, 1982. Cambridge: Cambridge University Library.

Mitchell, B.R., 1988. *British Historical Statistics.* Cambridge: Cambridge University Press.

Mitchell, W.J.T., 1986. *Iconology: Image, Text, Ideology.* Chicago: University of Chicago Press.

Morgan, V., 1979. The cartographic image of 'the country' in early modern England, *Transactions of the Royal Historical Society,* 29, 129–54.

Mukerji, C., 1983. *From Graven Images: Patterns of Modern Materialism.* New York: Columbia University Press.

Mukerji, C., 1984. Visual language in science and the exercise of power: the case of cartography in early modern Europe, *Studies in Visual Communication,* 10, 3, 30–45.

Munby, A.N.L., 1973. *Sale Catalogues of Libraries of Eminent Persons*. London: Mansell with Sotheby Parke-Bernet Publications.

[Munby, L.M., 1967]. *Village History in the Staploe Hundred*. [Soham: Soham Village College].

Munby, L.M., 1989. *How Much is that Worth?* Chichester: Phillimore for the British Association for Local History.

Munro, T., 1970. *Form and Style in the Arts: An Introduction to Aesthetic Morphology*. Cleveland: Case Western Reserve University Press.

Murphy, J., 1978. Measures of map accuracy and some early Ulster maps, *Irish Geography*, 11, 88–101.

Murphy, M.J., 1977. *Cambridge Newspapers and Opinion 1780–1850*. Cambridge: Oleander Press.

Myers, J.N.L., 1958. Oxford libraries in the seventeenth and eighteenth centuries, In: *The English Library: Studies in its History Before 1700*, edited by F. Wormald and C.E. Wright. London: Athlone Press, 236–55.

National Trust, 1983. *Wimpole Hall: The Park*. [London]: National Trust.

National Trust, 1986. *Little Moreton Hall, Cheshire*. [London]: National Trust.

Newton, K.C., 1969. The Walkers of Essex, *Bulletin of the Society of University Cartographers*, 4, 1–6.

Nichols, H., 1980. *Local Maps of Derbyshire to 1770: An Inventory and Introduction*. Matlock: Derbyshire Library Service.

Nichols, H., 1987. *Local Maps of Nottinghamshire to 1800: An Inventory*. [Nottingham]: Nottinghamshire County Council Leisure Services.

Nichols, J., 1812. *Literary Anecdotes of the Eighteenth Century: Comprising Biographical Memoirs of William Bowyer, Printer, F.S.A. and Many of his Learned Friends ... Vol. 1*. London: Printed for the author by Nichols, Son and Lentley.

Nuti, L., 1988. The mapped views by Georg Hoefnagel: the merchant's eye, the humanist's eye, *Word and Image*, 4, 545–70.

Oates, J.C.T., 1958. The libraries of Cambridge 1500–1700, In: *The English Library: Studies in its History Before 1700*, edited by F. Wormald and C.E. Wright. London: Athlone Press, 213–35.

O'Day, R., 1982. *Education and Society 1500–1800: The Social Foundations of Education in Early Modern Britain*. London: Longman.

Oschinsky, D., 1971. *Walter of Henley and Other Treatises on Estate Management and Accounting*. Oxford: Clarendon Press.

Owst, G.R., 1949. Iconomania in eighteenth-century Cambridge: notes on a newly-acquired miniature of Dr Farmer and his interest in historical portraiture, *Proceedings of the Cambridge Antiquarian Society*, 42, 67–91.

Palmer, W.M., 1935. *William Cole of Milton*. Cambridge: Galloway and Porter.

Pannett, D., 1985. The manuscript maps of Warwickshire 1597–1880, *Warwickshire History*, 6, 69–85.

Panofsky, E., 1939. *Studies in Iconology: Humanistic Themes in the Art of the Renaissance*. New York: Oxford University Press.

Parker, R.A.C., 1975. *Coke of Norfolk: A Financial and Agricultural Study 1707–1842*. Oxford: Clarendon Press.

Parsons, C.E., 1948. Horseheath Hall and its owners, *Proceedings of the Cambridge Antiquarian Society*, 41, 1–50.

Paulson, R., 1975. *Emblem and Expression: Meaning in English Art of the Eighteenth Century*. London: Thames and Hudson.

Pearce, E.H., 1928. *The Sons of the Clergy: Some Records of Two Hundred and Seventy-Five Years*. 2nd ed. London: Murray.

Peddie, R.A., ed., 1914. *English Catalogue of Books 1801–36*. London: Publishers' Circular.

Pell, O.C., 1888. A new view of the geldable unit of assessment of Domesday, In: *Domesday Studies. Vol. 1*, edited by P.E. Dove. London: Longman, 227–385.

Pevsner, N., 1970. *Cambridgeshire*. 2nd ed. Harmondsworth: Penguin.

Pevsner, N., 1972. *Dorset*, by J. Newman and N. Pevsner. Harmondsworth: Penguin.

Phelps Brown, E.H. and Hopkins, S.V., 1962. Seven centuries of the prices in consumables compared with builders' wage rates, In: *Essays in Economic History. Vol. 2*, edited by E.M. Carus-Wilson. London: Arnold, 179–96.

Phillips, A.D.M., 1979. The Staffordshire maps of William Fowler, *South Staffordshire Archaeological and Historical Society Transactions*, 21, 15–24.

Phillips, A.D.M., 1980. The seventeenth century maps and surveys of William Fowler, *Cartographic Journal*, 17, 100–10.

Pigott, S., 1956. Antiquarian thought in the sixteenth and seventeenth centuries, In: *English Historical Scholarship in the Sixteenth and Seventeenth Centuries: A Record of the Papers Delivered at a Conference Arranged by the Dugdale Society to Commemorate the Tercentenary of the Publication of Dugdale's Antiquities of Warwickshire*, edited by L. Fox. London: Oxford University Press for the Dugdale Society, 93–114.

Pollard, G. and Ehrman, A., 1965. *The Distribution of Books by Catalogue from the Invention of Printing to A.D. 1800 Based on Material in the Broxbourne Library*. Cambridge: Roxburghe Club.

Porter, R., 1982. *English Society in the Eighteenth Century*. Harmondsworth: Penguin.

Porter, W., 1889. *History of the Corps of Royal Engineers. Vol. 1*. London: Longman.

Prince, H., 1988. Art and agrarian change, 1710–1815, In: *The Iconography of Landscape: Essays on the Symbolic Representation, Design and Use of Past Environments*, edited by D. Cosgrove and S. Daniels. Cambridge: Cambridge University Press, 98–118.

Quarrie, P., 1986. The Christ Church collections book, In: *The History of the University of Oxford. Vol. 5: The Eighteenth Century*, edited by L.S. Sutherland and L.G. Mitchell. Oxford: Oxford University Press, 493–511.

Quinn, D.B., 1986. Artists and illustration in the early mapping of North America, *Mariner's Mirror*, 3, 244–76.

Rackham, O., 1968. The armed ponds of Cambridgeshire, *Nature in Cambridgeshire*, 11, 25–7.

Rackham, O., 1986. *The History of the Countryside*. London: Dent.

Ravenhill, W., 1972. Joel Gascoyne: a pioneer of large-scale county mapping, *Imago Mundi*, 26, 60–70.

Ravenhill, W., 1973. The mapping of Great Haseley and Latchford: an episode in the surveying career of Joel Gascoyne, *Cartographic Journal*, 10, 105–11.

Ravenhill, W., 1984. The plottes of Morden Mylles, Cuttell (Cotehele), *Devon and Cornwall Notes and Queries*, 35, 165–74, 182–3.

Ravenhill, W. and Gilg, A., 1974. The accuracy of early maps? Towards a computer aided method, *Cartographic Journal*, 11, 48–52.

Reaney, P.H., 1943. *The Place-Names of Cambridgeshire and the Isle of Ely*. Cambridge: Cambridge University Press.

Rees, R., 1980. Historical links between geography and art, *Geographical Review*, 70, 60–78.

Reitan, E.A., 1985. Expanding horizons: maps in the *Gentleman's Magazine* 1731–1750, *Imago Mundi*, 37, 54–62.

Richeson, A.W., 1966. *English Land Measuring to 1800: Instruments and Practices*. Cambridge, Mass.: Society for the History of Technology and MIT Press.

Robinson, A.H. and Petchenik, B.B., 1976. *The Nature of Maps: Essays Towards Understanding Maps and Mapping*. Chicago: University of Chicago Press.

Robinson, E., 1962. The profession of civil engineer in the late 18th century: a portrait of Thomas Yeoman, F.R.S. 1704(?)–1781, *Annals of Science*, 18, 195–215.

Robinson, F.J.G. and Wallis, P.J., 1975a. *Book Subscription Lists: A Revised Guide*. Newcastle Upon Tyne: Harold Hill for the Book Subscriptions List Project.

Robinson, F.J.G. and Wallis, P.J., 1975b. Some early mathematical schools in Whitehaven, *Transactions of the Cumberland and Westmorland Antiquarian and Archaeological Society*, 75, 262–74.

Rodger, E.M., compiler, 1972. *The Large Scale County Maps of the British Isles 1596–1850: A Union List*. 2nd rev. ed. Oxford: Bodleian Library.

Rogers, D., 1953. The Holkham collection, *Bodleian Library Record*, 4, 255–67.

Rosenthal, M., 1982. *British Landscape Painting*. Oxford: Phaidon.

Royal Commission on Historical Monuments, 1968. *An Inventory of Historical Monuments in the County of Cambridge. Vol. 1: West Cambridgeshire*. London: HMSO.

Royal Commission on Historical Monuments, 1972. *An Inventory of Historical Monuments in the County of Cambridge. Vol. 2: North-East Cambridgeshire.* London: HMSO.

Royal Commission on Historical Monuments, 1975. *An Inventory of Historical Monuments in the County of Dorset. Vol. 5: East Dorset.* London: HMSO.

Sack, R.D., 1986. *Human Territoriality: Its Theory and History.* Cambridge: Cambridge University Press.

Sambrook, J., 1986. *The Eighteenth Century: The Intellectual and Cultural Context of English Literature, 1700–1789.* London: Longman.

Schofield, B., ed., 1949. *The Knyvett Letters 1620–1644.* Fakenham: Norfolk Record Society.

Schofield, J., ed., 1987. *The London Surveys of Ralph Treswell.* London: London Topographical Society.

Schulz, J., 1978. Jacopo de' Barbari's view of Venice: map making, city views, and moralized geography before the year 1500, *Art Bulletin*, 60, 425–74.

Schulz, J., 1987. Maps as metaphors: mural map cycles of the Italian Renaissance, In: *Art and Cartography: Six Historical Essays*, edited by D. Woodward. Chicago: University of Chicago Press, 97–122.

Scott, J., 1982. *The Upper Classes: Property and Privilege in Britain.* London: Macmillan.

Selwyn, D.G., 1981. The Lumley library: a supplementary checklist, *British Library Journal*, 7, 136–48.

Seymour, W.A., ed., 1980. *A History of the Ordnance Survey.* Folkestone: Dawson.

Shelby, L.R., 1967. *John Rogers: Tudor Military Engineer.* Oxford: Clarendon Press.

Shirley, R.W., 1988. *Printed Maps of the British Isles 1650–1750.* Tring: Map Collector Publications Ltd, and London: British Library.

Sibley, J.L., 1873. *Biographical Sketches of Graduates of Harvard University, in Cambridge Massachusetts. Vol. 1: 1642–1658.* Cambridge, Mass.: Charles William Sever.

Silvester, R.J., 1989. William Haiwarde and the fens, *Fenland Research*, 6, 38–42.

Simmons, J., ed., 1978. *English County Historians.* East Ardsley: E.P. Publishing.

Simon, J., 1966. *Education and Society in Tudor England.* Cambridge: Cambridge University Press.

Skelton, R.A. and Harvey, P.D.A., eds., 1986. *Local Maps and Plans From Medieval England.* Oxford: Oxford University Press.

Smith, A.G.R., 1972. *Science and Society in the Sixteenth and Seventeenth Centuries.* London: Thames and Hudson.

Smith, B.S., 1967. The Dougharty family of Worcester: estate surveyors and mapmakers 1700–60, *Worcestershire Historical Society [Publications]*, 5, 138–80.

Smith, D., 1988. *Maps and Plans for the Local Historian and Collector: A Guide to Types of Maps of the British Isles Produced Before 1914 Valuable to Local and Other Historians and Mostly Available to Collectors.* London: Batsford.

Smith, M.H., 1974. Some humanist libraries in early Tudor Cambridge, *Sixteenth Century Journal*, 5, 15–34.

Snow, V.F., 1966. An inventory of the Lord General's library, 1646, *The Library*, 21, 115–23.

Somerville, R., 1953. *History of the Duchy of Lancaster. Vol. 1: 1265–1603.* London: Chancellor and Council of the Duchy of Lancaster.

Spring, D., 1963. *The English Landed Estate in the Nineteenth Century: Its Administration.* Baltimore: Johns Hopkins University Press.

Spufford, M., 1968. *A Cambridgeshire Community: Chippenham from Settlement to Enclosure.* Leicester: Department of English Local History, University of Leicester.

Spufford, M., 1974. *Contrasting Communities: English Villagers in the Sixteenth and Seventeenth Centuries.* Cambridge: Cambridge University Press.

Steer, F.W., 1962. *A Catalogue of Sussex Estate and Tithe Award Maps. [Vol. 1].* Lewis: Sussex Record Society.

Steer, F.W., 1968. *A Catalogue of Sussex Estate and Tithe Award Maps. [Vol. 2].* Lewis: Sussex Record Society.

Steer, F.W., ed., 1969. *Farm and Cottage Inventories of Mid-Essex 1635–1749.* 2nd ed. Chichester: Phillimore.

Stone, J.C., 1972. Techniques of scale measurement of historical maps, In: *International Geography*, edited by W.P. Adams and F.M. Helleiner. Toronto: University of Toronto Press, 452–4.

Stone, J.C. and Gemmell, A.M.D., 1977. An experiment in the comparative analysis of distortion on historical maps, *Cartographic Journal*, 14, 7–11.

Stone, L., 1965. *The Crisis of the Aristocracy 1558–1641*. Oxford: Clarendon Press.

Stone, L. and Stone, J.C.F., 1984. *An Open Elite? England 1540–1880*. Oxford: Clarendon Press.

Storey, E., 1982. *A Right to Song: The Life of John Clare*. London: Methuen.

Storrie, M.C., 1969. William Bald, F.R.S.E., c. 1789–1857: surveyor, cartographer and civil engineer, *Transactions of the Institute of British Geographers*, 47, 205–31.

Strype, J., 1820. *The Life of the Learned Sir Thomas Smith, Kt D.C.L. ...* New ed. Oxford: Clarendon Press.

Summerson, J., 1959. The classical country house in eighteenth-century England, *Journal of the Royal Society of Arts*, 107, 539–87.

Sylvester, D.W., 1970. *Educational Documents 800–1816*. London: Methuen.

Taylor, A., 1986. *Book Catalogues: Their Varieties and Uses*. 2nd ed. revised by W.P. Barlow jr. Winchester: St Paul's Bibliographies.

Taylor, C., 1973. *The Cambridgeshire Landscape: Cambridgeshire and the Southern Fens*. London: Hodder and Stoughton.

Taylor, E.G.R., 1929. The plane-table in the sixteenth century, *Scottish Geographical Magazine*, 45, 205–11.

Taylor, E.G.R., 1947. The surveyor, *Economic History Review*, 17, 121–33.

Taylor, E.G.R., 1954. *The Mathematical Practitioners of Tudor and Stuart England*. Cambridge: Cambridge University Press.

Taylor, E.G.R., 1966. *The Mathematical Practitioners of Hanoverian England 1714–1840*. Cambridge: Cambridge University Press.

Teversham, T.F., 1947. *A History of the Village of Sawston. Part II*. Sawston: Crampton and Sons.

Thomas, C., 1985. Land surveyors in Wales 1750–1850: the Matthews family, *Bulletin of the Board of Celtic Studies*, 32, 216–32.

Thompson, F.M.L., 1968. *Chartered Surveyors: The Growth of a Profession*. London: Routledge and Kegan Paul.

Thomson, G.S., 1937. *Life in a Noble Household 1641–1700*. London: Cape.

Thomson, G.S., 1940. *The Russells in Bloomsbury 1669–1771*. London: Cape.

Thomson, G.S., 1949. *Family Background*. London: Cape.

Thrower, N.J.W., 1972. *Maps and Man: An Examination of Cartography in Relation to Culture and Civilization*. Englewood Cliffs: Prentice-Hall.

Tibble, J.W. and Tibble, A., 1972. *John Clare: A Life*. London: Joseph.

Tipping, H.A., 1925. Crichel Dorset: the seat of Lord Alington, *Country Life*, 57, 766–74, 814–23, 874–81.

Tobler, W.R., 1965. Computation of the correspondence of geographical patterns, *Papers of the Regional Science Association*, 15, 131–9.

Tobler, W.R., 1966. Medieval distortions: the projections of ancient maps, *Annals of the Association of American Geographei., 56, 351–60.

Tooley, R.V., 1987. *Maps and Map-Makers*. 7th ed. London: Batsford.

Turner, A.J., 1973. Mathematical instruments and the education of gentlemen, *Annals of Science*, 30, 51–88.

Turner, G.L'E., 1986. The physical sciences, In: *The History of the University of Oxford. Vol. 5: The Eighteenth Century*, edited by L.S. Sutherland and L.G. Mitchell. Oxford: Oxford University Press, 659–81.

Twigg, J., 1987. *A History of Queens' College, Cambridge 1448–1986*. Woodbridge: Boydell Press.

Tyacke, S., 1984. Samuel Pepys as map collector, In: *Maps and Prints: Aspects of the English Booktrade*, edited by R. Myers and M. Harris. Oxford: Oxford Polytechnic Press, 1–29.

Tyacke, S. and Huddy, J., 1980. *Christopher Saxton and Tudor Map-Making*. London: British Library.

Tyson, B., 1986. Andrew Pellin's surveying career at Whitehaven 1688–1705, *Transactions of the Cumberland and Westmorland Antiquarian and Archaeological Society*, 86, 163–83.

Bibliography

Varley, J., 1948. John Rocque: engraver, surveyor, cartographer and map-seller, *Imago Mundi*, 5, 83–91.

Venn, J. and Venn, J.A., 1922–54. *Alumni Cantabrigienses: A Biographical List of All Known Students, Graduates and Holders of Office at the University of Cambridge from the Earliest Times to 1900. Part I: From the Earliest Times to 1751*, by J. and J.A. Venn. *Part II: From 1752 to 1900*, by J.A. Venn. Cambridge: Cambridge University Press. 4 and 6 vols.

Victoria History of the Counties of England. Cambridgeshire. Vol. 4, edited by R.B. Pugh, 1953. Oxford: Oxford University Press for the Institute of Historical Research, University of London.

Victoria History of the Counties of England. Cambridgeshire. Vol. 5, edited by C.R. Elrington, 1973. Oxford: Oxford University Press for the Institute of Historical Research, University of London.

Victoria History of the Counties of England. Cambridgeshire, Vol. 6, edited by A.P.M. Wright, 1978. Oxford: Oxford University Press for the Institute of Historical Research, University of London.

Victoria History of the Counties of England. Cambridgeshire, Vol. 8, edited by A.P.M. Wright, 1982. Oxford: Oxford University Press for the Institute of Historical Research, University of London.

Victoria History of the Counties of England. Cambridgeshire, Vol. 9, edited by A.P.M. Wright and C.P. Lewis, 1990. Oxford: Oxford University Press for the Institute of Historical Research, University of London.

Victoria History of the Counties of England. Hertfordshire. Vol. 2, edited by W. Page, 1908. London: Constable.

Vincent, W.A.L., 1969. *The Grammar Schools: Their Continuing Tradition 1660–1714*. London: Murray.

Waddington, J., compiler, 1934. *Who's Who in the Family of Waddington*. London: Wada Limited.

Wade Martins, S., 1980. *A Great Estate at Work: The Holkham Estate and its Inhabitants in the Nineteenth Century*. Cambridge: Cambridge University Press.

Wale, H.J., 1883. *My Grandfather's Pocket-Book: From A.D. 1701 to 1796*. London: Chapman and Hall.

Walker, E., 1866. *Terrestrial and Cosmical Magnetism*. Cambridge: Deighton Bell.

Wallis, H.M., 1990. Foreword, In: *Essex on the Map: The 18th Century Land Surveyors of Essex*, by A.S. Mason. Chelmsford: Essex Record Office, vii–ix.

Wallis, H.M. and Robinson, A.H., 1987. *Cartographical Innovations: An International Handbook of Mapping Terms to 1900*. Tring: Map Collector Publications Ltd.

Wallis, P.J., 1973. British philomaths: mid eighteenth-century and earlier, *Centaurus*, 17, 301–14.

Wallis, P.J., 1976. *An Index of British Mathematicians: A Check-List. Part 2: 1701–1760*. Newcastle Upon Tyne: Issued by the Project for Historical Bibliography at the University of Newcastle Upon Tyne.

Walne, P., 1969. *A Catalogue of Manuscript Maps in the Hertfordshire Record Office*. Hertford: Hertfordshire County Council.

Walters, G., 1988. The antiquary and the map, *Word and Image*, 4, 529–44.

Wardale, J.R., 1899. *Clare College*. London: F.E. Robinson and Co.

Warrand, D., ed., 1907. *Hertfordshire Families*. London: Constable.

Waterman, S. and Gordon, D., 1984. A quantitative-comparative approach to analysis of distortion in mental maps, *Professional Geographer*, 36, 326–37.

Watson, A.G., 1966. *The Library of Sir Simonds D'Ewes*. London: British Museum.

Way, A., 1847. *Catalogue of Antiquities, Coins, Pictures, and Miscellaneous Curiosities in the Possession of the Society of Antiquaries of London, 1847*. London: John Bowyer Nichols and Son.

Webster, D.C.F., 1989. Mony and diverse ways: surveying in Scotland before 1820, In: *Togail Tir Marking Time: The Map of the Western Isles*, edited by F. Macleod. Stornoway: Acair Ltd and An Lanntair, 79–88.

Welu, J.A., 1987. The sources and development of cartographic ornament in the Netherlands, In: *Art and Cartography: Six Historical Essays*, edited by D. Woodward. Chicago: University of Chicago Press, 147–73.

Whittington, G. and Gibson, A.J.S., 1986. *The Military Survey of Scotland 1747–1755: A Critique*. Lancaster: University of Lancaster for the Historical Geography Research Group of the Institute of British Geographers.

Williams, B.J., 1984. Mexican pictorial cadastral registers: an analysis of the Códice de Santa María Asunción and the Codex Vergara, In: *Explorations in Ethnohistory: Indians of Central Mexico in the Sixteenth Century*, edited by H.R. Harvey and H.J. Prem. Albuquerque: University of New Mexico Press, 103–25.

Williams, J.D., 1966. *Audley End: The Restoration of 1762–1797*. Chelmsford: Essex County Council.

Williams, R., 1973. *The Country and the City*. London: Chatto and Windus.

Williamson, T. and Bellamy, L., 1987. *Property and Landscape: A Social History of Land Ownership and the English Countryside*. London: George Philip.

Willis, R. and Clark, J.W., 1886. *The Architectural History of the University of Cambridge and of the Colleges of Cambridge and Eton*. Cambridge: Cambridge University Press. 4 vols.

Wills, G., 1984. A note on H. Copland, *Apollo*, 119, 421–3.

Wilson, C., 1965. *England's Apprenticeship 1603–1763*. London: Longman.

Woburn Abbey, 1987. Norwich: Woburn Abbey and Jarrold Publications.

Wood, D., 1977. Now and then: comparisons of ordinary Americans' symbol conventions with those of past cartographers, *Prologue, the Journal of the National Archives*, 9, 151–61.

Woodbridge, K., 1970. *Landscape and Antiquity: Aspects of English Culture at Stourhead 1718 to 1830*. Oxford: Clarendon Press.

Woodward, D.A., 1978. English cartography, 1650–1750: a summary, In: *The Compleat Plattmaker: Essays on Chart, Map and Globe Making in England in the Seventeenth and Eighteenth Centuries*, edited by N.J.W. Thrower. Berkeley: University of California Press, 159–93.

Woodward, D.A., 1974. The study of the history of cartography: a suggested framework, *American Cartographer*, 1, 101–15.

Woolgar, C.M., 1985. Some draft estate maps of the early seventeenth century, *Cartographic Journal*, 22, 136–43.

Wordie, J.R., 1982. *Estate Management in Eighteenth-Century England: The Building of the Leveson-Gower Fortune*. London: Royal Historical Society.

Wordsworth, C., 1877. *Scholae Academicae: Some Account of Studies at the English Universities in the Eighteenth Century*. New York: Augustus M. Kelley, 1969. Facsimile Reprint.

Wright, C.E., 1962. Edward Harley, 2nd Earl of Oxford 1689–1741, *Book Collector*, 11, 158–74.

Wrigley, E.A. and Schofield, R.S., 1981. *The Population History of England 1541–1871: A Reconstruction*. London: Arnold.

Yates, E.M., 1964. Map of Over Haddon and Meadowplace, near Bakewell, Derbyshire, c. 1528, *Agricultural History Review*, 12, 121–4.

Yates, E.M., 1982. Vernacular buildings on early maps of the Weald, *Transactions of the Ancient Monuments Society*, 26, 210–26.

INDEX

Personal names in *italic* refer to surveyors and cartographers. Page numbers in *italic* refer to illustrations, page numbers in **bold** refer to entries in the carto-bibliography. Parishes have not been given for places in Cambridgeshire or for county towns.

Bellamy, Thomas, 185
Bell and Sons, William, **278**
Bellingham, John, 102
Bendn, Mrs, **249**
Benese, Richard de, 124; surveying text by, 120, 121, 130 (ownership of) 144, 145
Bennington, Joseph, **324**
Benson, Edward, **218, 219**
Benson, Mary, **219**
Benwick, 153, 176, **200, 332**
Bermingham, James, 105
Bermondsey, Surrey, 51, 130
Bernard, Sir Robert, 154; maps for, 57, 149, **286**
Berry, Miles, **197**
Bessborough, 2nd Earl of, 41, *43*, 57, 153, **334**
Biggleswade, Bedfordshire, 138
binders, surveyors as, 125
binding of estate atlases, 180, **232**
Birdbrook, Essex, **211–12**
Bisterne, Hampshire, 97
Blackadder, John, 187
black-letter type, 120, 122
Blackstone, Worcestershire, 100
Blaeu, Willem Janszoon, 149
Blaikie, Francis, 113, 160
Blanch Lyon Pursuivant of Arms, 116
Bletchley, Buckinghamshire, **246–50**
Bletsoe, Thomas, 148
Blithe, Samuel, 148
Blunt, Henry Layton, 155, 176, **333**
Bluntisham, Huntingdonshire, **336**
Bodger, John, 106, 110
Boodle and Company, **319**
bookbinders: maps coloured by, 147–8; surveyors as, 98
bookcases, maps displayed in, 180, *181*
booksellers, 143–4, 148, 161; owners of surveying texts, 145; surveyors as, 98, 124, 125
borders to estate maps, 25, *26*, 46, 177, 192
Boswell, Mrs, **289**
Bosworth, Newton, 129
Bottisham, 95; maps of, 174, **200–3, 266, 306, 308** (accuracy of) 57, 58, 61, 62
boundaries, maps and surveys of, 157, 171, 172, 173, 176, **194, 202, 268–9, 275, 279, 289, 307, 315, 323, 327**
Bourn, 58, **203–4**
Bowen, Emanuel, ownership of atlas by, 149
Bowles, John, 56, 117, **328, 329**
Boxworth, 155; maps of, *42*, 134–5, *136*, 149, 155, 182, **204, 221, 273**
Boyce, Thomas, 171, **332**
Braintree, Essex, 156
Brampton Bryan, Herefordshire, 144
Brand, Jo., **276**
Brand, Robert, **276**

Brand, Thomas (d. 1794), 84, **208–9**
Brand, Thomas (1774–1851) *see* Dacre, Lord
Brand, William, **289**
Bransby, John, 154, **213, 334**
Brasenose College, Oxford, 82
Braun, Georg, 6
Brent, Nathanael, **249**
Bridgeman, Charles, **337–8**
Bridges, Benjamin, **292–3, 321**
Briggs, Rev. Thomas, 176, **280–1**
Brinkley, 155; maps of, **204, 205, 208–9**
Bristol, 126, 142, 145
British Museum, landowners as trustees of, 154
Britton, Mr, **212**
Bromley, Henry, 156
Bromley, John, 156
Bromley family *see* Montfort, Lords
Brooke, Susan, **269–70**
Brookes, Theophilus, 131
Broughton, Oxfordshire, 171
Brown, Mr, **232**
Browne, Richard, **312–13**
Browne, Thomas, 116
Browne, Thomas (farmer), 78
Brownrigg, John, 116
Brudenell, Catherine, **248**
Brunton, John, 134
Buckden, Huntingdonshire, 131
Bucke, Thomas, **279–80**
Buckingham, Duchess of, 105, 109–10
Buckinghamshire, 33, 35, 36
Buckland, William, 60, **220**
Buckle, Catharine, **334**
Buckle, Samuel, **289**
building sites, estate maps of, **219, 237, 270–1, 288**
buildings on estate maps, 49–50, 67–75; *see also* churches, houses
building surveyors, 95, 98, 101, **251**
Buller, James, **272**
Buller, John, **272**
Bun, Mr, **289**
Bundy, Thomas, **324**
Burcham, John, 92, 185, **227**
Burghley, Lord, 123
Burgoyne, John, **250, 263**
Burgoyne, Mary, **263**
Burman, Jo., **276**
Burns, A., 124; surveying text by, 120, 121, 122, 125, 130, 178, 180
Burrell, Mistress, 147
Burrough Green, 153, 158, **205–6**
Burton, Robert, 146
Burwell, 86, 113, **234**; maps of, 64, 115, 144, **206–7**